PAUL'S
METAPHORS

PAUL'S METAPHORS

THEIR CONTEXT AND CHARACTER

DAVID J. WILLIAMS

HENDRICKSON PUBLISHERS

Copyright © 1999 by Hendrickson Publishers, Inc.
P. O. Box 3473
Peabody, Massachusetts 01961-3473
All rights reserved
Printed in the United States of America

Second printing, softcover edition — April 2004

ISBN 1-56563-984-7

Library of Congress Cataloging-in-Publication Data

Williams, David John.
    Paul's metaphors: their context and character / David J. Williams
    Includes bibliographical references and indexes.
    ISBN 1-56563-287-7 (hardcover)
    1. Bible.   N.T.   Epistles of Paul—Socio-rhetorical criticism.
    2. Metaphor in the Bible.   I.   Title
    BS2655.M47W55   1999
    227'.066—dc21   98-54750
                                                                          CIP

To Audrey

Table of Contents

Preface

This book originated about twenty years ago in a series of lectures sponsored by Ridley College, Melbourne, and known as the Ridley College Learning Labs. These lectures were offered to the public as a way of promoting the work of the college. I chose as my subject the metaphors of the Apostle Paul largely because I had only recently penetrated the imagery of 2 Cor 2:14–15 to discover what was for me a new world—the world of Paul's day, the world of Rome. I had found myself caught up in the pomp and circumstance of a Roman triumph, and experiencing the excitement of that discovery, I wanted more. The metaphors became "windows" through which I could see Paul as a real man living in a real world, and he came alive for me as never before. And so I "collected" Paul's metaphors and made a hobby (pursued rather spasmodically) of reading social histories of the late Roman republic and early empire.

After I completed my Learning Lab lectures, my interest in Paul's metaphors might have remained simply a hobby but for two factors. The first was John Wilson (now Bishop John Wilson). The Learning Lab series was his brainchild, so I have to thank him for starting me on this course in the first place. And from that day to this he has never let up on his insistence that I should turn this material into a book. There were long periods when I did little about it. The more immediate demands of college and parish life leave little time for indulgence in hobbies. But John was diligent in his zeal for this project and kept my own zeal from flagging.

The second factor was the generosity of the council of Ridley College in granting me study leave in 1988. I spent four months at Tyndale House, Cambridge, writing the first draft of this book, which I brought to completion during another leave in 1996. Ridley is not a big college, nor is it a wealthy one. Study leave is a drain on the college's resources and a strain on the other members of the faculty who have to pick up the workload of their absent colleague. I place on record my indebtedness to all concerned for giving me this time off for writing.

I must also acknowledge a debt of gratitude to Ridley College librarians Ruth Millard and Kerri Hunter for their unfailing courtesy, kindness, and efficiency in tracking down obscure references and finding difficult-to-come-by journal articles for me. I wonder sometimes how I could have managed without them. I must thank my daughter-in-law, Jean Williams, too, for checking references for me at the University of Melbourne library in precious time taken from her own doctoral research.

From the time when I first raised with my publishers the possibility of a book on Paul's metaphors, they have encouraged me to get on with it, and I thank them for their support. Shirley Decker-Lucke, Associate Editor of Henrickson Publishers, whom I have never met but regard as a friend, has done much to transform my manuscript into this finished product. She deserves special thanks. The book, of course, is still mine, and Shirley cannot be held responsible for its faults. But she has worked hard to reduce them and to make what I have done as presentable and as useful as possible.

To facilitate my writing, Audrey, my wife, and I left our house in the city for a place of peace and quiet in the country. But the move cost Audrey hours of commuting to her own work in the city as a midwife and to all the other things that she does in church and community. In the give-and-take of married life, it has often been more of give on her part and of take on mine; the conditions and time needed for this work have been another instance of my taking and her giving. With all the other help that I have had, I still could not have done the work without her readiness to give yet again. I dedicate this book to her with gratitude and with love.

David J. Williams
Ridley College
Parkville, Victoria, Australia

Abbreviations

GENERAL ABBREVIATIONS

BCE	Before Common Era
ca.	circa
CE	Common Era
ch.	chapter
e.g.	for example
esp.	especially
f.	and following
lit.	literally
MS	manuscripts
MSS	manuscripts
n.	note
nn.	notes
par.	parallels

ANCIENT WRITINGS

OLD TESTAMENT APOCRYPHA AND PSEUDEPIGRAPHA

Apoc. Mos.	*Apocalypse of Moses*
Bel	Bel and the Dragon
1, 2, 3 En.	*1, 2, 3 Enoch*
Jub.	*Jubilees*
Let. Aris.	*Letter of Aristeas*
Odes Sol.	*Odes of Solomon*
Pss. Sol.	*Psalms of Solomon*
Sib. Or.	*Sibylline Oracles*
Sir	Sirach
T. Levi	*Testament of Levi*

T. Sol.   Testament of Solomon
Tob   Tobit
Wis   Wisdom of Solomon

DEAD SEA SCROLLS
1QS   Manual of Discipline
4QFlor   Florilegium

JOSEPHUS
A.J.   Antiquitates judaicae
B.J.   Bellum judaicum

MISHNAH, TALMUD, AND RELATED LITERATURE
b.   Babylonian Talmud
B. Qam   Baba Qamma
Ber.   Berakot
Ketub.   Ketubot
m.   Mishnah
Mek.   Mekilta
Qidd.   Qiddušin

ANCIENT CHRISTIAN AND CLASSICAL WRITINGS
Cod. justin.   Codex justinianus
Cod. theod.   Codex theodosianus
Gk. Anth.   Greek Anthology
Martyr.   Martyrdom of Perpetua and Felicity
P.Oxy.   Papyri Oxyrhynchus

Achilles Tatius
Leuc. Clit.   Leucippe et Clitophon

Aelius Aristides
Rome   To Rome

Aeschines
Tim.   In Timarchum

Aeschylus
Ag.   Agamemnon
Cho.   Choephori
Eum.   Eumenides
Pers.   Persae

Alciphon
Ep.   Epistles

Ammianus
Hist.   History

Antiphon
Chor.   On the Choreutes

Apostolic Fathers
1 Clem.   1 Clement
Herm. Vis.   Shepherd of Hermas, Vision
Ign. Rom.   Ignatius, To the Romans

Ign. *Smyrn.*	Ignatius, *To the Smyrnaeans*
Ign. *Trall.*	Ignatius, *To the Trallians*
Appian	
Hist. rom.	*Historia romana*
Apuleius	
Flor.	*Florida*
Metam.	*Metamorphoses*
Aristophanes	
Eq.	*Equites (Knights)*
Frag.	*Fragmenta*
Nub.	*Nubes (Clouds)*
Ran	*Ranae (Frogs)*
Vesp.	*Vespae (Wasps)*
Aristotle	
Eth. nic.	*Ethica nicomachea*
Gen. an.	*De generatione animalium*
Oec.	*Oeconomica*
Poet.	*Poetica*
Pol.	*Politica*
Rhet.	*Rhetorica*
Top.	*Topica*
Arnobius	
Nat.	*Adversus nationes*
Arrian	
Anab.	*Anabasis*
Artemidorus Daldianus	
Onir.	*Onirocritica*
Athenaeus	
Deipn.	*Deipnosophistae*
Augustus	
Res gest.	*Res gestae*
Caesar	
Bell. civ.	*Bellum civile*
Bell. gall.	*Bellum gallicum*
Calpurnius Fabatus	
Ep.	*Epistulae*
Cato	
Agr.	*De agricultura (De re rustica)*
Censorinus	
Die nat.	*De die natali*
Cicero	
Att.	*Epistulae ad Atticum*
Brut.	*Brutus*
Dom.	*De domo sua*
Fam.	*Epistulae ad familiares*

Fin.	*De finibus*
Leg.	*De legibus*
Leg. man.	*Pro Lege manilia*
Mil.	*Pro Milone*
Mur.	*Pro Murena*
Nat. d.	*De natura deorum*
Or.	*De oratore*
Phil.	*Orationes philippicae*
Quint. fratr.	*Epistulae ad Quintum fratrem*
Sen.	*De senectute*
Tusc.	*Tusculanae disputationes*
Verr.	*In Verrem*

Cleanthes
Hymn	*Hymn to Zeus*

Clement of Alexandria
Strom.	*Stromata*

Columella
Rust.	*De re rustica*

Cyprian
Ep.	*Epistles*

Demosthenes
Cor.	*De corona*
3 Philip.	*Philippica iii*

Dio Cassius
Rom. Hist.	*Roman History*

Dio Chrysostom
Disc.	*Discourses*
Melanc.	*Melancomas*

Diodorus Siculus
Hist.	*History*

Diogenes
Ep.	*Epistles*

Diogenes Laertius
Lives	*Lives of the Philosophers*

Dionysius of Halicarnassus
Ant. rom.	*Antiquitates romanae*

Dioscorides
Mat. med.	*De materia medica*

Epictetus
Diatr.	*Diatribae (Dissertationes)*
Frag.	*Fragmenta*

Euripides
Alc.	*Alcestis*
Bacch.	*Bacchae*

Eusebius
  Hist. eccl.   *Historia ecclesiastica*

Frontinus
  Aquaeduct.   *De aquaeductibus*
  Strat.   *Strategemata*

Fronto
  Am.   *Ad amicos*

Gaius
  Inst.   *Institutiones*

Galen
  Diagn.   *On the Diagnosis and Healing of Faults*
  Meth.   *On Methods of Healing*
  Mix.   *On the Mixing and Efficacy of Pure Drugs*

Gellius
  Noct. Att.   *Noctes Atticae*

Herodian
  Hist.   *Histories of the Emperors*

Herodotus
  Hist.   *History*

Pseudo-Hippocrates
  Ep.   *Epistles*

Hippolytus
  Haer.   *Refutatio omnium haeresium*

Homer
  Il.   *Iliad*

Horace
  Ars   *Ars poetica*
  Ep.   *Epistulae*
  Epod.   *Epodi*
  Sat.   *Satirae*

Irenaeus
  Haer.   *Adversus haereses*

Isocrates
  Paneg.   *Panegyricus (Or. 4)*

Isidorus
  Etym.   *Etymologiae*

Jerome
  Comm. Eph.   *Commentariorum in Epistulam ad Ephesios libri III*

Johannes Tzetzes
  Hist. var. chil.   *Historiarum variarum chiliades*

John Chrysostom
  Hom. 2 Cor.   *Homiliae in epistulam ii ad Corinthios*
  Hom. 1 Tim.   *Homiliae in epistulam i ad Timotheum*

Julian the Apostate
  Ep.   *Epistulae*

Justinian
   Inst.   *Institutiones*
Juvenal
   Sat.   *Satirae*
Libanius
   Or.   *Orationes*
Livy
   Ep.   *Epitomae*
   Hist.   *History*
Lucian
   Anach.   *Anacharsis*
   Fug.   *Fugitivi*
   Hermot.   *Hermotimus*
   Nav.   *Navigium*
   Peregr.   *De morte Peregrini*
   Philops.   *Philopseudes*
   Syr. d.   *De syria dea*
   Vit. auct.   *Vitarum auctio*
Lysias
   Or.   *Orations*
Macrobius
   Sat.   *Saturnalia*
Marcus Aurelius
   Med.   *Meditations*
Martial
   Epigr.   *Epigrams*
   Lib. spect.   *Liber spectaculorum*
Menander Rhetor
   Or.   *Orations*
Musonius Rufus
   Disc.   *Discourse*
Nag Hammadi Codices
   Gos. Truth   XII,*2 Gospel of Truth*
Nepos
   Att.   *Atticus*
Origen
   Cels.   *Contra Celsum*
Ovid
   Am.   *Amores*
   Her.   *Heroides*
   Metam.   *Metamorphoses*
Palladius
   Insit.   *De insitione*
Paulus
   Sent.   *Sententiae*

Pausanius
   Descr.   *Description of Greece*

Persius Flaccus
   Sat.   *Satirae*

Petronius
   Sat.   *Satyricon*

Phaedrus
   Fab.   *Fables*

Philo
   Conf.   *De confusione linguarum*
   Contempl.   *De vita contemplativa*
   Her.   *Quis rerum divinarum heres sit*
   Leg.   *Legum allegoriae*
   Legat.   *Legatio ad Gaium*
   Migr.   *De migratione Abrahami*
   Mos.   *De vita Moysis*
   Mut.   *De mutatione nominum*
   Opif.   *De opificio mundi*
   Post.   *De posteritate Caini*
   Praem.   *De praemiis et poenis*
   Sobr.   *De sobrietate*
   Spec.   *De specialibus legibus*
   Somn.   *De somniis*
   Virt.   *De virtutibus*

Philo of Byzantium
   Seven   *On the Seven Wonders*

Philostratus
   Vit. Apoll.   *Vita Apollonii*

Photius
   Bib.   *Bibliotheca*

Pindar
   Nem.   *Nemean Odes*
   Ol.   *Olympian Odes*
   Pyth.   *Pythian Odes*

Plato
   Alc. maj.   *Alcibiades major*
   Apol.   *Apologia*
   Leg.   *Leges*
   Lys.   *Lysis*
   Phaedr.   *Phaedrus*
   Prot.   *Protagoras*
   Resp.   *Respublica*
   Symp.   *Symposium*
   Tim.   *Timaeus*

Plautus
   Merc.   *Mercator*

Stich.	*Sticus*
Truc.	*Truculentus*

Pliny the Elder
Nat.	*Natural History*

Pliny the Younger
Ep.	*Epistulae*
Pan.	*Panegyricus*

Plutarch
Adol. poet. aud.	*Quomodo adolescens poetas audire debeat*
Adul. amic.	*Quomodo adulator ab amico internoscator*
Aem.	*Aemilius Paullus*
Alex.	*Alexander*
Amat.	*Amatorius*
Amat. narr.	*Amatoriae narrationes*
An virt. doc.	*An virtus doceri possit*
Apoph. lac.	*Apophthegmata laconica*
Caes.	*Caesar*
Cam.	*Camillus*
Cat. Maj.	*Cato Major*
Cat. Min.	*Cato Minor*
Def. orac.	*De defectu oraculorum*
Fab.	*Fabius Maximus*
Garr.	*De garrulitate*
Lib. ed.	*De liberis educandis*
Mor.	*Moralia*
Pomp.	*Pompeius*
Praec. ger. rei publ.	*Praecepta gerendae rei publicae*
Pyrrh.	*Pyrrhus*
Pyth. orac.	*De Pythiae oraculis*
Quaest. conv.	*Quaestionum convivialum libri IX*
Sull.	*Sulla*
Superst.	*De superstitione*
Ti. C. Gracch.	*Tiberius et Caius Gracchus*
Virt. mor.	*De virtute morali*
Virt. prof.	*Quomodo quis suos in virtute sentiat profectus*

Polybius
Hist.	*Histories*

Pomponius Mela
Chor.	*De chorographia*

Procopius
Hist.	*History of the Wars of Justinian*

Propertius
Eleg.	*Elegies*

Quintilian
Inst.	*Institutio oratoria*

Sallust
   Bell. Cat.   *Bellum catilinae*
   Bell. Jug.   *Bellum jugurthinum*

Seneca
   Ad Helv.   *Ad Helviam*
   Ben.   *De beneficiis*
   Clem.   *De clementia*
   Const.   *De constantia sapientis*
   Ep.   *Epistulae morales*
   Helv.   *Ad Helviam*
   Ira   *De ira*
   Nat.   *Naturales quaestiones*
   Prov.   *De providentia*
   Vit. beat.   *De vita beata*

Pseudo-Socrates
   Ep.   *Epistles*

Sophocles
   Phil.   *Philoctetes*

Soranus
   Gyn.   *Gynaecology*

Statius
   Silv.   *Silvae*

Strabo
   Geog.   *Geography*

Suetonius
   Aug.   *Divus Augustus*
   Cal.   *Gaius Caligula*
   Claud.   *Divus Claudius*
   Dom.   *Domitianus*
   Gramm.   *De grammaticis*
   Jul.   *Divus Julius*
   Tib.   *Tiberius*
   Tit.   *Divus Titus*
   Vesp.   *Vespasianus*

Synesius
   Ep.   *Epistles*

Tacitus
   Agr.   *Agricola*
   Ann.   *Annales*
   Dial.   *Dialogus de oratoribus*
   Hist.   *Historiae*
   Oct.   *Octavia*

Terence
   Phor.   *Phormio*

Tertullian
   Apol.   *Apologeticus*

Spect.	De spectaculis
Res.	De resurrectione carnis
Thucydides	
Hist.	History
Tibullus	
Corp.	Corpus
Valerius Harpocration	
Lex.	Lexicon
Valerius Maximus	
Memor.	Memorabilium
Varro	
Rust.	De re rustica
Vegetius	
Epit.	Epitome rei militaris
Velleius	
Rom. Hist.	Roman History
Vettius Valens	
Anth.	Anthologiarum libri
Virgil	
Aen.	Aeneid
Vitruvius	
Arch.	De architectura
Xenophon	
Anab.	Anabasis
Cyr.	Cyropaedia
Lac.	Respublica Lacedaemoniorum
Mem.	Memorabilia
Vect.	De vectigalibus
Xenophon Ephesius	
Eph.	Ephesiaca

PERIODICALS, JOURNALS, AND OTHER REFERENCES

AE	Année épigraphique
AHR	American Historical Review
AJA	American Journal of Archaeology
AJAH	American Journal of Ancient History
AJP	American Journal of Philology
AncSoc	Ancient Society
ANRW	Aufstieg und Niedergang der römischen Welt: Geschichte und Kultur Roms in Spiegel der neueren Forschung. Ed. H. Temporini, W. Haase. Berlin, 1972–
AV	Authorized Version (King James Version)
BA	Biblical Archaeologist

BAGD	Bauer, W., W. F. Arndt, F. W. Gingrich, and F. W. Danker. *Greek-English Lexicon of the New Testament and Other Early Christian Literature.* 2d ed. Chicago, 1979
BAR	*Biblical Archaeology Review*
BBR	*Bulletin for Biblical Research*
BC	*The Beginnings of Christianity.* Ed. F. J. Foakes Jackson and K. Lake. 5 vols. London, 1920–1933
Bib	*Biblica*
BTB	*Biblical Theology Bulletin*
BZ	*Biblische Zeitschrift*
CAH	*The Cambridge Ancient History.* Ed. J. B. Bury, S. A. Cook, F. E. Adcock (vols. 1–6), S. A. Cook, F. E. Adcock, M. P. Charlesworth (vols. 7–11) with N. H. Baynes (vol. 12). 12 vols. Cambridge, 1953–1965
CBQ	*Catholic Biblical Quarterly*
CIG	*Corpus inscriptionum graecarum.* Ed. A Boeckh. 4 vols. Berlin, 1828–1877
CIL	*Corpus inscriptionum latinarum*
CP	*Classical Philology*
CQ	*Classical Quarterly*
CSSH	*Comparative Studies in Social History*
DB	*Dictionary of the Bible.* Ed. J. Hastings. 5 vols. Edinburgh, 1898
DSS	Dead Sea Scrolls
EGT	*Expositor's Greek New Testament.* Ed. W. R. Nicoll. 5 vols. London, 1897–1910
EHR	*Economic History Review*
EMC	*Echos du monde classique*
EncJud	*Encyclopaedia Judaica.* 16 vols. Jerusalem, 1972
ERE	*Encyclopaedia of Religion and Ethics.* Ed. James Hastings. 12 vols. Edinburgh, 1908–1927
ExpT	*Expository Times*
Hesperia	*Hesperia: Journal of the American School of Classical Studies at Athens*
HTR	*Harvard Theological Review*
IDB	*Interpreter's Dictionary of the Bible.* Ed. G. A. Buttrick. 4 vols. Nashville, 1962
IG	*Inscriptiones graecae.* 1873–
IGR	*Inscriptiones graecae ad res romanas pertinentes.* Ed. R. Cagnat et al. Chicago, 1975
ILR	*Israel Law Review*
Int	*Interpretation*
JASA	*Journal of the Acoustical Society of America*
JB	Jerusalem Bible

JBL	*Journal of Biblical Literature*
JEBH	*Journal of Economic and Business History*
JETS	*Journal of the Evangelical Theological Society*
JRelS	*Journal Religion Studies*
JRS	*Journal of Roman Studies*
JSNT	*Journal for the Study of the New Testament*
JTS	*Journal of Theological Studies*
LSJ	Liddell, H. G., R. Scott, H. S. Jones, *A Greek-English Lexicon.* 9th ed. with revised supplement. Oxford, 1996
LXX	Septuagint
MAMA	*Monumenta Asiae Minoris antiqua.* Manchester and London, 1928–1993
MGLex	*A Manual Greek Lexicon of the New Testament.* G. Abbott-Smith. Edinburgh, 1954
MM	Moulton, J. H., and G. Milligan. *The Vocabulary of the Greek Testament.* London, 1930. Reprint, Peabody, Mass., 1997
MOFFATT	*The New Testament: A New Translation.* J. Moffatt
NIBC	New International Biblical Commentary
NIDNTT	*New International Dictionary of New Testament Theology.* Ed. C. Brown. 4 vols. Grand Rapids, 1975–1985
NIV	New International Version
NovT	*Novum Testamentum*
NT	New Testament
NTS	*New Testament Studies*
OCD	*Oxford Classical Dictionary.* Ed. N. G. L. Hammond and H. H. Scullard. 2d ed. Oxford, 1970
OT	Old Testament
PBSR	*Papers of the British School at Rome*
PG	Patrologia graeca. Ed. J.-P. Migne. 162 vols. Paris, 1857–1886
RAC	*Reallexikon für Antike und Christentum.* Ed. T Kluser et al. Stuttgart, 1950–
RIDA	*Revue internationale des droits de l'antiquité*
RSV	Revised Standard Version
RV	Revised Version
SBLSP	Society of Biblical Literature *Seminar Papers*
SBT	*Studia biblica et theologica*
SJT	*Scottish Journal of Theology*
ST	*Studia theologica*
TAPA	*Transactions of the American Philological Association*
TB	*Tyndale Bulletin*
TDNT	*Theological Dictionary of the New Testament.* Ed. G. Kittel and G. Friedrich. Trans. G. W. Bromiley. 10 vols. Grand Rapids, 1964–1976

TJ	*Trinity Journal*
TJT	*Taiwan Journal of Theology*
TLZ	*Theologische Literaturzeitung*
USQR	*Union Seminary Quarterly Review*
YCS	*Yale Classical Studies*
ZNW	*Zeitschrift für die neutestamentliche Wissenschaft*

Introduction

This is a book about metaphors. It is not a book about metaphor in the abstract, and it is not a philosophical discussion about the nature or function of metaphor as such. It is about the particular metaphors of a particular man—Paul. It has the practical interest of explaining them by describing the world from which they were drawn. In general, metaphor is a way of presenting a truth that is wholly or partly unknown by likening it to something that is known to the person or persons under instruction.[1] A metaphor is an aid to the perception of a truth (its intuitive recognition). It helps us to "get a handle" on a truth, but it does not necessarily furnish an explanation, certainly not a complete explanation, of the truth in question. Paul's forensic metaphor of justification, for example, illustrates and helps us to comprehend the great truth that through Christ God is able to accept the otherwise unacceptable. But it may not explain the actual process whereby he has been able to do it. Some, of course, say that it does—that justification is not a metaphor but describes what has actually happened. I prefer to regard it still as a metaphor,[2] although it does raise the possibility that one metaphor may stand closer to reality than another, that is, that it offers more in the way of explanation than another, and justification may well be a case in point. Insofar as a metaphor is a metaphor, it must always be distinguished in some degree from the truth to which it is pointing. It is an aid to understanding, but always, beyond the metaphor, there lies a reality that is more than the metaphor. This difference between understanding a truth, on the one hand (getting a handle on it), and explaining it, on the other, is sometimes the source of two errors (which we will try to avoid):

> First, there is the error of failing to perceive the distinction, which results in a distortion of our knowledge and appreciation of the truth. Secondly, the opposite error is to allow the distinction too much prominence, and to recoil from

analogies and metaphors as merely shadows, with a consequent impoverish-
ment of the understanding.[3]

Metaphor lies at the very root of our language. All language, it seems, like
the writing in which it is often expressed, began with the picture. Languages
live by adding new pictures to old. It is probably true to say that most of our
words started out as figures of speech that with use moved from the category of
conscious metaphor into the ranks of ordinary words.[4] A. T. Robertson asks,
"Is it not true that words are metaphors, sometimes with the pictured flower
still blooming, sometimes with the blossom blurred?"[5]—for example, in the
ideas "to owe" or "to reckon," images from the business world that, by constant use, have largely lost their metaphorical impact (see our discussion of these
images on pp. 180–84). The difficulty in attempting to identify and discuss the
metaphors of a man who lived so long ago is to know where to draw the line
between the "blooming" and the "blurred." There is a considerable body of
Pauline material that can be confidently regarded as metaphorical in the sense
that it was deliberately used as such by the apostle. But there is much that falls
into the category of the "blurred," and difficult decisions sometimes have to be
made as to what should and should not be discussed.

Regarding terminology, no distinction is intended, for example, between
the terms "metaphor" and "analogy," "image" and "figure," and so on. The
changes are rung simply for the sake of variety. If the term expresses a likeness
and appears to have been deliberately used by Paul for that purpose, then for
the purposes of this discussion it comes under the heading of metaphor.

Metaphors open a window on the world of those who employ them.
The prophet whose images were of pastures stricken by drought (Amos 1:2),
of the hungry lion roaring for prey, and of the shepherd finding the remains
of its prey—a few bones and an ear of a sheep (3:4, 12)—was himself a man
of the country, a shepherd. If metaphors are an index to their user's world, it
is equally true that a knowledge of that world is necessary to understand well
and appreciate his or her metaphors. Aristotle, rightly or wrongly, observed
that "everything said metaphorically is unclear."[6] To the extent that he was
right, it is incumbent on us, if we are to clarify what is unclear, to know the
context from which the image is drawn—to make ourselves as much at home
as we can with the image. We must try to keep in step, so to speak, with the
author and to see the matter of which he is speaking as he sees it himself.
Paul and the other biblical writers

> did not write independently of the circumstances with which they were sur-
> rounded, or of the tastes, pursuits, and habits of their time. If they had done so,
> they would have been unintelligible when they wrote. And they will only be ap-
> proximately intelligible to us, unless we have the means of re-setting the words
> in their true associations.[7]

This is the task before us—to understand as much of Paul's world as we
can in order to understand the metaphors that he employs. "Our her-
meneutical problem," as J. A. Harrill expressed it, "is how to direct social

history, now enjoying something of an upsurge in interest, back to the interpretation of texts, the main function of the exegete."[8]

With Paul we move, both culturally and geographically, from the East
to the West. The oriental ethos of the Old Testament, and even of the Gospels and some of the other New Testament letters, is in large part left behind
as we enter the mainstream of the Greco-Roman world.

> His figurative language, very different from that of Jesus, the Galilean, which
> . . . is full of country life, reflects the life of the great cities of antiquity; we see in
> it the games of the stadium, military affairs, slavery, legal practice and the law
> courts, then the theatre, home and family life, building, handicrafts, com-
> merce, sea voyaging. . . . Illustrations taken from country life are, on the other
> hand, but few and mostly more conventional than the others.[9]

Paul's Jewish roots are still evident and constitute the structure and
content of his theology, although the content of his theology was radically
reoriented by the Christ event (he "had found a new position with regard to God, not a new doctrine of God"[10]). Sometimes his medium—his
metaphors—reflects the Jewishness of his upbringing; for example, he portrays himself as the "friend" of the bride or sees the olive as a symbol of the
people of God. But in the main his figurative language is drawn, as
Deissmann observes, from the wider world into which he was born and to
which he was sent (cf. Acts 9:15). Much of this book, therefore, has to do
with the life and times of the Roman Empire. Yet it is not a social history as
such, nor is it an out-and-out commentary on the letters of Paul, although it
touches on both social history and commentary.

I have organized the metaphors thematically, moving from city life to
country life to family life, and so on, and have attempted (1) to outline
enough of the background to bring them to life and (2) to show how Paul
has applied them in his letters. The book is designed to be accessible to the
general reader, who may or may not have background in the Bible, as well as
useful to the scholar. The translations of Bible texts are my own. This has
sometimes allowed me to draw out the point that I want. I have tried to be
faithful to the Greek text and have gone for the "dynamic equivalent" translation rather than a word-for-word one. The endnotes help those who want
to go further. They include a great deal of additional information and serve
as a guide to further reading. They also presuppose a knowledge of New
Testament Greek. Where a word in the main text is shown in boldface, it is a
metaphor, presented in the English equivalent of the Greek word Paul used.
Because not all readers will be familiar with the history and the literature of
the ancient world, two appendices have been added: one giving a select
chronology of the Roman Empire, the other brief biographies of the ancient
authors cited in this book.

To write anything about Paul is to run the risk of stirring up the hor-
nets' nest of what precisely constitutes the Pauline corpus. I could have
avoided this, of course, by simply labeling my book *The Metaphors of the*

Letters Traditionally Attributed to Paul (with the exception of Hebrews). But I believe that there is a case for the Pauline authorship of those letters whose authorship is sometimes questioned, especially if one allows that authorship need not mean that the author himself set pen to paper. We know, for example, that Tertius penned Romans (Rom 16:22), and if, in some instances, the amanuensis, or scribe, was allowed a greater freedom of expression than may have been the case with Tertius, that would go some way to explaining the stylistic peculiarities of Ephesians and the Pastorals, while there is nothing in the matters treated in any of the supposedly doubtful letters or in their apparent circumstances that cannot be accounted for in Pauline terms. It is as much, then, a matter of conviction as of convenience that in this book I have accepted the traditional ascriptions of authorship to Paul. Additionally, I have made an occasional foray into the Pauline speeches of Acts, believing that they express the gist of what was said on their various occasions by the apostle and often preserve his actual words.

This book is historical and exegetical rather than philosophical. But it is also homiletical in purpose; that is, it is written with an eye to Christian preaching, taking preaching in the broadest sense to be the communication of the Christian gospel. All Christians have a responsibility to share what they know of the gospel, while recognizing that some, by virtue of their gifts and calling, are better placed than others to shoulder this responsibility. Christians especially should make every effort to understand the Bible and, at its heart, the gospel and to communicate that understanding clearly, intelligibly to their audience. Christian pastors, leaders, teachers, therefore, if they are worth their salt, must all the time be inventing new metaphors by which to present the gospel to the people of their own day (although old metaphors, in this case Paul's, can still do sterling service).[11] In short, our work is to move from understanding to intelligible communication—from exegesis to homiletics—otherwise we are no more than antiquarians, groping about among the dead and dusty facts of ancient history.

NOTES

1. C. E. Gunton, *The Actuality of Atonement: A Study of Metaphor, Rationality, and the Christian Tradition* (Grand Rapids: Eerdmans, 1989), 27, underlines the difficulty of defining a metaphor by referring to a book published in 1964 (before the debate on the role of metaphor in theology took off), which even then could list 125 definitions. I have chosen to work with Aristotle's classic definition of a metaphor (which has its own problems of ambiguity) as "the application of an alien name by transfer" (*Poet.* 1457b.7–8 = 21.7) and to allow "metaphor" to cover any comparison that appears to have been deliberately drawn.

2. This debate simply illustrates the way in which a word can move from being a metaphor to being accepted as expressing the literal meaning. What is the difference? Not that the word now mirrors its object as once it did not, but that *it has now come to be accepted as the primary use of the term.* The question is, Has justification, for Paul, made that transition, or is it still one of a number of conscious metaphors of

the way in which God has acted toward us? Would Paul have spoken of a human judge in these terms? Does he see justification differently from, say, adoption?

3. F. Lyall, "Of Metaphors and Analogies: Legal Language and Covenant Theology," *SJT* 32 (1979): 2. Cf. S. Sawatzky, "Church Images and Metaphorical Theology," *TJT* 6 (1984): 110:

> In our modern world where we are taught to discover things as they really are by the behavioral and empirical sciences, the metaphorical is suspected and disregarded for its connotation of non-empirical reality, its evocative, expressive and indirect manner of speaking. Doing theology metaphorically appears to be unsuited to the serious and propositional character of theological language, and further, the prejudice against metaphor views it as too subjective and emotional for yielding genuine insights.

See also, e.g., G. B. Caird, *The Language and Imagery of the Bible* (Philadelphia: Westminster, 1980), especially his section on metaphor, 131–97; Gunton, *Actuality of Atonement*, esp. his discussion of metaphor and theological language, 27–52; G. Backman, *Meaning by Metaphor: An Exploration of Metaphor with a Metaphoric Reading of Two Stories by Stephen Crane* (Uppsala: Almquist & Wiksell International, 1991), esp. 17–82.

4. Gunton, *Actuality of Atonement*, 34, cites the example of "muscle," from the Latin *musculus*, "a little mouse." "No-one now thinks of those associations," he says, "but that is because it has been so successful. When it first emerged as a metaphor it succeeded precisely because in an indirect way (i.e., as a picture) it enabled physiologists to name and begin to understand one part of the anatomy."

5. A. T. Robertson, *Word Pictures in the New Testament* (New York: Richard R. Smith, 1930–1933; repr. Nashville, Tenn.: Broadman & Holman, 1973), 1:1, x.

6. Παν γὰρ ἀσαφὲς τὸ κατὰ μεταφορὰν λεγόμενον (*Top.* 139b.34).

7. J. S. Howson, *The Metaphors of St Paul* (London: Strahan, 1868), 42. Cf. W. A. Meeks, *The First Urban Christians: The Social World of the Apostle Paul* (New Haven: Yale University Press, 1983), 1–2, who complains of "the air of unreality that pervades much of the recent scholarly literature about the New Testament and early Christianity. A clear symptom of the malaise is the isolation of New Testament study from other kinds of historical scholarship—not only from secular study of the Roman Empire, but even from church history." Similarly R. L. Wilken: "In the study of Roman history there has been a burgeoning interest in the religions of the Roman world, in Graeco-Roman philosophy, and in the social world of the early Roman Empire. Yet little of this material actually makes its way into the general accounts of early Christianity" (*The Christians as the Romans Saw Them* [New Haven: Yale University Press, 1984], xiv). Others too lend their voices in protest against the blindness of New Testament scholarship to the world of the New Testament (see, e.g., F. F. Bruce, "The New Testament and Classical Studies," *NTS* 22 [1976]: 229–42; A. J. Malherbe, *Social Aspects of Early Christianity* [Baton Rouge: Louisiana State University Press, 1977]; G. Kennedy, "Classical and Christian Source Criticism," in *The Relationships among the Gospels: An Interdisciplinary Dialogue* [ed. W. O. Walker; San Antonio: Trinity University Press, 1978], 125–55). In some part I hope to address this myopia.

8. J. A. Harrill, *The Manumission of Slaves in Early Christianity* (Tübingen: Mohr, 1995), 2.

9. A. Deissmann, *Paul: A Study in Social and Religious History* (London: Hodder & Stoughton, 1926), 71. Cf. W. A. Meeks: "The city breathes through [Paul's] language. Jesus' parables of sowers and weeds, sharecroppers, and mud-roofed cottages call forth smells of manure and earth, and the Aramaic of the Palestinian villages often echoes in the Greek. When Paul constructs a metaphor of olive

trees or gardens, on the other hand, the Greek is fluent and evokes schoolroom more than farm" (*First Urban Christians*, 9).

10. Deissmann, *Paul*, 188.

11. T. Williams, in reviewing C. E. Gunton's *The Actuality of Atonement*, suggests that "the question for another book is how far new metaphors can be developed to express the actuality of atonement now in ways that do not displace but complement those of the past" (in *Scottish Journal of Theology* 43 [3, 1990]: 403). In this connection, we note Aristotle's observation that to create good metaphors is a mark of genius (*Poet.* 1459a.7 = 22.17).

i

Life in the City

No century before the twentieth has been more urban in character than the first. Certainly, in the Mediterranean world of the first century, the world of Rome and its empire, the city was dominant. The Romans, it is said, "did not feel at home in the country. To feel at home they needed a city,"[1] and in this regard, Paul was a child of his time. He was preeminently a man of the city: a citizen of Rome, born in Tarsus, itself "no ordinary city" (Acts 21:39), and a missionary to most of the great urban centers of his world.[2]

THE THREAT OF THE CITY

The city was no place for the timid. Forty years after Paul met his end in Rome, Juvenal (ca. 50–127 CE) described that city as a grim, hostile, and dangerous place. Rome was no exception in this regard. Paul arrived in Corinth, as perhaps in other cities on his itinerary, in "fear and with much trembling" (1 Cor 2:3). There was probably a spiritual dimension to this trepidation, but there were also practical reasons for feeling afraid of the city—any city. It is true that Corinth had a particularly bad reputation, which may or may not have been deserved. To some extent, it was probably a hangover from a seamier past. There is also a suspicion that Athenian propaganda had something to do with it—the fruits of commerce are often envied by those who are devoted to culture. Nevertheless, Corinth was a rip-roaring town, in which, so Horace says (65–8 BCE), "none but the tough could survive."[3] And yet the Corinth that Paul knew was probably no worse than any other city of that time. All cities were dangerous places, and in them all fear was endemic.

DARKNESS AND LIGHT

The night especially was a time to be afraid. As dusk fell, the city shut down and anyone who ventured out after "closing" was at risk. Juvenal laments that to go out to supper in Rome without having first made your will was to be guilty of an act of gross negligence.[4] The pages of the *Digest* show how real and pervasive was the danger that Romans faced from murderers and housebreakers and muggers. At night the city's narrow streets were plunged into impenetrable darkness. Little or no attempt was made at lighting them.[5] Night fell over the city—any city—like the shadow of a great danger, and most people fled to their homes, shut themselves in, and barricaded their doors. But some welcomed the night as a cloak for their deeds.

Paul enlists their actions—orgies and drunkenness, sexual indulgence and debauchery—as a metaphor of immoral conduct in general, "the works of darkness," he calls them, "**darkness**" characterizing "the children of this age" and "**light**" the children of God.[6] At Christ's return "he will bring to light the things cloaked by darkness, that is, he will expose the inner thoughts of people's hearts" (1 Cor 4:5). We are "children of light, children of the day. We are not of the night or of darkness" (1 Thess 5:5). Christians, says Paul, were once "darkness," but now are "light in the Lord," a reference to their status. He follows with a plea concerning their practice: "Walk [live] as children of the light" (Eph 5:8).

He also employed "**the thief in the night**" as an image of Jesus' return (1 Thess 5:4). It was chiefly at night, of course, under the cover of darkness, that thieves did their work, but here the thought is more of the unexpectedness of Jesus' coming than of the time. Like the thief, he will come when people least expect him. This appears to be a reminiscence of a saying of Jesus himself.[7]

Doors were commonly barred against thieves and the like, but Paul spoke of doors that were sometimes, surprisingly, opened. When Paul and Barnabas returned to Antioch from what we call the first missionary journey, they gathered the church together and gave an account of what they had done. But they acknowledged that the achievement was not so much theirs as God's, for he "had opened **the door**[8] of faith to the Gentiles" (Acts 14:27; cf. 11:18). The focus of attention in this verse is on the hearers and their God-given response to the gospel. With this compare Acts 16:14, where God opened Lydia's heart to give heed to what Paul was saying (see also Rev 3:7). Elsewhere Paul uses the same figure, but with reference to the preachers. Thus, in describing his work in Ephesus, he declares that "a great door for effective work" had opened to him (1 Cor 16:9).[9] Again, in 2 Cor 2:12 he says that at Troas "a door had been opened"[10] to him "in the Lord" (this implies "by the Lord," but the sense is "in the course of his work for the Lord"). The same metaphor, but expressed in different terms, is found again in 1 Thess 1:9 and 2:1, as Paul speaks of his "**entrance**"[11] into Macedonia with the gospel. In Col 4:3 he asks for prayer that God would "open a door" for him and his colleagues in Rome that even there, in the imperial city, they might "proclaim the mystery of Christ." He wrote this letter, as far as we know, from behind a locked door in that city, a prisoner of Rome. He was not free to go in and out, but under God no door is barred to the gospel.

THE SQUALOR OF THE CITY

The urban sprawl is a modern phenomenon, the product of our ease of movement. But the cities of Paul's day, lacking our ability to transport people quickly over long distances, were condemned to remain within narrowly defined territorial limits (other factors, such as defense, were also important). People had to be within reasonable walking distance of all that they needed. Consequently, when their populations expanded, the cities could not match that expansion by extending their boundaries. They were driven instead to grow upwards rather than outwards, with the buildings crammed together and often reached by only the narrowest of streets. By the third century BCE, three-story buildings were not uncommon in Rome. By the first century CE, a height limit of six to eight stories was being imposed for reasons of safety.[12] Rome was a city of skyscrapers (to a greater extent than we usually imagine), as were many other cities of that time. There is evidence, for example, of multistory buildings in Ephesus,[13] while the height of the buildings in some of the more crowded cities of the East, such as Aradus and Tyre on the Syrian coast, drew the surprised comments of Strabo and Pomponius Mela. Strabo notes that the houses of Tyre were almost higher than those of Rome itself.[14]

For the most part, these high-rise developments were tenement buildings (*insulae*) containing many rooms (*cenacula*) into which were crowded the poor. These tenements might also include (not invariably) some larger apartments for the rich, probably on or near ground level. Only the wealthy had access to the few detached or semidetached houses to be found in the city (*domus*, plural *domūs*).[15] But there were no separate neighborhoods for rich and poor. The *domūs* of the rich and the *insulae* of the poor stood side by side, alternating oddly with public buildings, warehouses, and workshops. Rome was "continually forced to juxtapose her splendid monuments to an incoherent confusion of dwelling-houses . . . separated by a network of gloomy, narrow alleys."[16] Paul's reference in 1 Cor 3:12 implies that this confusion of buildings existed in other cities as well—a confusion that he saw as analogous to the quality of the work of Christian teachers and of the lives of those whom they taught.[17]

Burdensome rents ensured that the *insulae* were always teeming with people. The leasee of the upper floors would sublet, and those tenants would sublet in turn. The poorest people lived on the highest floors and were subject to a breathless overcrowding. In the Subura, the valley between the Viminal and the Esquiline hills of Rome, its poorest and most crowded district, people elbowed their way through presses of bodies so great that traffic through the narrow streets progressed at only a snail's pace. Dust, rubbish, and filth accumulated. The stench was overwhelming, and bugs ran riot. A character in Petronius's novel, hiding under his miserable mattress, was obliged to press his face against bedding that was black and crawling with lice.[18] And while the Subura may have been the poorest district of Rome, it was by no means the only district in which such conditions prevailed, nor was Rome the only city in which they could be found. The Christians meeting in a third-floor room in Troas (Acts 20:7–12) were almost certainly poor and living in an environment not unlike the Subura, crowded and dirty.

Other factors exacerbated the problems of overcrowding. One was a shortage of water. The Romans were skilled at bringing water into their cities. According to Frontinus (ca. 30–104 CE), in the time of Trajan eight aqueducts brought more than 200 million gallons of water a day into Rome.[19] Most other major cities would have had a comparable supply. This water went to public fountains, public toilets, and was then discarded into rivers and seas. Very little was channeled into people's homes, and then only to a favored few who lived at ground level. The poet Martial (ca. 40–140 CE) complains that his townhouse lacked water even though he lived close to an aqueduct.[20] The unfortunate tenants on the upper floors of the *insulae* had to draw their water from the nearest fountain or well and carry it to their rooms or buy it at the door from a carrier. Indeed, the water carriers *(aquarii)* were regarded (at least by the third century CE) as part of the *insula* itself—as a kind of human plumbing. Like the porters *(ostiarii)* and the sweepers *(zetarii)*, they were bought and sold with the building.[21] In short, "the lack of plentiful water for washing invited the tenants of many a Roman *cenacula* to allow filth to accumulate, and it was inevitable that many succumbed to the temptation."[22]

REFUSE

Another problem was the difficulty of sewage disposal. Rome had well-constructed sewers that were large enough to be traversed throughout their entire length by boat.[23] But the system only collected the outfall of a few private houses and of public lavatories that dotted its routes. Most people had either to use the lavatories (at a small fee) or to dispose of their sewage as best they could. They might clatter down the stairs to empty their pot in the vat provided by the landlord or find the nearest dung pit outside (travelers could reputedly smell Rome before reaching it). But there were always some who found the stairs too steep or the hour too late and, to save themselves further trouble, would empty their pots from a window into the street. So much the worse for the passerby who happened upon the wrong place at the wrong time! The evidence suggests that this occurred with some regularity.[24]

Filth was a fact of life in the city and Paul found illustrations in this fact. As the world regards them, he said, the apostles were the **scum**[25] of the earth, the **offscouring**[26] of the world (1 Cor 4:13). The apostle seems to be lifting the curtain on his own deepest feelings—the hurt that he felt at the negative response his ministry often elicited and perhaps at his current situation in Ephesus.[27] The Greek words that Paul employs here are rare, and they only occur in the New Testament in this passage. It has been suggested that "scum" *(perikatharma)* refers to the dust that is swept from the floor and that "offscouring" *(peripsēma)* refers to the dirt that is rubbed or scraped off an object. But this may be too fine a distinction. Probably, in general application, they both mean much the same, the dirt that comes from a good cleanup.

The "scum" and "offscouring" of Paul's metaphor may have been suggested to him by the condition of the cities in which he lived. But he may also have a quite different and specific reference in mind, in which the words point to the *process* rather than to the *product* of cleansing. In this sense, both words have an association with sacrifice—in particular, with human sacrifice for the expiation of sin. This may be the reference in LXX Prov 21:18: "A wicked man becomes a *perikatharma* [a purification (?)], for a good man."[28] The only other known occurrence of the word is in a context in which human lives were sacrificed on behalf of others. Epictetus tells of the custom in ancient Athens of throwing into the sea men who were deemed to be worthless, *perikatharma* (cf. Paul's "scum of the earth"), as an offering to appease the gods in times of plague or of some other disaster.[29] (Significantly, the second of Paul's two expressions in 1 Cor 4:13 was also used on such occasions: "Be a *peripsēma* [a purification] for us.")[30] The rationale behind this custom is further explained by B. H. McLean:

> When the normal functioning of a society was threatened by plague, draught, famine or military defeat, such threats were often interpreted as the manifestation of curses, a kind of pollution that resulted from transgression. Once in existence, a curse would work itself out on the society, unless a substitute victim was provided upon whom it may be discharged. A *pharmakos* was required to stand as substitute for the community and bear its curse in its place. The *pharmakos*, bearing this infectious pollution must either be banished or killed. In either case, the final goal of permanently excluding the *pharmakos* from society is accomplished.[31]

Something akin to the occasional practice outlined above took place on a regular basis. The Athenians annually, so we are told, expelled (slaughtered?) two *pharmakoi* during the month of Thargelion.[32] A similar ritual was practiced at Ephesus, where the *pharmakos*, who was deemed to be bearing that city's sins, was given a meal and then beaten. Wherever it was practiced and in whatever form it was found, for Paul the custom belonged to the distant past. And yet the memory of it still lingered. "On the subject of the common man's familiarity with these rituals, an examination of the sources will reveal that the textual witnesses to the *pharmakos* rituals are evenly spread over a period of more than eight hundred years, straddling, more or less evenly, the period of Paul's life."[33] Because 1 Cor 4:13 includes words associated with these ancient rituals, Paul may have intended his readers to see the connection. In the eyes of the world the apostles may have been "scum," but they were such "scum" or "offscouring" as the *pharmakoi* had been whose lives were spent for the good of others.

If Paul could apply the idea of the *pharmakos* to himself and his colleagues, why not also to Christ? The extent to which he was dependent on the sacrificial concepts of the Jewish cultus in forming and expressing his understanding of Christ's work is debated. Of course, the cultus played some part in his thinking—how could he not be influenced by something so fundamental to the culture in which he was nurtured? He certainly drew on sacrificial images for some of his metaphors. But in his proclamation of Christ Paul was not averse to borrowing from other cultures besides his own, and this may be the case with some of his most important soteriological statements, for example, that Christ "became a curse for us" (Gal 3:13) and "was made to be sin on our behalf" (2 Cor 5:21; cf. Rom 8:3). There are difficulties in squaring some of what he says here with his own Jewish tradition,[34] whereas a case can be made for his looking to the language and the lore of the *pharmakos* ritual:

> First, it presupposes an understanding of the eradication of curses and sin which was well suited to Paul's own gospel. . . . Secondly, Paul was motivated by the urgent need to make the significance of Christ's ignominious death intelligible to potential Gentile converts. This would have entailed drawing upon symbols and religious practices from Graeco-Roman culture which would have been recognisable to the Gentile converts. . . . Thirdly, Paul lived in a culture (that of the Graeco-Roman world) where the suffering and death of animals had no meaning. Even the slaughter of sacrificial animals was not considered to be part of the actual ritual, but merely a preparatory act that prepared the carcass for the ritual to follow. The fact of the animal's death had no meaning in and of itself. How then could Christ's suffering and death be meaningfully interpreted in the light of the suffering and death of animals?[35]

Thus, the figure of the *pharmakos* was a far more suitable metaphor for understanding Christ's death. The *pharmakos* was a human being, and his suffering and death did have meaning for others. Whether this was, indeed, the background to Paul's presentation of Christ's saving work must remain an open question. There is no question, however, that the figure of the *pharmakos* would fit well with his image of Christ—the Christ who died on behalf of us all.

The world might consider Paul and his colleagues to be "scum" and "offscouring," but Paul could speak no less harshly of the world, or at least of the things that were valued most by the world, than it did of him. In doing so, he drew his language from what was undoubtedly the most conspicuous of a city's problems: its refuse. Like Christ, Paul was no ascetic who turned his back on ordinary human life. But compared with Christ, the things of the world were to Paul as **refuse**.[36] The Greek word in question *(skybala)* most often refers to waste food in one form or another, either as scraps from the table or as excrement: dog's meat or dung. It is found in Phil 3:8. Philippians 3:7–9 is characterized by the threefold use of the verb "to consider."[37] The first refers to his conversion, which turned his life upside down. What had once been most important to him he now considered to be "loss for the sake of Christ" (the perfect tense suggests that this remained the case). The second (in the present tense) affirms that he was still of this opinion,[38] and the third (again in the present) reinforces this affirmation, substituting "refuse" for "loss." For Christ's sake, he says, "I have lost all things. I consider them as refuse, as nothing more than excrement, that I may gain Christ and be found in him not having a righteousness of my own."

FIRE

A third problem for the city dweller was fire. Timber was used extensively in most buildings, and open fires were used for heating, lighting, and cooking. In conditions of gross overcrowding, fire was a constant threat to rich and poor alike. The rich trembled for their mansions, the poor lived in constant fear of flames invading their attics.[39] Juvenal was prepared to quit the city to escape it. "No, no!" he cried, "I must live where there is no fire and the night is free from alarms!"[40] A century later little had changed. Ulpian (d. 223 CE) declares that not a day passed in the capital without several outbreaks of fire.[41] Those who were rich enough to have troops of slaves to do their bidding might save something from the holocaust.[42] Most people were glad simply to escape with their lives. There were some attempts at fire fighting. Augustus created a corps of *vigiles* in the capital, fire-fighting night watchmen under the command of the *praefectus vigilum*,[43] but there was little that they or anyone could do once a fire had engulfed a building.[44] There was one fire, however, that Paul hoped would not be put out. "Do not **quench** the fire of the Spirit,"[45] he warned (1 Thess 5:19). He was speaking of the gifts of the Spirit, which the church in Thessalonica was attempting to "dampen down," particularly, as it appears, the gift of prophecy. This image of "quenching the Spirit" fits well with the familiar figure of the Spirit as a fire (e.g., Exod 3:2; 19:18; Ezek 1:13).

Paul's metaphor in 1 Cor 3:10–15 refers to the ever present threat of fire that hung over the cities of his world. The passage begins as a metaphor for teachers and teaching (the "builders" and their "materials") and then turns its attention to those who are taught (the "buildings") and the quality of Christian lives. Undoubtedly teachers play a major role in shaping lives and will answer for their contribution. But in the last resort, the responsibility for what Christians are lies with themselves. All will be called on to give an account of what they have done. Some will have "fine structures" to speak of (in terms of their likeness to Christ); others will speak with shame of "miserable dwellings." The latter (the thought now shifts from the buildings to their occupants) Paul likens to desperate city dwellers who on almost any day or night might be observed dashing for safety through the flames engulfing their homes. In the judgment, all Christians will escape with their lives (thanks to the "foundation"); but some will escape "as through fire,"[46] carrying little or nothing with them to show for all the time they have been "in Christ."[47]

The architectural confusion of the city, its splendid monuments rubbing shoulders with its more modest buildings, becomes for Paul (1 Cor 3:10–15) a metaphor of the varying achievements of Christian teachers—the unevenness in the quality of what they taught. There is a penalty both for shoddy work (v. 15; sermons, lectures, books, teaching, all as dry as dust, go up in flames!) and for shoddy teachers (v. 17). By sound teaching or otherwise, it is possible to build on the one "foundation," Jesus Christ, impressive structures of "gold, silver, precious stones," on the one hand, or disappointing structures of "wood, hay, stubble," on the other—lavish palaces or wretched shanties made of mud. The ancients made free use of gold in their palaces. Their marble and granite pillars are still the wonder of those who view them. In contrast, the wooden huts had hay and stubble mixed with mud to fill their cracks, and reeds to thatch their roofs. But the day will come, says Paul, when **fire**[48] will sweep through these "buildings" that Christian teachers have erected; on that day the quality of their work will be manifest to all "because the day will bring their work to light." The "day" is the day of Jesus' coming, when all things will come under his scrutiny.[49]

FOUNDATIONS

Evidence relating to the Roman *insulae* shows that the ground plan usually ranged between 350 and 475 square yards. Even if there were none smaller, which is highly unlikely, it is clear that such foundations were inadequate for the structures that they were expected to carry. "The lofty Roman buildings possessed no base corresponding to their height and a collapse was all the more to be feared since the builders, lured by greed of gain, tended to economise more and more at the expense of the strength of the masonry and the quality of the materials."[50] Here, then, was another hazard that the city dweller had to endure. "We inhabit a city," cried Juvenal, "propped up for the most part by slats: for that is how the landlord patches up the crack in the old wall, bidding the inmates sleep at ease under the ruin that hangs over their heads."[51] Good foundations were at a premium and Paul certainly understood their value. He saw himself, figuratively speaking, as a specialist in this field: "I laid a **foundation**,"[52] he says, "as an **expert builder**,"[53] and someone else is building on it" (1 Cor 3:10). The "foundation" was Christ. Paul speaks of Christ in similar terms in Eph 3:17 (combining a botanical metaphor with an architectural metaphor). Here he prays that his readers may be "rooted and have their **foundations laid** in love"[54] by having Christ dwell in their hearts.[55]

This is not the first time in Ephesians that Paul uses this image. Earlier in this letter he describes his readers as **"built on**[56] the foundation of the apostles and prophets, Christ Jesus himself being the chief cornerstone,[57] in whom the whole building is joined together and grows [another mixed architectural and botanical metaphor?] into a holy temple" (Eph 2:20–21). These verses furnish a striking example of how one word seems to set off a train of thought in Paul's mind. He speaks of the "household"[58] in verse 19, and suddenly the house itself seems to rise before him, from the foundation to the roof, and then transforms itself into a temple. This flight of fancy is not without its exegetical problems. For example, what precisely does he see as the foundation? The genitive, "of the apostles and prophets" could mean that it was the foundation of which they had spoken, namely, Christ, who is at the same time "the chief cornerstone." This would bring the passage into line with those mentioned above (1 Cor 3:10; Eph 3:17). But Paul is quite capable of flexibility in the use of his metaphors, and here he probably means that the apostles and prophets[59] were themselves the church's foundation, in the sense that they were its founding members, whose work, moreover, was fundamental in maintaining the "building" and keeping it intact.

Paul's flexibility in applying his metaphors is further exemplified in 2 Tim 2:19, in which the church itself is said to be "God's solid foundation." Here the word "overturn" seems to set off a train of thought. Heretical teachers had made the spurious claim that the (general) resurrection had already occurred. This teaching had the effect of overturning the faith of some people. Yet, says Paul, "God's solid foundation **stands firm**."[60] Whatever else he may have had in mind in using this image (the commentaries reflect some uncertainty as to his meaning), he is certainly asserting God's ownership of the "building" and his own conviction that God will ensure that his church remains "standing" and is kept in good order, despite the loss of some members. The emphasis of the passage is on the faithfulness of God,[61] who has put his "seal" on his people.

It was customary for a building to bear the architect's seal—a medallion exhibiting his name or his mark. There might also be an inscription naming the purpose for which it had been built. So the church bears **the mark**[62] of its maker. On it are the words "the Lord knows those who are his," accompanied by **the inscription** "let everyone who names the name of the Lord depart from wickedness." This passage echoes the story of Korah,[63] whose insolence to Moses led to his untimely and dramatic death, and so the inscription sounds, perhaps, a note of warning to avoid a punishment like his. The church *must* turn away from iniquity. The primary thrust of verse 19, however, is not to threaten but to make a positive statement about the

church: it *has* turned away from iniquity, the heretical teaching of Hymenaeus, Philetus, and others (2 Tim 2:17). But wickedness has many
guises. It must be eschewed in all of its forms and at all times by God's foundation, the church.

When Paul describes the apostles and prophets as the church's "foundation" (Eph 2:20), he named Christ as its "**cornerstone**."[64] This word is
found only twice in the New Testament, here and in 1 Pet 2:6. In the latter,
it appears in a direct quotation from LXX Isa 28:16, and the same Old Testament passage may underlie Paul's use of the word. But its precise meaning is
one of the problems facing the exegete in this verse. The usual sense of the
word may be illustrated from *T. Sol.* 22:7–8 and 23:2,[65] in which it is the
final stone that completes the building. But LXX Isa 28:16 identifies it instead with the foundations. Was Paul guided in his reference by the latter or
by the more usual meaning of the word?

If he was thinking of Christ as the foundation, it was in terms of the
great blocks that were used (in Eastern rather than in classical architecture)
at the corners of buildings, generally arranged lengthways and endways alternatively, giving the building strength and direction. These blocks were
sometimes of great length, frequently measuring up to four yards, but in one
instance in Jerusalem, in the southern wall of the temple platform, more
than twelve yards. It was just such a stone as this that furnished Isaiah with
his image of the Messiah. But the thought of Christ as the copestone—the
stone that caps off the building—has much to commend it, especially in a
letter to the Ephesians. The great stones that capped the temple of Artemis
in their city went a long way to making that structure one of the so-called
wonders of the world.[66] Theologically, too, Paul was well aware of the importance that must be given to Christ's eschatological role. Until he returns,
the church remains unfinished, awaiting its final redemption.[67] It is possible,
of course, that Paul is being deliberately ambiguous to allow room for both
interpretations. Jerome, for one, accepts this possibility: Christ "is the foundation *and* the top because in him the church is founded and finished."[68]
Nor is it unprecedented for Paul to give a metaphor a double meaning. We
see another instance in his image of Christ as the head, by which he means
that he is both the *source* of the body's growth (Eph 1:22; 4:15; 5:23 = the
foundation) and the *objective* of its growth (Eph 4:13ff. = the copestone): he
is its beginning and its end.[69]

Paul also uses the metaphor of foundations in Rom 15:20 and 1 Tim
6:19. In Rom 15:20 he states, as his missionary principle, that he will not
build "on someone else's foundation." In 1 Tim 6:19, he describes how the
rich should conduct themselves in this world. They should hang loose, he
says (not in those words, of course), to their riches, being "generous and
willing to share" and so storing up for themselves "a fine foundation for
what lies ahead." This is not a quid pro quo doctrine of salvation—"You
scratch my back," says the rich man to God, "and I'll scratch yours." Paul is
simply making the point that worldly wealth is not the Christian's true trea-

sure. Our treasure lies elsewhere, in heaven. There is no loss, then, in giving away what we have in this world. On the contrary, there is gain, for so we "lay hold of [in the sense of making it real by expressing it in what we do] the life that is life indeed." In short, to store up a "fine foundation" simply means to get into practice for what lies ahead. It is instructive to compare this with the sayings of Jesus in Luke 12:32–33: "Your Father has been pleased to give you the kingdom" ("By grace you have been saved"). "Sell your possessions and give to the poor. *Lay up a treasure in heaven*" (our response to God's grace—"saved . . . to do good works," practicing in the present the life of the hereafter).[70]

It may be no accident that all of the passages in which Paul speaks of foundations are in letters written to or from Ephesus (with one exception, Rom 15:20). On the outskirts of that city, by way of the Magnesian Gate, stood that great temple of Artemis, on whose foundations immense labor and vast sums of money had been spent. Philo of Byzantium gives an account of the work:

> The architect loosened the bottom of the underlying ground, then dug out trenches to a great depth and laid down the foundations underground. The quantity of masonry expended on the structures below the ground amounted to whole quarries of mountains. He ensured its unshakeable steadiness and, having previously set Atlas under the weight of the parts that would support the building, first he set down on the outside a base with ten steps and on that base he raised [the rest of the structure].[71]

Although, the work was done well before Paul's time, in the fourth century BCE, we can safely assume that what had gone into those foundations was still common knowledge, so that there may have been a particular association in Paul's mind between foundations and Ephesus.

BUILDING AND DEMOLITION

From the foundations of great public buildings Paul's thoughts move to the structures raised upon them. The stones of such buildings were shaped according to precise specifications instead of being chosen, as for humbler dwellings, simply because they happened to fit. The process was an elaborate one. It entailed preparing surfaces by cutting and rubbing, and testing them for flatness by means of a "canon," a straightedge that could show up any unevenness on the stone.

The canon served also as a measuring stick—it had measurements marked on it—and so "canon" came to have the general sense of a standard for making any judgment, in our terms a "benchmark." In most instances in the New Testament, it must be doubted that any metaphor is intended in the word, but 2 Cor 10:12–16 may be an exception. Here in the space of five verses Paul uses "canon" three times, oscillating perhaps between its literal and metaphorical meaning and indicating that the metaphor was deliberate by using also the word "measure" (six times in one form or another). Paul refers to his competitors who measure themselves by their own standards. He then continues,

> We do not boast beyond measure, but measure ourselves by the **standard**[72] *[kanōn]* that God has set for us, namely, that of our coming all this way to you. . . . So we are not boasting beyond measure about other people's work. Our hope is that, as your faith grows, so our work will grow more and more by our standard *[kanōn]* and that we will preach the gospel in regions even further afield, rather than boasting about work done in someone else's territory [*kanōn*, i.e., the region *measured out* for another].

God's standard or canon—the job description by which Paul would be judged—was that he should carry God's name "before the Gentiles . . . and before his people Israel" (Acts 9:15), and Paul had measured up to that standard by carrying the name of God as far as Corinth and other places in which the gospel had not been preached. The increase in the Corinthians' faith would confirm that his coming was indeed God's will and would encourage him to venture farther into places where the gospel was unknown, rather than take the easier course (because the groundwork had been done) of preaching where someone else had gone before him.

Once the stones for a building had been shaped, bronze dowels and dowel holes were prepared, the dowels were fixed in place with molten lead, and the stones raised one upon the other, each held firmly in place by the dowel. Masons of that time had a word, *harmologeō*, that summed up this whole process.[73] Paul uses a compound in Eph 2:21 and 4:16, speaking of the "**fitting together**"[74] of all that went into the construction of the temple of God, but he has turned it into a compound to highlight the extraordinary integration into this building of such heterogeneous "materials" as the Jews and the Gentiles.

Metaphors of building and demolition abound in Paul's letters[75]—for example, with reference to his Christian principles. It would be folly, he says to the Galatians, to turn from the gospel of grace to the law (what he called the "works of the Law") for justification. To do so would be to "**build**"[76] again what has already been "**torn down**"[77] (Gal 2:18). He uses these metaphors to describe his commission. The Lord has given him authority, he tells the Corinthians, "for building[78] you up" and not "for tearing you down"[79] (2 Cor 10:8). He also speaks of his missionary principles in terms of not "building" on someone else's foundation, in the sense that he would not go as a church planter to where others had already gone. It was his ambition, rather, to preach the gospel where Christ was not known (Rom 15:20).

Sometimes Paul uses the notion of "building up" to express the goal of Christian conduct in relation to others, for example, in regard to eating meat that had been slaughtered in heathen temples. Most of the meat that came on the market was the residue of offerings to gods.[80] Some Christians, "the [morally] strong," as Paul calls them, could eat such meat without batting an eye, knowing that the gods of these temples were no gods at all (1 Cor 8:4–6; but cf. 10:20–22, where he argues that the demons were, in fact, the recipients of pagan sacrifices). But others, whom he designates "the weak," could not eat the meat with an easy mind. They found themselves unable to shake off the old associations of heathen worship, and eating such meat posed, for them, a moral dilemma. This situation could arise in a private home (10:27[81]) or in a public setting. It was not uncommon to use for gatherings of one sort or another the dining facilities attached to a temple.[82] These opened onto public areas. If the "weak" saw the "strong" eating in such a place,[83] they might be "built up," in the sense of feeling peer group pressure to eat contrary to the dictates of their own conscience. This would be to put them at risk; if the consciences of the weak could be overruled in this matter, why not in other matters also[84] (8:10–11)? It is better, said Paul, that the "strong" should defer to the scruples of the more susceptible. The "strong" are not harmed by this concession and the "weak" are kept safe from harm. This is love—a concern for the well-being of others that translates into action at whatever cost to oneself. "Not everything builds up" in a positive and Christian sense (10:23; cf. 6:12). But love builds community and Christian maturity (8:1–3).

Paul repeats this teaching in Romans. "We ought not to please ourselves. Each of us should please his neighbor for his good, to build him up" (Rom 15:1–2; cf. 14:19). He pleads, "Do not demolish the work of God for the sake of food" (14:20). The cities of the ancient world were filled with the noise of buildings collapsing or being demolished for fear of collapse. Paul wanted nothing of this kind for God's house, the church. His concern was with building up. "We have been speaking . . . for your upbuilding," he told the Corinthians (2 Cor 12:19). Speaking what? "The word of his grace [the gospel], which can build you up and give you an inheritance among all those who are sanctified" (Acts 20:32). "Build one another up" was his instruction to the Thessalonian Christians (1 Thess 5:11). Gifts of ministry serve the church to that end. They are the gifts of God through Christ to his church that it might "build itself up" in love (Eph 4:11–16). And here, in this word, we have the key to our own part in this process. The criterion of all Christian conduct is, Does it build up? Does it edify? Only where there is love is the answer truly, Yes! While probably not intended as a metaphor, it is interesting to note Paul's description of love in 1 Cor 13:7. It could be expressed in terms of "**putting a roof over**[85] everything," although the word is generally rendered here along the lines of "endures."

TENTS

In 2 Cor 5:1–5, Paul draws a contrast between the tent of the nomad and the (relatively) solid structures of the cities. Writing out of a sense of his own physical weakness and against the backdrop of the pressure that he was constantly under in ministry, Paul is looking forward to the good things that God has in store for the Christian. "If the **tent**,[86] which is our earthly dwelling, **is taken down**,"[87] he says, speaking of the body, "we have a **building**[88] from God, a **house**[89] in heaven, not made by hands." The context leaves us in no doubt that Paul is speaking of the resurrection of the believer. But it is possible, he thinks (mixing his metaphors), that a period of "nakedness"[90] may first intervene—a time between death and the resurrection when the believer does not have a body but is "like the souls in Sheol, without form, and void of all power of activity."[91] Paul is clearly uncomfortable with such a prospect, but in the end he consoles himself with the thought that ultimately our "nakedness" will be "clothed" with a heavenly "house," that what is mortal will be swallowed up by what he simply calls "life." Meanwhile, the Holy Spirit is given as God's guarantee that this will be so.

For the present, however, for such time as we still occupy this mortal "tent," Paul is of the opinion that "nothing good **lives within**."[92] Indeed, not to put too fine a point on it, "sin has taken up residence" (Rom 7:17, 18, 20). The most likely interpretation of Rom 7:7–25 (or at least vv. 14–25: the earlier verses may be a look back to what the law had meant to him as a Jew) is that it is Paul's account of his own Christian experience of wrestling with evil. He knows what he should do—live by God's rules—and to do so is the great desire of his life. But he finds himself forever falling short of that goal. Some commentators take the view that Paul reverts here to the theme of his earlier chapters (1:18–3:20) and is speaking of the human condition apart from Christ. In any case, the point remains that sin can and often does make itself the master of our "abode."[93] The only safe thing to do is to turn our "tent" over to God. Paul could say to the Roman Christians, "You, however, are controlled *not* by the sinful nature but by the Spirit, *if* the Spirit of God lives within you" (8:9; cf. v. 11; 1 Cor 3:16). Sin and the Spirit are incompatible "houseguests," and we must choose the one or the other to take up occupancy in our lives. But the warning of Rom 7 (understanding it to describe not just Paul's but a common Christian experience) is that even with the best will in the world and with the Spirit as our invited houseguest, sin can nevertheless infiltrate the dwelling and cause tension within.

HOUSEHOLD FURNISHINGS

Amid the confusion of buildings that marked the cities of the ancient world, here and there could be found a splendid *domus,* paved, it may be, with mosaics, its ceilings decorated with gilded stucco,[94] its pillared courtyards open to the sky. It has been estimated that in Rome there was one *domus* for every twenty-six tenement buildings. Among the buildings identified at Ephesus, J. Liversidge describes "a large house, built in the first century [CE] and spreading over five or more terraces, a storey on each. Here a first-century painting of Socrates and other treasures were discovered."[95] Although the house itself might be built on a grand scale and decorated richly, by our standards it would have seemed sparsely furnished. Wealth was displayed not in the number of items that filled the house but in their quality—in the designs and materials that bore witness to their owner's good taste.[96]

For every Roman the main item of furniture was the bed. Those who could afford it and had the space and the time to warrant it might have, in addition to the bed on which they slept at night, a day bed, or more than one, on which to take their siesta and to recline to eat, to read, to write, and to receive visitors. Beyond this, most Romans were content with benches or stools. Chairs with backs appear to have been especially favored by women of the upper classes,[97] whom Juvenal described as spending their days languidly lolling on these items of furniture.[98] Roman tables had little in common with the sturdy, four-legged kind commonly found in the modern house.[99] They might rather be a set of little shelves in tiers, supported on one leg and used to display objets d'art, or a low table of wood or bronze with three or four adjustable legs, or a simple tripod whose folding legs usually ended in the representation of a claw. Roman houses were supplied with cupboards of various sizes and designs and smaller items such as lamps, mirrors, weighing machines, candlesticks, clocks and braziers, and a variety of kitchen utensils to meet the varied needs of the household.[100] Only the poor were obliged to eat from earthenware dishes. Plain wooden or earthenware vessels were found in the great Roman houses but were only for the use of the slaves. The householder himself and his family might eat and drink from vessels, sparkling with gold and adorned with precious stones, made by a master craftsman. Silver table services were so common that Martial ridicules those patrons who were so niggardly in bestowing their Saturnalian gifts (the Saturnalia was an annual festival in December in honor of the god or planet Saturn) that they conferred on their clients less than five pounds weight of silverware.[101]

Clearly Paul was familiar with such domestic arrangements. "In a great house," he says, "there are **utensils**[102] not only of gold and silver but also of wood and clay; some are for noble purposes and some for ignoble" (2 Tim 2:20). The metaphor is of a building, but the idea of "house" merges easily with that of the "household."[103] The "great house" suggests the family within with its servants and slaves making good use of the gold and silver plate and the wooden and earthenware vessels. The former were reserved perhaps for meals on festive occasions ("for noble purposes," *eis timēn*), the latter for ordinary and often less seemly use, such as removing excrement or carrying garbage from the kitchen to the nearest point of disposal ("for dishonorable or shameful purposes," *eis atimian*). The idea of different vessels for different uses was a familiar one to biblical writers.[104] Paul himself uses it in Rom 9:19–24. But in the passage before us (2 Tim 2:20) his metaphor runs into difficulty. Strictly pressed, it would lead to a conclusion other than the one intended, suggesting that although they are different, all vessels have their own use (cf. 1 Cor 12:21ff.), or to the lesson of Jesus' parable, that different vessels exist side by side until the fire of judgment sorts them out (see Matt 13:24–30, 36–43). But as verse 21 and the wider context make clear, Paul's point is that there is only one vessel (or rather only one use of a vessel) that counts, whether the item in question is of gold, silver, wood, or clay. Those whom the Lord knows, who confess his name (v. 19), in an application of his metaphor, should **cleanse**[105] themselves from what is dishonorable (in this context, the false teaching of such people as Hymenaeus and Philetus; see vv. 14–18) and devote themselves to what is honorable—good conduct and sound teaching (vv. 21–26). Only thus will they be vessels "for noble purposes, made holy[106] [set apart, as the vessels in the temple had been, for sacred use], useful to the Master and made ready for any good work."

There is no better work than that of making the Master known. Paul himself had been called to be a "chosen vessel to carry [God's] name before the Gentiles and their kings and before the people of Israel" (Acts 9:15). Such work, in some measure, falls to us all. To us all is committed the "treasure," as Paul calls the gospel in 2 Cor 4:7, and to us all is given the task of sharing this treasure with others, no matter that, in our own case, it comes in a "clay vessel." Christians may feel that they are most unlikely "containers" of "the light of the knowledge of the glory of God," that is, of the good news about Christ (v. 6), that there is nothing fine or fancy about them that they should be given such a task by the Lord. Nevertheless, God sees fit to use unlikely people—even "clay vessels" such as ourselves—to carry the gospel into the world.

NOTES

1. P. Veyne, "The Roman Empire," in *A History of Private Life* (ed. P. Aries and G. Duby; Cambridge: Harvard University Press, 1987), 1:186. That the urbanization of its subject populations was, in fact, a deliberate policy of the Romans (as it had been of Alexander and his successors) is most clearly attested by Tacitus in describing the work of Agricola in Britain in 78–79 CE: "In order that a population scattered and uncivilized and proportionately ready for war might be habituated by comfort to peace and quiet, he would exhort individuals, assist communities, to erect temple, market-places, houses" (*Agr.* 21). The urbanization of the empire is highly praised by Aelius Aristides. He puts the rhetorical question: "When were there so many cities in the hinterland and by the sea?" (*Rome,* 93; cf. 94, 97, 98; see also Pliny, *Ep.* 10.37–42, 70f., 98f.). Seneca extols the civilizing influence of the cities (*Ep.* 90.25). For the place of cities in Paul's world, see, e.g., W. A. Meeks, *The First Urban Christians: The Social World of the Apostle Paul* (New Haven: Yale University Press, 1983), 9–16; for an estimate of the size and density of their populations and a discussion of their demographics, see, e.g., R. L. Fox, *Pagans and Christians* (Harmondsworth, U.K.: Penguin, 1988), 46ff.; cf. also R. Duncan-Jones, *The Economy of the Roman Empire: Quantitative Studies* (Cambridge: Cambridge University Press, 1982), 259–87; and R. MacMullen, *Roman Social Relations* (New Haven: Yale University Press, 1974), 63.

2. When Paul catalogued the places in which he had faced danger, he divided his world into city, wilderness, and sea (2 Cor 11:26). It did not include χώρα, the productive countryside, although he often traversed it of necessity. Outside the city, as far as his interest was concerned, there was nothing—ἐρημία.

3. Horace, *Ep.* 1.17.36. The character of the city is amply reflected in Paul's letters. See, e.g., 1 Cor 5:1–13; 6:9–20; 7:2, 5, 9; 10:8; 15:33f.

4. Juvenal, *Sat.* 3.268–314.

5. Much later, in the fourth century, the people of Antioch in Syria took great pride in their street lighting. But Antioch appears to have been the exception that proved the rule. Libanius speaks (in hyperbole) of the streetlights taking the place of the sun, "which leave the Egyptian festival of illumination far behind; and with us night is distinguished from day only by the difference of lighting" (quoted without reference by Lord Kinross, *Europa Minor: Journeys in Coastal Turkey* [London: Travel Book Club, n.d.], 3–4; see also A. H. M. Jones, *The Greek City* [Oxford: Clarendon, 1940], 214, 252).

6. Acts 26:18; Rom 2:19; 13:12–14; 2 Cor 4:6; 6:14; Eph 5:8–11; 6:12; Col 1:12–13; 1 Thess 5:4–8. Cf. ch. 4, nn. 72, 77; ch. 10, n. 70.

7. Cf. Matt 24:43/Luke 12:39; also 2 Pet 3:10; Rev 3:3; 16:15. See D. Wenham, *Paul: Follower of Jesus or Founder of Christianity?* (Grand Rapids: Eerdmans, 1995), 30, 307–11.

8. Θύρα "a door," is always used by Paul metaphorically of opportunities.

9. Θύρα . . . μοι ἀνέῳγεν μεγάλη καὶ ἐνεργής: Notice the perfect tense, suggesting that the "door" remained open, at least for the time being; in other words, there was a continuing opportunity for Paul to preach. He describes it as ἐνεργής ("a strange adjective to apply to a door," C. K. Barrett, *The First Epistle to the Corinthians* [repr.; Peabody, Mass.: Hendrickson, 1968], 389). This is understood to mean something like "working," "for effective work" (RSV, NIV), "active service" (MOFFATT). In the papyri a medical receipt has ἐνεργής for "tolerably strong" (cf. also Phlm 6; Heb 4:12) and MM shows that it can also mean "in working order." I find "effective work" the most likely sense. Paul had a *great* (μεγάλη) opportunity for *effective work* (ἐνεργής) in this city, although it is possible that the καί following should be given an adversative sense and that Paul was wondering whether the "many who opposed" would make it difficult for him to take up the opportunities that were offering. In the light of ἀντικείμενοι πολλοί "many who oppose," R. Strelan, *Paul, Artemis, and the Jews in Ephesus* (Berlin: de Gruyter, 1996), 163, for one, suggests that the door is rather "a door of opposition and even death." He points out that Epictetus uses the phrases ἤνοικται ἡ θύρα (*Diatr.* 1.9.20), ἡ θύρα ἤνοικται (1.24.19; 1.25.18; 2.1.19), and τὴν θυραν ἤνοιξεν (3.13.14), in each case as referring to death. In support of this interpretation he further notes that the defeated gladiator in the Roman arena was dragged off through the Porta Libitina— the "gate of death," Libitina being the goddess of funerals. Strelan may be right in supposing that Paul made only minor inroads in Ephesus with the gospel and met with much opposition; but he was determined to face that opposition, whatever the consequences. I think it more likely, however, that 1 Cor 16:9 expresses a more optimistic view of his prospects in this city, without his being blind, of course, to the difficulties that he would also encounter.

10. Again, notice the perfect tense, θύρας . . . ἀνεῳγμένης, the door "stood open" (so V. P. Furnish, *II Corinthians* [New York: Doubleday, 1984], 169). Here the statement is followed by an indisputably adversative conjunction (cf. the preceding note), ἀλλά, pointing to the fact that Paul did not "enter" but continued on his way to Macedonia.

11. Εἴσοδος (from εἰς "into" and ὁδός "a way"): (1) "a means of entering, place of entrance," (2) "a going in, entrance." Found only here in Paul. In 1 Thess 2:1 the "entrance" is qualified by the statement that "it has not become empty" (οὐ κενὴ

γέγονεν)—they had effectively introduced the gospel into that city. Cf. 1 Cor 15:14, 17, in which Paul speaks of preaching that is empty and faith that is a waste of time.

12. See Vitruvius, *Arch.* 2.8.17, and Strabo, *Geog.* 5.3.7.

13. See J. Liversidge, *Everyday Life in the Roman Empire* (New York: Putnam's, 1976), 64; A. K. McKay, *Houses, Villas, and Palaces in the Roman World* (Ithaca, N.Y.: Cornell University Press, 1975), 212–17.

14. Strabo, *Geog.* 16.2.13 and 23; Pomponius Mela, *De chorographia* 2.7.6. Cf. J. E. Packer, "Housing and Population in Imperial Ostia and Rome," *JRS* 57 (1967): 80–95, who shows that the standard height of apartment houses in Ostia, at the mouth of the Tiber, sixteen miles downstream from Rome, was four stories.

15. J. E. Packer's work in Ostia gives us some guide, perhaps, to the distribution of housing in other cities, including Rome itself. With two-thirds of the site excavated, Packer estimates that in the entire city there were perhaps thirty-three private mansions *(domūs),* accounting for 660 persons. Fifty-eight *insulae* with luxury apartments on the ground floor and perhaps on upper floors have been found. Packer estimates that 1,306 persons lived in this type of housing, i.e., in large apartments within *insulae* (*The Insulae of Imperial Ostia* [Rome: Memoirs of the American Academy of Rome 31, 1971], 70–71). In "Housing and Population," his estimate is somewhat higher but still accounts for less than 10 percent of the population. Out of a total estimated population of 27,000, then, less than 2,000 lived in either *domūs* or luxury apartments. The majority of the population lived in one or two rooms in the *insulae*. Finally, about 5,000 of Ostia's inhabitants were too poor to rent any kind of apartment and thus slept in and around public buildings and other structures (*Insulae*, 7–71; "Housing and Population," 84–86).

16. J. Carcopino, *Daily Life in Ancient Rome* (Harmondsworth, U.K.: Penguin, 1956), 31.

17. Although Paul is writing from Ephesus, it seems more likely that he is drawing a metaphor from the city to which he is writing (Corinth) than from the city in which he is at the time, although the same can be said of both. For a description of some well-to-do houses in Corinth of the first and second centuries CE and for factors relating to housing that throw light on some of the difficulties faced by the early church, not only in Corinth but elsewhere, see J. Murphy-O'Connor, *St. Paul's Corinth* (Wilmington, Del.: Michael Glazier, 1983), 153–61.

18. See Petronius, *Sat.* 98. Cf. Juvenal, *Sat.* 11.51, 141; Martial, *Epigr.* 2.17; 5.22.5–9; 7.31; 10.94.56; 12.18.2; Persius Flaccus, *Sat.* 5.32.

19. Frontinus, *Aquaeduct.* 65–73.

20. Martial, *Epigr.* 9.17.5–6.

21. Paulus, *Sent.* 3.6.58; cf. *Dig.* 33.7.12.42. In *Sat.* 6.332, Juvenal speaks of the water carriers as the scum of the slave population.

22. Carcopino, *Daily Life*, 47.

23. Pliny, *Nat.* 36.104–108.

24. See Juvenal, *Sat.* 3.269–272; *Dig.* 9.3.5.1–2.

25. Περικάθαρμα (from περικαθαίρω "to purify on all sides or completely"): "Sweepings, rinsings, cleansings around" and so "the refuse thrown off in cleansing," "scum." But the word might also be used of the process of cleansing, "purification," with a particular application to sacrifice. Found only here in the NT, once in OT (LXX Prov 21:18), and once elsewhere.

26. Περίψημα (from περιψάω "to wipe off all round"): "That which is wiped off, offscouring." A late word, only here in the NT but found in Tob 5:18. It later came to have a complimentary sense, being applied to those Christians who, in time of plague, gave their lives in caring for the sick. But in its original sense it was a bold figure for Paul to use, of a piece with περικάθαρμα. Like περικάθαρμα, it might also have the sense of "purification."

27. For the view that Paul had only a very limited success in Ephesus, see, e.g., R. Strelan, *Paul*.

28. It is difficult to know precisely what the writer meant by this. Some commentators find in it a reference to the scapegoat.

29. Epictetus, *Diatr.* 3.22.78. See further ch. 1, n. 31.

30. Cited without reference by A. T. Robertson, *Word Pictures in the New Testament* (New York: Richard R. Smith, 1930–1933; repr. Nashville, Tenn.: Broadman & Holman, 1973), 4:109.

31. B. H. McLean, "Christ as Pharmakos in Pauline Soteriology," *SBL Seminar Papers, 1991* (SBLSP 30; Atlanta: Scholars Press, 1991), 201. Φάρμακος is properly an adjective, "devoted to magical arts," but used as a substantive (= φαρμακεύς), "magic man." Cf. φάρμακον: "Healing, medicine, poison," etc., all with magical connotations. Thus, in connection with human expiatory rites, φάρμακος seems to mean "one who heals the people." In the above quote, McLean draws on three sources: (1) Diogenes Laertius explains that a pestilence that had devastated Athens was in fact the manifestation of a curse resulting from a transgression committed by a man named Cylon. He goes on to describe the remedy: "In consequence two young men, Cratinus and Ctesibus, were put to death and the city was delivered from the scourge" (R. D. Hicks, trans., *Diogenes Laertius: Lives of Eminent Philosophers* [London: Williams Heinemann, 1959], 1:110). (2) Helladios writes, "It was the custom at Athens to lead in procession two *pharmakoi* with a view to purification [καθαρμός], one for the men, one for the women. . . . This purification was of the nature of an apotropaic ceremony to avert diseases. . . . When the Athenians suffered abnormally from a pestilential disease, the custom was observed of constantly purifying the city by φάρμακοι" (cited by Photius, *Bibliotheca* 534A). (3) A scholiast, or commentator, on Aristophanes, *Eq.* 1136, testifies that certain people were kept for this ritual at public expense: "The δημόσιοι are those who were called φάρμακοι, and these φάρμακοι purified cities by their slaughter . . . for the Athenians maintained certain very ignoble and useless persons, and on the occasion of any calamity befalling the city, I mean a pestilence or anything of that sort, they sacrificed these persons with a view to purification from pollution, and they called them purifications [καθάρματα]."

32. So Istros, referred to by Valerius Harpocration, *Lexicon* 1.298. The reason for this expulsion is not known. It may have been a form of insurance against future disaster.

33. McLean, "Christ as Pharmakos," 202.

34. B. H. McLean, "The Absence of an Atoning Sacrifice in Paul's Soteriology," *NTS* 38 (1992): 531–53, argues the case for only a minimal role for OT in shaping Paul's soteriology, at least as it is expressed in his letters. McLean maintains the following: (1) There are no explicit textual references in Paul's letters to Christ's death as an atoning sacrifice. The noun θυσία is applied to Christ only once, in Eph 5:2, with no clear reference to the atonement. He is likened to the paschal lamb in 1 Cor 5:7, but the lamb of the Passover was never understood to effect atonement. But the idea of Christ as the ἱλαστήριον in Rom 3:25 presents a much greater obstacle for McLean's case than he allows. He argues, on the evidence of LXX, that it meant for Paul no more than *the sphere* (the "mercy seat") in which expiation took place, but this is to overlook the considerable weight of scholarship in favor of the view that in Romans ἱλαστήριον signifies that Christ himself was *the means* of expiation and, indeed, of propitiation. (2) The references to Christ's blood in Paul's letters are not necessarily references to atoning sacrifice. (3) Sacrifice in OT does not atone for personal sin but only effects the cleansing of the sanctuary. Again, this runs counter to widely held scholarly views on the role of sacrifice in OT. (4) A sacrificial victim in OT is never said to have become either sinful or accursed, and yet this is precisely what Christ is said to have become on our behalf. This is perhaps the most telling point in support of his argument.

35. McLean, "Christ as Pharmakos," 205f.

36. Σκύβαλον: A late word of uncertain etymology, either connected with σκῶρ "dung" or from ἐς κύνας βάλλω "to fling to the dogs," and so refuse of any kind. It occurs in the papyri, but only here (in the plural, σκύβαλα) in the NT.

37. Ἡγέομαι: (1) "to lead, rule, be a leader," (2) "to suppose, believe, consider, think." See also 2 Cor 9:5; Phil 2:3, 6, 25; 1 Thess 5:13; 2 Thess 3:15; 1 Tim 1:12; 6:1.

38. Five particles introduce the statement in v. 8, ἀλλὰ μενοῦνγε καί, which are difficult to translate individually but together show the force and passion of his conviction even after so many years.

39. See Juvenal, Sat. 3.199–207.

40. Ibid., 3.197–198.

41. Dig. 1.15.2.

42. See Juvenal, Sat. 3.305–308.

43. Part of this officer's duty was to warn tenants to always keep water ready in their rooms to quench any outbreak of fire. Dig. 1.15.3, 5.

44. The biographer who wrote the Historia augusta records that during the reign of Antoninus Pius a fire in Rome consumed 340 dwellings in one day—apartment buildings and private houses (Pius 9.1). A large part of the city was destroyed in the notorious fire of 64 CE. There were many other recorded fires in Rome.

45. Σβέννυμι: Of fire or things on fire, "to quench." The prohibition of 1 Thess 5:19 is expressed by a present imperative, with the sense "stop quenching." For the verb, see also Eph 6:16, and for the issue addressed by Paul in 1 Thess 5:19–22, see D. J. Williams, 1 and 2 Thessalonians (NIBC; Peabody, Mass.: Hendrickson, 1992), 100ff.

46. Ὡς διὰ πυρός: Not "by means of fire" (ἐν πυρί) but "enwrapped in fire." Paul describes the fire as "testing" its victims. Here the verb δοκιμάζω approaches its primary application, to the testing of metals, which was generally done by fire. See ch. 7, n. 8.

47. See D. J. Williams, The Promise of His Coming (Homebush West, Australia: Anzea, 1990), 93ff., for the judgment of Christians.

48. Πῦρ: "Fire," used also as a metaphor of the coming of Christ in 2 Thess 1:7. Cf. Dan 7:9f.; Mal 4:1; Matt 3:11; Luke 3:16; see also Luke 12:49 and Acts 2:3. It expresses the notion of testing. For Paul's use of the noun elsewhere, see Rom 12:20.

49. In 146 BCE Corinth fell to the Romans. Because of the leading role that the city had played as a member of the Achaean League's war against Rome, the consul Mummius burned it, putting its men to the sword and selling its women and children into captivity. The site was probably not entirely abandoned, but Corinth was certainly reduced to insignificance for a hundred years. But then, in 44 BCE, the city was reestablished by Julius Caesar and rose once more to importance. In writing 1 Cor 3:10–15, Paul may have had this particular history of fire and rebuilding in mind. He may have been thinking of the houses of new Corinth, built, no doubt, with whatever materials came to hand—ancient columns, perhaps, being made to support roofs thatched with reeds cut from the marshes nearby. In its early days, new Corinth may have been little more than a shantytown and may still have had something of that character in Paul's day (mid-50s CE)—a city of makeshifts and of contrasts. On the other hand, he may have had in mind in this passage a very different image, that of Solomon's temple, in the construction of which gold, silver, marble, and the better sort of timber was used (cf. 1 Kgs 6). The allusion would then prepare us for the mention of the temple in v. 16 (cf. Isa 54:12). The more perishable materials were used for huts and private houses of even some pretensions, the more enduring for temples and the like. In this case, the apostle is not thinking of contrasting

buildings so much as of the use of inappropriate materials in one "building" in particular, namely, the "temple" of God in the Spirit.

50. Carcopino, *Daily Life*, 40.

51. Juvenal, *Sat.* 3.190–196.

52. Θεμέλιος and θεμέλιον (from τίθημι "to lay, establish"): "A foundation stone, a foundation." In Paul, found in Rom 15:20; 1 Cor 3:10–12; Eph 2:20; 1 Tim 6:19; 2 Tim 2:19. In 1 Cor 3:10, Paul uses the cognates θεμέλιον ἔθηκα (aorist active indicative of τίθημι), "I founded a foundation," θεμέλιον being the accusative of the masculine form θεμέλιος (not the neuter, as is clear from v. 11). Presumably Paul chose the masculine because his reference was to Christ. He continues, "No one is able to lay another foundation *alongside* [παρά] the one that has been laid [τὸν κείμενον]." This leaves no room to question the uniqueness of Christ in Paul's estimation. Elsewhere, his use of the preposition ἐπί "upon" sometimes expresses the same thought as here in "foundation" (cf., e.g., Rom 4:5, 24). Wenham, *Paul*, 205, wonders whether the building imagery in 1 Cor 3 owes anything to the story of Peter the rock and/or to the parable of the two builders (Matt 7:24–27; 16:18). For the verb θεμελιόω, see ch. 1, n. 54.

53. Ἀρχιτέκτων (from τέκτων, itself from τίκτω "to beget," meaning "a begetter," then "a worker in wood and stone, a carpenter or mason," as in Mark 6:3): "A master builder, architect." In the papyri and inscriptions, the term has a wider application than our "architect," including what we might call the chief engineer and the building contractor. But we may suppose that in Paul's metaphor he wanted to place some emphasis on the ἀρχι-; he claimed primacy as pastor of the church in Corinth, and for the "building" to amount to anything worthwhile, all subsequent workers (τέκτονες) should work in accord with what he had done and not to the contrary. "Another builds *upon*" (ἐποικοδομέω; see ch. 1, n. 76) what he has already laid. It is a shame if a later minister digs up the sound foundation that has already been laid. It is equally a shame if a minister is obliged to dig up and replace what has not been well laid.

54. Θεμελιόω (cf. θεμέλιος, θεμέλιον, ch. 1, n. 52): "To lay the foundation of, to found." See also Col 1:23. The two perfect passive participles, "being rooted and founded," being in the nominative case, are to be taken with ἵνα ἐξισχύσητε "that you might be able," although placed before the conjunction. It is a question whether ἐν ἀγάπῃ "in love" should be read with "rooted and founded" or with the preceding phrase "that Christ may dwell in your hearts through faith." The reading adopted here is the one generally accepted—that love is the soil into which the roots grow and on which the foundation has been laid. For the contrary view, see, e.g., J. A. Robinson, *St Paul's Epistle to the Ephesians* (London: Macmillan, 1909), 175, and for a similar mixing of metaphors, cf. 1 Cor 3:9, Col 2:6–7, and possibly Eph 2:20–21. On the metaphor of being "rooted," see p. 38.

55. Κατοικέω: See ch. 1, n. 92. Used elsewhere by Paul of God indwelling Christ (Col 1:19; 2:9).

56. Ἐποικοδομέω: See ch. 1, n. 76.

57. Ἀκρογωνιαῖος: See the discussion below.

58. Οἰκεῖοι: See ch. 1, n. 89.

59. Some commentators take "prophets" to mean those of OT, but the word order, "apostles and prophets," makes it more likely that the author has NT prophets in mind. Cf. Acts 11:27ff.; 1 Cor 12:28, 29; 14:1–5, 24ff. Both offices are mentioned again in Eph 3:5; 4:11 with a clear reference to the NT era.

60. Paul's verbs are ἀνατρέπω "to overturn" and ἵστημι "to stand firm" (see ch. 10, n. 105), and he describes the foundation as στερεός "firm." Cf. Acts 15:24, 32; the church in Antioch had been "disturbed" (ταράσσω) by the incursion of a new teaching but was subsequently "made firm" (ἐπιστηρίζω) by James's letter and the teaching of Judas and Silas.

61. This passage speaks, on the one hand, of the faith of some being overturned and, on the other, of the faithfulness of God and the security of God's church. Thus it poses the perennial problem of whether a person can cease to be saved. NT evidence may suggest that, as individuals, we are secure *as long as we choose to remain* in the hand of God (see John 10:28–29) and that nothing external to ourselves can separate us from God (see Rom 8:38–39). But we can choose to separate ourselves (see Heb 6:4–6). Yet God will always ensure that there are some who are faithful and that God's church will endure (see Matt 16:18).

62. Σφραγίς: An old word for (1) "a seal, signet," (2) the impression of a seal or signet, "a seal." In Paul, in Rom 4:11 (circumcision the seal of righteousness—the outward sign of a God-given status); 1 Cor 9:2 (the Corinthians are the seal of Paul's apostleship—living proof that he was Christ's minister among them; cf. 2 Cor 3:1–3); 2 Tim 2:19. For the verb, σφραγίζω "to seal," see ch. 8, n. 4.

63. See Num 16:5, 26; cf. 2 Tim 2:17–18. For such danger that ever threatens God's people, see, e.g., Lev 24:16; Josh 23:7; Ps 6:8; Isa 52:11; and Paul's warning to the Ephesian elders in Acts 20:29–30.

64. Ἀκρογωνιαῖος (from ἄκρος "extreme" and γωνία "an angle"): Properly an adjective, "at the extreme angle." But with λίθος "a stone" understood, it becomes, in effect, a substantive, "a cornerstone." This word occurs only here in Paul. Jesus had spoken of himself, in terms of Ps 118:22–23, as the stone rejected by the Jewish builders (the experts) but chosen by God as the head of the corner, εἰς κεφαλὴν γωνίας (Mark 12:10; cf. Acts 4:11; 1 Pet 2:7). Paul may be deliberately echoing the image suggested by Jesus, albeit in the words of Isaiah.

65. Cf. also 2 Kgs 25:17.

66. Describing the earlier temple (and the same would have applied to the temple that Paul saw, for it was built to much the same design), Pliny states that the most amazing thing about it was the architraves, the beams supported by the columns, that such massive blocks could be lifted to such a height. He describes how it was done and reports that the greatest problem had been presented by the lintel above the door: "That, you see, was the heaviest block of them all" (*Nat.* 36.95–97).

67. See, e.g., Rom 8:18ff.

68. Jerome, *Comm. Eph.* 1.2.19ff.

69. This exegesis is the more likely if we accept the Pauline authorship of Ephesians, for the eschatology expressed here is certainly in keeping with that of his other writings.

70. Cf. Eph 2:8–10, and see the discussion on 1 Tim 3:13 below (pp. 245–46), which makes the point that as we serve God by doing his will, so we grow in Christian maturity, and so too (and this is the point made here in 1 Tim 6:19) we enlarge our capacity for the enjoyment of what is to come. Cf. 1 Tim 4:8.

71. Philo of Byzantium, *Seven* 6.2.

72. Κανών: (1) "a rod or bar," (2) "a measuring rule," (3) hence "a rule, standard, limit" (2 Cor 10:13, 15–16; Gal 6:16; Phil 3:16). In masonry, to test the flatness of a stone, the κανών, a wooden bar, was coated with ruddle (red ochre) and then drawn across the stone. The ruddle (or its absence) on the stone highlighted any unevenness. Stones failing that test were ἀδοκίμαστος "rejected." Paul uses the kindred term ἀδόκιμος of some people and of his fears for himself. See further ch. 7, n. 8; ch. 12, n. 115. In 2 Cor 10:12–16 Paul has three words used in measuring: the verb μετρέω (1) "to measure," of space, number, etc. (in Paul found only here in v. 12); (2) "to measure out"; the noun μέτρον "a measure" or that which is measured (v. 13; also in Paul in Rom 12:3; Eph 4:7, 13, 16); (3) the adjective ἄμετρος "without measure" (in the NT only here in vv. 13, 15, where it is twice used adverbially).

73. Ἁρμολογέω (from ἁρμός "a joint" and λέγω "to join together"): Not found in this form in the NT.

74. Συναρμολογέω (cf. preceding note): "To fit or frame together." In Eph 2:21 Paul uses the phrase πᾶσα οἰκοδομή, which is usually translated "the whole building," but which in ordinary Greek idiom is more likely to mean "each building," although it is not unknown to find such a phrase with the sense "the whole." In this connection, notice the use of the plural, οἰκοδόμαι "buildings," in Mark 13:1, with reference to the temple (ἱερόν, singular), and perhaps that is the idea here: Each believer is a "building" that is integrated into the one sacred precinct. The difficulty with this interpretation is that Paul then speaks of believers as comprising the ναός "the sanctuary," which in the Jewish temple distinguished the central structure from the whole temple complex.

75. See Wenham, *Paul*, 206–10, on the possible origin of these metaphors in Jesus' saying in John 2:19 about destroying and building.

76. Οἰκοδομέω (from οἰκοδόμος "a builder," itself from οἶκος and δέμω "to build"): "To build a house, to build," always in Paul metaphorically. See Rom 15:20; 1 Cor 8:1, 10; 10:23; 14:4, 17; 1 Thess 5:11. See also the compound ἐποικοδομέω (1) "to build upon," (2) "to build up," again, in the NT (not only in Paul) always metaphorical. See 1 Cor 3:10 (2x), 12, 14; Eph 2:20; Col 2:7.

77. Καταλύω: (1) "to destroy," (2) "to unloose, unyoke." In Paul, found in Rom 14:20; 2 Cor 5:1 (where it has the common meaning "to strike [a tent]"); Gal 2:18.

78. Οἰκοδομή: See ch. 1, n. 88.

79. Καθαίρεσις (from καθαιρέω "to take down, put down, destroy"): "A pulling down, destruction." In the NT found only in 2 Cor 10:4, 8; 13:10.

80. The practice in most animal sacrifices of antiquity was that part of the animal was burned on the altar, part was eaten by the worshipers at a solemn meal in the temple, and part was given to the priests for their own use or to be sold ἐν μακέλλῳ "in the meat shop." Μάκελλον is only in 1 Cor 10:25 in the NT, a transliteration of the Latin *macellum*. The discoveries at Pompeii give us some idea of how these shops were arranged. They generally had a masonry counter and the meat was suspended from a bar hung in the entrance (on shops in general, see pp. 169–71). As for the source of the meat, the temple of Artemis at Ephesus, for example, has been described as "a grandiose slaughter house." Excavations have revealed stalls for twenty oxen. "Here all the city's meat was slaughtered under the eye of the great goddess, the altar being carefully aligned to take the evening sunlight, shining alike upon the bloody stone and the gilded lips of the smiling statue high above" (J. Romer and E. Romer, *The Seven Wonders of the World* [London: Michael O'Mara, 1995], 153). In Corinth, the vaulted northwest shops of the agora, or some of them at least, are thought to have been cooling rooms for the storage of meat for sale from the ancient temple of Apollo, onto which they back.

81. Cf. Plutarch, *Mor.* 696E (*Quaest. conv.* 6.10.1): "Aristion's cook made a great hit with the dinner guests not only because of his general skill, but because the cock that he set before the diners, though it had just been slaughtered as a sacrifice to Heracles, was as tender as if it had been a day old."

82. See H. C. Youtie, "The Κλίνη of Seraphis," *HTR* 41 (1948): 14–15.

83. An examination of the Asclepeion at Corinth reveals how easily this could happen. Constructed in the fourth century BCE, the facility included three dining rooms built below the *abaton* (the antechamber of the temple proper) opening onto the courtyard by which the temple was approached. Each had couches around the wall that could accommodate eleven people. In front of them were seven small tables and in the center of the room a slab on which the cooking was done. The whole facility was destroyed when the city was sacked in 146 BCE, and it is not certain that these dining rooms were rebuilt when the temple was restored in the year 44. But there would have been others associated with other temples in Corinth. See Murphy-O'Connor, *St. Paul's Corinth*, 161–65; J. Wiseman, "Corinth and Rome

I," *ANRW* 7:487, 510. Similarly, in the Greek period, the temple of Demeter was equipped with a number of small dining rooms for the use of the worshipers. But again it is uncertain whether meals were associated with this temple in the Roman period. As R. S. Stroud ("The Sanctuary of Demeter on Acrocorinth in the Roman Period," in *The Corinthia in the Roman Period* [ed. T. E. Gregory; Ann Arbor: Cushing-Malloy, 1994], 69) notes, "Conceivably, there was still some kind of communal dining in the open air, but it seems clear from the excavated remains that in the Roman period small groups of segregated worshippers no longer assembled indoors for ritual dining as they had in Greek times." Nevertheless, it is not unlikely that the design of these earlier temples was perpetuated in the Roman period in other precincts, if not in these, and certainly the practice continued of eating in the temple precinct. B. W. Winter (*Seek the Welfare of the City: Christians as Benefactors and Citizens* [Grand Rapids: Eerdmans, 1994], 173–74) suggests that Paul's references in 1 Cor 8–10 are to feasts associated with the Isthmian games, which, like all Greek games, had a religious basis, and that the issue in Paul's mind was the dining "right" (Winter argues, 166–68, that ἐξουσία in 1 Cor 8:9 has this sense rather than that of "freedom") of Christian Roman citizens to attend such feasts.

84. See A. Booth, "The Art of Reclining and Its Attendant Perils," in *Dining in a Classical Context* (ed. W. J. Slater; Ann Arbor: University of Michigan Press, 1991), 105. He speaks of the "unholy trinity" of "eating and drinking and sexual indulgence" that often marked these festal occasions. There were peripatetic brothel keepers who "dragged their stock about to . . . festive gatherings" (Dio Chrysostom, *Disc.* 77, 78.4), and it may have been this risk of sexual immorality in particular that Paul feared.

85. Στέγω: (1) properly, "to cover closely, to protect by covering, to roof" (hence the noun στεγή "a roof"), (2) "to cover, keep secret, conceal," (3) "to endure." In the NT found only in Paul, in 1 Cor 9:12; 13:7; 1 Thess 3:1, 5.

86. Σκῆνος = σκηνή "a tent." In the phrase ἡ . . . οἰκία τοῦ σκήνους, the genitive is appositive; the dwelling is the tent. Σκῆνος appears only here in vv. 1, 4 in the NT.

87. Καταλύω: See ch. 1, n. 77.

88. Οἰκοδομή (from οἶκος "a house" and δέμω "to build"): (1) = the classical οἰκοδομία and οἰκοδόμησις "the act of building," always in the NT metaphorical, (2) = οἰκοδόμημα "a building." In Paul, found in Rom 14:19; 15:2; 1 Cor 3:9; 14:3, 5, 12, 26; 2 Cor 5:1; 10:8; 12:19; 13:10; Eph 2:21; 4:12, 16, 29.

89. Οἰκία "a house, dwelling": In Paul, found in 1 Cor 11:22; 16:15; 2 Cor 5:1 (2x); Phil 4:22; 1 Tim 5:13; 2 Tim 2:20; 3:6. Cf. οἶκος (1) properly, "a house, dwelling" (Rom 16:5; 1 Cor 11:34; 14:35; 16:19; Col 4:15; 1 Tim 5:4; Phlm 2), (2) by extension, "household, family" (1 Cor 1:16; 1 Tim 3:4, 5, 12, 15; 2 Tim 1:16; 4:19; Titus 1:11). Οἶκος is probably used of the "household" of the church in 1 Tim 3:15, and this use is implied in 1 Tim 3:5. Cf. also οἰκεῖος, properly an adjective, "in or of the house," but as a substantive (οἱ οἰκεῖοι), "family, household" (1 Tim 5:8 and metaphorically of the church in Gal 6:10; Eph 2:19).

90. Γυμνός "naked, without clothing." See also 1 Cor 15:37 and the discussion of the related words γυμνάζω and γυμνασία, ch. 12, n. 127.

91. A. Plummer, *Second Epistle of St Paul to the Corinthians* (Edinburgh: T&T Clark, 1915), 147. C. M. Pate, *Adam Christology as the Exegetical and Theological Substructure of 2 Corinthians 4:7–5:21* (Lanham, Md.: University Press of America, 1991), suggests that "Adam theology" explains the problem of the mixed metaphor in this passage.

92. Οὐκ οἰκεῖ ἐν ἐμοί . . . ἀγαθόν: "A good thing does not live in me." Οἰκέω (from οἶκος "a house, household"; see ch. 1, n. 89): "To inhabit, dwell." See also Rom 8:9, 11; 1 Cor 3:16; 7:12, 13; 1 Tim 6:16. Cf. ἐνοικέω "to dwell in" (Rom 8:11; 2 Cor 6:16; Col 3:16; 2 Tim 1:5, 14), ἐγκατοικέω "to dwell among,"

κατοικέω "to dwell in" (Eph 3:17; Col 1:19; 2:9), παροικέω "to dwell beside, among, near," περιοικέω "to dwell round about," συνοικέω "to dwell together."

93. But with differing consequences for the non-Christian and the Christian—condemnation for the one, acceptance still for the other, although perhaps with some sense of disappointment all around for a poor performance. See on 1 Cor 3:10–15 above (pp. 13–14); for a more detailed discussion of the interpretation of Rom 7:7–25, see p. 117 and notes.

94. Pliny, *Nat.* 33.57. See also Petronius, *Sat.* 60.

95. Liversidge, *Everyday Life*, 64.

96. Juvenal, *Sat.* 14.305–308.

97. See G. M. A. Richter, *Ancient Furniture, Greek, Etruscan, and Roman* (Oxford: Oxford University Press, 1926), 119–24, 127–29.

98. Juvenal, *Sat.* 6.91. See also Seneca, *Clem.* 1.9.7, and Pliny, *Ep.* 2.17.21; cf. 7.21.2.

99. See Richter, *Ancient Furniture*, 137–42.

100. See Richter, *Ancient Furniture*, and U. E. Paoli, *Rome: Its People, Life, and Customs* (London: Gerald Duckworth, 1990), 78–85.

101. Martial, *Epigr.* 2.43.11; 5.53; 6.94.1; 11.29.7; 14.97; and the passage in Cicero, *Mur.* 36.75, describing the funeral feast of Scipio Aemilianus. "Reading some of the ancient descriptions, one seems to relive a scene out of the *Arabian Nights*, set in spacious, unencumbered rooms where wealth is revealed only by the profusion and depth of the divans, the iridescence of damask, the sparkling of jewellery and of damascened copper" (Carcopino, *Daily Life*, 44).

102. Σκεῦος: "A vessel, implement." This is an old word with a wide variety of applications. In Paul, found in Rom 9:21–23 (with the same double use—noble and ignoble—as here); 2 Cor 4:7; 1 Thess 4:4; 2 Tim 2:20–21.

103. See ch. 1, n. 89.

104. Cf. Jer 18:1–11; Wis 15:7.

105. Ἐκκαθαίρω: Old verb, "to cleanse thoroughly, cleanse out," the language of ritual cleansing. In the NT, only here and in 1 Cor 5:7, in which it is used of purging a house of yeast at the time of the Passover. See ch. 11, n. 33.

106. Ἁγιάζω (hellenistic form of ἁγίζω, from ἅγος "religious awe" and ἄζω "to venerate"): (1) "to dedicate, separate, set apart for God," of things (e.g., 2 Tim 2:21, as a perfect passive participle, as also the following verb, "made and remaining dedicated and ready for his use"; see also 4:5) and of persons, (2) "to purify," make conformable in character to such dedication, forensically (e.g., 1 Cor 6:11; Eph 5:26), ceremonially (e.g., 2 Tim 2:21), morally (e.g., Rom 15:16; 1 Cor 1:2; 7:14 [2x]; 1 Thess 5:23), (3) "to treat as holy."

Life in the Country

OXEN

The ox was the most important working animal of Paul's world. Columella, a contemporary of Paul, gives an account of how the ox should be trained to walk at the steady pace required for either wagon or plow. It had to be accustomed to the yoke and set to work with an animal that already knew what to do. An ox that proved to be obstinate, he said, should be yoked between two other beasts until it had been trained.[1] The goad, a sharp-ended pole eight to ten feet long, was a useful aid to the beast's education and is the source of the proverb "It hurts to kick against **the goad**,"[2] which Paul cites in Acts 26:14 describing his conversion experience. Some have seen in these words a witness to an already troubled conscience, which he had tried to suppress by relentlessly pursuing the followers of the Way. But it is unwise to assess Paul's state of mind on the basis of a proverbial saying. He may simply have included the words on this occasion (they do not appear in the earlier accounts of his conversion, 9:1–9; 22:5–16) to stress, with the wisdom of hindsight, the absurdity of what he had been doing (cf. 5:39). The sense of the proverb is that it is foolish to fight against the odds—what must be must be, in Paul's case to "serve and bear witness" to Christ.

Each ox in a pair has its preferred side. Thus, a right-hand or a left-hand ox that dies may be difficult to replace. Paul may have known this when he urged the Corinthians not to be **yoked incompatibly**[3] with unbelievers (2 Cor 6:14). No other example of this verb is known, but the adjective from which it is apparently formed *(heterozygos)* is found in LXX Lev 19:19, in a passage that prohibits harnessing together different species of animal.[4] The same prohibition (but not the word) is found in Deut 22:10. The context of 2 Cor 6:14 suggests that Paul was considering a wider range of associations than simply that of husband and wife. There was something incongruous, he thought, in Christians having any close ties with the heathen.[5] In Phil 4:3 he mentions his own association with an unidentified Christian man, whom he describes as his **partner in harness** (NIV "loyal yokefellow").[6] He wants this man to help two women, Euodia and Syntyche, to patch up their quarrel. Evidently Paul and this person had worked well together—they had made a fine "left- and right-hand pair," which Paul remembered with appreciation, bestowing on his companion the epithet "loyal."

In defense of the principle that the preacher's needs should be met by the church, Paul twice appeals to the biblical injunction "Do not muzzle an ox while it is treading out grain" (1 Cor 9:9; 1 Tim 5:18; cf. Deut 25:4).[7] His question in the second half of 1 Cor 9:9, "Does [the Scripture] say this because God cares for the oxen?" anticipates a negative answer. But this does not mean that God is indifferent to the welfare of animals. On the contrary, Paul's point is that God *does* care for them but cares even more for his ministers. As the ox is permitted to have its share of the grain, so the preacher should be able to make a living from the work of the gospel (vv. 11, 12, 14). Paul makes this point already in verse 7, when he refers to the soldier, **the vineyard owner**,[8] and the shepherd,[9] and he returns to it again in verses 10 and 13 with **the plowman**,[10] **the thresher**,[11] and the priest at the altar. Each deserves a fair return from work done: the soldier, pay; the farmworker, a share of the produce; the priest, a cut from the offering.[12]

SHEPHERDING

Sheep were valued for their wool, their milk, the cheese that was made from their milk, and their manure. Ancient literature mentions several breeds and makes distinctions between hairy and woolly sheep and sheep of various colors. From Columella and other authorities we learn something of how sheep were managed (or of how they should be managed if the experts had their way), while a number of mosaics, reliefs, and inscriptions depict the life of the shepherd. One of the scenes of the Oudna (Uthina) mosaic in Tunisia shows a shepherd milking while another beguiles him with a pipe. At Mainz (Moguntiacum), in Germany, the landowner Marcus Terentius put up a tombstone for his freedman and shepherd, Jucundus, which shows him with his dog leading his sheep out to pasture. Another shepherd is mentioned in an inscription from Tugia, Spain. This man appears to have had management as well as veterinary skills, for he had to organize and provide for his workers, keep accounts, and give advice on tending the sheep. In these management skills, he and Paul had much in common.

In Acts 20:17–35 we find Paul giving advice to "his workers," the elders, on the care of their "sheep." The church, he says, is the **"flock**,"[13] a familiar figure for the people of God in both OT and NT. They are its **shepherds**[14] and overseers (v. 28), and the danger threatening the sheep is

fierce **wolves**,[15] which will not spare the flock (v. 29). This is Paul's reference to teachers coming into the church with a so-called gospel, other than
the one he had preached. He was probably thinking of the Judaizers who
had troubled the Galatian churches and others.[16] But danger threatened
from within the church no less than from outside. Teachers would arise from
among the Ephesians themselves who would "draw away the disciples after
them" (as sheep follow a shepherd, v. 30). Maintaining the metaphor, he
urged the elders "to watch," "to be on their guard" (v. 31). This group of
images probably came to Paul by way of the synagogue, which required of its
elders that they be "feeders, overseers, and shepherds" of God's flock.[17]

A very different application of the pastoral metaphor is found in 2 Tim
2:17. Paul likens the effect of the heretical teaching, which was now threatening Ephesus (Paul's worst fears for this church had been realized!), to a
gangrene **"eating its way"**[18] into the church. The picture is of a flock of
sheep fanning out (advancing) into the pasture. Each sheep eats its way forward. The emphasis in the text is not on the sheep but on their eating. Bad
teaching was gnawing at the life of the church.

TRAPPING

Hunting kept under control the wolves and other wild beasts that har-
ried the flocks. It also provided meat for the table. In Roman society, what
might be described as professional hunting was usually restricted to slaves.
This is reflected in Sallust's statement that hunting was a *servile officium*.[19]
Regardless of Sallust's opinion, however, hunting and fishing became two
popular Roman pastimes. Horace[20] compares them with the less manly
sports of the Greeks, perhaps unaware that hunting had been widespread in
Greece for a long time. As a sport, it appears to have been introduced to the
Romans by Greeks in the second century BCE[21] (hunting had been practiced
in rural districts from time immemorial as a matter of course). Roman
women also engaged in the sport.[22] An inscription puts hunting among the
greatest pleasures of life: "To hunt, to bathe, to gamble, to laugh, that is
life."[23] Cicero mentions it as a suitable pastime for the elderly.[24] Even Pliny
the Younger, whose life seems to have revolved around literature more than
anything else, amused himself in the country by hunting, although he did
take his writing gear with him to ensure that he would have something at
least to show for his day if he came home from the chase empty-handed.[25]

Hunting was of two kinds. *Venatio,* the pursuit of wild animals such as
wolves, bears, boars, and hares, was an active and sometimes dangerous
sport. *Aucupium,* the hunting of birds, was a largely sedentary occupation,
requiring skill rather than effort and courage. The art of the *auceps* lay in de-
ception, whether by simply concealing snares among bushes or in branches
of trees or by more elaborate means involving baits and blind birds as decoys
and hidden nets that could be instantly triggered. **Bait**[26] became a metaphor

of deceit, not so much for Paul as for others against him. In 1 Thess 2:3, he appears to be answering the charges of his detractors who accused him of (among other things) deceit, perhaps of the ulterior motive of making money out of the Thessalonians. A similar charge seems to lie behind 2 Cor 12:16. The words of this text should properly be shown as Paul quoting, with irony, what others were saying about him (only he has changed their third person to first): "Crafty fellow that I am, I caught you by deceit." The suggestion was probably that although he made a great show of not accepting maintenance from the church, he had intended to siphon off some of the collection for his own use. The collection was the "bait" by which he would trap them into something that would feather his own nest.

In the same way as bait took on a wider meaning, so a number of words for traps passed into use as figures of speech. Paul includes three of them in Rom 11:9–10, quoting from Ps 69:22–23 (LXX, slightly modified): "Let their table become **a snare**[27] and **a net**[28] and **a trap**[29] and a retribution for them, Let their eyes be darkened that they might no longer see and their backs bent forever."

Two of the three words used here for a trap are found elsewhere in Paul, *pagis* "a snare" and *skandalon* "a trap." In his correspondence with Timothy he twice warns about "the snare of the devil" *(pagis)*, which is set to catch both those who preach the gospel and those who resist it. For preachers, the snare is conceit (1 Tim 3:6–7), for those who resist the gospel, ignorance and an obsession with their own "stupid arguments" (2 Tim 2:23–26). He also warns of a snare that is set for us all (here he does not say who set the trap), namely, the desire to be better off than we are and to have all the things that money can buy. Even Christians, whose priorities should be other than these, have been known to be caught in this trap of obsession with wealth. The love of money has caused them to "wander away from the faith" and furthermore to wander into other troubles as well, which could lead to their "drowning" in a "sea" of destruction and ruin (1 Tim 6:9–10).

Skandalon, "a trap," occurs six times in Paul's writings. In three places it refers to Christ and, in particular, to his cross (Rom 9:33; 1 Cor 1:23; Gal 5:11). That God would save the world by a crucified Christ is such an odd proposition that many, including the wise of this world, fall into the trap of dismissing it. Its oddity is an offense, and its failure to fit preconceived notions an impediment to its acceptance (see 1 Cor 1:18–2:10). On a different tack, Paul warns that one Christian can be a *skandalon* to another by adopting a doctrinaire approach to sensitive issues (Rom 14:13), particularly in regard to the matter of eating meat from the temples,[30] an issue that was dividing the church. The solution was love—the readiness of one Christian (in a matter of moral indifference) to give way to another. Again, one Christian can be a *skandalon* to another by harboring a partisan spirit and teaching contrary to the gospel. "Avoid such a person at all costs!" Paul advises, who is a trap set to destroy the unwary (Rom 16:17).[31]

FARMING

Agriculture (the cultivation of the soil for the crowing of crops) was by far the biggest industry of the empire and *the* primary industry, in the sense that all else depended upon it. Time-honored methods continued to be practiced throughout the provinces, with little change under Roman rule except that some new crops were introduced and larger farming units were sometimes created. The chief benefits of Roman rule were indirect for farming communities. Peaceful conditions and the development of urban centers led to an increase in the population, which in turn led to an increased demand for food. Better roads made it easier for farmers to get their produce to market. Drainage and irrigation and cheaper and more plentiful tools also helped to boost the farm output.

More is known of agriculture in Italy than elsewhere, and we can only wonder about the extent to which Italian practice was typical of other parts of the empire. Farming manuals were produced by Cato, Varro, Columella, and Palladius (a span of five hundred years), but how extensive their circulation was and how influential they were in standardizing agricultural practice are matters of guesswork. Apart from these manuals (which may have been quite idiosyncratic), our knowledge of farming in general depends largely on the illustrations provided by reliefs and mosaics.[32] For the great majority of farmworkers, whether they were slaves on the large estates or peasants on their own plot of land, it was a life of unremitting hard work. And the farmer's best efforts cannot in themselves ensure the end product. Ultimately the outcome depends on processes of nature that are far beyond the farmer's control.

In 2 Tim 2:6 Paul speaks of **the hard-working farmer**[33] who deserves to have the first share of the crops. Paul was hoping, by this analogy, to encourage the young man Timothy to a wholehearted commitment to the ministry of the gospel by reminding him that the outcome of gospel ministry (under God) is new life for those who are "dead" (e.g., Eph 2:1). Paul's point is that there is something in this for the "farmer" as well. His "share of the crop" is the satisfaction of knowing even now that his hard work has counted for something—he has had a hand in the process of producing new life. It is possible, of course, that this "farmer" (the Christian minister) may not see the fruits of his work in this life. But in any case, he can expect his Lord's commendation: "Well done, good and faithful servant!" (Matt 25:21). Paul's emphasis (if the Greek word order means anything) is on the hard work. Successful farming, insofar as it lies with the farmer, depends as much on his sweat as his agricultural skill, and there is no public acclaim for this effort. H. C. G. Moule writes of the farmer's "strenuous and prosaic toil." Unlike the soldier and the athlete (see vv. 4 and 5), the farmer led a life that was "totally devoid of excitement, remote from all glamour of peril and of applause."[34] So did the minister.

At Corinth a partisan spirit had taken hold of the church. "I belong to Paul," one was saying, or "I belong to Apollos" or "to Cephas" or even "to Christ"—a piece of one-upmanship if ever there was one (1 Cor 1:12; cf. 3:1–4). In this situation it was imperative that Paul play down the part of the minister and draw attention, instead, to God's role in the matter. He does this in 1 Cor 3:5–9 by asking, "What, after all, is Apollos? And what is Paul?" They had done good work, of course, in growing the Corinthian church. Paul had **planted**[35] and Apollos had **watered**.[36] But God had given **the growth;**[37] that is, the telling factor was something other than the minister could contribute, try as hard as he might (v. 6). The tenses call for attention. The work of Paul and Apollos in "planting" and "watering" is expressed in the aorist, which describes their ministry in historical terms. They have done their work and have moved on. It is finished. God's work, on the other hand, is never done. It is referred to in the imperfect tense: God goes on giving the growth. In 2 Tim 2:6 ministry is considered subjectively, from the point of view of the minister, for whom (as for the hardworking farmer) there seems to be no end to the toil (the present participle[38]). But in fact, the only continuing and all-important factor is God.

In this discussion Paul makes three important points. First, "neither the one who plants nor the one who waters is anything, but the one who makes the 'plant' grow, namely, God" (v. 7). This is not to say that the human minister counts for nothing. "We are God's fellow workers," says Paul (v. 9). God is named first (in the Greek) to show where the emphasis lies, but the minister does have the status of partner.[39] Second, **the field**[40] belongs to God (v. 9, shifting the application of his agricultural metaphor from God as the force beyond the farmer's control to God as the farmer himself), but the minister works "the field" (the people to whom he is ministering) in partnership with the owner. Third, all human ministers serve the same end—"the one who plants and the one who waters are equal" (lit. "one," v. 8). Their tasks differ. Each makes his or her own contribution and each will be rewarded accordingly (v. 8). But it is God who determines what the "payment" will be. God's criterion is not the success of the worker, as we reckon success, not how one worker compares with another, but the worker's own "labor" (*kopos* "hard work"[41]). All that God asks of us is that we work as hard as we can, with all the skill that we have, in whatever field he has put us, at sowing the seed and nurturing what he brings to life (cf. Mark 4:2–20).

Meanwhile, God as farmer waters us with the Spirit. The idea of spiritual refreshment is often conveyed in the Bible through the metaphor of watering. We see it, for example, in Isa 44:3: "I will pour water on the thirsty land, and streams on the dry ground; I will pour out my Spirit."[42] Paul now declares that what God had once promised he has now carried out. The work of ministry may be hard and the ground may be dry, but God has **inundated**[43] us with God's Spirit (Titus 3:6), that is, has given us of himself, and is with us, therefore, in the work to the end of the age (cf. Matt 28:20).

Paul's second letter to the Thessalonians begins with a reference to his readers' faith **"growing abundantly"**[44] (2 Thess 1:3). Against the background of Old Testament references to the faithful as flourishing like trees planted near water (Ps 1:3) and as "oaks of righteousness, a planting of the Lord for the display of his splendor" (Isa 61:3), this might well be an intentional metaphor. The same Old Testament background might also explain his language in Ephesians and Colossians when he speaks of them as becoming strong in faith, **rooted**[45] and founded in Christ and his love (Eph 3:17; Col 2:6, 7).

SOWING AND REAPING

Paul applies the images of **sowing**[46] and **reaping**[47] in a number of ways. In Gal 6:6–10, from the principle expressed in the proverb that "a person reaps what he sows" (v. 7),[48] that is, gets some return from investment, he draws the conclusion that the minister, who has invested effort in teaching the word, deserves in return to have the church supply his material needs: "The one who is taught . . . should share all good things with his teacher" (v. 6).[49] I have taken the view that verses 6 and 7 belong together. But some prefer to take verse 7 with what follows. Perhaps it is a case of "both . . . and," the proverb illustrating the teaching about the minister's recompense and then suggesting the terms in which the warning of verse 8 is couched. At all events, Paul's thought moves now to Christian morality as he thinks of each Christian as comprising two "fields," the flesh (life lived as natural inclinations dictate) and the Spirit (life lived by God's rules). The harvest depends on which of the two fields is cultivated and on what is sown in that field. The "seeds" are our thoughts and deeds.

> Every time we allow our minds to harbour a grudge, nurse a grievance, entertain an impure fantasy, or wallow in self pity, we are sowing to the flesh. Every time we linger in bad company whose insidious influence we know we cannot resist, every time we lie in bed when we ought to be up and praying, every time we read pornographic literature, every time we take a risk which strains our self-control, we are sowing, sowing, sowing to the flesh.[50]

From such seed the harvest reaped is corruption, perhaps even destruction (the word can mean either[51])—the Christian is at best tainted and at worst lost, having allowed himself to lose sight of the Lord. On the other hand, if Christians set themselves to think as God thinks and to do as God does (guided by the pattern of Christ and the precepts of Scripture and empowered by the Spirit), the fruit of eternal life will be theirs (v. 8). Of course, life in Christ is life eternal *now*. But there is still room for growth. The closer Christians grow to God in their practice by "sowing to the Spirit," the greater their capacity to enjoy the life he has given them.[52]

The lesson of this passage can be summed up in the maxim that character is molded by conduct. As we bring our thinking and doing more and more into line with Christ, so our character takes on more and more the likeness of Christ. We show evidence of what Paul calls "the fruit[53] of the Spirit" (Gal 5:22–23). The cultivation of such "fruit" depends on a number of factors other than the Christian's own effort (the saving, sanctifying work of God in Christ and the Spirit[54]). And yet effort is also demanded from the Christian.[55] "Let us not become weary,"[56] therefore, "in well-doing [all that God expects of us as Christians], for in due season,"[57] says Paul, if we do not give up,[58] "we will reap the harvest" that we have been promised (Gal 6:9; cf. v. 8).

Paul speaks again of sowing in 2 Cor 9:6–11, with reference to financial matters. He appeals to the Corinthians to give generously to the collection (as they had earlier determined to do[59]) and, in this connection, affirms that "the one who sows sparingly will also reap sparingly and the one who sows bountifully will also reap bountifully."[60] The sense in which their "harvest" will be bountiful is explained in the verses that follow. For one thing, there will be a large sum of money for Paul and the others to take to Jerusalem. Beyond this, there will be thanksgiving to God for this evidence of God's grace in their lives (vv. 11b–13), and the grateful Judeans will pray for the Corinthians (v. 14). This, in turn, will add to the Corinthians' blessings. They have already experienced "God's grace abounding," not only in the spiritual realm but in the mundane and material also (some of the Corinthian Christians appear to have been well-off, and Paul believed that all, even the slaves in the congregation, had sufficient for their own needs and more[61]). In short, since God has supplied (in their material blessings) **the seed**[62] for this sowing (the collection for the Judeans) and will always give more than enough "bread for their food," they can afford to be generous (vv. 8–11a).[63] If further incentive is needed, they should know that "God loves a generous giver" (v. 7).[64]

Every year, thousands of Greeks took part in the mystery rites at Eleusis. These rites were based on the story of Demeter's search for Kore, her daughter. Hades had carried the girl off as his bride, and the goddess had come to Eleusis looking for her. In the guise of a crone she was received into the house of Celeus the king to be a nurse for his son. In time her identity was revealed and the Eleusians built her a temple. Meanwhile Zeus had constrained Hades to return Kore to her mother. But the girl had eaten the fruit of the underworld, which tied her to that realm, and she was doomed to go back to Hades each year. Her going and coming marked the cycle of winter and summer, of planting and harvest. On leaving Eleusis, Demeter gave Triptolemos, the child she had nursed, one grain of wheat. The seed grew and multiplied, and wheat became Demeter's gift to all people. The ritual of the Eleusian mystery had to do with the "death" and "rebirth" of wheat, its planting and growth into a staple of life, into which was interwoven the hope of human immortality. The initiates in the mystery underwent an annual rite of rebirth expressing that hope.

We may be sure that Paul knew the story of Demeter and Kore and was aware of the rite based upon it. It was, after all, a part of the cultural fabric of his Greco-Roman world, familiar to him, perhaps, from his childhood.[65] Corinth (in which he had lived for two years) was only forty miles from Eleusis, which lay on the road by which he had come from Athens to Corinth (Acts 18:1, 11). When Paul addressed the Corinthians on the subject of death and resurrection, of the perishable putting on the imperishable and the mortal, immortality (1 Cor 15: 53), he did so in terms of the familiar tale of the seed that "does not come to life unless it dies" (v. 36). "When you sow," he says, "you do not sow the plant in its final form [*to sōma to genēsomenon* "the body that will be"], but a bare "**grain**,"[66] perhaps of wheat, perhaps the seed of some other plant. But God gives it its "final form [*sōma* 'body'], according to his choice in creation, to each seed [*sperma*] its own form" (vv. 37–38). So in the resurrection. The body that is "sown in corruption, is raised in incorruption, that is sown in dishonor, is raised in glory, that is sown in weakness, is raised in power, that is sown a natural body, is raised a spiritual body" (vv. 42–44). If Paul is indeed expressing a Christian truth in terms that hint of the Eleusian mystery, he would not have been the first to have done so. Some twenty years earlier Jesus appears to have spoken of his death in similar terms: "Unless a seed of wheat falls to the ground and 'dies,' it remains alone. But if it 'dies,' it produces much fruit" (John 12:24). It may be no coincidence that Jesus, too, was speaking to Greeks.

FRUIT

If Paul shows an awareness of Greek culture in 1 Cor 15, he also shows his Jewish roots. Hebrews were required to give the firstfruits of the harvest to God in acknowledgment of God's ownership of the earth (e.g., Ps 24:1). And so they did. An annual offering of the first sheaf of the harvest was made at Passover time (on the day after the Sabbath, the very day on which our Lord rose), and of flour and loaves at Pentecost time.[67] Pentecost was sometimes called the Day of Firstfruits.[68] This notion of the firstfruits became for Paul a metaphor of the resurrection of Christ. At his coming, all those who are his will be raised, but before that, in anticipation of that eschatological "harvest," Christ himself has been raised as **the firstfruits**[69] (1 Cor 15:20–23; cf. "the firstborn from among the dead," Col 1:18).[70] When we, like Christ, are raised a "spiritual body," our salvation (as far as we know) will be complete. That will be the harvest of all the planting and watering of new life that God has been doing (with some help from others). Meanwhile, in anticipation of that day, we have its "firstfruits," the first taste of new life in relation to God, namely, the Spirit of God[71] (Rom 8:23), who brings to

God's people moral and spiritual gifts, gifts for ministry, gifts for growth.[72] Finally, Paul sometimes speaks of people as "firstfruits," meaning that they were the first in a particular place to have that new life in Christ—for example, Epenetus in the province of Asia (Rom 16:5) and the household of Stephanas in Achaia, by which he probably means Corinth, the capital of the province (1 Cor 16:15).

Bearing fruit is one of Paul's favorite metaphors for the Christian life. In Rom 15:28 he describes the collection for the Judeans as **a fruit**[73] of the Gentile churches, as he in one place describes a gift that he himself had received from the Philippians as their "fruit" in relation to him (Phil 4:17).[74] In each case the "fruit" was the product of God's grace in their lives. Compare this with Paul's direction to Titus that the Cretans should seek useful employment in order to meet their own needs and those of others.[75] In so doing they would not be **unfruitful**[76] (Titus 3:14). Unfruitfulness, by this definition, includes a failure to give aid to the needy, thus leaving the believer at odds with the Spirit, for the "fruit of the Spirit is . . . kindness and goodness" (Gal 5:22). This "fruit" has reference, as we have already seen, to Christian character (to the cultivation of which both the human and the divine must contribute), and it is in these terms of character that Paul most often speaks of bearing fruit.[77] But in Col 1:6 it is the gospel that "is **bearing** and growing."[78] The fruit that Paul has in mind here is people turning to Christ. In Phil 1:22, he speaks of his own ministry in particular as "fruitful" in winning converts and perhaps in the sense of building them up into Christian maturity.[79] To the Romans he expressed the hope that he would soon have the same "fruit" among them that he had had among others (Rom 1:13). Sometimes a little pruning is necessary to encourage fruitfulness or, in the case of the Cretan Christians, to correct "malformations." Paul instructed Titus to reprove sharply (a word suggestive of **pruning with a sharp knife**)[80] those church members who were in danger of being drawn away from the truth by the blandishments of the Judaizers (Titus 1:13).

THE OLIVE

If one symbol could express what all the countries through which Paul moved had in common, it would be the olive. His world was the world of the olive, valued for its fruit, its oil, its timber. But Paul would not have thought of this tree in ecumenical terms. For him it had a quite different significance. Like the fig and the vine, the olive was a symbol of Israel (see, e.g., Jer 11:16; Hos 14:6). From this perspective it might be considered a symbol of division rather than of unity, for the Jews regarded the Gentiles as "separate, excluded" from their theocratic commonwealth (Eph 2:12), having no part in the "olive tree" that was Israel.

But Paul's mission was to both Jew and Gentile. In Rom 11:16–24, he uses an analogy that allows us to see the olive as a symbol of both the Jews and the Gentiles and of the two as "one new man" in Christ (cf. Eph 2:14–18). Paul's analogy, however, reverses normal arboricultural practice. As with other fruit trees, a cultivated olive is grafted into wild stock; a wild sprig is not grafted into a garden tree. Paul's use of such a figure (Rom 11:17) has been seen as evidence that he knew nothing about the cultivation of trees. As C. H. Dodd once remarked, "He had not the curiosity to inquire what went on in the olive yards which fringed every road that he walked."[81] Both Columella[82] (first century CE) and Palladius,[83] however, speak of this very practice—the grafting in of a wild cutting—as a means of stimulating an unproductive tree into fruiting. There is evidence, moreover, that this remedy has been practiced in modern times as well.[84]

But the difficulty remains of Paul's reference to grafting back the branches that had earlier been removed to make room for the others (v. 23). In terms of actual practice, this is nonsense. Did Paul know that it was? (Not that it matters. His argument does not depend on the metaphor.) It is certainly possible that he knowingly pictured something contrary to practice in the interest of making his point. The incorporation of the Gentiles into the "Israel of God" (cf. Gal 6:16) was, after all, a matter of grace, not of nature.[85] "You were cut," he says to the Gentiles, "from **a wild olive tree**,[86] to which by nature you belonged, and **grafted**[87] [*para physin* "contrary to nature"] into **a garden olive**,[88] to which by nature you did not belong" (Rom 11:24). From this he draws the conclusion: You Gentiles must not be arrogant or complacent. You are what you are ("fellow citizens with God's people and members of the household of God," Eph 2:19) on no other grounds than those of God's sovereign grace. And if you have been grafted into this "tree" by grace, "how much more readily will the natural branches [the Jews] be grafted back into their own tree [if only they meet the condition of faith in Christ]?" (v. 24).[89] In Rom 6:5, he appears to employ the same metaphor (but a different word) to express the idea of the believer's union with Christ. "If we [Jews and Gentiles alike] have been **implanted**[90] into him in his death, so too shall we be in his resurrection."

NOTES

1. Columella, *Rust.* 2.
2. Κέντρον (from κεντέω "to prick"): (1) "a sting," metaphorically 1 Cor 15:55, (2) "a goad." Note the plural in Acts 26:14, κέντρα "goads," and λακτίζειν, the present active infinitive: "to keep on kicking against goads." The picture is one of an angry beast lashing out continually with its hooves. Λακτίζω is "to kick with the heel." The proverb is frequent in classical literature. See Pindar, *Pyth.* 2.94f. and the scholiast on 2.173; Aeschylus, *Ag.* 1624; Euripides, *Bacch.* 791; Terence, *Phor.* 1.2.27; Plautus, *Truc.* 4.2.59. There may have been a similar proverb among the Jews. See *Pss. Sol.* 16:4. The fact that Paul mentions this Greek and Latin proverb is an indication of his own broad culture and also of his awareness of the culture of his audience on this occasion. Cf. his citing of Greek poets in Acts 17:28 and our discus-

sion above (pp. 39–40) of his possible reference to the story of Demeter and Kore in 1 Cor 15.

3. Ἑτεροζυγέω (cf. σύνζυγος, ch. 2, n. 6): "To be yoked with a different yoke, to be misyoked." Note the present imperative: "Stop becoming misyoked." Evidently some Christians had already formed or were maintaining associations with nonbelievers.

4. The Hebrew text of Lev 19:19 prohibits not yoking but cross-breeding.

5. See, e.g., 1 Cor 5:9f.; 6:1–6; 7:12–16, 39; 9:21f.; 10:21, 27, 32; 14:23ff.; Gal 2:19; Eph 5:7; also Deut 7:3; Josh 23:12; Ezra 9:2; Neh 13:25. Such data suggest that the Christian must walk a fine line between withdrawal from and participation in pagan society. Close personal unions, such as marriage, should be avoided. Yet the Christian should be as involved as possible in society in order to change it (from within, as it were) for the better by bringing Christ into it and it to Christ. I take the ἄπιστοι of 2 Cor 6:14 in the general sense of "unbelievers" rather than in the narrower sense of Paul's opponents, contrary to D. Rensberger ("2 Corinthians 6:14–7:1," *SBT* 8 [1978]: 25–49). See further R. P. Martin, *2 Corinthians* (Waco, Tex.: Word, 1986), 196–97.

6. Σύνζυγος (from συνζεύγνυμι "to yoke together"; cf. ἑτεροζυγέω, ch. 2, n. 3): Many suggestions have been made for who this person was, including Lydia, who by this term is made Paul's wife! Unfortunately for this interesting suggestion, γνήσιε is a masculine form—the masculine vocative singular of the adjective γνήσιος (from γίνομαι "to become"), (1) properly, "lawfully begotten, born in wedlock," (2) "true, loyal, genuine, sincere" (cf. 1 Tim 1:2; Titus 1:4). It is used as a substantive in 2 Cor 8:8, "sincerity" (= γνησιότης). Some have suggested that σύνζυγος is a proper name ("I beseech you, who are a genuine Syzygus—in deed as well as in name—to help"), but as such it is rare, being known from only one inscription. J. B. Lightfoot (*Saint Paul's Epistle to the Philippians* [London: Macmillan, 1868], 158) suggests that the "true yoke-fellow" was Epaphroditus, the bearer of the letter, but it would seem to be an odd way in which to address him.

7. W. M. Ramsay (*A Historical Commentary on St Paul's Epistle to the Galatians* [New York: Putnam's, 1900], 457–59) points out that the priests of the pagan temples enjoyed a very lucrative arrangement, so much so that these positions were regularly auctioned by the state to the highest bidder. "One of the objects that Paul had most to heart," he suggests, "was to train his converts in voluntary liberality, as distinguished from payments levied on rituals (from which the pagan priests made their living)." In 1 Tim 5:18, Paul "yokes in tandem" two scriptures, one from Deuteronomy and the other, it would appear, from the sayings of Jesus (cf. Matt 10:10; Luke 10:7). On Paul's familiarity with the tradition of Jesus' teaching, see D. Wenham, *Paul: Follower of Jesus or Founder of Christianity?* (Grand Rapids: Eerdmans, 1995), and on this passage in particular, 192–93. The MSS of 1 Cor 9:9 have variously φιμόω (from φιμός "a muzzle") and κημόω (from κημός "a muzzle"), both meaning "to muzzle." The former appears in Aristophanes, *Nub.* 592, LXX, NT, and the papyri, but on the textual evidence, the latter (κημόω) is the better reading in 1 Cor 9:9. "Treading out grain" renders ἀλοῶντα, the present active participle of ἀλοάω "to thresh" (from ἅλως or ἅλων "a threshing floor"; cf. ch. 2, n. 11). An Egyptian hieroglyphic at Eileithyas reads, "Thresh O you oxen, measures of grain for yourselves, measures of grain for your masters." Egyptian monuments show oxen and sometimes donkeys pulling a drag over the grain. The Hebrews also employed this method (cf. 2 Sam 24:22), but sometimes the grain was threshed simply by having the oxen trample it (Mic 4:12–13).

8. Paul asks, "Who plants a vineyard?" Φυτεύω (from φυτόν "a plant," itself from φύω "to bring forth, produce, spring up"): "To plant." See also 1 Cor 3:6–8. Ἀμπελών (from ἄμπελος "a vine"): "A vineyard." For a similar analogy with a different application, see on 2 Tim 2:6 above (pp. 36–37).

9. See ch. 2, n. 14.

10. Ἀροτριάω (from ἄροτρον "a plow," itself from ἀρόω "to plow"): "To plow," here as a present active participle and infinitive, "The one plowing ought to plow in hope."

11. Ὁ ἀλοῶν: Present active participle of ἀλοάω "to thresh." See ch. 2, n. 7.

12. For details of the Jewish priests' entitlement, see Lev 6:8–7:38; Num 18:8–20.

13. Ποίμνιον: "A flock," properly of sheep but used metaphorically in Acts 20:28–29; cf., e.g., Gen 49:24; Ps 23:1; 80:1; John 10:1–18; Heb 13:20; 1 Pet 2:25; 5:4. See also ποίμνη "a flock" in 1 Cor 9:7.

14. Here is rendered as a noun what is in fact a verb. The Greek runs, "The Holy Spirit has appointed you overseers *to shepherd or tend* the church of God." Ποιμαίνω (from ποιμήν "a shepherd"): "To act as a shepherd, tend" flocks, elsewhere in Paul in 1 Cor 9:7. In John 21:16 ποιμαίνω is used synonymously with βόσκω, properly of a herdsman, "to feed," but of Christian pastoral care (John 21:15, 17). Cf. ποίμην "a shepherd," used of Christian pastors in Eph 4:11.

15. Λύκος: "A wolf." The adjective is βαρύς "heavy, burdensome, weighty, violent, cruel." Jesus had already described false teachers in these terms in Matt 7:15 and John 10:12; cf. its use for presumptuous and cruel rulers and judges in Ezek 22:27; Zeph 3:3. Cf. Matt 10:16; Luke 10:3 for the believers as "sheep among wolves," and see Rev 2:2 for "false apostles" at Ephesus.

16. See Gal 1:6–9. The Judaizers may also have been the problem at Corinth and the ones doing the threatening at Philippi (see Phil 3:2–3). With his reference in Acts 20:29 to false teachers as "wolves," cf. Paul's identification in Titus 1:10–12 (citing Epimenides) of the "many rebellious people, . . . especially those of the circumcision [the Judaizers]" with "evil beasts."

17. See A. Edersheim, *Sketches of Jewish Social Life in the Days of Christ* (London: Religious Tract Society, 1876), 282; F. J. A. Hort, *The Christian Ecclesia* (London: Macmillan, 1898), 100f.

18. Νομὴν ἕξει: "It [the gangrene] will have pasture." Νομή (from νέμω "to pasture, graze"): (1) "a pasture, pasturage," (2) "a grazing, feeding," used as a medical term for the consuming progress of a disease. See Plutarch, *Mor.* 165E (*Superst.* 3); Polybius, *Hist.* 1.81.6. H. Alford, *Greek Testament: An Exegetical and Critical Commentary* (London: Rivingtons & Deighton, Bell, 1871), 3:385, cites without reference Hippocrites and Galen as using this expression. For Paul's medical metaphors, see pp. 87–89.

19. Sallust, *Bell. Cat.* 4.1.

20. Horace, *Sat.* 2.2.9–13.

21. According to Polybius (*Hist.* 31.29.3), one of the earliest hunters in Rome was Publius Scipio Aemilianus. His Greek tutors presumably introduced him to the sport.

22. Juvenal, *Sat.* 1.22.

23. *CIL* 8.17938, found on a *tabula lusoria,* a kind of chessboard.

24. Cicero, *Sen.* 16.56.

25. Pliny, *Ep.* 1.6.1.

26. Δόλος: (1) "bait," (2) "a snare," (3) in the abstract, "craft, deceit." In Paul in Rom 1:29 (not in all texts); 2 Cor 12:16; 1 Thess 2:3. Cf. δολόω, ch. 7, n. 54.

27. Παγίς (from πήγνυμι "to make fast, fix"): A poetic and late form for πάγη "a snare" for birds or beasts. See also 1 Tim 3:7; 6:9; 2 Tim 2:26, in the first two of which and possibly also the third the trap is set by the devil. Cf. ch. 10, n. 74.

28. Θήρα: (1) "a hunting, chase," (2) "prey, game," and (3) "a net." Found only here in the NT.

29. Σκάνδαλον: Late form (more common in the LXX and the NT than anywhere else) of the rare word σκανδάληθρον, properly the "bait stick" of a trap. This

refers to the stick on which the bait was fixed. The animal for which the trap was set was lured by the bait to touch or step on the stick; the stick touched off a spring and so the animal was enticed to its capture or destruction. This word is used of the trap itself in the papyri and elsewhere. It is used metaphorically of anything that causes error or sin, sometimes a person, sometimes a thing. Aristophanes used it for "verbal traps" set to lure a person in argument into defeat. It is clear, therefore, that the original flavor of the word was not so much "a stumbling block" (as it is often rendered) to trip someone up as an "enticement" to lure someone to destruction. In Paul in Rom 9:33; 11:9; 14:13; 16:17; 1 Cor 1:23; Gal 5:11. Cf. σκανδαλίζω, properly, "to put a trap" in the way. In the NT this word is always metaphorical of something that hinders right conduct or thought, "to cause to fall into error" (as, e.g., 1 Cor 8:13 [2x]) and in the passive, "to be made to fall into error" (e.g., Rom 14:21; 2 Cor 11:29).

30. The source of most of the meat sold in the shops. See pp. 18–19 and notes.

31. There is a frequent association in Paul's writing between σκανδαλίζω/σκάνδαλον and προσκόπτω/πρόσκομμα (see ch. 9, n. 62). In his references to σκανδαλίζω/σκάνδαλον, Paul may have been indebted to the tradition (in a Greek form?) of Jesus' teaching in Matt 18:6–7; Mark 9:42–47; Luke 17:1–2.

32. See, e.g., J. Liversidge, *Everyday Life in the Roman Empire* (New York: Putnam's, 1976), 128–56.

33. Τὸν κοπιῶντα γεωργόν: "The toiling tiller of the earth." Γεωργός (from γῆ "earth" and ἔργω = ἔδρω "to do"): "A farmer," specifically "a vinedresser" in Jesus' parable (Matt 21:33–44 and par.). Found only here in Paul. For the kindred γεώργιον, see ch. 2, n. 40, and for κοπιάω (here as a present active participle) "to work with effort, toil," see ch. 7, n. 14. The use of κοπιάω in the analogy is particularly apt, as Paul seems to have employed it almost as a technical term for ministerial labor. See esp. Rom 16:6, 12 (2x); 1 Cor 15:10; 16:16; Gal 4:11; Phil 2:16; Col 1:29; 1 Thess 5:12; 1 Tim 4:10; 5:17. The analogy of the farmer is the same as in 1 Cor 9:7, but the application is different. There Paul was defending the minister's right to material support, whereas here he is talking more about the demands of the ministry itself. It involves hard work, although it is not without its rewards. This is the third of three illustrations (soldiering, athletics, and farming). The emphasis on the rewards is greater in the third than the first (his thought has been carried in this direction by the reference in his second illustration to the athlete's crown of victory), but the fact remains that the whole discussion, of which the three illustrations are all a part, is about the effort that must be put into ministry.

34. H. C. G. Moule, *The Second Epistle to Timothy* (London: Religious Tract Society, 1905), 77. R. A. Ward, *Commentary on 1 and 2 Timothy and Titus* (Waco, Tex.: Word, 1974), 163, sums up the lessons to be learned from vv. 4–6: "No distractions—concentration; no half-heartedness—exertion; no cessation—persistence. Good watchwords for the minister!"

35. Φυτεύω: See ch. 2, n. 8. For the historical circumstances, see Acts 18:1–18.

36. Ποτίζω (from πότος "a drinking bout," itself from πίνω "to drink"): "To give to drink, to irrigate." It may have as its object men, animals, or plants. See Rom 12:20; 1 Cor 3:2 (where Paul describes himself as giving the Corinthians milk to drink); 12:13. For the historical circumstances, see Acts 18:24–19:1. The metaphor of 1 Cor 3:6 bears out the historicity of Luke's account in Acts of Paul's preceding Apollos at Corinth.

37. Αὐξάνω: (1) "to make to grow," in passive, "to grow, increase, become greater," (2) "to grow, increase." In Paul in 1 Cor 3:6, 7; 2 Cor 9:10; 10:15; Eph 4:15; Col 1:10. The earlier form, αὔξω, occurs in Eph 2:21; Col 2:19.

38. See ch. 2, n. 33.

39. Συνεργός: See ch. 7, n. 21.

40. Γεώργιον (from γεωργός, see ch. 2, n. 33): (1) "a field," (2) "cultivation." Only found here in Paul.

41. See ch. 7, n. 14.

42. Cf. Ezek 36:26ff.; 39:29; Joel 2:23, 28–29; Zech 12:10; Mal 3:10; Sir 18:11.

43. Ἐκχέω (the forms ἐκχύνω and ἐκχύννω also occur; cf. Rom 5:5): "To pour out." The verb is found in Paul in Rom 3:15; Titus 3:6. In Titus 3:6 it is qualified by the adverb πλουσίως "richly, abundantly," giving the sense suggested above. In Rom 5:5, the subject of the verb is strictly love, but the sense is that we have the assurance of God's love precisely because we have the Spirit of God who "has been poured out in, and still floods, our hearts" (perfect tense). Historically, the Spirit was given in the events of the Pentecost described in Acts 2. But that once-for-all gift to the church is subsequently appropriated by each believer in the act of acknowledging Christ as Lord (see D. J. Williams, *Acts* [NIBC; Peabody, Mass.: Hendrickson, 1992], 44). Ἐκχέω is used in LXX Joel 3:1–2 (= 2:28–29) and so in Acts 2:17–18, 33 in reference to the pentecostal event.

44. Ὑπεραυξάνω (for αὐξάνω, see ch. 2, n. 37): "To increase beyond measure," only in 2 Thess 1:3.

45. Ῥιζόω (from ῥίζα "a root," metaphor of origin in Paul in Rom 11:16–18; 15:12; 1 Tim 6:10): "To cause to take root," metaphorically "to plant, fix firmly, establish." In the NT only in Eph 3:18; Col 2:7. Cf. ἐκριζόω "to pull out by the roots." On being "founded," see pp. 14–15 and ch. 1, n. 54.

46. Σπείρω: "To sow (seed)." In Paul in 1 Cor 9:11; 15:36–37 (2x), 42–43 (2x), 44; 2 Cor 9:6 (2x), 10; Gal 6:7–8 (2x).

47. Θερίζω (from θέρος "summer," itself from θέρω "to heat"): "To reap." In Paul in 1 Cor 9:11; 2 Cor 9:6 (2x); Gal 6:7–8 (2x), 9.

48. The following places use this metaphor to show that a person deserves to benefit from his labor: Plato, *Phaedr.* 260D; Aristotle, *Rhet.* 3.3.4 (citing Gorgias); Demosthenes, *Cor.* 159; Cicero, *Or.* 2.65; Plautus, *Merc.* 71; Plutarch, *Mor.* 394E (*Pyth. orac.* 1); Job 4:8; Prov 22:8; Hos 8:7; 10:12; Sir 7:3; *T. Levi* 13:6; *4 Ezra* 4:28–30; Philo, *Conf.* 21; *Mut.* 268–269; *Somn.* 2.76; 1 Cor 9:11; 2 Cor 9:6. The same thought is expressed in Matt 7:16–20; Luke 6:43; 19:21.

49. Κοινωνείτω ὁ κατηχούμενος τὸν λόγον τῷ κατηχοῦντι ἐν πᾶσιν ἀγαθοῖς: "Let the one who is taught [κατηχέω, late and rare verb; cf. Rom 2:18; 1 Cor 14:19] the word [the Christian faith] share with the one who teaches in all [the] good things [of life]." Κοινωνέω: "To have a share of, go shares in (something) with (someone), take part in." Cf. Rom 12:13; 15:27; Phil 4:15; 1 Tim 5:22 and, for similar teaching, 1 Cor 9:7–12; 1 Tim 5:17–18 (see p. 36); 2 Cor 11:7–8 (see p. 225).

50. J. R. W. Stott, *The Message of Galatians* (London: Inter-Varsity Press, 1968), 170. Paul has already expressed what he understands by "sowing to the flesh" in Gal 5:19–21. For further references to such "sowing," see Gal 5:15, 26; 6:1–2 (which implies an indifference to the needs of others); 6:3–4 (pride).

51. Φθορά (from φθείρω "to destroy"): "Destruction, corruption, decay." Cf. Rom 8:21; 1 Cor 15:42, 50; Col 2:22.

52. Cf., e.g., Rom 6:20–23 and 8:13 for the same idea expressed in other ways. Commenting on Gal 6:7–8, F. F. Bruce (*The Epistle to the Galatians* [Grand Rapids: Eerdmans, 1982], 265) suggests that the appearance of Christians "before the tribunal of Christ, to 'receive good or evil, according to the deeds done in the body' (2 Cor 5:10), is specially implied here." "Any one," he says, "who did not seriously believe in such a coming assessment, or thought that the law of sowing and reaping could safely be ignored, would indeed be treating God with contempt" (see v. 7).

53. Καρπός: See ch. 2, n. 73.

54. See, e.g., C. K. Barrett, *Freedom and Obligation* (London: SPCK, 1985), 77. The fruits of the Spirit, he says, "are not human products but the result of God's Spirit dwelling within. All are the consequences of the self-forgetfulness that looks away from itself to God."

55. The Epistles contain frequent imperatives, that imply freedom of choice on the part of the Christian and appeal to him or her to choose (1) in general, "not to conform to this age but to be transformed in attitude" and thereby in action (Rom 12:2), "to walk in the ways of the Spirit" (Gal 5:16, 25; cf. v. 18), "to have the outlook of Christ" (Phil 2:5), to "seek" and to "set the mind" on the things of God, namely, "the things that are above, not . . . things that are on earth" (Col 3:1, 2; cf. Phil 3:19), and (2) in particular, to avoid any hint of sexual impurity or, indeed, of any kind impurity, or of greed, obscenity, and the like (see, e.g., Eph 5:3ff.). A full list of directions, if drawn up, would be very long indeed, but they are gathered up in the one comprehensive command to love (see, e.g., Rom 13:9–10; Eph 5:1).

56. Ἐνκακέω (from κακός "bad" in a variety of senses, including "cowardly"): "To lose heart, be weary, tired." Cf. 2 Cor 4:1, 16; Eph 3:13; 2 Thess 3:13. On its own, this word might not be regarded as a metaphor but, rather, as a plain statement of fact. But it can be taken as part of the extended metaphor of sowing and reaping, the picture being that of workers worn out by their toil (see ch. 12, n. 86, which suggests that in 2 Cor 4:1, 16 it could equally be a metaphor drawn from the arena). Paul fears that the Galatian Christians, having begun well (cf. Gal 3:2–5; 5:7), were losing their enthusiasm for life lived "in step with the Spirit" (5:25) and were being enticed into a legalistic religion, a religion that was focused on self more than on the needs of others.

57. Καιρῷ ἰδίῳ: "At the appropriate moment," "at the proper time." In terms of the metaphor, this time is the harvest, and in terms of the meaning, probably the return of Christ and the final judgment. While the adjective ἴδιος and the noun καιρός occur frequently in Paul and elsewhere on their own, the only other instances bringing them together are 1 Tim 2:6 and 6:15 (both, however, in the plural). On ἴδιος as "appropriate," "due," or "proper" in Paul, see 1 Cor 3:8 and 15:23.

58. Ἐκλύω: Old verb, (1) "to loose, release," (2) "to unloose," as a bowstring, "to relax, weaken"; passive, "to be weakened, grow weary, be exhausted." Again, it is not necessarily a rural metaphor or even a conscious metaphor at all. But in this context it may be taken as part of the larger picture of sowing and reaping. It is found only here in Paul. The present passive participle (with μή) is conditional.

59. Προαιρέω: "To bring forth or forward," frequently in the middle, "to take by choice, prefer, propose." Here in the perfect middle (προῄρηται) and only here in the NT. They had proposed (and it remained their purpose) to take up a collection. The corresponding noun, προαίρεσις, is Aristotle's word in *Eth. nic.* 3.3.19 for a free act of moral choice.

60. See ch. 2, nn. 46, 47, 48; and cf. Prov 11:24–25 and Luke 6:38, which, like 2 Cor 9:6–11, relate to temporal blessing, and the discussion of Gal 6:7–10 above on the eschatological harvest (ch. 2, n. 57).

61. Paul has the expression πᾶσαν αὐτάρκειαν "all sufficiency," the noun being an old word from αὐτάρκης "self-sufficient, independent" (see Phil 4:11). Αὐτάρκεια is found only here and in 1 Tim 6:6 in the NT. Its use suggests that Paul had some acquaintance with the language of Stoicism. But whereas their ideal was to be indifferent to all circumstances, Paul's was to trust to God's grace in all circumstances. Notice the emphasis (it could be described as a pun) in this verse on "all." "God is able to make *all* grace [πᾶσαν χάριν] abound to you, that in *all* things [ἐν παντί], at *all* times [πάντοτε], having *all* that you need [πᾶσαν αὐτάρκειαν], you might abound in *every* good work [πᾶν ἔργον ἀγαθόν]."

62. Σπέρμα (from σπείρω; see ch. 2, n. 46): "Seed," either (1) of plants (e.g., 1 Cor 15:38; 2 Cor 9:10) or (2) metaphorically, of human or divine offspring (e.g.,

Rom 1:3; 4:13, 16, 18; 9:7 [2x], 8, 29; 11:1; 2 Cor 11:22; Gal 3:16 [3x], 19, 29; 2 Tim 2:8).

63. Πληθυνεῖ τὸν σπόρον ὑμῶν καὶ αὐξήσει τὰ γενήματα τῆς δικαιοσύνης ὑμῶν "[God] will increase your [store of] seed and will make the fruits of your righteousness grow." For αὐξάνω "to make to grow, to grow," see ch. 2, n. 37. Γένημα (from γίνομαι "to become"), a form not found in classical Greek but used in the LXX, the NT, and the papyri, as distinct from γέννημα ("offspring") "fruits, produce." Found only here in Paul. On δικαιοσύνη "righteousness," see ch. 6, n. 28.

64. Paul is showing his Jewish colors in all this. The duty of almsgiving played a large part in Hebrew ethics; the OT and Apocrypha often insist that it should be carried out ungrudgingly. See, e.g., Deut 15:10; Tob 4:7; Sir 35:9. In the early church the practice of having "all things in common" (Acts 2:44–45; 4:32–35) was a particular application of this ethic.

65. This does not at all mean that Paul's theology owed anything to the mystery religion, only that he may have used the story as illustration. On the cultural context of his childhood, he describes himself as "brought up in this city [Jerusalem], trained at the feet of Gamaliel" (Acts 22:3). The verb ἀνατρέφω "to nurse, nourish, bring up" generally relates to the upbringing of a *young* child. This suggests that Paul's childhood was spent not in Tarsus (as is commonly supposed) but in Jerusalem, in the home of Gamaliel. The Hillel family, of which Gamaliel was the head, had always had an interest in the Diaspora, so that a child from Tarsus might naturally have gone to them for training. But this is not to say that he was isolated at an early age from Hellenistic influences. On the contrary, this family had an interest in Greek language and culture (*b. Soṭa* 49b), and it may have been here, paradoxically in the heartland of Judaism and in the home of a great Jewish rabbi, that Paul began to acquire his Greek culture. See W. C. van Unnick, "Tarsus or Jerusalem," 259–320.

66. Κόκκος: Found only here in Paul.

67. See Exod 23:19; 34:22; Lev 2:12, 14; 23:9–21; Num 15:18–21; 18:12; 28:26; Deut 26:2, 10. In Prov 3:9–10 God's blessing is promised if the injunction to offer the firstfruits is observed. Cf. Jer 2:3, in which Israel is called the firstfruits of creation. The offering of a portion as firstfruits was deemed to consecrate the whole; Paul refers to this principle in Rom 11:16 in arguing for a place still for the Jews in God's purpose. "The whole lump [of dough]" (φύραμα, see ch. 4, n. 104) and "the branches" represent all Israel, and "the firstfruits" and "the root" the remnant who have believed in Jesus as the Christ. The fact that there is a faithful remnant is the basis of Paul's expectation that "when the full number of Gentiles has come in, all Israel [i.e., a significant number] will be saved" (Rom 11:25–26). See further N. A. Dahl, *Studies in Paul: Theology for the Early Christian Mission* (Minneapolis: Augsburg, 1977), 151; J. C. Beker, *Paul the Apostle: The Triumph of God in Life and Thought* (Edinburgh: T&T Clark, 1980), 90; D. G. Johnson, "The Structure and Meaning of Romans 11," *CBQ* 46 (1984): 98–99.

68. See Num 28:26–31; cf. Exod 23:16; 34:22; Lev 23:9–21; Deut 16:9–10. On the other hand, Philo (*Spec.* 2.162f.) refers to the day after the Passover Sabbath as ἀπαρχή "firstfruits." See the next note.

69. Ἀπαρχή (from ἀπάρχομαι "to make a beginning" in sacrifice, "to offer"; see ch. 11, n. 46): (1) "sacrifice," (2) "firstfruits."

70. This metaphor complements Paul's earlier reference to the Passover and to Christ as the Passover lamb in 1 Cor 5:6–8 (see ch. 1, n. 34).

71. There is some debate as to how best to render ἀπαρχή in the phrase τὴν ἀπαρχὴν τοῦ πνεύματος. The following suggestions have been made: (1) that ἀπαρχή means the "beginning" (implying more to come), (2) that the reference to the Spirit as ἀπαρχή is "not so very far from" the reference to Christ as the ἀπαρχή in 1 Cor 15:20, 23 (see A. T. Hanson, *Studies in Paul's Technique,* 109), which means

much the same as the first suggestion, that the new age has had its beginning, (3) that ἀπαρχή is used in the sense of "birth certificate" (see C. Spicq, " 'ΑΠΑΡΧΗ: Note de lexicographie néotestamentaire," in *The New Testament Age: Essays in Honor of Bo Reike* [ed. C. Weinrich; Macon, Ga.: Mercer, 1984], 2:501, following H. S. Jones, " 'Απαρχὴ πνεύματος," *JTS* 23 [1922]: 282–83; C. C. Oke, "A Suggestion with Regard to Romans 8:23," *Int* 11 [1957]: 455–60), which again amounts to much the same as the first two suggestions, and most commonly (4) that ἀπαρχή means "firstfruits" (still the meaning is not very much different) and is a metaphor from the harvest festival. Taken in the last sense, the genitive should *not* be interpreted partitively, for believers already have the Spirit in full, but rather appositionally—they have the "firstfruits," namely, the Spirit.

72. See, e.g., Rom 12:3–8; 1 Cor 12–14; Gal 5:22–23; Eph 4:7–13.

73. Καρπός: "Fruit" of trees, vines, fields, etc. (e.g., 1 Cor 9:7; 2 Tim 2:6), metaphorically (1) of converts won to Christ (Rom 1:13; Phil 1:22), (2) of a godly life (Rom 6:22; Gal 5:22; Eph 5:9; Phil 1:11; 4:17), (3) of an ungodly life (Rom 6:21; Eph 5:11), and (4) of the gift of the Gentile churches for those of Judea (Rom 15:28). Cf. καρποφορέω (see ch. 2, n. 78) and γένημα (see ch. 2, n. 63).

74. For the predominantly commercial metaphor of this verse, see ch. 8, n. 52.

75. Καλῶν ἔργων προΐστασθαι εἰς τὰς ἀναγκαίας χρείας: "To maintain good works for the necessary needs." The best commentary on this passage is 1 Thess 4:9–12, which (together with passages such as Eph 4:28 and 1 Tim 5:7) suggests that the "necessary needs" include maintaining oneself and one's family and helping others, especially those who belong to the "household of faith" (Gal 6:10) and are unable to help themselves.

76. Ἄκαρπος (cf. καρπός, ch. 2, n. 73): "Unfruitful, barren." See also 1 Cor 14:14; Eph 5:11.

77. See the references in ch. 2, nn. 73, 78.

78. Τοῦ εὐαγγελίου τοῦ παρόντος εἰς ὑμᾶς, καθὼς καὶ ἐν παντὶ τῷ κόσμῳ ἐστὶν καρποφορούμενον καὶ αὐξανόμενον: "The gospel that has come to you, as also in the whole world [so among you] it is bearing fruit and growing." Καρποφορέω (from καρποφόρος "fruitful," itself from καρπός, see ch. 2, n. 73, and φέρω "to carry, bear"): "To bear fruit," the periphrastic present emphasizing the on-going nature of the process and the middle voice (only here in the Greek Bible) denoting "the inherent energy" of the gospel. "The gospel is essentially a reproductive organism, a plant 'whose seed is in itself'" (J. B. Lightfoot, *Saint Paul's Epistles to the Colossians and to Philemon* [London: Macmillan, 1879], 133). Cf. the use of the active voice of the verb in Col 1:10, where it is used as a metaphor for godly conduct, as also in Rom 7:4, and for ungodly conduct in Rom 7:5. For αὐξάνω, see ch. 2, n. 37. Some commentators see these two terms ("bearing fruit" and "growing") as expressing qualitative and quantitative growth respectively, but it is more likely that Paul is simply piling up words to make the one point that there has been a significant result from preaching the gospel of Christ. Similarly, in Col 1:10, the two words together simply underline his hope that the Colossians will go on growing as Christians.

79. He describes it as "a fruit of work" (καρπὸς ἔργου, i.e., "the outcome of his effort"; cf. Ps 104:13 [LXX 103:13]; Wis 3:15). It is not clear whether Paul means by this the fruit of work already done—that he is following up in places where he has already preached to gather into the church any who have been touched by the gospel—or whether he is thinking of a new field of endeavor. Either way, the phrase is to be taken as a reference primarily to his evangelistic work. Paul characteristically refers to his missionary labors as "work" (see ch. 7, n. 14).

80. Ἔλεγχε αὐτοὺς ἀποτόμως: Ἀποτόμως (an old adverb from ἀπότομος "cut off," itself from ἀποτέμνω "to cut off") can read "severely, abruptly," literally, "cutting away as with a sharp pruning knife" (A. E. Humphreys, *The Epistles to*

Timothy and Titus [Cambridge: Cambridge University Press, 1895], 262). Cf. 2 Cor 13:10 (another reference to work done by Paul's proxy Titus?). It is unlikely that Paul used either this word or the corresponding substantive, ἀποτομία, in Rom 11:22 as conscious metaphors, although the latter is found in the context of his depiction of the pruning of the olive tree that is Israel (see pp. 41–42).

81. C. H. Dodd, *The Epistle of Paul to the Romans* (London: Hodder & Stoughton, 1932), 189.

82. Columella, *Rust.* 5.9.16.

83. Palladius, *Insit.* 53f.

84. See W. M. Ramsay, *Pauline and Other Studies in Early Church History* (New York: A. C. Armstrong, 1906), 219ff.

85. Thus H. M. Gale (*The Use of Analogy in the Letters of Paul* [Philadelphia: Westminster, 1964], 231) says that Paul's metaphors "provide no reliable clue as to his thought or understanding with respect to the phenomena or life situations that those pictures represent or from which they are drawn. Numerous pictures . . . simply do not conform to reality. The apostle has adjusted them in order that they might serve his purpose, sketching into them, so to speak, certain elements that may illustrate or reinforce his thought or argument."

86. Ἀγριέλαιος: Strictly an adjective, "of the wild olive," but as a substantive in Rom 11:17, 24, "a wild olive." Found only here in the NT.

87. Ἐνκεντρίζω (from ἐν "in" and κεντρίζω "to graft"): "To graft in." In the NT only in Rom 11:17, 19, 23–24. Both ἀγριέλαιος and ἐνκεντρίζω are found in Aristotle, although MM describes ἐνκεντρίζω as belonging to "the koine," albeit of the "higher" (i.e., literary) kind.

88. Καλλιέλαιος: "A garden or cultivated olive." Found only in Rom 11:24 in the NT.

89. Scholars debate about the terms on which "all Israel" will be saved. Some see it as by a *Sonderweg* "a special way of salvation" (for a summary of some earlier views, see R. Hvalvik, "A 'Sonderweg' for Israel: A Critical Examination of a Current Interpretation of Romans 11:25–27," *JSNT* 38 [1990]: 88). But to posit a *Sonderweg* would be to destroy the whole of Paul's argument thus far in Romans and, indeed, to run counter to the whole of NT. See further D. G. Johnson, "Structure and Meaning," 102–3. Hvalvik argues that what is special about Israel's salvation is that it will be *as a people* (pp. 87–107).

90. Σύμφυτος (from συμφύω "to make to grow together" rather than συμφυτεύω "to plant together"): "Grown along with, united with," found only here in the NT. This adjective "denotes the organic union in virtue of which one being shares the life, growth, and phases of existence belonging to another" (F. Godet, *Commentary on St Paul's Epistle to the Romans* [Edinburgh: T&T Clark, 1895], 1:412). W. Sanday and A. C. Headlam (*The Epistle to the Romans* [Edinburgh: T&T Clark, 1905], 157) believe that this word "exactly expresses the process by which a graft becomes united with the life of a tree."

Family Life

The family has always been the fundamental unit of society, with generally, not always, the man at the head. Certainly Roman society was patriarchal. At one time the husband (the *paterfamilias*) was deemed to be both the priest[1] and the proprietor of his household (the *familia*), the absolute master of all of its members: his wife, his sons (of any age), his unmarried daughters, his widowed mother, and his slaves.[2]

By the time of Paul, those days of the father's absolute power of life and death were almost passed, but Roman society still remained patriarchal. For example, only those relationships that had been established by male descent were formally recognized.[3] This was true also of most other ethnic groups within the Roman world, and not least of the Jews. It must be supposed, indeed, that Paul drew his analogy in Eph 3:14–15 from his own Jewish background. But so universal was the acceptance of the primacy of male descent that the analogy would have made good sense to any of his readers, whether familiar with Paul's own background or not. "I bow my knees to the Father," he says, "from whom every family in heaven and on earth is named." His expression *(patria)* translated "family" means strictly "lineage" or **"pedigree" on the father's side**.[4] On closer scrutiny, this passage is not without its problems. What, for example, does Paul mean by this description of God as giving God's name to every family? Given the context, which speaks of the unity of all peoples and refers to "angels, rulers, and powers," he probably means that every society, whether human or angelic, owes its origin to God and (assuming them all to be "father-headed") has its divine prototype in God.

MARRIAGE

It now seems certain that, as a rule, the people of Paul's world did not live in large, extended families, as has sometimes been supposed. The literary and epigraphical evidence from Rome, limited though it is, certainly gives no support to the view that Roman households usually included a number of smaller family units, all subject to the rule of a patriarch. Rather, the norm appears to have been the nuclear family, much as in our own day, with couples marrying and leaving their parental homes to make new homes of their own and to form their own families.[5]

The institution of marriage was fundamental to Greco-Roman society. To marry and to have children was regarded as the duty of all Roman citizens and no less of Greeks and of Jews. These peoples in particular—the Jews, the Greeks, and the Romans—were the chief constituents of Paul's world, and their cultures shaped his perception of marriage and gave rise to the metaphors that he drew from the rites and practices associated with it.

Greco-Roman Marriage Customs

Roman men usually married between the ages of twenty-five and thirty years (those of the senatorial elite a few years earlier). Most women married in their middle or late teens (girls from aristocratic families somewhat earlier, perhaps between twelve and fifteen). Thus, there was often a considerable age disparity between husband and wife, although not as great as was generally the case with the Greeks. Roman law allowed girls to marry at twelve years.[6] In republican times all three forms of marriage had the wife "under the hand *[manus]*," that is, under the authority, of her husband, the forms differing according to the couple's social class, whether patrician or plebian.[7] These older rites (some of which may have survived until as late as the second century CE) were replaced by a new form of marriage, in which the wife technically remained a member of her paternal household, subject to its *patria potestas,* instead of passing under the *manus* of her husband and the *patria potestas* of his family. In practice, this gave the woman a large measure of independence, making it possible for her to inherit, accumulate, and administer her own property and even to divorce her husband if she so desired.[8]

By the first century CE, under the "new" law of marriage, Roman women had come to enjoy a remarkable freedom compared with their former status.[9] Similar changes were also taking place among the Greeks. But Greco-Roman women were still subject to many restrictions—restrictions that were more the product of circumstance and custom than of any deliberate policy to keep them down. One such factor in their continuing secondary status was the customary difference in ages between men and women at the time of marriage.[10] A young girl marrying an older man, however much freedom she might notionally enjoy, would find it difficult in practice to assert her independence. Of course, not every wife was younger than her husband, nor were the consequences of the husband's usual seniority the same in every case. But a letter from Pliny about his third wife illustrates a situation that would not have been uncommon. Pliny was a man in his forties and his third wife, Calpurnia, was still in her teens. Writing to Calpurnia's aunt, he described his wife as shrewd, frugal, loving, and devoted. But it is clear from the tenor of his letter that he still regarded her as something of a child, and there is no suggestion that she was on an equal footing with her consular husband. She clearly took second place to his political interests and public achievements.[11]

Betrothal

The new form of marriage was preceded by a betrothal consisting of an agreement entered into by the couple[12] in the presence of their relatives and friends, some of whom acted, in a formal sense, as witnesses to the proceedings. At the betrothal, the man gave a number of gifts to the woman, the most important of which was a **ring**.[13] This was given as a pledge of his fidelity. In the presence of the witnesses the woman then placed the ring on the third finger of her left hand in acceptance of his pledge.[14] The ring was probably a survival of the ancient *coemptio,* the practice whereby the father "mancipated" his daughter to her husband by way of a notional sale, of which the *arra,* or pledge, was an important preliminary.[15] *Arra* (or *arrha*) is the Latin form of the Greek *arrabōn* (which, in turn, was probably Phoenician in origin). The word had a wide commercial application; the business of acquiring a wife was but one example.[16] We cannot be sure, then, whether it was from the rite of betrothal in particular or from business practice in general that Paul drew his metaphor, but three times he speaks of the Holy Spirit as an *arrabōn* (2 Cor 1:22; 5:5; Eph 1:14). Understood in commercial terms, he is picturing the Spirit as a pledge, perhaps the "part payment," of what will one day be "paid" in full (the final blessings of salvation). As a metaphor from marriage, on the other hand, the Spirit is portrayed as the token of our "betrothal," given in anticipation of our "marriage" at the return of Christ.

Jewish Marriage Customs

Jewish concepts of marriage are also evident in Paul's metaphors. Second Corinthians 11:2 is clearly Jewish in its origin: "I feel a divine jealousy for you," he says, "for I '**betrothed**'[17] you to Christ, to present[18] you as **a pure virgin**[19] to **one husband**."[20] In the Old Testament Israel is commonly depicted as the bride or the consort of God (a "bride" who often disappointed her "husband").[21] It was natural, then, for Paul to use this image of the church. Marriage among the Jews involved two separate steps: the betrothal and the wedding. Usually a year elapsed between the two, during which the woman was considered to be the man's wife. The contract of betrothal was binding and could not be dissolved except by death or divorce. The status of betrothal is exemplified in the law of adultery. If a betrothed woman was found to be unfaithful, she was held to be no less guilty than if she had been married, and she was punished accordingly.[22]

Two men played an important role in the formation of a Jewish marriage. One, known as **"the friend of the bridegroom,"** took the groom's part, and the other represented the bride.[23] They had a number of duties. They acted as liaisons between the bride and groom. To all intents and purposes, the representatives conducted the couple's wooing, and when the matter was settled, it was the "friends" who arranged the wedding and sent out the invitations. The **"friend of the bride"** had a particular duty to which Paul refers in this passage: he must ensure that the bride came to her wedding as a *virgo intacta*. Paul saw himself, vis-à-vis the Corinthians, in the role of the friend. He had wooed and won them for Christ. He had "betrothed" them to Christ, and now he was bound (so he felt) to present them as "a pure virgin" to their prospective "husband."[24] Recent events at Corinth, however, have made him nervous on that score: "I am afraid," he says, "that as the serpent deceived Eve by his cunning, so your thoughts will be turned away [corrupted] from the sincere and pure devotion which you have to Christ" (v. 3; cf. Gen 3:13). He fears that they might embrace "another Jesus"—a Jesus different from the one he had preached to them in Corinth (v. 4), from the Jesus of the apostolic tradition.[25] Of course, there was and is no other Jesus. But there were other claimants to the Corinthians' hearts and minds. Hence Paul's stress on the *one* "husband" to whom they are promised.

In Eph 5:27, he again portrays the church as a bride. No "friend of the bride" is mentioned because it is not part of the point that he is making. Christ is portrayed as presenting[26] the church to himself. The particular interest of this passage, from our point of view, lies in its possible reference to two features of marriage that Jews and Gentiles had in common and to a third feature that was peculiarly Jewish. First, his appeal to husbands "to nourish"[27] and "to nurture"[28] their wives may allude to **the marriage contract,** in which the husband is said to "owe" certain things to his wife (and she to him). In verse 28, husbands are said to "owe"[29] to their wives the duty of love, and the very words of verse 29, "to nourish and nurture," have been found in a marriage contract of that time.[30] Second, verse 26 may contain a reference to **the bridal bath.** A Greek bride, for example, would often bathe in a stream sacred to a god or goddess to be cleansed of impurity—in a moral or religious sense, the literal washing symbolizing the inner purification.[31] A Jewish bride would similarly bathe in a symbolic act of purification. This practice may have originated as a rite of passage—her being transferred as a piece of property from one man to another. But it had come to be seen as a religious rite signifying inner purification.[32] And so Paul says of Christ that he gave himself for the church to sanctify[33] it (set these people apart from all others) for himself, "having cleansed[34] it in the water of the [prenuptial?] bath[35] [and] with **[the spoken] word**" (vv. 25–26).[36] And herein may be a third reference to a facet of the marriage rite as it was practiced in Paul's day: in a Jewish marriage the spoken word was important—the legality of the marriage depended on what precisely the man *said*.[37]

But what does the metaphor mean? Paul's readers could hardly have failed to see in the bath an allusion to baptism—baptism being, as it were, the symbolic precursor to their union with Christ. This might lead us to suppose, then, that the "word" is the baptismal formula: "in the name of the Lord Jesus" or "in the name of the Father, the Son, and the Spirit."[38] But if the "word" is deemed to be a part of the metaphor and not simply Paul's added comment, it might be better understood as the gospel, represented in the metaphor by some such declaration of the bridegroom to the bride as "I love you." Or so, at least, Marcus Barth suggests:

> The "word" by which a man validly betroths a woman to himself and makes her his wife can have many forms, as the rabbinical examples . . . have shown. . . . Whatever be the specific form of the binding declaration made by a man—it has in all cultures and ages only one substance: "I love you." . . . It is probable that verse 26 describes the Messiah as the Bridegroom who says this decisive "word" to his Bride and thereby privately and publicly, decently and legally binds himself to her and her to him.[39]

Divorce and Remarriage

Once the bride and groom were married, they were bound to each other (in law) until death or divorce severed the connection. The romantic ideal undergirded the legal position; the expectation was that a marriage would last.[40] Often, of course, it did not. If a marriage ended in divorce,[41] Paul for one, would not countenance the remarriage of either the man or the woman. When a marriage ended by reason of the death of one of the partners, he had no objection to the other's remarrying, with certain qualifications.[42] In Rom 7:1–3 **marriage**, **death**, and **remarriage** illustrate what is involved in becoming a Christian:

> Do you not know, brothers (for I speak to those who are familiar with the law), that the Law has jurisdiction over a person only as long as he lives? Thus, by law, a married woman is bound to her husband as long as he lives. But if the husband dies, she is released from the marriage law. So then, if she becomes the wife of another man while her husband is still alive, she is declared to be an adulteress. But, if her husband dies, she is freed from that law and is not an adulteress if she marries another.

The analogy itself is plain enough. But what precisely is the point that Paul is making?[43] It is often supposed that the wife corresponds to the believer, the first husband to the law, and the second to Christ. But there are difficulties in this interpretation. The application in the verses that follow does not match the analogy. In verse 4, for example, the believer is said to have died. But verses 4–6 are reminiscent of 6:1–11 (in which Paul speaks of our "dying" and "rising" with Christ),[44] and herein may lie the clue to the interpretation of 7:1–3. It seems likely that the analogy reflects the "participatory soteriology" of the earlier passage, the wife's first marriage (and its

demise) picturing the believer's union with Christ in his death, and her second marriage the believer's union with Christ in his resurrection.

CHILDBIRTH

Birthing in the ancient world appears to have been generally done in a
seated position, in a chair designed for that purpose. The birthing woman
relied largely on the help of other women.[45] Midwives are frequently mentioned in the Old Testament, and the oldest known medical document in
existence, the Ebers Papyrus (ca. 1550–1500 BCE), refers to their ministra-
tions. It contains prescriptions for inducing labor, correcting uterine dis-
placements, and causing abortions. Men had little to do with obstetrics.
Hippocrates did show some interest and made some recommendations (his
oath denounces abortion), but generally physicians were only called in if the
fetus was dead or had to be killed in utero and extracted. Obstetrical writings, written mostly by men, had mainly to do with the instruments employed for this purpose. In the first century CE, in the medical school at
Alexandria, physicians began to develop techniques to benefit a mother and
child in a difficult birth. For most women, however, giving birth was both a
painful and a hazardous undertaking with little hope of remedy if anything
went wrong.[46]

In Gal 4:19, Paul speaks metaphorically of **pregnancy** and **labor pains**.
"My dear children,"[47] he writes, "for whom I am again in labor,[48] until
Christ has been formed[49] in you." He hoped that Christ might be formed in
them or, conversely, that they might be transformed into the image of
Christ. Until that was achieved, he was again enduring the pain of giving
birth to them. The metaphor is somewhat mixed in that he thinks of Christ
being formed in *them*, but of *himself* as suffering (for the second time!) the
trauma of birth. Indeed, he seems to envisage two "pregnancies": his with
them and theirs with Christ. But we must make allowances. The letter to the
Galatians is not a considered lecture on obstetrics. It is Paul at his most pas-
sionate. His present pain was exacerbated by the fact that he had "labored"
to give them "birth" at the time of their conversion. But now that labor was
in danger of having been wasted (cf. v. 11). A "different gospel" had been
preached in Galatia, and his converts were defecting or were threatening to
defect from the gospel of grace.[50] This was costing him his present "confine-
ment." He was "in labor" again with the Galatians, not simply to restore
them to the Christ of his gospel but to lead them on into Christian maturity.
His thought is not essentially different from that found elsewhere in his epistles. But nowhere is his plea for commitment and for Christ to be all in all
made with greater force than in this passage.[51]

The metaphor of childbirth is found again in 1 Thess 5:3, but with a
quite different focus. Here it is not so much the pains themselves that Paul
has in view, as in Galatians, but the suddenness of their onset, their unpre-

dictability in one sense (no one knows *when* they will start) and their certainty in another (they *will* start, whether people like it or not). Paul is discussing the Parousia, warning his readers that Christ will come at the very moment in which the scoffers are dismissing the possibility of his return with their slogan, "there is peace and security."[52] They will be caught out, taken unawares, "like a pregnant woman[53] overtaken by the sudden onset of her contractions."[54] In Rom 8:18–25, the focus of the metaphor is on what lies beyond the pain of birth, again referring to Christ's return. He will bring with him the "final installment" of our salvation, "the redemption of our bodies"—new bodies to match the new life that we already have.[55] But, for the present, nature itself seems to be yearning, just as we are, for that moment. "The whole creation," in Paul's words, "is crying with one voice" for an end to its present labor, for a quick delivery, for the birth of God's new creation from the womb of the old.[56]

ABORTION

Abortion was not uncommon. Because the fetus was not considered to be a person until it was born (it was regarded as a part of the maternal viscera),[57] abortion was not illegal in Roman law[58] (in Greek law it was). That is not to say that everyone approved of the practice.[59] In fact, a number of attempts were made to restrain it.[60] But it appears to have flourished at all levels of society. Both Suetonius and Juvenal refer, for example, to Domitian's affair with his niece Julia, which resulted in her conceiving a child. The emperor ordered that the pregnancy be terminated; the abortion cost Julia her life.[61] Contraception was practiced by both chemical and mechanical means, the simplest being the "pagan custom" of washing after sexual intercourse. A vase decorated with reliefs found in Lyons shows a man carrying a pitcher of water to a couple busily occupied in bed. If contraception failed, many of the same potions recommended in that connection, together with other expedients, were applied in the attempt to procure an abortion.

The physician Soranus, writing in the early second century CE, prescribed exercise: walking, riding, jumping, and carrying loads. Failing this (or as an alternative), various concoctions could be taken to bring on menstruation. "Laxatives are helpful," he suggested, "as well as pungent clysters [enemas]." He recommended bathing in a decoction of herbs and then applying a herbal poultice. If the pregnancy persisted, more drastic treatments, such as "bleeding" and the use of suppositories, were employed. Another physician, Dioscorides, writing a little earlier than Soranus, has many of the same prescriptions.[62] And they seem to have worked, so that abortions were very much a fact of life (or of death) in the ancient world,[63] but at what cost in the lives and the health of women we cannot tell.

Paul has a metaphor of abortion in 1 Cor 15:8. He was speaking of Jesus' postresurrection appearances, of which the appearance to him was the last. "He appeared," he says, "to James, then to all of the apostles, and last of all, to me, as to **an abortion**."[64] To be precise, he speaks of himself here as "*the* abortion" *(tō ektrōmati)*, as though he were the only one to whom such a name could properly be applied. In the light of verse 9, he may have been using the word as an expression of his disgust at what he had once been, a persecutor of the church. Or he may have been echoing an epithet coined for him by others—his Jewish or even his Jewish Christian opponents—as a term of abuse, the article indicating something that was commonly said: that "abortion of a man," as they call me. Or he may have been thinking of his lack (compared with the others named in 1 Cor 15) of a proper "period of gestation" in becoming what he now was, a leader in the church, an apostle. The Twelve had been disciples well before Jesus had appointed them to their office, and having called them, he trained them for their role before commissioning them and sending them out. But Paul had received none of these advantages.[65] His glimpse of the risen Christ had torn him, so to speak, like an aborted fetus, unformed, unprepared, from what he had been to what he became.

PARENTING

Passages such as 1 Cor 4:15, 2 Cor 12:14, and Phlm 10 refer to more general notions of birth and parenting. Here Paul describes himself as **the father**[66] or **the parent**[67] of his converts. He had **begotten**[68] them, he says, and so they are his **children**.[69] But among his many "children" there were a few, Timothy in particular, but Onesimus and Titus also, with whom he had a particularly close relationship. These he called his "sons."[70] The father and child images that Paul uses make two things clear: Paul's great affection for his converts and his claim to their affection. If affection is absent, as it was for a time with the Corinthians, he nevertheless claims their obedience. No matter how much they owed to others, such as Apollos, who had also been their teacher at Corinth, to Paul they owed much more. Their indebtedness, indeed, gave him every reason to expect and demand that they should heed his instruction. Thus the parenting metaphor in 1 Cor 4:15 is extended in verse 16 to include the notion of the parent as exemplar.[71] This father instructed his children not only by word but by example.

These images of parental affection and exemplary conduct are found again in 1 Thess 2:7–12. Here Paul uses an extraordinary mixture of metaphors. He reminds his readers, in verse 7, that he and his colleagues might have expected (according to Christian practice; see, e.g., 1 Cor 9:4–12) to be supported by the church for the duration of their ministry in that place. Or perhaps he meant that they as apostles could have demanded from the Thessalonians due deference to their status and authority.[72] But they had asked for nothing of the kind, neither kudos nor keep. Rather, says Paul, "we became **babes**[73] while we were with you," pointing perhaps to their "softly,

softly" approach or to the simplicity of their message, couched as it may have been in language that all could understand, "like a nurse talking baby talk to her children."[74]

"We [related] to you," he continues, "like **a mother suckling her children**"[75] (v. 7). Paul's word *(trophos)* is strictly "a nurse," not "a mother," but the reflexive pronoun in the Greek suggests that the image is of a nurse caring for *her own* children, not for someone else's. In short, the metaphor is of a nursing mother—as tender an image as one could find to represent the relationship of the pastor and the congregation (cf. Num 11:12). "We loved you so much[76] ['a term of endearment borrowed from the language of the nursery']"[77] that we were glad to share with you not only the gospel of God but ourselves" (v. 8). "We dealt with each one of you as a father does his children,[78] encouraging, comforting, and urging you to live lives worthy of God" (vv. 11–12). And then, for good measure, he calls them his **brothers** (v. 9)![79] Sadly, all too soon, Paul and the others had been forced to leave Thessalonica. Their enemies had effectively driven them out. This had been a devastating experience for Paul, which he could best describe now in terms of **a parent's loss of a child**: "We were bereft[80] of you" (v. 17), he tells his readers. His only consolation was that he was still with them in spirit and would, he hoped, be with them before long[81] in the flesh (it would be five years or more, however, as far as we know, before this hope was fulfilled). Meanwhile he had sent Timothy back to them to see how they were doing. Paul was left on his own in Athens, a prospect that he had not relished when he had first made the decision. Now, in retrospect, it seemed to him to have been a kind of **widowhood**[82] (3:1–2).

Children sometimes cause their parents much heartache, and this was certainly the case with Paul's "children" at Corinth. They were not "growing up" in the faith as he had expected that they should. What other assessment could he make of them? Their conduct was still barely distinguishable from that of their pagan associates. In the early days, when they had been "babes in Christ,"[83] he had taught them accordingly: "I fed you **milk**,[84] **not solid food**,"[85] he declared (1 Cor 3:1–4). This was as it should have been then, and there was nothing culpable in their being "babes." But there is something wrong if that condition persists, as it did at Corinth.[86] The Corinthians had remained infantile Christians. There is nothing so sad as having to go on speaking "as to babes," long after the time when those concerned should themselves have been teaching others. This was Paul's grief concerning the state of affairs at Corinth. His aim was always that "babes" grow up into "adults," but the Corinthians showed no signs of maturity. "Grow up!" was his plea (in effect). "Grow into Christ! Be Christlike in all your conduct and Christ centered in all your thoughts! Then, at last, you will be on solid food."[87] Incidentally, Paul was not implying that there is a higher teaching ("solid food") than the gospel he had preached to them from the first. The gospel provides all the nourishment that Christians can take, whether as "babes" or mature. He was speaking rather of their grasp of the gospel. In this they still had a lot of growing to do. In one respect only would Paul have his converts not grow, and that was in wickedness. "Stop being **children**[88] in your thinking [your grasp of the gospel]," he tells the Corinthians, "but go on **being babies**[89] in respect to evil" (14:20).

PARENTAL AUTHORITY

The most distinctive feature of the relationship between a Roman father and his children was his authority over them. In law, if not always in practice,[90] the *paterfamilias* (the oldest surviving male ascendant) had sweeping powers over his immediate family. He was, as we have already observed, their absolute master. As Gaius wrote in the *Institutes,* the *patria potestas* (the authority of the father) "is the special characteristic of Roman citizens; for virtually no other men have over their sons a power such as we have."[91] In Paul's day this power was already in decline, especially over a child who reached adult life.[92]

Fathers had the power of life or death over their newborn children as late as the fourth century CE. The newborn child was bathed (cf. Paul's reference to "the bath of rebirth," Titus 3:5[93]), carried to its father, and placed at his feet. If the father decided to keep his baby son, he would take him up into his arms. (A Roman did not "have" a child; he "took" a child, literally "raised" him up—*tollere.*) By so doing, he showed that he recognized the child as his offspring and undertook his care. At the same time he established his rights over him. If the baby was a girl and the father chose to accept her, he would simply give orders that she should be fed. In either case, the mother or the wet-nurse would then give the baby its first meal. If the child was sickly or deformed or if it seemed in any way retarded (or was simply unwanted), it was starved, suffocated, or exposed. If exposed, it died in the street or on a rubbish heap, food perhaps for the dogs. Or it may have been picked up by some passerby, almost certainly to spend the rest of its life as a slave.[94]

The *patria potestas* touched every aspect of the family life. The father bore all responsibility within the family. Thus he was held accountable for its members' behavior. The punishment of the head of the household for its misdemeanors (see the early Christian writing Herm. *Vis.* 7.3) reflects this legal structure. Again, the father was responsible for any debts his son might incur. We note that Paul, having named Onesimus his "son," offers to discharge his debt to Philemon, a euphemism perhaps for what he had stolen (Phlm 10, 18). The father possessed all authority within the family.[95] A daughter was subject to that authority until she married (the marriage was generally arranged by her father soon after she reached puberty[96]). But marriage offered her no independence. Under the earlier forms of marriage, she simply passed from one *potestas* to another.[97] True, the new form did give her a de facto independence, but only by holding her subject to her father.[98] A son was never free of the *patria potestas*,[99] except by emancipation[100] or death.

TEACHING OF CHILDREN

The *potestas* of the Roman father gave him (at least in law)[101] the final say in all matters relating to his children, although in practice the mother often played a role, in some cases a quite significant role, in the upbringing of both sons and daughters,[102] especially daughters.[103] More often than not, however, at least in the more affluent families, the children were entrusted for their day-to-day needs to the care of others: first the wet-nurse[104] and then, as they grew older, the private tutor or (increasingly in the first century CE) the schoolmaster.[105] Many boys and girls, from about the age of six, spent their days (seven out of eight[106]) in schooling, with only a short break for the summer holidays. Instruction was restricted at this level to reading, writing, and arithmetic. School began at dawn and continued without a break until noon. In some circumstances, it resumed after lunch for an hour or two. It was often conducted in a makeshift location—such as under an awning outside a shop—constantly invaded by the noise of the street. A more prosperous schoolmaster might rent a shop or a room.[107] Rarely, it would seem, were either the conditions under which the children were taught or the methods employed in their instruction designed to awaken in them a genuine love of learning.[108] For most children, formal education ended when they were about twelve years old. Those boys and the few privileged girls[109] who continued their schooling (the girls by means of a private tutor) did so under a *grammaticus,* who carried on the elementary work of the *litterator,* drilling his students in Latin and Greek literature. At sixteen, the boys might graduate to the school of the *rhetor,* who taught rhetoric and philosophy[110] and prepared his charges for public life. Classes at this level were usually conducted entirely in Greek. As for the Greeks themselves, they received no corresponding education in Latin. Unlike the Romans, they spent much of their school time (about half) on sport.

PEDAGOGUE

What caught Paul's imagination in all of this was the role of the **pedagogue**.[111] This was an ancient institution, Greek in origin. By Paul's day, it was common throughout Greco-Roman society and even found, it seems, in some Jewish households, since the word occurs as a loanword in Jewish sources. Certainly Josephus's son had a pedagogue.[112] The most noticeable function of the pedagogue was to accompany the child to school throughout the years of primary and secondary education (i.e., from about age six to sixteen). But there was more to the work of the pedagogue than this. He protected his charge and prevented him from experiencing physical and moral harm and educated him in all matters of conduct and speech. The pedagogue had to teach the child all that the Greek meant by *eukosmia:* good manners, good deportment, "decency" in every department of life.[113] To achieve these ends, the pedagogue was expected to discipline his charge, and by all accounts, he was generally found to do so, often with severity.[114] But his authority was necessarily short-lived. By the time the child reached adulthood, for better or for worse, the rule of the pedagogue was at an end.[115]

A household might have more than one pedagogue. The imperial households had at least one for each child. The use of multiple mentors is reflected in 1 Cor 4:15: "Though you have countless pedagogues in Christ, you do not have many fathers. For I [alone] begot you in Christ through the gospel." The respective importance of parents and pedagogues as an influence on their children was much discussed at the time,[116] as Paul may have been aware. Certainly, whether deliberately or not, he contributed to the discussion by asserting that, in the case of the Corinthian church, he is of much more importance to them as their "father" than any one could ever be as their pedagogue. The pedagogue "might be more capable, and even more affectionate, than the father, but he could never become father,"[117] for the father gave his children life, whereas the pedagogue was only their instructor for the time being.

In Gal 3:23–25, Paul speaks of the law as a pedagogue. His intention in using this image is evident in verses 15–25. He is concerned to show that the law cannot annul the earlier promise. God made a promise of blessing to Abraham—no strings attached—and the introduction of the law 430 years later changed nothing in respect to that promise (vv. 15–18). Why, then, was the law introduced? "Because of transgressions"[118] (v. 19). The pedagogue analogy in the verses that follow illustrates what he means (vv. 23–25). It draws attention to two facets of the law.

First, it is restrictive. In life, the pedagogue's preventative and protective role was, on the whole, a good thing. It kept the child from harm's way. This beneficial restrictiveness of the law is what Paul has chiefly in mind. The law was introduced to curb the human propensity to transgress. But the restrictive nature of the law contained negatives as well as positives. The law made it almost impossible for Jews to mix freely with Gentiles. Jewish writers such as Aristeas spoke of it as setting up a "fence" between themselves and others:

> Now our Lawgiver . . . fenced us round with impenetrable ramparts and walls of iron, that we might not mingle at all with any of the other nations, but remain pure in body and soul. . . . Therefore lest we should be corrupted by any abomination, or our lives be perverted by evil communications, he hedged us round on all sides by rules of purity, affecting alike what we eat, or drink, or touch, or hear, or see.[119]

Aristeas made these comments approvingly, an attitude that Paul did not share. That he disapproved of Jewish exclusivism is evident in Gal 3:23, in which he seems to parody the Jewish perception of the law by describing it as holding its adherents prisoner, behind a locked door.[120] Thus, although Paul was chiefly thinking of the beneficial aspects of the law—curbing transgressions—his image of the pedagogue also hints at the law's less desirable role, what might be called its negative restrictiveness.[121]

The second facet of the law to which the analogy draws attention is its temporary nature. The heir, if a child, is subject to the restraint of **a guardian**[122] and/or **an administrator**.[123] Until he comes of age, he is no better off than a slave (Gal 4:1–2).[124] So it is with those who are subject to the restraint of the law. But the power of the pedagogue eventually ends.[125] When the child becomes an adult, the dominance of supervisors is a thing of the past. The young man is now master de facto and not simply de jure. Likewise, the power of the law eventually ends: "The law was our pedagogue," says Paul, "*until* Christ"[126] (v. 24). Since the coming of Christ (his advent represents a sort of "coming of age" in the affairs of the world[127]), Jews need no longer be subject to the law (vv. 4–7), or Gentiles to the other "weak and miserable systems" that hold them in bondage (vv. 8–10). If we are "in Christ," we are free of such things. But, Paul hastens to add, not free in the sense of having an unfettered license to do as we please (5:1, 13ff.).

BECOMING A RESPONSIBLE ADULT

Once released from the restraint of the pedagogue, young men often indulged to the full their newfound freedom. Fathers would count themselves fortunate if their sons avoided the pitfalls of seduction and debauchery. Mark Antony affords a notorious, but by no means exceptional, instance of a wanton young man. Cicero gives this account of Antony's adolescence: "You assumed a man's gown and at once turned it into a harlot's."[128] Roman fathers feared for their children's moral well-being and Paul shared this concern for his "children." He was careful, therefore, to instruct them that freedom in Christ must not lead to the overthrow of the moral content of the law as it had led to that of its cultic and ritual demands—the "rules of purity, affecting alike what we eat, or drink, or touch, or hear, or see." (Strictly, of course, these had not been overthrown so much as fulfilled— they had served their purpose, but now Christ is our sacrifice and sanctification; cf. Rom 10:4; 1 Cor 1:30; Heb 7:27; 9:28; 10:10.) The moral law remains as a code of conduct—a set of guidelines—for the people of God. And the Spirit of God is given to help us to fit more and more within these bounds that God has set. The moral code is summed up, says Paul, in this one command: "Love your neighbor" (Gal 5:14; but see 5:13–6:10). Love, we are told, is not simply the product of our own will and work but also the "fruit" of the Spirit (Gal 5:22). We are to love and God is there to help us do it.[129]

ADOPTION

Sometimes an adult son (rarely a daughter) might exchange one *potestas* for another by way of adoption.[130] The practice had its roots in the religious basis of the Roman family. If the family cult was at risk because there was no male successor to act as priest, a family might adopt. This practice was also bound up with maintaining the family name and property.[131] But other reasons also encouraged the practice—reasons that may sometimes have assumed greater importance than the original religious and familial goals. Thus, by the time of the late republic and early empire, "adoption had the main purpose of establishing *patria potestas* over the adoptee. This authority, in turn, was used for social and/or political maneuvering, for avoiding the responsibility of raising one's own children, for helping a child, etc."[132] For the family giving up a child, monetary considerations were often primary—adopting out was a means of raising money. The adoptive father effectively bought the child. An adoption also allowed the family to save money for the support of other children, dowering the girls for marriage and underwriting the boys for public office, entry to which was subject to means tests. Whatever the reasons for an adoption, it was always a highly serious undertaking because it affected the status of the father in each of the families.

There were two steps to an *adoptio sensu stricto*:[133] (1) the release of the one to be adopted from his natural father's *potestas* and (2) the adopting father's assertion of his *potestas* over the adoptee. The first step was known as the *mancipatio*. It usually involved three people in addition to the adoptee— the natural father, the adopting father, and a third person (sometimes this intermediary was dispensed with), to whom the natural father "sold" his son three times (once in the case of a daughter), after which his *potestas* was deemed to be broken.[134] The *vindicatio* followed, in which the adopting father[135] laid a claim to the adoptee as son (or daughter) before the praetor (magistrate). If the intermediary or the natural father raised no objection, the praetor declared in favor of the claim, and the adopting father became the new *paterfamilias*.[136] For the adoptee, in law, this was a new birth. A new life had begun. The old life was behind. All rights in the old family were gone; all rights in the new family were now his (or hers). The adopted son was heir to his adoptive father's estate. If there were other sons, natural sons of his new father, he was treated as their equal. The debts of his old life were canceled, and no claim could be made against him in the courts on that account. In the eyes of the law, he was no longer the person he had been. He was a new man.[137]

Roman history provides many examples of adoption and the consequent change in status of the person concerned. The adoption of Nero by the emperor Claudius is a particularly good case in point. Claudius already had a son, Britannicus, but adopted Nero to be his successor (to be sure of the succession, Nero soon got rid of Britannicus). Claudius also had a daughter, Octavia, who was not otherwise related to Nero. But because of the adoption, Octavia and Nero were now legally brother and sister, and special enabling legislation was needed before they could be permitted to marry. It was this change in status accompanying the change in *potestas* that made adoption such a telling metaphor of our position as Christians.

Paul develops the metaphor most fully in Rom 8:12–17 (see also v. 23). The metaphor is not always apparent in English versions, which sometimes have something like "sonship," whereas the Greek has **"adoption."**[138] There was a time when we were under the *potestas* of sin (Paul has argued this, although not in these terms, in the earlier chapters), but God, in his mercy, has made us God's children by adoption. The past has no claim on us now.[139] Our adoptive Father, on the other hand, has an absolute claim (e.g., we have no right to our assets; they are rightfully his). The past is no more; our debts have been canceled; a new life has begun. We are **heirs,**[140] Paul declares, "heirs of God and fellow heirs with Christ"[141] (v. 17). Paul appears to think of Christ here as the natural son of the adoptive family (see v. 29), although some would argue from Rom 1:4 that Christ himself has been "adopted" and that our status as adoptees rides on his.[142] Either way we have great expectations! As with other concepts, such as redemption and justification, adoption has a future dimension, expressed in this notion of heirship.[143] But at this point, surely, the analogy fails, for "no one is the heir of the living." Does not an inheritance imply the death of the testator (e.g., Heb 9:15–17)? Not in Roman law (to which we believe Paul was referring). Here the heir was understood to be the embodiment of the testator[144]—the father lived on, so to speak, in the son—not from the time of the father's death but from the time of the son's birth or adoption. "The existence of heirs . . . was not conditional on the death of their ancestor, for they had existence and status already by virtue of their relationship with him. Birth not death constituted heirship."[145] As long as God is, we are his heirs, coheirs with Christ of all that God has,[146] but subject always, of course, to his *potestas.* Being heirs may entail suffering (we belong to a family that has always found the going hard), but it holds out the prospect of a glorious future (v. 17).

Meanwhile, it is our privilege as children to come without hindrance into the very presence of God and to address[147] God as *"Abba,* Father" (v. 15), even as Jesus had done. But how confident are we of this privilege? How certain do we feel of our "adoption"? How do we know that we are children of God who have the right to cry to him day or night? "The Spirit," Paul answers, "witnesses[148] to our spirit that we *are* the children of God" (v. 16; he is speaking of an inner conviction, the feeling that we *are* what the promises of the gospel declare us to be).[149] In so saying, he still has the metaphor of adoption in mind. The *mancipatio* was carried out in the presence of witnesses, to ensure that the legality of the adoption could be established beyond doubt by reference to one or more of the witnesses.[150] For

Christians seeking assurance, such proof may seem too subjective a testimony to carry any weight of conviction. Although what we feel is not unimportant, it is but one of a number of witnesses, others of which Paul has not taken the trouble here to name—the witness of Scripture; the testimony of the life, death, and resurrection of Jesus; the evidence of changed lives. These "proofs," in one way or another, give us every reason for confidence that God has indeed "predestined us to be his children by adoption through Jesus Christ, in accordance with his good pleasure and will, to the praise of his glorious grace" (Eph 1:5–6).

NOTES

1. Each family had its own cult or *sacra* ("sacred things"). The deities worshiped by each family varied from case to case but included the *Lares* and *Penates* (the gods of hearth and larder) and the *genius* of the family, a kind of spiritualization of the family itself, of which the *paterfamilias* was, in a sense, the embodiment, an embodiment that continued from generation to generation in father and son. The failure to provide a successor was, therefore, not simply a social tragedy but a religious one. In whom and by whom would the *sacra* be maintained?

2. Ulpian provides us with a number of definitions of the *familia* (*Dig.* 50.16.195): (1) The term can describe a man's estate in matters related to inheritance. This meaning, however, appears to be rare outside legal discussions (see R. P. Saller, "*Familia, Domus,* and the Roman Conception of the Family," *Phoenix* 38 [1984]: 336–55, esp. 338). (2) In another legal, rather than common, meaning, *familia* can denote those subject to the *potestas* of the *paterfamilias* (see Saller, "*Familia,*" 338; P. Garnsey and R. P. Saller, *The Roman Empire* [London: Gerald Duckworth, 1987], 127; S. Dixon, *The Roman Mother* [London: Croom Helm, 1988], 15; S. Dixon, *The Roman Family* [Baltimore: Johns Hopkins University Press, 1992], 1–3). This *potestas* was related to power over the estate, for the *paterfamilias* controlled all property and exerted power over his dependents on this basis (see T. E. J. Wiedemann, *Greek and Roman Slavery: A Source Book* [London: Croom Helm, 1985]; B. Rawson, "Adult-Child Relationships in Roman Society," in *Marriage, Divorce, and Children in Ancient Rome* [ed. B. Rawson; Oxford: Clarendon, 1991], 26–27). (3) *Familia* can also denote all those descended from the same male ancestor or those belonging to the same *gens* (see Saller, "*Familia,*" 339; Garnsey and Saller, *Roman Empire,* 127). (4) Finally, *familia* can refer to all slaves belonging to the household (see Pliny, *Ep.* 8.16; M. B. Flory, "Family in *Familia:* Kinship and Community in Slavery," *AJAH* 3 [1978]: 78–95, esp. 78; Garnsey and Saller, *Roman Empire,* 127). There was some overlap of meaning between *familia* and *domus,* but in the early empire *familia* was the broader term, whereas *domus* generally referred to the residential unit itself—what we would call the "family."

3. Under the empire, as never under the republic, a daughter's children might sometimes be spoken of as a man's "posterity." Fronto, who had no surviving son, wrote of his choice of Aufidius Victorinus to be his daughter's husband as a wise one "both for my own sake in regard to my posterity and for my daughter's whole life" (*Am.* 2.11). In the same vein, a letter from Pliny to his wife's paternal grandfather, Calpurnius Fabatus, indicates a desire on the part of Fabatus to extend his line through his granddaughter's children (*Ep.* 8.100). The preference, of course, was always for male descent.

4. Πατριά (an old word—πάτρα is the usual form—from πατήρ "father"; see ch. 3, n. 66): (1) "lineage, ancestry," (2) "a family, tribe." Found only here in Paul. In the Greek, there is a play on words between "father" (πατήρ) and "family" (πατριά) that is not obvious in the English. The precise meaning of πατριά in this passage is uncertain. Some understand it as "fatherhood," but this sense is not generally favored. The uncertainty is exacerbated by the phrase πᾶσα πατριά, which has been rendered "the whole family." This is a possible translation, although strictly, for such a meaning, it should have the article, πᾶσα ἡ πατριά. All things considered, "every family" appears to be the best rendering. See G. Schrenk, "πατήρ, κτλ," *TDNT* 5:982–1022, here 1017f.

5. At least this appears to have been the case in Rome and in the Latin-speaking West. See, e.g., P. Laslett, *Household and Family in Past Time* (Cambridge: Cambridge University Press, 1972); and R. Sieder and M. Mitterauer, *The European Family* (Cambridge: Cambridge University Press, 1982). Of course, exceptions can be found for all periods and in every class, with large, extended families sometimes living under the same roof. The striking example of the Aelii Tuberones is often cited: "For there were sixteen members of the family, all Aelii; and they had a very little house and one little farm sufficed for all, where they maintained one home together with many wives and children" (Plutarch, *Aem.* 5). In the East, on the other hand, the extended family may have been more in vogue. A recent study has shown that Egyptian towns and villages had more complex family structures, with "patriarchal households where grown brothers lived together, with their father if he is still living, and presumably with their own wives and children. . . . Families lived close to one another, perhaps in compounds with shared facilities" (D. W. Hobson, "House and Household in Roman Egypt," *YCS* 28 [1985]: 222).

6. See R. P. Saller, "Men's Age at Marriage and Its Consequences in the Roman Family," *CP* 82 (1987): 21–34; B. Shaw, "The Age of Roman Girls at Marriage: Some Reconsiderations," *JRelS* 77 (1987): 30–46. Cicero betrothed his daughter Tullia to Calpurnis Piso Frugi early in 66 BCE, and the marriage took place in 63. Tullia appears to have been born in 76, so that she was ten years old at the time of betrothal and thirteen at marriage. H. J. Leon (*The Jews of Ancient Rome* [Philadelphia: Jewish Publication Society, 1960], 230) notes six inscriptions that record the marriages of Jewish girls in Rome from twelve to seventeen years of age. Such early marriages were even more premature than they might at first appear, since girls reached puberty at a later age than they do today. There was, however, an inducement to marry as soon as possible. Augustan legislation penalized unmarried and childless women at age twenty and men at age twenty-five. See S. B. Pomeroy, *Goddesses, Whores, Wives, and Slaves: Women in Classical Antiquity* (New York: Schocken, 1975), 166. See also my discussion, p. 97 below.

7. There were (1) the patrician form of *confarreatio,* or solemn offering by the couple of a cake made of the old Italian grain called *far* to Jupiter Farreus in the presence of the *pontifex maximus* and the priest of the supreme god, the *flamen Dialis,* and ten other witnesses; the clearly religious nature of this rite was meant to qualify the bride to share in the *sacra* of her new family; (2) the *coemptio,* the fictitious sale whereby the plebian father "mancipated" his daughter to her husband; and (3) the *usus,* whereby uninterrupted cohabitation for a year produced the same legal result between a plebian man and a patrician woman. Of these, the *usus* was the first to go, probably abolished through law by Augustus. See further P. E. Corbett, *The Roman Law of Marriage* (Oxford: Clarendon, 1930), 68–106.

8. Technically it was the woman's paternal family rather than the woman herself who exercised independent power over against her husband. In a marriage without *manus,* she could divorce him, but only with the consent of her father or guardian, who was usually one of her male relatives. It was even possible for her *paterfamilias* to effect a divorce against her will. Moreover, although she could hold property that her husband could not control, she could not dispose of it herself without her guardian's

consent. Until the time of Hadrian (117–138 CE), she could not write a will without such approval. See J. A. Crook, *Law and Life in Rome* (London: Thames & Hudson, 1967), 99–107; Corbett, *Roman Law of Marriage;* and S. B. Pomeroy, "The Relationship of the Married Woman to Her Blood Relatives in Rome," *AncSoc* 7 (1976): 220, 224. Martial viewed this social phenomenon of relatively independent women (at least independent over against their husbands) with dismay: " 'Why am I unwilling to marry a rich wife?' do you ask? I am unwilling to take my wife as husband" (*Epigr.* 8.12). For the same reason (the woman's newfound independence), Juvenal complains, "There is nothing more intolerable than a wealthy woman" (*Sat.* 6.460). He declares that the typical wife "flits from one home *[domus]* to another, wearing out her bridal veil. . . . Thus does the list of her husbands grow; there would be eight of them in the course of five autumns" (*Sat.* 6.225ff.). But these recalcitrants were fighting a losing battle against women's liberation. So common had the new form become that Pliny reckoned it among the thousand and one trifles that uselessly encumbered the days of his contemporaries (*Ep.* 1.9).

9. See preceding note.

10. See p. 52 and ch. 3, n. 6.

11. Pliny, *Ep.* 4.19. For a more detailed account of Roman marriage, see Garnsey and Saller, *Roman Empire,* 130–36.

12. Properly speaking, it was the male head of each family who reached the agreement, sometimes only after protracted negotiations. One of Pliny's letters provides a glimpse of what must have been a typical procedure among the upper classes. The uncle of the prospective bride had asked Pliny whether he knew of anyone who would be a suitable match for her. Pliny responded with what amounted to a letter of recommendation for a friend, in which he gave information about his friend's hometown and his family, his career, his character, and his financial situation (*Ep.* 1.14). Older men and divorced men and women probably took more of the initiative themselves. A case in point was Valeria's direct approach to Sulla, which resulted in their marriage (Plutarch, *Sull.* 35). See S. M. Treggiari, *Roman Marriage:* Iusti Coniuges *from the Time of Cicero to the Time of Ulpian* (Oxford: Clarendon, 1998), 3–138. A union made without the consent of the *paterfamilias* was not a fully legitimate marriage *(justum matrimonium).* In the case of a father not knowing or approving of the marriage at the time, his subsequent approval was taken as his consent (*Cod. justin.* 5.4.5).

13. See Treggiari, *Roman Marriage,* 147–52. Other rites and customs could accompany a betrothal, but they depended solely on the wishes of the families concerned and not on any legal or religious requirements. The ring, however, was a legal requirement that reflected the commercial nature of this transaction.

14. Gellius (*Noct. Att.* 10.10) explains this practice, which still holds to this day: "When the human body is cut open as the Egyptians do and when dissections, or *anatomai* as the Greeks phrase it, are practiced on it, a very delicate nerve is found which starts from the annular [third finger of the left hand] and travels to the heart. It is, therefore, thought seemly to give to this finger in preference to all others the honor of the ring, on account of the close connection which links it with the principal organ."

15. Pliny, *Nat.* 33.28; Juvenal, *Sat.* 6.25; Justinian, *Dig.* 24.1.36; cf. Corbett, *Roman Law of Marriage,* 1–23.

16. For ἀρραβών, see ch. 8, n. 12. G. F. Abbott (*Songs of Modern Greece,* 258) draws attention to the modern Greek ἡ ἀρραβωνισμένη "the betrothed bride," "an interesting reminiscence," he remarks, "of the ancient custom of *purchasing* a wife." In the same way ἡ ἀρραβῶνα is used for "the engagement ring." See also W. E. B. Ball, *St Paul and the Roman Law* (Edinburgh: T&T Clark, 1901), 45–46.

17. Ἁρμόζω (from ἁρμός "a joining, a joint"): (1) "to fit, join," (2) of marriage, "to betroth." The middle voice expresses the subject's interest in the matter,

either "to join to oneself, marry," or "to give in marriage" (as in 1 Cor 11:2). An old verb, found only here in the NT.

18. Παρίστημι: See ch. 11, n. 50.

19. Παρθένον ἁγνήν: Παρθένος "a young woman or any unmarried woman," not necessarily a virgin, or "a virgin." In this context, the latter is clearly intended. See also 1 Cor 7:25, 28, 34, 36, 37. Ἁγνός (from ἄγος "religious awe," ἄζω "to venerate"): (1) "free from ceremonial defilement," i.e., in a condition prepared for worship, (2) "holy," (3) "pure, chaste, undefiled," of persons (e.g., 2 Cor 7:11; 11:2; 1 Tim 5:22; Titus 2:5) and things (e.g., Phil 4:8).

20. Ἀνήρ: "A man," (1) as opposed to a woman (Rom 11:4; 1 Cor 11:3 [2x], 4, 7 [2x], 8 [2x], 9 [2x], 11 [2x], 12 [2x], 14; Eph 5:23; 1 Tim 2:8, 12), a husband (Rom 7:2 [3x], 3 [4x]; 1 Cor 7:2, 3 [2x], 4 [2x], 10, 11 [2x], 13, 14 [2x], 16 [2x], 34, 39 [2x]; 14:35; 2 Cor 11:2; Gal 4:7; Eph 5:22, 24, 25, 28, 33; Col 3:18, 19; 1 Tim 3:2, 12; 5:9; Titus 1:6; 2:5), (2) as opposed to a child (Rom 4:8; 1 Cor 13:11; Eph 4:13). In general, the word expresses "maleness." In the phrase ἑνὶ ἀνδρί, the ἑνί underlines the notion of the exclusivity of marriage. The woman's commitment is to one man only (and, of course, the man's is to one woman).

21. See, e.g., Isa 54:5f.; 62:5; Jer 3:1; Ezek 16:23–33; Hos 2:19.

22. There was a slight difference in the way in which a betrothed and a married woman were treated if found guilty. A wife was strangled, a betrothed woman was stoned to death. See Deut 22:23–27 (cf. Lev 20:10). Where the woman was a consenting partner, both the man and the woman who committed the adultery were condemned to death; where the woman did not consent, only the man was put to death. But later Jewish law allowed that since the woman was no longer a virgin, she should be divorced; she is "forbidden" to both the husband and the paramour (m. Soṭah 5:1). Cf. Matt 1:18ff., and see further R. Batey, "Paul's Bride Image: A Symbol of Realistic Eschatology," Int 17 (1963): 176–82.

23. See Judg 14:20; John 3:29. Perhaps the two are collectively referred to in Mark 2:19 as "sons of the bridal chamber." L. Ginzberg draws together the picturesque traditions concerning these offices in The Legends of the Jews (Philadelphia: Jewish Publication Society, 1954), 68.

24. Cf. Matt 25:1–13; Rev 19:7; 21:2.

25. See, e.g., 1 Cor 15:1–8.

26. Παρίστημι: See ch. 11, n. 50. It was quite permissible, at least in later Jewish practice, for the groom to act for himself in this way. The Babylonian Talmud (Qidd. 41a–46b) expressly states that a man can betroth a woman to himself and that a father can give his daughter to a man without employing an intermediary. The implication of the analogy of marriage, particularly as it is presented here in Eph 5, is that Christ has acted as much for his own delight as for ours.

27. Ἐκτρέφω: Old compound with perfective sense of ἐκ, "to nourish up to maturity and on," properly with reference to children (cf. Eph 6:4) but also in a general sense, as here. Only here and in 6:4 in the NT.

28. Θάλπω: Late and rare word, "to heat, warm" and so "to cherish, nurture." In the NT, only here and in 1 Thess 2:7 (see below).

29. Ὀφείλω: See ch. 8, n. 16.

30. See A. T. Lincoln (Ephesians [Dallas: Word, 1990], 379), who cites evidence for both ἐκτρέφω and θάλπω occurring together in a marriage contract; and A. T. Robertson (Word Pictures in the New Testament [New York: Richard R. Smith, 1930–1933; repr. Nashville, Tenn.: Broadman & Holman, 1973], 4:546), who cites an example from the papyri. See also M. Barth, Ephesians (New York: Doubleday, 1974), 2:448; and Mek. on Exod 21:10, where it is said that a husband "owes" his wife food, clothing, and cohabitation. The Babylonian Talmud (b. Ketub. 47b–48a) adds to this list of marital obligations redemption from captivity and a funeral. A standard for the frequency of intercourse was set up according to the professional occupation of the

husband in the Talmud (*b. Ketub.* 62b and *b. Ber.* 22a), and with this we may compare Plutarch, *Mor.* 769A; *Amat.* 23, who claims that Solon prescribed to the men of Athens a minimum of three times a month. Paul in 1 Cor 7:3–5 speaks of the *mutual* indebtedness of the husband and wife in their sexual relationship. In Roman marriage, no written contract was regarded as necessary. But there was usually some sort of documentation, known in Latin as *tabulae nuptiales,* attesting the marriage—perhaps recording the dowry contributed by the bride or the property with which each partner entered the marriage, since, in imperial Roman society, under the "new" law, a married woman (or her *paterfamilias*) kept control of her property.

31. A reference in Plutarch's *Mor.* 772A (*Amat. narr.* 1) appears to attest the common use of this prenuptial rite.

32. See, e.g., Ruth 3:3; Ezek 16:8f.; 23:40; cf. Exod 19:10; Ezek 37:23 and the elaborate preparation for marriage to King Xerxes prescribed in Esth 2:12–13: the girl had to complete twelve months of beauty treatments, six months with oil of myrrh and six with perfumes and cosmetics. The goal of these preparations is depicted in Ps 45:13–14.

33. Ἁγιάζω: See ch. 1, n. 106.

34. Καθαρίζω: "To cleanse, make clean," (1) in a physical sense, (2) in a ceremonial sense, and (3) in an ethical sense (e.g., 2 Cor 7:1; Eph 5:26; Titus 2:14).

35. Τῷ λουτρῷ τοῦ ὕδατος: "In the bath of water." Λουτρόν (from λούω "to wash, bathe"): "A bath" or "a bathing place" (its common meaning from Homer to the papyri), rather than that of "an act of washing." If (as it seems) λουτρόν has its common meaning here, the dative will be locative: the church is cleansed *"in* the bath." Otherwise, it must be instrumental: "cleansed *by* the washing." Elsewhere in the NT only in Titus 3:5 (see ch. 3, n. 93).

36. Ῥῆμα: (1) properly of that which is spoken, "a word, a statement" (e.g., Rom 10:8 [2x], 17–18; 2 Cor 12:4; Eph 5:26; 6:17), but also (2) of that which is the subject of speech, "a thing, a matter" (e.g., 2 Cor 13:1). Whereas "bath" has the definite article (τῷ λουτρῷ), suggesting a particular bath, that of the prenuptial ceremony, ῥῆμα has none. This appears to militate against the interpretation adopted here, but the hymnic nature of the passage may sufficiently account for this form to allow the view that a specific "word" is in mind.

37. According to the Talmud, the legality of a betrothal or marriage depended, to a large extent, not only upon the fulfillment of certain conditions regarding money, the marriage contract, and intercourse but also upon what a bridegroom "says" to his bride in order to make her his wife. In *b. Qidd.* 2b–7b, the function of the right word at the right time is extensively discussed, and this tractate comes back time and again to this theme (e.g., 12b–13a; 60a; 65a). Betrothal or marriage is not valid when the man says only, "I am your husband, I am your lord, I am your betrothed," but is so when he says (whether in public or in private), "Be betrothed, be married, be my wife. . . . Be united with me, be destined for me, be my help, be my received one, be my counterpart, be my rib, be my attached one, be my complement, be my seized one, be taken" (*b. Qidd.* 5b, 6a). It is always a question to what extent the Talmud reflects earlier practice. But the later insistence on the importance of the correct "word" in sealing a marriage makes good sense of this Pauline passage. The gospel, announcing God's love in the person and work of Christ, is the "word" that is instrumental in sealing our union with him.

38. See, e.g., Acts 8:16; Matt 28:19. That the "word" is the baptismal formula is a widely held view.

39. Barth, *Ephesians,* 2:690f.

40. A recent discussion of literary and inscriptional references to marital and family life from the late republic and early empire concludes that already by the first century BCE Romans had a "sentimental ideal . . . focused on a standard of companionate (but not necessarily equal) marriage and a delight in children as indi-

viduals and as symbols of the home comforts" (S. Dixon, "The Sentimental Ideal of the Roman Family," in *Marriage, Divorce, and Children in Ancient Rome* [ed. B. Rawson], 111; see also Treggiari, *Roman Marriage*, 229–62). In the early third century CE, the Roman jurist Modestinus expressed the traditional Roman ideology of marriage as a consensual, lifelong union of two people: "Marriage is the joining of a male and female and a partnership *[consortium]* of all of life, a sharing of divine and human law" (*Dig.* 23.2.1; cf. Cicero, *Phil.* 2.77ff. for the romantic behavior of Pompey and Mark Antony toward their wives). Despite this clear ideal of romantic love, there remains ample evidence of marriages that were more a matter of convenience than of love. In Roman circles it was deemed to be indecent to make any public display of romantic affection. Cato the Censor expelled Manilius, a prospective candidate for consul, from the senate on the grounds that he had embraced his wife in broad daylight in front of their daughter (Plutarch, *Cat. Maj.* 17).

41. Cf. 1 Cor 7:10–11. In Jewish legal practice only a man could initiate a divorce. A woman, however, could achieve the same end by appealing to the court against her husband's treatment of her and having the court compel the husband to divorce her. In early Roman law it was also the case that only the man could initiate such proceedings, and only then on the grounds of the most serious fault (e.g., adultery). But by the first century BCE, women who had not come under their husband's legal power *(manus)* when they married could repudiate their husbands (but see our earlier discussion, p. 52 and ch. 3, n. 8). It is not certain whether this was possible for women who had come under their husband's *manus*, but in any case such marriages were becoming less common. See Treggiari, *Roman Marriage*, 441–46; S. M. Treggiari, "Divorce Roman Style: How Easy and How Frequent Was It?" in *Marriage, Divorce, and Children in Ancient Rome* (ed. B. Rawson), 31–46.

42. Cf. 1 Cor 7:39–40.

43. J. A. T. Robinson (*Wrestling with Romans* [London: SCM, 1979], 77) speaks for many when he asserts that the more closely one examines the details of this analogy, the more difficult they are to fathom. C. H. Dodd (*The Epistle of Paul to the Romans* [London: Hodder & Stoughton, 1932], 103) accuses Paul of lacking "the gift for sustained illustration of ideas through concrete images (though he is capable of a brief illuminatory metaphor). It is probably a defect of imagination." The defect, however, may lie with Dodd.

44. A number of scholars have reached the conclusion that there is a parallel in the underlying thought of Rom 6:1–11 and 7:4–6, e.g., A. Nygren, *Commentary on Romans* (Philadelphia: Fortress, 1949), 268–69; J. A. Little, "Paul's Use of Analogy: A Structural Analysis of Romans 7:1–6," *CBQ* 46 (1984): 82–83; J. D. G. Dunn, *Romans* (Dallas: Word, 1988), 1:359–61; J. D. Earnshaw, "Reconsidering Paul's Marriage Analogy in Romans 7:1–4," *NTS* 40 (1994): 66–88.

45. A midwife's sign in terra-cotta, now in the Archaeological Museum, Ostia, shows one midwife supporting a woman about to deliver, who clutches the chair while another midwife prepares to "catch" the child.

46. Childbirth and its aftermath appear to have carried off huge numbers of women between the ages of sixteen and thirty-five. In a time when the lives of relatively few women are recorded, the fact that it is possible to compile a substantial list of young women (including Tullia, Cicero's daughter, Emilia, Sulla's daughter-in-law, and Julia, Caesar's daughter) who died in childbirth is some measure of its frequency, although not enough to supply meaningful statistics. More eloquent, however, than any statistic is the evidence provided by Roman men complaining of the dearth of wives, especially when we take into account the general reluctance of Roman men to marry. On the basis of such data as we have, F. Dupont (*Daily Life in Ancient Rome* [Oxford: Blackwell, 1992], 110) supposes that "childbirth killed more women than wars did men."

47. Τέκνα μου: Some texts read τέκνα "my children" (plural of τέκνον, see ch. 3, n. 69), and some the diminutive, τεκνία (plural of τεκνίον) "my little or dear children." If the latter, it is the only instance in Paul, but most appropriate to the metaphor being employed. Τεκνία is the term more usual for maternal than for paternal endearment (although used also in 1 John 2:1 in that writer's address to his "children"). That Paul should have used it (if he did) is a further measure of the depth of his feeling.

48. Ὠδίνω: "To have birth pains." An old word, in the NT only here and in Gal 4:27 (used literally). For a general discussion of the metaphor of birth pains in the NT against the background of the OT, see C. Gempf, "The Image of Birth Pangs in the New Testament," *TB* 45 (1994): 119–35.

49. Μορφόω (from μορφή "form"): "To form." A late and rare word but an attested medical term for the formation of the fetus (see J. Behm, "Μορφή, κτλ.," *TDNT* 4:742–59, here 753). Found only here in the Greek Bible, but the compound μεταμορφόω "to transform" occurs in a similar sense in Rom 12:2; 2 Cor 3:18. The thought is that the life of Christ in the believer touches and changes everything that he (or she) is to the very roots of his being (cf. Rom 8:29). In contrast to σχῆμα "form" in the sense of external appearance, μορφή is "essential form, or nature," or perhaps the outward expression of what lies within.

50. See, e.g., Gal 1:6–7.

51. See, e.g., Rom 12:1–2; 13:14; 2 Cor 4:16; Eph 4:23; Col 3:10 for a similar plea in different words. There is something particularly apt in pregnancy as a metaphor of growth into Christian maturity. The period of gestation is a long one—Christ will not be fully formed in us while this age runs or while we live in this age—and there is about the whole process something that is both open and secret, both gift and task: it "just happens" once the relationship has been established, but it happens with greater felicity if we do what we can (with "diet" and "exercise") to help the process along.

52. Paul's language appears to be drawn from OT denunciations of those who cried "peace" when there was no peace. Cf. Jer 6:14; Ezek 13:10.

53. Τῇ ἐν γαστρὶ ἐχούσῃ: Literally, "the [woman] who has in belly," a technical term for pregnancy (e.g., Matt 1:18). Γαστήρ: "A belly" and, if the context so decrees, "a womb." Elsewhere in Paul, only in Titus 1:12, where it is used metaphorically for a glutton.

54. Ὠδίν (late form of ὠδίς): "A labor pain." Found only here in Paul, but a common metaphor for the onset of eschatological events. See Isa 13:6–8; 21:3; 37:3; Jer 4:31; 6:24; Mark 13:8; John 16:21.

55. Cf. 1 Cor 15:51; 2 Cor 5:2; Phil 3:21. For redemption in this future sense, see 1 Cor 1:30 and the discussion on pp. 122–24.

56. We have tried to give some feel here for what Paul has said in far fewer words: οἴδαμεν . . . ὅτι πᾶσα ἡ κτίσις συστενάζει καὶ συνωδίνει ἄχρι τοῦ νῦν "we know that the whole creation groans together and labors together until the present time." Συστενάζω: "To groan or lament together." Συνωδίνω: "To be in labor pains together" (cf. ὠδίν, ch. 3, n. 54). Both rare verbs, and both only here in the NT. Their subject is "the whole creation." The συν- of these compounds should not be taken to include humankind, since a clear distinction is made in v. 23 between it and (the rest of) creation: "Not only [does nature groan], but we ourselves groan" (στενάζω; see also 2 Cor 5:2, 4). We should not make too much of Paul's reference here to nature. He is simply resorting to the familiar literary convention of projecting the human drama onto the wide screen of the physical world in order to underline the point that *our* "pain" will, in time, give way to God's good things to come. Cf., e.g., Ps 114:4; Isa 13:10, 12; 34:4–5; 55:12; Mic 1:4, in all of which, and in many similar passages, nature is figuratively portrayed as being in sympathy with the acts of God. See further D. J. Williams, *The Promise of His Coming* (Homebush West, Australia:

Anzea, 1990), 46–47. Cf. also Paul's references to the "new creation" in 2 Cor 5:17; Gal 6:15 and to "new life" in Rom 6:4.

57. *Dig.* 35.2.9.1; 25.4.1.1. This was also the view of Alexandrian philosophers and physicians, according to Philo, *Spec.* 3.20.117.

58. The first Roman action against abortion as a crime in itself was a rescript enacted by the emperor Septimus Severus (193–211 CE) and continued by his successor, Antoninus Caracalla (211–217 CE). The concern of the rescript was only with the husband's rights and wife's duties. See further J. F. Gardner, *Women in Roman Law and Society* (London: Croom Helm, 1986), 158–59; and M. J. Gorman, *Abortion and the Early Church* (Downers Grove, Ill.: InterVarsity Press, 1982), 27–32.

59. Seneca lauded his own mother for not participating in unchastity, "the greatest evil of our time," and for never having "crushed the hope of children that were being nurtured in her body" (*Ad Helv.* 16.3). Ovid's sometimes nonchalant references to abortion show how common it was in his day (e.g., *Her.* 11.33–42), but he himself condemned it: "The first one who thought of detaching from the womb the foetus forming in it deserved to die by her own weapons" (*Metam.* 8; cf. *Am.* 2.14.1–8). He reproached his own mistress for having an abortion. Favorinus spoke of abortion as only one degree less criminal than the exposure of infants (in Gellius, *Noct. Att.* 12.1). Juvenal equates abortion with murder, *Sat.* 6.592–601. Soranus notes that some of his contemporaries held that abortion was improper. He himself held it to be improper only if it concealed adultery or was aimed at maintaining feminine beauty (*Gyn.* 3.19.60). The Stoic philosopher Musonius Rufus was opposed to it (*Disc.* 15).

60. Augustus's edict concerning cutthroats and poisoners may have been applied to sellers of abortifacients; the *lex julia de maritandis ordinibus* of 18 BCE and the *lex papia poppaea* of 9 CE promoted childbearing rather than abortion and similar practices. See J. T. Noonan, *Contraception: A History of Its Treatment by the Catholic Theologians and Canonists* (Cambridge, Mass.: Belknap, 1965), 21.

61. Suetonius, *Dom.* 22; Juvenal, *Sat.* 2.29–35.

62. Soranus, *Gyn.;* Dioscorides, *Mat. med.*. To access the details of these works, see J. M. Riddle, *Contraception and Abortion from the Ancient World to the Renaissance* (Cambridge: Harvard University University Press, 1992).

63. It is certainly the view of many scholars writing on the subject that abortion was commonly practiced in the Roman world (e.g., Riddle, *Contraception and Abortion*). But it is a view that has not gone uncontested. B. W. Frier ("Natural Fertility and Family Limitation in Roman Marriage," *CP* 89 [1994]: 318–33), on the basis of general studies of marital fertility rates, comes to the conclusion that "no general population practiced family limitation before the modern fertility transition" and that statistical evidence for the Roman world in particular shows that it conformed to the general pretransitional pattern. No one, however, questions that abortion was practiced and was sufficiently well known to serve Paul as a metaphor.

64. Ἔκτρωμα (from ἐκτιτρώσκω "to miscarry," itself compounded of ἐκ "out" and τιτρώσκω "to wound"): "An abortion, untimely birth." The earliest instance of this word is in Aristotle for an "abortion" or a "miscarriage" (*Gen. an.* 6.5). It is found also in LXX Num 12:12; Job 3:16; Eccl 6:3 and the papyri (for miscarriage by accident). It does not appear as a term of abuse until Johannes Tzetzes, *Hist. var. chil.* 5.515 (twelfth century CE). Cf. Paul's description of himself as one who died that he might live (Gal 2:19; see also Rom 7:4–6, 13, 24, 25; 8:2).

65. See, e.g., Mark 3:13ff. It must be said, however, that, providentially, he had had advantages that they did not. He was the best educated of the early church leaders, as far as we know, and the best qualified, humanly speaking, to formulate the faith that they all held in common. It could be argued, moreover, that the time he spent in Arabia (Nabatea) following his conversion (see Gal 1:17) and in Cilicia

following his expulsion from Jerusalem (see Acts 9:30) was for him the equivalent of the time spent by the Twelve with Jesus, a time of preparation for mission.

66. Πατήρ: "A father," (1) properly, of the male parent—the natural father or a forefather (e.g., Rom 4:17, 18; 9:5, 10; 11:28; 15:8; 1 Cor 10:1; Eph 5:31; 6:2, 4; Phil 2:22; Col 3:21; 1 Tim 5:1), (2) metaphorically, of the author or originator of something (e.g., Rom 4:11, 12 [2x], 16; 1 Cor 4:15), (3) frequently of God (e.g., Rom 1:7; 6:4; 8:15; 15:6; 1 Cor 1:3; 8:6; 15:24; 2 Cor 1:2, 3 [2x]; 6:18; 11:31; Gal 1:1, 3, 4; 4:2, 6; Eph 1:2, 3, 17; 2:18; 3:14; 4:6; 5:20; 6:23; Phil 1:2; 2:11; 4:20; Col 1:2, 3, 12; 2:2; 3:17; 1 Thess 1:1 [2x], 3; 3:11, 13; 2 Thess 1:1, 2; 2:16; 1 Tim 1:2; 2 Tim 1:2; Titus 1:4; Phlm 3). B. Winter suggests that Paul's image of father in 1 Cor 4:15 has a specific background: "Just as the secular authorities of the Roman colony of Corinth recorded on inscriptions that Julius Caesar was its founding father, and recognized the jurisdiction of the present emperor by attributing the same title to him, so too Paul uses the image of the founding father of the Christian community to commend imitation of himself" ("1 Corinthians," in *New Bible Commentary* [ed. D. A. Carson et al.; Leicester, U.K.: Inter-Varsity Press, 1994], 1161–87, here 1168).

67. Γονεύς (from γίγνομαι/γίνομαι "to become"): "A begetter, a father," mostly in the plural, οἱ γονεῖς "parents." In Paul in Rom 1:30; 2 Cor 12:14 (2x); Eph 6:1; Col 3:20; 2 Tim 3:2.

68. Γεννάω (from γένος "offspring, family, race," itself from γίγνομαι/γίνομαι "to become"): (1) of the father, "to beget," (2) of the mother, "to bring forth, bear," and in the passive, "to be begotten" or "to be born." In Paul in Rom 9:11; 1 Cor 4:15; Gal 4:23–24 (of the covenant "bearing children" for slavery), 29; 2 Tim 2:23 (of foolish disputes "giving birth" to strife); Phlm 10 (of Paul's having "given birth to Onesimus in prison").

69. Τέκνον (from τίκτω "to beget, bring forth"): That which is begotten, born, "a child" (e.g., 1 Cor 7:14; Gal 4:25, 27–28; Eph 6:1, 4; Col 3:20–21; 1 Thess 2:7, 11; 1 Tim 3:4, 12; 5:4; Titus 1:6). Used as a form of address (e.g., Gal 4:19; 2 Tim 2:1), metaphorically of disciples, of those who imitate an exemplar or follow a certain course (e.g., Rom 9:7; 1 Cor 4:14, 17; 2 Cor 6:13; 12:14 [2x]; Gal 4:31; Eph 2:3; 5:8; Phil 2:22; 1 Tim 1:2, 18; 2 Tim 1:2; 2:1; Titus 1:4; Phlm 10) and in relation to God (e.g., Rom 8:16–17, 21; 9:8 [3x]; Eph 5:1; Phil 2:15).

70. Again τέκνον, the word used of all his converts (see preceding note), but in the singular it marks these men out especially. See 1 Cor 4:17; Phil 2:22; 1 Tim 1:2, 18; 2 Tim 1:2; 2:1; Titus 1:4; Phlm 10. In the case of Onesimus, Paul goes a step further in expressing affection by calling him τὰ ἐμὰ σπλάγχνα (Phlm 12), lit., "my viscera." Although often translated "heart," as in vv. 7 and 20, σπλάγχνα may be employed as a synonym of παῖς "child," expressing the thought that the child is part of oneself and, therefore, dear to oneself. So Artemidorus: "Children [οἱ παιδές], like the inward parts of the body, are also called σπλάγχνα" (*Onir.* 1.44). Cf. Pindar's description of children as those who have "come from the womb" (e.g., *Ol.* 6.43; *Nem.* 1.35).

71. His plea: Μιμηταί μου γίνεσθε "become my mimics." Μιμητής (an old word from μιμέομαι "to imitate," itself from μῖμος "a mimic, actor"): In the NT always in a good sense, "an imitator." See also 1 Cor 11:1; Eph 5:1; 1 Thess 1:6; 2:14. Notice that the verb is in the present imperative, "keep on becoming imitators of me" (objective genitive).

72. His expression is, lit., we were "able, as apostles of Christ, to be in [or with] weight [ἐν βάρει]." Βάρος: "Weight," (1) in a literal or metaphorical sense, "a weight, a burden"; in this sense, ἐν βάρει could mean "burdensome" (cf. 2 Cor 4:17; Gal 6:2), but (2) also the further metaphorical sense of "dignity, authority."

73. Νήπιος: Strictly an adjective, "of a child, childish," but used as a substantive, "a child, a babe." Found in Paul in Rom 2:20; 1 Cor 3:1; 13:11 (5x);

Gal 4:1, 3; Eph 4:14; and possibly 1 Thess 2:7. There is a notorious textual problem in this verse. The weight of MSS evidence is in favor of the reading νήπιοι "babes." But the two possible readings differ only by one letter in the Greek (the letter ν), which happens to be the last letter of the previous word. Thus, the letter was either accidentally repeated, giving νήπιοι, or accidentally omitted because it had just been written, giving ἤπιοι "gentle." When we remember that all words were run together in ancient writing, we can see how easily such an accident, either way, could have occurred. The question is, What is Paul *most likely* to have said? "Gentle" is consistent with his metaphor of a mother caring for her children, but Paul was quite capable of mixing his metaphors and, indeed, of employing such a striking mixture as this, likening himself and his colleagues first to babes and then to a mother. See S. Fowl, "A Metaphor in Distress: A Reading of νήπιοι in 1 Thessalonians 2:7," *NTS* 36 (1990): 469–73. In the end, by a happy chance, the meaning is much the same whether he wrote "babes" or "gentle." The one would imply the other.

74. Origen and Augustine, cited without reference by L. Morris, *The Epistles of Paul to the Thessalonians* (Leicester, U.K.: Inter-Varsity Press, 1984), 57.

75. Ὡς ἐὰν τροφὸς θάλπῃ τὰ ἑαυτῆς τέκνα. Τροφός (from τρέφω "to rear, nourish"): "A nurse." See W. A. Meeks, *The Moral World of the First Christians* (Philadelphia: Westminster, 1986), 125–30. Θάλπω means strictly "to warm" but has the secondary sense "to care for, cherish" (cf. Eph 5:29) and in this context "to suckle." It may be noted, however, that it was customary among the elite of Roman society to entrust their children to slaves for wet-nursing and rearing, a custom lamented by Tacitus, *Dial.* 28–29. If this was Paul's metaphor, i.e., a *slave* rather than a mother suckling the children, it adds yet another dimension to his understanding of the role of the minister.

76. Ὀμείρομαι: "To desire earnestly, yearn after." Found nowhere else in the NT and only in the LXX in Job 3:21 and Ps 62:2. There is a fourth-century CE Lycaonian funerary inscription that speaks of parents ὀμειρόμενοι "longing for" their dead son. Compare this with Paul's reference below to being "bereft" of his children.

77. G. Milligan, *St Paul's Epistles to the Thessalonians* (London: Macmillan, 1908), 22.

78. See ch. 3, n. 66 (πατήρ "father") and ch. 3, n. 69 (τέκνον "child").

79. Ἀδελφός (from ἀ copulative and δελφύς "a womb"): "A brother," (1) lit. of one born of the same parent or parents, (2) of a neighbor, (3) of a member of the same nation. In the NT in each of these senses and also (4) of a fellow Christian. "Brothers" is one of the earliest names used by Christians of themselves and certainly the most frequent in the NT. The roots of the Christian use lay in the Jewish practice of calling one another "brother" (cf. Acts 2:37; 7:2; 13:15; 28:17), but for Christians it came to have a deeper meaning (cf. Matt 23:8; Mark 3:34). They were those whose new birth had made them members of the one heavenly family and children of the one heavenly Father. The name is a reminder that, despite our differences, we are one and there is "one God and Father of all" (Eph 4:6). The many occurrences of this form of address in the Thessalonian correspondence (28x), more than might have been expected even from its frequent use elsewhere, may be taken as a measure of Paul's affection for these people. Needless to say, "brothers" includes both men and women.

80. Ἀπορφανίζω (from ἀπό "from" and ὀρφανός "orphan, fatherless"): "To be bereaved," properly used of a parent who has lost a child. See J. B. Lightfoot, *Notes on the Epistles of St Paul* (London: Macmillan, 1895), 36. Found only here in the NT.

81. Πρὸς καιρὸν ὥρας: "For a season of an hour," i.e., "a short season," an idiom found only here in the NT.

82. This image might be implied from Paul's use of the verb καταλείπω: (1) "to leave behind, leave," (2) "to forsake, abandon." The verb itself is a forceful one (in Eph 5:31 used of a man leaving his parents) and is often used of dying. It expresses a

sense of desolation that is reinforced here by the emphatic μόνοι "alone." But it is not sufficiently specific for us to claim it as a conscious metaphor of bereavement. See also Rom 11:4; Titus 1:5.

83. Νηπίοι ἐν Χριστῷ: For νήπιος, see ch. 3, n. 73.

84. Γάλα ὑμᾶς ἐπότισα: Γάλα "milk," used literally in 1 Cor 9:7. Ποτίζω (from πότος "a drinking bout"): "To give to drink," of plants, "to water, irrigate," as often in the LXX and papyri.

85. Βρῶμα: "Food," here "solid food" in contrast to milk but not necessarily "meat" (flesh), although this is certainly the connotation in Rom 14:15 (2x), 20; 1 Cor 8:8, 13, where Paul is discussing the issue of meat from the temples. For its more general use, see 1 Cor 6:13; 10:3; 1 Tim 4:3. The metaphor of milk and solid food was used widely in ancient philosophical and other works. See, e.g., Epictetus, *Diatr.* 2.16.39.

86. Compare, e.g., 1 Cor 13:11 with 14:20. See also Heb 5:13–14.

87. Cf. Col 1:28–29; Eph 4:11–14. "The imperfection, the immaturity of children (νήπιοι, 'babes') is mentioned here in opposition to the perfection of the Perfect Man as described in verse 13" (M. Barth, *Ephesians* [New York: Doubleday, 1974], 2:441).

88. Παιδίον: Diminutive of παῖς "a young child." Common elsewhere in the NT but in Paul only in 1 Cor 14:20.

89. Νηπιάζω (from νήπιος; see ch. 3, n. 73): "To be a babe." Only in 1 Cor 14:20 in the NT.

90. "Reading the literature of the time [the period of the early empire—first and second centuries CE]," writes J. Carcopino, "we find it full of examples of fathers of families whose *patria potestas* was betrayed only in the indulgence shown to their children; and of children who in their father's presence behaved as they pleased, as though they were completely their own masters" (*Daily Life in Ancient Rome* [Harmondsworth, U.K.: Penguin, 1956], 84). In one of his letters, Pliny takes a father to task for reproving his son's excessive expenditure, as though he were acting both oddly and most unreasonably (*Ep.* 9.12), and Martial recounts the misadventures of Philomusus, whose father indulged him to such an extent that when the father died, the coffers were empty. "Your father has disinherited you, Philomusus!" (*Epigr.* 3.10).

91. See, e.g., Gaius, *Inst.* 1.55; 2.86–7; Justinian, *Inst.* 1.9; 2.9; *Dig.* 1.6; 28.2.11; 49.17. Cf. also Dionysius of Halicarnassus, *Ant. rom.* 2.26–7; Gellius, *Noct. Att.* 5.19. A useful discussion of these powers can be found in J. A. Crook, "Patria Potestas," *CQ* 17 (1967):113–22; and B. Nicholas, "Patria Potestas," *OCD* 789. That the power of the father over his children was still important to him is illustrated, for example, by the reluctance of fathers in the early empire to nominate their sons for the priesthood of Jupiter or to let their daughters marry into that priesthood (Tacitus, *Ann.* 4.16), for in both of these circumstances the father lost his *patria potestas* over his child.

92. The legitimacy of using this power to punish adult children was affirmed by Augustus but was later denied by Hadrian and later still by Ulpian. See *Dig.* 48.8.2.

93. This does not mean that the practice of washing a baby lay behind Paul's reference but simply that there is a suggestive parallel. It may be debated whether Paul's reference is metaphorical or literal. G. W. Knight, for example (*The Pastoral Epistles* [Grand Rapids: Eerdmans, 1992], 342), believes that it is metaphorical: "Λουτρόν, 'washing,' is used here as a metaphor for spiritual cleansing, i.e., the removal of one's sins." But if λουτρόν means "bath" rather than the act of washing, as seems most likely (see ch. 3, n. 35), the reference is lit. to the water of baptism as the outward and visible sign of the inward and spiritual grace of "renewal by the Holy Spirit."

94. On exposure as a source of slaves, see ch. 5, n. 58. In the literary sources, people such as the Jews, who did not expose unwanted children, were regarded as anomalies. See Tacitus, *Hist.* 5.5; Strabo, *Geog.* 17.824. Scholars debate the extent to which exposure was practiced in the Roman Empire. See Garnsey and Saller, *Roman Empire,* 136, for references. But some records from Trajan's reign are suggestive. Entries for public assistance to children, in the same town and in the same year, show that assistance was given to 179 legitimate children (145 boys and 34 girls) and only 2 bastards *(spurii),* a boy and a girl. These discrepancies are best explained by assuming that a large proportion of bastards and girls were disposed of by exposure (See *CIL* 11.1147). A. Deissmann (*Bible Studies* [Edinburgh: T&T Clark, 1901], 167–70) reproduces a letter from an Egyptian workman in Alexandria—part of the Roman Empire—to his pregnant wife in Oxyrhynchus telling her, in quite a matter-of-fact way, that if she was delivered of a girl, she should throw it out, whereas a boy could be kept. On the continuing practice, at least to the fourth century CE, of exposing children at birth, see *Dig.* 25.3.4.

95. For example, the father alone had the right to own property, even such property as might otherwise have come to the children, whether by gift or by their own effort. And he had the sole right to dispose of the property as he wished. See further ch. 3, nn. 2, 91.

96. See Garnsey and Saller, *Roman Empire,* 140.

97. Under the old laws, women were condemned to live in perpetual tutelage. See Gaius, *Inst.* 1.144; cf. Cicero, *Mur.* 27; and the discussion on pp. 52–53 above.

98. See further ch. 3, n. 8.

99. In estimating the effects of the *patria potestas,* account must be taken of the demographics of the Roman family. Those who survived the high rate of infant mortality might live to the age of fifty or longer (see further p. 86). As we have seen, men tended to marry in their late twenties, and women in their teens (see ch. 3, n. 6). Consequently, few fathers were alive to witness a son's marriage. It has been estimated that the average age gap between father and child was about forty years! "Only a fifth or so of men at the time of their marriage . . . were still in their father's power and had to tolerate their interference in a decision about marriage. . . . Obviously, no more than a small fraction of mature Romans . . . lacked the capacity to own property because they were still in their father's power" (Garnsey and Saller, *Roman Empire,* 138).

100. In the mid-republic and earlier, emancipation had been a punishment, less drastic than death or slavery, but severe nevertheless, for it condemned a son to an exclusion from the family that inevitably accompanied his being disinherited. By the end of the republic, emancipation had become a benefit. Thanks to the praetorian legislation of the *bonorum possessio,* introduced in the early days of the empire, emancipation enabled a son to acquire and administer his own property without being deprived of his paternal inheritance. No doubt this did much to change the "atmosphere" of the Roman family, in which the father-son relationship was often difficult.

101. See ch. 3, n. 91.

102. Since most of our sources were written by men, "our image of the Roman mother and of her relationship to sons and daughters is a fragmentary one, based on sporadic and sometimes conflicting evidence" (Rawson, "Roman Family," 30; cf. Gardner, *Women in Roman Law,* 146). We have taken Roman practice as in some measure representative of family life generally at the time, in which the father was responsible for the children but the mother undoubtedly played some part in their rearing, at least in their early years. Socrates in Plato's *Protagoras* (525C) says of the child, "*Mother* and nurse and father and *paidagōgos* [παιδαγωγός; see ch. 3, n. 111] are quarrelling about the improvement of the child as soon as he is able to understand them." Some Roman mothers had a

considerable influence on their sons, e.g., Corellia Hispulla, who educated her son in association with tutors until he was about fourteen years of age (Pliny, *Ep.* 3.3); Julia Procilla, mother of Tacitus's father-in-law, Agricola, who supervised Agricola's education until his early manhood (Tacitus, *Agr.* 4); Cornelia, the mother of the Gracchus brothers (Plutarch, *Ti. C. Gracch.* 1; cf. Cicero, *Brut.* 104; Quintilian, *Inst.* 1.1.6; Tacitus, *Dial.* 28); Caesar's mother Aurelia and Augustus's mother Atia (Tacitus, *Dial.* 28).

103. In his general discussion of the Mediterranean world of antiquity, J. J. Pilch ("Beat His Ribs While He Is Young [Sirach 30:12]: A Window on the Mediterranean World," *BTB* 23 [1993]: 104) comments that "girls were treated by their mothers harshly in their youth and socialised as soon as possible to adopt the life-long female-roles expected of them. In actuality Mediterranean girls have no childhood. They must assume domestic and other feminine tasks as soon as they are capable."

104. By the end of the first century CE most upper-class Roman mothers had abandoned the chore of breast-feeding their children, and wet-nurses were hired instead. See Varro, *Rust.* 2.10.8; Tacitus, *Dial.* 28.4; cf. Quintilian, *Inst.* 1.1.4, where the *nutrices* are probably wet-nurses. They should speak well and be of good character, he instructed, since a child's first impressions are lasting. Soranus, *Gyn.*, discusses what are the desirable qualities in a wet-nurse. See further K. R. Bradley, "Wet-Nursing at Rome: A Study in Social Relations," in *The Family in Ancient Rome* (ed. B. Rawson; London: Croom Helm, 1986), 201–29; and the discussion of 1 Thess 2:7 above (p. 59 and ch. 3, n. 75), in which Paul likens himself either to a wet-nurse or to a mother with her own children at the breast. For other aspects of infant care, see ch. 4, n. 1.

105. The decision was largely a financial one. A wealthy father might see his son through his whole education at home. Cato, for example, found time to do much of the work of instruction himself.

> As soon as the boy showed signs of understanding, his father took him under his own charge and taught him to read, although he had an accomplished slave, Chilo by name, who was a schoolteacher and taught many boys. Still, Cato thought it not right, as he tells us himself, that his son should be scolded by a slave or have his ears tweaked when he was slow to learn, still less that he should be indebted to his slave for such a priceless thing as education. (Plutarch, *Cat. Maj.* 20)

Aemillius Paullus had several teachers in his house for the purpose of educating his sons and, "unless some public business prevented him, would himself be present at their studies and exercises, for he had now become the fondest parent in Rome" (Plutarch, *Aem.* 5–6). Cicero was another who seems to have educated his son at home (Cicero, *Leg.* 2.59), although he himself is said to have attended a school.

106. The ancients observed the three natural divisions of time: the day, the lunar month, and the solar year. The week was little used. In Italy, however, it was customary to have market days at intervals of eight days, and this might be loosely called a week—a week of eight days. Similarly, Jews and Christians, strictly speaking, did not have a week but observed a religious festival (Sabbath and Sunday respectively) that occurred at intervals of seven days.

107. A relief in Narbonne appears to show a schoolroom lit by two windows with two seated schoolmasters and a dozen children sitting on benches.

108. Discipline was maintained by means of corporal punishment. Although a *grammaticus*, a teacher of older children, Orbilius may be cited as the best-known example of the tyrannical schoolmaster. See Horace (*Ep.* 2.1.70–71), who calls him *plagosus* "whacker," a "man of blows"; and cf. Suetonius, *Gramm.* 9. On his successors, see Juvenal, *Sat.* 1.15; Martial, *Epigr.* 10.62.10; 14.80; cf. Plutarch, *Caes.* 61.1. Quintilian (*Inst.* 1.3.16–17) deplores the effects of corporal punishment on the chil-

dren and its abuse by teachers, whose morals "no one has taken the trouble to investigate." He is equally condemnatory of the teaching methods of the day (see 1.1.24–26). See Pilch ("Beat His Ribs," 101–13), who puts corporal punishment into the cultural context of a society generally concerned to establish or maintain the father's authority.

109. By the time of Juvenal, some Roman women were benefiting from higher education and did not hesitate to enter into debates with men, as Juvenal notes (*Sat.* 6.398–412, 434–456).

110. In philosophy, some mathematics and astronomy would be learned. Professional studies such as jurisprudence and the art of war were only learned by attaching oneself to a practitioner.

111. Παιδαγωγός (from παῖς "a boy," ἀγωγός "a leader," itself from ἄγω "to lead"). Found only in 1 Cor 4:15 and Gal 3:24, 25 in the NT, an old word for "a kind of nursery-governor, who had charge of the child from tender years, looking after his food and dress, speech and manners, and when he was old enough taking him to and from school" (Findlay, "First Corinthians," 804). The papyri examples in MM illustrate well this description of the pedagogue. For a general discussion of the pedagogue in antiquity, see, e.g., H. I. Marrou, *A History of Education in Antiquity* (New York: Sheed & Ward, 1956), 220–22; S. Bonner, *Education in Ancient Rome: From the Elder Cato to the Younger Pliny* (Berkeley: University of California Press, 1977), 34–46; R. N. Longenecker, "The Pedagogical Nature of the Law in Galatians 3:19–4:7," *JETS* 25 (1982): 53–56; D. J. Lull, " 'The Law Was Our Pedagogue': A Study in Galatians 3:19, 25," *JBL* 105 (1986): 489–95; N. H. Young, "Παιδαγωγός: The Social Setting of a Pauline Metaphor," *Novum Testamentum* 29 (1987): 150–76; T. D. Gordon, "A Note on Παιδαγωγός in Gal. 3:24–25," *NTS* 35 (1989) 150–54; N. H. Young, "The Figure of the Παιδαγωγός in Art and Literature," *BA* 53 (1990): 80–86.

112. Josephus, *Vita* 429.

113. On the pedagogue's protective role, see Plato, *Lys.* 208C and *Symp.* 183C; also Aeschines (*Tim.* 9–10), who argued that the law legislated for a pedagogue to be present at school with the boy because of a basic distrust of the teachers' characters; and Lucian (*Vit. auct.* 15), who observes that good-looking lads in Athens and elsewhere needed constant protection. This was certainly the case in Rome. "As long as they were still beardless, Roman boys were pursued relentlessly by adult men. Girls too were much sought after, but since they went out less and tended to be surrounded by women, there was less risk of them being seduced. Few Roman boys escaped unscathed" (Dupont, *Daily Life,* 226; cf. Horace, *Sat.* 1.6.81ff.). On the pedagogue's role in guiding the child toward virtue, see Plutarch, *Mor.* 439F (*An virt. doc.* 2) and 452D (De *virtute morali* 12); Plato, *Prot.* 324D–325D; Aristotle, *Pol.* 7.15.5–10. And on the constant attention that he must give to the task, see Plutarch (*Fab.* 5), who likens Quintus Fabius Cunctator's dogging of Hannibal's armies up and down Italy to a pedagogue who never lets his charge out of his sight.

114. Alciphron (*Ep.* 3.7.3–5) tells of a pedagogue named Smicrines, a "fierce and mean old man," who, accompanied by "a gang of menials," put an end to the merrymaking of some youths by dragging off his ward, Charicles, "like the lowest slave" and putting the others in the stockade (cf. Paul's image of the law, as pedagogue, keeping its charges "locked up," Gal 3:23), intending to have them sent off to "the public executioner" Seneca (*Ira* 2.21.9) desired that pedagogues should be of a quiet disposition, but from Alciphron's account of Smicrines, this appears not always to have been the case. Cato the Younger was fortunate to have Sarpedon as his pedagogue, a cultured man who taught "with reasons rather than thrashings" (Plutarch, *Cat. Min.* 1.5). But thrashings were, apparently, more the rule than the exception. Philo refers to "the rod" as both the tool of the pedagogue and the very symbol of his educational style (*Post.* 97). He describes him as educating by means of

reproach, punishment, reviling, and accusation (see esp. *Migr.* 115–116; cf. Plutarch, *Mor.* 452C; *Virt. mor.* 12). The often unsatisfactory way in which the pedagogue went about his work was largely due to the fact that he was, in many cases, given the job of pedagogue because he was incapable of doing anything else. See Plato, *Alc. maj.* 122B and *Lys.* 223.

115. See Xenophon, *Lac.* 3.1: "Whenever they emerge from childhood to youth, they cease from παιδαγωγοί, they cease from teachers. No one governs them any more, but they let them go as masters of themselves." Epictetus (*Frag.* 97) contrasts the control of a pedagogue, when one is a child, with the arbitration of the conscience when one reaches adulthood. Martial protested to his pedagogue, Charidemus, that he gave him no liberty. Martial supported his claim to independence by appeal to the growth of his beard and his prowess with his mistress (*Epigr.* 11.39). In a word, he was too old, he believed, for the restraint of a pedagogue.

116. Plato, *Prot.* 325C–D; Epictetus, *Diatr.* 1.11.21–23; Lucian, *Anach.* 20; Plutarch, *Mor.* 36E (*Adol. poet. aud.* 14); Philo, *Her.* 295; *Virt.* 178; *Migr.* 116; *Mut.* 217; and *Legat.* 115.

117. A. Robertson and A. Plummer, *First Epistle of St Paul to the Corinthians* (Edinburgh: T&T Clark, 1914), 89f. See p. 58 for Paul's claim, on the basis of his "fatherhood," to the Corinthians' affection; and ch. 3, n. 66, for the possible analogy of Caesar's "fatherhood" of the Corinthians.

118. Τῶν παραβάσεων χάριν: Χάριν, accusative of χάρις "grace, etc.," is used (1) adverbially (per LSJ), "in favor of, for the pleasure of," and (2) as a preposition (= ἕνεκα), "because of, on account of, for the sake of." It can be causal (e.g., Luke 7:47; 1 John 3:12) or telic (e.g., Titus 1:5, 11; Jude 16). It is a moot point which is the best way to understand it here. The commentators are divided. (1) As telic, the law was introduced "for the purpose of transgressions." From Paul's statement that "the Scripture has locked in all things together under sin" (i.e., declares that all things have been locked in, v. 22; see ch. 10, n. 81) and that "we are . . . locked up under the law" (v. 23), it might be argued that the law was the instrument of sin in this matter, as in Rom 4:15; 5:20, reinforcing our predicament and, in that sense, increasing the offence (this may also be the understanding of the role of the law in Col 2:14; see p. 182 and notes). (2) As causal, the law was introduced "because of transgressions," presumably as a means of keeping transgression in check. Since vv. 24–25 are evidently explanatory of v. 19, the second meaning accords better with the role of the pedagogue.

119. *Let. Aris.* 139, 142. Cf. the images used by Libanius in depicting the pedagogue's role as guardian: "For pedagogues are guards [φρουροί, cf. φρουρέω, ch. 10, n. 80] of the blossoming youth, they are keepers [φύλακες, cf. φυλάσσω, ch. 10, n. 83], they are a fortified wall; they drive out the undesirable lovers, thrusting them away and keeping them out, not allowing them to fraternise with the boys, they beat off the lovers' assaults, becoming like barking dogs to wolves" (*Or.* 58.7). Later he speaks of those who wanted to get rid of the guardianship of their pedagogues (their "guards" φρουράς) that they might be free to do as they wished (58.31). In another passage he praises a pedagogue for being as a protective wall and a prison (φρουρά) (*Or.* 34.29). For Jewish exclusivism, see further, e.g., *Jub.* 22:16; Tob 1:10–11; J. N. Sevenster, *The Roots of Pagan Anti-Semitism in the Ancient World* (Leiden: Brill, 1975), 89–144.

120. On φρουρέω "to guard" and συνκλείω "to shut in on all sides," the verbs employed in this verse, see ch. 10, nn. 80, 81 respectively.

121. It is the view of Young and others (see Young, "Παιδαγωγός," 175, n. 249, for the support that he claims) that Paul's concern in Galatians in general, and in 3:23–25 more specifically, was to attack "religious nationalism and exclusivism." As a general proposition, there is no doubt that "the apostle was determined to oppose those who wished to make ethnic religious matters a test of Christian fellow-

ship" (p. 175), but in 3:24–25, his attack on Jewish exclusivism can only be regarded, at most, as a subsidiary theme. Verse 19 is the key to understanding these verses, and it appears to view the law as pedagogue in terms of the beneficial role of "keeping the child from harm's way."

122. Ἐπίτροπος (an old word from ἐπιτρέπω "to entrust"): (1) "an administrator, steward," (2) frequently in the papyri and elsewhere, "a guardian" of minors (e.g., Gal 4:2). Ἐπίτροπος had a more general role than the παιδαγωγός, who was specifically entrusted with the training up of the child and with his protection.

123. Οἰκονόμος (from οἶκος "a house or household," see ch. 1, n. 89, and νέμω "to manage"): An old word, (1) properly, of "a manager of a household or estate, a steward" (as in the papyri; Rom 16:23, of Erastus, the "steward" of Corinth [city treasurer] and 1 Cor 4:2), but (2) in a wider sense, "an administrator, steward" (as perhaps Gal 4:2). Used of Christian ministers (e.g., 1 Cor 4:1; Titus 1:7) and of Christians in general. D. Wenham (*Paul: Follower of Jesus or Founder of Christianity?* [Grand Rapids: Eerdmans, 1995], 312–13) argues that, in 1 Cor 4:1–5 in particular, with its eschatological reference (cf. also 1 Cor 3:13), Paul is echoing Jesus' eschatological parables of the faithful and unfaithful stewards (Matt 24:45–51/Luke 12:41–46). See further on οἰκονόμος, pp. 98–99, and for οἰκονομία "the office of steward," ch. 4, n. 118.

124. There are two main elements to this metaphor of the minor heir being under guardians and managers. (1) The first element is the double title ἐπιτρόπους καὶ οἰκονόμους, which is found elsewhere in an inscription (see *CIG* 3.4957), in Aristotle (*Pol.* 1315B.2), and in Vettius Valens (*Anth.* 9.73.7). On this basis, it has been suggested that Paul had in mind the Roman law *tutela impuberis* ("guardianship of a minor"), more specifically, *tutela testamentaria* ("guardianship established by testament"), according to which the son of a deceased father was under the supervision of a tutor nominated by his father until he was fourteen and then under a curator appointed by the *praetor urbanus* until he reached the age of twenty-five. See Gaius, *Inst.* 1.22–23 and the literature cited by H. D. Betz, *Galatians: A Commentary on Paul's Letter to the Churches in Galatia* (Philadelphia: Fortress, 1979), 202 n. 6. See also J. D. Hester, *Paul's Concept of Inheritance: A Contribution to the Understanding of Heilsgeschichte* (Edinburgh: Oliver & Boyd, 1968), 18–19, 59; and F. Lyall, "Roman Law in the Writings of Paul—Adoption," *JBL* 88 (1969): 465. Against this view are the following points: (a) we cannot be sure that Paul intended a distinction between the two titles (see E. de W. Burton, *The Epistle to the Galatians* [Edinburgh: T&T Clark, 1921], 213); (b) we cannot be sure that he would have drawn on a law that assumed the death of the father; and (c) in any case, since the law in question is much later than Paul, we cannot be sure that such a provision existed in his day.

(2) The second element under discussion is the phrase ἄχρι τῆς προθεσμίας τοῦ πατρός "until the day appointed beforehand by the father." W. M. Ramsay (*A Historical Commentary on St Paul's Epistle to the Galatians* [New York: Putnam's 1900], 391–93) assumes that Roman law of Paul's day prescribed the age at which the son of a deceased father came of age. Because Paul speaks of the father's appointing the age, Ramsey argues that Paul had in mind not the Roman but the Greek (Seleucid) law, as practiced in Phrygia, in which the father could state in his will at what age his son was to reach his majority (cf. also W. M. Calder, "Adoption and Inheritance in Galatia," *JTS* 31 [1930]: 372–74). But again, (a) it seems unlikely that Paul would have drawn on a law (whether Roman or Greek) that assumed the death of the father; and (b) in any case, we cannot be sure that the Greek/Syrian law (any more than the Roman) applied in Paul's day. A Semitic background has also been proposed for this metaphor (see W. H. Rossell, "New Testament Adoption— Graeco-Roman or Semitic?" *JBL* 71 [1952]: 233–34). In the end, these attempts to pin down the reference may prove to be fruitless. Longenecker is probably correct when he writes, "It is entirely possible . . . that Paul, being more interested in

application than precise legal details, made the specifics of his illustration conform to his purpose. No illustration is required to represent exactly every aspect of a situation in order to be telling or meaningful" (*Galatians,* 164).

125. The pedagogue might remain a trusted friend of his protégé long after childhood has passed. See, e.g., the story of the mutual affection of Habrocomes and his former pedagogue in Xenophon Ephesius, *Eph.* 1.14. Philo defends the harsh discipline of the pedagogue as that of a friend (*Migr.* 116).

126. In the phrase εἰς Χριστόν the preposition εἰς has this temporal force. Paul's references in Galatians to the law as a παιδαγωγός are generally read against a Greco-Roman background. A less likely suggestion has been made by A. T. Hanson, "The Origin of Paul's Use of ΠΑΙΔΑΓΩΓΟΣ for the Law," *Journal for the Study of the New Testament* 34 (1988): 71–76, who argues that Paul had in mind the reference to Moses as "nurse" in Num 11:11–12, which in the Targumim is rendered "guardian." By this allusion, Hanson claims, Paul was able to stress even more aptly the temporary nature of the law.

127. In verse 4, ῞Οτε ἦλθεν τὸ πλήρωμα τοῦ χρόνου "when the fullness of time had come," is an expression unique to Paul. Cf. Eph 1:10.

128. Cicero, *Phil.* 2.44–45. Such conduct was roundly condemned. See, e.g., Plutarch, *Mor.* 12A–B (*Lib. ed.* 16).To prevent the kind of depravity that Cicero attributes to Antony, some fathers kept their sons from the city long after they had assumed their *toga virilis* (on Roman dress, see p. 94 and ch. 4, n. 81). So Manlius Torquata, who imprisoned his grown-up son on a farm (Valerius Maximus, *Memor.* 5.4.4). Others, such as Cato, took more positive measures, "working hard at the task of moulding and fashioning their sons to virtue" (Plutarch, *Cat. Maj.* 20). For a general discussion of the father-son relationship in Roman society, see E. Eyben, "Fathers and Sons," in *Marriage, Divorce, and Children in Ancient Rome* (ed. B. Rawson), 114–43.

129. Notice the striking juxtaposition in Gal 5:13 of the ideas of freedom and slavery: "You are called to be free, but . . . through love be slaves to one another." On Christian "slavery," see ch. 5, n. 21. On the continuing role of the "moral law," see pp. 92–95 and also the discussion of Eph 5:2ff., pp. 247–48, and of Rom 13:8–10, pp. 181–82.

130. For instance, Gallio, mentioned in Acts 18:12ff., was adopted. He was first called Marcus Annaeus Novatus and was the son of Seneca the rhetorician. Born in Spain, he came to Rome during the reign of Tiberius, was adopted into the family of his father's friend, Lucius Junius Gallio, and took the name of his adoptive father (becoming Lucius Junius Gallio Annaeus). Most of the adopted sons of whom we know were already adults at the time of their adoption. By then, chances of survival were greater and the adopting father could see what he was getting. Most of the emperors of the first two centuries CE had to rely on adoption to secure for themselves an heir. Augustus's adoption of Tiberius is an interesting case in point. Tiberius was in his mid-forties and himself the father of an adult son when he was adopted. His adoption entailed, among other things, the surrender of all financial independence (Suetonius, *Tib.* 15). In exchange, he became Augustus's heir, and the emperor himself upon Augustus's death.

131. See Cicero (*Dom.* 35), who states the threefold reason for adoption: the maintenance of *nomen* (name), *pecunia* (property), and *sacrum* (religious rites). See further ch. 3, n. 1 (on *sacrum*) and ch. 3, nn. 2, 95 (on *pecunia*).

132. See J. M. Scott, *Adoption as Sons of God: An Exegetical Investigation into the Background of* ΥΙΟΘΕΣΙΑ *in the Pauline Corpus* (Tübingen: Mohr, 1992), 9. Cf. M. Kurylowicz, *Die adoptio, im klassischen römischen Recht* (Studia Antiqua 6; Warsaw: University Warszawskiego, 1981), 14, 17–18, 24, 26–27, 157. Note, however, that in subsequent pages Kurylowicz seems to say that the original purpose of adoption still held (see esp. pp. 76, 81).

133. This was the more common form of adoption. The other form was *adrogatio*. (*Ad* + *rogatio*, "request," refers to the fact that a motion had to be put before the *comitia curiata* for its approval. See Gaius, *Inst.* 1.99.) *Adrogatio*, the older of the two forms, applied in the case of a man (never a woman) who was *sui juris*—not under the legal authority (the *potestas*) of his father. Since *adrogatio* actually extinguished one *familia* (including possibly its *sacrum*) to perpetuate another, the institution required public approval and pontifical sanction. The pontiffs were obliged to inquire into the appropriateness of the proposal (see Cicero, *Dom.* 34–38; Gellius, *Noct. Att.* 5.19.5ff.) and, if satisfied, to bring the proposal to the *comitia calata*, that is, to a sitting of the *comitia curiata*, under the presidency of the high priest, the *pontifex maximus* (see Cicero, *Dom.* 34ff.; Gellius, *Noct. Att.* 5.19; Gaius, *Inst.* 1.99). Thus through elected officers the people effected the creation of *potestas* (see Gaius, *Inst.* 1.99, 100, 101, 105, 107; 2.138). The one adopted lost *patria potestas* over his own children, and he and his children came under the *potestas* of the adoptive father. In the process, all the previous debts of the adopted son were cancelled (see Gaius, *Inst.* 3.83–84; 4.38). For many years (until the time of Diocletian, 284–305 CE) *adrogatio* was only possible in Rome itself. Thus, this form was probably not what Paul had in mind in Rom 8–9, Gal 4, and Eph 1 (see the discussion below). In any case, the force of his metaphor rests, in part, on the transfer from one *potestas* to another, which was only the case in *adoptio sensu stricto*. For further discussion, see W. W. Buckland, *A Textbook of Roman Law from Augustus to Justinian* (Cambridge: Cambridge University Press, 1963), 124–28; H. F. Jolowicz, *Historical Introduction to the Study of Roman Law* (Cambridge: Cambridge University Press, 1972), 120; F. Schulz, *Classical Roman Law* (Oxford: Clarendon, 1951), 144–48; Gardner, *Women in Roman Law*, 8–9.

134. One of the powers of the *paterfamilias* was that of selling his offspring into slavery. In earlier days, if the son was subsequently released, he reverted to his father's *potestas*. To avoid this situation, the Twelve Tables (the law established about 450 BCE) laid down that when a son had been sold three times, his father ceased to have any authority over him. Hence the threefold *mancipatio* of the adoption procedure in the case of a son. Cf. Cicero, *Fin.* 1.7.24.

135. Only men could adopt, since only men had *potestas*. Ulpian, however, mentions in passing that women could not adopt "without the emperor's authorization," implying that by his time (third century CE) adoption by women was allowed by imperial rescript, although only one instance is known from the end of the third century CE (*Dig.* 5.2.29.3).

136. See Gellius, *Noct. Att.* 5.19.3; Gaius, *Inst.* 1.87–107, 132, 134. For a more detailed account of *adoptio*, see W. J. Woodhouse, "Adoption (Roman)," *ERE* 1:111–14. See also Buckland, *Textbook*, 121–24; Jolowicz, *Historical Introduction*, 119; Schulz, *Classical Roman Law*, 146; J. A. C. Thomas, *Textbook of Roman Law* (Amsterdam: North Holland, 1973), 439–41; F. Lyall, *Slaves, Citizens, Sons*, 95–99; Scott, *Adoption*, 11–13.

137. The privileges that were now his were matched by responsibilities. In both forms of adoption, adopted sons were obligated to perpetuate the *nomen*, the *pecunia*, and the *sacrum* of the new family (see ch. 3, n. 131). The first duty was accomplished by taking the full name of the adoptive father (except for non-hereditary *agnomina* such as Africanus or Numidicus) and by retaining only the previous *gentilicium* (the *nomen* or clan name ending in -*ius*) in a modified form (ending in -*ianus*) as a *cognomen* or *agnomen* (that is, as an additional name). See D. R. S. Bailey, *Two Studies in Roman Nomenclature* (New York: American Philological Association, 1976), 81.

138. Υἱοθεσία: "Adoption" (cf. the classical and Hellenistic phrases υἱὸν εἰσποιεῖν/ἐκποιεῖν/τίθεσθαι, υἱὸν ποιεῖσθαι, υἱοποιεῖσθαι, υἱοθετεῖν, and θετὸς υἱός "to be made into, appointed, etc., a son, an appointed son"; and see

Scott [*Adoption*, 13–57] for his study of the "semantic field" of υἱοθεσία). Used only by Paul in the NT in Rom 8:15, 23; 9:4 (of Israel's relationship with God); Gal 4:5; Eph 1:5. The metaphor is widely held to have been drawn from Greco-Roman, more specifically from Roman, practice. Some provision appears to have been made for adoption in the legal systems of the Greek city-states, but it seems not to have been as developed a concept as in Roman law (see F. Lyall, *Slaves, Citizens, Sons*, 88–95; and Scott, *Adoption*, 3–7). The unprovable suggestion has been made that Paul got the idea from Galatian law (See Calder, "Adoption," 372–74). It is, at all events, highly unlikely that he got it from Jewish law, as there is little evidence that the Jews practiced adoption, at least in the formal sense, although it was not unknown for someone to raise the child of another (e.g., Gen 15:2ff.; Exod 2:10; Esth 2:7). There are, of course, passages in which Israel is said to be God's "son" (e.g., 2 Sam 7:14), which Paul cites in 2 Cor 6:18, and these might be deemed to be metaphors of adoption. Philo has one clear instance of such a metaphor in *Sobr.* 56, in which he speaks of the wise as God's adopted sons; but he was probably influenced, as Paul was, by non-Jewish practice. Paul, however, gives theological input to the metaphor from his Jewish background, for he links adoption with inheritance and that with the promise to Abraham (see further ch. 3, nn. 140, 142). For a discussion of what little evidence there is of Jewish adoption, all of it questionable, see G. Fohrer, "υἱός," *TDNT* 8:340–54, here 344; H. Tigay and H. J. Tigay, "Adoption," *Enc Jud* 2:298–301; F. Lyall, *Slaves, Citizens, Sons*, 70–81. For a denial, based (in part) on the absence of the practice among the Jews, that Paul used υἱοθεσία in the sense of "adoption," see B. Byrne, *"Sons of God"—"Seed of Abraham": A Study of the Idea of the Sonshp of God of All Christians against the Jewish Background* (Rome: Biblical Institute Press, 1979). Scott, *Adoption*, esp. 175–76, has a critique of Byrne's arguments.

139. For the canceling of past debts, see, e.g., Col 2:14 (discussed on pp. 182–83).

140. Κληρονόμος (from κλῆρος "a lot" and νέμομαι "to possess"): (1) "an heir," (2) "a possessor." Cf. Rom 4:13–14; Gal 3:29; 4:1, 7; Titus 3:7. In Rom 4 and Gal 3 the idea of inheritance is linked with the promise to Abraham, and this might warrant the conclusion that κληρονόμοι in Rom 8:17 takes up from 4:13 this theme of our being heirs to the Abrahamic promise, although Abraham is not mentioned in this passage (but see 9:4, 6ff.) and the text does speak rather of κληρονόμοι θεοῦ "heirs of God." In Romans and Galatians, the thought of inheritance is linked with that of adoption, in Titus 3:7 with that of justification.

141. The implication of this analogy from Roman law of an equality between Christ and the believer should be balanced with other passages in the NT that make a clear distinction between Christ's sonship and our own, e.g., Mark 12:1–12, where the Son is differentiated from the servants; Mark 13:32, where Jesus distinguishes between the angels and humankind, on the one hand, and himself, as Son, on the other. He calls God "my Father" (Matt 11:27; Luke 2:49) or "your Father" (Matt 5:16, 45; Luke 12:30), but never "our Father," as though including himself. See esp. John 20:17, "I am returning to my Father and your Father, to my God and your God." See also C. F. D. Moule, *The Phenomenon of the New Testament* ((London: SCM, 1967), 52. In an earlier day, adoption was not permitted when there was a natural son, since an heir was already in existence to continue the family. But the very fact of Paul's analogy and Claudius's adoption of Nero argues that this rule had by this time gone by the board.

142. "The correlation of Rom 8 with Rom 1:4 is . . . complete and unmistakable: believers will share in the destiny of him who was 'appointed Son of God' " (Scott, *Adoption*, 244–45). Cf. Gal 3 and 4, in which the Abrahamic heirs are those who participate in Christ, who is the "seed" of Abraham and, strictly, the sole heir of the promise. Paul's word in Rom 1:4 is ὁρίζω (from ὅρος "a boundary") (1) "to separate, mark off by boundaries," (2) "to determine, appoint," the sense that it has in

all of its other occurrences in NT and arguably the sense here, its only occurrence in Paul. Irenaeus (*Haer.* 3.19.1) held that Jesus became the Son of God by receiving υἱοθεσία; Cyril of Alexandria appears to have held the same view, assuming that in Rom 1:4 ὁρίζω means "to adopt" (see P. E. Pusey, *Sancti patris nostri Cyrilli archiepiscopi alexandrini in D. Joannis evangelium* [Oxford: Clarendon, 1872], 3:175). Doctrinal considerations, however, have generally suggested some other rendering, such as "to designate." What we make of the word will depend on a variety of factors, such as whether we regard it as metaphorical, whether we regard it as reflecting Paul's conversion experience—his encounter with the risen Christ convinced him that Jesus was the Son of God—what we make of the qualifying phrase ἐξ ἀναστάσεως, etc. At least we can hardly doubt that Paul held Jesus to have been the preexistent Son of God and not to have become such only on his resurrection from the dead.

143. This future dimension was already adumbrated in Gal 4:1–7. On redemption as both present and future, see pp. 122–24 and ch. 5, n. 118 (cf. also ch. 3, n. 55), and on justification, pp. 144–47 and ch. 6, n. 41.

144. Again this notion had its roots in the religious basis of the family, the heir maintaining the patriarch's conduct of the family cult (see ch. 3, n. 1). Each successive father-priest was the *persona* in the root sense of that word (*per-sonare* "to speak through"), the one through whom the family "spoke" in its *sacra*. The individual was, as it were, the "personification" of the family, with a continuity of that personality from father to son.

145. Lyall, *Slaves, Citizens, Sons,* 110f. Cf. Gaius (*Inst.* 2.157), who says that the *sui heredes,* the children, "even in their father's lifetime are considered in a manner owners." Similarly Paulus (*Dig.* 28.2.11), "On the death of the father the heirs are not seen to inherit the property as rather to acquire the free control of their own property." Sometimes, of course, the death of the testator might find the heirs still in their minority, and although technically the estate might be theirs, in practice they might be subject to an administrator until they reached a responsible age. This is Paul's metaphor in Gal 3:23–4:11. See pp. 62–63.

146. When there were joint heirs, they held the estate in common on the death of the testator, in Jewish law and probably in Roman. It was not automatically divided between them, although subsequently it might be divided on the initiative of the heirs. See G. Horowitz, *The Spirit of Jewish Law* (New York: Central Book, 1963), 398–99; Z. W. Falk, *Introduction to Jewish Law of the Second Commonwealth* (Leiden: Brill, 1972), 2:347–49; Thomas, *Textbook,* 323–26; Buckland, *Textbook,* 318; Crook, "Patria Potestas," 113–22.

147. Κράζω: An old (though rare in the present tense, as here and Gal 4:6) onomatopoeic word of the croak of the raven, (1) "to scream, cry out," and then (2) "to cry, call out" with a loud voice, but in an articulate fashion. Used here of prayer—"an urgent and sincere crying" to God (C. E. B. Cranfield, *The Epistle to the Romans* [Edinburgh: T&T Clark, 1979], 1:399). See also Rom 9:27; Gal 4:6, and cf. the "inarticulate groanings" of Rom 8:26.

148. Συνμαρτυρέω: "To bear witness with." See also Rom 2:15; 9:1.

149. The very fact that we think of God as Father and call on God as such is evidence both of the Spirit's presence and of our relationship with God as Father. Cf. 1 Cor 12:3. Cranfield puts it this way: the Spirit's witness lies in "his whole work of enabling us to believe in Jesus Christ, through whom alone we may rightly call God 'Father' " (*Romans,* vol. 1, 403).

150. Generally, in Roman law, the certification of any matter required seven witnesses. See A. N. Sherwin-White, *Roman Society and Roman Law in the New Testament* (Oxford: Clarendon, 1969), 149.

Providing for Physical Needs

ILLNESS

Comparative evidence for preindustrial societies suggests that the average life expectancy at birth in the Roman world was twenty to thirty years. Infant mortality was high, with a quarter or more of those born not surviving their first year and perhaps only a half living beyond the age of ten. Those who did survive childhood diseases and the rigors of their upbringing[1] faced a somewhat less hazardous future and could expect to live to the age of fifty or longer, their chance of longevity improving the farther they lived from the city, any city, for in the cities disease of every kind was endemic.[2] But no one was ever safe from the threat of disease or sickness or accident.[3] And those affected by such disasters found little help. There were medical schools and some skilled doctors,[4] but such doctors were not accessible to most people. Many, in desperation, resorted to practitioners who were doctors in name only, "charlatans with a . . . smattering of superstitious medical knowledge,"[5] like the cobbler in Phaedrus's tale, who was so incompetent with his needle that no one entrusted him with their shoes, but so persuasive with his tongue that people let him do what he would with their bodies.[6] But for most people (for better or for worse) there were no doctors at all. "There are thousands," writes Pliny, "who live without doctors, but do not live without medicine."[7] They used remedies that had been passed down from father to son and were largely herbal in nature,[8] derived from leaves, roots, and the like, and from bread (a common ingredient in these ancient potions)[9]—medicines that sometimes proved to be fatal to a patient who might otherwise have survived and recovered![10]

Paul had some medical advice to give as a "father" to his "son." "Stop drinking water," he said, and take "a little wine for the sake of your stomach" (1 Tim 5:23). He was speaking to Timothy, who (it seems from Paul's evidence) was frequently ill. Paul appears to have attributed Timothy's condition to the water supply,[11] which in Ephesus was as likely a cause as any.[12] Paul himself was no stranger to sickness. In 2 Cor 12:7 he speaks of **a thorn in [his] flesh**."[13] "Flesh" implies that the reference is to a physical ailment of an unknown nature. Sickness and disease loomed large in Paul's world and find their way into his metaphors. In Eph 5:27, he speaks of Christ as presenting his bride (the church) to himself "free from **spot**[14] or **wrinkle**[15] or any such thing." A "spot" could refer to a minor blemish, or it could apply to the symptoms of certain conditions (for example, venereal diseases) that were regarded as the result of divine retribution. "Wrinkle" could also refer to such diseases or to leprosy or to the aftermath of major surgery (among a range of possible meanings "borrowed from a medical book, a beautician's parlour, the slang of the gutter, or a disreputable 'house' "[16]). Neither term, as used in Eph 5:27, merely describes the outcome of old age. Longevity is not the issue, but the defilement of sin and its purification by Christ in "the bath of water."[17]

In Eph 4:16 and its parallel, Col 2:19, Paul appears to be thinking of the crippling effect of arthritis when he describes the church as a body that can only function as well as its **"joints"**[18] will allow. Emphasis should not be given to the joints in this metaphor, as though they signified a particular group, such as the apostles, without whose contribution the church cannot grow. Rather, Paul's emphasis is on the more general point that the church only grows optimally when *the body as a whole* is functioning well, *each member* doing its bit (this is the human side of the process; Col 2:19 refers to God's role). Paul is thinking here of its growth into love (Eph 4:16).

TREATMENT

Earlier we canvassed the possibility that Paul's metaphors of sickness came either from his own experience or from his observation of the experience of others. But this would hardly account for the extraordinary number of medical metaphors that are found in the Pastoral Epistles. In these Epistles Paul seems to have drawn his inspiration from the language of contemporary philosophy. Philosophers often spoke of themselves as "physicians" whose role was, by their teaching, to "heal" vice and to promote the "good health" of virtue.[19] Their diagnosis of the "patient's" condition might sometimes demand radical treatment: not only diet and drugs, so to speak, but the knife and a hot iron to cauterize wounds.[20] Dio Chrysostom believed that the philosopher as "physician" had to be frank with his "patient," informing him at once that his soul was corrupt[21] and that "surgery" was required. The philosophers may have moved the metaphor a step beyond the original world of the physician when they affirmed that the physician/philosopher should look to himself.[22] Seneca asked, "Why do you tickle my ears? Why do you entertain me? There is other business at hand; I myself [a philosopher] am to be cauterized, operated upon, or put on a diet."[23]

The treatment the philosopher offered must fit the condition. Sometimes it had to be severe (plainspoken reproof of the person at fault), but sometimes a more gentle approach was required. Cynics tended to prefer the harsh remedy. They saw the human condition as so corrupt that only the most painful "treatment" would do—a frankness (*parrēsia*) concerning the fault to the point of downright abuse. Cynics of this kind scoffed at the masses,[24] whom they considered beneath their contempt.[25] They hated those whom they abused.[26] Their disdain for society at large is epitomized in a letter attributed to Diogenes (fourth century BCE), in which he condemns Greek civilization as exemplified at Sinope. Of Greeks, he said, their laws were a delusion, they did nothing by reason, their ignorance was profound and he hated them. They were "tickled by pleasure" (cf. the "itching ear" in 2 Tim 4:3), and if they went on in this way, they would have judges who, as "physicians," would cut and cauterize them and prescribe drugs for the people. Personally, he intended to steer clear of them all, except, of course, for those who recognized his worth as a Cynic.[27]

The Cynics were so belligerent that other philosophers, Lucian (second century CE) for example, took them to task. Since the Cynics posed as physicians of the soul, he would address them in those terms. Such physicians, he declares (tongue in cheek), should be impudent, bold, and abusive. Only then would they earn the respect of their patients and be considered by them real men. No education, of course, was necessary for the kind of healing offered by Cynics.[28] How strange it was, then, he observed, that their treatments seemed to be so well accepted and that the people appeared to delight in their "therapy."[29]

Lucian was a master of gentle irony. Paul was not always so gentle. But the terms of Paul's attacks on his opponents were not dissimilar to those employed by Lucian and other philosophers. This is not to say that he was confronting the Cynics or any other philosophical school, only that he was familiar with the language of the cut and thrust of contemporary debate—as, of course, were also his readers, who would have heard this kind of thing any day in the streets of their city.

Paul's opponents were teachers who taught "another gospel." He charges them, as Lucian did the Cynics, with being ignorant, abusive, immoral, and antisocial, exploiting those who were as ignorant as they were and who, in their ignorance, had welcomed them into their homes (1 Tim 6:4–10; 2 Tim 3:2–4, 6; Titus 1:10, 11, 16; 3:9–10). He charges them with being "deluded,[30] understanding nothing, but **diseased**[31] in their debates and word-battles" (1 Tim 6:4). Their word battles, he says, did nothing to promote the cause of (moral) good health. On the contrary, they produced "envy, strife malicious talk, evil suspicions—the **infectious sickness**[32] of men of corrupt or **disabled**[33] mind" (1 Tim 6:5). Those who liked their itching ears to be tickled (2 Tim 4:3) were at risk of contracting disease. Because they could not endure sound teaching, they choose instead to listen to these men and were infected with a contrary teaching.[34] These teachers were men whose consciences were **cauterized**[35] (1 Tim 4:2). They were **contaminated**[36] (Titus 1:15), Paul declared, and their teaching devoured their hearers like a **gangrene**[37] (2 Tim 2:17). The only **antidote**[38] to their sickness was "the man Christ Jesus" (1 Tim 2:5–6); the only safeguard against their pernicious doctrine, the **healthy**[39] word of "the glorious gospel of the blessed God, which he entrusted," said the apostle, "to me" (1 Tim 1:11).[40]

BODY

The excavation of the Asclepeion at Corinth (the temple of Asclepius, the god of healing) yielded an enormous number of terra-cotta votive offerings representing heads, hands and feet, arms and legs, breasts and genitals, eyes and ears. These represent the afflicted members supposedly cured by the god or those parts for which a cure was sought.[41] In Paul's day these ex-votos would have been on display in the temple precinct, an area open to the public and probably a popular place of retreat in the lower city (with the added attraction of a large swimming pool, the Lerna, nearby[42]), away from the bustle and noise of the city center. Paul himself may sometimes have gone there, and his observation of these offerings, against the background of his undoubted awareness of the philosophers' predilection to likening the universe to the human frame,[43] may have contributed to the formation of his concept of the church as a "**body**,"[44] especially as expressed in 1 Cor 12. For here alone (significantly in a letter addressed to Corinth), among all the instances in which he employs the metaphor, does he speak of hands, feet, eyes, genitals, and so on, in asserting that not only do all church members have a part to play but each has his or her own part, without which the function of the "body" as a whole is impeded.

Apparently the church in Corinth had a tendency to favor certain gifts above others (and therefore those who possessed them). Paul corrects this immature outlook by explaining that all Christians have God-given gifts. Not all persons have the same gift, but all gifts (because they are given by God) have the same value (see vv. 1–11). Although there are different gifts and therefore different roles for all members in the life of the church, the church is still one. As with the body, so with the church, there is a unity in diversity: a unity that stems from God's grace and redounds to God's glory (vv. 12–13).[45] As members of the church, we should respect each other's gifts and the part that each plays in the life of the whole and, indeed, have a proper estimate of, and respect for, our own role in the church (see vv. 14–26; cf. Rom 12:3),[46] the more so as the church is "[the] body *of Christ*" (v. 27; cf. v. 12). But what does Paul mean by "[the] body of Christ"?

First, the genitive "of Christ" is not one "of identity but one of possession and authority; not, the body which is Christ, of which Christ consists,
but, the body that belongs to Christ, and over which he rules."[47] Second,
"body" has no definite article (Paul's phrase is simply *sōma Christou*). A
noun, qualified by a genitive, may be regarded as definite, but not necessarily so and perhaps not in this case. But how, then, do we translate the phrase?
Neither "*a* body" (as though there were others) nor "*the* body" (as though
there were no others besides the Corinthians) quite gives the sense of the
Greek. "Body" is perhaps best understood as characterizing the church. We
are of the nature of "body"; we are "body" in relation to Christ; we lend to
Christ a corporeal presence. This being so, it behooves us to work well as a
body and to work together as parts of the body, respecting each other's gifts
and what each of us does within the life of the whole, for we are the body
that gives Christ a face to the world; his voice, as it were, his hands and
his feet.

HEAD

Sometimes the metaphor of the body occurs in conjunction with Christ
as the "**head.**"[48] These are two separate but complementary metaphors.
Each metaphor stands on its own; each has its own meaning. Paul does not
picture the church as a headless body or Christ as a bodiless head. But when
the two metaphors are found side by side, the association of "body" with
"head" does give to "head" a particular meaning. Of the passages in which
these images are found together, the most important for ascertaining the
meaning of "head" are Eph 4:15–16 and Col 2:19.[49] Each contains the extraordinary statement that the body *grows* (into love, into Christian maturity) *from the head*.[50] Herein lies the clue to both the meaning of the
headship of Christ in these verses and the origin of the metaphor by which
this meaning is expressed. But before we go any further down this track, we
should first clear the ground of another concept of headship that is sometimes applied to these and related verses.

A number of Old Testament and nonbiblical passages use "head"
(*kephalē*) in the sense of "ruler."[51] In 2 Chron 13:12 "head" refers to God
as the ruler of Israel.[52] This concept of headship as ruler best accounts for
Eph 1:20–22 and Col 2:10, in which Christ is said to be "head" over "all
[other] rule and authority, power and dominion."[53] But these passages do
not refer to those ruled by the "head" as its "body" and do not say that they
have "grown from the head." Thus, such passages have little to offer in the
quest for an understanding of headship in Eph 4:15–16 and Col 2:19.

In these and their kindred passages it appears that the metaphor of
headship derived from the current understanding of the physiology of the
human body. It was commonly supposed among the medical writers of
Paul's day that the head was the source and center of the life of the body—all

that was needed for the proper functioning of the body derived from the head. No doubt it was this same understanding that lay behind the "secular" use of the metaphor. When the philosophers conceived of the universe as a body, it was often with some entity or divinity such as Zeus or Aion or Reason as its head (sometimes but not always using the term *kephalē*), in the sense of the source of its life and power.[54]

Paul's metaphor shares with these others the salient feature of growth from the head. In Paul's case it opens the way for him to say something more than the Old Testament notion of head as ruler would allow. He speaks of Christ as the source of our life and, more than that, as the one who sustains and nurtures that life. He "enables the church to grow; he knits her into a unity; he nourishes her by caring for each member; he gives her strength to build herself up in love."[55] As against the headship of authority (Old Testament), this physiological metaphor presents what might be described as "the headship of source and of service" (the head sustaining the life of which it is the source), anticipated by Jesus himself: "The Son of man came, not to be served, but to serve" (Mark 10:45).

Such "headship" becomes a model for others, specifically for the husband as "head of the wife," as in Eph 5:23.[56] Here Paul speaks again of Christ as "head" of "the body," the church—the "headship of source." He then draws from this the analogy that the husband is "head of the wife." This headship, like Christ's, is one of source and service. It is possible that this verse expresses more than merely an *analogy* with Christ in the conduct of the man; it may be *a mandate* that the man should be Christlike: "Let wives be subject to their own husbands . . . , because the husband is [= must be] head of the wife, as[57] Christ is also head of the church." This is a command to reciprocal service. That Paul had in mind the physiological notion of headship may be borne out by his reference to the creation story of Gen 2, in which the woman is made *from* the man.[58] Of course, Eph 5:22–33 is not intended to be a discussion of headship as such. This language has only been introduced to underline the man's primacy in creation—he was made first, and from him the woman was made—as giving an historical/theological basis for the wife's submission to her husband. Equally, the husband is to submit to the wife (v. 21), only here the argument rests not on the order of creation but on the nature of redemption. The man should give place to the woman; that is, he should love his wife as Christ loved the church and gave himself for it (v. 25).

First Corinthians 11:3–11 is another passage often referred to in discussions of headship. But here headship is even less the real issue than in Eph 5. The issue is dress—how, as Paul perceived it, a person is honored or dishonored by the covering or uncovering of the head when praying or preaching in church. In defending this proposition (and Paul's language may be, in some part, a deliberate play on the word "head"), he mentions that "the man is [the] head of [the] woman" (v. 3). The reference is only incidental, but again he employs the physiological metaphor, as is seen from the explanation in verse 8. The man, says Paul, is the "head" of the woman *because* "the woman [in the Genesis story] came *from* the man."[59] His intention is simply to appeal to Gen 2, in this shorthand fashion by reference to the man as the "head," with a view to urging the women to remain true to their creation— women are women and should honor their femininity by wearing a veil, the traditional mark of their gender.[60]

VEIL AND MIRROR

In 2 Cor 3 Paul contrasts the old and new covenants, in verses 12–18 by reference to Exod 34. When Moses came down from Mount Sinai with the law, having met with God, his face was radiant and the people were afraid to come near him. Therefore Moses put a veil over his face. The Exodus story does not say so, but Paul supposes that in time the veil served also to hide the fading of that radiance. This becomes a metaphor for the fading glory of the old covenant. It was destined to be superseded.

The idea of the veil now takes hold of Paul's mind, and he uses it in different ways. When the Jews hear the old covenant being read (the Old Testament), it is as though a **veil**[61] hangs between them and their understanding of what they hear. Christ is the key to that understanding; it is to Christ as its fulfillment that the Old Testament points. In Christ that veil of misunderstanding is taken away. Similarly, Paul speaks of the gospel **being veiled**[62] to those who have been blinded by "the god of this age"—they do not see "the glory of God in the face of Christ" and are therefore blind to the gospel (cf. 2 Cor 4:3–6). On the other hand, those who are enlightened by Christ now find that **the veil is drawn over**[63] their sins (see Rom 4:7). As Moses' face reflected the glory of God, so Christians with **unveiled**[64] faces—there is no need to hide it—**reflect**[65] Christ, in whom that glory is seen. The more they look on Christ, the more they reflect him, the Holy Spirit working this transformation within them (cf. Rom 12:2).

In 2 Cor 3 Paul is thinking of the relative clarity of the Christians' vision of God because they see Christ, who is "the radiance of God's glory and his exact representation" (Heb 1:3). Nevertheless not all is seen. "For the present," says Paul (relative to what is to come), "we see but **a poor reflection** [of God] **in the mirror**,[66] but one day we will see him face to face" (1 Cor 13:12). Ancient mirrors were of polished metal, not glass, Corinth being famous for their manufacture. But even the best of such mirrors gave only a poor reflection. The best is yet to come.

WAKING AND DRESSING

Generally speaking, the people of Paul's world were early risers. This was due in great part to the very imperfect lighting of houses, which made it difficult to carry on work, especially reading and writing, after dark.[67] The rich were as eager as the poor to be up and about at sunrise. Paul repeatedly refers to his own working "night and day." The order of the words indicates that he rose early, while it was still dark, to make the most of the daylight hours.[68] Early rising may also have resulted from the noise of the city. Martial laments that he was a martyr to the deafening din of the streets and squares of the city, in which the metalworkers' hammers blended with the bawling of the children at school: "The laughter of the passing throng wakes me and Rome is at my bed's head. . . . Schoolmasters in the morning do not let you live; before daybreak, bakers; the hammers of the coppersmiths all day."[69] Only the roisterers of the night before or drunkards reduced to a state of stupor might manage to sleep through the noise of the day.[70]

Getting up in the morning was a straightforward matter. Most people spent little or no time on washing.[71] Since they did not undress for bed, they had only to take up their cloak, which may have served as an extra blanket during the night, and begin the new day. Paul would have the Christians in Rome **wake up**[72] and **"fling off"**[73] the coverings of the night ("the works of darkness" that belonged to their past), for "the night" (of this present age) was almost over and "the day" (of Christ's return) was at hand (Rom 13:11–14).[74] The new age, the age of God's kingdom, had already dawned. Christ had already come, and before long it would be "the full light of day," that is, of *the* day, the day when Christ would return. They must look, then, to their conduct. They must not live as though it were still night. "Put on the armor of light," he demands (portraying his readers as soldiers[75]), "**dress yourselves**[76] with the Lord Jesus Christ" (in the sense of recalling anew every morning that they were "in Christ"), and make no concession to your sinful desires. Similarly Eph 5:14, apparently a free adaptation of Isa 26:19 and 60:1, now perhaps some lines of a Christian hymn: "Wake up sleeper, get up from the dead, and Christ will shine on you." The same thought is expressed in 1 Thess 5:5–8, with the images of night and day, **sleep**[77] and waking, representing moral conditions made urgent by the imminence of Christ's return. "We are not of the night, not of darkness. So then, let us not sleep as do others. . . . We belong to the day."

CLOTHING

The metaphors of waking and dressing refer to practice—how Christians should live. In Col 3:9–10 and Eph 4:22–24, the image of dressing (or better, of changing one's clothes) refers rather to position—our change of status with regard to God. We have "**taken off**[78] the old man" (what, by nature, we were) and "**put on**[79] the new" (what, by grace, we are in Christ, the tense in each case pointing to something decisive).[80] Expressed differently, in terms of the verses leading up to this passage, we have died with Christ to sin (Col 2:20), we have risen with him to new life

(3:1), we sit with him, so to speak, beside God (3:1–3), and we shall be with him when he returns (3:4).

Paul may have adopted the figure of putting off old clothes and putting on new ones from Roman and Greek practice. When a boy grew to manhood, he exchanged (in the Roman context) the *toga praetexta* for the *toga virilis*.[81] No longer was he under the control of his pedagogue. He was now considered old enough to act responsibly and look after himself. Much was made of his investiture with the new toga, the sign that he had now come of age. The ceremony took place on the festival of Liber (17 March). His *toga praetexta* and *bulla* (the childhood amulet designed to ward off evil) were set aside and dedicated to the family god, the *Lar familiaris*. Clothed in the toga of manhood, he was conducted by his father or guardian to the Capitol (or to the corresponding place of enrollment in a municipal town), where his name was entered on the list of citizens. The choice of place was significant. Capitoline Jupiter himself would receive him. The whole city was buzzing on this day as family processions crisscrossed Rome, making their way, with their young men, to the Capitol. In the streets old women sold special cakes made with honey, a fragment of which would be offered to the god. As the Romans donned their togas of manhood, so have Christians been invested with Christ, of which baptism is the outward sign (Col 2:12; cf. Gal 3:27).[82] But would they act responsibly? It was always possible that the new man would turn his freedom into license.[83] Having "put on" Christ, Paul counsels, you must now live up to what is expected of you in that "dress." It behooves you to be renewed, that is, changed into the likeness of God (this is God's own specification for the new life that God has given us; notice the present tense—the renewal is an ongoing process). As the process continues, says Paul, so you will know God more and more (Col 3:10; cf. Eph 4:23).

Christian practice remains the theme in Col 3:12–14. Paul urges his readers to clothe themselves[84] with certain virtues. People in Paul's world distinguished two types of clothing: underwear, which they put on first and wore most of the time, and their street clothes, which they put on over the other.[85] The first item of underwear was the loincloth, usually a strip of linen worn to keep one's private parts private (decency, together with the demonstration of rank, was the primary objective of clothing, not protection or comfort). In earlier days the loincloth had been the only item of underwear, but by the first century CE most people were also wearing and sleeping in a tunic, a long shirt of linen or wool consisting of two strips of material sewn back-to-back. It was slipped over the head and tied by a belt. A man's tunic differed from a woman's in that the man's was generally longer. Over this went the outer garment, a cloak (Greek *himation*) or a toga. As Christians, Paul urged, "put on [as '**underwear**'] compassion, kindness, humility, meekness, and patience" (he names these five virtues to match the five vices named in vv. 5, 8). These virtues find outward expression in our "putting up with each other and forgiving each other." Over these items of "underwear," let us put on the "**outer garment**" of love.[86] Or perhaps Paul imaged love as **the belt**[87] that fastened the tunic. Either way, he conceived of it as something that added the finishing touch to one's dress. The metaphor is somewhat strained in that love is not simply one of a number of virtues but the root (to use another image) of all virtues, without which it is hard to imagine how compassion, kindness, humility, and the like could exist. But the meaning is clear. This is simply Paul's way of saying that "the greatest of these [Christian virtues] is love."[88]

Five times in the Corinthian correspondence Paul uses the verb "to put on"[89] of the body with which Christians will be clothed at the coming of Christ. In 2 Cor 5:1–10 he longs that it might be "put on" immediately after we divest[90] ourselves of the old, but he fears that a period of "nakedness" may well intervene. Nevertheless, he holds on to the thought that in the end either our "nakedness" or our present body (before the inconvenience of its death has ensued) will have "the heavenly dwelling" (mixing his metaphors[91]) **put on over**[92] it, so that "what is mortal may be swallowed up by life." This will be the final outcome of our salvation, at the center of which stands the cross of Christ, where he **stripped himself bare**[93] of the powers of evil (Col 2:15). This verb has been variously understood. It can mean, for example, "to strip or despoil another," but here I think it is better understood in the reflexive sense, "he stripped himself," which J. B. Lightfoot explains in the following terms:

> Christ took upon himself our human nature with all its temptations (Heb. 4:15). The powers of evil gathered about him. Again and again they assailed him; but each fresh assault ended in a new defeat. . . . Then the last hour came. This was the great crisis of all, when "the power of darkness" made itself felt (Luke 22:53), when the prince of the world asserted his tyranny (John 12:31). The final act in the conflict began with the agony of Gethsemane; it ended with the cross of Calvary. The victory was complete. The enemy of man was defeated. The powers of evil, which had clung like a Nessus robe about his humanity, were torn off and cast aside for ever. And the victory of mankind is involved in the victory of Christ.[94]

In 1 Cor 1:10 Paul may be making a play on the notion of torn clothes being repaired. Separately the words would not suggest a deliberate metaphor, but together they might. "I appeal to you, brothers, in the name of our Lord Jesus Christ that you all agree so that there may be no **tears**[95] among you, but that you may be **mended**,[96] having the same mind and the same judgment in everything."

COOKING AND CLEANING

Paul's own experience embraced all sorts and conditions of domestic life. In the humbler homes in which he must sometimes have stayed, he would have seen the housewife stir up the embers of the fire to cook a meal (the standard fare in poorer homes was cereal, made into either porridge or bread, a few vegetables, cheese, and fish). He may have recalled one kitchen scene in particular, with the mother Eunice or the grandmother Lois standing over the fire, when he later urged the young man of that household to **rekindle**[97] his gift, which had nearly "gone out" (2 Tim 1:6). Paul's arrest at Ephesus had evidently had a dampening effect, to say the least, on his protégé (see vv. 4–7, 8, 15–16)! This should be compared with Paul's warning to the Thessalonians not to **put out** (**the fire**)[98] of the Spirit (1 Thess 5:19). Both passages refer to the gifts of the Spirit.

Paul wanted people to be spiritually **on the boil**[99] (Rom 12:11), like a kettle over the fire. In Rom 12:20 he counsels his readers against taking revenge. Leave that to God, he says. Instead do something good to the person concerned. "In so doing [and here he is quoting Prov 25:21–22] you will heap **burning coals**[100] on his head"—a metaphor for making him feel what Moffatt calls "the burning sense of shame." Such kindness may lead to repentance.

Often, perhaps, he had seen the housewife season a dish with a pinch of salt, and he urged the Colossians to do the same with their conversation: "Let your speech be always gracious, **seasoned with salt**"[101] (Col 4:6). Among classical writers, "salt," *hals*, expressed the wit with which conversation was flavored ("Attic salt" = witty conversation).[102] But Paul may have had in mind the secondary meaning of wholesomeness, derived from the function of salt to preserve from corruption. That Christian speech should be wholesome is the thrust of the parallel in Eph 4:29.[103] Thus in Col 4:6 he was looking for a "polished courtesy" in the Colossians that would give them an acceptance among their pagan neighbors and friends. Perhaps he was also looking for wholesomeness in their speech and for the wisdom that knows what to say to inquirers.

In 1 Cor 5:6 he warned, by means of analogy, of the effect that one (public) sin can have on the moral tone of the church if the church does not act immediately in the matter: "Don't you know," he asked, "that **a little yeast leavens the whole lump of dough?**"[104] Some Corinthian church members may have argued that one such case did not affect the church as a whole—a specious excuse for negligence. In Paul's response the emphasis is on the "little" (note the position of *mikra*). Even a small amount of yeast causes an entire loaf of bread to rise; even one "small" sin can be detrimental to the entire church. This catalog of Paul's homely images concludes with one taken from Acts. When his friends tried to dissuade him from making the journey up to Jerusalem, which they all knew was fraught with danger, Paul accused them of "pounding his heart," that is, of weakening his determination to go. Some commentators have suggested that he employs in these words the metaphor of **a washerwoman pounding the clothes**[105] (Acts 21:13), an image that emphasizes the persuasive force of his friends' words.

HOUSEHOLD MANAGEMENT

Pliny described his young wife, Calpurnia, as shrewd and frugal.[106] In this she lived up to the ideal of the Roman wife, whose traditional role was to manage the home while her husband concerned himself with matters outside the home. In his discussion of estate management Columella upholds this ideal, condemning the current practice of consigning to slaves much that had once been done by the wife.[107] But Columella and other traditionalists were swimming against the tide on this issue. Despite their disapproval, wives who could afford slaves (or whose husbands could afford them) were in fact delegating their responsibilities to them. One wonders, then, how much scope Calpurnia actually had to practice the virtues and skills attributed to her by her husband when he maintained an establishment of five hundred slaves to do the work for her.[108] Calpurnia's situation was not exceptional among rich upper-class women, and this may go some way to explaining the difference in the age at which rich and poor women usually married. In a poor family, without the backup of slaves, an inexperienced wife of twelve or thirteen years of age would have been more of a liability than an ornament to her husband, whereas in the homes of the rich, her age would not have mattered at all as long as the household was properly managed.

The proper management of the "household," the church, was important to Paul. His reference to "**good order** and **firmness**" in Col 2:5, while most often understood as a military metaphor, could be an image drawn from the good management *(oikonomia)* of the state or of a private estate.[109] (There is, however, nothing in the context to suggest that this was the case. But neither is there anything in the context to suggest a military association.) The situation that he commends in these terms at Colossae had its opposite at Thessalonica. Here there was an element of "**disorderliness**"[110] in the church that caused Paul a great deal of anxiety (1 Thess 5:14; 2 Thess 3:6–7, 11). Some members were refusing to work and were living on support given by others.

The guest of a rich man or woman would never witness the homely scenes mentioned above of the housewife cooking and cleaning, and sometimes Paul was such a guest—certainly of Lydia in Philippi, perhaps also of the Asiarchs in Ephesus, and perhaps of Erastus, Corinth's director of public works and a member of the church in that city[111] (Paul's family circumstances and his life in the home of Gamaliel may have prepared him more for the rich man's table than for the poor). In these homes slaves or hired servants would do the bidding of their mistress or master, and no guest would ever be permitted to sit in the kitchen watching the meals being prepared. Ausonius's poem *Ephemeris* ("The Daily Round"), although written some centuries after Paul, conveys something of the manner of life in such an establishment. The poem begins in the morning, with Ausonius reproaching his servant for oversleeping. He demands water and his clothes. Then the chapel is opened for prayers (Ausonius is a Christian), and next the servant brings his cloak, as Ausonius intends to visit his friends. He realizes, however, that it is already past 10 o'clock (as we would call it; in his terms the forenoon),[112] so he sends the servant instead to invite five friends to lunch (six was considered the ideal number for an informal meal). Ausonius meanwhile calls on his cook and tells him to taste and season carefully the dishes already bubbling on the kitchen fire. We may be sure the kitchen is full of servants helping with the preparation of the meal. Our last glimpse of Ausonius finds him with his secretary, dealing with correspondence and business matters. From other sources we may guess that this rich man spent his afternoon talking with his friends or being outside, and ended his day with a visit to the baths and a pleasant meal at home, again with his friends.

In these larger households, much of the day-to-day management of the estate was in the hands of the steward, who controlled the staff (sometimes running into hundreds of workers) and issued supplies. Here was a ready illustration of the role of church leaders. They were **"stewards"**[113] of the mysteries of God (1 Cor 4:1; Titus 1:7). These references should be coupled with those that speak of the church as the "household" of God.[114] Within the *familia*,[115] the steward stood, as it were, in his master's place, transmitting his master's instructions and distributing his rations to the household (on Roman estates, daily, weekly, or monthly). The plural "mysteries" in 1 Cor 4:1 ("think of us in this way, as servants of Christ and stewards of God's mysteries") suggests that the **"storeroom"** from which these "stewards" draw their supplies is well stocked with the good things of God's revelation of himself and of his purpose in Christ (the general sense of "mystery" in the New Testament is of a secret about God which has now been revealed).

Although the steward was over others, he was himself under authority. He was usually a slave or a freedman[116] answerable, in either case, to his master for all that he did. And yet he was given a great deal of latitude. He was free to act responsibly. His work was not closely supervised, since a large part of his function was to free his master from these household duties. Above all else, then, the steward had to be a man on whom the master could depend. Varro has an interesting chapter advising that the *vilicus (oikonomos)*, the steward, be carefully selected. His faithfulness can be assured by allowing him to take a wife and to have the means of accumulating property *(peculium)* of his own.[117] Without suggesting incentives as Varro did (but he does mention that the Lord will judge him, v. 4), Paul certainly agrees with him that "it is looked for in a steward that he be found to be faithful" (1 Cor 4:2). To this he adds, in respect to the "steward of the mysteries of God," that he is not to be "arrogant, nor quick-tempered, nor a heavy drinker, nor a brawler, nor a man out to make a quick [and suspect] buck, but hospitable, a man who loves what is good, is sensible, upright, holy, disciplined, and true to the gospel" (Titus 1:7–8). All of these virtues are subsumed under faithfulness; the steward must answer to "the God and Father of our Lord Jesus Christ."

Paul was well aware of his own responsibility in this regard. He speaks of himself in 1 Cor 9:17 as **"entrusted with a stewardship"**[118] and in a similar vein in Eph 3:2 and Col 1:25. In 1 Tim 1:3–4 he instructs his protégé to warn the Ephesians against those who were teaching contrary to the gospel and neglecting what he calls their "stewardship of God which is in faith." The precise meaning of *oikonomia* in this verse is much debated, since the word can sometimes mean "plan" (the program according to which the steward orders the work of the household) as well as the office of steward. Were these people neglecting God's plan, or was it the stewardship (ministry) that God had given them that they were neglecting (the genitive "of God" being either possessive or subjective respectively)? It is unlikely that Paul would describe their "ministry" as a stewardship from God. He probably meant God's plan. The contrary teaching of these people was frustrating the divine plan of salvation—a plan (Paul adds) that is only made effective to its beneficiaries in the context of faith.[119] Ephesians 1:10 supports this understanding of *oikonomia* as "plan" in 1 Tim 1:4. The thesis of Eph 1:3–14 is that the whole of history (spanning all of time and touching all of creation) is the outcome of God's *oikonomia*—God's plan and careful management. God is "working his purpose out as year succeeds to year," with Christ the agent and our redemption the goal.

NOTES

1. At birth, the Roman child was regarded as barely human and as something that needed yet to be formed; such formation was especially important in the case of a boy. For the first few months the baby was imprisoned in its cradle, wrapped in swaddling bands tied particularly tight around its elbows, wrists, knees, hips, and ankles. Its hands were kept open and splints were used to keep its legs straight. Its arms were strapped straight against its body. After two months of this regime, the bands were loosed a little, and the right hand was freed to ensure that the child grew up right-handed. It was bathed only in cold water, and at bath time, its various parts were manipulated in an attempt to give them the desired shape, including kneading the head and stretching the foreskin. Bath time was never popular with Roman children! For the father's acceptance of the child at birth, see pp. 60–61; for wet-nursing, see p. 59, ch. 1, n. 99, and ch. 3, n. 104.

2. These data on life expectancy are taken from P. Garnsey and R. Saller, *The Roman Empire* (London: Gerald Duckworth, 1987), 138. See also T. G. Parkin, *Demography and Roman Society* (Baltimore: Johns Hopkins University Press, 199), 291ff. For all cities up to the 1870s for which evidence is available, the death rates of those born in the cities exceeded the birth rates, presumably because urban populations were more often exposed to virulent communicable diseases than were rural populations. The cities, of course, were constantly being replenished by the urban drift from the countryside. See T. McKeown and R. G. Record, "The Reasons for the Decline of Mortality in England and Wales during the Nineteenth Century," *Population Studies* 16 (1962): 94–122; B. Benjamin, "The Urban Background to Public Health Changes

in England and Wales, 1900–1950," *Population Studies* 17 (1964): 225–48; D. V. Glass, "Some Indicators of Differences between Urban and Rural Mortality in England and Wales and Scotland," *Population Studies* 17 (1964): 263–67.

3. It is difficult to ascertain the diseases to which the ancient world was prone. The Romans seem to have been mainly subject to eye infections (which they treated with ointments), stomachaches, skin diseases, and summer and autumn fevers (Horace, *Ep.* 1.1.29–31). Insomnia was also a problem, for which Horace prescribed a swim in the Tiber followed by a large dose of wine (*Sat.* 2.1.7).

4. For a brief history of Greek and Roman medicine, see H. C. Kee, *Medicine, Miracle, and Magic in New Testament Times* (Cambridge: Cambridge University Press, 1986), 27–65.

5. U. E. Paoli, *Rome: Its People, Life, and Customs* (London: Gerald Duckworth, 1990), 210. Only state doctors—those appointed by the magistrates to care for the poor—were required to provide proof of training and qualification (*Cod. theod.* 13.3.8; *Cod. justin.* 10.53.c9).

6. Phaedrus, *Fab.* 1.14.

7. Pliny, *Nat.* 29.11.

8. Traditionally, in both Greek and Roman circles, the *paterfamilias* prepared the medicines for the entire household, including women, children, and slaves. In the *Il.* 2.728–733, Homer mentions the two sons of Asclepius (the renowned healer) among those assembled for the attack on Troy and notes that they were "both good healers themselves," for Asclepius, like any father, had bequeathed to them his medical knowledge. Similarly, Cato was the latest custodian of a medical tradition passed on from father to son. Deeply suspicious of professional doctors, all of whom were Greeks in his time, he believed that they were out to poison the people. He looked after his own household with advice culled from a huge book— which had long been in his family—about medical treatments (see Pliny, *Nat.* 29.4–16). He treated sciatica, for example, with juniper wood wine (Cato, *Agr.* 123) and always kept a pomegranate extract at the ready to combat colic and worms (126). But best of all was cabbage (157). It aided digestion, facilitated urination, made a powerful diuretic, an emetic, and a cure for colic. As a poultice it could heal ulcers, open sores generally, and dispel any tumor. It was good for infected wounds. Eating it could soothe most aches and pains. Fried in hot fat and taken on an empty stomach, it helped to induce sleep. Dried, it could be taken as snuff. Its juice, dropped into the ears, was a sure cure for deafness. Incantations generally accompanied the treatment and might even be used on their own (see Horace, *Ep.* 1.1.36–37). Cato had an astonishing procedure for healing dislocations and fractures:

> Any kind of dislocation may be cured by the following charm. Take a green reed four or five feet long and slit it down the middle and let two men hold the two pieces to either side of your hips. Begin to chant: *"motas uaeta daries dardaries astataries dissunapiter"* and continue, advancing the ends until they meet. Brandish a knife over them and, when the ends of the reeds are actually touching, grasp them and cut right and left. If the pieces are applied to the dislocation or the fracture, it will heal. And none the less chant every day and, in the case of a dislocation, in this manner, if you wish: *"haut haut haut istasis tarsis ardannabou dannaustra."* (*Agr.* 160)

9. Pliny, *Nat.* 22.138.

10. In fifth-century BCE Athens, a young singer died from a draught that was supposed to improve his voice (Antiphon, *Chor.* 15). Suetonius tells us that the emperor Caligula was driven mad by a love philtre given him by his wife (*Cal.* 50).

11. Since the time of Hippocrates, the Greeks and Romans had understood that drinking contaminated water caused disease (an understanding forgotten in later times). See Hippocrates, *De flatibus* 1.71–117; Aristotle, *Pol.* 7.11.2–3; Frontinus, *Aquaeduct.* 2.88–94.

12. Ephesus was an ancient and decaying city. Its harbor was silting up, and a sewage system is often the first casualty in such an event. This, in turn, can lead to pollutants infiltrating the groundwater in wells (although Greek and Roman cities took as much of their water as possible from natural springs). So disease spreads. Moreover, we know that in Rome lead piping was used for reticulation and that this was the cause of poisoning. This, too, could have been a source of Timothy's problems. See E. M. Blaiklock, *The World of the New Testament* (London: Ark, 1981), 25.

13. Σκόλοψ τῇ σαρκί: Σκόλοψ, an old word for anything pointed, (1) in classical Greek, "a stake," (2) in the Hellenistic vernacular (as in papyri and inscriptions), "a splinter, a thorn." Found only here in the NT. All sorts of theories have been advanced as to what the "thorn" was: malaria, insomnia, migraine, etc. Galatians 4:15 is often appealed to in this connection and the "thorn" identified, on this basis, as an eye problem. But this is a precarious exegesis. Probably all that Paul meant in Galatians was that there had been a time when they would have given him their most precious possession. Although the most likely explanation is that Paul's "thorn" was a physical ailment, it always remains possible that it was something spiritual. He does call it a "messenger of Satan" sent to buffet him (κολαφίζω, ch. 12, n. 107).

14. Σπίλος: (1) "a rock, cliff," (2) in later Greek apparently the equivalent of the Attic κηλίς "a spot or stain," including the symptoms of the (disreputable) diseases that were considered to have been visited on their victims by the gods, such as syphilis. But to what extent σπίλος covers the whole range of meaning embraced by κηλίς remains uncertain. The word is found only here in Paul.

15. Ῥυτίς: "A wrinkle." Found only here in the whole Greek Bible and rare elsewhere. For the prenuptial purificatory rites to which Paul alludes in Eph 5:27, see p. 54 and notes.

16. M. Barth, *Ephesians* (New York: Doubleday, 1974), 2:627.

17. See ch. 3, n. 35.

18. Ἀφή (from ἅπτω "to fasten, fit"): "A joint, ligament," occurring on its own in Eph 4:16 and with σύνδεσμος (from συνδέω "to bind together") in Col 2:19, "that which binds together, a bond" (see also Eph 4:3; Col 3:14). That ἀφή was used in the sense of "ligament" in ancient physiology is suggested by an entry in Galen's list of words that were used by Hippocrates (*An Explanation of the Words of Hippocrates* [under A]; see further J. A. Robinson, *St Paul's Epistle to the Ephesians* [London: Macmillan, 1909], 186).

19. The description of the philosopher as a physician was an apt one, since the two professions were, in fact, historically related. Cf. the title of one of the works of Galen: *That the Best Physician Is Also a Philosopher*. See Seneca, *Ep.* 22.1; 40.5; 50.4; 64.8; 72.5f.; 94.24; 95.29; and Epictetus, *Diatr.* 2.15.3; 3.21.20; 3.23.27f., 30; 3.25.7f. See also G. W. Bowerstock, *Greek Sophists in the Roman Empire* (Oxford: Clarendon, 1969), 19, 59–75, esp. 67f.; and S. Dill, *Roman Society from Nero to Marcus Aurelius* (New York: Meridian, 1956), 292.

20. See Seneca, *Ep.* 75.6f.; Epictetus, *Diatr.* 3.22.72f.; Dio Chrysostom, *Disc.* 77–78.

21. Διεφθαρμένη is the perfect passive participle of διαφθείρω. See ch. 4, n. 33.

22. Dio Chrysostom, *Disc.* 43, 45, 77, and 78.

23. Seneca, *Ep.* 75.6f. Cf. the similar image of the "itching ear" in 2 Tim 4:3.

24. E.g., Pseudo-Hippocrates, *Ep.* 17.26ff and 47ff.

25. E.g., Pseudo-Socrates, *Ep.* 8.

26. E.g., Pseudo-Socrates, *Ep.* 24.

27. Diogenes, *Ep.* 28. Cf. *Ep.* 29, which denounces Dionysius, the tyrant of Sicily. Diogenes threatens to send him someone (a Cynic) to purge him; his disease was far gone and required surgery, cautery, and medication for healing. And what had Dionysius done? He had brought in "grandparents" and "wet-nurses," that is, philosophers who had sometimes been gentle in their instruction!

28. Lucian, *Philops.* 8 and 10f. Cf. Plutarch, *Mor.* 61D–62C (*Adul. amic.* 20–21); 80B–C (*Virt. prof.* 9). He accused them of parading a specious παρρησία and took exception to their arming themselves with arguments "as with boxing gloves or brass knuckles, with which to contend against their opponents, and who take more delight in scoring a hit or a knockout than in learning something useful and passing it on to others."

29. Lucian, *Fug.* 12.

30. Τυφόω (from τῦφος "smoke"): Properly, "to wrap in smoke," but metaphorically, "to puff up, cloud" with pride, which Epictetus saw as a danger confronting all philosophers (*Diatr.* 1.8.6f.). Found only in Paul in the NT, in 1 Tim 3:6; 6:4; 2 Tim 3:4. The word could also mean "to be mentally ill, demented." See Demosthenes, *3 Philip.* 9.20, where it is contrasted with being in one's right mind (ὑγιαίνω; see ch. 4, n. 39). Plutarch, *Mor.* 81F (*Virt. prof.* 10), assures the young man that as he takes a firmer hold on reason, he will lay aside τῦφος. He then goes on to expand a medical metaphor. In the light of this, it is not unlikely that the τετύφωται of 1 Tim 6:4 is intended to describe mental illness.

31. Νοσέω (from νόσος "disease, sickness"): "To be sick." Found only here in the NT.

32. We have drawn a long bow here in the translation of 1 Tim 6:5. Διαπαρατριβή is most often trans. "mutual irritation, wrangling." The word occurs only here in the NT, but cf. 1 Tim 6:4–5; 2 Tim 2:14; Titus 3:9 for a description of the problem in other words. Παρατριβή is found with the same meaning as διαπαρατριβή in Polybius and others. But Chrysostrom (*Hom. 1 Tim.* 17) proposes an alternative meaning for these words. The false teachers, he says, are like scab-covered sheep that infect the healthy sheep when they rub against them. He evidently thinks that παρατριβή is related to παράτριμμα, which is used by medical writers of (infected?) abrasions. Since διαφθείρω in 1 Tim. 6:5 is also used sometimes in a medical sense (see the next note), it is possible that we have here a cluster of medical terms and that Chrysostom rightly includes διαπαρατριβή among them. His suggestion has been taken up here. But M. Dibelius and H. Conzelmann dismiss Chrysostom's explanation as "much too learned" (*The Pastoral Epistles*, 83 n. 3).

33. Διαφθείρω: (1) "to destroy," passive (as here) "to be destroyed, disabled," used sometimes in a medical sense, (2) in a moral sense, "to corrupt, deprave." See also 2 Cor 4:16 and cf. 2 Tim 3:8 for the similar καταφθείρω: (1) "to destroy," passive "to be destroyed," (2) "to corrupt."

34. Cf. Dio Chrysostom, *Disc.* 33.15f.: "Man's ears are dainty when reared on flattery and lies; they cannot endure demanding preaching."

35. Καυστηριάζω (or καυτηριάζω): "To mark by branding, brand." A rare verb, found only here in the NT.

36. Μιαίνω: Old verb, (1) "to dye, stain," (2) "to stain, defile, soil." Found only here in Paul.

37. Γάγγραινα: "A gangrene, an eating sore" that leads to mortification. A late word found in medical writers and Plutarch, but only here in the NT. Sulla's death, as described by Plutarch, was brought about by a gangrene that was as much moral as physical:

> He consorted with actresses, harpists and theatrical people, drinking with them on couches all day long. These were the men who had most influence on him now: Roscius the comedian, Sorex the archmime and Metrobius, the impersonator of women. . . . By this mode of life he aggravated a disease that was insignificant when it began, so that for a long time he did not know that his bowels were ulcerated. This disease corrupted his whole flesh. (*Sull.* 36–37)

38. Ἀντίλυτρον: "Ransom" (see further ch. 5, n. 122). But in *Orphica* 588, the word is used for "antidote" and "remedy." Taken in this sense, Christ's death is

seen as the antidote for poisonous teaching, to say nothing of the remedy for sin. But this sense is less likely than "ransom."

39. Ύγιαίνω (from ὑγιής): "To be sound, healthy." Old word for well-being. The expressions "sound (healthy) teaching" (1 Tim 1:10; 2 Tim 4:3; Titus 1:9; 2:1), "sound words" (1 Tim 6:3; 2 Tim 1:13; Titus 2:8), and being "sound in the faith" (Titus 1:13; 2:2) appear in the NT only in the Pastorals and represent a major theme of these letters. In all of the above references, with the exception of Titus 2:8, the verb in some form is employed. In Titus 2:8 we have the adjective ὑγιής "healthy."

40. Much of the material of this section has been drawn from A. J. Malherbe, "Medical Imagery in the Pastoral Epistles," in *Texts and Testaments* (ed. W. E. March; San Antonio: Trinity University Press, 1980), 19–35, and this article should be consulted for a more detailed discussion. For further evidence of Paul's awareness of the philosophical language of the day, see the discussion of his metaphors of body and head, pp. 89–92 and notes; his military metaphors, pp. 215–16 and notes; and his athletic metaphors, pp. 268–70 and ch. 12, n. 106. See also J. N. Sevenster, *Paul and Seneca* (Leiden: Brill, 1961).

41. See M. Lang, *Cure and Cult in Ancient Corinth: A Guide to the Asklepieion* (Princeton: American School of Classical Studies at Athens, 1977), 14. For a further description of the Asclepeion at Corinth, see ch. 1, n. 83.

42. See Pausanius, *Descr.* 4.5.

43. See, e.g., Plato, *Tim.* 30B–34B; Cleanthes, *Hymn to Zeus* (no. 537 in J. von Arnim, *Stoicorum veterum fragmenta, I* [Leipzig: Terbner, 1903], 119–24); Cicero, *Nat. d.* 1.35; 3.9; Seneca, *Nat.* 6.14.1; Seneca, *Ep.* 92.30; 95.52. The likeness of the universe to the human body is found also in some religious texts, such as the magic papyri (e.g., Papyrus Leiden 5 in K. Preisendanz, *Griechische Zauberpapyri, I–II* [Leipzig: Teubner, 1928, 1931], 1:243); the so-called Naassene Sermon, cited by Hippolytus, *Haer.* 5.7.3–5.9.9; *Odes Sol.* 17:14–17; and certain Mandaean texts, for which see H. Schlier, "κεφαλή, κτλ," *TDNT* 3:673–82, here 678. See also Ign. *Trall.* 11.2. The Stoic moralists in particular appear to have had a liking for the imagery of the body. For a discussion of Paul's similarity to, and difference from, them in his use of the analogy, see J. N. Sevenster, *Paul and Seneca*, 170–73. Since there is nothing comparable with this concept in the Jewish literature of the time (unless we see the germ of the idea in the rabbinic notion that Adam's body contained within it the whole of the human race), it is fairly certain that Paul did not draw the analogy from here but from the wider world in which he now moved. Some scholars, however, suggest that it was not Greek philosophy but Christ himself who sowed in Paul's mind the seed of the idea of the church as Christ's body, when he identified himself with his followers in Acts 9:4: "Why do you persecute *me?*" See Bruce, *Paul,* 421.

44. Σῶμα: "A body," (1) properly, of the human body but also (2) of the bodies of animals, (3) of inanimate objects ("the heavenly bodies"), and (4) of any corporeal substance (as opposed to σκία "a shadow" in Col 2:17), thus metaphorically, of the church (e.g., in Rom 12:5; 1 Cor 10:16, 17; 12:13, 27; Eph 1:23; 2:16; 4:4, 12, 16; 5:23, 30; Col 1:18, 24; 2:19; 3:15). In one sense or another, the word occurs ninety-one times in Paul.

45. Notice in v. 12 the reiterated "one" (ἕν) and "many" (πολλά), also the emphatic "all" (πάντα) of the second clause: "But *all* the members of the body, many as they are, are *one* body." See also Rom 12:3–8; 1 Cor 6:15; 10:16–17; Eph 1:22–23; 2:16; 4:4; Col 1:24; 3:15, all of which, either expressly or by implication, reflect the more detailed teaching of 1 Cor 12. To this list might also be added 1 Cor 11:29, a notoriously ambiguous passage. Alternatively, 1 Cor 11:29 might refer to the bread of the Lord's Supper, the sacramental body of Christ. For such an explanation of Paul's body language, see J. A. T. Robinson, *The Body* (London: SCM, 1952); E. P.

Sanders, *Paul and Palestinian Judaism* (London: SCM, 1977), 453–63. See also
E. E. Ellis, "Traditions in 1 Corinthians," *NTS* 32 (1986): 487–88; idem, "Soma in
First Corinthians," *Int* 44 (1990): 132–44. For Christ as the "head of the body," see
below on Eph 4:15–16; 5:23; Col 1:18; 2:19.

46. Cf. Marcus Aurelius (*Med.* 2.2), who says that we are made to cooperate
with one another, as feet and hands and eyelids and upper and lower jaws. To act in
opposition to one another is unnatural. Earlier, Socrates had remarked how mon-
strous it would be if hands and feet, which God made to work in harmony, were to
thwart and impede one another (Xenophon, *Mem.* 2.3.18).

47. C. K. Barrett, *A Commentary on the First Epistle to the Corinthians* (London: Adam & Charles Black, 1971), 292. Paul does not assert "an ultimate substantial or essential identity of Christ and the church. The use he makes of three other
images reveals this clearly: the keystone is not identified with the building (Eph
2:20–22); the inhabiting power is something other than the inhabited heart (Eph
3:16–17); the bridegroom has a bride but is not bridegroom and bride at the same
time (Eph 5:22–23)." Furthermore, the church is called the "new person created in
him" and "by him." It is his "bride," his "beloved" (Eph 2:15; 5:22–23). That is to
say, the church is always his partner and is always seen "over against" Christ, never as
Christ himself. See M. Barth, *Ephesians* (New York: Doubleday, 1974), 1:185f.,
195; and, for a recent defense of this position, G. L. O. Yorke, *The Church as the
Body of Christ in the Pauline Corpus* (Lanham, Md.: University Press of America,
1991).

48. Κεφαλή: "A head." In Paul in Rom 12:20; 1 Cor 11:3 (3x), 4 (2x), 5 (2x),
7, 10; 12:21; Eph 1:22; 4:15; 5:23 (2x); Col 1:18; 2:10, 19.

49. Cf. also Eph 5:23; Col 1:18 for the conjunction of "head" and "body."

50. Eph 4:15–16: ἡ κεφαλή, Χριστός, ἐξ οὗ πᾶν τὸ σῶμα . . . τὴν αὔξησιν τοῦ
σώματος ποιεῖται: "The head, namely, Christ, *from whom* the whole body makes
the growth of the body"; Col 2:19: τὴν κεφαλήν, ἐξ οὗ τὸ σῶμα . . . αὔξει τὴν
αὔξησιν τοῦ θεοῦ: "The head, *from whom* the whole body . . . grows with the
growth [that comes from] God."

51. See, e.g., Deut 33:5; Judg 10:18; 11:8–9; 1 Sam 15:17; 1 Kings 21:12
(LXX 3 Kings 20:12); Job 29:25; Ps 18:43; Isa 7:8–9; Jer 31:7 (LXX 38:7); Lam 1:5;
Hos 1:11 (LXX 2:2). Some LXX MSS occasionally translate the Hebrew *rosh* by the
Greek ἀρχή "rule" or ἄρχων "ruler." J. A. Fitzmyer draws mostly from Philo and
Plutarch other instances of "head" in this sense. See "Another Look at ΚΕΦΑΛΗ in
1 Corinthians 11:3," *NTS* 35 (1989): 506–10; idem, "Κεφαλή in 1 Corinthians
11:3," *Int* 47 (1993): 52–59; and the critique of Fitzmyer's reading of the data by
A. C. Perriman, "The Head of a Woman: The Meaning of ΚΕΦΑΛΗ in 1 Corinthi-
ans 11:3," *JTS* 45 (1994): 602–22.

52. Cf. 1 Cor 11:3, in which God is described as "head of the Messiah."

53. In Eph 1:22 it is difficult to know how precisely to understand Paul's statement ἔδωκεν κεφαλὴν ὑπὲρ πάντα τῇ ἐκκλησίᾳ: "He [God] gave Christ as head
over all things *to* the church"? or "He gave him to be head over all things *for* the
church"? in the sense that he rules all things generally for the particular benefit of his
people. At all events, the notion of Christ as head *of the church* is only incidental to
this passage, if present at all. The parallel in Col 2:10 makes no mention of the
church. Even so, not all commentators are agreed that these verses speak only of the
headship of authority. Some understand "head" here in the sense suggested below,
as "source," and others as combining the ideas of source and authority; e.g., A. L.
Williams, *The Epistle of Paul the Apostle to the Colossians and to Philemon* (Cambridge: Cambridge University Press, 1928), 90: "Even over them (the principalities
and powers) Christ is supreme, even to them He is the source of their original and
continued existence." Cf. H. C. G. Moule (*Ephesian Studies* [London: Hodder &

Stoughton, 1900], 54), who sees Christ's headship in Eph 1:22 as primarily one of source and only secondarily as one of authority.

54. See Barth, *Ephesians*, 1:185. Barth adds, "According to this notion Zeus is not only the highest part of the universe, but its very life. Philosophers preferred to ascribe this function to the soul rather than to the head, but both conceptions can also be combined: 'The soul of the universe is located in the head.' " Perriman ("The Head of a Woman"), while questioning the interpretation of "head" as "authority," is equally cautious in accepting "source" as its meaning. Recently, however, W. Grudem ("Does ΚΕΦΑΛΗ Mean 'Source' or 'Authority over' in Greek Literature? A Survey of 2,336 Examples," *TJ* 6 [1985]: 38–59) has argued that the statistical evidence favors "authority." Where "head" has been understood as "source," it would be better understood as "extremity," the beginning or the end point of the thing in question. But this is open to argument, and R. S. Cervin ("Does ΚΕΦΑΛΗ Mean 'Source' or 'Authority over' in Greek Literature? A Rebuttal," *TJ* 10 [1989]: 85–112) has revealed the somewhat tendentious nature of Grudem's work, showing that in some instances κεφαλή does mean "source," although it is hardly a common meaning. On the other hand, he argues that it *never* means "authority over" or "leader." In any case, the facts still remain that (1) Paul speaks of growth *from* the head and (2) this does fit with an understanding of the physiology of the (literal) head current in that day. For a useful summary of Hippocrates and Galen on this point, see Barth, *Ephesians*, 1:187–88, and his conclusion, 190:

> By his acquaintance with physiological insights Paul could ascribe to the head more than a representative and dominating function. He could attribute to it the power to perceive, to interpret, to coordinate, and to unify all that went on in the body and its several members. Because the head is the "greatest power" of the body, causation and coordination can be ascribed to nothing else. There is but one source, throne, and acropolis of all members, including their movements and perceptions—the head.

55. Barth, *Ephesians*, 2:614. Cf. Eph 5:29, where Paul speaks of a man as "nourishing and caring for his body, just as Christ does the church."

56. The question of whether marriage is meant to be a hierarchical arrangement today is too large a question to discuss fully here. But Paul sees the Christian as operating in two different orders—the order of creation and the order of redemption. Insofar as we are still in the old order of creation, there is a hierarchy, and he defends this on the basis of the creation story. Woman was made from man: headship of source. Thus, if you will, the headship of source becomes a headship of authority. But this is only his argument in defense of the status quo. He doesn't want Christians "rocking the boat" of accepted social norms. Insofar as we belong to the order of redemption, we are all one—male and female—there is no hierarchy.

57. Ὡς καί, in most versions, is rendered "as also." But ὡς can introduce a dependent clause of reason, and some commentators prefer this rendering here, "*because* Christ is also head of the church."

58. Gen 2:21–24. Paul quotes v. 24 in Eph 5:31.

59. Γὰρ . . . γυνὴ ἐξ ἀνδρός: This statement, however, is counterbalanced in v. 12 by the observation that subsequently every man has come from a woman (ὁ ἀνὴρ διὰ τῆς γυναικός).

60. It appears to have been generally the case, at least of the lands of the eastern Mediterranean, that women wore a head covering of some sort when in public, κάλυμμα "a covering, a veil" (see the following notes). Paul likens the uncovered woman to a woman whose head has been shaved (1 Cor. 11:5). This refers to the practice, under Roman law, of shaving the head of an adulteress. Such a woman was deemed to have repudiated her relationship with her husband, and so also, in the eyes of some, had the woman who prayed or prophesied with her head uncovered. In that Roman world it was generally only a woman who was looking for a man—a

virgin or a prostitute—who publicly uncovered her hair, although social status was also a factor, a woman of higher class having greater liberty to go uncovered and to sport the latest hairstyle in public (e.g., C. S. Keener, "Man and Woman," in *Dictionary of Paul and His Letters* [ed. G. Hawthorne and R. P. Martin; Downers Grove, Ill.: InterVarsity Press, 1993], 585). A woman praying with head uncovered, Paul argues, has denied the role given to her in creation, namely, that of the woman/wife, by abandoning the icon of that role, the κάλυμμα. As for Christian men covering their heads (v. 4), "it was the pagan custom for the priests of a cult who were drawn from the elite of society to distinguish themselves from other worshippers by praying and sacrificing with their heads covered. Is it[, then,] that there were some among the minority of Christians from the social elite who wished to draw attention to their status by praying and prophesying with their heads covered?" To do so would be to draw attention to themselves and so to dishonor Christ, their "head," who should, at all times, be the center of Christian attention (B. W. Winter, "1 Corinthians," in *New Bible Commentary* [ed. D. A. Carson et al.; Leicester, U.K.: Inter-Varsity Press, 1994], 1178). Cf. Virgil (*Aen.* 3.545): "our heads are shrouded before the altar with a Phrygian vestment."

61. Κάλυμμα (from καλύπτω "to cover"): "A covering veil," in the NT only in 2 Cor 3:13–16. Cf. the adjective ἀκατακάλυπτος "uncovered, unveiled," in the NT only in 1 Cor 11:5, 13, from κατακαλύπτω "to cover up," middle voice, "to cover or veil oneself," 1 Cor 11:6.

62. Καλύπτω: (1) "to cover," (2) metaphorically, "to veil, conceal," in Paul only in 2 Cor 4:3.

63. Ἐπικαλύπτω: "To cover over, cover up," only in Rom 4:7 in the NT.

64. Ἀνακαλύπτω: "To unveil," in the NT only in 2 Cor 3:14, 18.

65. Κατοπτρίζω (from κάτοπτρον "a mirror"): "To show as in a mirror," here in middle voice, "to see oneself mirrored," "to reflect as a mirror." Only in 2 Cor 3:18 in the NT.

66. Ἔσοπτρον: "A mirror." In the NT only in 1 Cor 13:12; Jas 1:23. Paul's expression is βλέπομεν γὰρ ἄρτι δι᾽ ἐσόπτρου ἐν αἰνίγματι, "For we see now through [= by means of] a mirror in a riddle [= in an obscure fashion]." Αἴνιγμα (from αἰνίσσομαι, an old word expressing obscurity): "A dark saying, riddle." In the NT only in 1 Cor 13:12. Mirrors were an ancient and common phenomenon. The Hebrew women of the exodus, for example, or more specifically those who did duty at the entrance of the Tent of Meeting, had enough of them to supply the metal for the bronze basin and its stand (Exod 38:8).

67. The use of lamps fueled by olive oil had spread from the East through Greece to Rome, so that by Paul's day the oil lamp was in universal use in houses and public places such as baths. Even in the small old baths of Pompeii there were found about a thousand lamps, obviously used for illumination after dark. Despite this and the invention of candelabra for extending the use of candles, close work at night remained a difficult exercise.

68. Acts 20:31; 1 Thess 2:9; 3:10. The habit of getting up at dawn, inherited no doubt from their rural past, was so deeply ingrained with most people that, even if they stayed in bed, they still woke before daybreak and, when it was feasible to do so, would work in bed, by lamplight, at their reading and writing. Thus we find Cicero on a February morning writing to his brother before sunrise (*Quint. fratr.* 2.3.7); it is not unlikely that the soreness of the eyes of which he sometimes complains may have been the result of reading and writing before the light was good. Horace describes himself calling for pen and paper before daylight (*Ep.* 2.1.112). The elder Pliny would end one day by lamplight and begin the next in attendance upon Vespasian before daybreak, dealing with reports and opening the emperor's correspondence, for Vespasian also liked to be on the job early (Pliny, *Ep.* 3.5.8; cf. Suetonius, *Vesp.* 21).

69. Martial, *Epigr.* 12.57.

70. Persius Flaccus, *Sat.* 3.1–7; Horace, *Sat.* 1.6.122; see ch. 4, n. 3, for Horace's cure for insomnia.

71. Martial, *Epigr.* 12.18.17–18; cf. Arnobius, *Nat.* 2.68. By the first century CE, the better-appointed homes of the rich generally sported the modern innovation of a bathroom or set of bathrooms, providing every accommodation according to the season and the bather's taste. In the old days the Romans washed their arms and legs daily and took a bath every market day, i.e., every eighth day. This is told us by Seneca (*Ep.* 86), who gives a description of the bath in the villa of the elder Scipio at Liternum; it consisted of a single room without a window and was supplied with water (which was often dirty after rain).

72. Ὥρα ἤδη ὑμᾶς ἐξ ὕπνου ἐγερθῆναι: "[The] hour has come for you to be aroused from sleep." Ὕπνος "sleep," found only here in Paul, is used as a metaphor of one's moral condition. Cf. καθεύδω, ch. 4, n. 77.

73. Ἀποτίθημι: "To put off or aside," in the NT always middle voice, "to put off from oneself," as with a garment or the like. See also Eph 4:22, 25; Col 3:8.

74. For "the day," see the discussion of 1 Cor 3:13, pp. 13–14. For the city at night, see p. 8.

75. See pp. 219–20 for a further discussion of this passage as a military metaphor.

76. Ἐνδύω, middle voice ἐνδύομαι "to put on oneself, be clothed with." Found in Paul in Rom 13:12, 14; 1 Cor 15:53 (2x), 54 (2x); 2 Cor 5:3; Gal 3:27; Eph 4:24; 6:11, 14; Col 3:10, 12; 1 Thess 5:8. The word (appearing in the best texts as ἐνδύνω) is used in a rather different sense, "to enter, press into," in 2 Tim 3:6.

77. Καθεύδω: "To sleep," in Paul metaphorically, (1) of moral and spiritual insensibility in Eph 5:14; 1 Thess 5:6–7 (see p. 8 and cf. ὕπνος, ch. 4, n. 72) and (2) of death in 1 Thess 5:10. With the latter, cf. κοιμάω "to lull to sleep, put to sleep," and in middle and passive, "to fall asleep," commonly as a metaphor of death among Greeks and Romans and generally in the NT, e.g., 1 Cor 7:39; 11:30; 15:6, 18, 20, 51; 1 Thess 4:13–15. In the NT, however, it was not, as it was elsewhere, simply a euphemism for death but an expression of the conviction that physical death was not the end—it was only a "sleep" from which the Christian would "wake." Jesus, on the other hand, is never said to sleep but always to have died. Because he died, we need only "sleep."

78. Ἀπεκδύω: "To strip off" clothes or arms, middle voice (as here in Col 3:9), "to strip off from oneself." In Col 2:15, the only other instance of this word in the NT (elsewhere it occurs only once in Josephus), the middle voice is sometimes thought to be used for the active in the sense of "to strip or despoil" another, in this case "the powers and authorities" although there too it is more likely reflexive, Jesus stripping himself (see further on this passage, p. 95). Both of the single compounds ἀποδύω and ἐκδύω (see ch. 4, n. 90) occur in ancient writers. Paul has simply combined the two probably in order to express, by means of the double compound, the idea of *complete* removal. Clearly he is not speaking here (Col 3:9) of Christian practice, which sadly retains much that belongs to the old nature (e.g., Rom 7:7–24 and the discussion of this passage on pp. 117, 214), but of Christian status. Before God we are deemed to be absolutely new people. In the parallel in Eph 4:22 the verb is ἀποτίθημι. See ch. 4, n. 73.

79. Ἐνδύω, see ch. 4, n. 76.

80. The thought is akin to that in Rom 5:12–21, in which Paul sees humankind as identified with either Adam or Christ. In those terms, Adam is "the old man" (ὁ παλαιὸς ἄνθρωπος) that must be discarded, and Christ the "new man" that must be put on. This will lead to both the renewal of knowledge and the restoration of the image of the Creator within us (Col 3:10), an obvious allusion to the Adam story. Cf. Gen 1:27 and 2:17.

81. The *toga virilis* was assumed between the ages of fourteen and seventeen years. The two young Ciceros seem to have assumed it at sixteen, Octavian and Virgil at fifteen, Mark Antony's son at fourteen. The toga of childhood, the *toga praetexta*, was worn by children of both sexes. The same name, *toga praetexta*, was also applied to the purple-bordered toga of the curule magistrates.

82. There is an obvious correspondence between this figure of "putting on Christ" at baptism and the later practice of investing catechumens with white robes at their initiation. But the symbolism of the later practice differed from what Paul had in mind. The white robes corresponded rather to the wedding garment in the parable. They were an emblem of purity and signified the cleansing effect of baptism or, rather, of what it signified, whereas the context in Galatians especially points to the emancipation of those concerned from past restraints and to their new status as "sons" and "heirs."

83. See the discussion of liberty and license, p. 63 and notes.

84. Ἐνδύω: See ch. 4, n. 76.

85. This is the difference between the Greek ἔνδυμα ("a garment" in general) and ἐπίβλημα ("that which is thrown over," particularly "an outer garment") and, similarly, between the Latin *indumentum* which was worn day and night, and the toga or *amictus* (which, in Paul's day, had succeeded the toga in popular favor) for the street. For details, see J. Carcopino, *Daily Life in Ancient Rome* (Harmondsworth, U.K.: Penguin, 1956), 157–60; F. A. Wright and L. B. Lawler, "Dress," *OCD*, 364–65; Dupont, *Daily Life*, 258–62.

86. Ἐνδύσασθε . . . ἐπὶ πᾶσιν τούτοις τὴν ἀγάπην: Ἐπί is interpreted here locally, "put *on* [i.e., on top of] all these love," but some take the preposition as meaning "in addition to." In any case, a garment put on in addition to others will be over them. This phrase is assumed here to be still part of the construction with the verb in v. 12. It has been suggested, however, that the metaphor of clothing has been left behind in v. 14 and that this is a separate charge: "In addition to all these things [which I have said], [have] love." But this seems less likely than the interpretation that we have adopted. Love is described as the "bond of perfection" (σύνδεσμος τῆς τελειότητος). For σύνδεσμος, see ch. 4, n. 18. The genitive "of perfection" has been regarded as either (1) descriptive (love is the perfect bond) or (2) telic (love is the bond that leads to the goal of perfection). See, e.g., P. O'Brien, *Colossians, Philemon* (Waco, Tex.: Word, 1982), 203–4.

87. So, e.g., A. T. Robertson, *Word Pictures in the New Testament* (New York: Richard R. Smith, 1930–1933; repr. Nashville, Tenn.: Broadman & Holman, 1973), 4:504. Cf. Eph 4:3, where peace is the "bond" that holds the outfit together, in this case the church. But there is no peace without love.

88. Cf. 1 Cor 13:13.

89. Ἐνδύω: See ch. 4, n. 76. The notion of "putting on" the resurrection body may have been already current in Jewish literature. See, e.g., *1 En.* 62:16 and the discussion in G. E. Ladd, *A Theology of the New Testament* (Grand Rapids: Eerdmans, 1974), 323.

90. Ἐκδύω: "To take off, strip." Found only here in Paul. Cf ἀπεκδύω, ch. 4, n. 78.

91. See pp. 19–20 for the discussion of this passage as a building metaphor.

92. Ἐπενδύω: "To put on over," in the middle voice (as in 2 Cor 5:2, 4), "to put upon oneself, be clothed upon." Found only in these verses in the NT. Cf. ἐπενδύτης in John 21:7, "the fisherman's linen blouse or upper garment" (so Robertson, *Word Pictures*, 4:228).

93. Giving full weight to the middle voice, ἀπεκδυσάμενος. On ἀπεκδύω and the alternative interpretation of Col 2:15, see ch. 4, n. 78.

94. J. B. Lightfoot, *Saint Paul's Epistles to the Colossians and to Philemon* (London: Macmillan, 1879), 188.

95. Σχίσμα (from σχίζω "to tear"): (1) "a tear," (2) metaphorically, "a dissention, division." In Paul in 1 Cor 1:10; 11:18; 12:25.

96. Καταρτίζω: "To render ἄρτιος, i.e., fit, complete," "to mend, repair, complete, equip, prepare." Galen used it for a surgeon mending a joint, Herodotus for resolving divisions, Matt 4:21 and Mark 1:19 for mending torn nets. In Paul in Rom 9:22; 1 Cor 1:10; 2 Cor 13:11; Gal 6:1.

97. Ἀναζωπυρέω (an old double compound, ἀνά and ζώπυρον "a live coal," itself from ζωός "alive, living" and πῦρ "fire"): "To kindle afresh" or "to keep in full flame." Found only here in the NT; cf. Paul's use of πυρόω, ch. 10, n. 119. Cf. also ἀνάπτω "to kindle," not used by Paul.

98. Σβέννυμι: See ch. 1, n. 45.

99. Ζέω, an old and common verb, "to boil, be hot," is often used metaphorically of anger, love, zeal. In the NT only here and in Acts 18:25.

100. Ἄνθρακας πυρὸς: "Coals of fire." Ἄνθραξ: An old word for "coal, charcoal," found only here in the NT. The metaphor in Proverbs may have been from the practice of heaping red-hot charcoal over crushed ore, which, as it melted, ran out into a collecting pit. There was also an Egyptian rite in which a person carried glowing embers in a bowl on the head or, in another case, carried a tray of burning coals to express repentance. For πῦρ see ch. 1, n. 48, and for a discussion of the meaning of the proverb, see W. Klassen, "Coals of Fire: Sign of Repentence or Revenge? [Rom 12:20; Prov 25:22]," NTS 9 (Jl 1963): 337–50.

101. Ὁ λόγος ὑμῶν . . . ἅλατι ἠρτυμένος: Ἀρτύω (1) "to arrange, make ready" (Homer, etc.), (2) of food, "to season." This is an old verb found also in Mark 9:50 and Luke 14:34 in connection with salt.

102. Cf., e.g., Plutarch, Mor., 514F (Garr. 23) and 669A (Quaest. conv. 4.3).

103. W. Nauck ("Salt as a Metaphor in Instructions for Discipleship," ST 6 [1952]: 165–78) draws attention to rabbinic parallels for the figurative use of salt as wisdom. D. Wenham (Paul: Follower of Jesus or Founder of Christianity? [Grand Rapids: Eerdmans, 1995], 254) sees here another instance of Paul's familiarity with the Jesus tradition. Cf. Matt 5:13.

104. On ζύμη "leaven" and ζυμόω "to leaven," see ch. 11, n. 32. Φύραμα (from φυράω, a late word, "to mix," in papyri of mixing a medical prescription): "That which is mixed (with water) or kneaded, a lump," used of dough in Rom 11:16; 1 Cor 5:6–7; Gal 5:9; of clay in Rom 9:21. Here is another instance of a word setting off a train of thought. Leaven had a particular association with the Passover, thus the paschal metaphor of 1 Cor 5:7–8 (see the discussion on p. 248).

105. Συνθρύπτω: A late form of ἀποθρύπτω "to break in pieces, crush." F. F. Bruce (The Acts of the Apostles [Grand Rapids: Eerdmans, 1986], 388) notes without reference J. A. Findlay's rendering, "bleaching my heart by pounding it like a washerwoman," and T. Zahn's inference from the metaphor that Paul meant, "Why do you try to make me soft?"

106. See Pliny, Ep. 4.19, for Pliny's glowing description of his wife, who lives up to the conventional ideals for the virtuous Roman wife.

107. Columella, Rust. 12.8–10.

108. Another random example of the size of a rich man's household is afforded by Tacitus (Ann. 14.42–45), who mentions that there were about four hundred slaves in the house of L. Pedanius Secundus, a sometime urban prefect in Rome.

109. On τάξις and στερέωμα, see ch. 10, nn. 12, 15, respectively. Both words are used in a military sense, but that sense is suggested by the context. "Here the context suggests nothing of the kind. . . . The idea of a well-ordered state lies much nearer than that of an army. The apostle rejoices in the orderly arrangement of the Colossian Church" (T. K. Abbott, Epistles to the Ephesians and to the Colossians [Edinburgh: T&T Clark, 1897], 243; cf., e.g., O'Brien, Colossians, Philemon, 99).

110. The Thessalonian correspondence employs three related forms to express this idea of disorderliness: the adjective ἄτακτος, the adverb ἀτάκτως, and the verb ἀτακτέω. See ch. 10, n. 131, which considers them as a possible military metaphor.

111. See Acts 16:15; 19:31; Rom 16:23.

112. Thanks to the advent of sundials, it was possible to reckon time by hours, i.e., twelve divisions of the day. But as they continued to reckon the day from sunrise to sunset on the principle of the old agricultural practice, these twelve hours varied in length at different times of the year. For the ordinary Roman, however, without easy access to a sundial or a water clock, the day fell into four convenient divisions: (1) *mane,* or morning, from sunrise to the beginning of the third hour, (2) *ad meridiem,* or forenoon, (3) *de meridie,* or afternoon, and (4) *suprema,* from about the ninth or tenth hour to sunset (see Censorinus, *De die natali* 23.9; 24.3).

113. Οἰκονόμος: See ch. 3, n. 123.

114. See ch. 1, n. 89, on οἰκία, οἶκος, and οἰκεῖοι.

115. On the range of meanings of this term, see ch. 3, n. 2.

116. See the discussion of the relationship between the freedman and his patron, pp. 120–21.

117. Varro, *Rust.* 1.17.

118. Εἰ ἄκων, οἰκονομίαν πεπίστευμαι: A. T. Robertson (*Word Pictures,* 4:147) expresses Paul's thought as follows: "I have been entrusted with a stewardship and so would go on with my task like any οἰκονόμος (steward) even if ἄκων (unwilling)." Πιστεύω: (1) intransitive, "to have faith, believe," (2) transitive, "to entrust." Paul has the verb fifty-four times, here in the perfect passive, "I have been entrusted." Οἰκονομία (from οἰκονόμος, see ch. 3, n. 123): In classical Greek it had two meanings: (1) "an administration," the management of a house or property, and, from this, "a plan of management, a dispensation," and (2) "the office of the administrator, a stewardship." It has the same twofold sense in the NT. It is found in Paul in 1 Cor 9:17; Eph 1:10; 3:2; Col 1:25; 1 Tim 1:4.

119. In the phrase οἰκονομίαν θεοῦ τὴν ἐν πίστει, the definite article τήν ties ἐν πίστει to οἰκονομίαν to indicate the sphere in which the οἰκονομία is accomplished. Πίστις can have (1) the active sense of "faith, belief, trust, confidence" or (2) the passive sense of "fidelity or faithfulness." The ambiguity of Paul's phrase in 1 Tim 1:4 may be allowed to cover both possibilities, namely, (1) the response of faith (both initially and continually) in those to whom God's salvation is offered and (2) the faithfulness of the "stewards" in making that offer to them on God's behalf.

Slavery and Freedom

Slavery formed an integral part of the Roman way of life. Slaves had been a large part of the workforce that had served the wealthy in Italy and Sicily ever since the period of overseas expansion had begun at the end of the third century BCE. According to the best modern estimates, there were about two (but some estimates go as high as three) million slaves in Italy by the end of the first century BCE. Thus, slaves made up 35 to 40 percent of the total estimated population of the country.[1] The evidence for slavery in the more distant provinces is less easy to come by.[2] Archaeology, sculpture, inscriptions, and occasional literary references provide us with some data, but the scanty nature of the evidence makes it difficult to generalize. Slavery was certainly a fact of life, as familiar to Paul as to his readers, a number of whom were either slaves or slave masters.[3] Slaves could be found everywhere—in the countryside, in the towns, in the houses, in the shops, and in every corner of state administration. There was no work in which they were not employed, from the most menial of tasks to key positions in business and government, and they mingled at all levels with the free population.[4]

JOBS PERFORMED BY SLAVES

There is a tendency to assume that slaves were either agricultural workers and miners or (in an urban context) menial household servants. This may have been the case for most slaves, but not for all. Slaves could be found doing almost any job that a free person might do.[5] Evidence from Greece shows them working as tradesmen of various kinds, including builders,[6] shoemakers, and linen workers. They were involved in banking,[7] book publishing,[8] shopkeeping, clerical work, entertainment, medicine,[9] teaching, and philosophy.[10] Many towns and cities in the East had public slaves who performed all kinds of jobs, from temple maintenance[11] to policing.[12] In the West there appears to have been an even greater diversity of slave jobs—for example, barbers, mirror makers, goldsmiths, cooks,[13] architects,[14] innkeepers,[15] agents, tradesmen of all kinds, fishermen, foremen, laborers, gladiators, personal servants, painters, prostitutes, janitors, cooks, waiters, cleaners, couriers, child minders, wet-nurses, and general factotums whose duties might sometimes include providing sexual favors for the owner or for his or her guests.[16]

The lot of the urban slaves was generally easier than that of their rural counterparts. Their work was lighter, and the conditions under which they lived and worked were incomparably better. Sometimes a slave might even be allowed to have a de facto family life.[17] Those who ran workshops or commercial enterprises for their masters often had a great deal of freedom in the conduct of the business. Some controlled large sums of money through their *peculium* and apparently were able to call much of that money their own. Greek and Roman authors complained constantly about high-flying slaves who were richer than they were. In the first century CE, men such as Pallas, Narcissus, and Callistus, slaves who later became freedmen of the imperial household, amassed enormous fortunes and exercised the power that often accompanies great wealth. There are a number of other examples, both inside and outside the bureaucracy, of slaves who made money.[18] For them in particular, as for most urban slaves, freedom was always a possibility. In most cases this was not so for rural slaves.

THE LEGAL CONDITION OF SLAVERY

In Roman law the head of the household held complete power over his slaves. It was known as *dominica potestas* "the power of ownership." Legally, every slave was absolutely subject to the will of his or her master. Slaves were classed as chattels, not persons,[19] and could be bought and sold and punished[20] at the will of the master. It was this status that prompted Paul's description of our human condition as a form of **slavery**.[21] The human race is, by nature, in service to sin (which in Romans he personifies for dramatic effect: sin reigns [5:21; 6:12]; sin has a mastery [6:14], which is the counterpart of God's mastery [6:13, 22]; either we serve sin [6:6, 16, 17, 20] or we are set free to serve God [6:22]). We may differ in other respects, but we have in common one master: "Jews and Gentiles alike are all under sin"[22] (3:9). The word "slave" does not occur in this particular verse, but the image is certainly one of subjection to **an absolute master**, the latter conceived of (e.g., in Rom 5–6) as perhaps a king but more likely as the owner of slaves, given the use of that metaphor elsewhere in this section of Romans.[23] This notion of thralldom to sin is developed at length in 6:12–23. The ideas of **dominion**, on the one hand (dominion properly implies ownership, not merely domination), and **obedience**, on the other, run through this passage.[24] A slave had no choice but to do as his (or her) master instructed. He was at all times at the beck and call of his master. In practice, of course, it was not always like this,[25] but Paul's point in Romans rests more on the theory than on the practice of slavery—on the legal status of slaves, which was unquestionably one of utter subjection. From this he argues that we, no less than a slave to his master, are subject to sin[26] and in a service, moreover, that could end in our death.[27]

With no rights in law, the only recourse for a slave oppressed by a tyrannical master was to flee,[28] risking terrible punishment if caught, or to seek sanctuary in a temple[29] (not allowed in Roman law[30]) or at a statue of the emperor (allowed, but with an uncertain outcome for the slave[31]). A number of important rulings, made over a period of time, gave tacit recognition to the slave's humanity and imposed some restrictions on the cruelty of the master. For instance, Claudius (41–54 CE) decided that masters who abandoned sick slaves to avoid the cost of caring for them could not reclaim the slaves if they recovered. Domitian (81–96 CE) forbade the castration of male slaves (the punishment inflicted on those who did castrate their slaves was severe—the loss of half of the owner's property), and by the reign of Hadrian (117–138 CE) laws were established that prohibited *ergastula* (private prisons on country estates in which slaves were habitually kept in chains and treated no better than beasts), regulated the punitive sale of slaves, and severely curtailed the master's right of life and death,[32] although the right of masters to kill their slaves appears to have remained on the books until the time of Justinian (527–565 CE).[33] Such laws undoubtedly suppressed some of the worst abuses of slavery, but they did nothing to mitigate its hardship or to modify the slave's complete legal subjugation to his or her master.[34]

CRUELTY TO SLAVES

Roman literature abounds in examples of incidental cruelty to slaves. The emperor Augustus, for example, ordered that the legs of a trusted slave be broken because he had abused his trust.[35] Galen the physician noted that many slaves had their teeth broken and their eyes blackened by blows, and reported a particular instance in which the emperor Hadrian stabbed a slave in the eye with a stylus in a moment of anger.[36] Seneca portrayed a master at dinner, surrounded by slaves: "The unfortunate slaves are not allowed to move their lips, let alone talk; the birch keeps murmuring down. A cough, a sneeze, a hiccup is rewarded by a flogging, with no exceptions. Any break in the silence is severely punished. They stand at the ready all night, tense and mute."[37]

If the lot of domestic or urban slaves was a hard one, that of rural slaves who labored on the estates or in the mines was infinitely worse. Diodorus wrote of slaves in the Spanish mines, where forty thousand are said to have worked: "The slaves . . . produce incredible profit for their masters, but they themselves wear out their bodies, digging underground by day and by night, and many of them die under the strain of such terrible conditions. They are not allowed any pause or rest from their work, but are forced by the blows of their overseers to endure sheer misery."[38] Apuleius describes what he saw in a flour mill:

> I inspected . . . this highly undesirable mill with a certain degree of pleasure. The men there were indescribable—their entire skin was coloured black and blue with the weals left by whippings, and their scarred backs were shaded rather than covered by tunics which were patched and torn. Some of them wore no more than a tiny covering around their loins, but all were dressed in such a way that you could see through their rags. They had letters branded on their foreheads, their hair had been partly shaved off, and they had fetters on their feet. They were sallow and discoloured, and the smoky and steamy atmosphere had affected their eyelids and inflamed their eyes. Their bodies were a dirty white because of the flour dust.[39]

"All slaves are enemies" *(Quot servi, tot hostes),* ran a Roman proverb,[40] and by and large they were treated as such by their masters. K. Hopkins sums up their plight as follows:

> Tens of thousands of slaves were systematically exploited on farms and in mines; even talented and responsible slaves in the households of senators and knights were liable to suffer from the cruel caprice or normal disciplinary practices of a master. Slaves were at the mercy of their masters. They could be overworked, neglected, thrown out when old, beaten, or even killed, and mostly had no realistic chance of protecting themselves. . . . Slaves must often have feared maltreatment, and that fear must have affected even more than those who actually suffered.[41]

BRANDING

Branding the slave's forehead was regarded as a particularly humiliating procedure, inflicted either as a punishment[42] or as a mark of ownership.[43] But such marks, or *stigmata,* were not always penal or proprietorial and not always restricted to slaves. Soldiers are known to have had themselves tattooed or branded with the name of their general, as an expression of their loyalty to him and their devotion to his cause. Paul mentions *stigmata* in Gal 6:17 when he speaks of himself as bearing in his body "**the marks**[44] of Jesus." Doubtless he carried a number of literal scars from wounds suffered in the course of his ministry,[45] and taking his metaphor either from the voluntary practice of soldiers (expressing his commitment to Christ) or, as seems more likely, from the common practice of branding slaves, he calls them his *stigmata,* "the badges" of his belonging to Christ. In particular, he may have thought of them as his *stigmata hiera,* his "sacred badges" of office. The *hierodouloi,* a class of slaves with whom his Galatian readers were no doubt familiar, were attached for life to the Phrygian temples and branded with the name of the god whom they served.[46] Paul may have seen himself as the *hierodoulos* of Jesus, sealed by his scars for the service of Christ in perpetuity. These marks are the ground of his plea "Let no one give me a hard time," that is, "Let no one question my authority, for my body testifies to whom I belong."

One reading of 1 Cor 13:3 has, "give my body to be burned."[47] This has been seen as another reference to the *stigmata hiera,* the sense being, "If I devote myself to Christ's service (by submitting to be branded as his slave), but do not have love, that service is worthless."[48] But this reading, and certainly this interpretation of the reading, is open to question. Allowing that Paul did speak of giving his body "to be burned" and not of "boasting," he may have meant "burned" in the ordinary sense, simply making the point that, no matter how great the sacrifice (burning being the most painful death that he could think of at the time[49]), no credit is deserved if the one who makes the sacrifice is not motivated by love.

CRUCIFIXION

If Paul is referring metaphorically to the branding of slaves in Gal 6:17, his references to crucifixion in the same letter may also be drawn from a practice related to slavery (but by no means restricted to it). "The world has been 'crucified'[50] to me [through the cross of Christ] and I to the world," he declares (Gal 6:14), applying to himself the general statement of 5:24 that all "those who belong to Christ Jesus have crucified the flesh with its passions and desires." Crucifixion was the most common form of execution for slaves. With his arms outstretched and tied to the *patibulum* (originally a fork-shaped yoke but now the term for what would become the crossbeam), which he carried on his neck, the victim was made to walk (under the blows of a whip) to the place of execution, where the *patibulum* was fixed to an upright post already in place. He was nailed through the wrists to the *patibulum,* then his feet were raised, twisted sideways, and nailed to the post. Here he might linger for hours, even days, before death put an end to his sufferings. On the face of it, Paul's references in Galatians to crucifixion were suggested entirely by what had happened to Jesus. But the fact remains that only here does he speak of crucifixion in a figurative sense and he does so in a context in which the metaphor of slavery is much to the fore.

THE PURCHASE OF SLAVES BY NEW MASTERS

A slave might pass into the possession of a new master through inheritance or through the sale of the property to which he or she was attached.[51]

A slave could also be put on the market as a "commodity" (and be stripped, handled, trotted about, and treated with every kind of indignity in the course of being sold). Writing to the Corinthians (whose city had a flourishing slave trade), Paul twice uses the language of such a transaction: "**You were bought**," he says, "at a price" (1 Cor 6:20; 7:23).[52] The image is of believers "changing hands," passing by purchase from the hand of one master (sin) to that of another (God). This transaction was only possible "at a price," and the implication of this phrase is that it was at a considerable price; we know that Paul is speaking of Christ and his crucifixion (cf., e.g., 15:3). This does not appear to be a metaphor of manumission, portraying believers as being "purchased" ("redeemed") for freedom. Rather, a new master is buying them for a new service. Notice the context in which these statements are set: "*You are not your own*," says Paul, "you were bought" (6:19); you are "*Christ's slave*. You were bought" (7:22). In the Christian context, the concept of slavery is always balanced by the concept of freedom. Christians are free in a number of respects, not least from the trammels of sin. But our freedom is with a view to our service. "The glorious liberty of the children of God" releases us, paradoxically, to be slaves: "slaves of God," "slaves of Christ," bound "to serve in the new way of the Spirit," to serve "as slaves of obedience," "slaves of righteousness," and "slaves of each other" for God's sake and for Christ's. Notice, for example, the striking juxtaposition in Gal 5:13 of the ideas of freedom and slavery: "You are called to be free, but . . . through love be slaves to one another."[53]

The thought of service to God as our new master is also expressed in the phrase "under grace"[54] (Rom 6:14–15, cf. 6:1), the counterpart to Paul's description of our former condition as "under sin" (3:9). Slavery may not be the most appropriate figure for the Christian life, as Paul acknowledges in 6:19. But he employs it, he says, because it expresses an important truth that his readers were inclined to forget, namely, that they owe their total commitment to God. Their lives had been forfeit, but God has given them new life—eternal life—and they owe it to God to live that life to its full potential (6:19–23). In Eph 2:8–10 Paul says that we have been saved "to perform the tasks[55]—the good works—that God has set down for us to do." The metaphor of slavery helps to bring home that truth.

SLAVERY AS A RESULT OF WAR

In a little over two hundred years Rome conquered the entire Mediterranean basin. In 260 BCE, Rome was a relatively poor (but politically strong) city-state that controlled central and southern Italy. By the end of the first century BCE, Rome had control of an empire that stretched from the English Channel to the Red Sea, from Algeria to the Black Sea. It covered a land area equal to more than half of the United States and contained a population of fifty to sixty million. Slavery in Roman Italy (including Sicily) was a product of that era of conquest. Defeated soldiers were the largest single source of slaves over those many years.[56] This supply was augmented from other sources such as piracy, brigandage, kidnapping,[57] the exposure and sale of unwanted children,[58] the enslavement of criminals, the self-enslavement of the freeborn,[59] and children born into slavery.[60]

Paul refers to slavery as a result of war and conquest in Rom 7:23. He is speaking of the Christian experience. Each Christian belongs to God, and on that basis each Christian is, in a sense, a microcosm of God's larger domain. Sin invades that domain, waging war[61] within us and **taking captive**[62] not all but some part of what rightly belongs to God. Put differently, Christians still sin. Romans 7 is a very personal chapter coming out of Paul's own experience, but it also reflects a common Christian experience. "I am **sold as a slave** to sin,"[63] he laments (7:14). Paul constantly finds himself succumbing to sin despite his desire to do otherwise and to be subject to God in all things. But what he wants and what he does are two different things. This chapter is about *doing*. Paul is speaking about Christian *practice*, not status. The discussion is not about his loss of salvation but about his dissatisfaction, indeed his disgust, at his failure to live Christianly, that is, to be like Christ in all things.[64]

Paul did not consider the body *(sōma)* to be sinful in itself. But if sin did get the upper hand in his life, he knew that it would be through his "flesh" *(sarx)*—his physical needs and natural desires. He understood very well that the body "becomes a bad master, if it is not made to be a good servant,"[65] and so he declares his policy in 1 Cor 9:27: "I beat my body black and blue[66] [figuratively speaking] and make it my slave."[67] His image is of the victor leading the vanquished into slavery. In Rom 7, he felt that sin had taken him captive; in 1 Cor 9:27, he fights back, so to speak, by making his body his slave, but the metaphor is the same in each case. In 9:27, Paul's fear is that his lack of "training"—his failure to maintain a strict discipline and to curb his natural desires—might lead to "disqualification" from the "event." It is not the loss of his salvation that he fears but of something less than that, howbeit bad enough—some diminution, perhaps, either now or at the coming of Christ, of all that it means to the Christian to be "in Christ."[68]

It used to be thought that slavery, especially on the country estates, diminished as the era of Roman expansion came to an end. But the literary evidence suggests, to the contrary, that the number of slaves hardly diminished at all throughout the period of the early empire and well beyond that.[69] Slavery had created a need for itself. It had created a dependent society, an economy that was built upon slavery.[70] And the need could be met. The supply was still abundant. Wars continued, if on a reduced scale, and other sources made up any shortfall in the number of prisoners of war.[71] In short, the slave trade continued to flourish, and always there was the reproductive capacity of those who were already slaves. In most cases, the child of a slave mother assumed its mother's status at birth[72] (this appears to have been so in most other cultures; cf. the Old Testament references to "house-born slaves"[73]).

Paul makes use of this universally understood principle—of the child assuming its mother's slave status—in Gal 4:21–31 in reference to the two sons of Abraham. He is addressing those who were attracted (thanks to "another gospel" being preached in their churches) to a system that, as Paul saw it, was more Jewish than Christian. Its basis was obedience to the Old Testament law (v. 21), with particular emphasis on circumcision and other Jewish distinctives, which had the effect of keeping the Jews and the Gentiles apart. Paul meets the advocates of this nascent Judaism on their own ground with an argument from the Old Testament (no doubt the Judaizers boasted of their faithfulness to the Scriptures). First, he reminds them that Abraham had two sons, Ishmael, the son of a slave woman, and Isaac, the son of his wife (vv. 22–23). He then draws an allegory from this historical fact by suggesting that the two sons represent the two options that now lay before the Galatian Christians: either the "slavery" of Judaism or the freedom of Christ (vv. 24–27). Finally, Paul applies the allegory to his readers. If they opted for the legalism of the Jewish religion, they would be of the order of Ishmael; if for Christ, they would be of Isaac. "Brothers," he says, "we [Christians] are not children of the slave woman, but of the free" (vv. 28–31). Compare this passage with 1 Cor 7:14, in which the same presupposition, that children inherit their mother's status at birth, lies behind the argument for accepting children into the church as members of the household of God.

A SLAVE'S MONEY

It was sometimes possible for a slave to earn money. Indeed, it was not unusual for a master to fund a slave in some enterprise. The disabilities of a slave's legal status as a mere chattel were circumvented by means of the *peculium,* capital made available to the slave against which the slave could contract obligations. The *peculium* seems originally to have denoted a small herd, or part of a herd, that a master set aside for the slave. With time this pastoral practice became a model for a more widespread arrangement. *Peculium* came to denote any form of capital entrusted by a master to his slave: money, goods, land, sometimes even other slaves *(vicarii)*. It might include what could be described as intellectual or artistic capital; a master might have his slave trained as an actor, a poet, or an accountant, either for his own benefit or to hire out to others. The *peculium* (at least in its more tangible forms) was assigned to the slave for his use, and within certain limits he could dispose of it as he saw fit. If the slave was freed, it might be given to him in whole or in part on his manumission.[74] Meanwhile, there is also evidence that some masters paid their slaves a regular wage.[75] When Paul uses the imagery of slavery, he portrays sin (personified) as paying his slaves a wage. "**The wage**[76] that sin pays," says Paul, "is death" (Rom 6:23)—death in the sense of exclusion from God, who is the source and center of life. Physical death is but a symptom of this spiritual death, a symptom that unfortunately lingers on (until "the redemption of our bodies," Rom 8:23) even when the underlying cause has been cured.

MANUMISSION

One of the most striking aspects of Roman slavery was the frequency with which masters freed their slaves. The sources suggest that many thousands of ex-slaves mingled with the freeborn population of Rome. Sulla alone, for example, is said to have manumitted ten thousand of his slaves.[77] The fire brigade, formed by Augustus in 6 CE, comprised, at the time of its establishment, seven thousand men, all of them ex-slaves.[78] The fact that the same emperor passed a law prohibiting masters from freeing more than one hundred slaves in their wills[79] leads us to suppose that many more than that number had commonly been manumitted en masse by their masters. On the other hand, no effective limit was ever placed on the number of slaves that could be freed in a master's lifetime.[80] Of all the tombstones of ancient Rome (there are some twenty-two thousand recorded), about seven thousand bear inscriptions indicating the status of the deceased. By a three-to-one ratio they commemorate freedmen.[81] This suggests that ex-slaves made up a large part of the population of Rome, and may point to the makeup of the population elsewhere in the empire.

Historians of ancient slavery have often supposed that the emancipation of slaves sprang from humanitarian considerations. Altruism was, no doubt, sometimes a factor.[82] But manumission was more often the product of the owner's self-interest than of any consideration for his slaves.[83] He may have wanted to marry his slave, or may have hoped to get a name in society as a benefactor of the oppressed by releasing his slave.[84] There were financial benefits also. He could demand a manumission price from his slave, which might be paid from his *peculium* or from whatever other resources on which the slave might be able to draw (such as the common fund of an association[85] or even money borrowed from the owner). This would compensate the owner for his loss and contribute to the cost of a younger, abler replacement. Meanwhile, with the "carrot" of freedom dangling before him, the slave was generally more manageable and productive than he would have been otherwise.[86] When the slave was freed, the master lost his slave but acquired a new client from whom much was still to be gained.

Manumissio Justa *and* Manumissio Minus Justa

In Roman law manumission was broadly of two kinds: *manumissio justa* and *manumissio minus justa*. Of *manumissio justa* (complete freedom) there were four forms: adoption (rarely resorted to), testament (*manumissio testamento,* the master bequeathing freedom to his slave in his will), census, and *vindica*. Manumission by census *(manumissio censu)* was an ancient republican form, not quite obsolete in New Testament times, in which the slave's name was entered in the census lists. It is tempting to see this behind Paul's reference to "**those whose names are registered in the book** of life" (Phil 4:3). This metaphor, however, is more likely to have been Jewish than Roman in origin.[87] The most common form of manumission was *vindica,* which simply required the master, in the presence of the praetor, to turn his slave around uttering the words *Liber esto,* "Let him be free," while the praetor, or his lictor (attendant), struck the slave with his rod.

The *manumissio minus justa,* on the other hand, was effected by the master's making some demonstration or statement of his intention to set his slave free, perhaps in a letter to a friend *(manumissio per epistulam),* or by declaring him (or her) to be free in the presence of friends *(manumissio inter amicos),* or by putting the little conical cap of liberty (the *pileus*) on the slave's head.[88] The *manumissio minus justa* gave the slave a freedom of sorts, but he was not fully enfranchised as a Roman citizen and had only the status of a Junian Latin.[89] In certain circumstances (depending on the slave's age and legal relationship to the former master) even slaves granted *manumissio justa* had only this status. A Junian Latin had *commercium,* the right to enter into Roman contracts, but neither *conubium,* the right to a legal marriage with a Roman citizen, nor *testamenti factio,* the right to make a Roman will. Lacking this right, the estate of the freedman reverted to the former master.[90]

Patron-Client Relationship between Former Master and Slave

A freedman or freedwoman with only partial enfranchisement could never be totally independent. But even with *manumissio justa* and full citizenship certain ties of a semiformal nature remained between the ex-slave and the former master. Freed slaves (unless freed by the state because of the master's misconduct) became the clients of their former master for as long as they lived, and he became their *patronus,* literally, "the one who takes the place of a father."[91] This relationship between patron and client imposed obligations on each party. The freedman owed his patron deference *(obsequium),* as a son owed his father, aid *(officium),* and perhaps other duties *(operae),* specified at the time of release.[92] Neglect of these duties might be punished, in an extreme case, by reenslavement.[93] The patron, for his part, was bound to consider the welfare of his clients. Generally, of course, the patron benefited from the arrangement. In addition to the benefits already mentioned, there was often a monetary gain. If, for example, the freedman died intestate and without natural heirs, the patron inherited. The freedman was allowed to bequeath only half of his property; the other half went to the patron. But the duty of care could sometimes tip the balance of benefit to the client. Certainly, without it manumission would have been nothing more than a convenient way of discarding unwanted slaves. Under Greek law the relationship between master and freedman appears to have been far more one-sided, with the master able to impose all sorts of conditions.[94]

The distinctive relationship between the Roman *patronus* and his freedman is the basis (in part) of Paul's comments in 1 Cor 7:20–22:

> Each should remain in the class *[hē klēsis]* in which he was when called [to be a Christian].[95] Were you a slave when called? Never mind. But if you can gain your freedom, take the opportunity to do so *[mallon chrēsai]*.[96] Howbeit, the slave who has been called by the Lord is "his freedman." And, in the same way, 'the free man' who has been called is Christ's slave.[97]

Broadly, what Paul is saying is that, in the long run, the outward circumstances of our lives do not matter. What really matters is our relationship with Christ. But notice the details of these verses. Paul addresses as slaves those of his readers who were free men and women, bringing home the need for them to be subject to Christ. But when he addresses Christian slaves, he does not call them free, since doing so would have suggested that they were cut off from all care and protection. Instead, he calls them the freedmen of Christ, on whose patronage they could always depend and to whom they were bound to give *obsequium* and *officium,* deference and aid. In short, all Christians, however placed in the world, owe to Christ their wholehearted service. And in their vulnerability they are assured of his wholehearted care.

Sacral Manumission

Long ago, Adolf Deissmann drew attention to another form of manumission that is best described as sacral, involving the notional sale of the slave to a god.[98] The most abundant evidence for this is contained in the inscriptions at Delphi. But Deissmann points out that it was by no means peculiar to Delphi, as it was practiced nearby on Mount Parnassus and "probably throughout ancient Greece" and beyond. There is evidence that this kind of manumission was practiced by the Jews of Asia Minor and perhaps made its way into the practice of the church by this route.[99] Deissmann explains the process of sacral manumission:

> Among the various ways in which manumission of a slave could take place by ancient law we find the solemn rite of fictitious purchase of the slave by some divinity. The owner comes with the slave to the temple, sells him there to the god, and receives the purchase money from the temple treasury, the slave having previously paid it in there out of his savings. The slave is now the property of the god; not, however, a slave of the temple, but a protégé of the god. Against all the world, especially his former master, he is a completely free man; at the utmost a few pious obligations to his old master are imposed upon him. The rite takes place before witnesses; a record is taken.[100]

Because these transactions were often perpetuated on stone, we have a wealth of detail concerning them. They were commonly recorded in the following form: Date. X sold, e.g., to the Pythian Apollo, e.g., a male slave named Y *at a price* of so many minae, *for freedom* (or on condition that he shall be free, etc). Then follow any special arrangements and the names of the witnesses. A less commonly used form saw the god as trustee. Deissmann cites an inscription from Delphi as an example:

> Date. Apollo the Pythian *bought* from Sosibius of Amphissa, *for freedom,* a female slave, whose name is Nicaea, by race a Roman, *with a price* of three minae of silver and a half-mina. Former seller [that is, to Sosibius, thus establishing the latter's ownership] according to the law: Eumnastus of Amphissa. The *price* he has received. The purchase [price], however, Nicaea has committed to Apollo, *for freedom*.[101]

Clearly Paul was familiar with the terms in which these transactions were recorded, as well as with the concept itself. He repeatedly describes the Corinthian Christians as bought "**at a price**."[102] Even if he was thinking more of the exchange of slaves between masters than of their manumission (although the latter cannot be ruled out), the Delphic inscriptions demonstrate that he was using the language of slavery. Other echoes of the inscriptions in Paul's letters are more specific to manumission, especially in his letter to the Galatians: "**For freedom** Christ has set us free," and "you have been called **to freedom**"[103] (Gal 5:1, 13). Further, in numerous inscriptions the slave's newly won freedom is characterized in terms of his "doing what he wants." Paul warns the Galatians, who were being tempted into a "slavery" to another gospel, that if they yielded, they would no longer be **able to do what they wanted**[104] (5:17), for they would be thrown back on their own resources, which would inevitably fail them. They could never please God (Paul supposes that this is what they wanted to do) because the obedience to the law that their "new gospel" demanded was beyond our human capacity. (Whatever the Judaizers said, Paul argued that it had to be a *total* obedience, that anything less than this was sin and rendered the sinner liable to the curse.) Many of the Delphic inscriptions expressly forbid reenslaving the newly enfranchised man or woman. Such a warning adds color to Paul's complaint that the Judaizers had attempted "to spy on our freedom, which we have in Christ Jesus, in order **to make us slaves**"[105] (2:4). The same prohibition against reenslavement may lie behind his plea in 5:1: "Stand firm [in your freedom] and do not **submit again to the yoke of slavery**."[106] Compare 1 Cor 7:23: "You were bought at a price; do not become slaves of others."[107]

REDEMPTION

"Redemption" is the term applied to the process whereby something or someone is rescued from forfeiture by the payment of a price. Most of Paul's readers undoubtedly associated redemption with the manumission of slaves, and on the evidence above, it seems likely that this image was uppermost in

Paul's own mind. He certainly shows a predilection for metaphors drawn from the practice of slavery and a familiarity with the vocabulary of the trade; this suggests that he spoke of redemption primarily in these terms.

But for Paul and his Jewish readers (or for any reader who was familiar with the Old Testament), what was already a telling metaphor from the "secular" world must have been greatly enhanced by the added color of the biblical concept of redemption, especially insofar as this concept concerned a person's life or freedom.[108] For example, in the OT, if an ox that was known to be dangerous killed a free man or woman, its owner was liable to the death penalty but could redeem his life by paying a ransom.[109] Also, first-born males, human or animal, were deemed sacred to God, but they could be "bought back" by the payment of the appropriate price.[110] And so on. Redemption could be applied to a number of contingencies,[111] all of them sanctioned by the fact that God had "redeemed" the Hebrews from slavery in Egypt.[112] Common to most (if not all) of these provisions for redemption was the payment of a ransom. Whether, then, it derived from the Old Testament or from the common practice of the manumission of slaves or even, as some have suggested, from the practice of the repatriation of prisoners of war[113] (or perhaps from an amalgam of all of these images), the idea of redemption carried with it, for Paul, the connotation of cost. There was no redemption without a ransom. It was precisely this notion of cost that made redemption such an appealing metaphor of the work of Christ, and it may have been suggested to Paul in the first place by his awareness that Christ himself had taught in this vein.[114]

When Paul speaks of "**redemption**[115] through his blood" in Eph 1:7, he means that the blood of Christ was the cost at which the freedom of Christians was bought. In Rom 3:24–25, he declares that believers "are justified by [God's] grace . . . through the redemption which is in Christ Jesus, whom God intended . . . as a propitiation by his blood." This statement employs three metaphors: one legal (justification), one sacrificial (propitiation), and one (it is supposed) from the manumission of slaves. The latter speaks of redemption (at no cost to the redeemed; it is a "gift") as being achieved at the cost of Christ's "blood."[116] Christ's death (for that is the meaning of "blood") was accepted in the place of us "slaves," that we might be free.[117]

The price of redemption is not always mentioned. In 1 Cor 1:30 Paul simply says that Christ is our wisdom (all that we need to know as far as God is concerned), for Christ is our "righteousness from God, our holiness and our redemption." In Col 1:14 he asserts that in Christ "we have redemption, the forgiveness of sins." These verses say nothing of what it cost Christ to redeem us. Nor is there any mention of the cost in Rom 8:23 and Eph 1:14; 4:30. In each passage the thought is of the future. The notion of cost is overshadowed by the prospect of what is to come: "the redemption of our bodies" and the consequent "glorious freedom of the children of God" from the change and decay of our present condition (Rom 8:21, 23; cf. Phil 3:20–21; Col 3:4; 1 John 3:2).[118] Still, Paul never entirely loses sight of the cost in his use of the word "redemption." Sometimes, indeed, it is the cost rather than redemption that he mentions, although the thought is still of the latter. Thus in Gal 3:13 (cf. 4:5), Christ is said to have "**bought**[119] us from the curse of the law [i.e., from the curse of God on those who do not keep the law, the curse that the law pronounces][120] by becoming for us a curse." The cost of our freedom was his bearing the penalty that was rightfully ours.

In one passage, Paul appears to echo Jesus' own words when he speaks of "the man Christ Jesus, who gave himself as **a ransom** for all"[121] (1 Tim 2:6). In another, he expresses much the same thought but uses the verb instead of the noun: "Christ," he says, "gave himself for us **to redeem**[122] us from all wickedness"[123] (Titus 2:14; cf. Gal 3:13). And in all of these references to Christ having "redeemed" us or "bought" us or become a "ransom" for us, Paul's thought is surely wide enough to include the biblical figure of the redeemer, the one who acts on behalf of the needy. There was no legal obligation for a redeemer to act. But there was a familial obligation, for a redeemer was generally the next of kin to the person concerned.[124] Nor was it only a matter of his acting after the event to redeem the lost person or property: he would take a proactive role in pleading his kinsman's cause as soon as the matter was raised. Thus Job took comfort from the thought that his redeemer was alive and would surely come to his aid (Job 19:25–27). This thought of the kinsman-redeemer may lie behind the statement of Hebrews that Christ was "not ashamed to call us his brothers" (Heb 2:11; cf. Rom 8:16–17, 29) and of John that he now "pleads our cause" at the tribunal of God (1 John 2:1–2; cf. Rom 8:26–27). At all events, it anticipates Paul's legal metaphors, to be discussed in the chapter that follows.

NOTES

1. See, e.g., K. Hopkins, *Conquerors and Slaves* (Cambridge: Cambridge University Press, 1978), 9. A study of ancient slavery is impeded by these factors: (1) most of the authors of the primary sources were slave owners themselves, so that it is only their view that is reflected, (2) most of the evidence relates to urban slavery, and (3) the evidence is, in any case, fragmentary. The secondary literature on ancient slavery is immense. J. Vogt and H. Bellen (*Bibliographie zur antiken Sklaverei: Im Auftrag der Kommission für Geschichte des Altertums der Akademie der Wissenschaften und der Literatur* [rev. E. Herrmann and N. Brockmeyer; Bochum, Germany: N. Brockmeyer, 1983]) list 5,162 books and articles. Further data are added by J. C. Miller, *Slavery: A Worldwide Bibliography, 1900–1982* (White Plains, N.Y.: Kraus International, 1985), esp. 249–306 (ancient slavery) and 387–88 (ancient slave trade); and J. C. Miller, *Slavery and Slaving in World History: A Bibliography, 1990–1991* (Milford, N.Y.: Kraus International, 1993). The classic study, however, remains M. I. Finley, ed., *Slavery in Classical Antiquity: Views and Controversy* (Cambridge: Heffer, 1974), esp. 1–66. See also A. H. M. Jones, "Slavery in the Ancient World," *EHR* 9 (1956): 185–99; Hopkins, *Conquerors and Slaves,* 1–132; T. E. J. Wiedemann, *Slavery* (Oxford: Clarendon, 1987); M. Grant, *A Social History of Greece and Rome* (New York: Scribner's, 1992), 85–122; Y. Thebert, "The Slave,"

in *The Romans* (ed. A. Giardina; Chicago: University of Chicago Press, 1993), 138–74; J. Andreau, "The Freedman," in ibid., 175–98.

2. For a bibliography relating to slavery in the eastern provinces, see Finley, *Ancient Economy*, 222 n. 17, 245 n. 11.

3. See, e.g., 1 Cor 7:21ff.; 12:13; Gal 3:28; Eph 6:5, 8; Col 3:11, 22; 4:1; 1 Tim 6:1; Titus 2:9; Phlm 16. English versions often use the word "servant," but in all of these reference the Greek word is δοῦλος "slave" (see ch. 5, n. 21). Paul's references to "Chloe's people" and to the household (οἶκος; see ch. 1, n. 89) of Stephanus (1 Cor 1:11, 16; 16:15; cf. other "households" in Acts 16:15, 34; 18:8) suggests the presence of slaves in the homes of some of his converts.

4. On the ubiquity of slaves in the Roman world, see, e.g., D. B. Martin, *Slavery as Salvation* (New Haven: Yale University Press, 1990), 1; and F. Dupont, *Daily Life in Ancient Rome* (Oxford: Blackwell, 1992), 56–57.

5. M. Maxey (*Occupations of the Lower Classes* [Chicago: University of Chicago Press, 1938]) found listed in inscriptions twenty-three different household occupations alone that a slave might be called on to perform. For further references and discussion, see M. N. Tod, "Epigraphical Notes on Freedmen's Professions," *Epigraphica* 12 (1950): 3–26; C. A. Forbes, "The Education and Training of Slaves in Antiquity," *TAPA* 86 (1955): 321–60; S. M. Treggiari, "Urban Labour in Rome: *Mercennarii* and *Tabernarii*," in *Non-slave Labour in the Graeco-Roman World* (ed. P. Garnsey; Cambridge: Cambridge University Press, 1980), 48–64; H. W. Pleket, "Urban Elites and Business in the Greek Part of the Roman Empire," in *Trade in the Ancient Economy* (ed. P. Garnsey, K. Hopkins, and C. R. Whittaker; Berkeley: University of California Press, 1983), 131–41; L. Casson, *Ancient Trade and Society* (Detroit: Wayne State University Press, 1984), 39, 46, 59 n. 21, 61 n. 31, 108–10; A. Kirschenbaum, *Sons, Slaves, and Freedmen in Roman Commerce* (Washington, D.C.: Catholic University of America Press, 1987), 157–58; Dupont, *Daily Life*, 56–57.

6. *IG* 1.374.

7. *Dig.* 14.3.19.1; Hippolytus, *Haer.* 9.12.1ff.

8. Cornelius Nepos, *Att.* 13.4.

9. *AE* 1929.215; *IGR* 1.283.

10. Gellius, *Noct. Att.* 2.18; Macrobius, *Sat.* 1.11.41–44.

11. *MAMA* 7.135.

12. Pliny, *Ep.* 10.19.

13. Columella, *Rust.* 1.5.

14. Cicero, *Quint. fratr.* 2.2.

15. Varro, *Rust.* 1.2.23; *Dig.* 14.3.8.

16. Petronius, *Sat.* 75.11; Horace, *Sat.* 1.2.116–119; Dio Chrysostom, *Disc.* 15.5.

17. See S. Treggiari, "Jobs in the Household of Livia," *PBSR* 43 (1975): 48–77; M. Flory, "Family in *Familia:* Kinship and Community in Slavery," *AJAH* 3 (1978): 78–95. The slave was sometimes "allowed," writes U. E. Paoli, "to choose from among the female slaves a *conserva* as his companion, and to live with her in a form of servile marriage called *contubernium;* although it had no legal status or effect and the children born of such a union were the slaves of the *paterfamilias,* this form had the master's approval, and in the Empire it even found legal protection when masters were forbidden to sell the partners of the *contubernium* separately" (*Rome: Its People, Life, and Customs* [London: Gerald Duckworth, 1990], 125). But that was later. In the early empire families could be and were broken up at the whim of the master. Juvenal (*Sat.* 11.152–153) notices the homesick slave boy, and the papyri give the impression that familial disruption was common. See K. R. Bradley,

Slaves and Masters in the Roman Empire: A Study in Social Control (New York: Oxford University Press, 1987), 47–80; Finley, *Ancient Slavery*, 93–122.

18. See, e.g., Athenaeus, *Deipn.* 13.593–596, in which the diners talk for pages about famous rich slaves of classical history. Most appear to have been prostitutes, such as Pythionike, who, according to Theopompus, was a famous Athenian whore. See also the *Gk. Anth.* 6.332 for the wealthy prostitute Polyarchis.

19. See, on the slave as *res*, W. W. Buckland, *The Roman Law of Slavery: The Condition of the Slave in Private Law from Augustus to Justinian* (New York: AMS Press, 1969), 10–72. Finley (*Ancient Slavery*, 74–75) notes that "the uniqueness of slavery . . . lay in the fact that the labourer himself was a commodity, not merely his labour or labour-power. His loss of control, furthermore, extended to the infinity of time, to his children and his children's children." (This was true in theory, at least. But see p. 119 on the frequency of manumission.) The Delphic manumission inscriptions (see pp. 121–22) clarify the four basic elements of slavery: lack of legal rights, liability to seizure, inability to choose one's activities, and lack of freedom to determine one's residence (see W. L. Westermann,"Slavery and the Elements of Freedom in Ancient Greece," in *Slavery in Classical Antiquity: Views and Controversy* [ed. M. I. Finley], 17–32).

20. The punishments inflicted on slaves could be merciless: transfer to the *villa rustica* (the country estate), sentence to hard labor in the *ergastulum* (a kind of private prison) or at the mill wheel—both of which normally involved being kept in chains—were at the least severe end of the spectrum of penalties. The more severe punishments progressed from whipping, aggravated in various ways, to some of the most unbearable tortures: branding with hot metal rods *(laminae)*, racking by the *eculeus* (a wooden instrument that stretched the body and broke the joints), mutilation, and *crurifragium* (the violent breaking of legs). Runaways, liars, and thieves were branded *(stigma, nota)* on the forehead with a hot iron with the letters *FUG, KAL, FUR* (see pp. 114–15). For the most serious offences, the slave was condemned to death, normally by crucifixion (see p. 115) but sometimes by exposure to wild animals (see p. 264) or by burning alive in a cloak impregnated with pitch *(tunica molesta)*. See Paoli, *Rome*, 125–26.

21. Δοῦλος: Strictly an adjective, "in bondage to, subject to" (e.g., Rom 6:19), but most commonly as a substantive, "a slave," either feminine (ἡ δούλη) or masculine (ὁ δοῦλος). In Paul this word is used of literal slaves in 1 Cor 7:21–23; 12:13; Gal 3:28; 4:1; Eph 6:5, 8; 1 Tim 6:1; Titus 2:9; Phlm 16 (2x) and as a metaphor (1) of our human or sinful condition (e.g., Rom 6:16–17, 20; 1 Cor 7:23[?]; Gal 4:7; Phil 2:7; Col 3:11, 22; 4:1 and (2) of our new life in Christ (e.g., Rom 1:1; 6:16 [2x]; 1 Cor 7:22; 2 Cor 4:5; Gal 1:10; Eph 6:6; Phil 1:1; Col 4:12; 2 Tim 2:24; Titus 1:1). Cf. δουλεύω (from δοῦλος): "To be a slave, be subject to, serve," of mundane service in Rom 9:12; Eph 6:7; 1 Tim 6:2 and metaphorically, (1) of serving sin (e.g., Rom 6:6; Gal 4:8–9, 25; Titus 3:3 and (2) of Christian service to God and to others (e.g., Rom 7:6, 25; 12:11; 14:18; 16:18; 1 Cor 9:19; Gal 5:13; Phil 2:22; Col 3:24; 1 Thess 1:9). Martin argues that it is not so much the slave's subjugation to his (or her) master that lies behind Paul's use of this metaphor as the fact that slavery proved sometimes to be (paradoxically) a first step toward a better social position. The slave was often educated and put into a position of trust in which he enjoyed the reflected status of his master. As far as his humbler readers were concerned, Martin asserts, Paul's use of this metaphor presented a "positive soteriological image" (*Slavery as Salvation*, 137). As for Paul's upper-class readers, the image may have taught them something about their duty of service. There is no denying that slavery was sometimes the means of social and economic advancement, but Martin's argument that it was this, rather than the idea of subjection, that Paul had in mind is not convincing.

22. Ὑφ᾽ ἁμαρτίαν: This construction of ὑπό with the accusative is used "of power, rule, sovereignty, command, etc." (see BAGD). The same phrase, or its like, with the same suggestion of a slave's subjection to his or her master, is found in Rom 7:14; Gal 3:22; cf. 1 Tim 6:1, where Paul speaks of literal slaves being "under the yoke" (ὑπὸ ζυγόν). Cf. also the related ideas of being "under the elemental spirits of the world" (ὑπὸ τὰ στοιχεῖα τοῦ κόσμου), Gal 4:3, and "under the curse [of God because we are subject to sin]" (ὑπὸ κατάραν), Gal 3:10. Paul speaks also of our being "under the law" (ὑπὸ νόμον); again the image is of a bondage from which Christ has set us free (Rom 6:14–15; 1 Cor 9:20; Gal 3:23; 4:4–5, 21; 5:18). In Gal 3:25; 4:2, he likens this condition to that of the child, subject to his pedagogue and guardian and thus no better off than a slave (discussed on pp. 61–63). Cf. the use of the same grammatical construction in the phrase "under grace" (ὑπὸ χάριν), discussed on p. 116.

23. Βασιλεύω (from βασιλεύς "a king"): "To be king, to reign, rule." This word appears in Paul in Rom 5:14, 17 (2x), 21 (2x); 6:12; 1 Cor 4:8 (2x); 15:25; 1 Tim 6:15. The use of this verb might suggest the imagery of a king reigning over his subjects rather than an owner exercising his authority over his slaves. Either way Paul's point would still stand, since both a king and a slave master ruled absolutely. But βασιλεύω can apply to the rule of others besides kings. Since Paul speaks of our being "slaves to sin" in Rom 6:6, 17, 20 and "slaves to impurity and wickedness" in 6:19 and uses the analogy of slaves in 6:16, it is best to maintain this metaphor throughout. See J. D. G. Dunn, *Romans* (Dallas: Word, 1988), 1:148.

24. In addition to βασιλεύω, Paul employs the verb κυριεύω (from κύριος "lord, master") "to be lord or master of, to rule (over)" (Rom 6:9, 14; see also 7:1; 14:9; 2 Cor 1:24; 1 Tim 6:15) and associated terms such as ὑπακούω "to obey" (Rom 6:12, 16–17; see also 10:16; Eph 6:1, 5; Phil 2:12; Col 3:20, 22; 2 Thess 1:8; 3:14), ὑπακοή "obedience" (Rom 6:16 [2x]; see also 1:5; 5:19; 15:18; 16:19, 26; 2 Cor 7:15; 10:5, 6; Phlm 21), δουλεύω (Rom 6:6), and δοῦλος (Rom 6:16 [2x], 17, 20). On δουλεύω and δοῦλος, see ch. 5, n. 21.

25. There are indications, however, that not all slaves were as obedient as their masters wished. Incidental remarks in Roman and Greek literature stereotype slaves as lazy, deceitful, dishonest, and in need of constant coercion. Laziness may have been the only weapon of defense for slaves who were otherwise quite powerless. See Hopkins, *Conquerors and Slaves,* 121. Whether or not most slaves were lazy, this issue does not seem to be part of Paul's metaphor.

26. This not to say that the "subjects" of sin are incapable of doing good but, rather, that sin is the controlling factor of their lives. "Man experiences (consciously or unconsciously) a power which works in him to bind him wholly to his mortality and corruptibility, to render impotent any knowledge of God or concern to do God's will, to provoke his merely animal appetites in forgetfulness that he is a creature of God" (Dunn, *Romans,* 1:149).

27. See Rom 5:21; 6:16, 21, 23; 7:9, 11.

28. The sources indicate that runaway slaves were a major problem for owners, who might take precautionary measures such as chaining slaves or fixing tags around their necks (see Xenophon, *Mem.* 2.1.16). A slave collar in bronze, found around the neck of a skeleton in southern Rome, bore this inscription: "If captured, return me to Apronianus, minister in the imperial palace, at the Golden Napkin on the Aventine, for I am a fugitive slave." The collar is now in the Dutuit Collection, Petit Palais, Paris, together with a bronze plaque of the third or fourth century CE with a similar inscription: "I am Asellus, slave of Prejectus attached to the ministry of markets, and I have escaped the walls of Rome. Capture me, for I am a fugitive slave, and return me to Barbers' Street, near the temple of Flora." In the event of a slave's escape, the owner could post "wanted" notices or employ slave catchers to help find

him. For "wanted" notices, see P.Oxy. 1423 and 1643. For the employment of *fugitivarii*, see Finley, *Ancient Slavery*, 111–12, and Westermann, "Slavery," 77.

29. Thus Cicero writes of a Roman quaestor (official concerned with financial administration) of his time who was prevented by a high-ranking city official from removing his slave from the temple of Artemis in Ephesus, in which he had sought sanctuary (*Verr. Act.* 2.1.33.85). On the authority of Achilles Tatius, *Leuc. Clit.* 7.13.3, who states that any slave with a complaint against her master could find refuge in the temple, it appears that the Artemisium offered such asylum as late as the third century CE. T. E. J. Wiedemann (*Greek and Roman Slavery: A Source Book* [London: Croom Helm, 1988], 195) explains how temple asylum functioned in the ancient world: "In theory, running away was a crime which deserved no mercy; but in practice there had to be scope for compromise. One way out was for the slave to appeal to a god. While a master could not give way to his slave, there was no disgrace in giving way to a god and it presented no threat to property rights or to slavery as an institution." One did not cease being a slave for having taken refuge in a temple; it was simply a way of replacing the human master with a divine one. On runaway slaves, see also E. R. Goodenough, "Paul and Onesimus," *HTR* 22 (1929): 181–83; and J. D. M. Derrett, "The Function of the Epistle to Philemon," *ZNW* 79 (1988): 74. Goodenough points out that in Athenian law places of sanctuary included the hearths of private houses—and this provision seems to have extended throughout much of the eastern empire. On this basis, he suggests that it was to Paul's "hearth" in Rome that Onesimus had fled (Phlm 8ff.). See further B. M. Rapske, "The Prisoner Paul in the Eyes of Onesimus," *NTS* 37 (1991): 187–203. However, it is not certain that Onesimus was a runaway slave. He may have been with Paul quite legitimately, having been sent by Philemon. See ch. 7, n. 27.

30. See W. L. Westermann, *The Slave System of Greek and Roman Antiquity* (Philadelphia: American Philosophical Society, 1955), 108. In later imperial law the slave was allowed to demand sale out of the possession of a cruel master. The Roman law in question is *De servo corrupto*, cited by Apuleius (*Metam.* 6.4).

31. Thus, it became standard practice in buying a slave to demand a guarantee that he had not fled to the statue (*Dig.* 21.1.19.1). Such a slave was obviously considered to be a bad investment.

32. For a detailed account of the various legislative measures that were gradually introduced, see A. Watson, *Roman Slave Law* (Baltimore: Johns Hopkins University Press, 1987), 120ff.

33. See Justinian, *Inst.* 1.8.1.

34. Even in the republican period there was some slight mitigation of the master's power to be cruel to his slaves. "During the Republic there was no legal limitation to the power of the *dominus*. . . . It must not, however, be supposed that there was no effective protection. The number of slaves was relatively small, till late in that era, and the relation with the master far closer than it afterwards was. Moreover, the power of the Censor was available to check cruelty to slaves, as much as other misconduct" (Buckland, *Roman Law of Slavery*, 36). Others, too, write of censorial intervention, but it is open to question how effective it was. There is little evidence that it ever took place. But see Dionysius of Halicarnassus, *Ant. rom.* 20.13, and the discussion in Watson, *Roman Slave Law*, 115ff.

35. Suetonius, *Aug.* 67. On another occasion Augustus is said to have punished an ex-slave procurator in Egypt, who ate a prize fighting quail, by having him nailed to a ship's mast (Plutarch, *Mor.* 207B [*Apoph. lac.—Caesar Augustus* 4]).

36. Galen, *Diagn.* 4.

37. Seneca, *Ep.* 47.

38. Diodorus Siculus, *Hist.* 5.38. See also 3.12–14. Ancient descriptions of working conditions for slaves in quicksilver mines in central Asia Minor or gold mines in Egypt make it clear that slave miners there did not survive long. See Strabo,

Geog. 12.3.40: "In addition to the harshness of the work, it is said that the air in the mines is deadly . . . so that workmen very soon die." Cf. Cyprian, *Ep.* 76, for an account of conditions in mines for condemned Christians. For numbers in the Spanish silver mines in the second century BCE, see Strabo, *Geog.* 3.2.10, and for an overview, see O. Davies, *Roman Mines in Europe* (Oxford: Clarendon, 1935).

39. Apuleius, *Metam.* 9.12. See also F. G. B. Millar, "The World of the Golden Ass," *JRS* 71 (1981): 65–75.

40. Festus (epitomizer of the *De significatu verborum* of Verrius Flaccus) 314L, Seneca (*Ep.* 47.5), and Macrobius (*Sat.* 1.11.13) all call it a proverb. The memories of the slave revolts did not fade quickly. In Rome in particular there is evidence of a certain paranoia concerning their possible repetition. In a senate debate in 61 CE, Cassius expresses a basic insecurity in respect to slaves (Tacitus, *Ann.* 14.42–45).

41. Hopkins, *Conquerors and Slaves,* 119–20. On the psychologically devastating insecurity of the slave, see Finley, *Ancient Slavery,* 74, and on the role of fear in the social control of slaves, see Bradley, *Slaves and Masters,* 113–37. Hopkins remarks (p. 121) that "the viciousness of Roman slavery, the exploitation, cruelty and mutual hostility are worth stressing because modern accounts often focus instead on those elements in Roman philosophy, literature and law which point to the humanitarian treatment of slaves, and to the willing loyalty of some slaves to their masters" (for the latter, see, e.g., Tacitus, *Hist.* 1.3; Seneca, *Ep.* 47.4; and the well-known story of Epicharis in Tacitus, *Ann.* 15.57). Since the institution of slavery involved millions of people, any generalization is precarious, to say the least. Clearly slavery was not always a terrible condition to be in. Epictetus can imagine a man who had recently been freed looking back wistfully on the days when "someone else kept me in clothes and shoes and supplied me with food and nursed me when I was sick" (*Diatr.* 4.1.37). But generally, it appears that disdain tending to brutal cruelty, on the one side, and indifference leading to dislike and often murderous hatred, on the other, were more the rule in master-slave relations than otherwise. Seneca (*Ep.* 4.6), whose remarks on slavery are particularly humane (see above in this note), and the equally mild Pliny (*Ep.* 3.14.5) regarded being murdered by slaves as a risk to which everyone was exposed.

42. See, e.g., Pliny, *Nat.* 18.4; Petronius, *Sat.* 103; Macrobius, *Sat.* 1.19; Gaius, *Inst.* 1.13; and ch. 5, n. 20. Cf. Herodotus's account of Xerxes sending tattooers to brand the Hellespont as a mark of its disgrace when a storm destroyed the pontoon bridge he had constructed across it. He also ordered the sea to be scourged with three hundred lashes (*Hist.* 7.35).

43. Xenophon, *Vect.* 1.21. Of particular interest, in light of the discussion that follows, is Artemidorus Daldianus (*Onirocriticus* 1.8), who mentions the marking of slaves as a peculiarity of the Galatians.

44. Στίγμα (from στίζω "to prick, stick, sting"): "A tattoo, mark, or brand." Found only here in the NT.

45. See, e.g., Acts 14:19; 16:22; 2 Cor 6:4–6; 11:23–25; perhaps also Gal 4:13–14. It has sometimes been suggested, largely on the basis of Gal 6:17, that early Christians generally and Paul in particular bore tattoo marks to signify that they were Christians—perhaps the Greek letter X for Χριστός. But the phrase "in my body" (ἐν τῷ σώματι) makes it more likely that he is referring to scars.

46. See Herodotus (*Hist.* 2.113); Lucian (*Syr. d.* 59) refers to the same practice in Syrian Hierapolis, which W. Ramsay takes as proof of a general custom (see *Galatians,* 473). This practice of branding temple slaves lies behind the reference in Rev 13:16–17 to the Beast putting his mark on the right hand or the forehead of those who serve him.

47. Καίω: "To kindle, light," passive "to be lighted, to burn." Broadly speaking, there are two readings in the Greek from which to choose in this verse. Since

they are similar—(1) ἵνα καυθήσωμαι or καυθήσομαι (future passive subjunctive [Byzantine] or indicative of καίω) "that I may be burned," and (2) ἵνα καυχήσωμαι (aorist middle subjunctive of καυχάομαι) "that I may glory"—the error, one way or the other, is easily understandable. For the related word, καυστηριάζω "to mark by branding, brand," understood as a medical term, "to cauterize," see ch. 4, n. 35.

48. So J. Jeremias, *The Central Message of the New Testament* (London: SCM, 1965), 37.

49. Lucian (*Peregr.* 21–25) describes the self-burning of the Christian charlatan Peregrinus, and there was a well-known case of an Indian who had ended his life in this way (Plutarch, *Alex.* 69; Strabo, *Geog.* 15.1.73; Dio Cassius, *Rom. Hist.* 54.9).

50. Σταυρόω (from σταυρός, an upright "stake, a cross"): (1) "to fence with pales," (2) "to crucify." Elsewhere in Paul of Christ's crucifixion (1 Cor 1:23; 2:2, 8; 2 Cor 13:4; Gal 3:1) and, by implication, of Christ's death in 1 Cor 1:13, where he asks, "Was Paul crucified for you?" Because the word originally had to do with fencing, it is possible that Paul is making a play on its two senses in Gal 6:14: "I will only boast in the *cross* of our Lord Jesus Christ, through which the world has been *fenced* off from me." In Rom 6:6 and Gal 2:20 he uses the compound συσταυρόω (or συνσταυρόω) "to crucify with" of his own or others' identification with Christ in his death. On the punishment of slaves generally, see ch. 5, n. 20 above. On the punishment of enemies by crucifixion, see ch. 10, n. 26.

51. Water carriers, porters, and sweepers of third-century apartment buildings were inherited or sold with the building. See p. 10.

52. Ἀγοράζω (from ἀγορά "an assembly, a place of assembly, a forum or marketplace"): (1) "to frequent the ἀγορά," (2) "to buy in the market," as in 1 Cor 7:30. In 1 Cor 6:20 and 7:23, Paul has qualified the verb with the noun τιμή "a valuing," hence (1) "a price" paid or received and (2) "esteem, honor." This word is commonly used in the context of manumission, and on this basis, it has been argued that ἀγοράζω should be included in the vocabulary of redemption (e.g., A. Deissmann, *Light from the Ancient East* [London: Hodder & Stoughton, 1908], 324 n. 2; cf. 2 Pet 2:1; Rev 5:9; 14:3–4). Nevertheless, I hold that the emphasis here is not on redemption for freedom but on purchase for slavery, following, e.g., L. Morris (*The Apostolic Preaching of the Cross* [London: Tyndale, 1965], 51) and I. H. Marshall ("The Development of the Concept of Redemption," in *Reconciliation and Hope: New Testament Essays on Atonement and Eschatology Presented to L. L. Morris on His 60th Birthday* [ed. R. Bank; Exeter, U.K.: Paternoster, 1974], 157). On the other hand, the compound of this verb, ἐξαγοράζω, does appear to belong with the words for redemption in Gal 3:13; 4:5 (see ch. 5, n. 119). It is used metaphorically in a broader commercial sense in Eph 5:16; Col 4:5 (see the discussion on p. 170).

53. For these and other references to δοῦλος "a slave" and δουλεύω "to be or to serve as a slave," see ch. 5, n. 21. With reference to "slavery" to others, there might appear to be a contradiction between 2 Cor 4:5, where Paul speaks of the apostles as the "slaves" of those to whom they preach, and 1 Cor 7:23, where he warns, "Do not become [or 'stop becoming,' as the present tense implies] slaves of men." The contexts, however, are quite different. In the latter he is probably referring to literal slavery, entered into voluntarily for economic reasons (see further ch. 5, n. 59), or, if it is a figurative reference, to their bondage to the fads and fashions of this present evil world (cf. 2 Cor 11:20; Gal 5:1; Col 2:20–23). In 2 Cor 4:5, on the other hand, he is speaking of the Christian duty of service to others. Cf. 1 Cor 9:19, where Paul speaks of making himself a slave to others in this same sense but with particular reference to ministering the gospel to them.

54. Ὑπὸ χάριν: Cf. ch. 5, n. 22.

55. The phrase is ἐπὶ ἔργοις ἀγαθοῖς. The preposition ἐπί with the dative commonly has the sense "on, on the basis of" but here appears to have the less common sense of purpose. For this use, cf. Wis 2:23; Gal 5:13; 1 Thess 4:7; 2 Tim 2:14. Certainly the context leaves us in no doubt that salvation is "with a view to good works," *not* "on the basis of good works."

56. According to Dio Chrysostom, slaves were originally obtained by capture in war and by land or sea brigandage (*Disc.* 15.25). Ever since the time of Alexander and the wars of his successors with each other and their neighbors, it is probable that the supply of captives sold as slaves had been increasing. Under the Romans the stream feeding into the slave market became a flood. After the campaign at Pydna, for example, and the overthrow of the Macedonian kingdom, Aemilius Paullus sold into slavery 150,000 free inhabitants of communities in Epirus, which had sided with Perseus in the war (Livy, *Hist.* 45.34). After the war with the Cimbri and Teutones, 90,000 of the latter and 60,000 of the former are said to have been sold (Livy, *Ep.* 68). On the single occasion of the capture of Aduatuci, Caesar sold 53,000 prisoners on the spot (Caesar, *Bell. gall.* 2.33). In his campaigns in Gaul between 58 and 51 BCE alone he shipped back to peninsular Italy nearly one million enslaved Gallic prisoners of war (Plutarch, *Caes.* 15.3; Appian, *Hist. rom.* 4.1.2). See further W. V. Harris, *War and Imperialism in Republican Rome, 327–70 BC* (Oxford: Clarendon, 1979), 74–75; J. A. Harrill, *The Manumission of Slaves in Early Christianity* (Tübingen: Mohr, 1995), 30–42.

57. Cicero, in his speech in support of the appointment of Pompey to suppress the pirates of Cilicia, mentions that well-born children had been carried off from Misenum under the very eyes of a Roman praetor (Cicero, *Leg. man.* 12.23). Plutarch (*Pomp.* 24) adds that Romans of good standing would join in the pirate business in order to make a profit. In Italy itself, where there was no police protection until Augustus took the matter in hand, kidnapping was by no means unknown. The kidnappers, called *grassatores,* who were often slaves escaped from the prisons of the great estates, haunted the public roads for unsuspecting travelers (Suetonius, *Aug.* 32; see ch. 9, n. 66). Slave merchants seem to have been constantly carrying on their trade in regions in which no war was going on and desirable slaves could be procured. The kingdoms of Asia Minor, for example, were ransacked by them (see Varro, *Rust.* 2.10; Diodorus Siculus, *Hist.* 26.3.1).

58. The literary sources reveal a clear expectation that the exposed child would not die immediately but would be picked up and enslaved (see ch. 3, n. 94). Often the unwanted child would be left at a place known for foundlings, such as a temple of Asclepius or an area in which slave dealers were known to linger. Some scholars have suggested that, especially in Greco-Roman Egypt, the public dunghill (κοπρία) often served as one such place, as attested by the frequency of slave names beginning with the prefix κοπρ- (Κοπρεύς, Κοπριαίρετος). See E. Eyben, "Family Planning in Graeco-Roman Antiquity," *AncSoc* 11–12 (1980–1981): 25; J. E. Boswell, "*Expositio* and *oblatio:* The Abandonment of Children and the Ancient and Medieval Family," *AHR* 89 (1984): 10–33; H. W. Harris, "Towards a Study of the Roman Slave Trade," in *Roman Seaborne Commerce* (ed. J. H. D'Arma and E. C. Kopff; Rome: American Academy, 1980), 117–40.

59. This was a common source of slavery at various periods of Roman history, sometimes as an act of desperation—the failed farmer, or the like, was at least guaranteed his keep as a slave—sometimes, paradoxically, as a means of advancement. Slaves were sometimes employed in businesses and government bureaucracies where it was possible to acquire both wealth and power. They could then expect, by manumission, to return with their capital to the "free market." Paul may be referring to this practice in 1 Cor 7:23, suggesting (according to D. B. Martin, *Slavery as Salvation,* 66) that "because they are now slaves of Christ, they should not willingly become slaves of any human being. To do so would be to pass from high status in a

highly placed household to a position in a lesser household." Martin's interpretation is somewhat strained. B. W. Winter has the more likely suggestion that Paul opposed the practice on religious grounds: "Those who voluntarily sold themselves into slavery would have been expected to swear by the *genius* of their master. It was a veiled form of worship" (*Seek the Welfare of the City: Christians as Benefactors and Citizens* [Grand Rapids: Eerdmans, 1994], 159; cf. J. Rives, "The *iuno feminae* in Roman Society," *EMC* 36 [1992]: 39–42). If indeed Paul was opposing literal self-enslavement, given the economic and social benefits that sometimes accrued from this status, he may have found himself fighting a losing battle on the issue. See Petronius, *Sat.* 57, and J. A. Crook, *Law and Life in Rome* (London: Thames & Hudson, 1967), 60. See also ch. 5, n. 53.

60. Sometimes children were born into slavery as a matter of course, sometimes as a result of deliberate breeding (see Varro, *Rust.* 1.17; 2.10.3; cf. Horace, *Epod.* 2.65). See further the discussion below of Paul's metaphor in Gal 4:21–31 (p. 118).

61. Ἀντιστρατεύομαι: "To make war against." A rare word, found only here in the NT (cf. ch. 10, n. 30). Since much of the material discussed in this section belongs also with Paul's military metaphors, it will be treated again later in that connection. Slavery was one of the inevitable outcomes of defeat in war, and thus the subjects overlap.

62. For a further discussion of this theme of captivity, see pp. 217–18. Αἰχμαλωτίζω (from αἰχμάλωτος "a captive," itself from αἰχμή "a spear" and ἁλίσκομαι "to be taken"): "To take or lead captive," a "late and vivid word for capture and slavery" (A. T. Robertson, *Word Pictures in the New Testament* [New York: Richard R. Smith, 1930–1933; repr. Nashville, Tenn.: Broadman & Holman, 1973], 4:370). Its strict meaning is "to take prisoner in war," but BAGD adds that "the figure may fade" so that the word comes to signify "carry away, i.e., mislead, deceive." It is found in Rom 7:23; 2 Cor 10:5; 2 Tim 3:6. In Eph 4:8 the similar verb αἰχμαλωτεύω is used, with the same meaning as αἰχμαλωτίζω. Also in that passage occurs the noun αἰχμαλωσία "captivity." Cf. the adjective αἰχμάλωτος "captive" (not in Paul) and the compound συναιχμάλωτος "a fellow prisoner" (see ch. 10, n. 66). See also p. 218 on "passing under the yoke," i.e., "passing under an arch of spears."

63. Ἐγὼ . . . εἰμι πεπραμένος ὑπὸ τὴν ἁμαρτίαν: For ὑπὸ τὴν ἁμαρτίαν, lit., "under sin," see ch. 5, n. 22. Πεπραμένος is the perfect passive participle of πιπράσκω, an old verb, "to sell." Paul portrays the deal as over and done with (the sense of the perfect tense). Sin owns its slave.

64. It must be said that this is only one of a number of interpretations of Rom 7:7–25. C. Kruse (*Paul, the Law, and Justification* [Leicester, U.K.: Inter-Varsity Press, 1996], 208–10) asks,

> Is he speaking autobiographically, and, if so, is he speaking of his own experience before he became a Christian (either representing how he felt then about his moral failure, or how he thought later as a Christian about those failures), or is he speaking of his experience as a Christian, or both? If he is not speaking autobiographically, then is he speaking rhetorically in order to portray the experience of humankind in general, or of religious Jews in particular, or of both? Is Paul speaking of Adam's encounter with the commandment of God in the Garden, or is he speaking redemptively-historically of Israel's encounter with the law at Sinai?

See Kruse's documentation of each of these positions. His own view is that Rom 7:7–25 is best understood as both redemptive-historical and autobiographical, the aorist tenses of vv. 7–13 marking Israel's encounter with the law at Sinai and the present tenses and more intensely personal tone of vv. 13–25 marking Israel's and his own subsequent struggle with the law. It is certainly hard to rule out any autobiographical element. The progression of the argument of the letter in which he has dealt with sin (1:18–3:20), salvation (3:21–5:20), and now appears to be dealing with aspects of Christian life (6:1–8:39, perhaps as part of his response to various objections, 6:1–11:36), suggests that these verses are autobiographical specifically of his Christian experience, as reflecting the common Christian experience. The body is not yet redeemed (cf. 8:18–25), and until it is, there will always be a tension between the propensity to sin and the desire not to do so.

65. A. Robertson and A. Plummer, *First Epistle of St Paul to the Corinthians* (Edinburgh: T&T Clark, 1914), 197.

66. Ὑπωπιάζω: See ch. 12, n. 107.

67. Δουλαγωγέω (from δοῦλος "a slave" and ἄγω "to lead"): A late verb, "to make a slave, bring into bondage," unique to this passage in biblical Greek. It is found, however, in Diodorus Siculus and Epictetus; the substantive δουλαγωγία "enslavement" occurs in the papyri. See also ch. 12, n. 108.

68. But see, e.g., C. K. Barrett (*A Commentary on the First Epistle to the Corinthians* [London: Adam & Charles Black, 1971], 218), who takes the contrary view that, in 1 Cor 9:27, it is his very salvation that Paul fears is at risk. See p. 269 for a further discussion of this passage as a metaphor from the Greek games.

69. See P. Garnsey and R. Saller, *The Roman Empire* (London: Gerald Duckworth, 1987), 72–73.

70. See Hopkins (*Conquerors and Slaves,* 112), who discusses the importance of slavery not simply as a means of producing wealth but as a means of displaying it. In both the Greek and the Roman worlds, especially the latter, in which there were so many slaves, to have no slave was the benchmark of the very poor. A house, a field, a slave—such were the possessions of even the poorest peasant as imagined by Virgil in *Moretum.* See also Lysias, *Or.* 24.6; Xenophon, *Mem.* 2.3.3; Catullus, *Poems* 23–24; and M. I. Finley, "Was Greek Civilization Based on Slave Labour?" in *Slavery in Classical Antiquity: Views and Controversy* (ed. M. I. Finley), 53–72, esp. 58. Slave owning was an important status indicator and an important factor, therefore, in raising the social standing of those who were not slaves, apart from any economic value that the institution of slavery may have possessed. But for all that, archaeological and other evidence suggests that a large proportion of the population (perhaps as high as 75 percent) had neither the means to buy slaves nor, if it had, the room to accommodate them. See D. C. Verner (*The Household of God: The Social World of the Pastoral Epistles* [Chico, Calif.: Scholars Press, 1983], 56–63) on lower-class households; and R. Duncan-Jones (*The Economy of the Roman Empire: Quantitative Studies* [Cambridge: Cambridge University Press, 1982), 348–50] on the price of slaves in Rome and Italy.

71. There is no evidence that the capture of slaves was ever a primary objective in wars fought by the Romans. Nevertheless, the hope of booty, including saleable captives, was often, it can be assumed, an important motive in their going to war.

72. See Buckland, *Roman Law of Slavery,* 397; W. W. Buckland, *A Textbook of Roman Law from Augustus to Justinian* (Cambridge: Cambridge University Press, 1963), 68–69; J. A. C. Thomas, *Textbook of Roman Law* (Amsterdam: North Holland, 1973), 390, and, on the right of the master to dispose of slave children, see ch. 5, n. 17.

73. See I. Mendelsohn, *Slavery in the Ancient Near East: A Comparative Study of Slavery in Babylonia, Assyria, Syria, and Palestine from the Middle of the Third Millennium to the End of the First Millennium* (Oxford: Oxford University Press, 1949), 57–58. Houseborn slaves are mentioned in Scripture from patriarchal times onward, e.g., Gen 15:3; 17:12–13, 27; Eccl 2:7; Jer 2:14.

74. See Plautus, *Stic.* 751; Pliny, *Ep.* 8.16. Sometimes the very wording of laws relating to the *peculium* shows that the Romans seemed to think of the *peculium* as in some sense the slave's, although from a strictly legal point of view the master

owned all of the slave's assets; e.g., *Dig.* 15.1.17. Ulpian poses the following question: "If my ordinary slave *[ordinarius]* has *vicarii*, may I deduct from the *peculium* of the *ordinarius* whatever the *vicarii* owe me?" That such a question should be asked suggests that there was some uncertainty on whose precisely the *peculium* was. See Watson, *Roman Slave Law*, 90–101, esp. 99; also Buckland, *Roman Law of Slavery*, 187–206; Buckland, *Textbook*, 65, 533–35; Crook, *Law and Life*, 188–89; Kirschenbaum, *Sons, Slaves, and Freedmen*, 31–38.

75. Sometimes they were paid on a daily basis, sometimes by the month. Seneca (*Ep.* 80.7) indicates that some of his urban slaves received five *modii* of wheat and 20 sesterces cash per month. See further S. S. Bartchy, *Mallon Chresai: First-Century Slavery and the Interpretation of 1 Corinthians 7:21* (Missoula: Scholars Press, 1973), 42, 74.

76. Ὀψώνιον (from ὄψον, ὀψάριον "cooked meat, fish" and ὠνέομαι "to buy"): (1) "provisions, provision money, soldiers' pay" (e.g., 1 Cor 9:7; cf. Luke 3:14), (2) generally, "wages, hire" (e.g., 2 Cor 11:8). The use of this word for a soldier's pay makes it possible that Paul has reverted here to the military metaphor of Rom 6:13 ("weapons of wickedness"), although the more immediate context of vv. 15–22 does have slavery as its motif. Note the contrast in v. 23 between "wages" and "gift." Wages are something earned—they are ours by right. A gift, on the other hand, by its very nature is not something earned and in this case is certainly not deserved. "Man has rights only in relation to sin, and these rights become his judgment. When he throws himself on God without claim, salvation comes to him" (H. W. Heidland, "ὀψώνιον," *TDNT* 5:591–92, here 592). For the discussion of both "wages" and "gift" as possible military metaphors, see p. 224.

77. Appian, *Hist. rom.* 1.100, 104.

78. Dio Cassius, *Rom. Hist.* 55.26.

79. Gaius, *Inst.* 1.42–43.

80. See S. M. Treggiari, *Roman Freedmen during the Late Republic* (Oxford: Clarendon, 1969), 31–36; and A. N. Sherwin-White, *The Roman Citizenship* (Oxford: Clarendon, 1973), 322–24.

81. On Roman tombstones recording the death of slaves in the period of the republic, see Treggiari, *Roman Freedmen*, 32. For later evidence, see L. R. Taylor, "Freedmen and Freeborn in the Epitaphs of Imperial Rome," *AJP* 82 (1961): 113–32. Only about one-third of twenty-two thousand tombstone inscriptions from Rome, however, provide clear indication of the dead person's status, whether slave, ex-slave, free citizen, or alien. On the basis of names typically given to slaves (e.g., Eutyches; cf. Acts 20:9) and from the marriage of men and women with the same name taken from their common master, Taylor deduces that, among those whose deaths were recorded and whose status is uncertain, the proportion of slaves and ex-slaves was as high as among the minority whose status was certain. But some of these data may relate to the children of ex-slaves who were themselves born free. T. Frank ("Race Mixture in the Roman Empire," *AHR* 21 [1916]: 689–708) concludes that most people living in Rome were of slave extraction.

82. A special sentiment that was neither friendship nor love but a sort of grateful compassion was often evident in the slave owner, as borne out by the numerous funerary inscriptions expressing a master or a mistress's regret over the loss of a servant or a child of the house. A corresponding loyalty and even love might sometimes be found in a slave for his master, as in Philocrates, the slave of Gaius Gracchus, and in the slaves of Mark Antony and Urbinus Panopio, who bore torture and suffered death in the interests of their masters. See Valerius Maximus, *Memor.* 6.7.4; 6.8.1; 6.8.6; cf. Rom 5:7.

83. See the discussions in Treggiari, *Roman Freedmen*, 11–22; and A. M. Duff, *Freedmen in the Early Roman Empire* (Oxford: Clarendon, 1928), 15–21.

84. See Dionysius of Halicarnassus, *Ant. rom.* 4.24.6.

85. The freedom of association was strictly controlled. Throughout the period of the empire, no association *(collegium)* could legally exist without specific governmental permission, and no organization was authorized that might conceivably serve as a focus of political agitation. In the main, only religious and benevolent (usually burial) societies were tolerated. *Dig.* 47.22.1–3 allows that "slaves . . . may be admitted into societies of the lower classes with the consent of their masters." See Harrill, *Manumission of Slaves*, 129–57, on the role played by the funds of these societies, and 159–92, on the early Christian practice, in particular, of manumitting slaves from the common fund.

86. See Philo, *Spec.* 2.67; cf. Pseudo-Aristotle, *Oec.* 12.5.6; Aristotle, *Pol.* 1330a.32–33. Hopkins (*Conquerors and Slaves*, 131) writes, "For the masters, manumission was economically rational, partly because it tempted slaves to increase their productivity and lowered the cost to the master of supervising his slaves at work, and partly because the slave's purchase of freedom recapitalised his value and enabled the master to replace an older slave with a younger one." See further ibid., 117–18, 128–32, for illustrations of how "humanity was complemented by self-interest"; and Bradley, *Slaves and Masters*, 108–12.

87. Cf. Rev 3:5; 13:8; 17:8; 20:12, 15; 21:27; 22:19. Registration is first mentioned in the Bible in Dan 12:1 and Ezek 13:9 (but cf. Exod 32:32; Ps 69:28). G. Schrenk ("βιβλίος, βιβλίον," *TDNT* 1:615–20, here 620) suggests that the notion of the Book of Life may have stemmed from the establishment of genealogies, family lists, and national registers in Israel; e.g., Neh 7:5–6, 64; 12:22–23. It signifies those who are truly God's people. On the other hand, it may have been a commercial metaphor. See, e.g., the discussion of God's keeping his "books" in Col 2:14 and Rom 4:1–25, pp. 182–84. On the Roman census lists, see A. N. Sherwin-White, *The Roman Citizenship* (Oxford: Clarendon, 1973), 314–16; on manumission by census, see Buckland, *Roman Law of Slavery*, 439–41; and Buckland, *Textbook*, 72–73.

88. See Buckland, *Roman Law of Slavery*, 437–597; Bradley, *Slaves and Masters*, 81–112.

89. By a *lex junia* of either 17 BCE or 19 CE, a slave of a Roman citizen manumitted informally or in violation of certain rules of Augustus became not a Roman citizen but a *Latinus* (this seems not to have had any reference to nationality—it was not that he was made a member of one of the Latin tribes). There is no way of knowing how numerous the *Latini juniani* were, nor is it entirely clear why the status was established in the first place; presumably it was to limit the number of ex–slave citizens. See Gaius, *Inst.* 1.17; Duff, *Freedmen*, 75ff., 210ff.; P. R. C. Weaver, "Where Have All the Junian Latins Gone? Nomenclature and Status in the Early Empire," *Chiron* 20 (1990): 275–305.

90. See B. Nicholas, *An Introduction to Roman Law* (Oxford: Clarendon, 1987), 64–65, 74–75.

91. For a discussion of patronage as "an asymmetrical exchange relationship," see J. K. Chow, *Patronage and Power: A Study of Social Networks in Corinth* (Sheffield, U.K.: Sheffield Academic Press, 1992), 30–33. See also P. Marshall, *Enmity in Corinth: Social Conventions in Paul's Relations with the Corinthians* (Tübingen: Mohr, 1987), 157–64; and B. Levick, *The Government of the Roman Empire: A Sourcebook* (Totowa, N.J.: Barnes & Noble, 1985), 137–51. A. Weingrod ("Patrons, Patronage, and Political Parties," *CSSH* 10 [1968]: 377–400; repr. in *Friends, Followers, and Factions* [ed. F. W. Schmidt, L. Guasti, C. H. Landé, and J. C. Scott; Berkeley: University of California Press, 1977], 325) suggests that patron-client ties tend "to arise within a state structure in which authority is dispersed and state

activities limited in scope, and in which considerable separation exists between the levels of village, city and state." On this basis, it appears that the Roman Empire was an ideal breeding ground for patron-client ties. Indeed, G. E. M. de Ste. Croix goes so far as to say that patronage was the secret to the integration of the empire (*The Class Struggle in the Ancient World from the Archaic Age to the Arab Conquest* [London: Gerald Duckworth, 1987], 364). R. P. Saller, although not prepared to go quite as far as de Ste. Croix, believes that the institution of patronage does certainly explain how Roman rulers were able to administer the empire with a minimal number of officials (*Personal Patronage under the Early Empire* [Cambridge: Cambridge University Press, 1982], 205–6).

92. These obligations, which had had a long history among the social customs of Roman society, received the force of law under Augustus. *Obsequium* proscribed certain kinds of behavior against one's patron, such as bringing a lawsuit (unless the claimant could obtain special permission from the praetor) or criminal charges (except for treason). *Officium* obligated the freedman to undertake a certain number of days in service. *Dig.* 38.1.16.1 explains that "such days of work are given to the patron as ought to be estimated in accordance with age, dignity, health, needs, and other such factors, with regard to both parties." But other unscheduled claims might be made on the client as occasion demanded. The patron, e.g., might ask his freedman to take care of his children or to give him financial assistance (Watson, *Roman Slave Law*, 40). Other clients were expected to attend the morning "greeting" *(salutatio)* at the patron's house, at which they might be favored by a gift of food, money, or some other benefit. It is not certain whether the freedman-client was also expected to attend. On the other hand, he might be invited to dinner together with those other dependents. Dinnertime brawls between the two classes of client were not unknown. See Juvenal, *Sat.* 3.129–130, on paying morning respects to the patron; and cf. 1 Cor 7:35, where Paul would have the Corinthians live "in a seemly way, giving *constant and single-minded attention* to their Lord." For a general discussion of the obligations of the client, see Duff, *Freedmen*, 36–49. Those whom Paul castigates as "idle" in 1 and 2 Thessalonians and sought to wean from their state of dependency may well have been clients of a wealthy member of their church, an Aristarchus, say, or a Jason (see Acts 17:7; 19:29; 20:4; cf. also Acts 17:4). See Winter, *Seek the Welfare of the City*, 45–60.

93. For the reenslavement of a freedman for ingratitude toward his patron, see Buckland, *Roman Law of Slavery*, 422ff.

94. A large percentage of the Delphic contracts (see pp. 121–22), e.g., restrict the freedom of the freedman in his employment or movement at least for a specific period of time to guarantee some benefit to the owner or his descendants. He might be bound, e.g., to the house in which he had served as a slave. According to 1 Cor 7:24 (in a context that uses the metaphor of the freedman) each person, whether slave or freed, should "remain where he is with God." See Hopkins, *Conquerors and Slaves*, 133–71.

95. Martin (*Slavery as Salvation*, 65–66) rightly observes that "Paul's language . . . clearly reflects the Graeco-Roman preoccupation with status and the place of persons . . . within society." For a more detailed discussion of class in Roman society, see Winter, *Seek the Welfare of the City*, 159–64.

96. For a full discussion of this difficult clause, see Harrill, *Manumission of Slaves*, 68–128. It has been read to mean either that those who are slaves should "keep on in slavery" or that they should take the opportunity to secure their freedom. The fact that χρῆσαι (from χράομαι "to use, make use of") is an aorist infinitive has determined our acceptance of the latter meaning. The present would have supported the alternative view.

97. The key words here are ἐλεύθερος (from ἔρχομαι "to go"), strictly an adjective, "free," but sometimes used as a noun (in Paul in Rom 6:20; 7:3; 1 Cor

7:21–22, 39; 9:1, 19; 12:13; Gal 3:28; 4:22–23, 26, 30–31; Eph 6:8; Col 3:11) and ἀπελεύθερος (from ἔρχομαι and ἀπό "to go [free] from [bondage]"), an old word for a manumitted slave, "a freedman," found only here in the NT. The analogy of the freedman does not quite hold up, since in life it was to the former master that the freedman owed his duty, whereas here it is to Christ, who is not the former owner but someone new in the equation (see, e.g., Marshall, "Concept of Redemption," 158 n. 7, who makes this objection). But this is to quibble. It is enough for Paul that Christ has freed us from sin by paying the ransom (see p. 124, and he is therefore not unlike the patron to whom the freedman owes his new status. For the substantive, ἐλευθερία, see ch. 5, n. 103. On the application of Roman law in Corinth and the Roman character of the colony, see D. W. J. Gill, "Corinth: A Roman Colony of Achaea," *BZ* 37 (1993): 259–64, esp. 264: "Classicists are in no doubt as to the Roman nature of the colony." For the institution of patronage in Corinth, see Chow, *Patronage and Power*, 38–82. Chow raises the possibility that patronage functioned within the church in Corinth no less than within Corinthian society, thus giving a particular edge to Paul's metaphor (pp. 83–112).

98. Deissmann, *Light*, 318ff.

99. See ibid., 321–22, for details of the geographical range of sacral manumission.

100. Ibid., 322. The analogy between sacral manumission and Paul's idea of release from "slavery" has been deemed to fail on the grounds that, in sacral manumission, it was the slave who raised the price of freedom, whereas in Paul's metaphor it is not the "slave" who pays but Christ. Further, it has been pointed out that the slave's relationship with the god was merely a legal fiction, which can hardly be said of us (e.g., J. D. M. Derrett, *Law in the New Testament* [London: Darton, Longman & Todd, 1970], 399 n. 4). But the analogy does not have to be complete to be valuable. There was enough in sacral manumission to provide Paul with an apt illustration, and he simply took what served his purpose. Indeed, Marshall ("Concept of Redemption," 158) speculates that the early Christian preachers would have delighted in making the very differences between the analogy and the real thing a talking point, contrasting the price paid by the slave in the secular world with the free gift of God in Christ.

101. Deissmann, *Light*, 323. Italics his.

102. 1 Cor 6:20; 7:23. See ch. 5, n. 52.

103. Ἐλευθερία reads as "freedom" in Paul in Rom 8:21; 1 Cor 10:29; 2 Cor 3:17; Gal 2:4; 5:1, 13 (2x). In the two passages under discussion, we have the phrases τῇ ἐλευθερίᾳ and ἐπ' ἐλευθερίᾳ respectively. The latter is particularly common at Delphi and elsewhere. In illustration of the extent to which it had passed into common speech, Deissmann (*Light*, 324 n. 5) cites a letter, written in the time of Augustus by a freedman to his patron, which uses precisely this phrase: "As a slave *for* [the sake of] *freedom* desires to please [his lord], so have I also, desiring thy friendship, kept myself blameless" (italics mine). That the phrase was a common one does not, of course, make it any less a conscious metaphor from manumission. For ἐλεύθερος and ἀπελεύθερος, see ch. 5, n. 97.

104. The context is one in which Paul is contrasting our natural inclinations with those produced with the help of the Spirit. But the Spirit is only present to help where Christ is Lord (see, e.g., Gal 3:1–2), and these people, by turning to "another gospel," were in danger of disclaiming that lordship. Behind this discussion, then, lay the ultimate issue: would the Galatians opt for some form of Judaism, which (despite its biblical roots) issued from the "natural person," or would they opt for Christ? Notice in 5:18 the phrase "under the law," which is suggestive of slavery (see ch. 5, n. 22).

105. Καταδουλόω: "To enslave." In the NT, only here and in 2 Cor 11:20. In the latter, notice the verbs in the five conditional clauses. Paul speaks of those who "enslave" the Corinthians, "exploit" them (κατεσθίω; see also Gal 5:15), "take" them (λαμβάνω; take them captive? take advantage of them?), "exalt" themselves over them (ἐπαίρω; see also 2 Cor 10:5; 1 Tim 2:8), and, as the final insult, "slap" them in the face (δέρω; see also 1 Cor 9:26)—a graphic description of the lot of the slave!

106. See ch. 10, n. 75.

107. See ch. 5, nn. 52 and 53.

108. For the biblical background of the concept of redemption, see, e.g., D. Daube, *Studies in Biblical Law* (Cambridge: Cambridge University Press, 1947), 1–73; Morris, *Apostolic Preaching,* 9–59; D. Daube, *The New Testament and Rabbinical Judaism* (London: Athlone, 1956), 389–460; Marshall, "Concept of Redemption," 151–69.

109. See Exod 21:28–30. See further ch. 5, n. 111.

110. There was a special provision for the redemption of the firstborn, which allowed parents to buy back their son for five shekels, paid to the priest. See Num 18:15–16; cf. Exod 13:2, 12–13; 34:20. This payment is regularly called a λύτρον (LXX Num 3:12, 46, 48–49, 51; 18:15). See further ch. 5, nn. 121 and 122.

111. These were as follows: (1) Redemption of a person from bondage to a resident alien (Lev 25:47–55; cf. Exod 21:1; Deut 15:12–18, where bondage to a fellow Hebrew is envisaged; in theory, it should terminate after six years). For an instance of redemption from threatened bondage, see 2 Kgs 4:1–7. See further R. Westbrook, "Jubilee Laws," *ILR* 6 (1971): 206–26; and B. Cohen, *Jewish and Roman Law: A Comparative Study* (New York: Jewish Theological Seminary of America, 1966), 1:159–78. (2) Redemption of a property (Lev 25:23–34; cf. Ruth 4:1–6; Jer 32:6–15; R. Westbrook, "Redemption of Land," 367–75). (3) Redemption of something devoted to God (Lev 27:15–33; cf. Judg 11:29–40). (4) Levirate marriage as a form of redemption whereby a family was saved from extinction (Gen 38:1–30; Deut 25:6; Ruth 3:10–4:12; cf. Mark 12:18–27; G. Horowitz, *The Spirit of Jewish Law* [New York: Central Book, 1963], 283–85; M. Burrows, "The Marriage of Boaz and Ruth," *JBL* 59 [1940]: 445–54). (5) There was also a sense in which the "avenger of blood," in killing the killer, "redeemed" the one who was slain (Num 35:9–34; Deut 19:1–13; M. Cohn, "Blood-Avenger," in *The Principles of Jewish Law* [ed. M. Cohn; Jerusalem: Ktav, 1975], 530–31; M. Cohn, "City of Refuge," in ibid., 531–32; F. Lyall, *Slaves, Citizens, Sons: Legal Metaphors in the Epistles* [Grand Rapids: Zondervan, 1984], 161–63). In some circumstances there was no provision for redemption, such as deliberate murder (Num 35:31–32; cf. Prov 6:35). See further ch. 5, nn. 121 and 122.

112. See, e.g., Exod 6:6; 15:13; Num 3:13; Deut 7:8; 9:26; 15:15; 24:18; Ps 25:22; 26:11; 31:5; 55:18; 69:18; 77:15; 103:4; 106:10; 130:8; Isa 43:1; 44:22; 63:9; Jer 15:21; 50:34.

113. See ch. 10, n. 71.

114. See D. Wenham, *Paul: Follower of Jesus or Founder of Christianity?* (Grand Rapids: Eerdmans, 1995), 149–50.

115. Ἀπολύτρωσις (ἀπό and λύτρωσις, from λυτρόω [see ch. 5, n. 122], itself from λύτρον [see ch. 5, n. 121]): This is the normal NT word for redemption. It occurs ten times, always in connection with the work of Christ, sometimes explicitly with his death. Seven of the occurrences are in the letters of Paul (Rom 3:24; 8:23; 1 Cor 1:30; Eph 1:7, 14; 4:30; Col 1:14). In Greek literature generally, the word (but not the idea) is both late and rare, being found only about ten times outside the NT and only once in the LXX (Dan 4:30).

116. Strictly, the phrase ἐν τῷ αὐτοῦ αἵματι "by his blood" qualifies the statement that God intended Christ as a propitiation, emphasizing the idea of sacrifice already associated with the word ἱλαστήριον. But it is legitimate to extend this and,

indeed, the other qualifying phrase, "through faith" (διὰ τῆς πίστεως), to each of the concepts expressed here—justification, redemption, propitiation—viewing them as constituting one complex statement of our salvation. This passage serves, moreover, to illustrate an important association of ideas between redemption and sacrifice found elsewhere in the NT, an association that "is strongly rooted in the Old Testament and Judaism"; see further Marshall, "Concept of Redemption," 159–60. Finally, the metaphor has served its purpose when it has drawn attention to the redeemer and the cost of redemption. It does not point to a third party to whom the payment is made. We are not obliged, e.g., to name Satan as the payee, as the early church fathers often did.

117. Notice, e.g., the connection between redemption and freedom from bondage (δουλεία) in Rom 8:21–23. For the contrast between the Christian's former and present states and Christ's role in making the difference, see, e.g., Rom 6:23; 2 Cor 5:21.

118. Eph 1:7 and 14 provide a particularly good example of the accomplished and yet future character of our redemption: "In him we *have* redemption" (v. 7), and the Spirit is the "downpayment on our inheritance *looking ahead to* [εἰς] the redemption" that will one day be ours (v. 14). Other concepts also, such as adoption (which also figures here in Eph 1:5) and justification, have this future as well as accomplished dimension. For adoption, see p. 65 and ch. 3, n. 143; for justification, see pp. 146–47 and ch. 6, n. 41.

119. Ἐξαγοράζω (cf. ἀγοράζω; for both verbs, see ch. 5, n. 52): "To buy," middle "to buy up for oneself." Although not technically the verb "to redeem," it can hardly be doubted that in Gal 3:13; 4:5 Paul has the metaphor of redemption in mind. Notice in 4:5 that those bought were "under the law," i.e., "slaves to the law" (see ch. 5, n. 22), and were earlier described as "no different" from slaves (4:1). "The accent lies," writes I. H. Marshall, "on the deliverance of sinners and their entry into freedom, and the metaphor used is that of the ransoming of slaves" ("The Concept of Redemption," 157; cf. Morris, *The Apostolic Preaching*, 52–56). Diodorus Siculus (*Hist.* 36.2.2) used ἐξαγοράζω of the redemption of slaves. For its use elsewhere in Paul as a more general commercial metaphor, see the discussion of Eph 5:16 and Col 4:5, p. 170.

120. The genitive in ἡ κατάρα τοῦ νόμου is not to be construed as an epexegetical genitive, "the curse which is the law itself," as does, e.g., H. D. Betz (*Galatians: A Commentary on Paul's Letter to the Churches in Galatia* [Philadelphia: Fortress, 1979], 149), since elsewhere Paul extols the goodness of the law (cf. Rom 7:7–12). Moreover, κατάρα here recalls κατάρα in v. 10, which states that there is a curse on those who do not keep the law. It seems better to construe the τοῦ νόμου of v. 13 as a subjective genitive, "the curse which the law pronounces," especially as κατάρα frequently occurs with such a genitive in the LXX (cf. Judg 9:57; Prov 3:33; Sir 3:9). The whole section of vv. 10–14 should be studied. We were under a curse (ὑπὸ κατάραν, v. 10) in the sight of God (παρὰ τῷ θεῷ, v. 11; παρὰ "by the side of," i.e., from God's point of view), for the simple reason that no one except Jesus has ever kept *all* of God's law. But Christ paid to get us out from (ἐξηγόρασεν ἐκ) under the curse, having become a curse for us (ὑπὲρ ἡμῶν). The primary sense of ὑπέρ is "over," but its use to express substitution, "for, on behalf of," is common in the papyri and in secular Greek generally where benefit is involved, as also in the NT. In short, the curse of God hung like a Damocles sword above us, but Christ interposed himself, as it were, between us and the sword, and the sword fell on him. His death was the price of our freedom. For the Hebraic background of the idea of substitution expressed in such a passage as this, see J. B. Lightfoot, *Saint Paul's Epistle to the Galatians* (London: Macmillan, 1884), 139.

121. Ἀντίλυτρον ὑπὲρ πάντων: Ἀντίλυτρον "a ransom" occurs only here in the NT and, as far as we know, nowhere else before this time in Greek literature. The

word may have been coined by Paul himself. See the preceding note for ὑπέρ "on behalf of." Ἀντί is not unlike it in meaning but has more the idea of exchange, "instead of." Ἀντίλυτρον ὑπέρ combines the two ideas. "The addition of the prep[osition] ἀντί, 'instead of,' is significant in view of the prep[osition] ὑπέρ, 'in behalf of,' used after it. Christ is conceived of as an 'exchange price' " (D. Guthrie, *The Pastoral Epistles: An Introduction and Commentary* [Grand Rapids: Eerdmans, 1990], 82; cf. Morris, *Apostolic Preaching,* 48, who sees little difference between ἀντίλυτρον and λύτρον, except that the preposition in the former "emphasises the thought of substitution; it is a 'substitute-ransom' that is signified." The notion of substitution implies the exchange of something of equal value, in this case the "new man" for the "old." All that Adam lost for the human race when he sinned, the right to life with God both for himself and for his offspring, Jesus' ransom bought back. "The last Adam" (1 Cor 15:45), as the original Adam had been at first, was without sin and so was a "corresponding ransom"—an appropriate "exchange price"—for Adam's race. For the less likely sense of ἀντίλυτρον as "antidote," see ch. 4, n. 38; and on the prepositions, see further M. J. Harris, "Prepositions and Theology in the Greek New Testament," *NIDNTT* 3:1171–1215). Cf. λύτρον, *NIDNTT* 3:1215. Λύτρον appears only in the reports of Jesus' teaching in Matt 20:28; Mark 10:45 in the NT (in the phrase λύτρον ἀντὶ πολλῶν "a ransom for many") but is the common word in classical Greek and LXX (about 18x) for "a ransom," often in the plural, λύτρα. Nearly always the word is used in its literal sense: "the price paid to effect someone's deliverance." The tenth-century CE lexicographer Suidas defined λύτρον as simply μισθός "pay" or "price" and explained it further as "those things that are offered for freedom in order to ransom a man from barbarian slavery." Occasionally it has a semimetaphorical sense, as in Aeschylus, *Cho.* 48, "What λύτρον can there be for blood that has fallen upon the ground?" For Paul's familiarity with the Jesus tradition in respect to redemption, see Wenham, *Paul,* 149–50.

122. Λυτρόω (from λύτρον "a ransom"; see the preceding note): (1) In classical Greek it means (a) in the active, "to hold to ransom," (b) in the passive, "to be ransomed," and (c) in the middle, "to ransom for oneself," i.e., "to redeem" or "to rescue by the payment of a price." The context is always one of "captivity," and the word always refers to the rescue of someone or something from the (usually hostile) possession of another. (2) In the papyri it commonly means "to redeem a pledge" that is in the possession of another. (3) In the LXX, where the word occurs sixty-five times, it commonly means "to redeem" something or someone in the possession of another (see ch. 5, n. 111), hence the figurative sense of God rescuing Israel in times of need (see ch. 5, n. 112), so common that the present participle ὁ λυτρούμενος "the redeeming one" became almost a name for God. This shaped Israel's expectation of the future (e.g., Luke 1:68–69; 2:25, 38; 24:21), and as this future unfolded, Jesus was found to have assumed the mantle of the redeemer. (4) In the NT the verb occurs (a) in the middle, "to release by the payment of a price, to redeem" (Luke 24:21; Titus 2:14, in which ὑπέρ is used again: ἔδωκεν ἑαυτὸν ὑπὲρ ἡμῶν; see ch. 5, n. 120), and (b) in the passive, "to be ransomed" (1 Pet 1:18).

123. Ἀνομία (from ἄνομος "without law, lawless, wicked"): "Lawlessness," disobedience to God's law (cf. Rom 4:7; 6:19 [2x]; 2 Cor 6:14; 2 Thess 2:7).

124. See, e.g., Lev 25:25, 47–49; Ruth 4:4–6; Isa 59:12–20; 63:1, 16 (such expressions as "vindicate" and "acknowledge," which are found in these verses, are technical terms expressing the duties of the kinsman-redeemer); Jer 32:6–12. See also Deut 25:9 for the obloquy that falls on the kinsman who will not act for his relative. For the portrayal of the ideal redeemer, see, e.g., Ps 35:1; 72:12–14; 119:153–154; Prov 23:10–11; Lam 3:55–66. For a recent discussion of the role of the redeemer, see R. L. Hubbard, "The *Go'el* in Ancient Israel: Theological Reflections on an Israelite Institution," *BBR* 1 (1991): 3–19.

Citizens and Courts of Law

THE ROMAN PRACTICE OF THE LAW

The Romans' greatest achievement and their greatest bequest to those who succeeded them were their law and their sense that life should be lived according to law. At first the law was administered by the priests, but by 450 BCE it was codified in the Twelve Tables and thus became more accessible. The Tables comprised a series of terse commands dealing with court actions, family law, wills, property rights, and the public behavior of citizens. Roman law began as civil law—the *jus civile*—the law as it pertains to citizens. It was not until much later, under the emperors, that a specific body of criminal law made its appearance. In general terms the *jus civile* can be characterized as upholding the rights of citizens to contract marriages, which gave the husband *potestas* over wife and child, to acquire, hold, and dispose of property, and to be party to a legal suit for the enforcement of these rights.

Only Roman citizens had access to the law—the distinctive mark of their citizenship. But access to the law was not an easy matter. With its roots in religion, legal practice was not unlike the performance of a liturgy. Things had to be done in precisely the right way. Scrupulous attention was paid to form: the correct formulae had to be used, and the proper days had to be observed in bringing matters before the courts. At first all such knowledge was esoteric and belonged exclusively to the college of pontiffs. (By the time of Caesar, the pontiffs numbered sixteen, presided over by the *pontifex maximus*. The *collegium pontificum* included others—the *flamines*, a group of fifteen priests, the six vestals, and the *rex sacrorum*. Its role was to supervise the state cult and to advise the magistracy on its sacral functions.) But the practice emerged of publishing lists of the necessary forms (the first in 304 BCE) and then of producing more elaborate treatises that discussed specific points of law. This made litigation easier and served to restrict the somewhat arbitrary power of the pontiffs.

Legislation also aided this process. Various meetings of citizens, chaired by magistrates, would approve or reject proposals that the magistrates put forward. In particular, matters touching on public law were dealt with in this way—the powers of the magistrates themselves, the rights of citizens, taxation, suffrage, and so on. Such laws as evolved by this process were concerned, as a rule, not with principle but with practice. They addressed specific grievances and met specific needs. As the law evolved, so did the magistracies that administered it.[1] The most important magistrate was the praetor until the end of the republic. When the office was created in 367 BCE, there was only one praetor, the *praetor urbanus,* who administered the *jus civile.* In 242 BCE a second magistrate was added, the *praetor peregrinus,* who handled cases in which one or both of the parties were foreigners. He would draw on the *jus civile* but would enlarge it by reference to other legal systems. Thus evolved the *jus gentium,* the "law of the nations," which by the second and third centuries CE had a considerable influence on Roman law.[2] Over time, the number of praetors rose to sixteen, partly because of an increase in the work in Rome itself and partly because of the growth of the empire. As judge, the praetor's function was to give permission to bring a suit, to name the arbitrators (who were like the jurors in our system), to explain to them the law as it related to the case, and to pass sentence when their decision had been reached. The number of arbitrators varied from case to case. There might be one or there might be a hundred or more, as in the court of the centumviri.

As Rome expanded, it brought the whole of Italy within the ambit of its law. In Italian communities either prefects (delegates representing the praetors) or municipal magistrates exercised jurisdiction. Important cases could be appealed to the praetors' courts in Rome and later to the emperors, who gradually replaced the praetors. Roman law did not establish itself in the more distant provinces to the same extent as in Italy. There were not enough personnel to implement a single legal system throughout the empire, had such a scheme ever been proposed (and it never was, as far as we know).[3] Where local law and judicial procedures were already well established, as in most of the eastern provinces, the Romans were content to leave them in place, their own courts serving as courts of appeal, except, of course, in the case of Roman citizens, whose right it was to be heard in a Roman court. In the West, on the other hand, the introduction of Roman law was a matter of policy and was carried out with determination. The emperor himself or his deputies, not the praetors, heard appeals from these western courts.

But if the Romans were the great exponents of the rule of law, they were also its victims, falling prey, as they did, to their passion for litigation. This mania is already discernible in the speeches of Cicero, and it is an unhappy coincidence that it seized the city at just about the time when the emperors were proscribing political debate. Thus the courts became a forum, and litigation became a medium, of public expression. From the reign of one emperor to another, the rising tide of cases threatened to overwhelm the courts altogether. The work was more than anyone could master.[4]

To get some feel for the practice of the law, let us consider for a moment the court of the centumviri, who exercised their jurisdiction in the Basilica Julia, beside the Forum in Rome. The great hall was divided into three naves, the widest of which, the central nave, measured about twenty yards by ninety yards. There were 180 centumviri (not 100, as their name seems to imply), and they were divided into four groups.[5] They took their seats either in their groups in separate "chambers" or all together, according to the nature of the case. When they sat together, the *praetor hastarius* himself presided, sitting on an improvised βῆμα *(bēma),* or platform, with the 180 arbitrators beside him. At their feet, on benches facing the *bēma,* sat the parties to the suit with their supporters. Behind them stood the public, hoping for some entertainment. When the four chambers sat separately, each had 45 of the centumviri with a *decemvir* as president and with the same arrangement of the personnel found in the full court. Each chamber was divided from the other by a curtain or a screen.

Whether sitting in the divided chambers or in the full court, all concerned—the magistrates, the arbitrators, the litigants, and the public—were likely to find themselves packed as tightly as sardines. The atmosphere was stifling. To make the discomfort complete, the acoustics of the hall were deplorable, forcing advocates to strain their voices, arbitrators their attention, and the public their patience. It was not uncommon for the thunder of one counsel to fill the entire building and to drown out other cases in progress. On one notorious occasion, Galerius Tracalus (a contemporary of Paul's), whose voice was extraordinarily powerful, was applauded by all chambers, three of which could not see him and should not have been listening to him.[6] Matters were sometimes made even worse by a "low rout of claquers [professional scoffers] whom shameless advocates, following the example of Larcius Licinus, were in the habit of dragging round after them to the hearing of any case they hoped to win, as much to impress the jury as to enhance their own reputation."[7]

THE ADVOCATE

A party to a trial conducted in a Roman court could be assisted by a legal adviser, his *advocatus,* who was something akin to today's lawyer. Under the emperors this term signified anyone who assisted in the conduct of a case; often the orator or *patronus* who addressed the court on behalf of his client would function in this role.[8] There was a time when Paul needed such a person,[9] when he was again a prisoner of Rome. "At my first defense,"[10] he told Timothy, "no one took my part;[11] they all deserted me" (2 Tim 4:16). The occasion was the *primo actio,* the preliminary investigation of his case, which resulted in his being remanded to await a formal trial.[12] He was writing in the interval between the two proceedings, lamenting to his colleague that no one, as a friend or as his *patronus* or *advocatus,* was prepared to speak in his defense. He had no option but to plead his own cause.[13] The charges against Paul are not known, but Christians in general at about that time were called atheists (because they eschewed idolatry and emperor worship), cannibals (because they spoke of eating the body and blood of their Lord), and haters of the human race (because they renounced the so-called delights of sin).[14]

But if Paul felt the absence of a human defender, he was compensated by the divine presence. "The Lord stood at my side,"[15] he said, "and so strengthened me that through me the gospel was preached in full and all those Gentiles present got to hear it" (2 Tim 4:17).[16] The Lord was his **legal adviser**.[17] The notion of a divine *advocatus* may also lie behind Paul's references in Rom 8:26–34. In our weakness, he says, we do not know how to pray, whether in terms of the content of our prayer or of its expression—how best to frame what we want to say (is this a hint of the importance of the use of proper formulae in the practice of Roman law?). But we need not despair, for the Spirit **intercedes**[18] for us (vv. 26–27). If someone (Satan) brings a charge against us, we have **one who pleads our cause**[19] in the court of heaven—Christ (v. 34), who died for our sins and was raised. There is (our Lord would argue) no case to answer. He himself has settled the score. The defendant is exonerated, therefore, and the charge is dismissed (vv. 30, 33). Perhaps the common Pauline formula "through Christ" *(dia Christou)* belongs also, in both origin and intention, with this notion of Christ as advocate.

JUSTIFICATION

Pliny provides another glimpse of proceedings in a Roman court. He speaks of a session in which he himself had taken part during one of Trajan's visits to his Centumcellae villa. It had lasted only three days. The three cases on the list, cases that had been appealed to the emperor, were of no great importance (at least to Pliny). The first was an unfounded accusation against a young Ephesian, Claudius Ariston, "a nobleman of great munificence and unambitious popularity," who was acquitted. The next day, Gallitta was tried on a charge of adultery. The third day was devoted to an inquiry "concerning the much discussed will of Julius Tiro, part of which was patently genuine, while the remainder was said to be forged."[20] Scenes such as these were repeated over and over again, day after day, throughout the empire: courts hearing cases, finding for or against the plaintiff, acquitting or condemning the accused. From such a context, not necessarily Roman but certainly forensic, Paul drew his metaphor of justification.

Paul uses the noun **"justification"**[21] only twice (Rom 4:25; 5:18), but he uses the verb[22] repeatedly. Of its thirty-nine occurrences in the New Testament, twenty-seven are in Paul's letters, fifteen in Romans. It is his most characteristic way, in Romans at least, of expressing the truth that God forgives sinners. The verb means "to acquit, to declare a person to be not guilty," that is, to declare a person righteous, in the common biblical sense of this word as "innocent." "To justify" is the opposite of "to condemn" and has reference to the judge's role in pronouncing the final verdict. "To be justified" means "to get the verdict of acquittal" (e.g., LXX Deut 25:1). In some places the forensic sense of the verb is not prominent (if it is present at all), and it takes on the more general sense (in the passive) "to be saved," "to experience God's grace."[23] But in Paul's hands the forensic sense is generally present. It is a legal metaphor that makes a quasi-legal point. It speaks of a change in a person's status in relation to God, not of an inner change in the person concerned (Paul has other ways of expressing that thought). The metaphor pictures God as the judge who has reached a decision in favor of the accused, who had been brought before God's court, so to speak, on a charge of unrighteousness.[24] But God acquits the accused. And yet, paradoxically, the charge has been upheld, for we *are* all sinners; we are all, as judged by the benchmark of God's righteousness, unrighteous.[25]

This notion that God justifies the unrighteous was at the center of Paul's understanding of the gospel. But it was also at the center of the misunderstanding that dogged him as he preached the gospel to Gentiles and Jews. Many of his Jewish contemporaries simply could not come to terms with the concept. As they saw it, to treat the unrighteous as though they were righteous was the mark of a wicked judge. Does not the Scripture say (they would argue), "He who pronounces the unrighteous righteous and the righteous unrighteous is unclean and an abomination before God"?[26] The Lord himself declares, "I will not acquit the guilty."[27] But this is precisely what Paul says God has done. The critical point is that God's justification is not an arbitrary decision—God is not dismissing sin as if it were a matter of little importance. Rather, God deals with it as thoroughly as a just God should deal with such an offence. Sin is a most serious matter in God's eyes. The Bible is clear on this point. Sin is an abomination to God and cannot be dismissed. God's righteous nature demands that he do something about it. And so he has. In one act, God has both condemned sin and made possible the justification of the sinner. The classic statement of this doctrine is in Rom 3:21–26:

> But now, apart from law, the righteousness of God has been made apparent— [the righteousness] to which the law and the prophets bear witness, namely, the righteousness of God which comes through faith in Jesus Christ to all who believe. There is no difference [between people], for all have sinned and fall short of the glory of God [and all] are justified by his grace as a gift through the redemption which has come about by Christ Jesus. As for Christ, God put him forward as a means of propitiation through faith in his blood. God did this as a

demonstration of his righteousness, because in his forbearance he had let the sins committed beforehand go unpunished. [He did this, I say again,] to demonstrate his righteousness at this present time, that he might be both just and the one who justifies the person who has faith in Jesus.

Paul begins by declaring that "the 'righteousness'[28] of God" has been manifested. This phrase, "the righteousness of God," could mean one of two things: either the *status* of righteousness that God confers (in certain circumstances) on the sinner ("the gift of righteousness," 5:17) or God's own nature as righteous—the righteousness that is expressed in God's actions. The phrase is used in each of these senses in 3:21–26, but Paul begins with the first. God confers on the sinner the *status* of righteousness—God acquits him (or her) of the charge of sin and declares him to be righteous or innocent (vv. 21–22). How can this be? Paul has spent the best part of three chapters demonstrating that the whole human race, Gentile and Jew alike, is anything but innocent. We have "all sinned," he declares, "and fall short of the glory of God"[29] (v. 23). This is the bad news. The good news is that we are nevertheless "justified[30] by [God's] grace as a gift" (v. 24). And God has done it in a way that does not compromise God's own righteousness, for God has acquitted us (or will do so) on the grounds that the penalty due to our sin has been paid by another.[31] Sin has put us all under a curse,[32] as Paul explains elsewhere (Gal 3:10–14). Each of us is liable to God's wrath (Rom 1:18, etc.),[33] to be "punished with everlasting destruction and shut out from the presence of God" (2 Thess 1:9). In short, "the 'wage' that sin pays us is death" (Rom 6:23), but Christ has accepted that "payment" on our behalf. He has died for our sins (e.g., 1 Cor 15:3).[34] His death has been taken for our death. In Rom 3:24–25 Paul speaks of it in sacrificial terms as effecting propitiation,[35] that is, as turning away the wrath of God by taking away its cause. Again he speaks of it in terms of manumission as achieving our redemption,[36] and yet again in forensic terms as securing our justification— the death of Christ is the grounds of our acquittal at the tribunal of God. All that God asks of us is that we trust that it is so, resting our confidence in Jesus Christ (vv. 22, 26).[37]

What Christ did was "to demonstrate God's righteousness" (v. 25). Here we have the second of the two meanings of Paul's phrase "the righteousness of God." Christ's death shows God to be righteous and to have acted rightly in the matter of our sin. We might say, indeed, that Christ was God not "taking it out" on another but "taking it out" on himself. There was a time, Paul suggests, when it might have been thought that God was indifferent to sin. For a long time, certainly, God appeared to do little about it (v. 25), so that people might have been forgiven for thinking that God was more kind than just. Would not a just God have punished sin long since? But that, says Paul, is precisely what God has now[38] done in Christ (v. 26). God has treated Christ, who had not sinned, as though he had.[39] God has deemed Christ to be bearing our sin and, as a consequence, damned him for doing so, in a sense therefore damning himself. So God proved to be just (in dealing with sin) and kind (in dealing with us). "He did it," says Paul, "that he might be both just and the one who justifies the person who has faith in Jesus."[40] God declares all believers to be righteous. We know very well that we are not yet good in ourselves, in our practice; we are still working on that. "The Divine verdict of acquittal runs in advance of the actual practice of righteousness."[41] But in terms of status, righteousness is ours already. God has accepted us, and nothing other than an act of our own volition can change that status of acceptance (cf. Rom 5:9; 8:33–39). God's verdict of acquittal has been given, and all that will happen on the last day (in respect to our salvation), when we stand before God's tribunal, is that God's decision will be ratified—not reviewed and revised but simply ratified.

OTHER COURTROOM TERMS

Paul uses a number of other courtroom terms. "To call," for example, is the word commonly used in secular Greek for summoning a witness or a defendant to appear in court. The word had many other associations as well, but it is possible that Paul had its forensic connection in mind in Rom 8:30: "Those whom [God] **summoned**,[42] these also he justified." In Rom 14:10 and 2 Cor 5:10, he speaks of **the judgment seat**[43] *(bēma)*, the term commonly employed for the platform on which magistrates sat when a court was in session. In Romans it is the *bēma* of God; in 2 Corinthians it is the *bēma* of Christ, who acts as God's executor in giving judgment. Romans 8:33–34, takes us, in thought, to that heavenly tribunal (but this passage, with its legal terminology, should be read against the background of charges that have been laid and judgments that have been given against Christians in the mundane courts of the Roman provinces[44]). It is the day of judgment and someone asks, "Who will **bring a charge**[45] against the elect?" No answer is heard, for no charge can be laid. The elect have long since been acquitted by God of any charge that impinges on their salvation.[46] Again, "Who will **condemn?**"[47] (v. 34, effectively the same question). But there is no condemnation, for only the judge can condemn, and in this case he does not, having condemned our sin already in Christ, who died for our sin and rose again (see vv. 1–4, 34). The judge, says James Denney, "is so far from condemning that he has done everything to deliver us from condemnation."[48] Compare Rom 5:18: "So then, as through one man's misdeed **condemnation**[49] came to all, so also through one man's righteous deed, a life-giving sentence of acquittal came to all."

Sometimes Paul enlists a word from the group "to avenge," "vengeance," and "avenger."[50] When he uses such terms—as in his description of God as "**an avenger**" (1 Thess 4:6) and as wreaking "**vengeance**" on wrongdoers (Rom 12:19; 2 Thess 1:8)—it is not always certain whether he is doing so against the backdrop of the courtroom (that is, metaphorically) or is speaking in plain language. In Rom 13:4, however (as in the papyri), "avenger" does have the connotation of the courtroom, being used of the human magistrate who is "God's servant, his avenger, to execute God's wrath on the person who does wrong." This suggests that in the former passages the divine activity is indicated by means of forensic metaphors.

Finally, Paul often uses words that have to do with witnessing.[51] Galatians 4:15 is a good example ("**I bear you witness**"; cf. Rom 10:2; 2 Cor 8:3; Col 4:13 for a similar use of the verb in the first person). The whole clause, says F. F. Bruce, "is in origin a forensic form of words ('I am ready to go into the witness-box and swear . . . ')."[52] In Rom 1:9 he calls on God as **his witness** (cf. 1 Cor 1:23; Phil 1:8; 1 Thess 2:5, 10 for a similar appeal to the divine). In many cases there is uncertainty whether Paul is using the language of witness as a conscious legal metaphor. But in 2 Tim 4:1 he is clearly drawing an analogy from the courts. He was thinking of his own trial (vv. 16–18) as well as of the judgment of God (v. 1). With this in mind, he puts Timothy, as it were, on oath before God's *bēma* to preach "the word" in season and out. The courtroom imagery underlines his "solemn and emphatic" call (the sense here of the verb *diamartyromai*; cf. MM) to the younger man to be about the work of his ministry.

THE WILL

Many Jews, brought up in a religion whose basis had become justification by obedience to the law, found it hard to accept the proposition that we are justified by grace through faith in Jesus Christ. Even some Jewish Christians, who believed that Jesus was the Christ, felt that there must still be a place for obedience in the process of salvation. It was probably with this kind of thinking, rather than with Judaism itself, that Paul had to contend in Galatia, and we find him parrying the Judaizers' attack on his gospel with what he calls the "human example" of **a will**[53] (Gal 3:15). Once a person's last will and testament has been executed, he says, it cannot be **annulled or amended**;[54] its provisions stand. So with God's promises. They cannot be changed.

Some scholars have questioned the Roman, Greek, or Jewish customs behind Paul's thinking here. In Roman law, the testator could change the provisions of a will at any time, either by making a new will or by adding a codicil to the current will. Greek law, on the other hand, as practiced in many of the cities of the East, appears not to have allowed even the testator, much less anyone else, to change a will once it had been duly registered and lodged in the office of public records. On this basis, W. M. Ramsay supposed that Paul must have had the Greek rather than the Roman law in mind in Gal 3:15, where he speaks of the inviolability of God's promises.[55] But this makes too much of the metaphor—there is no need to suppose that Paul is drawing a detailed analogy from either Greek or Roman practice. Nor is it relevant to point out that a will needs the testator's death to activate its provisions,[56] whereas God (the testator of Paul's analogy) is not dead. Paul's point is simply that wills are generally (in all cultures) regarded as unchangeable. From this premise he argues a fortiori that if human wills cannot be changed, neither can the promises of God be annulled or amended. But what has this to do with his defense of the gospel?

Long ago God promised the land to Abraham and his posterity (Gen 12:7; 13:15, 17; 17:8; cf. 26:3–5; 28:13; Rom 4:13). But the land became a symbol of something else—God's ultimate blessing[57]—and the ultimate inheritor of that blessing, says Paul, is Christ[58] and all who are "in Christ" by faith (Gal 3:28–29; cf. the promise of blessing to Abraham's "seed" and the parallel promise of blessing to the nations through Abraham in Gen 12:3; 18:18; 22:18). And here is the nub of the argument. It was a promise made with no strings attached—the land or the blessing would be theirs, with no suggestion that their possession of it would depend on their obedience to the law. The law, of course, had (and still has) a place in God's purpose, but its introduction subsequent to the promise did not negate the promise. Like the provisions of a will, the promise stands unchanged and remains unconditional[59] (Gal 3:17–18).

CITIZENS AND ALIENS

Gaius, a Roman jurist who wrote in the second century CE, states that the basic distinction in the law of persons is that all men are either free or enslaved.[60] Thus all who were free *(ingenui)*, whether citizens of Rome or of some other place, belonged, on the principle expounded by Gaius, to the one category. In practice, however, among the free there was a clear distinction between the Roman citizen, whom the law protected, and the noncitizen, who was merely subject to the law.

The privileges of Roman citizenship included *conubium*, the right to make a marriage recognized by Roman law, which ensured the legitimacy of the children born within the marriage and their right to inherit, and *commercium*, the right to conduct a business under the protection of Roman law, with access to Roman courts if required. There were other advantages also. Roman citizens in trouble were less liable to suffer torture and other summary ill-treatment in the event of their arrest. Paul himself claimed this protection more than once.[61] In time the privilege of Roman citizenship was extended until, under Caracalla (212 CE) it was granted to virtually all in the empire who were free. The old distinction between the citizen and the noncitizen was replaced by a distinction between the elite *(honestiores)* and the others *(humiliores)*.[62]

But in Paul's day citizenship was still a privilege that the large majority of the free population of the empire did not enjoy. From the point of view of the Romans, noncitizens were *peregrini*, aliens, who came from (1) territories that were part of the empire or (2) territories not part of the empire but allied in some way to Rome. Complete outsiders, who came from countries with which Rome had no alliance, were treated as enemies and were liable to be enslaved if they came within the ambit of Roman authority. In the eastern provinces, by and large, peoples whose lands had been incorporated into the empire retained their own forms of government and their own laws, subject always to compliance with Roman interests and to the maintenance of peace. Such peoples were Roman subjects but not Roman citizens. They were exempted from military service, but were taxed and had no rights in terms of Roman law. Similar conditions applied to those whose countries were allied to Rome.

In certain circumstances, however, the position of the alien was somewhat ameliorated. In Rome itself, for example, aliens were so numerous that the office of *praetor peregrinus* was created to address their legal needs. Where resident aliens of a common origin were present in large numbers, the local authorities might allow them to form a πολίτευμα *(politeuma)*, a self-sufficient and, to some extent, self-governing body within the larger community. The Jews were thus constituted in a number of cities, most notably in Alexandria. The same principle worked in reverse for the Romans, except that they were not dependent, as other peoples were, on the goodwill of the local government for the establishment of their *politeumata*. These Roman enclaves, or colonies *(coloniae)*, were scattered throughout the empire,[63] often enjoying special privileges, of which the *jus italicum* was the most prized—the right to be governed as though on Italian soil.[64] The colonists were proudly Roman, and their community, especially if it possessed the "Italian right," might fairly be described as "a miniature likeness" of Rome itself.[65] Philippi was such a place. It was certainly a Roman colony— Luke describes it as "a city of the first district of Macedonia, a colony" (Acts 16:12, according to the most likely reading of the text; Macedonia had been divided by the Romans into four regions), and it appears to have possessed the *jus italicum*.[66] Not surprisingly, in Acts 16 and in Paul's letter to the church at Philippi, we are brought face-to-face with Roman life and with the Philippians' pride and sense of privilege in being Roman.[67]

Paul appeals to the Christians of Philippi in terms that clearly reflect their colonial status. In Phil 1:27, where he says, "Let your manner of life be worthy of the gospel of Christ," the verb is literally **"to be or to live as a citizen"**[68] *(politeuō)*. Paul is making a play on their civic pride. Bring the same pride, he is implying, that you have in your Roman citizenship to your Christianity. Live as citizens of heaven; live, as colonists do, by the laws of another place. He makes this point again in 3:20: "Our **citizenship** *[politeuma]*,"[69] the place where people have rights and a home and from which they are ruled, "is in heaven." A Roman *colonus,* no matter how distant he lived from Rome, could be identified by such things as dress, language, the laws that he lived by—his lifestyle. Similarly, Christians should be identified in terms of the place to which they belong, the person to whom they owe their allegiance.

A similar metaphor, but based on Jewish polity rather than Roman and referring to status rather than conduct, is found in Paul's letter to the Ephesians. The Jews, like the Romans, made a clear distinction between themselves and other peoples, a clearer distinction, indeed, than their law would strictly allow. The Old Testament insisted on fair dealing with foreigners,[70] including aliens ("strangers") and resident aliens ("sojourners"). Foreigners who lived where Hebrew law was in force were subject to Hebrew law in all civil and in criminal matters.[71] Thus, the law protected foreigners, who, for their part, were bound to respect it for as long as they lived under its jurisdiction.[72] But principle and practice often diverge.[73] In the first century CE Jewish courts consistently discriminated against Gentiles, imposing far harsher sentences on them than on Jews,[74] to the point that Roman officials complained.[75] Jews saw Gentiles as **"alienated**[76] from **the commonwealth**[77] of Israel."** But in the Christian context, says Paul, the Gentiles are "no longer **aliens**[78] or **resident aliens**,[79] but **fellow-citizens**[80] with the saints" (Eph 2:12, 19). Paul is referring not to their standing with the Jews but to their status with God, made possible by Christ's death for their sins (2:13). It is a sociopolitical metaphor of their salvation. Elsewhere Paul makes the point that Jews and Gentiles alike are personae non gratae with God. Sin has made us so. But here, referring to the Gentiles in particular, he describes their position in terms of contemporary Jewish attitudes. Apart from Christ, they are foreigners, excluded from all the rights and privileges of Israel. But in Christ they are "fellow citizens," in possession of all that properly belongs to those who are "the Israel of God" (cf. Gal 6:16).

THE AMBASSADOR

The image of Christians as *coloni,* living at a distance from their capital and their king but demonstrating their allegiance by their manner of life, leads us to the related thought of the Christian as an ambassador,[81] one who represents one sovereign or state to another. The word in Greek means literally "an old man."[82] Paul uses the word in that sense of himself in Phlm 9 and of others in Titus 2:2. A related word, "elder,"[83] is used in both secular and biblical Greek of leaders of one sort or another, including, in the New Testament, church leaders. The verb *presbeuō,* in line with the basic meaning of this word group, can have the sense "to be the older or the eldest," but it is commonly rendered "to be **an ambassador**."[84] Paul uses it twice in this sense as a metaphor of ministry (2 Cor 5:20; Eph 6:20). Both the verb and the corresponding noun[85] were "the proper terms in the Greek East for the emperor's legate."[86] Thus, the Christian minister may be thought of as the emissary of his emperor, a king far greater than Rome's.

In 2 Cor 5:20 Paul describes his preaching in terms of an embassy: "We act as ambassadors on behalf of Christ, as though God were making his appeal through us."[87] The divine appeal through his legate is this: be reconciled to God. "The use of the solemn official term *presbeuo* is justified by the apostle on the ground that the divine act of reconciling the world in Christ entails also the ministry of reconciliation."[88] Reconciliation (God's part) and the ministry of reconciliation (our part) go hand in hand. The structure of the sentence shows that the ministry is not a mere addendum but is as much a part of the reconciliation as the work of Christ itself. The whole package is from God (see v. 18), but God graciously allows us to act for him. Our role is to be ambassadors for Christ, commending his message as well as we can by our conduct (an ambassador has to be persona grata both with his principal and with those to whom he is sent[89]).

Ephesians 6:20 also refers to the apostle's preaching. Here he names the gospel—or, perhaps, "the mystery of the gospel"[90]—as his principal. Either way, he considers himself to be an emissary of the message. And now he is asking the Ephesians for prayer that he might boldly speak the message for which he is "an ambassador in a chain." With this final phrase, "in a chain," Paul may have been deliberately maintaining the metaphor. More than once, during this Roman imprisonment, he had referred to his literal chains.[91] On a state occasion an ambassador would wear a chain of office, such insignia serving to enhance both his own and his master's dignity. Paul has identified the message as his master, but behind the message stood the Christ who had been crucified. Might not a prison chain be a fitting badge of office for the representative of such a king?[92] The metaphor is spiced with irony. No ordinary representative would ever have been circumstanced as Paul was.[93] If he was, his mission was clearly at an end. But a chain was no impediment to this "ambassador." It was, rather, a decoration to be worn with distinction, marking a new "posting" in which his service to the gospel would continue despite his unpromising circumstances.[94]

NOTES

1. See H. F. Jolowicz, *Historical Introduction to the Study of Roman Law* (Cambridge: Cambridge University Press, 1952), 43–55; H. F. Jolowicz and B. Nicholas, *Historical Introduction to the Study of Roman Law* (Cambridge: Cambridge University Press, 1972), 45–57; T. R. S. Broughton, *The Magistrates of the Roman Republic* (2 vols.; New York: American Philological Association, 1951–1952).

2. See R. H. Barrow, *The Romans* (Harmondsworth, U. K.: Penguin, 1949), 208.

3. See Jolowicz and Nicholas, *Historical Introduction*, chs. 21–23; F. Schulz, *History of Roman Legal Science* (Oxford: Clarendon, 1963), part 3; H. Galsterer, "Roman Law in the Provinces: Some Problems of Transmission," in *Sources for Ancient History* (ed. M. H. Crawford; Cambridge: Cambridge University Press, 1983), 13–28.

4. To mitigate the congestion of the courts, Augustus, as early as 2 BCE, was obliged to hand over to them the use of the forum that bears his name (Suetonius, *Aug.* 29). Seventy-five years later, Vespasian wondered how to manage the flood of

suits so numerous that "the life of the advocates could scarce suffice" to deal with them (Suetonius, *Vesp.* 10). J. Carcopino (*Daily Life in Ancient Rome* [Harmondsworth, U.K.: Penguin, 1956], 189) writes,

> In the Rome of the opening second century the sound of lawsuits echoed throughout the Forum, round the tribunal of the *praetor urbanus* by the *Puteal Libonis,* and round the tribunal of the *praetor peregrinus* between the *Puteal* of Curtius and the enclosure of Marsyas; in the Basilica Iulia where the centumviri assembled; and justice thundered simultaneously from the Forum Augustus, where the *praefectus urbi* exercised his jurisdiction, from the barracks of the Castra Praetoria where the *praefectus praetorio* issued his decrees, from the Curia where the senators indicted those of their peers who had aroused distrust or displeasure, and from the Palatine where the emperor himself received the appeals of the universe in the semicircle of his private basilica.

5. See Pliny, *Ep.* 6.33.3; cf. 1.18.3; 4.24.1; 2.14; 5.9.

6. Quintilian, *Inst.* 12.5.6.

7. Carcopino, *Daily Life,* 191. Cf. Pliny, *Ep.* 2.14.9.

8. See Acts 24:1 for the hiring of Tertullus by Paul's Jewish adversaries as an *advocatus* to argue their case against him before Felix at Caesarea. A painting in the Archaeological Museum, Ostia, shows two orators arguing the case of a broken amphora.

9. Probably not for the first time. He had faced Roman courts in the provinces several times (Acts 16:19–24; 18:12–17; 24:1–23; 25:7–12) and once before in Rome itself (by implication, Acts 28; but see the next note). It is not unlikely that 2 Cor 1:8–11 refers to a trial in Asia, by which Paul probably means Ephesus. "We despaired even of life," he says, and "in our hearts had already passed sentence of death [upon ourselves]." The use of the legal term ἀπόκριμα "a judicial sentence" (found only here in the NT) suggests that the context was that of a trial. He likened his acquittal on this occasion to resurrection from the dead (v. 9). Cf. 1 Cor 15:32 and the discussion of that passage in ch. 12, n. 60. Paul's sometimes negative experience of Roman justice may have colored his remarks in 1 Cor 6:1–8 but did not prevent his admonition of Rom 13:1–7.

10. The reference to his "first defense" (ἀπολογία "a speech in defense"; cf. Acts 22:1; 25:16; 1 Cor 9:3; 2 Cor 7:11; Phil 1:7, 17) is either to the first stage of his current trial, which seems the most likely view—the sentence reads as a piece of fresh information—or to his previous trial and acquittal at the end of his first Roman imprisonment (Acts 21:22–28:31; so Eusebius, *Hist. eccl.* 2.2).

11. Παραγίνομαι: (1) "to be beside or at hand," hence "to stand by, support," used in the sense of appearing in court as a witness or serving as an advocate; cf. Aeschylus, *Eum.* 309, (2) "to come or arrive," e.g., 1 Cor 16:3.

12. Evidently the court had not been able to reach an immediate decision. In such an event, the judge would pronounced the verdict *Non liquet* or *Amplius.* When this happened, Roman legal practice required that a further investigation, or *secunda actio,* take place. Strictly, the process was not so much one of an investigation and a formal trial (although in effect that is what it was) as of the one trial being conducted in two stages. "If the matter was one of difficulty the hearing might be adjourned as often as was necessary: such a respite was called *ampliatio*" (A. E. Humphreys, *The Epistles to Timothy and Titus* [Cambridge: Cambridge University Press, 1895], 200; cf. J. N. D. Kelly, *The Pastoral Epistles* [London: Adam & Charles Black, 1963], 218).

13. As A. Plummer puts it, "Among all the Christians in Rome there was not one who would stand at his side in court either to speak on his behalf, or to advise him in the conduct of his case, or to support him by a demonstration of sympathy" (*The Pastoral Epistles* [London: Hodder & Stoughton, 1888], 420).

14. See, e.g., Tacitus (*Ann*. 15.44), who describes the Christians as "loathed for their crimes"; Suetonius, *Nero* 16; Pliny, *Ep*. 10.96–97.

15. Παρίστημι: See ch. 11, n. 50. Cf. παραγίνομαι, ch. 6, n. 11.

16. On the assumption that he was referring to his present trial, those who heard the gospel were the people in the court. If the reference was to his former imprisonment and release, the Gentiles who heard were those in the courts of Felix and Festus and perhaps his subsequent audiences in Spain and Crete and wherever else he had gone in his remaining years of freedom. He goes on to speak of being delivered "from the lion's mouth." This is probably a proverbial saying based on passages such as Ps 7:2; 22:21, 35:17; Dan 6:20ff.; etc. See further p. 265 and notes.

17. Cf. Matt 10:19–20; Mark 13:11.

18. Paul uses two striking expressions in describing the Spirit's work on our behalf: (1) συναντιλαμβάνομαι (only here and in Luke 10:40 in the NT) "to lend a hand together with, at the same time with," on which A. T. Robertson (*Word Pictures in the New Testament* [New York: Richard R. Smith, 1930–1933; repr. Nashville, Tenn.: Broadman & Holman, 1973], 4:376) writes, "Here beautifully Paul pictures the Holy Spirit taking hold at our side at the very time of our weakness and before too late"; (2) ὑπερεντυγχάνω (found only here in the NT), "a picturesque word of rescue by one who 'happens on' [ἐντυγχάνω; see the next note] one who is in trouble and 'in his behalf' (ὑπερ) pleads" (ibid., 4:377).

19. Ὅς καὶ ἐντυγχάνει ὑπὲρ ἡμῶν: Ἐντυγχάνω (1) "to fall in with," (2) "to meet with in order to converse," (3) "to petition, make petition." In Paul in Rom 8:27, 34; 11:2. Cf. the preceding note.

20. Pliny, *Ep*. 6.31.13.

21. Δικαίωσις: "The act of pronouncing righteousness, justification, acquittal." In the NT found only in Paul, Rom 4:25; 5:18. This is one of a group of words that stem from the adjective δίκαιος "righteous," i.e., conforming to the divine standard of right, itself from δίκη "custom, right, a judicial hearing," hence "justice." Basically, this word group refers to a status or a relation. Other words of the group are discussed below (δικαιόω, the next note; δικαιοσύνη, ch. 6, n. 28; ἐκδικέω, ἐκδίκησις, and ἔκδικος, ch. 6, n. 50). Here may be noted δικαίωμα, a concrete expression of righteousness, the expression and result of the act of δικαίωσις, "a declaration that a thing is δίκαιον, or that a person is δίκαιος" (MGLex), hence (1) "an ordinance" (e.g., Rom 1:32; 2:26; 8:4), (2) "a sentence," of acquittal (e.g., Rom 5:16) or of condemnation, (3) "a righteous act" (e.g., Rom 5:18).

22. Δικαιόω (see the preceding note): (1) "to show to be righteous," (2) "to declare to be righteous." It is sometimes argued that verbs ending in οω always have the sense "to *make*." But this is not the case when a moral quality or the like is in mind, as in the case of δικαιόω. Morris cites a number of examples to bear this out and concludes, "There should be no doubt that δικαιόω means 'to declare righteous,' not 'to make righteous.' Usage is decisive," he says. "It is the ordinary word for 'to acquit,' 'to declare not guilty.' When the accused is acquitted he is not 'made righteous' but declared to be righteous" (*Romans*, 145 n. 175). Cf. C. K. Barrett (*A Commentary on the Epistle to the Romans* [New York: Harper & Row, 1957], 50), who similarly states that δικαιόω "does not mean 'to make virtuous,' but 'to grant a verdict of acquittal.' " The verb is found in Paul in Rom 2:13; 3:4, 20, 24, 26, 28, 30; 4:2, 5; 5:1, 9; 6:7; 8:30 (2x), 33; 1 Cor 4:4; 6:11; Gal 2:16 (3x), 17; 3:8, 11, 24; 5:4; 1 Tim 3:16; Titus 3:7.

23. See, e.g., J. Jeremias, *The Central Message of the New Testament* (London: SCM, 1965), 51–57.

24. Ἀδικία (from ἄδικος, itself from δίκη; see ch. 6, n. 21): (1) "injustice" (e.g., Rom 9:14), (2) "unrighteousness" (e.g., Rom 1:18 [2x], 29; 2:8; 3:5; 6:13; 1 Cor 13:6; 2 Thess 2:10, 12; 2 Tim 2:19), (3) = ἀδίκημα "an unrighteous act" (e.g., 2 Cor 12:13).

25. Ἄδικος (from δίκη; see ch. 6, n. 21): (1) "unjust" (e.g., Rom 3:5), (2) "unrighteous" (e.g., 1 Cor 6:1, 9). Cf. ἀδικέω (1) intransitively, "to do wrong" (e.g., 1 Cor 6:8; 2 Cor 7:12; Col 3:25), (2) transitively, "to wrong (someone)" (e.g., 1 Cor 6:7; 2 Cor 7:2, 12; Gal 4:12; Col 3:25).

26. Ὅς δίκαιον κρίνει τὸν ἄδικον [= δίκαιοι τὸν ἄδικον "justifies the unrighteous"], ἄδικον δὲ τὸν δίκαιον, ἀκάθαρτος καὶ βδελυκτὸς παρὰ θεῷ, LXX Prov 17:15.

27. Exod 23:7. LXX has, "*you* will not justify" (οὐ δικαιώσεις).

28. Δικαιοσύνη (see ch. 6, n. 21): (1) in a broad sense, "righteousness," conformity to the divine standard of right, (2) in a narrower sense, "justice." For the Hebrews generally and for Paul in particular, righteousness is primarily a legal standing, not an ethical virtue. It does have an ethical dimension (the righteous will be righteous in their conduct; e.g., Rom 5:21?; 6:13, 16, 18–20; 14:17; 2 Cor 6:7?, 14; 9:9–10; 11:15; Eph 5:9; 6:14; Phil 3:6; 1 Tim 6:11; 2 Tim 2:22; 3:16; Titus 3:5), but first and foremost it speaks of status or relation (the righteous are those who have "secured the verdict"; they have been declared to be in good standing). Nowhere is this more apparent than in Isa 5:23, where a woe is pronounced on those who "take away the righteousness of the righteous." They could not be robbed of their moral character, but they could lose their status, their good standing in the community. Isaiah was addressing human judges, but the ultimate judge is God and the ultimate righteousness is God's acquittal and declaration of good standing. The word occurs about sixty times in Paul, thirty-three times in Romans. Of particular importance is the phrase "the righteousness of God" or the like (e.g., Rom 1:17; 3:5, 21–22, 25–26; 10:3 [2x]; 2 Cor 5:21; Phil 3:9), in which the genitive could be possessive: the righteousness that belongs to God's very nature. God, by God's very nature, does what is right (cf. Rom 9:28). Even here the forensic association of the word can sometimes be seen in the descriptions of God as a righteous judge (e.g., Gen 18:25; Ps 50:6; 96:13). Not that God is subject to any law that stands apart from and over God, as a human judge is. Rather, he is "a law unto himself." To speak of God as a "righteous judge" is simply to say that God does what is right in terms of God's own nature—is consistent within himself. Or the genitive could be subjective (the "genitive of origin"): the righteousness that comes from God and is God's gift of status, God's declaration that the recipient is a person in good standing with himself or herself. This notion of righteousness as a gift from God is particularly evident in Phil 3:9, where what is implicit in the genitive elsewhere is made explicit by the preposition ἐκ. Paul writes, μὴ ἔχων ἐμὴν δικαιοσύνην τὴν ἐκ νόμου ἀλλὰ τὴν διὰ πίστεως Χριστοῦ, τὴν ἐκ θεοῦ δικαιοσύνην ἐπὶ τῇ πίστει "not having my own righteousness that is from [obedience to] the law, but the righteousness that comes through faith in Christ [or the faithfulness of Christ; cf. ch. 6, n. 37], the righteousness that is conferred by God on the basis of faith." Cf. Rom 5:17, which speaks of the "gift of righteousness." For a review of the debate on the meaning of δικαιοσύνη θεοῦ in Rom 3:21–26, see D. A. Campbell, *The Rhetoric of Righteousness in Romans 3:21–26* (Sheffield, U.K.: Sheffield Academic Press, 1992), 139–56. For other instances in which the noun expresses a status conferred by God, see Rom 4:3, 5–6, 9, 11 (2x), 13, 22; 5:21?; 8:10; 9:30 (2x), 31 (2x); 10:3 (3x); 10:4–6, 10; 1 Cor 1:30; 2 Cor 3:9; 6:7?; Gal 2:21; 3:6, 21; 5:5; Eph 4:24; Phil 1:11; 2 Tim 4:8.

29. In the first statement, πάντες ἥμαρτον "all have sinned," the verb in the (timeless) aorist gathers up the whole race and its sinful activity over the whole of time into one damning statement. In the second, καὶ ὑστεροῦνται τῆς δόξης τοῦ θεοῦ "and all fall short of the glory of God," the verb in the present expresses the thought that the whole race *continues* to fall short. "Glory" is what can be seen of God. It was God's intention that we should reflect God's image, but both as a race and individually, we have failed to do so and have therefore forfeited this reflected glory that might have been ours. Some commentators, however, have understood

Paul to mean that we have failed to give God the glory due to God's name and, for this, are condemned, the point made in Rom 1:18–23. See, e.g., J. A. Ziesler, *Paul's Letter to the Romans* (London: SCM, 1989), 110; J. Piper, "The Demonstration of the Righteousness of God in Romans 3:25, 26," *Journal for the Study of the New Testament* 7 (1980): 28–29.

30. Δικαιούμενοι: Present passive participle of δικαιόω (see ch. 6, n. 22). The present tense points to the repeated action in each case. As each turns to Christ, so each is justified. As far as the individual is concerned, the matter is completed: he or she is acquitted. As far as the race is concerned, the process of justification continues.

31. See, e.g., Piper, "Demonstration," 28–32.

32. Κατάρα: "A curse." See the discussion of Gal 3:10–14 in ch. 5, n. 120.

33. Ὀργή: (1) "impulse, propensity, disposition," (2) "anger, wrath," of man (e.g., Eph 4:31; Col 3:8; 1 Tim 2:8) or of God ("That reaction of the divine nature against sin which in anthropomorphic language is called 'anger' " [MGLex]; e.g., Rom 1:18; 2:5 [2x], 8 [ὀργή and θυμός, the latter expressing "passion, anger, indignation"]; 3:5; 4:15; 5:9; 9:22 [2x]; 12:19; 13:4–5 [of rulers as executors of God's wrath]; Eph 2:3; 5:6; Col 3:6; 1 Thess 1:10; 2:16; 5:9).

34. Cf. Gal 3:13, where Christ is said to have become "a curse for us."

35. See discussion at p. 247 and ch. 11, n. 20.

36. See discussion at pp. 122–24 and ch. 5, n. 115.

37. I take the genitives Ἰησοῦ Χριστοῦ (v. 22) and Ἰησοῦ (v. 26) to be objective, faith "in Jesus Christ," rather than subjective, the faith "of Jesus Christ" (i.e., his faithfulness), and, similarly, the phrase διὰ πίστεως (v. 25) to be "through the faith" of the believer rather than "the faithfulness" of Jesus Christ. This understanding is supported by the qualifying phrase in v. 22, εἰς πάντας τοὺς πιστεύοντας "to all who believe." Cf., e.g., Gal 2:16; Col 2:5; 1 Tim 3:13, where the objective nature of saving faith is made clear by the use of the prepositions εἰς and ἐν—it is a faith "directed toward" or "resting in" Jesus Christ. Some, however, opt for the faithfulness of Christ in these references. This view leaves the doctrine of justification by grace through (our) faith intact while it adds to it the other dimension of what was demanded of Christ. It is only a question of which exegesis is most likely. See, e.g., L. T. Johnson, "Rom 3:21–26," 78–80; Davies, *Faith and Obedience*, 106–8; B. W. Longenecker, "Πίστις in Romans 3:25: Neglected Evidence for the 'Faithfulness of Christ'?" *NTS* 39 (1993): 478–80. Cf. S. K. Stowers ("ΕΚ ΠΙΣΤΕΩΣ and ΔΙΑ ΤΗΣ ΠΙΣΤΕΩΣ in Romans 3:30," *JBL* 108 [1989]: 667–68), who interprets διὰ πίστεως in v. 25 as the faithfulness of God; Campbell, *Rhetoric of Righteousness*, 58–69.

38. Literally, "in the now season" (ἐν τῷ νῦν καιρῷ) in contrast to what was "done beforehand." Acting when God did was something done in God's own good time. God was under no external constraint. Cf. Gal 4:4.

39. Cf. 2 Cor 5:21.

40. "Nowhere has Paul put the problem of God more acutely or profoundly. To pronounce the unrighteousness righteous is unjust by itself (Rom 4:5). God's mercy would not allow him to leave man to his fate. God's justice demanded some punishment for sin. The only possible way to save some was the propitiatory offering of Christ and the call for faith on man's part" (Robertson, *Word Pictures*, 4:348).

41. W. Sanday and A. C. Headlam, *The Epistle to the Romans* (Edinburgh: T&T Clark, 1905), 30. Cf. A. Deissmann (*Paul: A Study in Social and Religious History* [London: Hodder & Stoughton, 1926], 170): "In the apostle's thought on justification, as elsewhere, we see the peculiar . . . tension between the consciousness of present possession and the expectation of future full possession." Justification is, strictly, an eschatological event. It is the judgment of the last day "brought forward" into the present. But it still has a future as well as an accomplished dimension. This is reflected in Rom 3:30, where "the future tense (δικαιώσει) is not simply a logical future, but, as so often with this verb, and as appropriate when the one God, Creator

and Judge, beginning and end, is in view, it looks forward also to the final judgment" (J. D. G. Dunn, *Romans* [Dallas: Word, 1988], 1:189; cf. C. E. B. Cranfield, *The Epistle to the Romans* [Edinburgh: T&T Clark, 1979], 1:222, for a different understanding of the future tense of the verb). The same thought is expressed in Gal 5:5, where Paul speaks of "the hope of righteousness." The hope (= expectation, not merely wishful thinking) is of a favorable verdict in the Last Judgment (Rom 2:5–16), which, for believers, is assured in advance. They know the verdict already: "Not guilty!" Cf. Rom 5:1–2 ("the hope of the glory of God") and 1 Thess 5:8 ("the hope of salvation") and our discussion of the future aspect of adoption, p. 65 and ch. 3, n. 143, and redemption, p. 123 and ch. 5, n. 118.

42. Καλέω: "To summon, invite, call by name." The verb occurs thirty-three times in Paul, and the noun κλῆσις "a calling" or "a call" nine times. Both noun and verb (cf. Acts 4:18; 24:2) are associated with being cited to appear before a judge in court, but this notion cannot be said to be prominent in Paul's usage, if present at all.

43. Βῆμα (from βαίνω "to step"; cf. βαθμός, ch. 11, n. 5): Originally, "a step, stride, pace" but then "a raised place or platform" (reached by steps), frequently used of the tribune or tribunal, the raised floor for the magistrate's chair, perhaps in the apse of a Roman basilica, but wherever magistrates held court, as in Acts 18:12, 16–17; 25:6, 10, 17.

44. See ch. 6, n. 9.

45. Ἐγκαλέω (cf. καλέω, ch. 6, n. 42): (1) "to call in, demand," (2) as a legal term referring to the formal process of laying charges against someone, "to accuse, prosecute, take proceedings against," as in Acts 19:38, 40; 23:28–29; 26:2, 7. "Clearly envisaged is the final judgment scene at the close of history. Though the rhetorical form renders it unnecessary to seek a reference to a particular accuser, a Jewish reader would think naturally of (the) Satan (in view of Job 1–2; Zech 3:1–2), even though the role of Satan had become much elaborated in Jewish thought in the meantime" (Dunn, *Romans,* 1:502). Cf. the use of the corresponding noun ἔγκλημα "an accusation, charge" in Acts 23:29; 25:16.

46. Δικαιόω; see ch. 6, n. 22. Here as a present participle, θεὸς ὁ δικαιῶν "it is God who justifies." The tense makes the point that God still stands by God's initial act of justification. The verdict God gave then (at whatever time we first entrusted ourselves to Christ) God still maintains and will continue to maintain until it is ratified on the day of judgment. As far as God is concerned, a person who is "in Christ" is ἀνέγκλητος (α and ἐγκαλέω; see the preceding note) "unaccused, blameless." See 1 Cor 1:8; Col 1:22; cf. 1 Tim 3:10; Titus 1:6–7.

47. Κατακρίνω: "To give judgment against, condemn." Cf. Rom 2:1; 8:3, 34; 14:23; 1 Cor 11:32.

48. Denney, "Romans," 653.

49. Κατάκριμα (from κατακρίνω; see ch. 6, n. 47): "Penalty, condemnation." In the NT found only in Paul in Rom 5:16, 18; 8:1. See ch. 6, n. 21, for δικαίωσις "acquittal" and ch. 9, n. 62, for παράπτωμα "misdeed."

50. The words in question are ἐκδικέω (1) "to vindicate," (2) "to avenge (e.g., Rom 12:19; 2 Cor 10:6), ἐκδίκησις "vindication, vengeance" (e.g., Rom 12:19; 2 Cor 7:11; 2 Thess 1:8), and ἔκδικος, the latter (from which the other two are in turn derived) from ἐκ "out of" and δίκη "right" (see ch. 6, n. 21), meaning "outside of what is right," "unjust," and then, in later Greek, "exacting penalty from the unjust" (e.g., Rom 13:4; 1 Thess 4:6).

51. Μαρτυρέω: (1) properly, "to be a witness, bear witness, testify" (e.g., Rom 3:21; 10:2; 1 Cor 15:15; 2 Cor 8:3; Gal 4:15; Col 4:13; 1 Tim 6:13), (2) in late Greek, "to witness favorably, give a good report, approve" (e.g., 1 Tim 5:10). Cf. μαρτύρομαι "to summon as witness," hence, "to solemnly affirm," "to beseech" (cf. Gal 5:3; Eph 4:17); διαμαρτύρομαι, an intensive form of the other, "to solemnly

affirm" (cf. 1 Thess 4:6; 1 Tim 5:21; 2 Tim 2:14; 4:1). On this verb, J. R. W. Stott (*Guard the Gospel* [Leicester, U.K.: Inter-Varsity Press, 1973], 105) writes, "Διαμαρτύρομαι has legal connections and can mean to 'testify under oath' in a court of law or to 'adjure' a witness to do so." Μαρτυρία "testimony, evidence" (cf. 1 Tim 3:7; Titus 1:13); μαρτύριον "a testimony, witness, proof" (cf. 1 Cor 1:6; 2:1; 2 Cor 1:12; 2 Thess 1:10; 1 Tim 2:6; 2 Tim 1:8); μάρτυς (or μάρτυρ) "a witness" (cf. Rom 1:9; 2 Cor 1:23; 13:1; Phil 1:8; 1 Thess 2:5, 10; 1 Tim 5:19; 6:12; 2 Tim 2:2).

52. F. F. Bruce, *The Epistle to the Galatians* (Grand Rapids: Eerdmans, 1982), 210.

53. Διαθήκη (from διατίθημι "to arrange, dispose," and so "to make a covenant"): Used for both (1) "a will" and (2) "a covenant." A. Deissmann (*Light from the Ancient East* [London: Hodder & Stoughton, 1908], 337) maintains that "no one in the Mediterranean world in the first century CE would have thought of finding in the word διαθήκη the idea of 'covenant' (in the sense of a mutual agreement). St Paul would not, and in fact did not. To St Paul the word meant what it meant in his Greek Old Testament, 'a unilateral enactment,' in particular 'a will or testament.' " Cf. Philo (*Mut.* 6.52), who says that "a διαθήκη is a symbol of grace, which God has placed between himself, who proffers it, and man, who receives it." This is precisely Deissmann's point. When God enters into a relationship with an individual or with a group of people, it is not an agreement between equals. It is always a gracious condescension on God's part, with the notion of acceptance and of agreement on the part of the other wholly subordinate. In secular Greek, a bilateral agreement or covenant was strictly a συνθήκη (σύν "together with"), although in the LXX διαθήκη was sometimes used in this sense (e.g., Josh 9:6; Judg 2:2; 1 Sam 23:18). It is, however, in Deissmann's sense of "a unilateral disposition" on God's part that διαθήκη is used in Rom 9:4; 11:27; 1 Cor 11:25; 2 Cor 3:6, 14; Gal 3:17; 4:24; Eph 2:12, although it is generally spoken of here as a "covenant," despite the risk of misunderstanding (convention dictates the terminology). Where the disposition is made by a man, the unilateral idea is more easily expressed. It is clearly "*his* last will and testament," as in Gal 3:15.

54. Two distinct methods of superseding a will are suggested by the verbs ἀθετέω and ἐπιδιατάσσομαι. It might be expressly annulled (ἀθετέω "to set aside, nullify, reject," cf. 1 Cor 1:19; Gal 2:21; 1 Thess 4:8; 1 Tim 5:12), or it might be overlaid by new stipulations (ἐπιδιατάσσομαι "to add provisions to" a document). In v. 17 Paul substitutes for ἀθετέω the probably stronger verb ἀκυρόω "to revoke, invalidate." In using these terms, whether consciously or not, Paul appears to have been maintaining the legal metaphor, for the equivalent nouns, ἀθέτησις and ἀκύρωσις, were certainly technical legal terms (cf. "null and void"). See A. Deissmann, *Bible Studies* (Edinburgh: T&T Clark, 1901), 228–29.

55. According to W. M. Ramsay (*A Historical Commentary on St Paul's Epistle to the Galatians* [New York: Putnam's 1900], 352f.), the validation of a will, in many cities throughout the Greek world, depended on its being duly registered and deposited (either in original or in a certified copy) in the public records office. Once this was done, not even the testator was permitted to alter it unless such permission had been expressly written into it. This irrevocable character attached to a will especially where the inheritance of sons was concerned—above all (and this is particularly important in view of the reference to υἱοθεσία in 4:5) where the inheritance of *adopted* sons was concerned.

56. This is not the point at issue for Paul. In any case, under Roman law, according to Gaius (*Inst.* 2.157), a son became an heir at birth (or adoption), rather than on the death of the father. The children "even in their father's lifetime are considered in a manner owners." See further p. 65 and ch. 3, n. 145.

57. This interpretation of the land as representing something else was not peculiar to Paul. Although the original promise was limited to the possession of the land, it was coupled with a perpetual covenant between God and Abraham and his posterity: "I will be their God. . . . You [Abraham] must keep my covenant, you and your descendants after you for the generations to come" (Gen 17:8ff.). On this basis, Hebrew prophecy imported into the promise the idea of a spiritual inheritance, which Paul now adopted. We see it also in Heb 4:1–11: "If Joshua had given them rest [in the land], God would not have spoken later about another day. There remains, then, a Sabbath rest for the people of God."

58. The argument in Gal 3:16 from the singular "seed" (τῷ Ἀβραὰμ . . . καὶ τῷ σπέρματι αὐτοῦ) that the promise was ultimately fulfilled in Christ is more than mere verbal criticism. It contains the germ of the doctrine of continuous divine election within the posterity of Abraham that is developed in Rom 9 and comes to its apogee in the recognition that the Jewish nation has been rejected in favor of Christ and his church. Cf., e.g., Mark 12:1–12.

59. Notice the verb χαρίζομαι (from χάρις "grace"; cf. χάρισμα, ch. 10, n. 146): (1) "to show favor, kindness," (2) "to give freely" (e.g., Rom 8:32; 1 Cor 2:12; Gal 3:18; Phil 1:29; 2:9; Phlm 22), (3) in late Greek, "to forgive" (e.g., 2 Cor 2:7, 10; 12:13; Eph 4:32; Col 2:13; 3:13). Paul is speaking of God's blessing as a *gift* (the sense of the verb), offered, in a sense, once for all in Christ but still on offer in the gospel (the sense of the perfect tense).

60. Gaius, *Inst.* 1.9.

61. Acts 16:37–39; 22:25–29; 25:11. On the occasion reported in Acts 22:25–29, "as far as the centurion was concerned what mattered was that Paul had Roman citizenship. It was irrelevant that he was a Greek-speaking Jew from southern Asia Minor who had never set foot in Italy, let alone Rome, and whose knowledge of Latin was probably no better than the centurion's" (M. Hassall, "Romans and Non-Romans," in *The Roman World* [ed. J. Wacher; London: Routledge & Kegan Paul, 1987], 2:685).

62. See P. Garnsey, *Social Status and Legal Privilege in the Roman Empire* (Oxford: Clarendon, 1970), esp. ch. 11; G. E. M. de Ste. Croix, *The Class Struggle in the Ancient World from the Archaic Age to the Arab Conquest* (London: Gerald Duckworth, 19874), 55–62; P. Garnsey and R. Saller, *The Roman Empire* (London: Gerald Duckworth, 1987), 115–18.

63. Philippi alone is referred to in the New Testament as a "colony" (Acts 16:12), but a number of other cities named in Acts are known to have enjoyed that status, e.g., Antioch of Pisidia (13:14), Iconium (14:1), Lystra (14:6), Troas (16:8), Corinth (18:1), Ptolemais (21:7), Syracuse (28:12), and Puteoli (28:13). There were, of course, many others beyond those mentioned in Acts. Roman colonies were of three kinds and of three periods: those of the earlier republic, before 100 BCE, established in conquered towns as guardians of the frontier and centers of Roman influence; those of the Gracchan period (the agrarian colonies) established to provide land for the poorer citizens of Rome; and those of the Civil Wars and the empire, intended for the resettlement of soldiers at the end of their service. Unlike the earlier colonies, which were established by formal law and ruled by a commission, these "military colonies" were simply set up by the emperor, who would nominate a legate to give effect to his will. To this class, Philippi belonged.

64. The possession of the *jus italicum*, the "Italian rights," gave the right of freedom *(libertas);* that is, the colony was self-governing, independent of the provincial government; the right of exemption from tax *(immunitas)*. It also gave the right of holding land in full ownership and of transferring land, as under Roman law, and the right of using Italian legal procedures and precedents. But "it was not given universally to colonial settlements, and was not reserved for especially favoured groups, since the dispossessed Antonians of Italy whom Augustus settled in Macedonia held

it [but see further ch. 6, n. 66], but the great Julian colonies of Corinth and
Carthage did not." See the detailed discussion of this issue in A. N. Sherwin-White,
The Roman Citizenship (Oxford: Clarendon, 1973), 316–22.

65. J. B. Lightfoot, *Saint Paul's Epistle to the Philippians* (London: Macmillan,
1868), 51.

66. D. W. J. Gill ("Macedonia," in *The Book of Acts in Its First Century Setting*
[ed. D. W. J. Gill and C. Gempf; Grand Rapids: Eerdmans, 1994], 2:411–12) ex-
presses some uncertainty on when Philippi received the *jus italicum*, although it cer-
tainly had that privilege by the third century CE. Most commentators assume that
Philippi had the "Italian right" from the time that it was constituted a colony by
Octavian in 42 BCE (see, e.g., Sherwin-White, *Roman Citizenship*, 316; also A. N.
Sherwin-White, *Roman Society and Roman Law in the New Testament* [Oxford:
Clarendon, 1969], 76).

67. For example, the city is administered by στρατηγοί (v. 20)—presumably
Roman *praetores*—and the citizens emphatically describe themselves as 'Ρωμαίοις
οὖσιν ("being Roman," v. 21). Furthermore, the authorities are depicted as very
careful (at least by the end of the story) to follow Roman law in detail (vv. 20–24,
35–40; see C. J. Hemer, *The Book of Acts in the Setting of Hellenistic History* [Tü-
bingen: Mohr, 1989], 115). Beyond this (and in addition to the matters discussed in
the text above), notice Paul's use of the Latinized vocative form Φιλιππήσιοι (Phil
4:15) and his unique references to τὸ πραιτώριον "the praetorium" and οἱ ἐκ τῆς
Καίσαρος οἰκίας "those of the household of Caesar" (1:13; 4:22) in speaking (presumably for the encouragement of the Philippians) of the progress of the gospel in
such areas of particular interest to Romans as the imperial guard and the domestic
and administrative establishment either of the emperor himself or of his provincial
representative (in Ephesus?). Moreover, the military and athletic images (e.g.,
1:27–30) as well as Stoic terminology (4:8, 11) all play on ideas and images highly
intelligible to a church in a predominantly Roman environment. The juxtaposition
of συναθλέω and ἀγών (1:27, 30; see ch. 12, nn. 71, 125) refers to some sort of military or athletic contest. Such contests were popular in Roman society generally and
certainly in Philippi, where games and festivals were regularly held in honor of
Roman gods and the emperor and in demonstration of the city's loyalty to Rome
(see M. Tellbe, "The Sociological Factors behind Philippians 3:1–11 and the Conflict at Philippi," *Journal for the Study of the New Testament* 55 [1994]: 111 n. 54).
Again, terms such as στήκω (1:27; 4:1; see ch. 10, n. 105; ch. 12, n. 70), συν- or
συστρατιώτης (2:25; see ch. 10, n. 141), and φρουρέω (4:7; see ch. 10, n. 80) all
carry military connotations and were probably deliberately employed to communicate to a church in a military colony. Finally, Tellbe ("Sociological Factors,"
111–14) suggests that the distinctive "κύριος Christology" of the letter is determined by the Roman character of Philippi.

68. Πολιτεύω or, more frequently, πολιτεύομαι (from πολίτης "a citizen," itself from πόλις "a city"), is found only here and in Acts 23:1 in the NT, but see
H. A. A. Kennedy ("The Epistle of Paul to the Philippians," *EGT* 3:430), who cites a
number of inscriptions from Pergamon, employing this verb in a manner not unlike
Paul's, with a qualifying adverb expressing worthiness. There is some discussion as to
what Paul intended by the verb, but the fact that he has used it at all instead of his
preferred term for "living," namely, περιπατέω "to walk" (see ch. 9, n. 57) suggests
that he had in mind its original meaning and was deliberately drawing a parallel between a *colonus* and a Christian. But a number of scholars take this further, suggesting that Paul was instructing his readers to be good colonists as well as good
Christians. They understand it as an instruction, lit., "to take an active part in the affairs of the state," not as a metaphor of Christian living. See, e.g., R. Roberts, "Old
Texts in Modern Translation: Philippians 1:27," *ExpT* 49 (1937–1938): 325–26;
R. R. Brewer, "The Meaning of *politeuesthe* in Philippians 1:27," *JBL* 73 (1954):

76–83; A. T. Lincoln, *Paradise Now and Not Yet* (Cambridge: Cambridge University Press, 1981), 100–101; E. C. Miller, "Πολιτεύεσθε in Philippians 1:27: Some Philological and Thematic Observations," *Journal for the Study of the New Testament* 15 (1982): 86–96; and G. F. Hawthorne, *Philippians* (Waco, Tex.: Word, 1983), 55–56. B. W. Winter (*Seek the Welfare of the City: Christians as Benefactors and Citizens* [Grand Rapids: Eerdmans, 1994], 82–104) argues that Paul's language reflects his concern that discord within the church could easily spill over into a more public dispute waged in the local courts, i.e., that Christian conduct has implications in the realm of πολιτεία. A number of scholars also draw attention to the possible OT and Jewish background to Paul's use of the word πόλις, in the way in which the "city" (Jerusalem) had become a symbol of a spiritual fellowship into which the nations of the world would eventually enter to worship the God of Israel (cf. Ps 87; Isa 66:20; Amos 9:11–12; Zech 14:8–11; and see further Hawthorne, *Philippians*, 55–56; and P. T. O'Brien, *The Epistle to the Philippians* [Grand Rapids: Eerdmans, 1991], 146–47).

69. Πολίτευμα (from πολιτεύω, see the preceding note): (1) "an act of administration," (2) "a form of government," (3) = πολιτεία "citizenship, commonwealth" (see ch. 6, n. 77). Found only here in the NT, but a word in common use at the time, signifying a colony of foreigners or relocated veterans. For the range of meaning of this word, see, e.g., O'Brien (*Philippians*, 459–61): "The meaning that is best attested in Hellenistic times and that is most suitable for our context is 'state' or 'commonwealth' in an active and dynamic sense, a connotation that may be compared to βασιλεία as 'reign' " (p. 460). In using this and the kindred verb πολιτεύομαι, against the background of the Roman Empire with its πολιτεύματα scattered throughout the lands of its conquests, Paul

> pictures the world as an empire over which Christ rules de jure, though not yet de facto. Each local church is a colony of heaven, its members enjoying full citizenship of the heavenly city (cf. Gal 4:26; Eph 2:19), but charged with the responsibility of bringing the world to acknowledge the sovereignty of Christ. Neither the Roman colonist nor the Christian depended for the meaning, character, and purpose of his life on the ethos of his alien environment, nor did he allow that environment to determine the quality of his behaviour. (G. B. Caird, *Paul's Letters from Prison* [Oxford: Oxford University Press, 1976], 147–48)

But see, e.g., H. Strathmann ("πόλις, κτλ," *TDNT* 6:516–35, here 535) for a different view. It is striking that only in Phil 3:20 does Paul use the title "Savior" of Christ, a title often associated with the rulers of this world.

70. See, e.g., Exod 22:21; 23:9; Lev 19:33–34; Deut 10:18–19; 24:14, 17–18.

71. See, e.g., Lev 24:22; 25:35, 47; Num 35:15; Deut 14:29; 24:19; 26:11–15.

72. See, e.g., Exod 20:10; Lev 17:8–16; 18:26; 20:2; 24:16; also Num 9:14; 15:14–16.

73. See, e.g., Josh 9:27; Judg 1:28–36; 1 Kgs 9:20–21; 1 Chron 22:2; 2 Chron 2:17–18.

74. F. Lyall (*Slaves, Citizens, Sons: Legal Metaphors in the Epistles* [Grand Rapids: Zondervan, 1984], 53–54) writes,

> In practice the Gentile was at a disadvantage before Jewish courts. . . . Talmudic opinion was that in a situation involving a choice of law, the court should apply either the Jewish law or the law of the Gentile's country of origin; where it was clear the Gentile had resorted to the Jewish courts and their rules because these might be more favourable to his case, the court should apply whichever law was less favourable to the Gentile.

Cf. G. Horowitz, *The Spirit of Jewish Law* (New York: Central Book, 1963), 234–35; Z. W. Falk, *Introduction to Jewish Law of the Second Commonwealth* (Leiden: Brill, 1972), 2:273–74. M. Barth (*Ephesians* [New York: Doubleday,

1974], 1:269) remarks that "the hospitality offered to strangers by, e.g., Abraham, Rahab, and Job (Gen 18; Josh 2; Job 31:32) was not frequently imitated, and the reminders in Deuteronomy that Israel herself was a stranger were not followed with sufficient enthusiasm to spare the Jews the reproach of *miso-xenia* and *a-mixia* (fear and hatred of foreigners, lack of hospitality, opposition to intermarriage)."

75. The Babylonian Talmud itself preserves a criticism by Roman officials of the administration of Jewish law. They objected to the fact that a Gentile could not sue the Jewish owner of an animal that had done him damage, whereas the Jew, if the situation were reversed, could bring an action for damages against the Gentile owner of the beast. See *b. B. Qam.* 38a; *m. B. Qam.* 4:3; Horowitz, *Jewish Law,* 236; B. Cohen, *Jewish and Roman Law: A Comparative Study* (New York: Jewish Theological Seminary of America, 1966), 1:1, 24–27; S. W. Baron, *A Social and Religious History of the Jews* (New York: Columbia University Press, 1962), 2:300–301, and notes on 430–31.

76. Ἀπαλλοτριόω: "To alienate, estrange." In its three occurrences in the NT, Paul appears to restrict the term to Gentiles, certainly in Eph 2:12 and 4:18 and almost certainly in Col 1:21. It would be difficult to imagine him describing Jews in the terms that he uses here (so O'Brien, *Colossians, Philemon,* 66). The word does not imply a previous unity. "To alienate," therefore, may be a misleading translation, although I have retained it to preserve the idea of "alien." It may be better to translate, "excluded from the commonwealth." See Barth (*Ephesians,* 1:257): "In Ephesians 2:12 a *status* of strangership is described, not an *event* leading to estrangement."

77. Πολιτεία (from πολιτεύω; see ch. 6, n. 68): The word has two main senses: (1) "citizenship or the rights of a citizen (e.g., Acts 22:28, the only other instance of the word in the NT) and (2) "a state or commonwealth" (as in Eph 2:12; cf., e.g., 2 Macc 4:11; 8:17).

78. Ξένος: As an adjective, "foreign, alien, strange." As a substantive, (1) "a foreigner, stranger" (e.g., Eph 2:12, 19), (2) one of the parties bound by ties of hospitality, "a guest" or "a host" (= ξενοδόκος, e.g., Rom 16:23). See further the next note.

79. Πάροικος: (1) in classical Greek, as an adjective, "dwelling near, neighboring," as a substantive, "a neighbor," (2) in late writers, "foreign, alien," as a substantive "an alien, sojourner." Here it represents the classical μέτοικος, which is not found in the NT and means one who comes from one country or city and settles in another but does not rank as a citizen: a "resident alien." The two words together, ξένοι καὶ πάροικοι, constitute one comprehensive expression, including "all who, whether by natural and territorial demarcation, or by absence of civic privilege, were not citizens" (S. D. F. Salmond, "The Epistle of Paul to the Ephesians," *EGT* 3:298)—an out-group that was formally segregated from an in-group.

80. Συνπολίτης: "A fellow citizen." An old but rare word, found only here in the NT.

81. M. M. Mitchell ("New Testament Envoys in the Context of Graeco-Roman Diplomatic and Epistolary Conventions," *JBL* 4 [1992]: 644) writes,

> One most pervasive concepts in all New Testament literature is that of the envoy, one who is sent by another to represent him or her in the carrying out of certain functions. In fact, very few teachings or practices cut across the different corpora of New Testament documents . . . as do commonplaces about envoys, and particularly the Christian theological developments based on them. The general principle governing all social relations, formal and informal, in the first century is that ὁ λαμβάνων ἄν τινα πέμψω ἐμὲ λαμβάνει (John 13:20, "he who receives whomever I send receives me").

82. There are, in fact, two words with this meaning in Greek: πρέσβυς and πρεσβυτής, each of which strictly means "an old man." They become confused with πρεσβευτής, which strictly means "an ambassador" (Latin *legatus*), so that all three are used of an ambassador and two of an old man. Many commentators, following

J. B. Lightfoot (*Saint Paul's Epistles to the Colossians and to Philemon* [London: Macmillan, 1879], 336–37), have supposed that in Phlm 9 Paul was referring to himself as an ambassador, but in this verse "old man" is probably to be preferred. See the discussion in M. R. Vincent, *A Critical and Exegetical Commentary on the Epistles to the Philippians and to Philemon* (Edinburgh: T&T Clark, 1945), 184; G. Bornkamm, "πρέσβυς, κτλ," *TDNT* 6:651–83, here 683. See also J. N. Birdsall ("ΠΡΕΣΒΥΤΗΣ in Philemon 9: A Study in Conjectural Emendation," *NTS* 39 [1993]: 625–30) for the unlikelihood of πρεσβευτής having been corrupted to the πρεσβυτής of this verse. As for what constitutes an old man, Hippocrates (or Pseudo-Hippocrates, quoted by Philo, *Opif.* 105) calls a man πρεσβυτής from the age of forty-nine to fifty-six years and γέρων after that, but neither the papyri nor NT appear to maintain that distinction, so that a πρεσβυτής is an old man of any age (Luke 1:18; Titus 2:2; Phlm 9).

83. Πρεσβύτερος: Strictly a comparative adjective, "elder." As a substantive, used (1) of age, the opposite to νεανίσκοι "young men" in Acts 2:17 and νεώτερος "a younger man" in 1 Tim 5:1–2, and (2) of dignity, rank, office, as in the papyri and inscriptions of civil and religious offices, including priesthood (see Deissmann, *Bible Studies*, 154–57, 233–35), and in 1 Tim 5:17, 19; Titus 1:5 (the Pauline examples) of Christian leaders.

84. Πρεσβεύω: (1) "to be the older or the eldest, to take precedence," (2) "to be an ambassador." When used in the latter sense, the one who gives the authority or commissions the ambassador is often introduced (in the genitive case) by the preposition ὑπέρ "for, on behalf of." This is so in both instances discussed here. Paul is an ambassador ὑπὲρ Χριστοῦ "for Christ" (2 Cor 5:20) or ὑπὲρ οὗ (τὸ μυστήριον τοῦ εὐαγγελίου) "for the mystery of the gospel" (Eph 6:20).

85. Πρεσβευτής: See ch. 6, n. 82.

86. Deissmann, *Light*, 374. He refers to "innumerable examples" of this use in the inscriptions.

87. The function of the envoy, in both carrying a written message and conveying a message orally, is plentifully attested in Greco-Roman letters (see Mitchell, "New Testament Envoys," 650). Cf. Menander Rhetor (*Or.* 2.425), "The word of the ambassador is the word of the city."

88. Bornkamm, *TDNT* 6:682. This idea of the ministry as part of the total divine "package" is further expressed in 2 Cor 6:1 by the verb συνεργέω (1) properly, "to work together with," in this instance the human ministers "working together with [God]" in making the appeal (cf. Rom 8:28; 1 Cor 16:16), (2) in Hellenistic writers a transitive sense, "to cause to work together" (cf. Rom 8:28).

89. See 2 Cor 6:3–10. A. Plummer (*Second Epistle of St Paul to the Corinthians* [Edinburgh: T&T Clark, 1915], 185) has the following quotation from J. B. Lightfoot's *Ordination Addresses:*

> The ambassador, before acting, receives a commission from the power for whom he acts. The ambassador, while acting, acts not only as an agent, but as a representative of his sovereign. Lastly, the ambassador's duty is not merely to deliver a definite message, to carry out a definite policy; but he is obliged to watch opportunities, to study characters, to cast about for expedients, so that he may place it before his hearers in its most attractive form. He is a diplomatist.

90. The antecedent of the pronoun οὗ could be either the mystery contained in the gospel or the gospel itself. In terms of the meaning, it makes little difference. Paul explains what he means by "mystery" (God's "open secret") in 3:6. Cf. Col 4:3.

91. See Acts 23:29; 26:29; 28:20; Col 4:3, 18; Phlm 10, 13 and, if it belongs to this period, Phil 1:7, 13–14, 16. Cf. Acts 20:23; 21:33; 22:30; 26:31. He would again be in Roman chains some years later, 2 Tim 1:16; 2:9. These references employ two words for "chain," δεσμός and ἅλυσις, the latter used sometimes of the

handcuff by which a prisoner was attached to his guard. That may be its meaning here in Eph 6:20. But ἅλυσις is also used sometimes of "the (golden) adornment(s) worn around the neck and wrists by rich ladies or high ranking men. On festive occasions ambassadors wear such chains in order to reveal the riches, power, and dignity of the government they represent" (Barth, *Ephesians*, 2:782).

92. The parallel in Col 4:18 has δεσμός. If it is accepted that Paul wrote Ephesians and wrote it after Colossians, the change to ἅλυσις in Eph 6:20 may be seen as deliberate, perhaps to make the wordplay suggested here.

93. On the proper reception of Greek envoys, see D. J. Mosley (*Envoys and Diplomacy in Ancient Greece* [Wiesbaden: Steiner, 1973], 79, 89): "A state was always pleased to hear that its ambassadors had been well received while abroad"; Mosley gives inscriptional evidence. It was a familiar Greek saying that "an ambassador is neither beaten nor insulted," which appears to have been corroborated in actual practice: "Ambassadors fared comparatively well and were usually treated with considerable respect. The traditional codes of hospitality were largely honoured." For further examples in Greco-Roman writings, see Mitchell, "New Testament Envoys," 647–49. The relation between this principle in Greco-Roman social and diplomatic practice and Paul's own practice in sending envoys in his name (as exemplified in 2 Cor 8:24) is demonstrated by H. D. Betz, *2 Corinthians 8 and 9: A Commentary on Two Administrative Letters of the Apostle Paul* (Philadelphia: Fortress, 1985), 82–85. See esp. his notes on page 85: "For Paul asked that their love should be demonstrated in concrete action, first by the reception of the envoys, then by the collection for Jerusalem. . . . The *peroratio* (8:24) envisages the welcome that should take place at the time of the arrival of the delegates."

94. Cf. Acts 9:15–16; Phil 1:12–14; 2 Tim 4:2.

VII

CHAPTER

Manufacturing and Marketing

Little is known in detail about the economy of the Roman world. There are no government accounts, no official records of production, trade, or taxation. The number of people who were engaged in the various occupations and industries of the time is unknown. It is therefore impossible to give a systematic account of the Roman economy.[1] Nevertheless, the combined evidence of archaeology, literature, and inscriptions conveys the impression that the economy of the early empire was in a generally healthy condition. A process of decentralization and industrialization was under way. By the second century CE, "most of the cities in the provinces which had been originally centres of agricultural life and headquarters of the administration of a larger or smaller agricultural territory developed an important local industry. Every larger territory, too, every province, had its own commercial and industrial centres, which produced goods not merely for the local, or even the provincial market,"[2] but for trade throughout the empire and beyond. And at the hub of this busy commercial world, of which it was also the political and administrative capital, stood Rome itself.

Both the size of the city (estimates of Rome's population in the first century CE put it at about one million) and its political dominance condemned Rome to an intense and unremitting activity, not only in trade but in some manufacturing also—value adding to the raw products that poured into the city. All roads led to Rome, and into Roman warehouses poured the tiles and bricks, the wines and fruits of Italy; the wheat of Egypt and northern Africa (also, to a lesser extent, Gaul, Spain, Sardinia, Sicily, and Cyprus; wheat was Rome's largest single import);[3] the oil of Spain; the venison, the timbers, the wool of Gaul; the cured meats of Baetica; the dates of the oases; the marble of Tuscany, Greece, and Numidia; the porphyries of the Arabian desert; the lead, the silver, the copper of the Iberian Peninsula; the ivory of the Syrtes and of the Mauretanias; the gold of Dalmatia and of Dacia; the tin of the Cassiterides (the Scilly Isles); the amber of the Baltic; the papyri of the Nile valley; the glass of Phoenicia and Syria; the stuffs of the Orient; the incense of Arabia; the spices, the corals, the gems of India; and the silks of the East.[4] Rome was not an industrial city in the modern sense, but it mobilized a vast army of artisans to toil in its workshops, to say nothing of the office workers, the shopkeepers, the laborers on its building sites, the dockers and storemen on its wharves and in its warehouses, manufacturing, servicing, selling, unloading, handling, and housing the enormous quantity of its imports.[5]

THE LABORER

The building industry was perhaps Rome's single largest employer. Among the products carried upriver from Ostia were bricks in great quantity, marble, granite, and timber, for Rome was always building and rebuilding itself. Writing from Rome (albeit from prison) and familiarity with the city may have colored Paul's counsel to Timothy to present himself before God "as one approved, **a workman**[6] who had no need to be ashamed, cutting the word of truth [like a stone] to the required dimensions"[7] (2 Tim 2:15). Commentators differ as to what precisely Paul's metaphor was in this final injunction (and, therefore, how best to translate it) and whether it was a conscious metaphor at all. But the very fact that Paul calls Timothy a "workman" rather than a teacher or something of that kind suggests that this is a conscious metaphor, and since the context is already rich in images drawn from the building industry, it is at least possible that Paul was thinking of Timothy as **a mason** cutting and squaring stones.[8] (In one place Paul speaks of himself as a builder, indeed, as an "expert" in this trade.[9]) The "material" with which Timothy was working was "the word of truth." Paul urged him, as a good workman, to comply with the "specifications"—to present the truth about Christ as set out in the gospel,[10] in contrast to the useless "word battles" (v. 14) and "godless chatter" (v. 16) of others; perhaps also to present the truth in such a way that it could be readily understood. As J. R. W. Stott puts it, he was "to be accurate on the one hand and plain on the other" in presenting the word of God.[11]

If Timothy is the "workman," God himself must be the master builder or (if the image is not that of building) the "boss" in the enterprise, whatever it is (cf. v. 21). And Paul does, in fact, speak of Timothy as being in some such relation to God (cf. v. 15). In 1 Thess 3:2, he goes so far as to elevate him to the status of "God's fellow worker,"[12] a status that he also allows to himself and Apollos (1 Cor 3:9). He uses different terms, but to the same effect, of Barnabas and himself in describing their working together "with" God on the first missionary journey (Acts 14:27; 15:4).[13] These references draw attention to the importance of the human in the divine-human partnership that God has set up for the advancement of the gospel. It is not an inherent importance but one given by grace. Salvation and service are two sides of one coin; they are together God's gift to his people. On the other hand, this notion of partnership reminds us that nothing we do for the gospel can succeed without God: "Without us, he will not; without him, we cannot." But there is certainly work for us to do, often hard work, often repetitious and tedious work. In most cases this is all that Paul means when he speaks of his work and working, but sometimes there is the hint of a metaphor.

Adolf Deissmann suggests that Paul's statement **"I labored**[14] **more than them all"** (1 Cor 15:10) has the sound of a pieceworker boasting on payday that he has produced more than his colleagues, and that Paul's frequent references to **"laboring in vain"**[15] are "a trembling echo of the discouragement resulting from a piece of work being rejected . . . and therefore not paid for."[16] Paul was himself a tradesman who worked at his trade from time to time. He would have been familiar with the laborers' boasts and complaints.[17]

Paul often refers to the **wage**[18] paid to a workman. In Rom 6:23, sin is said to pay the "wages" it owes; in Rom 4:4, salvation is not a thing to be "earned"; in 1 Cor 3:8, 14, a teacher will be "paid" by God in accordance with what he has done; in 1 Cor 9:17–18, there are "rewards" for the preacher in terms of personal satisfaction. In 1 Cor 9:7, 2 Cor 11:8; and 1 Tim 5:18, Paul invokes a series of images from farming, priestly service, and military service to suggest that the preacher or teacher of "the word" has earned the right to be supplied with his material needs by the church.[19] As one whose own needs had been met in this way by the Philippian church, Paul ends his letter to them with a form of receipt, simulating the business documents of his day: "I have **received payment in full**"[20] (Phil 4:18). This should probably be seen as an analogy, not as an actual receipt. Deissmann thinks that Paul is writing in "a gently humorous way."

THE PARTNER

On a number of occasions Paul speaks of his "fellow workers" in a literal sense—people such as Priscilla and Aquila, Urbanus and Timothy, all named as such in Rom 16, who worked in ministry (and sometimes in the workshop) alongside the apostle. But in 2 Cor 8:23, in a reference to Titus, he combines **"fellow worker"**[21] with **"partner."**[22] "Partner" is certainly used here in a figurative sense, and in this combination, "fellow worker" must also be understood as metaphorical. The concept of partnership was known to both Romans and Jews,[23] although how it worked under Jewish law is uncertain. Among the Romans the concept appears to have had its origin in *consortium,* the community of property among brothers,[24] which continued to exist in a limited form well after New Testament times. *Consortium* appears to have given rise to the *societas omnium bonorum,* the general partnership, which was the only form of commercial association in Roman law in the first century CE.[25] Partnership was (and is) a voluntary association of persons for profit. It involves a common purpose and a contribution of time, money, and/or effort by each of the partners, with profits and losses being divided among them either by mutual agreement or as determined by law. As a metaphor, it was probably intended to express the particular bond that Paul felt between himself and Titus as together they went about the "business" of Christ in their ministry to the Corinthian church.[26] Each had invested much of himself in the work, each had worked hard, and each would suffer much if the Corinthian "enterprise" should fail. The same metaphor is more clearly developed in Phlm 17–19. In returning the (runaway?) slave Onesimus (now a Christian) to his master (also one of Paul's converts) or perhaps in asking that he be allowed to stay with him,[27] Paul requests that Onesimus be treated as he would be himself, that is, as Philemon's partner. If Philemon was owed anything because of Onesimus, he should **debit Paul's account,**[28] so to speak, in the partnership books. Paul would cover the loss. The apostle thought it worth mentioning, however, that Philemon was himself in his debt.[29]

GOD AS MASTER CRAFTSMAN

In Rom 9:21, Paul likens God to **a potter**[30] who, from the one lump of clay,[31] makes both "a vessel for noble purposes [*eis timēn*] and another for ignoble" (*eis atimian* "for dishonorable or shameful purposes"). This image is suggested by a number of Old Testament and related passages that depict God as a potter,[32] but the application is distinctive to Paul. As a potter makes pots of all kinds, so God is at liberty to do as God pleases with creation—God "has mercy on whom he wants to have mercy and he hardens whom he will" (v. 18). Paul is arguing here for the sovereign freedom of God. There is nothing capricious about God's freedom, however. God has a purpose (a beneficent purpose that includes our salvation), and all that God does is to that end.[33]

Both the original creation (Rom 1:20) and the new creation (Eph 2:10), the latter being those who are made new in Christ,[34] are described as God's **products** *(poiēmata),*[35] the work of God's "hands." *Poiēma* does not differ much in meaning from *ergon,* which usually refers to work as an activity but can also apply to the outcome of work, "that which is made."[36] If there is any difference between the two words, it is that *poiēma* can have the sense of not just any work but of a work of art.[37] The association of the word with the thought of God's creative activity in each of the texts mentioned here suggests that this sense might not be out of place in these verses, especially in Eph 2:10. The new creation in Christ is God's latest, greatest achievement (at least as we perceive it), a veritable work of art, a showpiece of grace. But it is a fine line in these verses between metaphor and plain speaking. Paul may have intended (as suggested here) to picture God as a master craftsman producing a work of art, or he may simply have been making (as he understood it) a matter-of-fact statement about the creative activity of God.

The Marketplace

Rome's "warehouses *(horrea)* stretched out of sight. Here accumulated the provisions that filled Rome's belly, the stores that were the pledge of her well-being and of her luxury."[38] An example of the retail environment of Paul's time is preserved in a row of vaulted rooms at Tomi, on the western shore of the Black Sea. In these were found, besides one hundred amphorae (large two-handled storage jars) containing resin, dyes, bitumen, and so on, iron ingots and anchors, candlesticks, the head of a bronze statue, and seven large weights. Such warehouses were the penultimate link in the chain of commerce that ended with the retailers, who could stock and restock their shelves from them. The 119 retail shops identified in one area alone of Volubilis (Morocco) exemplify the final link in the chain, as does the series of small shops that have come to light in the excavations at Corinth. The shopping complex of the North Agora was only recently completed when Paul came to Corinth and illustrates well the conditions under which he himself had often worked.[39]

But Pompeii provides the clearest impressions of the world of the small trader in Paul's day. The main commercial area was the forum. On its western side was the basilica, outside which, under the colonnade, many small traders set up their businesses. At the northeastern corner of the forum was an enclosed area with a fish market at its center and other shops around its perimeter. Nor was retailing restricted to the forum. There is hardly a street in Pompeii without its share of small shops. Wherever the public tended to congregate, as at the baths, the whole of the outer facade of the building was turned over to shops. Food shops had masonry counters with large earthenware pots *(dolia)* set into them. Grain, dried fruits, and liquids were kept in these pots. Meat and poultry were suspended from a bar hung in the entrance. Other shops probably had a table or wooden counter at the entrance.[40] From France a series of stone reliefs from funeral monuments gives some idea of the life that once filled these establishments. At Metz a scene in a patisserie shows a seated shopkeeper and a standing customer, who is pointing to some small cakes on the shelves. Larger cakes and loaves are arranged on the counter. A scene from Dijon shows a wine seller with a customer holding a jug that is being filled from a pipe. A row of six more jugs may be measures. The wine is probably kept in barrels under the counter. Part of a tombstone from Autun shows a man walking with a small cask on his shoulder. The Dijon relief also depicts part of a butcher's shop, with sausages on display and what may be a pig's head on the counter. A large barrel in the foreground may contain lard.[41] A second(?)-century CE tomb from Rome (now in the Dresden Museum) shows a butcher cutting chops on a three-legged chopping block like ones that can be seen in butcher's shops to this day.

Food selling was not limited to storefronts. For example, a stall comprising a trestle table set up in the forum can be seen on one of the Arlon reliefs. Apples and pears are spread out on the table; in front stand three baskets containing fruit, and more may be hanging at the back; a young assistant watches the stall owner as he attempts to attract the attention of a passerby. The potential customer is feeling the wares, seeming to suspect their quality. A Bordeaux relief shows fruit being offered for sale in four open sacks and a woman with her hand in a sack of grain. These everyday scenes were repeated throughout the empire. They were so familiar that Paul could aptly invite his readers, metaphorically, to go into the market to **buy up**[42] time, that most precious of all commodities (Eph 5:16; Col 4:5)—his way of saying, "Make the most of your opportunities" for the advancement of the gospel because time is running out. "The days are evil," he adds in Eph 5:16. Paul must have seen sufficient evidence that the church was heading for hard times to make him doubt that there would ever be a better time for Christians to propagate their faith. Christ himself may be thought of as being in the market for people's hearts. Paul prays that we "might know the love of Christ that surpasses knowledge" (Eph 3:19)—the most likely sense of the verb *hyperballō*, "to throw over or beyond." But the verb can also mean "to **outbid at auction**,"[43] and that sense cannot be ruled out here. Knowledge increases its bid, but Christ can always up the ante. His love will always do more, pay more, give more than knowledge or anything else that competes in the market for our devotion.

SHOPKEEPERS AND PEDDLERS

The image of **the retailer selling his wares** may have colored Paul's description of the household of Stephanas in 1 Cor 16:15. Its members "appointed[44] themselves," he says, using a common expression for taking up a trade or profession, "to the service of the saints." J. Moffatt describes it as a trade metaphor, their "trade" consisting of voluntary, unofficial service to others. Retailers sometimes went to the front of the shop to engage customers. The verb, which means literally "to stand before," thus took on the sense "to stand in front of a shop selling goods" and then, generally, "**to practice a profession or trade**."[45] Paul uses this verb in Titus 3:8 and 14, in each case with the qualifying phrase "good works" *(kalōn ergōn)*, possibly intending the verb to be understood in the latter sense. These verses, then, are a straightforward plea to believers to take up only respectable lines of business when it comes to choosing their mundane occupations,[46] or—and this seems more likely—they are Paul's instruction, by means of a commercial metaphor, to live the whole of their lives as those who have trusted in God, to make it their business, so to speak, to retail only good works (with no shoddy products and prices ridiculously low![47]).

A Roman street cry survives inscribed on a stone fragment found at Narbonne. The carving depicts a man with a basket of apples suspended round his neck and a flyswatter in his hand. The caption reads, "Apples, ladies!"[48] He was a peddler, a common sight on the streets of that day, and a representative of a calling not always trusted by prospective customers. Peddlers were typically suspected (no doubt with good reason) of using false weights and resorting to other devious practices. Wine peddlers in particular were often accused of diluting their product. Against this background Paul repudiates any suggestion that he and his colleagues were "**peddlers**[49] of God's word," as were some others—teachers who "watered down" the gospel. "On the contrary," he declares, "we speak with sincerity, as men sent out by God" (2 Cor 2:17). Similarly in 1 Thess 2:1–12 Paul is probably distinguishing himself from such people. He is certainly careful to mention his work as an artisan (v. 12). He wasn't out to sponge off the church. The standard of sincerity that Paul set for himself was something he looked for no less in others. Thus he bade Roman and Philippian Christians to be "pure" (Rom 16:19; Phil 2:15). The word is literally "unmixed, **unadulterated**."[50] The positive form of this word (as a verb) was often used of mixing or diluting wine. Like pure wine, Paul wanted his readers to be free from "dilution" or "additives"—no compromise, no taint of insincerity or moral impurity.

The lampooning of teachers as peddlers was a commonplace in Paul's world.[51] He resorts to this stratagem again in 2 Cor 4:2, still denying that he and his colleagues were guilty of the underhanded, shady practices employed by others. "We have renounced their disgraceful deceptions,"[52] he says, adding that they had never used cunning[53] and had never tampered with God's word. The verb "to tamper"[54] was frequently applied to watering down wine. Paul may have been addressing a specific criticism (which is still being leveled at him today) that he was misreading the Scriptures by reading them from his Christian perspective (thus "tampering" with them). But only so, he would argue, is "the veil" of misunderstanding taken away (see 2 Cor 3:16). He is determined "to present the truth openly" and to allow his hearers to judge what he says on its merits.

NOTES

1. M. Rostovtzeff, *The Social and Economic History of the Roman Empire* (2 vols.; Oxford: Clarendon, 1957), is the standard work on this subject. But see also K. Hopkins, *Death and Renewal* (Cambridge: Cambridge University Press, 1983); M. I. Finley, *The Ancient Economy* (London: Hogarth, 1985); P. Garnsey and R. Saller, *The Roman Empire* (London: Gerald Duckworth, 1987), 43–63.

2. Rostovtzeff, *Social and Economic History*, 1:174.

3. See Josephus (*B.J.* 2.386; 4.605) for the importance of Alexandria and Egypt in supplying grain.

4. Cf. Aelius Aristides, *Rome* 10–13: "Here is brought from every land and sea all the crops of the seasons and the produce of each land, river, lake, as well as of the arts of the Greeks and barbarians, so that if someone should wish to view all these things, he must either see them by travelling over the whole world or be in this city." "The city of Rome," he adds, "is like a common market for the whole world." Cf. Pliny (*Pan.* 29), who is similarly impressed by the flow of goods into Rome. But not all viewed this commerce with approval: "Triumphing luxury has long with greedy hands been clutching the world's unbounded stores—that she may squander them" (Seneca, *Oct.* 434f.; this work is attributed to Seneca but was clearly not written by him). Seneca often refers to Rome's "bottomless and insatiable maw, which explores on the one hand the seas and on the other the earth, with enormous toil hunting down [its] prey" (*Ep.* 89.22; cf. *Ad Helv.* 10.2–7; *Vit. beat.* 11.4). For a general discussion of Roman commerce, see, e.g., H. J. Loane, *Industry and Commerce of the City of Rome* (Baltimore: Johns Hopkins University Press, 1938), 11–59.

5. See J. Carcopino, *Daily Life in Ancient Rome* (Harmondsworth, U.K.: Penguin, 1956), 180.

6. Ἐργάτης (from ἐργάζομαι; see ch. 7, n. 14): (1) properly, "a field laborer" (2) but generally, "a workman, laborer." Cf. 2 Cor 11:13; Phil 3:2 for its use by Paul for teachers—in both cases, perhaps of the Judaizers, whom Paul describes as "deceitful" and "evil" workmen.

7. Ὀρθοτομέω (from ὀρθός "straight" and τέμνω "to cut"): A late and rare compound, found only here in the NT, "to cut straight." It occurs in LXX Prov 3:6; 11:5 (cf. Heb 12:13) for making straight paths. This appears to have determined the definition of the word given by BAGD, "to cut a path in a straight direction" or "to cut a road across country [that is forested or otherwise difficult to pass through] in a straight direction." Theodoret explains this word as being used of a plowman who drives a straight furrow, Chrysostom of cutting away what is spurious or bad, Beza of the correct cutting up of a sacrificial victim, Calvin of a father cutting portions for the food of the household (all these cited without references by N. J. D. White, "The First and Second Epistles to Timothy and the Epistle to Titus," *EGT* 4:165). A. T. Robertson (*Word Pictures in the New Testament* [New York: Richard R. Smith, 1930–1933; repr. Nashville, Tenn.: Broadman & Holman, 1973], 4:619) asks, "Since Paul was a tent-maker and knew how to cut straight the rough camel-hair cloth, why not let that be the metaphor?" Many feel, however, that the original sense of the metaphor has been lost and that the emphasis lies simply in doing something correctly. Thus the word is sometimes rendered, "to handle accurately, rightly, correctly," or the like. See further ch. 7, n. 11.

8. Some support for this interpretation may be found in the fact that the adjective δόκιμος (from δέκομαι = δέχομαι "to receive") "tested, accepted, approved," used here of Timothy, had an association with the building industry (although not exclusively; it referred primarily to the testing of metals). It is the word used for a stone that had been cut and tested and was approved to be used in the building. For its use elsewhere by Paul, see Rom 14:18; 16:10; 1 Cor 11:19; 2 Cor 10:18; 13:7. Cf. Paul's frequent use of the verb δοκιμάζω: (1) primarily of metals, "to test, try, prove" (see ch. 1, n. 46 for fire as a means of testing; for testing generally [metaphorically], see Rom 12:2; 1 Cor 11:28; 3:13; 2 Cor 8:8; 13:5; Gal 6:4; Eph 5:10; 1 Tim 3:10); (2) as a result of testing, "to approve" (see Rom 1:28; 2:18; 14:28; 1 Cor 16:3; 2 Cor 8:22; Phil 1:10; 1 Thess 2:4). A stone that had not been cut truly or was flawed in some way was marked with a capital *A* (for ἀδόκιμαστος "not approved"). Cf. Paul's use of the kindred word ἀδόκιμος in Rom 1:28; 1 Cor 9:27; 2 Cor 13:5–7; 2 Tim 3:8; Titus 1:16. Also see ch. 1, n. 72. For the work of a mason in "fitting together" the stones of a building, see p. 18 and notes.

9. For Paul as ἀρχιτέκτων "master builder, architect," in 1 Cor 3:10, see ch. 1, n. 53.

10. In Eph 1:13, "the word of truth" is defined as "the gospel" (τὸν λόγον τῆς ἀληθείας, τὸ εὐαγγέλιον; cf. Col 1:5), and on this basis I so define the phrase here. "The gospel" is, moreover, a recurring theme of this letter (cf. 2 Tim 1:8, 10; 2:8).

11. J. R. W. Stott, *Guard the Gospel* (Leicester, U.K.: Inter-Varsity Press, 1973), 67. Cf. R. A. Ward (*Commentary on 1 and 2 Timothy and Titus* [Waco, Tex.: Word, 1974], 172), who suggests that the preacher should not give "great slabs of truth . . . rough-hewn from the quarry of the gospel" (understanding the metaphor as I have) but should rather give one block at a time, "rightly proportioned and fitting easily with the [blocks] which have already been given." It is noteworthy that Sophocles used the verb ὀρθοτομέω in the sense of "to expound accurately" (see MM). It was probably on the basis of 2 Tim 2:15 that the corresponding noun ὀρθοτομία was used in both Clement of Alexandria (*Strom.* 7, 16) and Eusebius (*Hist. eccl.* 4.3) to mean "orthodoxy."

12. Συνεργός: See ch. 7, n. 21. There are a number of variants to this text, but the very boldness of the reading that makes Timothy "God's fellow worker" is the best test of its authenticity. But even on this reading differences of interpretation remain. Was Timothy a fellow worker with others in God's work? Or was he a fellow worker with God? From time to time, Paul speaks of others as his (or our) fellow worker(s), where the qualifying genitive indicates with whom he worked. On this analogy, the genitive "of God" indicates with whom Timothy worked. He and God were partners (see ch. 7, n. 23).

13. Strictly, the reports are of "all that God had done with them" (ὅσα ἐποίησεν ὁ θεὸς μετ' αὐτῶν), the "senior partner" being named first. The force of the preposition μετά, expressing companionship, "with," is sometimes missed in English versions by their rendering of "through."

14. Κοπιάω (from κόπος/κόπτω; see below in this note): (1) "to grow weary," (2) "to work with effort, toil." In Paul in Rom 16:6, 12 (2x); 1 Cor 4:12; 15:10; 16:16; Gal 4:11; Eph 4:28; Phil 2:16; Col 1:29; 1 Thess 5:12; 1 Tim 4:10; 5:17; 2 Tim 2:6. The verb seems to have become something of a technical term in Paul's vocabulary for ministerial labor (see also ch. 2, n. 33). Cf. κόπος (from κόπτω "to beat"): (1) "a beating," (2) "laborious toil, trouble" (e.g., 1 Cor 3:8; 15:58; 2 Cor 6:5; 10:15; 11:23, 27; Gal 6:17; 1 Thess 1:3; 2:9; 3:5; 2 Thess 3:8); ἔργον: (1) "work, employment" (e.g., Phil 1:22; 2:20; 1 Thess 5:13), (2) "a deed, action" (e.g., Rom 2:6–7, 15; 3:20, 27–28; 4:2, 6; 9:11, 32; 11:6 [4x]; 13:3, 12; 15:18; 1 Cor 5:2; 15:58; 16:10; 2 Cor 9:8; 10:11; 11:15; Gal 2:16 [3x]; 3:2, 5, 10; 5:19; 6:4; Eph 2:9, 10; 4:12; 5:11; Phil 1:22; 2:30; Col 1:10, 21; 3:17; 1 Thess 1:3; 5:13; 2 Thess 1:11; 2:17; 1 Tim 2:10; 3:1; 5:10 [2x], 25; 6:18; 2 Tim 1:9; 2:21; 3:17; 4:5, 14, 18; Titus 1:16 [2x]; 2:7, 14; 3:1, 5, 8, 14). Paul characteristically refers to his missionary labors as an ἔργον (see, e.g., Rom 15:18; 2 Cor 10:11; Phil 2:30). Ἔργον also refers to (3) "that which is made, a work" (e.g., Rom 14:20; 1 Cor 3:13 [2x], 14–15; 9:1; Phil 1:6). Ἐργάζομαι (from ἔργον): (1) intransitive, "to work, labor" (e.g., Rom 4:4–5; 1 Cor 4:12; 9:6, 13; 1 Thess 2:9; 4:11; 2 Thess 3:8, 10–12), (2) transitive, "to produce, perform" (e.g., Rom 2:10; 13:10; 1 Cor 16:10; 2 Cor 7:10; Gal 6:10; Eph 4:28; Col 3:23). Cf. ποίημα "that which is made, a work" (see. ch. 7, n. 35).

15. Expressed in a variety of ways: ὁ κόπος ὑμῶν οὐκ ἔστιν κενός "your work is not empty" (1 Cor 15:58), εἰκῆ κεκοπίακα "I have labored in vain" (Gal 4:11), οὐδὲ εἰς κενὸν ἐκοπίασα "nor did I labor for nothing" (Phil 2:16). The second of these references, however, may be better understood as a part of his metaphor of childbirth (see pp. 56–57), and the third as a part of his metaphor from the Greek games (see p. 268).

16. A. Deissmann, *Light from the Ancient East* (London: Hodder & Stoughton, 1908), 313–14. In line with this, Deissmann suggests that the maxim "If someone won't work, let him do without food" (2 Thess 3:10) was probably "a bit of good old workshop morality, a maxim applied no doubt hundreds of times by industrious workmen as they forbade a lazy apprentice to sit down to dinner."

17. In Acts 18:3, Paul and his hosts, Aquila and Priscilla, are described as "tentmakers" (σκηνοποιοί). This probably meant that they were, in a general way, leatherworkers. See R. Hock, *The Social Context of Paul's Ministry: Tent Making and Apostleship* (Philadelphia: Fortress, 1980), 21. Rabbis were expected to learn and practice a trade, and Paul must have been glad of this in later life as he worked to support his ministry (cf. Acts 20:34; 1 Cor 4:12; 9:3–19; 2 Cor 11:7–12; 1 Thess 2:9; 2 Thess 3:8), although in 2 Cor 11:7 he gives the impression that he felt himself to be somewhat demeaned by having to do so. On this point again, see p. 225 and ch. 10, n. 150, and on the conditions under which Paul may have worked, ch. 7, n. 39.

18. He has two words: μισθός (1) properly, "wages, hire" (e.g., Rom 4:4; 1 Tim 5:18) and (2) generally, "reward" (e.g., 1 Cor 3:8, 14; 9:17–18), and ὀψώνιον (see ch. 5, n. 76).

19. See pp. 33, 37 for discussion of the priest's and farmer's reward and not muzzling the ox, and pp. 224–25 for the spoils of war and the soldier's reward.

20. Ἀπέχω (from ἔχω, with ἀπό giving to the compound a "perfective" force): (1) transitive, "to hold back, keep off" or "to have in full" (e.g., Phil 4:18; Phlm 15), (2) intransitive, "to be away, distant," in middle, "to abstain" (cf. 1 Thess 4:3; 5:22; 1 Tim 4:3). Paul's words, ἀπέχω πάντα, lit., "I have all," echo those that appear regularly in ancient receipts, e.g., (1) for rent: "Asclepiades, the son of Charmagon, to Portis, the son of Permamis, greeting. I have *received* from you the fruits that fall to me (rents were paid in kind) and the increase of the lot that I have let to you, for the sowing of the year 25, and I have no further claims to make on you"; "I have *received* from you the rent of the olive press that you have from me on hire"; (2) for payment of taxes: "Pamaris, the son of Hermodorus, to Abos. I have *received* from you the alien tax for the months of Thouth and Phaophi. In the year 19 of Tiberius Caesar Augustus"; (3) for the payment of religious dues: "Psenamunis, the son of Pekusis, to the laborer under contract, Pibuchis, the son of Pateesis, greeting. I have *received* from you 4 drachmas and 1 obol being the collection of Ibis, on behalf of the public works"; and (4) for the sale of a slave: "I have *received* the whole price." See A. Deissmann, *Bible Studies* (Edinburgh: T&T Clark, 1901), 110–12; Deissmann, *Light*, 110–12; and MM for these and other examples from the papyri and ostraca. C. S. Wansink (*Chained in Christ: The Experience and Rhetoric of Paul's Imprisonments* [Sheffield, U.K.: Sheffield Academic Press, 1996], 129–46) draws an analogy between Philippians and a letter of Cicero to his brother (*Quint. fratr.* 1) that goes a long way toward explaining certain features of Philippians and, not least, why Paul's formal acknowledgment of the church's gift was left to the last.

21. Συνεργός: "A fellow worker," with genitive of person, Rom 16:3, 9, 21; 1 Cor 3:9; Phil 2:25; 4:3; 1 Thess 3:2 (see ch. 7, n. 12); Phlm 1, 24. See also 2 Cor 1:24; 8:23; Col 4:11.

22. Κοινωνός (from κοινός "common"): (1) as an adjective = κοινός "common," in the sense of general (= Latin *communis*) and in the sense of ordinary (= Latin *vulgaris*), (2) as a substantive, "partner, associate, companion" (e.g., 2 Cor 8:23; Phlm 17), and in a more general sense, "partaker, sharer" (e.g., 1 Cor 10:18, 20; 2 Cor 1:7). F. Lyall (*Slaves, Citizens, Sons: Legal Metaphors in the Epistles* [Grand Rapids: Zondervan, 1984], 144) appears to agree that 2 Cor 8:23 is a metaphor.

23. On partnerships in Jewish practice and law, see, e.g., Prov 29:24; Luke 5:10; G. Horowitz, *The Spirit of Jewish Law* (New York: Central Book, 1963), 557–64; I. H. Hertzog, *The Main Institutions of Jewish Law* (New York: Soncino, 1967), 1:213–33 on joint property and 2:155–66, on partnership; J. D. M. Derrett, "The Footwashing in John 13 and the Alienation of Judas Iscariot," *RIDA* 24 (1977): 3–19, esp. 10–13.

24. Cf. Rom 8:17, 29, in which Paul conceives of believers (male and female) as "brothers" of Christ. By coincidence, he also speaks of "brothers" in 2 Cor 8:23, in the same context in which he names Titus his "partner."

25. See W. W. Buckland, *A Textbook of Roman Law from Augustus to Justinian* (Cambridge: Cambridge University Press, 1963), 506–14 and index; H. F. Jolowicz, *Historical Introduction to the Study of Roman Law* (Cambridge: Cambridge University Press, 1952), 309–11; H. F. Jolowicz and B. Nicholas, *Historical Introduction to the Study of Roman Law* (Cambridge: Cambridge University Press, 1972), 295–97 and index; J. A. C. Thomas, *Textbook of Roman Law* (Amsterdam: North Holland, 1973), 300–304 and index; F. Schulz, *Classical Roman Law* (Oxford: Clarendon, 1951), 549–54; J. A. Crook, *Law and Life in Rome* (London: Thames & Hudson, 1967), 229–336. For the developed law, see C. H. Monro, *Digest 17.2: Pro Socio* (Cambridge: Cambridge University Press, 1902). For an extended treatment of Paul's understanding of partnership, centering on the concept of *societas*, see J. P. Sampley, *Pauline Partnership in Christ* (Philadelphia: Fortress, 1980).

26. See F. Hauck, "κοινωνός, κτλ," *TDNT* 3:797–809, here 804. R. P. Martin (*2 Corinthians* [Waco, Tex.: Word, 1986], 277) comments that "Paul looks on [Titus] as an intimate associate" and, in using κοινωνός, describes a "personal relationship with a nuance of confidence and joy-in-service."

27. It is generally assumed that Onesimus had run away from Philemon and had somehow contacted Paul in Rome and been converted. There is no question about the conversion, but a case can be made that he had been sent by Philemon to succor Paul while he was a prisoner (cf. the sending of Epaphroditus to him by the Philippians in similar circumstances, Phil 2:25–30) and that Paul is now requesting that Onesimus be permitted to stay on for longer than had been intended, perhaps indefinitely. See, e.g., S. Winter, "Methodological Observations on a New Interpretation of Paul's Letter to Philemon," *USQR* 35 (1984): 3–12; S. Winter, "Paul's Letter to Philemon," *NTS* 33 (1987): 1–15; Wansink, *Chained in Christ,* 175–99. For slaves seeking refuge, see ch. 5, n. 29, and for letters of recommendation, ch. 9, n. 18.

28. Ἐλλογάω: "To charge to one's account, impute." A late word found in inscriptions and papyri. In the NT only in Rom 5:13; Phlm 18. See Deissmann (*Light,* 84), and for a general discussion of debt as a metaphor see pp. 180–84.

29. F. Lyall (*Slaves, Citizens, Sons,* 144–45) draws out the metaphor as follows: "Paul and Philemon as Christians were in partnership, working for a common purpose. The contributions to the partnership made by Paul and Philemon clearly differed: the one travelled and preached, the other provided a centre for a local church (Phile 2), but both were devoting themselves to the same 'business.' " An interesting parallel to this letter is found in a papyrus of the second century CE, written in Latin by a freedman, Aurelius Archelaus, to the military tribune Julius Domitius, recommending to him one Theon, his friend. See Deissmann, *Light,* 197–98. Deissmann (pp. 330–32) also shows that Paul was using a stereotyped acknowledgment of debt in the expression ἐγὼ ἀποτίσω (future of ἀποτίνω "to pay, repay," and stronger than the more common ἀποδώσω) "I will repay" (v. 19).

30. Κεραμεύς (from κεράννυμι "to mix, mingle"): "A potter," only here and Matt 27:7, 10 in the NT.

31. Φύραμα: See ch. 4, n. 104.

32. See, e.g., Isa 29:16; 45:9; Jer 18:1–11; and esp. Wis 15:7. Cf. also 2 Tim 2:20.

33. Paul's imaginary interlocutor might well have raised the objection that there is a world of difference between a potter and his clay and God and God's human creation. To deny this difference is to concede the point that moral significance is taken out of life and that God has no room any longer to pronounce moral judgments or to speak of human beings in terms of praise or blame.

> Paul's argument . . . has got into an *impasse*. He is not able to carry it through and to maintain the sovereign freedom of God as the whole and sole explanation of human destiny. . . . He does, indeed, assert that freedom to the last, against the presumptuousness of man; but (as his theodicy continues), he begins to withdraw from the ground of speculation to that of fact and to exhibit God's action, not as a bare unintelligible exercise of will, which inevitably provokes rebellion, but as an exercise of will of such a character that man can have nothing to urge against it. (J. Denney, "St Paul's Epistle to the Romans," *EGT* 2:664)

It is at least hinted at in the following verses that God's sovereignty has a beneficent purpose in view. See further the discussion in J. D. G. Dunn, *Romans* (Dallas: Word, 1988), 2:564–66.

34. Cf., e.g., 2 Cor 5:17; Gal 6:15; Col 3:10; Eph 2:15; 4:24.

35. Ποίημα (old word from ποιέω "to make, produce, do"): "That which is made or done, a work." At times it has the particular meaning of "poem," so that we might interpret Paul's statement as "we are God's poem," having in mind all that poetry can mean to some people: the music of words, the pictures that speak, the balm that soothes every mood of the human heart. In the NT, only in Rom 1:20; Eph 2:10, but in the LXX often used of the creation, e.g., Ps 91:4; 142:5.

36. See ch. 7, n. 14.

37. See, e.g., JB on Eph 2:10. Starting from this verse, L. Williamson has aptly summarized the whole message of Ephesians under the title *God's Work of Art*.

38. Carcopino, *Daily Life*, 179.

39. The North Agora comprised a series of shops built around the central square. They had a uniform height of about 4.5 yards and were about the same depth; the width varied from about 3 to 4.5 yards. Frequently they had a communicating door or window to the shop next door (see F. J. de Waele, "The Roman Market North of the Temple at Corinth," *AJA* 34 [1930]: 439–41). As was generally the case in the ancient world, these shops no doubt housed the entire operation of the business concerned. Here the work of manufacture was done and the raw materials stored, here the wares were displayed, from here they were sold, and here the proprietor and his household might even have eaten and slept. Since the doorway was the only source of natural light, it would have had to stand open all day, making conditions very trying sometimes for those working within. A. Deissmann (*Paul: A Study in Social and Religious History* [London: Hodder & Stoughton, 1926], 49) suggests that Paul's working conditions left him with the legacy of a "clumsy hand" when it came to writing his letters. The hours worked were long. If the apprentice contracts from Egypt are any guide, shops were open from sunrise to sunset. But the pace of life may have been such as to allow for some kind of social life during these hours. Several stories about Socrates in Athens take place in the cobbler's shop of Simon the shoemaker, where people gathered to discuss philosophy and politics. One imagines that Paul similarly found time for discussion in the leather shops in which he worked in Corinth and elsewhere. On Paul as a workman, see further ch. 7, n. 17.

40. See P. Connolly, *Pompeii* (Oxford: Oxford University Press, 1990), 54. Paul Veyne ("The Roman Empire," in *A History of Private Life* (ed. P. Ariès and G. Duby; Cambridge: Harvard University Press, 1987], 1:123) reproduces a shop

sign (without stating its provenance) that shows all of this—poultry suspended from a bar and other produce on wooden counters. It appears that this shop was called Two Monkeys and a Snail, no doubt reflecting the characters of its sales personnel.

41. See J. Liversidge, *Everyday Life in the Roman Empire* (New York: Putnam's, 1976), 101–2.

42. Ἐξαγοράζω. See ch. 5, n. 52.

43. Ὑπερβάλλω. "To outbid at auction" is one of a number of metaphorical meanings for this verb (see, e.g., Lysias, *Or.* 22.8; Herodotus, *Hist.* 5.51; Thucydides, *Hist.* 8.56; P.Oxy. 513.25; 1633.5). In the NT this occurs only in Paul in 2 Cor 3:10; 9:14; Eph 1:19; 2:7; 3:19. Eph 3:19 is commonly, and I think correctly, regarded as an oxymoron: a seemingly absurd combination of opposites designed to emphasize a point (cf. Phil 4:7). Paul should be seen not, then, as denigrating knowledge (revealed knowledge is, in fact, highly regarded in this letter; cf. Eph 1:9, 17, 18; 3:3–5, 9; 4:13; 5:17) but only as exalting the love of God that is encountered in Christ Jesus our Lord.

44. Τάσσω. See ch. 10, n. 17. Although generally regarded as having a military connotation more than anything else, "to appoint oneself" to some role was a recognized idiom in a number of other connections, not least in the commercial world. Plato (*Resp.* 2.371) uses the term of tradesmen who "set themselves to the business of serving the public" by retailing farm produce, since they "saw the need of this." See J. Moffatt, *The First Epistle of Paul to the Corinthians* (London: Hodder & Stoughton, 1938), 278; G. G. Findlay, "St Paul's First Epistle to the Corinthians," *EGT* 2:950.

45. Προΐστημι (1) transitive, "to stand (a person or thing) before, set over," (2) intransitive, "to stand (oneself) before, preside, rule, manage," and so in the senses mentioned above. In Paul in Rom 12:8; 1 Thess 5:12; 1 Tim 3:4–5, 12; 5:17; Titus 3:8, 14.

46. Cf., e.g., AV and RV margins, "profess honest occupations," RSV margin, "enter honorable occupations," MOFFATT, "practicing honorable occupations." The difficulty with such a reading is that καλὰ ἔργα everywhere else in the NT, as well as in secular authors, means "good works" in the religious or moral sense.

47. From R. A. Ward, *Commentary on 1 and 2 Timothy and Titus* (Waco, Tex.: Word, 1974), 277. Cf., e.g., J. N. D. Kelly (*The Pastoral Epistles* [London: Adam & Charles Black, 1963], 254), who also sees this as a conscious commercial metaphor on Paul's part.

48. See Liversidge, *Everyday Life*, 102.

49. I have expressed the Greek as a noun, but Paul has the verb καπηλεύω (from κάπηλος "a huckster, peddler") "to make a trade of" and so (given the character of these traders) (1) "to dilute, corrupt" and (2) "to make a profit by selling shoddy goods." Found only here in the NT. Robertson (*Word Pictures,* 4:219) notes that there has been an association of corruption with peddling throughout the history of these words (noun and verb): "It is curious how hucksters were [always] suspected of corrupting by putting the best fruits on top of the basket." Cf. H. Windisch, "καπηλεύω," *TDNT* 3:603–5. In LXX Isa 1:22, peddlers (οἱ κάπηλοι) are accused of watering down their wine, while Sirach observes that they "will not be judged to be free from sin" (Sir 26:29). Plummer (*Second Corinthians,* 73) cites the Talmud (without reference) as accounting the peddler to be one whose business involved robbery and as interpreting Deut 30:13 to mean that the law cannot be found among hucksters and merchants.

50. Ἀκέραιος (from κεράννυμι "to mix, mingle," chiefly of diluting wine but also of alloying metals with baser material): "Unmixed, pure," hence "sincere, guileless," see Lightfoot (*Saint Paul's Epistle to the Philippians* [London: Macmillan, 1868], 117). G. Kittel ("ἀκέραιος," *TDNT* 1:209–10, here 209) notes that this

word is used in the Hellenistic period in combination with "wine," "gold," etc., but also, as in Paul, metaphorically.

51. Plato (*Prot.* 313) used the figure of those who made a pretence of wisdom: "The sophist is a merchant or retailer [κάπηλος] in knowledge"; Philostratus (*Vit. Apoll.* 1.13), using the verb καπηλεύω, speaks of teachers "hawking wisdom around"; Lucian (*Hermot.* 59) says that philosophers dispose of their wares just as hucksters (κάπηλοι) do, most of them giving bad measure after adulterating and falsifying what they sell. In *Vit. auct.* 2.449–511, Lucian offers a humorous account of the hawking of philosophy in the great cities of the Roman Empire. R. L. Wilken (*The Christians as the Romans Saw Them* [New Haven: Yale University Press, 1984], 74) sums up these data as follows:

> Philosophers became hucksters, salesmen marketing the ideas and beliefs of their respective schools. Addressing crowds on street corners and in the market place, they offered advice on how to live one's life and deal with personal problems. Appealing less to reason and logic than to emotion and feeling, philosophers appeared as travelling evangelists, directing their hearers to the wondrous accomplishments of the founder of the school, its venerable tradition, or the high regard in which many people viewed it.

Cf. V. P. Furnish, *II Corinthians* (New York: Doubleday, 1984), 566: "On the streets of Corinth, as of other large cities, charlatans and cheats passing themselves off as philosophers were a familiar sight . . . and the apostle will not allow himself to be classified with them." For all that, Lucian regarded Christian preachers as not unlike these others (see *Peregr.* 11; cf. also Origen, *Cels.* 5.61–62).

52. Τὰ κρυπτὰ τῆς αἰσχύνης: "The hidden things of shame." The stress is on τὰ κρυπτά "the hidden things." It is the openness and candor of his ministry on which he insists.

53. Πανουργία (from πανοῦργος "ready to do anything," chiefly in a bad sense, "crafty," as in 2 Cor 12:16; sometimes a good sense, "clever"): "Cleverness," usually in a bad sense, "cunning," the "unscrupulous readiness to adopt any means in order to gain one's ends" (Plummer, *Second Corinthians*, 111). See 1 Cor 3:19; 2 Cor 4:2; 11:3; Eph 4:14.

54. Δολόω (from δόλος, see ch. 2, n. 26): (1) strictly, "to trap, snare" but (2) as applied to wine (frequently) and to metal, "to adulterate," and so metaphorically, "to corrupt," as commonly in the papyri and inscriptions. Found only here in the NT.

The Business World

A GUARANTEE

It is especially fitting that 2 Corinthians, a letter addressed to Corinth, a great center of commerce, opens with a cluster of metaphors from the business world (1:21–22), beginning with the statement "it is God who establishes [guarantees] us and you [lit., 'us together with you'] in Christ." The verb translated "establishes" is used in a legal sense, in the papyri and elsewhere, of **a guarantee**[1] that certain commitments will be carried out. The sense is that God guarantees (note the present participle—"goes on guaranteeing") that Paul and his colleagues, on the one hand ("us"), and his readers, the Corinthian Christians, on the other ("together with you"), belong to Christ. The phrase "in Christ" (rendered thus by most English versions) is literally "into *[eis]* Christ" and may be regarded as another in this group of metaphors. It probably represents the notion of being **"entered into an account"**—the believer is "credited [as it were] to Christ."

The same metaphor may help explain the terminology of Christian baptism, according to which we are baptized "in or into the name."[2] The rite may have been seen as a deed of transfer whereby we are "made over" to the one named, to Jesus or the triune God. The problem at Corinth was that too many Christians were behaving as though they had been "made over" to Paul or to Cephas or to Apollos and not to Jesus, in whose "account" alone they belonged (cf. 1 Cor 1:10–17).

In 2 Cor 1:21–22, Paul goes on to say, "God has anointed[3] us; moreover, it is he who has **sealed**[4] us." Sealing is another commercial metaphor. The practice is mentioned in the Old Testament, in both a literal[5] and a figurative sense,[6] and was still common in Paul's day, especially in commercial and legal circles.[7] In a world in which not everyone could read or write, a seal was an easily recognizable sign. It could indicate ownership, and it also served to validate documents. A will, for example, was deemed valid only when it was sealed and presented to the authorities with the seals still intact. Sometimes a seal served as a trademark indicating the particular brand of a product. Galen refers to an eye ointment from Lemnos that could be identified in this way.[8] Goods on consignment were sealed as a mark of ownership and a guarantee that they had not been interfered with in transit. Paul uses this metaphor of "sealing" to say that believers belong to God.[9] Of the four participles in these verses (2 Cor 1:21–22), the first is a present (*bebaiōn*, "guarantees"; see n. 1) and the others are aorists (*crisas, sphragisamenos, dous,* "has commissioned, sealed, put"), all pointing to something already accomplished. There is a sense in which God goes on guaranteeing our position in Christ (the present tense), and there is a sense in which this position has been established once for all and the matter is ended (the aorist). Although the Spirit strictly belongs with the last of these aorist participles ("who . . . put his Spirit in our hearts"), the syntax of the sentence allows us to link the Spirit no less with the sealing.[10] (In Eph 1:13–14 and 4:30 believers are said to be "sealed with the Spirit.") The Spirit, then, is evidence of God's ownership. The Spirit's presence tells us (and perhaps tells others also) to whom we belong, with the added assurance (clearly expressed in Eph 1:13–14) that this "seal" will guarantee our safety in transit.[11]

Finally, "God . . . has given **an installment**"[12] of what is to come: "He has put his Spirit in our hearts" (2 Cor 1:22). This is one of three places in which believers are said to have the installment or "the earnest" of the Spirit (cf. 2 Cor 5:5; Eph 1:13–14). The concept of the earnest was a familiar one, and the same word was used by Jews, Greeks, and Romans (originally derived, it seems, from the Phoenicians). It was something given in anticipation of payment for goods, services, and so on. F. Lyall points out that there was a significant difference between Greek and Roman law in the precise definition of the earnest. In Roman law the earnest was simply a token of goodwill, not an essential part of the contract. It might be money, but it might also be a gift of some other kind, not uncommonly a ring (e.g., a betrothal ring). To the Greeks, however, the earnest was a part of the price to be paid—a downpayment—with the balance to follow.[13] Instead of pressing the metaphor along either Greek or Roman lines, it is of more value to explore the idea of not yet having received the "full payment" of our salvation.[14] We are redeemed—there is no question of that—but we await our final redemption.[15] God's Spirit is with us in anticipation of that day (as *arrabōn*) and to see that we arrive there intact (as "seal").

DEBT

Sometimes the nouns **"debt"** and **"debtor"** and more often the verb **"to owe"**[16] are employed by Paul in a figurative sense. Thus Paul describes the Jews and the Judaizers (in Galatians he probably had in mind the latter specifically) as "debtors" to the law. They believed that their only hope of salvation lay in obedience to the injunctions of the Old Testament. As Paul saw it, walking that path required of them a total obedience. They were obliged, he says (and in that sense they were debtors—they "owed it" to their chosen course), to keep the whole law or to suffer the consequence of any breach of the law (Gal 5:3; cf. 3:10). He makes the same point with the analogy of Rom 4:4–5: "Wages are not credited as a gift, but as something owed" (the employer's debt to his workmen). Either we seek to earn our salvation, as we earn our wages (and inevitably fail in the attempt), or we accept it as something unearned, as God's gracious gift. But even a gift may involve obligations.

Those who are saved by grace, Paul declares, owe it to God to live their lives in a manner pleasing to God (cf. Eph 2:8–10). "We are debtors," as he puts it in Rom 8:12, "but not to the flesh [our sinful nature], as though we were bound to live by that standard." Clearly, Paul intended to complete the sentence by adding "but [debtors] to the Spirit, to live by God's standard." But he was sidetracked by the warning in verse 13 and never brought the sentence to its proper conclusion. What he would have said was something he never tired of telling his readers. In a letter now lost he had told the Corinthians, for example, not to associate with the ungodly. Either they had not understood him or they had not acted decisively on his instruction, so he spelled it out for them again in the letter that followed (1 Cor 5:10). They owed it to God, he said, to dissociate themselves, *in terms of their practice,* from the ways of the world. They should not, for example, accept sexual immorality as a matter of course, as did the ungodly. They could not avoid the ungodly, but they could and should avoid their practices. On the other hand, there was a case, he believed, for their distancing themselves from Christians who did not toe the ethical line (v. 11).

In public worship Christians owed it to God to conduct themselves and to dress themselves in a way that expressed what they were by creation. They were made male and female, so let the man be seen to be male and the woman female by the signs of their sexes: the uncovered head for the man, the veil for the woman (1 Cor 11:7, 10; cf. Gen 1:27). In effect, Paul is saying, we have a duty to acknowledge God's work in creation.[17] Beyond this, Paul felt a particular obligation to thank God for the spiritual recreation of the Thessalonian Christians—"we owe it always," he wrote, "to thank God for you" (2 Thess 1:3; 2:13).[18] He always felt that he owed it to God to fulfill his commission (Acts 9:15). But this had put him under an obligation to others no less than to God. Thus he described himself in Rom 1:14–15 as a debtor both to the Greeks and to others,[19] to the wise and to the ignorant. He owed it to them all to "carry God's name before them." "That is why," he explained, "I am so eager to preach the gospel also to you who are at Rome."

In Rom 13:7 Paul speaks of literal debts (the word for debts, *opheilē,* is commonly used in the papyri but not in literary works; Paul is writing in the vernacular). His reference is to the taxes that we ought to be paying. In verse 8 (also see Phlm 18) he uses the verb in the literal sense: "Owe nothing to anyone" (NIV "let no debt remain outstanding"). But (moving now from the literal to the figurative) there is one debt that Christians are bound to incur. "Owe nothing," he says, "*except* to love one another," in the sense of wanting the best for the other and trying hard to achieve it. Such love, Paul explains, is the fulfillment of the moral law, for love is antithetical to adultery and murder and theft and covetousness and the like (Rom 13:8–10).[20] Constrained by such love, the "strong," for example, owe it to the "weak" to make allowance for their scruples (Rom 15:1; cf. 1 Cor 8:1–13); husbands owe it to their wives, and wives to their husbands, to satisfy their sexual desires (1 Cor 7:3, cf. v. 36); husbands owe it to their wives to care for them (Eph 5:28); parents owe it to their children to meet all their needs (2 Cor 12:14); churches owe it to the likes of Paul ("full-time" ministers) to support them in their ministry (1 Cor 9:10). To cite a particular case, the Gentile churches owed it to those of Judea to help them in their economic necessity. "They were pleased to do it," said Paul. After all, they were their debtors. The Gentiles had shared in spiritual blessings that had come to them through the Judean churches, and now they owed it in return to those churches to be of service to them in material things (Rom 15:27).

Paul recognizes here that love should be reciprocal (not that we love in order to be loved in return). The kind of love that we are called on to practice—God's kind of love—does not operate on a quid pro quo basis but on the basis of the other person's need for our help. Nevertheless, within "the household of faith" each member should expect to be loved as well as to love. Paul was disappointed on one occasion when the Corinthians failed in their duty of love. "You owed it to me," he complained, "to come to my defense," and yet you did not (2 Cor 12:11). He felt badly let down. He felt the pain of unrequited love that God must often feel in connection with us.

A funerary relief (ca. second century CE) now in the Landesmuseum, Trier, shows a landowner checking his accounts in a large ledger (a polyptych consisting of five wooden tablets covered with wax). It graphically illustrates Paul's metaphors of debit and credit and keeping accounts.[21] In these terms God might be pictured as the landowner, poring over his "books" or checking his files and discovering our name there as his "debtors" by reason of sin. This is certainly the picture suggested by Col 2:14, in which Paul speaks of the "document that stood against us,"[22] using a term *(cheirographon)* that was often used in secular Greek of "**an acknowledgment of debt**" (an IOU) signed by the debtor and now in the creditor's hand. Adolf Deissmann cites a number of examples of such documents from the papyri, but there is one closer at hand in Phlm 18–19. The signature, of course, is all-important on an IOU, and thus Paul says to Philemon, "I, Paul, *am writing this with my own hand:* I will repay."[23] *Cheirographon* does not necessarily mean a debtor's note to his creditor, but this is probably the best way to explain the word in Colossians. It is our IOU, so to speak, acknowledging our debt to God. But then Paul describes it as comprising the "ordinances" or "decrees,"[24] and this appears to be a reference to Old Testament law, which the Jews accepted as binding[25] and to which, according to Paul, the Gentiles also, unawares, gave their assent.[26] Was he thinking of the Old Testament as a kind of tally of sins—not intended as such, of course, but, in effect, a written acknowledgment of our failure to give God God's due?[27] Jeremias, for one, renders Paul's phrase along these lines as "the writ issued against us which enumerated the statutes we had violated."[28] At any rate, the "document," whatever Paul meant by it in detail,[29] is a metaphor of our sin. We have "defaulted" in the matter of obedience to God, but God has cancelled the *cheirographon* and forgiven the "debt."

The usual practice was to cancel a document by simply crossing it out. The Greek word for this was *chiazō*, "to make the letter chi" across the page. The papyri afford numerous examples of documents that have been canceled in this way. But Paul has chosen to use a different word, which means "to wash over" and so "to wipe off."[30] He uses it metaphorically, but it was possible to wipe off a debt literally by **expunging the record**. Writing that was only crossed out remained visible, but the ink used on a papyrus could be wiped with a sponge so that all traces of the writing were removed.[31] So Paul avers that when God forgives, God forgets.[32] Nothing remains to impair our credit rating with God.

God's forgiveness rests on Christ's death. In this passage (Col 2:14) Paul's reference to the cross makes that clear. But the details of the imagery—what exactly he pictured as occurring on the cross—are not easy to fathom. He appears to identify the *titulus* that Pilate had written (John 19:19–22) with the "document that stood against us," which, he says, God nailed to the cross.[33] Or is the document to be identified with Christ himself? Has it become, in Paul's mind, the sinful flesh, in the likeness of which Christ came and for which he died on the cross (cf. Rom 8:3)?[34] The questions come easier than the answers. But the fact remains that God can justly "wipe off" our "debts" because Christ died for our sins.

The same truth, of a gracious forgiveness, is sometimes expressed in the notion of **reckoning**.[35] "To reckon" was originally the word for keeping accounts. But it had long since passed into general use as "to consider," and in some cases it cannot be claimed as a conscious metaphor. But in some cases it can be; in Paul's writings, "to reckon" occurs with greatest frequency in Rom 4 (eleven times), where it seems to have retained its commercial links. For example, after introducing this metaphor in verse 3, Paul goes on to speak of people working for wages. After his exposition of the doctrine of justification by faith in 3:21–31, he is attempting to show that, far from being something newfangled, this doctrine exemplifies a principle on which God has always worked, his dealings with Abraham being a case in point. "What does the Scripture say?" Paul asks. It says, "Abraham believed God and it was reckoned to him for righteousness" (4:3; cf. Gen 15:6). In commercial terms Abraham's faith was entered **on the credit side** of God's ledger in lieu of another entry, his righteousness.[36] Abraham was not righteous in himself; he had done nothing to warrant God's kindness (v. 2). Yet he was credited by God with righteousness on no other grounds than his belief that God would do what God said he would do. **A debit entry**, of course, is always possible in that ledger. In Ps 32:2 the man is blessed whose sin is *not* taken into account (v. 8). Taking verse 3 and verse 8 in conjunction, the image of "reckoning" pictures our sins as a debit entry, against which God sets God's own generous provision, a gift no less (vv. 4–5), which more than balances the books. All God asks of us is that we trust God's accounting!

God has settled our "debt" in Christ, winning the eternal gratitude of all who understand and accept what he has done. Paul, for one, could never forget how much he owed to God, Father and Son, and his gratitude is expressed in the central place that he now gives to Christ in all that he does. From the moment he met Christ on the road to Damascus, other things ceased to matter for Paul in the way that they once mattered. They paled by comparison with Christ, who mattered most of all. In Phil 3:7–11 Paul attempts to express his sense of indebtedness to the God who, in Christ, had cleared the "debt" of his sin. He turns again to the language of commerce: "Whatever had been **profit**,"[37] he says, thinking of all that had once been the ground of his confidence (vv. 4–6), "I now think of as **loss**"[38] (v. 7). He has "written them off" and, indeed, is still "writing them off" (v. 8). The only profit[39] that he now takes is Christ (v. 8); his overriding interest now is to know Christ, to be in him and to be like him (vv. 8–10). As he later tells Timothy, "Godliness with contentment [the contentment that one finds in Christ] paid the **best dividend**[40] of all" (1 Tim 6:6).

BANKING

In Paul's day banks were a well-established and integral part of government and business life. Under the Ptolemys a network of royal banks had spread across Egypt, with a central bank in Alexandria, provincial banks in all district capitals, and branches in smaller towns. Some private banks also functioned under state control. Thousands were employed in the banking industry. Similar developments had also taken place in most of the Greek city-states. Roman banks of the second and first centuries BCE appear to have been smaller and to have offered less in the way of services to their customers than did the Egyptian banks.[41] Much of what was done elsewhere by banks was done in Roman society by the *equites* and other such men of wealth.[42] Nevertheless, the banks had their role, facilitating bills of exchange and so on. The so-called *permutatio,* a method of clearing between banks in and outside Rome, allowed banks to make payments to provincials, and vice versa, without the actual transfer of money.[43] Cicero, for example, availed himself of this service when providing for his son's education in Athens.[44] As the empire spread, so did the Roman banking system (with local variations).

There was, however, no significant increase in the range of its products, except that by the second or third century CE the payment of interest on investment accounts appears to have become normal practice.[45]

In earlier times temples had functioned as banks, and some continued to do so, offering their services alongside other financial institutions.[46] In Paul's day the temple of Artemis at Ephesus appears to have been used as a depository by both individuals and corporations, most notably by the city itself. It is possible that the temple functioned as the treasury of the city of Ephesus, receiving income on its behalf and making payments. Certainly the sources give little indication that the city had its own department of finance.[47] An inscription from the time of Claudius tells how one city official siphoned off the vast wealth of the temple by corrupting its priests.[48] Ironically, at just about this time a charge was laid (or at least hinted at) against certain Christians in Ephesus of "robbing the temple" and "blaspheming the goddess" (see Acts 19:37). Interestingly, the city boss was quick to quash these accusations. He may not have relished the prospect of a closer inquiry into the temple's affairs.

In his letter to the Ephesians Paul speaks of the church as a temple (Eph 2:19–22) and employs the metaphor of riches more often than in any other of his letters. He could hardly have been unaware of the wealth of the Artemisium and may have been particularly struck by it. Time and again, he assures his Christian readers in Ephesus of their own "**immeasurable riches**"[49] in Christ (Eph 1:7, 18; 2:7; 3:8, 16). And it was to them, or at least to those of their number "who were rich in this present world," that he later gave this advice: "Be rich [rather] in good deeds" (1 Tim 6:18). In this way, he said, mixing his metaphors, they would "**treasure up**"[50] for themselves "a fine foundation" for what lay ahead (6:19). He meant that good deeds done in the present—their practice of love—would enlarge their capacity for love and for life in the hereafter, "the life that is truly life," as he calls it, whose author is love.[51] On a similar note, enlisting another metaphor of financial growth, Paul expresses his hope that the Philippians' gift to him would be credited to their account in God's ledger with **interest accruing**[52] (Phil 4:17).

Paul speaks of "treasuring up" in Rom 2:5, in the negative sense of adding entry to entry on the debit side of the ledger, in his warning to those who expect forgiveness without expressing repentance. They are **treasuring up**[53] wrath, he says, for themselves on the day of God's wrath. He uses the same verb in its literal sense in 1 Cor 16:2 and 2 Cor 12:14, with reference to the collection. Behind the latter verse there probably stands an unkind suggestion that Paul had his eye on the money himself. He met this slur with the maxim that the children (in this case, the Corinthian Christians) do not "treasure up" for the parents (Paul), but the parents for the children. It was not for himself, he assured them, that he wanted the money. So far was he from any such thought that he would gladly **spend**[54] and be spent[55] to the uttermost on their behalf (v. 15).

Finally, employing what has been described as a "figure from banking,"[56] the apostle again writes to Ephesus, **"depositing"**[57] with Timothy, as he puts it, a number of important instructions. "Follow these," he says, and you will be fully equipped to "fight the good fight," that is, to exercise an effective ministry in that city (1 Tim 1:18–19). At the end of the letter he again calls on Timothy to guard the deposit (6:20; cf. the "good deposit" of 2 Tim 1:14). Here he is referring to the truth of the gospel itself on which the church had been founded, not to his earlier instructions concerning church polity. He must maintain the integrity of the gospel at all costs but not "guard" it in the sense of keeping it hidden from others. On the contrary, he is to pass the truth on, "depositing" the gospel, as he had received it, with other "trustworthy people," who, in their turn, would transmit it to others (2 Tim 2:2).

One more reference to a "deposit" is found in this correspondence: "I know whom I have trusted and I am convinced that he is able to guard my deposit until [*eis*, with a view to] that day" (2 Tim 1:12). Who has deposited what and with whom? Is the deposit something that God has entrusted to Paul? Or Paul to God? Or Paul to Christ? The antecedent of the pronoun "whom" *(hō)* in the statement "I know whom I have trusted" is not expressed in the immediate context; both God and Christ have been named in the preceding verses. But since there has been some emphasis on God's power in verses 6–8, it seems that God the Father is in view in this verse. And it seems to be Paul who has deposited. God is certainly the one who is doing the guarding, and this idiom surely demands that God be guarding something entrusted *to* rather than *by* God. Moreover, Paul's reference to "my deposit" *(tēn parathēkēn mou)* and his expressions of trust[58] fit this view better. The same is true of his eschatological reference to "that day."[59] As to the deposit, it must be his life—his eternal well-being, which stands or falls on his commitment to Christ.[60] Bengel aptly sums up the matter: "Paul, on the point of his departure, had two deposits, one to be committed to the Lord and the other to Timothy."[61] The apostle had no doubt about the security of the first, and he hoped that the second would be in good hands.

NOTES

1. Βεβαιόω: "To confirm, establish, secure," as a legal term "to guarantee" the validity of a purchase, "to establish or confirm" a title, etc. Cf. Rom 15:8; 1 Cor 1:6, 8; Col 2:3; see A. Deissmann, *Bible Studies* (Edinburgh: T&T Clark, 1901), 104–9. From βέβαιος (adjective) "firm, secure, sure" (esp. "in the sense of a legally guaranteed security," ibid., 109); cf. Rom 4:16; 2 Cor 1:7. See also βεβαίωσις (noun) "confirmation," frequently in the papyri of a guarantee in a business transaction (see Deissmann, *Bible Studies*, 104ff.); cf. Phil 1:7.

2. For this use of εἰς "into," see Matt 28:19; Acts 8:16; 19:3 (2x), 5; Rom 6:3; 1 Cor 1:13, 15; 10:2; 12:13; Gal 3:27; for ἐν "in," see Acts 10:48; 1 Cor 6:11.

3. Χρίω (found only here in Paul): "To anoint." This is best seen as a general reference to all believers, although he speaks only of "us" and no longer of "us together with you" (see further ch. 8, n. 9). This and the following two participles (all three participles are aorists) should probably be understood as referring broadly to the same event—the beginning of Christian life. This word in particular suggests that all Christians begin their new life with a commission; i.e., from the outset, all have a ministry given by God. Appointment to a theocratic office in Israel (prophet, priest, judge, king) was generally marked by a literal anointing, from which this is a metaphor.

4. Σφραγίζω: "To seal," in Paul in Rom 15:28 (see ch. 8, n. 43); 2 Cor 1:22; 11:10; Eph 1:13; 4:30. For the noun σφραγίς "a seal," see ch. 1, n. 62.

5. E.g., 1 Kgs 21:8; Dan 6:17.

6. E.g., Deut 32:34; Job 14:17; Isa 8:16; Dan 12:4.

7. See, e.g., MM and Deissmann, *Bible Studies*, 238–39.

8. Galen, *Mix.* 9.2.

9. How should the repeated "us" of 2 Cor 1:22–23 be interpreted? Does it still imply the "together with you" of v. 21, or is Paul now restricting his comments to himself and his ministerial colleagues? I have assumed the former (see ch. 8, n. 3), taking what he says in these verses as applicable to believers in general.

10. This exegesis takes account of the fact that the two participles of v. 22 ("who sealed us and put") are bound together under the one definite article. Indeed, A. Plummer (*Second Epistle of St Paul to the Corinthians* [Edinburgh: T&T Clark, 1915], 41) links the Spirit (in sense, not syntactically) with all three aorist participles: "The Spirit is the anointing, the sealing, and the first instalment of eternal life; and the three metaphors are perhaps meant to form a climax."

11. Many commentators mention baptism in their discussion of these verses as the "outward and visible sign" of our "sealing," since that rite was later spoken of sometimes in these terms. See, e.g., the discussion in R. P. Martin, *2 Corinthians* (Waco, Tex.: Word, 1986), 28.

12. Ἀρραβών: Sometimes spelled ἀραβών, a word of Semitic, probably Phoenician, origin, "an earnest," part payment in advance for security, a first installment. In the phrase τὸν ἀρραβῶνα τοῦ πνεύματος, I take the genitive to be one of apposition; the earnest *is* the Spirit. See also ch. 3, n. 16.

13. See F. Lyall, *Slaves, Citizens, Sons: Legal Metaphors in the Epistles* (Grand Rapids: Zondervan, 1984), 145–48. On the Roman law, see further Gaius, *Inst.* 3.139; F. de Zulueta, *The Roman Law of Sale* (Oxford: Clarendon, 1966), 22–24; W. W. Buckland, *A Textbook of Roman Law from Augustus to Justinian* (Cambridge: Cambridge University Press, 1963), 481–82; H. F. Jolowicz, *Historical Introduction to the Study of Roman Law* (Cambridge: Cambridge University Press, 1952), 525–26; H. F. Jolowicz and B. Nicholas, *Historical Introduction to the Study of Roman Law* (Cambridge: Cambridge University Press, 1972), 290–91; J. A. Crook, *Law and Life in Rome* (London: Thames & Hudson, 1967), 220–21; J. A. C. Thomas, *Textbook of Roman Law* (Amsterdam: North Holland, 1973), 280–81. On the Greek law, see F. Pringsheim, *The Greek Law of Sale* (Weimar: Bohlaus Nachfolger, 1950), 333–439 (includes a comparison with the Roman law); J. W. Jones, *The Law and Legal Theory of the Greeks: An Introduction* (Oxford: Clarendon, 1956), 229–31. MM gives a number of instances of the Greek practice of a "down payment." For example, a woman selling a cow received 1,000 drachmas as ἀρραβών (97 CE); a second- or third-century CE letter writer reports: "Regarding Lampon the mouse catcher, I paid him for you as earnest money [ἀρραβών] eight drachmas in order that he might catch the mice while they are with young"; and in 237 CE a number of dancing girls were hired for a village festival and were paid an advance by way of earnest money

(ὑπὲρ ἀρραβῶνος), which was to be taken into account in the final reckoning of what was owed to them.

14. This is an awkward concept to apply to a salvation that is not, in any sense, "earned."

15. See p. 123 and ch. 5, n. 118.

16. Ὀφειλή: "A debt" (e.g., Rom 13:7; 1 Cor 7:3); ὀφείλημα "that which is owed, a debt" (e.g., Rom 4:4); ὀφειλέτης "a debtor" (e.g., Rom 1:14; 8:12; 15:27; Gal 5:3); ὀφείλω "to owe, to be a debtor" (e.g., Rom 13:8; 15:1, 27; 1 Cor 5:10; 7:3, 36; 9:10; 11:7, 10; 2 Cor 12:11, 14; Eph 5:28; 2 Thess 1:3; 2:13; Phlm 18). See also the discussion of ἐλλογάω, ch. 7, n. 28.

17. For a further discussion of this passage, see p. 92 and ch. 4, n. 60.

18. Thessalonica was the first major city to which Paul had come on his missionary journeys. The fact that the gospel had taken root and was flourishing here was a matter of great encouragement to him, especially as he was now writing from Corinth, perhaps early in his stay in that city and at a time when he was oppressed by misgivings about the Corinthian mission (see Acts 18:9–11). This may account for the special sense of obligation that he felt to give thanks for the Thessalonians. Nowhere else does he employ this form of thanksgiving ("we owe it to thank").

19. Paul's phrase is Ἕλλησίν τε καὶ βαρβάροις "to Greeks and to barbarians," but "barbarians" did not connote quite what it does to us. They were people whose speech, from the point of view of the Greeks, sounded like "bar bar." Barbarians might be as civilized as Greeks, but their language seemed odd. Paul means by the phrase "the whole human race."

20. See p. 63 (on Gal 4:8–6:10) for the distinction between the "moral law" and the "ritual or cultic law." Cf. also pp. 247–48 on Eph 5:2ff.

21. In using these metaphors, Paul presumably had at least the layman's awareness of contemporary accounting procedures (see, e.g., G. E. M. de Ste. Croix, "Greek and Roman Accounting," in *Studies in the History of Accounting* [ed. A. C. Littleton and B. S. Yamey; Homewood, Ill.: Association of University Teachers of Accounting/American Accounting Association, 1956], 14–74; and R. H. Macve, "Some Glosses on Greek and Roman Accounting," in *Crux: Essays Presented to G. E. M. de Ste. Croix on His 75th Birthday* [ed. P. A. Cartledge and F. D. Harvey; London: Imprint Academic, 1985], 233–64). At the same time, his thinking may have been colored by the ancient notion of the "book of remembrance." If oriental monarchs could keep files on their people (see, e.g., Esth 6:1ff.), why not God? Thus God was conceived of as maintaining a book in which he noted all the good and evil that people had done (e.g., Ps 56:8; Isa 65:6; Mal 3:16; see W. S. Sanday and A. C. Headlam, *The Epistle to the Romans* (Edinburgh: T&T Clark, 1905), 100; see also ch. 5, n. 87.

22. Τὸ καθ' ἡμῶν χειρόγραφον: Perhaps the root idea of κατά could be brought in "the document that sent us *down*." Χειρόγραφος (from χείρ "a hand" and γράφω "to write"): Strictly an adjective, "written by hand," but used as a substantive (neuter, χειρόγραφον), "a handwriting," very common in the papyri for a certificate of debt. See Deissmann, *Bible Studies*, 247. Such a χειρόγραφον Gabael had given to Tobit, acknowledging that he held ten talents of his, and Tobit had subsequently entrusted it to his son, Tobias, in order that he might receive the money (Tob 4:1, 20; cf. 9:2, 5). E. Lohse ("χείρ, κτλ," *TDNT* 9:424–37, here 435) suggests that Paul has in mind the familiar Jewish idea of God as keeping an account of each person's debt, which God calls in through his angels (at death) and for which he imposes the appropriate penalty. Cf. Rabbi Akiba's illustration of God as a shopkeeper (*b. ʾAbot* 3.20). Others have seen this as a legal metaphor, the χειρόγραφον being an indictment presented at the heavenly court. See, e.g., A. J. Bandstra, *The Law and the*

Elements of the World: An Exegetical Study in Aspects of Paul's Teaching (Grand Rapids: Eerdmans, 1964), 158–63.

23. On ἐγὼ ἀποτίσω, see ch. 7, n. 29.

24. Δόγμα (from δοκέω, "to be of opinion," itself from δόκος "opinion," and that from δέχομαι "to receive"): (1) "an opinion," (2) a public "decree, ordinance," as of the emperor in Luke 2:1, of the apostles and elders in Acts 16:4, and of the Jewish law in Eph 2:15. The latter is decisive for the interpretation of Col 2:14 that I have adopted. The word is used in Col 2:14 in the dative (τοῖς δόγμασιν), and it is difficult to know what precisely to make of the case. It could be understood as instrumental: "The document was against us [i.e., it condemned us] *by means of* its ordinances." But perhaps the dative has the more unusual sense of indicating the contents of the χειρόγραφον: "the document *comprising* the ordinances." This is the sense in which I have taken it. To object that the law was not written by "the debtors," as a χειρόγραφον should strictly have been, is to ask too much of the metaphor. See ch. 2, n. 85.

25. See, e.g., Exod 24:3; Deut 27:14–26.

26. See Rom 2:14–15.

27. I have interpreted the "us" of καθ' ἡμῶν "against us" in the broad sense of the human race, although it is possible that Paul meant "us Jews." On the effect of the law in highlighting human sinfulness and thereby condemning us, see, e.g., Rom 4:15; 5:20; Gal 3:19–22.

28. J. Jeremias, *The Central Message of the New Testament* (London: SCM, 1965), 37.

29. R. Yates ("Colossians 2:14: Metaphor of Forgiveness," *Bib* 71 [1990]: 248–56) lists six different interpretations: the law of Moses, a pact with Satan, an IOU from mankind to God, the heavenly book (see ch. 5, n. 87), penitential stellae, and theophanic visions.

30. Ἐξαλείφω: (1) "to plaster, wash or wipe over," (2) "to wipe off, wipe out." Found only here in Paul.

31. The ink was generally made of soot and gum and did not, as with modern inks, eat into the texture of the paper. MM, in its discussion of ἐξαλείφω, refers to a third-century BCE papyrus in which the writer complains, "I could not read your letter because it had been obliterated" (διὰ τὸ ἐξηλεῖφθαι), and to the common practice of "washing out" the ink on papyrus so that the sheet might be used for other purposes. See also G. Milligan (*The New Testament Documents: Their Origin and Early History* [London: Macmillan, 1913], 16), who cites a reference to a decree that had been "neither washed out nor written over."

32. This truth is reinforced by Paul's further statement that "he [God] has taken it out of the way" (v. 14, αὐτὸ ἦρκεν ἐκ τοῦ μέσου). The verb αἴρω "to take up, take away" was used by the Baptist of Jesus, "The Lamb of God *takes away* the sin of the world" (John 1:29). There it is in the present tense, here in the perfect, the tense emphasizing the permanence of the removal. The bond has been cancelled and removed from the file, so to speak, and that remains the case. It cannot be re-presented. The phrase "out of the way" (ἐκ τοῦ μέσου) was a common expression for "the decisive removal of a certificate of indebtedness" (so P. T. O'Brien, *Colossians, Philemon* [Waco, Tex.: Word, 1982], 126).

33. So, e.g., J. Jeremias (*Central Message,* 37): "Don't you see . . . that there is a hand which removes this *titulus* [written by Pilate] and replaces it with another one, with lines of writing crowded upon it? You will have to draw near if you want to decipher this new *titulus*—it is your sins and mine that are inscribed upon it." The thought of the *titulus* may have conditioned Paul's expression in Gal 3:1, where he speaks of Christ as having been "placarded as one who has been crucified." The verb is προγράφω: (1) "to write before," Rom 15:4; Eph 3:3, (2) "to write in public, placard," Gal 3:1, (3) = ζωγραφέω "to portray."

34. This is the argument proposed by O. A. Blanchette, "Does the *Cheiro-graphon* of Col. 2:14 Represent Christ Himself?" *CBQ* 23 (1961): 306–12. Support for this view comes from *Gos. Truth* 20.22–28, which speaks of Jesus "wearing a book" as his own and as being nailed to the cross and affixing the ordinance of the Father to that cross. That the "book" is the "sinful flesh" is made clear in 20.34: "Having divested himself of these perishable rags [his flesh], he clothed himself with incorruptibility, which it is impossible for anyone to take away from him."

35. Λογίζομαι (from λόγος "a word, saying, account, etc."): Basically, "to think logically," applied (1) properly of numerical calculation, "to count, reckon," but also (2) without reference to numbers, "to reckon, take into account, consider, suppose." As a metaphor, Paul appears to have retained the commercial sense in the following: Rom 2:26; 4:3–6, 9–11, 22–24; 9:8; 2 Cor 5:19; 12:6; Gal 3:6; 2 Tim 4:16, where the sense is "to reckon to the credit of," and Rom 4:8; 2 Cor 10:7, where it is "to reckon to the debit of." Notice in 2 Cor 10:7 the bookkeeping terms: "If someone [Paul is referring to his opponents] thinks that he belongs to Christ, *let him make a counter entry* [in his ledger, λογιζέσθω πάλιν] to the effect that we also are Christ's." Πάλιν was the Greek equivalent of the Latin *per contra* "on the opposite side of the ledger." Beyond this, λογίζομαι is used in a general sense (without particular reference to debit or credit) in Rom 2:3; 3:28; 6:11; 8:18, 36; 14:14; 1 Cor 4:1; 13:5, 11; 2 Cor 3:5; 10:2 (2x), 11; 11:5; Phil 3:13; 4:8.

36. Ἐλογίσθη αὐτῷ εἰς δικαιοσύνην: "(Faith) was reckoned to him for righteousness." Εἰς, as often, should be understood as "for." Cf. the commercial phrase εἰς λόγον "to the account of" (see ch. 8, n. 52).

37. Κέρδος: "Profit, gain," in the papyri used of interest on capital; cf. Phil 1:21; Titus 1:11. The word is used here (Phil 3:7) in the plural (κέρδη). Humanly speaking, he had enjoyed many advantages (gains) in terms of position and prospects. He had been the rising star of Gamaliel and the Sanhedrin and the like. All these advantages, however, he now totals up as a single loss. For the verb κερδαίνω, see ch. 8, n. 39.

38. Ζημία: Originally, "disadvantage," but in a commercial context (as commonly), "damage, loss, forfeit," the debit side of the ledger. W. Hendriksen, *Philippians* (Grand Rapids: Baker, 1962), 162, has drawn attention to the interesting parallel in the sea voyage of Acts 27, where the only other occurrences of ζημία in the NT are found. The cargo of wheat on board the ship bound for Italy represented potential gain for many. Yet it had to be thrown into the sea; otherwise "great loss" (πολλῆς ζημίας, v. 10) would have resulted, in terms not only of the ship but also of those on board (cf. v. 21). Cf. the verb ζημιόω "to damage," and in the passive (as in Phil 3:8), "to suffer loss, forfeit, lose." Cf. 1 Cor 3:15; 2 Cor 7:9.

39. Κερδαίνω: "To gain, make a profit." Elsewhere in Paul in 1 Cor 9:19, 20 (2x), 21, 22, 22, where it is used as a missionary term, "to win." In Phil 3:8 it is clearly a commercial metaphor. G. F. Hawthorne describes it as "a strange expression that must be understood in the light of the imagery Paul uses throughout this section of a profit and loss system and the balancing of accounts. The verb κερδαίνω is a play on the noun κέρδη. Paul has given up all other forms of 'gain,' in order that he might get the true 'gain' which is Christ" (*Philippians* [Waco, Tex.: Word, 1983], 139).

40. Πορισμὸς μέγας: Πορισμός (from πορίζω "to procure") (1) "a providing," (2) "a means of gain." Only in 1 Tim 6:5–6 in the NT. The whole section 1 Tim 6:3–10 should be studied for Paul's warnings against an obsession with wealth. In so wealthy a city as Ephesus the temptation would be very great for Christians to fall in with the ethos of the place and to set their own sights on the acquisition of wealth, even Christian teachers using their position as a means to that end (see 1 Tim 6:5). For a further discussion of this passage, see pp. 35, 197, and ch. 9, n. 47.

41. See F. G. B. Millar, "The World of the Golden Ass," *JRS* 71 (1981): 70, 72. The standard monograph on Greek banks remains R. Bogaert, *Banques et banquiers dans les cités grecques* (Leiden: A. W. Sijthoff, 1968). See also Bogaert, "Gelt (Geldwirtschaft)," *RAC* 9 (1976): 797–907, esp. 862–907. Nothing of its scope has been written for the Roman world, but see W. L. Westermann, "Warehousing and Trapezite Banking in Antiquity," *JEBH* 3 (1930–1931): 30–54; F. M. Heichelheim, "Banks," *OCD*, 160–61; P. Garnsey and R. Saller, *The Roman Empire* (London: Gerald Duckworth, 1987), 52; W. E. Thompson, "Insurance and Banking," in *Civilization of the Ancient Mediterranean: Greece and Rome* (ed. M. Grant and R. Kitzinger; New York: Scribner's, 1988), 2:829–36. From their name, the *argentarii*, it appears that bankers evolved out of money changers.

42. See, e.g., Plutarch (*Cat. Maj.* 21.5–6); Pliny (*Ep.* 3.19); Dio Chrysostom (*Disc.* 7.104).

43. Money was transferred under seal, and in Rom 15:28 Paul uses the technical term for sealing sacks of money for delivery: σφραγισάμενος αὐτοῖς τὸν καρπὸν τοῦτον "having sealed to them this fruit," i.e., "having safely delivered to them the proceeds of the collection." See Deissmann, *Bible Studies*, 238–39; and H. D. Betz, *2 Corinthians 8 and 9: A Commentary on Two Administrative Letters of the Apostle Paul* (Philadelphia: Fortress, 1985), 141. On σφραγίζω, see ch. 8, n. 4, and on καρπός, ch. 8, n. 52.

44. Cicero, *Att.* 12.24, 27.

45. "The Principate saw no major developments in the Roman law of banking. The only sign that lawyers were shifting their position to take account of commercial realities is in the rather halting movements they made towards recognising deposit banking as a specific institution. *Depositum* was traditionally gratuitous; the receiver held the object on trust and returned it on demand. But texts of Antonine and Severan jurists recognise an investment account at a bank as a category of *depositum* and admit the payment of interest to the depositor" (Garnsey and Saller, *Roman Empire*, 55; see *Dig.* 16.3.28; 24; 26.11).

46. The only temple in ancient Greece for which sufficient evidence exists to reconstruct its finances over time is the temple of Apollo at Delos, which derived revenues from investments, real-estate rentals, and loans. See J. H. Kent, "The Temple Estates of Delos, Rheneia, and Mykonos," *Hesperia* 17 (1948): 243–338. For the financial operations of temple banks in general, see Bogaert, *Banques et banquiers*, 279–304. On the Roman institution of *depositum* into temple banks, see J. Ranft, "Depositum," *RAC* 3 (1957): 778–84.

47. See W. M. Ramsay, "Ephesus," *DB* 1:724. This appears to have been the case in Athens, where the Parthenon housed, among other things, the city treasury. In Rome, the temple of Saturn on the Capitol seems to have served a similar purpose. See Tacitus, *Ann.* 3.51, and H. N. Couch, *The Treasures of the Greeks and Romans* (Menasha, Wis.: George Banta, 1929).

48. See A. H. M. Jones, *The Greek City* (Oxford: Clarendon, 1940), 181.

49. His phrase is τὸ ἀνεξιχνίαστον πλοῦτος τοῦ Χριστοῦ (Eph 3:8). Πλοῦτος (masculine and neuter): "Riches, wealth" is used of literal wealth in 1 Tim 6:17 and metaphorically of moral or spiritual qualities in Rom 2:4; 9:23; 11:12 (2x), 33; 2 Cor 8:2; Eph 1:7, 18; 2:7; 3:8, 16; Phil 4:19; Col 1:27; 2:2. Ἀνεξιχνίαστος (α privative plus a verbal adjective formed from ἐξιχνιάζω "to trace out by footsteps," itself from ἐκ and ἴχνος "a track") "that cannot be tracked" and so "unsearchable, unfathomable, immeasurable, inexhaustible." The word first appears in Job 5:9; 9:10, from where Paul probably got it. Nowhere else in the NT except Rom 11:23.

50. Ἀποθησαυρίζω (from ἀπο and θησαυρίζω, see ch. 8, n. 53): A late and literary word, "to treasure up, store away," found only here in the NT.

51. See further pp. 16–17.

52. In thanking the Philippians for their gift, Paul explains that he did not look for this kind of support for himself (although he maintained the principle that the church should support its ministry; see, e.g., ch. 7, n. 19). He appreciated what they had done, but it was more important for them than for him. (Cf. Acts 20:35: "It is more blessed to give than to receive.") He says, "I am looking for *the fruit that goes on growing* to your account." Καρπός is lit. "fruit" as from trees, etc. (see ch. 2, n. 73), but in the light of its cognates, the noun καρπεία and the verb καρπίζω (neither in the NT), and in a context such as this, in which other commercial terms are employed, καρπός must be understood as "profit" or "credit" (see MM). It is qualified by the present active participle πλεονάζοντα, of the verb πλεονάζω (from πλέον "more"): (1) intransitive, "to abound, increase" (e.g., Rom 5:20; 6:1; 2 Cor 4:15; 8:15; Phil 4:17; 2 Thess 1:3), (2) transitive, "make to abound" (e.g., 1 Thess 3:12). The present tense of the participle gives the sense "that goes on increasing," as though Paul had in mind compound interest. Finally, we have the phrase εἰς λόγον ὑμῶν. Εἰς λόγον was a technical term used in business to signify "to the account of." Cf. Phil 4:15, and see Thucydides, *Hist.* 3.46; Polybius, *Hist.* 11.28.8; P.Oxy. 275.19, 21. See also P. Marshall, *Enmity in Corinth: Social Conventions in Paul's Relations with the Corinthians* (Tübingen: Mohr, 1987), 157–64; G. Kittel, "λέγω, κτλ," *TDNT* 4:69–143, here 103–4.

53. Θησαυρίζω: "To lay up, store up." In Paul in Rom 2:5; 1 Cor 16:2; 2 Cor 12:14. For the compound ἀποθησαυρίζω, see ch. 8, n. 50. Cf. θησαυρός: (1) "a place of safekeeping, a treasure chest, a treasury, a storehouse," (2) "a treasure," metaphorically of knowledge or wisdom in 2 Cor 4:7; Col 2:3.

54. Δαπανάω: An old verb, (1) "to spend, expend," (2) "to consume, squander." Found only here in Paul.

55. Ἐκδαπανάω: A late compound making a strengthened form of δαπανάω (see the preceding note), "to spend wholly," and in the passive, as here, "to spend oneself wholly." Found only here in the NT. The juxtaposition of this notion of spending with that of saving up in the previous verse suggests a deliberate play on the words.

56. So A. T. Robertson, *Word Pictures in the New Testament* (New York: Richard R. Smith, 1930–1933; repr. Nashville, Tenn.: Broadman & Holman, 1973), 4:565.

57. Παρατίθημι: An old and common verb, (1) in the active voice, "to place beside, set before" (e.g., 1 Cor 10:27), (2) in the middle voice, "to have set before one" and so "to deposit" (e.g., 1 Tim 1:18; 2 Tim 2:2). See the noun παραθήκη "a deposit, trust," discussed on p. 186.

58. Πεπίστευκα καὶ πέπεισμαι: "I have believed and am persuaded." Both verbs common in Paul (πιστεύω "to believe, trust, entrust" [52x]; πείθω "to persuade, be persuaded, trust" [23x]). Notice the perfect tense in each case: His trust has not wavered. He remains convinced.

59. For the contrary view, see, e.g., J. R. W. Stott (*Guard the Gospel* [Leicester, U.K.: Inter-Varsity Press, 1973], 46), who argues on the grounds of consistency that if the metaphor is of the gospel in v. 14, it must also be so in v. 12. "The sense, then, is this. The deposit is 'mine,' Paul could say, because Christ has committed it to him. Yet Paul was persuaded that Christ would himself keep it safe 'until that Day' when he would have to give an account of his stewardship." See G. W. Knight (*The Pastoral Epistles* [Grand Rapids: Eerdmans, 1992], 379–80) for a survey of the literature and of the arguments on both sides.

60. Cf 1 Pet 4:19: "Let them deposit [middle voice of παρατίθημι; see ch. 8, n. 57] their lives with a trustworthy Creator."

61. J. A. Bengel, *Gnomon Novi Testamenti* (Edinburgh: T&T Clark, 1877).

CHAPTER

Travel

REASONS FOR TRAVEL

In Paul's world the movement of people was as extensive as the movement of goods. The emperor might be traveling with his entourage, making **an official visit**,[1] with dignitaries **coming out to meet**[2] him (a scenario that supplied Paul and others with metaphors for Christ's coming). Military leaders and their troops often marched on important (or less important) business.[3] Roads were peopled by envoys from the provinces, couriers of the *cursus publicus,* the imperial post,[4] and other civil servants. Merchants traveled in search of sales or supplies,[5] and itinerant craftsmen, seasonal laborers, and actors traveled in search of work. Cynics begged their way from town to town, and wealthy Greek Sophists traveled in style.[6] Poets such as Martial traveled in search of patrons. Oculists, doctors, astrologers, and miracle workers went in search of clients. On the roads could be found students, runaway slaves, missionaries of all sorts (including Christians like Paul), litigants, mourners in a funeral procession,[7] courtesans,[8] migrants and exiles, members of the guild of traveling athletes, and pilgrims.[9] The sick journeyed in search of health, whether to a shrine of Asclepius, to drink medicinal waters, or to breathe fresh country air.[10] Some were in search of an oracle, as was Tiberius when he met groups of wandering priests and a host of quacks.[11] Some traveled to satisfy their curiosity (such as Polybius, Pliny the Elder, Plutarch, and Cleombrotus; according to Plutarch, Cleombrotus "wandered about Egypt" and sailed "far down the Red Sea"[12]). Others roamed merely for pleasure (such as Pliny the Younger[13]). All of these and many more thronged the roads or plied the sea routes of the central sea, which was a more comfortable yet no less dangerous way to travel. The travelers attracted many other people, who provided the range of services de-manded by travelers.[14]

People's mobility made the cities (Rome especially, but also Antioch in Syria, Alexandria, Ephesus, and Corinth) great cosmopolitan melting pots. Syrians and Greeks, Spaniards and Africans, and scores of other na-tions and races, not least among them the Jews, were drawn to these cen-ters. They could be found mixed together in the same offices and warehouses, the same workshops and shops, the same government de-partments and private households. The New Testament itself bears wit-ness to the mobility of people in the ancient world: Lydia sells cloth in Philippi, six hundred miles from Thyatira, her home (Acts 16:14); Aquila travels from Pontus on the Black Sea to Rome and from there with his wife, Priscilla, to Corinth and Ephesus (Acts 18:2, 19); Apollos, the Alex-andrian scholar, arrives in Ephesus, transfers to Corinth, and then goes back to Ephesus (Acts 18:24–28; 1 Cor 16:12); Phoebe sets off some-where (Rome? Ephesus? Rom 16:1–2); Erastus and Timothy are sent from Ephesus to Macedonia (Acts 19:22); Stephanus with Achaicus and Fortunatus travel from Corinth to Ephesus (1 Cor 16:15–18). So too do Chloe's people (1 Cor 1:11) and perhaps Sosthenes, if he is the person of that name in Acts 18:17 (1 Cor 1:1). Then there are the businessmen whom James takes to task for their restless quest for money, which takes them from one place to another (Jas 4:13). And Paul himself, of course. Paul's journeys took him to almost every province and major city between Syria and Spain.[15]

LETTERS OF RECOMMENDATION

Most travelers carry certain documents. A Roman citizen, such as Paul, might find it useful to have evidence of his (or her) status,[16] and someone relocating to a new city might take with him (or have sent ahead) a letter of introduction. The Papyri Oxyrhynchus[17] include six ex-amples of such letters, and there are seven in the New Testament, as well as a number of other references to them.[18] In 2 Cor 3:1–3 Paul speaks fig-uratively of the Corinthians as his **letter of recommendation**.[19] His op-ponents, who had come to Corinth armed with such documentation, appear to have charged Paul with an unwarranted, perhaps overweening commendation of self (v. 1).[20] He denied the charge. He, who had first brought the gospel to Corinth, needed no such commendation either to or from this church. But if such a commendation *were* needed, the Corin-thians themselves would be his "letter" (vv. 2–3).[21] Their very lives (sig-nificantly changed, for all their many failings) would speak louder than any words penned on papyrus or inscribed in stone—the latter a reference to the self-serving monuments that could be found in any city of that time and not least in Corinth itself (cf. v. 1).[22] To be precise, the Corinthians were Christ's letter, not Paul's. It was Christ (in and through "the Spirit of the living God") who had changed them and had made them what they were. Paul was merely the "scribe" (a lesser but important role), doing as his master dictated (v. 3).

SEA TRAVEL

Sea travel was common. The wall paintings of Pompeii and Herculaneum provide some idea of the ships that plied the rivers and seas of the Roman world.[23] One of the most distinguishing features of these ships was the stern shaped like the stem. Both swept high and often terminated in a structure like the backward-bent neck of a goose.[24] Vessels were of all sizes; some of them were quite large and fast.[25]

Lucian describes a grain ship from Egypt called the *Isis Geminiana*, which was driven off course for seventy days by unusually severe summer storms until it reached the safety of Piraeus. It was 177 feet long, a quarter as wide, and 44 feet deep from deck to keel. Estimates of its tonnage vary from twelve hundred (about the size of Nelson's *Victory*) to nineteen hundred. It was equipped with flame-colored sails and an anchor with windlass and capstan. The Athenians optimistically estimated that its cargo of wheat was enough to supply Attica for a year. "And all this," says Lucian, "a little old man had kept safe by turning the huge steering oars with a tiny tiller."[26] The image of the helmsman controlling the ship was a favorite way of portraying the statesman's skill in administration and government. Paul uses the term that describes the helmsman's function, "**helmsmanship**,"[27] probably in the metaphorical sense of "administration," in his list of gifts of the Spirit in 1 Cor 12:28. In the light of the popular image of the statesman as "helmsman," it may be assumed that he was speaking of one of the gifts of leadership in the church—the ability to steer the congregation on a safe course, so to speak, avoiding the hidden rocks and negotiating the wild waves of the sea. But did Paul consciously picture church leaders in these terms, or was he simply using an accepted term with no metaphor intended? The same uncertainty attaches to his use of the word "**underrowers**"[28] (1 Cor 4:1).

Merchant vessels, such as the *Isis Geminiana* and the ships on which Paul himself made his voyages,[29] depended chiefly on sail, although the sail was sometimes augmented by the use of long sweeps.[30] Warships carried sail but depended chiefly on oars. Before the invention of the trireme, the standard Greek warship was the penteconter *(pentēkonteros)*, with twenty-five rowers in a single bank on each side. The trireme, introduced in the sixth century BCE, is generally thought to have had three banks of rowers on each side. The later Greek period saw many experiments in multiple-banked warships, two of which, the quadrireme and the quinquereme, were adopted and used with some success by the Romans. These ships appear not to have had more than three banks of rowers but to have increased the number of rowers on each oar, the bottom and second banks sitting and the third, because of the length of the sweeps, probably standing.[31]

The word describing the rowers on the bottom bank, the "under-rowers," came to mean a servant, and Paul employs it in this sense for the apostles in 1 Cor 4:1. Whether he was deliberately drawing an analogy with those toiling in the bilge of a trireme or was not even aware of the origin of the word is open to question. He may have employed the term because it, more than the familiar *diakonos*,[32] expresses the thought of their subordination to God. In the same breath he also names the apostles stewards,[33] thus asserting their authority within "the household of God" while maintaining their servant (or even slave) status vis-à-vis the Master himself.

Paul had considerable experience of the sea. Writing to the Corinthians, even before the events outlined in Acts 27, he could claim, "Three times I have been shipwrecked; a night and a day I have spent adrift on the open sea" (2 Cor 11:25). Clearly he was familiar, at least as an observer, with ships and their handling. He may also have had some hands-on experience. Ship passengers were sometimes recruited to help in an emergency.[34] Having recently disembarked at Miletus, Paul may have been employing as a metaphor the word "to **furl** or **reef [a sail]**"[35] when he assured the Ephesian elders that he had held nothing back from them—he had not shortened sail, as it were—in respect to any facet of the counsel of God (Acts 20:20; cf. v. 27). On another occasion Paul had to speak to Peter about his inconsistent behavior in Antioch. Peter had been eating unreservedly with Gentile Christians, but when some hard-line Jewish Christians arrived, he pulled back. In Paul's words, he "began to trim his sails and to separate himself" from the Gentiles (Gal 2:12).

The familiar sight of seamen casting off the moorings and setting their ship's course for a distant port may have colored Paul's choice of language in Phil 1:23. He was writing from prison, possibly facing death. He could accept or even embrace the prospect of death, but in the interest of others, he thought it better that he continue to live and to serve: "My desire is to **depart**[36]—to let go the rope that holds me to this shore and to ride out with the tide—to be with Christ." The same image, again with reference to his death, is found in 2 Tim 4:6: "The time for my departure[37] has come," he declares. "Departure" was then, as now, a euphemism for death, and Paul may simply have been observing this conventional usage. It is also possible that he deliberately pictures death as a voyage to another shore (or, since the word can also have this meaning, as the folding up of his tent for another trek; see 2 Cor 5:1–5). He may have thought, on other occasions, of new life in Christ as a ship coming into harbor. Three times, in describing the access to God and God's grace that Christ gives us, he uses a word *(prosagōgē)* that was sometimes used of a **haven for ships**[38] (Rom 5:2; Eph 2:18; 3:12).

DANGERS OF SEA TRAVEL

Paul knew only too well the dangers of a journey by sea. Perhaps out of his own experience, his memory of the events described in Acts 27 still fresh,[39] he wrote to the Ephesians urging that they "grow up" as Christians—that they stop being "children," immature, "**tossed to and fro by the waves**,"[40] as it were, "and **whirled about by every wind**"[41] of theological fad (Eph. 4:14). He was thinking, perhaps, of the unsettling effect of the teaching that was currently being aired in Colossae and was looming as a threat to all the churches of that region (the province of Asia). In 2 Thess 2:2 he uses a similar metaphor with reference to another piece of errant theology, namely, that "the day of the Lord had already come." Paul begs the Thessalonians not to be **unsettled**[42] in their mind; that is, they should keep their wits about them, remembering all that he had taught them (v. 5). His expression properly refers to the action of the wind or the waves. It suggests a restless tossing, as of a ship adrift at sea.[43]

Paul also associates troubles at sea with bad doctrine in 1 Tim 1:19 as he urges Timothy to "hold on to faith and a good conscience." The association between faith and conscience is that the one forms the other—faith in Christ sets the boundaries of what we now know to be right and wrong. This is essentially what he says to the Philippians, "Have the same attitude that you see in Christ Jesus" (Phil 2:5), to the Romans, "Be transformed by the renewing of our mind" (Rom 12:2), and to the Ephesians (in a letter that antedates his present letter to Timothy in that city), "Be renewed in the attitude of your mind" (Eph 4:22; cf. Col 3:5–10). Faith and conscience go hand in hand. Faith looks to Christ "out there," and conscience is a contributing factor to his formation "in here." Because faith and conscience are linked, to reject[44] the dictates of our conscience is to run the risk of losing our faith. So, "when the life is corrupt (conscience having been rejected), it engenders a doctrine congenial with it."[45] Thus certain people in the church in Ephesus had, in Paul's words, "made **shipwreck**[46] of their faith"—they had repudiated faith in Christ and conscience in matters of conduct. As Paul saw it, they were no longer Christians. A lesson may be taken from this: if you get rid of the pilot (take Christ from the center of your Christianity), your ship (your Christianity) will run aground. Paul's warning in 1 Tim 6:9, that those who love money are in danger of "**drowning**" in a "sea" of destruction and ruin,[47] is a case in point. Something other than Christ was looming as the dominant interest of their lives, and they were at (spiritual) risk.

LAND TRAVEL

How did Paul get from one place to another when he traveled by land? One passage in Acts hints that he and his colleagues may have been riding on a mule or horse when they made their journey from Philippi to Thessalonica. Had their finances been subject to audit, they could certainly have justified the expenditure. Paul and Silas had been savagely beaten only a day or two earlier and were probably in no shape to travel.[48] Each stage of their journey, Philippi to Amphipolis, Amphipolis to Apollonia, and Apollonia to the Macedonian capital, is approximately thirty miles.[49] If Luke means us to understand from Acts 17:1 that this was the distance covered each day, the party must have had access to horses or mules,[50] thanks possibly to Lydia's generosity.[51] Thirty miles was about as far as a horse could manage in one day. But how the missionaries made their way to Thessalonica—whether mounted or carried or walking—is speculation. The only explicit reference anywhere in the New Testament to Paul's means of getting about occurs in Acts 20:13, which speaks of his going "by foot"[52] from Troas to Assos, and even that reference may not be as clear-cut as it seems. It stands in contrast to his companions' going to Assos by ship, and in this case "by foot" could indicate any means of travel on land.[53] Nevertheless, it seems likely that Paul did go by foot on most occasions. Considering the distances that he covered and the courage and endurance demanded by those many miles,[54] his frequent references to life as a "walk" take on added interest. Indeed, this metaphor may have appealed to Paul because he did so much walking himself.[55]

Paul was by no means the first to have used this figure of speech. It occurs often in the LXX, which more than anything else (or so it seems) dictated Paul's use of the figure.[56] But he made it his own. His letters contain more than thirty references to **walking**[57] as a metaphor for the Christian life. The verb is usually qualified in some way:[58] (1) Sometimes he expresses the distinctiveness of the "walk" (e.g., its "newness" [Rom 6:4] or its different standards from those of the world [Rom 8:4; Eph 5:8]). In 2 Cor 10:2–3 Paul has the expression twice, each time metaphorically, but in each case with a different application. He speaks of some people "who think that we walk according to the flesh [live by the world's standards]. But though we walk in the flesh [live in the world], we do not make war as the flesh does [use the world's ways in our ministry]." (2) Sometimes he mentions distinguishing marks of the "walk," such as "good deeds," "wisdom," "love," "faithfulness," and so on (e.g., Rom 5:7; 13:13; 14:15; 2 Cor 5:7; Eph 5:2, 15; Col 1:10; 4:5; 1 Thess 2:12; cf. Eph 4:1; 1 Thess 4:12), in contrast to former "trespasses and sins" (e.g., 1 Cor 3:3; 2 Cor 4:2; Eph 2:1–2; 4:17; 5:15; Col 3:5–7; 2 Thess 3:6, 11). (3) Sometimes he names its dynamic. The Christian "walk" is only possible because of Christ. It begins with Christ and can continue only with Christ. This is the point of Paul's extraordinary mixture of metaphors in Col 2:6: "Since you have accepted Christ Jesus as Lord, go on walking in him [present imperative—a command to make this walk their life's work], keeping your roots deep in him, building your lives upon him, becoming stronger in [your] faith [in him]."

Other ways of saying that Christianity is Christ from first to last are the expressions to "walk in the Spirit" (or perhaps the dative in Gal 5:16 is instrumental—to "walk by means of the Spirit's power"; cf. v. 26, "live in or by the Spirit") and to "**keep in step**[59] with the Spirit" (v. 26). The Spirit's whole purpose is to focus our attention on Christ and to make us more and more like him as we move from our beginning in him to whatever God has in store at the end. If Christ is the road we travel ("the way and the truth and the life," John 14:6), it is essential that we **walk a straight line** (Gal 2:14), avoiding any deviation from that road. Paul himself may have coined the Greek word used here to express the idea of "straightforward, unwavering, and sincere conduct in contrast with the pursuing of a crooked, wavering, and more or less insincere course."[60] The metaphor refers to the incident in Antioch in which Peter had not acted well in his dealings with Gentile Christians and Paul had had to do some straight talking to "pull him back into line." Finally, it sometimes helps in the Christian "walk" to follow the example of others. So Paul speaks of believers as walking **in the footsteps**[61] of Abraham in the matter of faith (Rom 4:12). In defending himself against a suggestion that he had exploited the Corinthian church, he speaks of himself as walking strictly where Titus had earlier trod in respect to his fair dealing with them (2 Cor 12:18).

OBSTACLES TO LAND TRAVEL

Travel by land, as by sea, always entailed risk, if only **stumbling**[62] on badly made roads. (Paul makes this a metaphor for giving or taking offense, especially of the Jews taking offense at Christ crucified and of some Christians taking offense at eating meat from the temples.) Travelers also risked finding **the road blocked**.[63] (This is Paul's image, in 1 Thess 2:18, of Satan's hindering him from returning to the Macedonian capital.) But if these were the only hazards that the traveler encountered, he would reckon his prayers to have paid off.[64] Notice Paul's prayer in 1 Thess 3:11: "May God himself . . . **clear the way**[65] for us [to come] to you." He uses the same word again in 2 Thess 3:5 (*kateuthynō*) to express his hope that God would keep their hearts clear as they progress in love and loyalty to Christ.

Of Paul's own journeys by land, perhaps none was more dangerous than his crossing and recrossing of the mountains between Perga and Pisidian Antioch (Acts 13:14; 14:24). When he later wrote of dangers from rivers and bandits, these journeys were most likely in his mind (2 Cor 11:26). The floods of the Pisidian highlands were notorious, and the Romans were far from suppressing the bandits who made the Taurus Mountains their home.[66]

The traveler who survived the human terrors of the road and the often rugged terrain still had to endure the "hospitality" of such wayside accommodation as he might happen to find.[67] The archaeological and literary evidence indicates that the establishments catering to travelers were generally cramped and undecorated. They were frequented by carters, drunkards, prostitutes, and the riffraff of society. The beds they offered seemed to harbor every known insect, and the proprietor, as likely as not, was a rogue.[68] Yet the fact remains that travel was generally easier in the first century CE than it had been before and has been for much of the time since, thanks to the Pax Romana (the achievement and maintenance of peace both at home and abroad that was Augustus's and his successors' great gift to the world[69]) and to the network of roads that covered the empire.

TRANSPORTATION AND ROMAN ROADS

Passenger vehicles ranged from light two-wheeled chariots to large coaches. Among the lighter two-wheeled types were the *essedum* (a luxurious vehicle used by officials), the *cisium,* and the *covinnus.* The latter were simpler, smaller vehicles for single travelers with little luggage. The Romans also adapted the Etruscan *carpentum,* a cabriolet drawn by a span of mules. The *carruca* was a larger four-wheeled wagon capable of carrying four passengers and a coachman. The largest vehicle in this category was the *raeda,* which was drawn by two to four horses and somewhat resembled the stagecoach of later periods. A tombstone from Moesia, now in a Belgrade museum, shows a *raeda* being drawn by three horses and carrying L. Blassius Nigellio, a courier of the *cursus publicus,*[70] with an urgent message in his hand. He sits behind the driver, and behind him, surrounded by luggage, sits his servant.

Heavier vehicles were used to transport agricultural products and other goods. These were not usually horse-drawn. The method of harnessing horses had not yet been perfected, and it was the ox that did most of the heavy work. Paul mentions oxen from time to time in his letters, giving little evidence, however, of a detailed knowledge of how they were used. He was a man of the city.[71] But oxen were the prime movers of the ancient world. It is difficult to imagine how that world would have functioned without them. They hauled a variety of carts, such as the *plaustrum,* which was the most common type used by farmers. Another vehicle mentioned in the sources is the *sarracum.* It was heavier than the *plaustrum* and had closed wheels, making it especially suitable (because stronger) for the transportation of building materials. Others were the *carrus* and the *clabulare,* used by the army to move goods and personnel over long distances.[72]

By the time of Diocletian, Rome had built fifty-three thousand miles of roads,[73] which served the whole of society, enabling people to trade, travel, and communicate with each other more easily. Mention has already been made of the diversity of people seen out and about on the roads, walking or mounted, borne on litters or carried in carriages, alone or accompanied by a host of retainers.[74] Still, the benefit of the roads to ordinary people was an incidental result. In most cases they were built not for them but for military use, often by the army itself. Their primary purpose was to facilitate the rapid movement of troops and to otherwise serve the interest of the central administration.[75]

NOTES

1. Παρουσία: (1) "a being present, presence" (e.g., 2 Cor 10:10; Phil 2:12), (2) "a coming, arrival, advent" (e.g., 2 Cor 7:6–7; Phil 1:26; 2 Thess 2:9). In the papyri and in Hellenistic Greek generally, παρουσία was the technical term for the coming of a king, a governor, or the like. Such a coming always entailed preparation for that person's reception, and it often marked (for dating purposes) the beginning of a new era. Cos dated a new era from the παρουσία of Gaius Caesar in 4 CE, as did Greece from the παρουσία of Hadrian in 124 CE. Sometimes coins were struck to commemorate such a παρουσία. The word was also applied to a divine visitation. And whether of a king or a god, a παρουσία was often an occasion for healing of one sort or another (see A. Deissmann, *Light from the Ancient East* [London: Hodder & Stoughton, 1908], 368). The term was aptly applied by Christians to the coming of Christ. See 1 Cor 15:23; 1 Thess 2:19; 3:13; 4:15; 5:23; 2 Thess 2:1, 8.

2. Ἀπάντησις (from ἀπαντάω "to go to meet, to meet"): "A meeting." In Paul, this word is found only in 1 Thess 4:17 in a context in which he is discussing the παρουσία of our Lord. When the emperor or some other dignitary paid an official visit (παρουσία) to a city, the action of the leading citizens in going out to meet him and escorting him back on the final stage of his journey was called the ἀπάντησις. So Cicero, describing Julius Caesar's progress through Italy in 49 BCE, says, "Just imagine what ἀπαντήσεις he is receiving from the towns, what honors are paid to him!" (*Att.* 8.16.2). Five years later he says much the same about Caesar's adopted son, Octavian (Augustus): "The municipalities are showing the boy remarkable favor. . . . Wonderful ἀπαντήσεις and encouragement!" (16.11.6). It is this picture of the king coming and being met by his people (the dead being raised and the living being caught up with them to meet the Lord in the clouds) that Paul is invoking in 1 Thess 4:13–18. The analogy, incidentally, would suggest that they then accompany the Lord *back to earth,* from where they came. Perhaps earth will be heaven.

3. For instance, sailors were regularly rostered to march up from Ostia to the capital to hoist awnings in the amphitheater. See Suetonius (*Vesp.* 8.5); on amphitheaters, see p. 264 and ch. 12, n. 57.

4. See ch. 9, n. 70.

5. These travels include the picturesque camel caravans that the Roman world gradually came to know. See Pliny, *Nat.* 24.183.

6. Teachers such as Apuleius (of *Metamorphoses* fame) journeyed widely. Demetrius of Tarsus had roamed as far afield as Britain, perhaps to investigate the educational possibilities of that land (Plutarch, *Mor.* 410 [*Def. orac.* 2]). This may be the same Demetrius who dedicated two tablets with Greek inscriptions at York (discovered in 1860).

7. Such as for Drusus the Elder, whose body Augustus accompanied from Ticinum to Rome (Tacitus, *Ann.* 3.5.2).

8. See Propertius (*Eleg.* 2.32; 4.8.15) for his description of Cynthia's journeys to Praeneste, Tusculum, Tibur, and Lanuvium along the Appian Way.

9. See, e.g., R. L. Fox (*Pagans and Christians* [Harmondsworth, U.K.: Penguin, 1988], 41ff.) for his account of pagan pilgrimages.

10. Pliny, *Ep.* 5.9.

11. Suetonius, *Tib.* 14.

12. Plutarch, *Mor.* 410 (*Def. orac.* 2).

13. Pliny traveled primarily to visit his estates (*Ep.* 1.3.2; 3.19.4; 4.14.8; 9.15.3) but saw travel as also providing exercise and inspiration (4.14; 7.4–8; 8.8.20; 9.36). Cf. Apuleius, *Metam.,* who lists people's reasons for traveling: sightseeing (2.21), religious purposes (8.24; 11), and business (1.2, 5). If Pausanius's

guidebooks of the second century CE are any indication, tourism was a not unimportant motivation for travel.

14. Renters of horses and vehicles, innkeepers, and the like (see further ch. 9, n. 68), blacksmiths, people selling produce beside the road, as Pliny (*Nat.* 23.95) notes in respect to the Via Flaminia. For communications, transport, and supplies generally, see B. Levick, *The Government of the Roman Empire: A Sourcebook* (Totowa, N.J.: Barnes & Noble, 1985), 99–115.

15. See Acts 9:1–30; 11:29–30; 13:1–14:28; 15:1–35; 15:36–21:17; 27:1–28:16; Rom 15:19–29; Gal 1:17; Titus 1:5. Mention might also be made of the travels of Mary (Luke 1:39–56; 2:1–5, 22–39), of Jesus and the disciples (e.g., John 2:13; 5:1; 7:1–10), of Philip to Samaria, Gaza, and Caesarea (Acts 8:5, 26, 40), and of Peter to Samaria, Lydda, Joppa, Caesarea, Antioch in Syria, possibly Pontus, Galatia, Cappadocia, Asia, Bithynia, and Achaia (Corinth), and probably Rome (Acts 8:14; 9:35–39; 10:1–24; 1 Cor 1:12; Gal 2:11; 1 Pet 1:1).

16. When an auxiliary soldier was enfranchised, a special document, known as *diploma civitatis Romanae* or *instrumentum,* was issued. It contained a copy of the man's certificate of citizenship, which could be used as a card of identity. To what extent private persons carried such certificates is uncertain. "They were convenient in shape and size, being small wooden diptychs. But it is more likely that they were normally kept in the family archives" (A. N. Sherwin-White, *Roman Society and Roman Law in the New Testament* [Oxford: Clarendon, 1969], 146–49, here 149; cf. H. J. Cadbury, "Roman Law and the Trial of Paul," *BC* 5:316). An itinerant like Paul, however, might well have carried his certificate with him.

17. P.Oxy. 292, 746, 787, 1162, 1219, 1587. See A. Deissmann, *Light,* 171, 197ff., 235; H. G. Meecham, *Light from Ancient Letters* (London: George Allen & Unwin, 1923), 122. Diogenes refers to the practice of Greek teachers giving ἐπιστολαὶ συστατικαί or γράμματα συστατικά, "letters of commendation" (Diogenes Laertius, *Lives of the Philosophers* 8.87), although he himself considered them useless. Nothing but personal experience of men, he said, was of any real value (cited by Epictetus, *Diatr.* 2.3.1). Nevertheless, such letters were extensively employed and apparently regarded as serving a useful purpose. See further C. W. Keyes, "The Greek Letter of Introduction," *AJP* 56 (1935): 28–44; W. Baird, "Letters of Recommendation: A Study of 2 Cor. 3:1–3," *JBL* 80 (1961): 166–72; S. K. Stowers, *Letter Writing in Graeco-Roman Antiquity* (Philadelphia: Westminster, 1986), 153–65.

18. For references to such letters, see Acts 9:2; 18:27; 22:5; 1 Cor 16:3; Col 4:10; for actual letters of recommendation, see Acts 15:25–26; Rom 16:1–2; 1 Cor 16:10–11; 2 Cor 8:22–23; Phil 2:19–24; Col 4:10; Phlm (see ch. 7, n. 27). The apparently abrupt opening to the commendation of Phoebe in Rom 16:1 (συνίστημι δέ) is typical of such letters. "There is no lack of analogies for a letter of recommendation plunging at once *in medias res* and beginning with 'I commend' " (Deissmann, *Light,* 235).

19. Συστατικὴ ἐπιστολή: The adjective συστατικός (from συνίστημι "to commend, approve, establish"; see the next note) has the sense (1) "for putting together, constructive" and (2) "for bringing together, introductory, commendatory." Found only here in the NT.

20. The order of the words ἑαυτοὺς συνιστάνειν "ourselves to commend" is significant. The particular phrase is found four times in 2 Corinthians, always in a bad sense, the prominent position of the pronoun signifying that there has been an undue promotion of self (2 Cor 3:1; 5:12; 10:12, 18). On the other hand, the same words in the reverse order, συνιστάνειν ἑαυτόν, occur three times in the same letter in a good sense of the legitimate commendation of oneself (2 Cor 4:2; 6:4; 7:11). Beyond this, the verb, in its various forms, συνιστάνω, συνιστάω, συνίστημι, meaning (1) transitive, "to commend" or "to show, prove, establish," (2) intransitive, "to

stand with, near," or "to be composed of consist, cohere," is found also in Rom 3:5; 5:8; 16:1; 2 Cor 10:18; 12:11; Gal 2:18; Col 1:17.

21. The application of the metaphor is somewhat confused by the words "written in our hearts." They are best treated as a parenthesis (they arise from the memory of all the labor and pain the Corinthians had cost him). There is a variant reading, "your hearts," which, however, is not as well attested and should not be accepted. The opening words of v. 2 have already made the point that the Corinthians themselves are the "letter." The parenthesis, although it certainly muddies the exegetical waters, is typical of Paul in allowing his heart to run away with his logic. The true application of the metaphor lies in the words "known and read by all." A letter written on Paul's heart could not be read by others, but a letter written on their hearts by Christ through his ministry was patent to the whole world. Cf. 1 Cor 9:2, where he describes the Corinthians as the "seal of his apostleship" (see ch. 1, n. 62), and 2 Cor 11:21–23; 12:12, where he appeals to his sufferings as the "signs of an apostle."

22. A feature of the agora at Corinth, which Paul could not have missed when he was there, was a small monument bearing the inscription "Gnaeus Babbius Philinus, aedile and pontifex, had this monument erected at his own expense, and he approved it in his official capacity as duovir." For this and other examples, see J. Murphy-O'Connor, *St. Paul's Corinth* (Wilmington, Del.: Michael Glazier, 1983), 170–72.

23. A mosaic at Medeina, Tunisia, provides further examples. It shows a variety of river and seagoing vessels. The river craft include types seen on the reliefs from Mainz and Cabrières d'Aigues. The seagoing ships include the most common varieties, the *ponto* and the *corbita*. Similar vessels appear on other African mosaics in the Bardo Museum, Tunisia. Meanwhile underwater archaeologists are recovering from the waters of the Mediterranean a series of wrecks that fill out our knowledge of the ships of this period and of the products that they carried.

24. Hence the term χηνίσκος for the stern of a ship, from the Greek χήν "a goose." In one of the Pompeii tombs, the device expands into the head of Minerva to form something like the figurehead of more recent times. Paul's ship from Malta to Puteoli appears to have been similarly decorated with Castor and Pollux, the twin brothers who protected seamen (Acts 28:11).

25. As shipping developed during the period of the empire, two or three masts are sometimes found, with triangular sails above the main yard. Such sailing vessels apparently made three to four knots in good conditions and up to six knots in ideal conditions (see Pliny, *Nat.* 19.3–4). But two to three knots was probably about the average speed of a merchantman. From various literary sources it has been calculated that voyages from Rome to Carthage averaged four to six days, to Marseilles one to two days, and to Narbonne three days. From Ostia or Carthage to Gibraltar the voyage took an average of seven days, Corinth to Puteoli four to five days. With a northwest Etesian wind blowing from behind, i.e., in ideal conditions, the time from Rome to Egypt or Palestine was about 30 days. See C. G. Starr, "Ships," *OCD*, 984; J. Liversidge, *Everyday Life in the Roman Empire* (New York: Putnam's, 1976), 171. The difficulties of a square-rigger in contrary winds is well described by Achilles Tatius, *Leuc. Clit.* 3.1.3–6.

26. Lucian, *Nav.* 5. This ship appears to have been unusually large, but it was not unique. The obelisk that now stands in St. Peter's Square was brought to Rome during the reign of Caligula. It weighs 322 tons, and its base 174 tons. A special ship was constructed for its transport. The mainmast was made of one very large pine tree (Pliny, *Nat.* 16.201–202). We may note also that Josephus claims to have been on a ship for Rome that carried six hundred passengers. "Our ship foundered," he writes, "in the Sea of Adria and our company of six hundred souls had to swim all night." Not for the first time in his life Josephus survived where others did not. He was one of the eighty picked up by a ship of Cyrene (*Vita* 13–16). Ships were steered by a

large oar at the stern or, on larger vessels, two, one on either side of the stern. A second- or third-century CE mosaic from Tebessa, Algeria, shows a somewhat overladen *ponto* thus equipped. A relief from Sidon depicts a *corbita*, also with two steering oars, and likewise a painting of a *corbita* from Ostia, now in the Vatican Library, Rome. Coincidentally, the Ostia ship was named *Isis Geminiana*.

27. Κυβέρνησις: (1) "steering, pilotage," (2) metaphorically, "government," as in 1 Cor 12:28 (found only here in the NT). Cf. κυβερνήτης: (1) "a steersman, helmsman" (Acts 27:11; Rev 18:17); his work is that of κυβέρνησις "steering"; (2) metaphorically, "a guide, governor" (both nouns from κυβερνάω "to steer," like the Latin *gubernare*, from which we get "to govern"). For examples of the metaphorical application of κυβέρνησις and κυβερνήτης elsewhere in Greek literature, see H. W. Beyer, "κυβέρνησις," *TDNT* 3:1035–37.

28. Ὑπηρέτης (from ὑπό and ἐρέτης "rower"): Properly, "an underrower," but generally of anyone who does anything under another, "an underling" and so "a servant, attendant, minister," used of various officers such as those of the synagogue or the Sanhedrin. John Mark is described as the ὑπηρέτης of Barnabas and Paul in Acts 13:5, and Paul himself was appointed as God's ὑπηρέτης in Acts 26:16. Luke acknowledges his indebtedness to ὑπερέται λόγου "ministers or servants of the word," in the preface to his Gospel (Luke 1:2). Like our word "minister," the context in which ὑπηρέτης was used sometimes lent to it a certain respectability, even an authority. It is found only here in Paul.

29. Acts 13:4, 13; 16:11; 18:18, 21; 20:6, 13–16; 21:1–8; 27:2–44; 28:11–13. A number of these references make it clear that the ships concerned were entirely dependent on sail.

30. A mosaic from Sousse, Tunisia, shows a Roman freighter fitted with both sails (a mainsail and a large foresail) and oars.

31. There is much uncertainty about the arrangements of oars and rowers in these multiple-banked fighting ships; I have adopted a widely accepted view. For a different view, see C. G. Starr, "Trireme," *OCD*, 1095. One thing that appears to be certain is that the quinqueremes were kept in the same sheds as the triremes, which means that they were no broader in the beam and therefore no higher, for otherwise they would have been quite unstable. On this basis it has recently been suggested that the only difference between all of these multiple-banked vessels lay in the provision of extra rowers to the oar, the quinquereme having two to the oar on each of the two upper banks and the quadrireme having two banks with two rowers to each oar on each bank. See further J. S. Morrison and R. T. Williams, *Greek Oared Ships* (Cambridge: Cambridge University Press, 1968). For a description of the performance of a quinquereme during the Second Punic War (206 BCE), see Livy, *Hist.* 28.30. For details of the construction of both merchant ships and warships, see K. D. White, *Greek and Roman Technology* (London: Thames & Hudson, 1984), 141–56.

32. Διάκονος (derivation unknown): (1) in general, "a servant, attendant, minister" (e.g., Rom 13:4 [2x]; 15:8; 1 Cor 3:5 [this might make it difficult to draw a sharp distinction between the ὑπηρέτης of v. 1 and the διάκονος of v. 5]; 2 Cor 3:6; 6:4; 11:15 [2x], 23; Gal 2:17; Eph 3:7; 6:21; Col 1:7, 23, 25; 4:7; 1 Thess 3:2; 1 Tim 4:6), (2) as a technical term for a church officer, "a deacon" (e.g., Rom 16:1; Phil 1:1; 1 Tim 3:8, 12).

33. Οἰκονόμος: See ch. 3, n. 123. The two terms οἰκονόμος and ὑπηρέτης were applied by Epictetus to the Cynic preacher who, as responsible to God, did not shrink from speaking the truth that he had received (*Diatr.* 3.22.3, 95).

34. See, e.g., Acts 27:16, where Luke's use of "we" should be noted. In vv. 10–12, Paul's advice, whether invited or volunteered, was at least taken seriously, presumably on the grounds that he was an experienced sea traveler. It was, perhaps, a pity that his advice was not heeded.

35. "To furl" is to roll up the sail completely and tie it to the yard or boom; "to reef" is to shorten the sail (reduce the sail's surface) by taking a tuck in it. Either sense is conveyed by the verb ὑποστέλλω: (1) "to lower, draw in," as of a sail, and so (2) "to draw back, hold back, withdraw" (Acts 20:20, 27; Gal 2:12). A. T. Robertson (*Word Pictures in the New Testament* [New York: Richard R. Smith, 1930–1933; repr. Nashville, Tenn.: Broadman & Holman, 1973], 3:349) thinks it possible that this is a deliberate metaphor, although it must be conceded that the middle voice, used in the two Acts references, frequently has the sense "to withdraw oneself, to cower, to shrink, to conceal." Such a use makes good sense here without any reference to ships. Cf. the simple verb στέλλω: (1) properly, "to set, place, arrange, fit out," in the middle voice "to set oneself for, prepare," (2) "to bring together, gather up," used of furling sails, hence "to restrain, check," in the middle voice "to restrain, withdraw oneself." See 2 Cor 8:20; 2 Thess 3:6. Cf. also the compound συνστέλλω: (1) "to draw together, contract, shorten," used of time in 1 Cor 7:29, perhaps as a nautical metaphor, "the time has been reefed like a sail," i.e., "shortened," (2) "to wrap up."

36. ’Αναλύω: (1) "to unloose," (2) "to unloose for departure, depart," (3) "to return." Only here and in Luke 12:36 in the NT. Used elsewhere of weighing anchor and putting out to sea and of soldiers breaking up camp. Commonly used in the LXX and late Greek in the sense "to depart."

37. ’Ανάλυσις (from ἀναλύω, see the preceding note): "A loosing," either in terms of striking a tent (see, e.g., W. Lock, *The Pastoral Epistles* [Edinburgh: T&T Clark, 1924], 111), releasing from shackles (see, e.g., E. K. Simpson, *The Pastoral Epistles* [London: Tyndale, 1954], 154), or untying a boat. "The ship reminds us of the other shore; the tents . . . tell us of the temporary nature of our life. The best is yet to be!" (R. A. Ward, *Commentary on 1 and 2 Timothy and Titus* [Waco, Tex.: Word, 1974], 211). The word is found only here in the NT. It may be no more than coincidence (if it is more, I cannot explain it), but Paul confines his references to death as "departure" (verb and noun) to letters connected in some way with Timothy.

38. Προσαγωγή (from προσάγω "to bring, lead, draw near"): (1) "a bringing to," (2) "an approach, access," and so a harbor for ships. Plutarch speaks of an army drawn up on the shore where there was no προσαγωγή—no place for ships to put in (*Aem.* 13). In Sophocles (*Phil.* 236) the question is asked: "What need made you put in [προσάγω] to Lemnos?" For the word as a conscious metaphor, however, most commentators are inclined to understand it in terms of access to a king rather than of a haven for ships. Xenophon tells how prisoners in chains were "brought into the presence" of Cyrus the king (*Cyr.* 3.2.12) and how Cyrus expected anyone who wanted anything from him to get into favor with his friends and, through them, to ask for a προσαγωγή "an introduction to the royal presence" (7.5.45). He tells also how Sacas, the cupbearer, had the office of "introducing" (προσάγω) to Astyages those who had business with him and of keeping out those whom he thought it not expedient to admit (1.3.8). There was an official at the Persian court known as the προσαγωγεύς, whose function it was to introduce people into the royal presence. Either image is an attractive one: Christ, the "bringer" of the suppliant into God's presence, and Christ, the "safe haven" for those "all at sea."

39. Or else simply drawing on literary images. See, e.g., Isa 57:20–21. A less well-known but hardly less interesting account of a sea voyage (than Acts 27) has come to us from the hand of Synesius. In a letter of 404 CE (*Ep.* 4) he writes about a turbulent journey from Alexandria to his hometown in Libya. The text is reproduced in F. Meijer and O. van Nijf, *Trade, Transport, and Society in the Ancient World: A Sourcebook* (London: Routledge, 1992), 170–76. Cf. also Apuleius (*Metam.* 7.6–7), who tells of "the thousand and one difficulties" of sea travel and of the terrors that can even come upon a ship hugging the coastline.

40. Κλυδωνίζομαι (from κλύδων "a wave"): "To be tossed by waves." Found only here in the NT.

41. Περιφέρω: "To carry about," passive "to be carried about" (2 Cor 4:10; Eph 4:14). In the phrase περιφερόμενοι παντὶ ἀνέμῳ τῆς διδασκαλίας, the dative ἀνέμῳ is instrumental, "*by* every wind." The "wind" is defined by a genitive of apposition, "the wind which is the teaching." In the singular and with the definite article, "*the* teaching" is difficult but must be read, in the light of both Col 2:22 ("teachings," plural) and the "every" of this verse, as indicating "any and all kinds of teaching" in contrast to the true faith. Specifically, in the context of Asia Minor and against the background of the "Colossian heresy," it is "a reference to false teaching in the guise of various religious philosophies which threatened to assimilate, and thereby dilute or undermine, the Pauline gospel" (A. T. Lincoln, *Ephesians* [Dallas: Word, 1990], 258). The metaphor lies in the whole picture of waves and wind: "Stop being babies, tossed high by waves and blown all about by every gust of teaching in this sea of human trickery."

42. Σαλεύω (from σάλος, "a tossing," as of an earthquake or the sea): Found only here in Paul. Properly of the action of wind, storm, etc., "to agitate, shake," and so of making people feel insecure, unsettled, even depressed. It also has the sense "to stir up," as of a crowd.

43. Luke uses the same verb of an incident also associated with Thessalonica. He speaks of the Jews of that city as "agitating" the Bereans, "shaking them like an earthquake," as one writer puts it, "and disturbing them like a tornado" (Acts 17:13). Robertson, *Word Pictures*, 3:275.

44. Ἀποθέω: "To thrust away," and in the middle voice as here "to thrust away from oneself, refuse, reject." The verb is a strong one. It suggests a deliberate spurning of conscience rather then mere carelessness. Cf. Rom 11:1–2.

45. Chrysostom, cited without reference by N. J. D. White, "The First and Second Epistles to Timothy and the Epistle to Titus," *EGT* 4: 101.

46. Ναυαγέω (from ναῦς "a ship" and ἄγνυμι "to break"): "To suffer shipwreck," as in 2 Cor 11:25. The qualifying phrase is περὶ τὴν πίστιν "concerning the faith," where the definite article may be taken as the possessive pronoun, as commonly in Greek. But see, e.g., G. D. Fee (*1 and 2 Timothy, Titus* [NIBC; Peabody, Mass.: Hendrickson, 1984], 58), who takes it as "the faith"—the conduct of these people has brought the gospel itself into disrepute. Cf. "missing the mark" of faith and good conscience (1 Tim 1:6; 6:21; 2 Tim 2:18), being "cauterized in their conscience" (1 Tim 4:2), "corrupted in mind" (1 Tim 6:5), and "rejected as far as the faith is concerned" (again περὶ τὴν πίστιν, 2 Tim 3:8).

47. Paul's warning is against an obsession with wealth. It leads, he says, to "a temptation and a trap [παγίς; see ch. 2, n. 27] and to many foolish and harmful desires, which are of such a kind [αἵτινες] as to drown" those who are of this mind. Βυθίζω (from βυθός "the bottom, the depth" of the sea): (1) transitive, "to cause to sink," (2) intransitive in the passive, "to sink." Only here and in Luke 5:7 in the NT. For a further discussion of this passage, see p. 35 and ch. 8, n. 40.

48. See Acts 16:22–23 (note the "many blows" that were laid on them, presumably by the lictors using the rods that were their badge of office). Note the reference in v. 33 to their "wounds."

49. To be precise, Philippi to Amphipolis is thirty-three Roman miles; Amphipolis to Apollonia is thirty, and Apollonia to Thessalonica is thirty-seven. The Western text has the variant "taking the road through Amphipolis, they came down to Apollonia and from there to Thessalonica." On this reading it appears that they made a longer stay at Apollonia than we might otherwise have thought. The road by which they traveled was, of course, the Via Egnatia.

50. Strict Jews such as the Pharisees seldom used horses. If Paul retained his Pharisaic predilections in this matter and if they were mounted, then we must suppose that it was on mules or even on asses.

51. Travel was expensive. When Lucius went to Rome, his outlay "melted away his humble inheritance" (Apuleius, *Metam.* 11.28). What was the financial cost of Paul's journeys? His general policy was to pay his own way, at least never accepting support from the people to whom he was ministering at the time (see Acts 20:34; 1 Cor 4:12; 9:3–19; 2 Cor 11:7–12; 1 Thess 2:9; 2 Thess 3:8). Nevertheless, he seems to have been glad to accept support from elsewhere when it came (see Phil 2:25; 4:15–16).

52. Πεζεύω (from πεζός, an adjective, "on foot, by land"): "To travel by foot or on land."

53. The only other explicit reference in Acts (8:28–29, 38) to the means by which anyone traveled is to the Ethiopian's ἅρμα (from ἀραρίσκω "to join"), which is generally translated "chariot." But in this case it was probably a covered wagon drawn by horses or even oxen, not the light war chariot, which in any case was by now obsolete, except for its use in the circus. See further the discussion of vehicular transport on p. 200. Such a wagon would go at about walking pace. The lack of springs made vehicles slower, and often the condition of the roads, at least away from the main thoroughfares, further impeded their progress. For the hazards of travel, including the state of the roads and the methods of their construction, see ch. 9, nn. 66, 73.

54. From the schematic itineraries of the book of Acts alone, R. Hock (*The Social Context of Paul's Ministry: Tent Making and Apostleship* [Philadelphia: Fortress, 1980], 27) has estimated that Paul traveled nearly ten thousand miles in the course of his reported career.

55. Some of Paul's metaphors arose from his own experience, and this may be another case in point. It should be noted, however, that the terms used for his comings and goings do not include περιπατέω, the verb employed in this metaphor. This may suggest that the metaphor had its origin elsewhere than in his own means of locomotion. See the discussion that follows. For details of the verb, see ch. 9, n. 57.

56. H. Seesemann argues that "though instances of this [metaphorical] use are less common in the LXX than in later Old Testament translations, it is impossible that Paul should have taken it from any other source" ("πατέω, κτλ," *TDNT* 5:943–45, here 944). But G. Bertram ("πατέω and Compounds in the LXX," *TDNT* 5:941–43, here 943) is less certain. The metaphor of walking is also found in DSS, but R. Banks ("Walking as a Metaphor of the Christian Life," in *Perspectives on Language and Text* [ed. E. W. Conrad and E. G. Newing; Winona Lake, Ind.: Eisenbrauns, 1987], 303–13) finds little in common between the DSS and Paul in this regard and thinks it more likely that Paul's use came from his Pharisaic background. Another possibility is that it was already a Christian idiom, going back to Jesus' use of the figure (John 8:12; 11:7–10). A similar idiom is found in many other cultures.

57. Περιπατέω: "To walk" and, from this, "to live, to pass one's life, to conduct oneself." See Rom 6:4; 8:1, 4; 13:13; 14:15; 1 Cor 3:3; 7:17; 2 Cor 4:2; 5:7; 10:2–3; 12:18; Gal 5:16; Eph 2:2, 10; 4:1, 17 (2x); 5:2, 8, 15; Phil 3:17–18; Col 1:10; 2:6; 3:7; 4:5; 1 Thess 2:12; 4:1 (2x, but the parenthetical clause καθὼς καὶ περιπατεῖτε is lacking in some MSS), 12; 2 Thess 3:6, 11. To this and the metaphors of "keeping step" and "stumbling" discussed below (ch. 9, nn. 59, 62) should be added Paul's use of ὁδός: (1) "a way, path, road," (2) "a journey," as a metaphor of conduct in 1 Cor 4:17; 12:31 (cf. Rom 3:16–17; 11:33; 1 Thess 3:11); δρόμος "a course, a race," (see ch. 12, n. 100); and τρέχω "to run" (see ch. 12, n. 97). Note should also be taken of the various terms for "coming" and "going" and of the verbs formed from the root στρέφω "to turn, bring back" (the simple verb is not found in Paul), such as ἀναστρέφω "to overturn, turn back, turn hither and thither, dwell, behave" (see 2 Cor 1:12; Eph 2:3; 1 Tim 3:15); ἀποστρέφω "to turn away, turn back" (see Rom 11:26; 2 Tim 1:15; 4:4; Titus 1:14); διαστρέφω "to distort, twist, pervert"

(see Phil 2:15); ἐπιστρέφω "to turn about, toward" (see 2 Cor 3:16; Gal 4:9; 1 Thess 1:9); ὑποστρέφω "to turn about, return," only used literally (see Gal 1:17).

58. These qualifications highlight the fact that in this metaphor Paul places emphasis more on the *process* than on the destination of the Christian life. This may also explain his preference for περιπατέω over πορεύομαι "to go," which is the more common word of the two for the metaphor in the LXX. More than περιπατέω, it emphasizes the intention and destination.

59. Στοιχέω (see. ch. 10, n. 19): "To be in rows (as of waves, plants, etc., as well as of people), to walk in line," especially of marching into battle. From this, it has the sense "to walk by rule, to act according to a standard, to behave properly," as in Gal 5:26.

60. E. de W. Burton, *The Epistle to the Galatians* (Edinburgh: T&T Clark, 1921), 110. Paul's word is ὀρθοποδέω (from ὀρθος "straight," πους "foot"; = the classical εὐθυπορεω): "To walk straight." Found only here in Gal 2:14 and in later ecclesiastical writers, whose use of the word may be traced to this passage, and in one instance in a third-century CE papyrus. But ὀρθόποδες βαίνοντες "going in a straight line" does occur in texts earlier than Paul.

61. Ἴχνος: "A track, footstep." In Paul in Rom 4:12 (where also he uses στοιχέω; see ch. 9, n. 59); 2 Cor 12:18.

62. There are three nouns: First, πρόσκομμα (from προσκόπτω; see this note below) (1) "a stumble, stumbling" (the phrase λίθος προσκόμματος "a stone of stumbling" is used figuratively in Rom 9:32–33 of a cause of offense), (2) = προσκοπή "an occasion of stumbling, a barrier, a hindrance, a roadblock" (πρόσκομμα is the word that would be used, e.g., of a tree that had been felled and laid across a road to block it), used metaphorically in Rom 14:13, 20; 1 Cor 8:9. Second, προσκοπή (also from προσκόπτω) "an occasion of stumbling, offense," 2 Cor 6:3. The verb, προσκόπτω, has the sense (1) transitive, "to strike (e.g., hand or foot) against," (2) intransitive, "to stumble," and of wind, "to rush against, beat upon," metaphorically "to take offense at, stumble at." In Paul found only in Rom 9:32; 14:21. Cf. πταίω: (1) "to cause to stumble," (2) "to stumble," found only in Paul in Rom. 11:11 (again metaphorical). Cf. also προκοπή "progress" (Phil 1:12, 25; 1 Tim 4:15) and the verb προκόπτω "to cut forward, advance" (in Paul in Gal 1:14; 2 Tim 2:16; 3:9, 13). This could be deemed to be an agricultural image from cutting through undergrowth or the like, but in any case was probably not used as a conscious metaphor. Thirdly, from a different root but in its literal meaning not unlike some of the words of the κόπτω group, παράπτωμα (from παραπίπτω) (1) "a false step, a blunder," (2) metaphorically of conduct, "a misdeed." In Paul in Rom 4:25; 5:15 (2x), 16, 17, 18; 11:11, 12; 2 Cor 5:19; Gal 6:1; Eph 1:7; 2:1, 5; Col 2:12.

63. Ἐνκόπτω: See ch. 10, n. 20. For the state of the roads, see ch. 9, n. 66.

64. Superstition was rife, and travelers took care to ascertain the most propitious day on which to set out and to propitiate the gods before doing so. Archaeology provides ample evidence of altars built in thanks for a safe journey. See, e.g., J. Liversidge, *Everyday Life in the Roman Empire* (New York: Putnam's, 1976), 171–72; and Apuleius, *Metam.* 1.5; 2.12–13; 9.8. Cf. Acts 13:3.

65. Κατευθύνω: "To make or keep straight, direct, guide." In Paul only in 1 Thess 3:11; 2 Thess 3:5.

66. See W. M. Ramsay, *The Church in the Roman Empire* (London: Hodder & Stoughton, 1897), 23–24. Describing Paul's crossing of the Taurus, Ramsay makes the general observation that "the roads all over the Roman Empire were apt to be unsafe, for the arrangements for insuring public safety were exceedingly defective." Apuleius bears this out. He tells of brigands attacking a merchant in Macedonia (*Metam.* 1.6f.), of a farmer on his way to town being robbed of his ass by a soldier (9.39ff.), of encounters with dogs and wolves (8.15–17). Sometimes there were meetings with police patrols (9.9), more often with robbers. ("Don't you realize

that the roads are swarming with brigands," 1.15; cf. Propertius [*Eleg.* 3.16.1]: "Shall I go off into complete darkness and risk some night attack?" Diodorus Siculus [*Hist.* 34.38] tells of a Sicilian slave owner whose slaves complained that they were insufficiently clothed. He told them that the remedy was to rob any traveler they happened to meet. See further ch. 5, n. 57.) Physical hazards included the occasional river crossing (Apuleius, *Metam.* 7.18) and the poor condition of some roads. The track was sometimes "heavily rutted, now a morass of stagnant water, now covered by a layer of slippery mud." Elsewhere, writes Apuleius, there was "a lane that was a mass of stones and obstructed by tree stumps of every kind" (9.9). Galen remarks that "even today we see that some of the ancient highways of the world are in part swampy, in part covered by stones or thickets; that they are difficultly steep or dangerously sloping, infested with wild animals, impassable because of the width of the rivers, long, or rough" (*Meth.* 10.632–633). See also Apuleius, *Flor.*, and Pliny, *Ep.* 2.17.

67. From the catalog of his difficulties in 2 Cor 11:26–27 it appears that Paul did not always find even the poorest of places to stay overnight. He speaks of the lack of food, water, clothing, and shelter, as well as the weariness induced by sleepless nights.

68. See Horace, *Sat.* 1.1.5; 1.5.4. In addition to the stations that served the *cursus* (see ch. 9, n. 70), various privately run establishments offering hospitality to the traveler might be found both in the towns and by the roadside (themselves often becoming the nuclei of new villages and towns). The hostelries offering board and lodging were known by the terms *deversorium* (sometimes a private abode built by the wealthy on the way to their estates), *hospitium,* and *caupona.* The latter seems to have been a somewhat pejorative term. A *stabulum* was an inn with a stable. Inns and other places for eating and drinking were called by the names *taberna* (cf. Acts 28:15) and *popina,* but one also finds the words *cenatio* (the normal meaning is "dining room"), *ganeum,* and *gargustium,* mere hovels, and loanwords from Greek, such as *thermopolium,* a place for the sale of hot drinks, and *xenodochium,* a cheap rooming house for foreigners. A typical inn complex has recently been excavated at Chameleux in Belgium on the road from Rheims to Trier. Built in the first century CE, it was altered and reconstructed several times after fires and flooding. Rebuilding always followed on the same site. Buildings were found on either side of the road, and the largest had a court with a gate wide enough for the entrance of carriages and wagons. Stables and an inn were ranged around it. A large cellar down a wooden staircase had a sanded floor and oak supports to keep upright a number of wine jars. A forge repaired harnesses and made horseshoes (from Liversidge, *Everyday Life,* 164–65; see also R. Chevallier, *Roman Roads* [London: B. T. Batsford, 1976], 185–91).

69. For a critique of the Pax Romana, see K. Wengst, *Pax Romana and the Peace of Jesus Christ* (London: SCM, 1987), 7–54.

70. This was a government postal-cum-intelligence service. Suetonius describes the original arrangements: "So that there might be swifter news of what was going on in each province, he [Augustus] organized relays of runners, then of chaises, at intervals along the military roads. The second proved a more satisfactory idea, since when the letter arrived at its destination, the bearer could be cross-examined on the situation if needed" (*Aug.* 49.5–50). The normal speed of the couriers was about fifty Roman miles a day, a Roman mile being about ninety-five yards shorter than the English mile.

71. On Paul as a man of the city, see p. 7 and ch. 1, n. 2. On Paul's mention of oxen, see pp. 32–33.

72. This is but a short selection of the vehicles that could be found on the roads. See the list of vehicle types in Chevallier, *Roman Roads,* 178–79.

73. Most of the roads of the empire were constructed in the first two centuries of our era. Archaeology provides the best information about their methods of construction, to which may be added brief descriptions by Plutarch (*Ti. C. Gracch.* 7), Statius (*Silv.* 4.3; 5.40–55), and Procopius (*Hist.* 5.147). From these data, it appears that where major roads were concerned, the method of their construction was generally as follows: First the route was laid out by trenches, and then the area between them was excavated and filled with slabs of stone set in mortar, perhaps above a layer of sand. On this was laid a concrete of crushed stone and mortar, and on this the surface of stone slabs. The roadbed might be forty to fifty-five inches deep, a "wall in the ground," as someone has put it. Drainage ditches were constructed on both sides, and stone curbs laid, separating the ditches from the road. Marshy areas were crossed on wooden causeways, steep slopes were sometimes negotiated with zigzags, and mountains were pierced by tunnels (see also Strabo, *Geog.* 5.3.8 and book 4, for his description of the mountain passes across the Alps). In the provinces, these fully paved roads were found mostly in or near cities. Elsewhere road construction was a bit less extensive; roads were cobbled or surfaced with gravel on a gravel or rammed-earth foundation. Minor roads were sometimes nothing more than a thin layer of gravel without any foundation. The construction varied depending on the materials at hand. The straightness of Roman roads is proverbial, but in fact they are made up of a series of straight alignments from one intermediary point to another. The alignment was generally determined by the terrain. See further Chevallier, *Roman Roads,* esp. 65–177.

74. Apuleius (*Metam.* 10.18) describes the progress of Thiasus, who traveled with "beautifully appointed carriages" and a considerable retinue (Thiasus, however, was an eccentric who used to turn his nose up at his carriages and his Thessalian steeds and Gallic teams, and preferred to ride ahead on his mule). Horace gives a detailed account of an uneventful but delightful journey that he made from Rome to Brundisium (Brindisi) by the Appian Way (*Sat.* 1.5).

75. Livy has a number of references to roadworks carried out by civil magistrates for civil purposes, mostly in Rome itself. But in *Hist.* 39.44 he records that the censor Flaccus had a highway built "in the interests of the people," leading to the waters of Neptune (cf. 9.29, 43; 10.23, 47; 38.28; 41.32). The fact remains, however, that most of the road building had a military purpose. See Livy, *Hist.* 39.2, for the army itself building roads, and 4.41; 22.11, 55; 26.8; 39.2 for incidental references to the army's use of the roads. Roads of strategic importance (not necessarily built or paid for by the army but constructed with the needs of the army in view) were known as *viae militares,* of which the roads built in Gaul by Agrippa (16–13 BCE), in Dalmatia-Pannonia by Tiberius (6–9 CE), in the Rhine and Danube basins by Claudius, and in Asia Minor by the Flavians are examples. The *viae militares* were always, at the same time, *viae publicae,* open to all. Not all Romans, however, saw these roads as a public benefit. Pliny the Elder, for example, blamed them as instrumental in corrupting society: "Which way was vice introduced if it was not by the public road? Which other way indeed could ivory, gold, and precious stones have passed into private use?" (*Nat.* 36.5). Moreover, the roads were sometimes an aid to the enemy. See Livy, *Hist.* 2.39; 9.43; 10.36; 26.8.

Warfare and Soldiering

THE ARMY

The Roman army was a citizen militia. Service was compulsory for all citizens who held property (although in a crisis even slaves might be enrolled). Evidently the best soldiers were thought to be those who had a vested interest in the defense and advancement of their city and its territories. This arrangement is attributed to Servius Tullius in the sixth century BCE. It can be assumed that Roman soldiers at this time resembled their opponents in their accouterment and their military tactics. Wars were won and lost on the clash of the phalanxes (a tactic borrowed from the Greeks)—solid masses of heavily armed infantry, the hoplites, thrusting forward with long spears.

In the centuries following the overthrow of Etruscan rule (traditionally dated 509 BCE, but possibly as late as 475[1]), the circumstances of war brought many changes to the Roman militia. A number of these, affecting the organization of the army, are attributed to the hero Furius Camillus,[2] but, in fact, they were probably introduced over a longer period during the second half of the fourth century BCE. Further changes were forced by the wars with Carthage. In the Second Punic War in particular (218–201 BCE), the Romans, facing a highly trained and brilliantly led army, had to adopt different tactics to counter the threat. The elements of speed and surprise became important. The phalanx (already modified by the Romans) was now too cumbersome, and a citizen militia, raised and trained for a specific campaign, was no longer adequate. Successful armies needed longer and better training. A professional army was needed.

In 152 BCE, in light of the growing reluctance of qualified Romans to serve in the army (especially in Spain, which offered little in the way of reward), the time-honored method of enlistment was modified and men were chosen by lot to serve for a fixed period.[3] Greater use was made of auxiliaries, troops recruited from non-Roman forces.[4] Marius (157–87 BCE) undertook further reforms. He abolished the property qualification (which had already been overlooked on occasion), opening the army to the lowliest of Roman citizens, the *capite censi* "counted by the head," who were too poor to belong to one of the five economic classes of property-owning and/or income-earning people. This "head count" army he equipped and supported at a cost to the state, unlike earlier soldiers, who had to be largely self-supporting. Marius is also credited with making the cohort the basic military unit (nominally 600 men in six centuries but usually about 480 men, with ten cohorts to a legion)[5] and with standardizing the soldiers' equipment.

The period between Marius and Augustus saw little change in either the organization or the tactics of the army, but there were important changes in its character. As citizenship was granted to most of the peoples of Italy, including Cisalpine Gaul, additional human resources became available. Volunteers were plentiful, and conscription was only used to fill occasional gaps. But volunteers from the newly enfranchised Italians, as indeed from the *capite censi,* did not share the loyalties of the former militia. The shift of allegiance from the state to the commander was to have far-reaching consequences. Meanwhile, under Caesar, the army became a highly efficient and thoroughly professional organization. To Caesar's successor, Augustus, fell the task of maintaining on a permanent peacetime basis what Caesar had made of Rome's armies. The success of Augustus's policy and its gradual consolidation under his successors can be measured by the remarkable survival of the empire despite conflicts within and pressures without. It stands as a military monarchy without parallel in the history of the world.

TACTICS

The most important change in the Roman army during the early republic was the abandonment of the phalanx as a tactical weapon. This solid mass of men, heavily armed with long, thrusting spears, had been invincible in its day. But the phalanx was too ponderous to be effective against lightly armed, fast-moving opponents. Livy describes the new Roman tactic.[6] There were basically three lines of soldiers, the *hastati* at the front[7] (cf. the description of Paul in Acts 24:5 as a **"front liner"**[8] of the sect of the Nazarenes), behind them the *principes,*[9] and behind them the *triarii.*[10] The first two ranks made up the main fighting force,[11] each having fifteen *manipuli* consisting of 120 to 200 men each. This subdivision into smaller tactical units provided the flexibility that the phalanx had lacked. The *hastati* would engage the enemy first. If they failed, they retired between the maniples of the second rank, leaving the battle to the *principes.* Meanwhile, the third rank, the *triarii,* unseen, knelt down with their spears at the ready. If the second rank failed, the third rose to the attack. The impact of these successive waves of fresh troops could be decisive in turning the battle. In addition, 300 cavalry were attached to each legion and could be called on as needed.

With some modification in the composition of the ranks outlined above and in their accouterment, this remained, broadly speaking, the Roman battle order throughout the remaining period of the republic and into the first century CE. With their training, discipline, and flexibility in battle, the Roman army was unequalled. Paul encouraged his Christian readers to emulate the legions in their discipline and order. He urged the Corinthians, whenever they met together for worship, to do everything in a decent and orderly manner (1 Cor 14:40), **"in proper battle array,"**[12] a phrase that occurs nowhere else in biblical Greek but is used by Herodotus to describe the Greek lines at Salamis as opposed to the disorderly ranks of the Persians.[13] Paul rejoiced to "see" (actually to hear; he had not been to their city) the **"good order**[14] and **firmness"**[15] of the church in Colossae (Col 2:5). Both terms may be supposed to express a military metaphor, the latter of an army drawn up and holding its ground, immovable, against the shock of an enemy onslaught.

The image of troops moving forward in line of battle lies behind the language of 1 Cor 15:23, with its reference to the *tagmata*,[16] the **"ranks"** of the believers. Paul is thinking of a new force, the "resurrection army," advancing like the legions on the spent force of this world. The first line is Christ in his solitary glory; the second, the army comprising all those who are his. Whether "asleep" in the grave or awake in the world, they will be summoned by the sound of God's trumpet to rally to Christ (1 Cor 15:52). The same metaphor of troops in line of battle (perhaps used with less deliberation) occurs in Acts 13:48 in regard to God's appointing the Gentiles to eternal life. They had been **ordered into line,**[17] so to speak, to receive what God would gladly hand out. In Rom 13:1 the same term is employed for God's instituting ("putting into place") the benefit of human government. In 1 Cor 16:15 members of the household of Stephanas are said to have "put themselves in line" for service.[18] Finally, in Gal 5:25 Paul enjoins all Christian "soldiers" to **keep in step**[19] with the Spirit (as though the Spirit were taking them towards the likeness of Christ and setting a pace that would get them well on their way), and in 1 Thess 2:18 Paul warns that Satan is ever ready to throw up **a roadblock**[20] to hinder their progress.

WARFARE

In 2 Cor 7:5 Paul speaks of a time (his return to Macedonia) when he felt himself to be more like a soldier at war than anything else—"on the outside, **battles;**[21] on the inside, fears." His fears were for Titus, his envoy to the church in Corinth, whose return from that city was long overdue, and for that church, with whom his relationship had been strained almost to breaking point over the past several months. The battles of which he speaks were probably mundane, battles with human antagonists[22] rather than spiritual, and may have amounted to nothing more dangerous than "wars with words."[23] But they may have been more serious, even life-threatening. Paul was no stranger to physical threat. Such "battles," however, were occasional. A **conflict**[24] from which there is no respite, an internal conflict that is known to all Christians, is the one between the flesh (NIV "our sinful nature") and the Spirit of God. Paul speaks of it in Gal 5:16–25. There is no doubt as to its outcome. God has already won. The decisive battle was "out there" on the cross. But "in here," in terms of our thoughts and words and deeds, the battle still rages. The flesh will not "lay down its arms" and is fighting a stubborn rearguard action. Thus, we must strive, under the command of God's Spirit, to overcome the flesh by refusing to carry out its desire (v. 16).[25]

The decisive battle has been won: the big issues of sin and its consequences and our acceptance with God are behind us. In this sense, "those who belong to Christ have already **crucified**[26] the flesh with its passions and desires" (v. 24). In terms of our eternal well-being in relation to God, there is nothing more to be done. But in practical terms, there is much to be done—much ground still to be won. The hortatory form of v. 25 (although the metaphor has changed to that of walking) implies this. In practice, the flesh still has to be "nailed" by our refusing to do the kinds of things mentioned in verses 19–21 and by doing those mentioned in 22–23.[27] To the extent that we follow these guidelines, we anticipate and are prepared for the perfection that will one day be ours. When Christ comes, our practice will, at last, conform to our status.

This thought of inner conflict occurs again in Rom 6:12–14. The flesh, or as Paul now names it in verse 6, the "old nature,"[28] has been crucified in our identification with Christ ("crucified with," *synestaurōthē;* notice both the aorist tense and the passive voice). Thanks to Christ, the war against the flesh has been effectively won, but the flesh and the Spirit continue to skirmish. Paul returns to this theme yet again in 7:23. There are, he says, "two principles[29] **at war**[30] within me" and he laments that the flesh so often has the upper hand. He knows—and in this he speaks for us all—that the flesh ("the principle of sin," as he calls it here) would long since have won and made him "**a prisoner of war**" had it not been for Christ.[31] Again, in 8:5–9, he speaks of this conflict. Here the flesh is identified as God's **enemy**,[32] for it **does not submit**[33] to God's law (v. 7).

In short, the Christian is a theater of war and is summoned to fight "manfully under Christ's banner against sin, the world, and the devil," as the *Book of Common Prayer* has it. Sin, for which the flesh has a proclivity, must not be allowed to have that upper hand: "Let not sin continue to reign[34] [present imperative] . . . Let not sin be your master"[35] (Rom 6:12, 14). Our faculties are the "weapons"[36] of this warfare and must not fall into enemy hands: "Stop yielding [as you have done] your faculties to sin as weapons of wickedness, but rather yield yourselves once and for all to God . . . and your faculties, therefore, to God as weapons of righteousness"[37] (v. 13). Paul's warning to the widows of Ephesus in 1 Tim 5:14 is applicable to us all: in matters of conduct, "give the enemy no **base of operations**"[38]—no beachhead—from which to launch further attacks.

Paul lived under the shadow of Rome's military might and spent much of his time in the presence of soldiers. No doubt the military presence was more conspicuous in some parts of the empire than in others. For example, when Paul and Barnabas visited Pisidian Antioch, the city was the center of operations against the clans who held the highlands between it and the Pamphylian coast. The province of Syria, in which Paul spent so much of his time, was held by a standing army of four legions plus auxiliary forces.[39] But wherever he was, there was no escaping the presence of soldiers. As he traveled, he was likely to meet them on the march or pursuing bandits or escorting prisoners. And there were times when he himself was a prisoner of Rome: in the garrison of the Antonia (Acts 21:33ff.), in the *praetorium* of Caesarea (Acts 23:31ff.),[40] and twice (apparently) in Rome itself in the custody of the Praetorian Guard (Acts 28:16, 30; 2 Tim 1:15–18). Thus, it is not surprising that he laced his writings with military metaphors. But it was also something of a literary convention to do so.

Long before Paul, at least from the time of Socrates' immediate followers,[41] spiritual or intellectual struggle was commonly portrayed in military terms. This practice was certainly popular among the Stoics and Cynics of Paul's own day. Seneca's dictum "Life is a battle" expressed a view held by many and in terms that many others would endorse.[42] Of particular interest is the metaphor of the impregnable fortress—the soul "fortified" against misfortune by logical arguments—found in Epictetus[43] and Seneca.[44] Paul uses a similar metaphor in 2 Cor 10:3–6. But where the philosophers looked for an inner impregnability—the soul untouched by "the slings and arrows of outrageous fortune"—Paul speaks of even the strongest keep of the soul being breached by the weapons that God has put into the hands of his "soldiers." Paul is probably more indebted to biblical and extrabiblical Jewish writings, such as Prov 21:22, Eccl 9:14–16, 1 Maccabees, and even Philo,[45] than to the Stoics and Cynics for the images that he employs in this passage, but the coincidence of language is such that some influence must be allowed to these philosophers. Some scholars maintain that their influence is primary.[46] Paul writes,

> Though we live [lit., "walk"] in the world ["flesh"], we do not make war as the world ["flesh"] does, for the weapons of our warfare are not worldly ["fleshly"], but have divine power to destroy strongholds. We destroy arguments and every obstacle raised against the knowledge of God and take captive every thought to make it obedient to Christ. We are ready to punish every disobedience, once your obedience is complete.

He is referring metaphorically to a military campaign as he speaks of **"making war"**[47] (v. 3) and of **"warfare"**[48] (v. 4), words that are often used of specific campaigns, such as Rome's campaign against the pirates of Paul's native Cilicia. Their strongholds lining the coast had to be destroyed if the Romans were ever to succeed against them. Paul's family may have lived in close proximity to these events and may have discussed in a young Paul's hearing how the Romans tore down these fortresses.[49] The pirate strongholds were laid under siege, a method of warfare in which, in the opinion of Tacitus,[50] the Romans were especially skilled.

LAYING SIEGE

Siegecraft had evolved in Roman warfare, much as it had among the Greeks, with blockade giving way more and more to assault. To this end the Romans had developed the *testudo* ("tortoise"), by which interlocking shields formed a screen under which a scaling party or sappers could attain to the walls.[51] Other devices also protected those working at the base of the walls,[52] such as the *musculus,* a long gallery on wheels with a pitched roof to deflect missiles hurled down from above. If the walls of the stronghold were protected by a ditch, a causeway *(agger)* might be constructed across it to allow access to the walls. A moveable tower could be brought up to the walls across the *agger,* or a tower could be erected in situ. From these towers the assailants could drive off the defenders and gain access to the walls by means of a fixed bridge thrusting out from the tower *(exostra)* or a drawbridge let down from the tower by pulleys (*sambuca,* so called because it resembled a harp).[53] There was also a kind of crane *(tolleno)* that hoisted the attackers onto the walls. The chief battering engine was the ram *(aries),* a beam tipped with a heavy iron head in the shape of a ram's head, sometimes suspended on a wheeled frame with a roof and swung by means of ropes (this contrivance was also known as a tortoise *[testudo arietaria]* because of its "shell" and "head," which moved in and out).[54] Other weapons of assault were the catapults *(catapultae)* of various sizes. The smaller were known as *scorpiones* or *ballistae,* and the largest as *onagri*.[55] The lines of the besieging force might be protected at their front by trenches and pits and at their rear—if there was any likelihood of a relieving army coming at them from that direction—by a circumvallation, that is, a defensive wall and ditch.[56]

In 2 Cor 10:3–6 Paul does not identify the siege **weapons**[57] employed in the campaign that he has in mind beyond describing them as having "divine power"[58] (in answer, perhaps, to his critics, who may have represented him as unspiritual and therefore ineffectual, unlike themselves). It seems likely, however, that all of his "weapons" are comprehended in one, namely, the gospel of Christ. The "**strongholds**"[59] (v. 4) and the "**obstacles**"[60] (v. 5, lit., "every high thing lifted up," like the walls of a citadel) are the arguments by which the gospel of Christ is resisted. But the gospel can overcome even "the cleverness of the clever."[61] And once these citadels of sophistry have been breached, **the defenders are taken captive**[62]—those who resist the gospel are at last conquered by the gospel. Still working with this metaphor but shifting its application a little, Paul states that his objective is to "take every thought captive to make it obedient to Christ" (v. 5).[63] That is, in those who are won for Christ, he wants no half measures. He is looking for a commitment of the mind as well as of the heart. He is **"at the ready,"**[64] he adds (with the church in Corinth especially in view), like a soldier on standby, "to punish every act of disobedience" (v. 6). Here the image is of **the pacification of a region**—the aftermath of breaching its strongholds. There were still "pockets of resistance" in the congregation at Corinth—people who repudiated Paul's authority and held to "a Jesus other than the one whom he had preached" (11:4). Paul regarded them, or at least their teachers, as the servants of Satan (11:13–15). He would deal with that problem in due course, but first he must be sure of the Corinthians' general obedience both to the gospel and to himself as Christ's legate.

TAKING PRISONERS

In the Roman world, war and slavery went hand in hand, slavery being the inevitable outcome of defeat in war. It is open to question, then, whether Paul's metaphors of imprisonment are best discussed in this chapter or under slavery. The idea of enslavement may be uppermost when he calls himself the **prisoner**[65] of Christ (Eph 3:1; 4:1; 2 Tim 1:8; Phlm 1, 9) and three times describes his colleagues as his **"fellow prisoners"**[66] (Andronicus, Junias, Aristarchus, and Epaphras in Rom 16:7; Col 4:10; Phlm 23). Or is he only making a play on the fact that he was literally a prisoner of Rome when he uses this terminology (Rom 16:7 being the only exception)? At all events, by calling himself a "prisoner," Paul was declaring his subjection to Christ. Like slavery, imprisonment is a metaphor of unconditional allegiance.

In Col 1:13, on the other hand, the idea of the prisoner of war may be uppermost,[67] although slavery is part of the image. God is said to have **rescued**[68] and **removed**[69] us from one authority to another that we might no longer be subject to darkness[70] (as our former oppressor is called) but to the light. The kingdom to which God has brought us, in which God has made us citizens,[71] is the kingdom of God's Son. The similar notion of a prisoner escaping is found in 2 Tim 2:26. Here Paul suggests that the good conduct of Christians might provide the context in which God will bring their opponents to a better mind. Their opponents, he says, "have been **taken alive as captives**[72] by the devil to do his bidding" (i.e., they are his slaves). If only God will grant them repentance, they will "come to their senses[73] and spring the devil's trap."[74] Strictly speaking, it is not so much that the devil takes prisoners as that we are born into his service— by nature we belong to "the authority of darkness," and only by grace do we come to the light. But the metaphor should not be pressed. It is

simply a graphic description of our human condition and another reminder of our dependence on grace.

Roman conquerors compelled their prisoners to march under an arch
made of three spears lashed together. This was a symbol of their defeat and
was known as "passing under the yoke" (was this a Roman metaphor from
the harnessing of beasts?). Thus, slavery in all of its forms came to be described as a "yoke," as in 1 Tim 6:1, where Paul is addressing literal slaves. In
Gal 5:1, on the other hand, he speaks in these terms of those who were in
danger of submitting (if they had not already done so) to the metaphorical
"yoke" of Judaism, which saw salvation as vested in obedience to God's law,
contrary to the Christian gospel, which offers salvation by the grace of God
and freedom from that other "slavery" (i.e., from the necessity of obedience
as the *grounds* of salvation, not, of course, from that necessity as our *response*
to the gift of God). "For freedom," Paul declares (with reference to the obligations that the Judaizers sought to impose), "Christ has set us free. Stand
therefore [on the gospel of grace] and do not submit again to **the yoke** of
slavery."[75]

SIGNALS AND SETTING WATCH

Once the army was encamped and the watches set, a trumpet call signaled each change of watch. When the army struck camp and prepared to
move, everything was done in a certain sequence, each step signaled by the
trumpet. At the first sound, the tents were struck and the baggage was gathered up; at the second, the baggage was loaded on the pack animals or (at a
later date) into the wagons; at the third, the ranks moved forward at the
march. In battle the trumpet signaled the advance or retreat,[76] and Paul pictures the resurrection of the last day in these terms. Christ has led the advance with his own resurrection, but others will follow at **the sound of the
trumpet**[77] and on **the word of command**[78] that God will utter (1 Cor
15:23, 52; 1 Thess 4:13–18, esp. v. 16). It was crucial that the trumpet
sound clearly and be understood in the face of the enemy. "If the trumpet
gives an uncertain sound," asks Paul, "who will prepare himself for the
battle?" (1 Cor 14:8). With this analogy he makes the point that the church
is better served in its public meetings by the gifts of intelligible speech,
which address the mind, than by the unintelligible "tongues" so highly valued by the Corinthians.

The Roman army, when encamped, took great care in setting the
watch. Sentries were posted within the camp and on its perimeter, and the
sentries themselves were kept under surveillance by regular patrols throughout the night.[79] The Greek word *phroureō* "to guard,"[80] which covers this
range of activities, has two applications: keeping the enemy out and (with
reference to prisons and the like) keeping the enemy securely within. The
second sense is found in 2 Cor 11:32 in Paul's account of his escape from

Damascus. "In Damascus," he says, "the governor under king Aretas had the city guarded in order to seize me, but . . . I slipped through his hands." This sense is found again in Gal 3:23, where Paul speaks in a figure of the law as **holding** its subjects **in custody**, confining them[81] until faith in Christ came along to give them a way of escape.

Paul uses the verb in the other sense of **keeping the enemy at bay** in Phil 4:7. There was a Roman garrison at Philippi in Paul's day, making this metaphor particularly apt for the readers there. The Philippians' "enemy" in this instance was anxiety, and it appears to have been making some perhaps serious inroads into their general well-being. "Stop being anxious," he writes (present imperative). "The peace of God . . . will garrison your hearts and minds." This peace is the peace that we have with God, a peace established by God and located "in Christ Jesus." It is primarily a matter of status with God (see, e.g., Rom 5:1). But status shades into experience, and this appears to be what Paul has in mind in this passage.[82] Philippians 4:6 explains how that peace can be had: "In everything, by prayer and intercession, with thanksgiving, let your requests be made known to God." The peace of God can be experienced through prayer, and this passage shows how important prayer is in terms of "realized Christianity," of believers knowing God's peace in practice ("on earth as it is in heaven").

In 2 Thess 3:3 Paul speaks again of our divine protection. He makes the statement "The Lord [i.e., God] is faithful," in the sense that God is utterly dependable. He then describes the Lord as "the one who will strengthen you and guard you from the evil one." The verb *phylassō* "**to guard** or protect,"[83] used here, is not necessarily a military term. But in this one instance, in which God is said to protect his people from their enemy,[84] it sits well with the other references to the cosmic war in which Christians are engaged.

THE SOLDIER'S ARMOR

Paul probably wrote his letter to the church in Rome during the three-month stay in Corinth to which Luke refers in Acts 20:3. The seat of the provincial government of Achaia, Corinth would have had a military establishment of some sort,[85] and the sight of Roman soldiers in Corinth would be nothing unusual. Imagine the following scene: The morning light glances off the burnished armor of a soldier as the business of the day begins. Sounds of revelers from the previous night can still be heard somewhere nearby. Paul turns from the window and resumes his dictation to Tertius (see Rom 16:22), incorporating into his letter the sights and sounds of the new day: "Wake up [he tells the Romans], for the night is nearly over and the day is at hand. Let us, therefore, cast aside the works of darkness and put on **the armor**[86] of light; let us conduct ourselves in a manner that befits the day, not in reveling and drunkenness" (Rom 13:11–13; cf. 1 Thess 5:5–8).[87]

The precise meaning of the genitive in the phrase "the armor of light" is not clear. It could be possessive: the armor belongs to the light in the sense that it is the proper dress for the "new day" of God's kingdom. Or it could be subjective: the armor is issued by God, who is the light.[88] Either way, it comes down to this: we are to put on the Lord Jesus Christ (v. 14) in the sense of recalling new every morning that we are "in Christ" and thus ought to live Christ every day.[89]

Paul returns to the theme of the soldier's armor in 2 Cor 6:7 with his reference to "the weapons of righteousness." Again, it is not clear what Paul meant by the genitive. It could be descriptive: the weapons are themselves righteous. It could be objective: the weapons are given for the defense and promotion of righteousness. Or it could be subjective: the weapons are those that come with the righteousness that God reckons to all whom God justifies (in a sense, the weapons are given by righteousness). Whatever the phrase means in detail, Christians are assured in these words that they are equipped for the work to which they are called—the work of ministering the divine reconciliation to others—God making his appeal, as Paul puts it, through the minister (5:18–20). The weapons of righteousness enable the Christian to contend for the gospel both offensively, by taking the initiative in making it known, and defensively, by parrying the argumentative thrusts of those who oppose it, for the Christian is armed both "on the right hand" (i.e., the offensive sword and javelin) and "on the left" (i.e., the defensive shield).[90] What are these "weapons of righteousness"? They are the power of God, given to all who are in Christ by his Spirit (cf. 2 Cor 10:4).

The body armor of the Roman soldier varied from time to time. In the late republic and early empire, legionaries wore an armor of mail *(lorica hamata)*. By the time of Claudius, mail had been replaced by a more complex suit *(lorica segmentata)*[91] comprising (1) a pair each of back and front metal plates, (2) sets of curved metal strips over the shoulders, and (3) a leather apron, covered on the outside by six or seven horizontal strips of metal. The apron hung from a belt at the waist.[92] The armor could be taken apart or put on as a complete unit and laced up at the front. A scarf (the origin of the necktie) was worn around the neck to protect it from chafing. The head was covered by a metal helmet, with a projecting plate at the back to protect the neck. The face was protected by cheek plates hinged at the top to the helmet. A short woolen tunic[93] and a loincloth were worn beneath the armor. Sandals *(caligae)* studded with hobnails completed the outfit.[94] The thongs of the sandals were wound halfway up the shin and tied. In cold climates the legionaries were permitted to wrap their feet in wool and to wear knee-length leather trousers *(bracae)*.[95] The trousers, however, were generally frowned on as a foreign and effeminate innovation. Occasionally, a heavy cloak *(sagum)* was worn also.

Each man carried on his left arm a large shield *(scutum)* that was curved to cover the body. It was made of wood edged with metal, and the handgrip on the inside was protected on the outside by a metal boss. The outside surface of the shield was covered with leather and embellished with metal decorations. "The weapons for the right hand" were the javelin *(pilum)*, of which each man had two, and the sword *(gladius)*, a short, two-edged weapon (the shorter the sword, the quicker the draw).[96] The tactic in battle was (1) to discharge the two javelins[97] and (2) to draw swords, close ranks, and charge, using the sword as a thrusting weapon.[98] The target was the opposing soldier's lower abdomen or groin—the part of his body least well protected by armor. It was probably such hand-to-hand fighting that Paul had in mind in Eph 6:10–18. He uses a word that means "to wrestle" but can be applied to a conflict of any kind—here, it would seem, to soldiers closing in battle. "Our **fight**,"[99] he says, "is not [primarily] against flesh and blood"— the conflict of which he had written in Romans and Galatians[100]—but against spiritual powers.[101] For such a conflict, which is ours even now but will come to its apogee on "the evil day" (presumably the period immediately preceding the second coming of Christ[102]), we must **put on**[103] **the full armor**[104] of God to be able to **hold our ground**[105] and to **withstand**[106] the foe.

Before battle is joined, the Christian's armor must be in place. (As the aorist tense of the participles in vv. 14–16 clearly shows: "Stand . . . having [already] girded . . . put on . . . shod . . ." These participles are in effect aorist imperatives). Paul itemizes the armor selectively (the legionaries carried far more than he mentions) and adds an interpretation to each of the items. This passage should be compared with 1 Thess 5:8, and both should be compared with the descriptions of the divine warrior in Isa 11:4–5, 59:17 and Wis 5:17–22, passages to which Paul no doubt owed much for his metaphor.[107] An important clue to the proper interpretation of Eph 6:10–18 lies in the fact that all of the terms mentioned—truth, righteousness, peace, faith, the Spirit, and the word of God—have their setting in the Old Testament covenantal relationship between God and God's people. A new covenant, based on Christ's death for our sins and entered into by faith in Christ, is now on offer. But truth, righteousness, peace, faith, the Spirit, and the word of God still characterize this new relationship. To have "put on Christ," therefore, is to have "put on" these things and to be clothed with "the armor of God."[108] This passage should be read in conjunction with Eph 4:23–24 and Col 3:10. There it is "the new man" *(ho kainos anthrōpos)* that is to be put on. In Gal 3:27 the new man is seen to be Christ, and in Rom 13:12–14 Christ is seen to be the armor of light. Thus Paul's intention in Eph 6:10–18 is to remind his readers that they have "put on" Christ, that they are "in Christ," and that they should live Christ, overcoming *in practice* the evil that Christ has overcome on the cross.[109] Thus Eph 6:10–18 is about Christians bringing Christ's victory into their day-to-day lives.

In practice, Christians should be distinguished by their truthfulness, their integrity in word and in deed.[110] If Paul is following the normal sequence by which a soldier put on his armor, he identifies this with **the belt**[111] from which hung the protective apron (v. 14). The virtue of righteousness[112] he identifies with **the breastplate,**[113] the Greek word being the general term for armor that covers the area between the shoulders and the abdomen (v. 14). Two meanings are possible for **the sandals,**[114] either "the preparedness" or "the readiness[115] of the gospel of peace" (v. 15). The latter suggests that Christians should be on the alert, in offensive mode, ready to make the gospel known "in season and out" (2 Tim 4:2), as though Paul's thought had shifted from the armor of Isa 59:17 to the announcement of good news in Isa 52:7 (a passage to which he had already referred in Eph 2:17). "Preparedness," on the other hand, suggests that Christians should have such a grasp of the gospel that they can defend their position against any assault. This notion of defense best suits the context, as Paul calls on his readers to "hold their ground" in the face of the enemy. It is noteworthy that Paul discusses a "gospel of peace" in the context of a military metaphor. His reference is to peace with God. The genitive is objective—the peace about which the gospel makes its announcement.

In addition to their "body armor," Paul's Christian readers are instructed to take up[116] **"the shield**[117] of faith."** His thought is of the *scutum,* the shield carried by the legionaries. When its outside leather covering was soaked in water, as it should have been before any battle, it protected the soldier from incendiary missiles—arrows or spears tipped with fibrous material of some kind, impregnated with pitch, set alight, and discharged. For Christians, faith—their trust in God and conviction that God can be trusted—is the best protection[118] against "the **incendiary missiles**[119] of the evil one" (v. 16). The assurance of salvation,[120] which is the product of this trust in God, is **"the helmet"**[121] that Christians wear. In their hands the Spirit has put **"the sword,"**[122] which is "the word of God"[123] (v. 17). The imagery is still of defensive warfare,[124] in which Paul sees the Scriptures (the Old Testament and perhaps the Christian tradition, soon to become the New Testament) as an important part of the Christian's armory.[125]

The passage ends with an injunction to pray (v. 18). Paul does not liken prayer to any item of armor and may have finished his military metaphor. But isn't prayer **the battle cry** of the Christian? The tactic of sound was sometimes decisive in ancient warfare. In verse 18 there is a significant change of tense (from the Greek aorist to the present). Earlier the call had been to decisive action (the aorist): "Stand . . . girded . . . put on . . . shod. . . ." The call is now to ongoing activity. Prayer (aided as it is by the Spirit of God) should be made *throughout* the battle (the force of the present). A Christian should remain *constantly* **on the alert**[126] (again, the force of the present). Nowhere is the scope of prayer more clearly stated than here. The word "all" is repeated four times in the Greek, each time expressing a comprehensive concern: (1) for every circumstance of life, (2) for the duration of life, (3) for every facet of life, and (4) for all the saints.

The Soldier's Discipline and Commitment

Constant training was the secret of the legions' success. "They allow no truce from their military training," Josephus reports.

> Each soldier tests his strength and courage every day; thus battles are neither new nor difficult to them. Accustomed to keep their places, disorder never arises, fear never troubles their minds, fatigue never exhausts their bodies. They are certain to conquer, because they are certain to find enemies unequal to them and one may say without fear of mistake that their exercises are battles without bloodshed and their battles are bloody exercises.[127]

If the training was hard, so was the discipline that enforced it. In battle a soldier who failed to keep his place in the line or allowed his weapons to fall into the hands of the enemy was condemned to the *fustuarium*—that is, to be set upon by his colleagues with cudgels and stones. The victim was usually killed. If he survived, he was discharged ignominiously. A whole unit that failed in its duty was paraded before the legion. Every tenth man, selected by lot, was condemned to the *fustuarium*. The practice of decimation (taking one in ten) appears to have happened often enough not to be particularly remarked upon.[128] Roman soldiers as a matter of course killed each other for their common good.[129] The remainder of the unit were put on rations of barley in place of wheat and were made to pitch their tents outside the camp. Thus they were constantly brought to the notice of others and made to endure their contempt.[130]

When Paul experienced a disciplinary problem with certain members of the church in Thessalonica, he remarked that **they had not** (as "soldiers" of Christ) **held their place in the line of battle**.[131] A modern military metaphor would call them "deserters." The problem was that they were idle. They were not merely unemployed—there is no fault in that—but were actively refusing to work (*"will* not work," 2 Thess 3:10) and were sponging off others, thus "breaking ranks" and undermining the good order of the Christian community.[132] The problem appears to have worsened during the interval between the writing of Paul's two letters to that church. In the second letter, as a last resort, he recommends to the church that it withhold "rations" from these "mutinous troops"[133] (2 Thess 3:10). Yet he continues to regard them as "brothers in Christ" (see v. 15). They are to be disciplined, not jettisoned.

G. R. Watson notes,

> Theoretically, an army may be more efficient if its members are celibate and wedded only to the idea of discipline. There is then no heart-searching when a unit is suddenly posted from one end of the empire to another, there is no attached civilian population to defend and to take into account in the siting and construction of camps and forts, and the soldier's only ties are to the army in which he serves.[134]

It was probably such a theory as this that inspired the requirement, dating from the early empire, that a soldier should remain unmarried for the duration of his military service.[135] A man who was married at the time of enlistment was expected to sever the relationship.[136] This ban covered all ranks up to centurion.[137] Similarly, no soldier was permitted to moonlight by conducting his own business on the side, probably to keep him focused on his commitment to his military calling. The issue of commitment prompted Paul to cite the rule in 2 Tim 2:4: **"No one on military service**[138] **gets entangled in the affairs of ordinary life."** Such entanglements must be avoided, he says, "in order to please **the commander under whom he has enlisted."**[139] In short, he would have Timothy conduct his life under the principle that ruled his own: "For me to live is Christ" (Phil 1:21) and therefore to be always on active service.

The fact that Paul describes himself as a "soldier," and other "front liners"[140] such as Epaphroditus and Archippus as his **"fellow soldiers"**[141] (Phil 2:25; Phlm 2), and invites Timothy, who apparently had charge of the church in Ephesus, "to share hardship with him as **a good soldier**[142] of Christ Jesus" (2 Tim 2:3) and "to wage the good warfare"[143] (1 Tim 1:18) might suggest that the injunction of 2 Tim 2:4 is addressed to church leaders only—that only a select few in the church are to make the kind of commitment that the soldier was expected to make. But this would be a misreading of what Paul had in mind. In other circumstances, what he had occasion to say here to Timothy he may well have said to others who were not in the "front line" and yet whose responsibility as "rank and file" Christians was no less to serve Christ. There is a sense in which we are all "soldiers" of Christ, to whom we owe the soldier's single-minded devotion.[144]

THE SOLDIER'S PAY

In Rom 6, the military image of verses 11–13, with their reference to "weapons," merges into the image of slavery in the verses that follow. Slavery was, as mentioned, often the outcome of war, but at the end of the chapter Paul may return to a military metaphor in his reference to the "wages" of sin (v. 23). This word (*opsōnion*, derived from *opson*, meaning "cooked meat or fish") means "provisions, provision money" and so "wages" generally, but specifically **the wages paid to a soldier**.[145] And the metaphor may continue in the second half of the verse, for *charisma*, "a free gift,"[146] was also a military word, although not exclusively so. Tertullian recognized the association when he translated Paul's Greek by the Latin *donativum*, **the largesse given by the commander** to his troops.[147] Sin pays its soldiers precisely what they have earned; God gives God's soldiers largesse—something over and above anything that they have earned or deserved. There is in the word *charisma* a recognition that all is from God, whether the grace that covers sin or every grace with which life is adorned.

In republican times, Roman generals customarily distributed part of the spoils of war among their troops at the conclusion of a successful campaign. By the first century BCE the prospect of plunder had become a major incentive to enlistment and was probably the underlying reason for the commanders themselves wanting to raise an army and take to the field. Many a consul and proconsul amassed his fortune in this way.[148] Under the emperors, however, the payment of special bounties was uncoupled from the outcome of a campaign, and other occasions for gifting the soldiers were found. This was to discourage the army from supporting an aggressive foreign policy with an eye simply to plunder.[149] Nevertheless, the thought of plunder must always have been at the back of the soldier's mind. It was certainly the image in Paul's mind when he was defending himself to the Corinthians for preaching the gospel to them free of charge. He was able to do it, he says, by "lowering" himself to make leather goods for a living[150] and by "**plundering**[151] other churches," that is, by allowing them to contribute more than their fair share of his "soldier's pay"[152] (2 Cor 11:7–8). The same metaphor (and almost the same word) is found in Paul's warning to the church in Colossae not to let anyone **carry it off as the spoils of war**[153] by means of a specious but deceptive philosophy (Col 2:8).

In 1 Cor 9:7 Paul, using the professional soldier as an analogy, defends the right of church leaders (himself included) to have their material needs met by the church: "Who **serves as a soldier**," he asks, "**at his own expense?**" He is referring to the Roman soldier. As mentioned at the beginning of this chapter, in the early days of the citizen militia, when campaigns had been confined to the spring and summer (before harvest), the Roman soldier had served at his own expense. Payments are first mentioned at the siege of Veii, in 396 BCE, when the campaign was drawn out into the winter.[154] By the second century BCE the Roman soldier was on a regular rate of pay.[155] The sources give some idea of how much he grossed, but how much he cleared after expenses remains a matter of some dispute because the amount deducted for rations and for equipment is unknown.[156] But the fact remains that he was paid. On the principle that the laborer is worthy of his hire, Paul argues that the congregation should similarly support its ministers or at least those whose ministry is their chief occupation.[157]

NOTES

1. A. Momigliano, "Procum Patricium," *JRS* 56 (1966): 21.
2. See Livy, *Hist.* 8.8; Plutarch, *Cam.* 40; also Dionysius of Halicarnassus, *Ant. rom.* 14.9.
3. The total liability was sixteen years, but under this new regulation, men serving in Spain had to be returned to Italy after only six years. These men could, however, be reenlisted for service elsewhere.
4. See ch. 10, n. 98.

5. For many years, the old tactical unit, the maniple, notionally a double century, i.e., perhaps 120 or 60 soldiers (see further ch. 10, n. 7), had proven to be too small to contend with the massive, undisciplined armies that the legions had often to face, and the cohort—three times the size of the maniple—had been gradually supplanting it in practice. According to Polybius (*Hist.* 2.23), the cohort had already been used by Scipio (236–184 BCE) as a tactical division against Hasdrubal, but Polybius only mentions it on this one occasion. Both Livy (*Hist.* 22.5.7; 25.39.1) and Sallust (*Bell. Jug.* 51.3; 100.4), however, refer to its existence as a military unit well before the time of Marius. Nevertheless, Gaius Marius may be credited with recognizing its value and structuring his army around it. See further G. R. Watson, *The Roman Soldier* (London: Thames & Hudson, 1969), 13–15, 21–24; G. Webster, *The Roman Imperial Army* (London: Black, 1979), 21. For a detailed discussion of the vexed question of the actual size of the legions, see J. Roth, "The Size and Organization of the Roman Imperial Legion," *Historia* 43 (1994): 346–62.

6. Livy (*Hist.* 8.8) describes the army as it was constituted in the second half of the fourth century BCE. Some details are not certain, but the general picture is clear enough. Other authorities for the changes introduced by (or around the time of) Camillus are Plutarch, *Cam.* 40, and Dionysius of Halicarnassus, *Ant. rom.* 14.9. Polybius (*Hist.* 6.19–42) provides a detailed description of the army of the late third century BCE. This summary is indebted to Webster (*Army*, 5–15) for his interpretation of these sources. See also ch. 10, n. 127.

7. The *hastati* were younger men and comprised two kinds of troops. In each maniple (*manipulus*, a double century; it is referred to more frequently in republican times than later, although the pairing of centuries continued and probably had some administrative or ceremonial significance, "a pretty parade-ground unit," as one writer describes it) there were twenty lightly armed men, each carrying a spear and javelins. (Livy speaks of these as *hasta* and *gaesum*, the latter being a heavy type of javelin.) The remainder of each unit carried body armor and a rectangular shield, the *scutum*, which now replaced the smaller round *clipeus*. This change of shield is confirmed by Dionysius of Halicarnassus (*Ant. rom.* 14.9). There is much dispute about the origin of the *scutum*, but Diodorus believed that it was a Roman invention (*Hist.* 23.2).

8. Πρωτοστάτης (from πρῶτος "first" and ἵστημι "to stand"): Of soldiers, "one who stands in the first rank," and so metaphorically, "a leader."

9. The *principes* were older, experienced men equipped with *scutum* and armor. Their weapon was the sword.

10. The *triarii* were, in fact, only the first of *three* further ranks behind the *principes*, each rank being of fifteen companies (a total of forty-five companies) of some 180 men each. Livy calls them "companies" (*ordines*) rather than maniples. The *triarii* were veterans, the *rorarii*, the second of the three ranks, were younger men, and the *accensi*, the third rank, were the least dependable men in the legion. For greater detail, see Webster, *Army*, 5–6.

11. They were known at this stage as the *antepilani*, not from *pilum* "a spear" but from *pilus* "a closed rank." See H. M. D. Parker, *The Roman Legions* (Cambridge: Cambridge University Press, 1958), 13 n. 1.

12. Κατὰ τάξιν: Τάξις (from τάσσω; see ch. 10, n. 17) (1) "an arranging" and, in a military context, "a disposition" of an army, "battle array," as in Xenophon, *Anab.* 1.2.18; Plutarch, *Pyrrh.* 16, (2) generally, "an arrangement," (3) "due order," (4) "office, order." In 1 Cor 14:40, Paul is expanding on his statement in v. 33 that God is not a God of disorder (ἀκαταστασία). In Stoic use, "disorderliness" referred to the state of a mind ruled by passion. Here it is to the state of a church in which the exercise of gifts was out of control. In this context, the κατὰ τάξιν of v. 40 suggests "a strict . . . method and rule of procedure" in the exercise of the gifts (G. G. Findlay, "St Paul's First Epistle to the Corinthians," *EGT* 2:917).

Both here in 1 Cor 14:40 and in Col 2:5, the only other instance of τάξις in Paul, it is commonly supposed that the metaphor is a military one. Thus E. Lohmeyer comments on Col 2:15, "The apostle is 'with them' as a field commander standing before his troops and arranging the ranks for battle once more" (*Die Briefe an die Philipper, Kolosser, und an Philemon* [Göttingen: Vandenhoeck & Ruprecht, 1964] 95), while R. P. Martin interprets Paul's words to mean that he viewed with approval their steadfast intent to close ranks and stand firm, without yielding to erroneous propaganda from an intruding enemy (*Colossians and Philemon* [London: Oliphants, 1981], 76–77). See also, e.g., C. F. D. Moule, *The Epistles of Paul the Apostle to the Colossians and to Philemon* (Cambridge: Cambridge University Press, 1957), 89.

13. Herodotus, *Hist.* 8.86.

14. Τὴν τάξιν: See ch. 10, n. 12.

15. Στερέωμα (from στερεόω "to make firm, solid, to strengthen, make strong"): "A solid body," thus "a support, foundation" and, from this, "strength, steadfastness, firmness." Found only here in the NT. 1 Macc 9:14 is often quoted in support of the military sense of στερέωμα. But στερέωμα is not necessarily a military term, as is also the case with τάξις (see the discussion of τάξις, ch. 10, n. 12, and of τάξις and στερέωμα together in Col 2:5 as a possible domestic metaphor, p. 97 and notes). With τάξις, however, the military association is much stronger. The context must always determine the precise sense of either word, and it could be argued that nothing in this context demands that these words be understood as a military metaphor. Most commentators, however, do understand them in these terms and I have followed their lead (see references, ch. 10, n. 12), supposing, on this basis, that Paul rejoiced to see that their "line" (τάξις) had remained unbroken and that they had held firm (στερέωμα) under the attack of the new teacher with his curious doctrine. A few stragglers had gone over to the enemy, but the church as a whole had remained true to the teaching that it had received at the outset.

16. Τάγμα (from τάσσω; see the next note): "That which has been arranged or placed in order," especially as a military term (which it nearly always is), "a company, troop, division, rank." It was commonly applied to divisions of the Roman legion. Found only here in the NT.

17. Τάσσω: Primarily in a military sense, then generally, "to draw up in order, arrange" in place, "assign, appoint, order." See also ch. 7, n. 44.

18. Here the language may be more that of trade than of troops lining up. See p. 170 and ch. 7, n. 44.

19. Στοιχέω (from στοῖχος "a row"): (1) "to be in rows (as of waves, plants, etc., as well as people), to walk in line," especially of soldiers marching into battle, (2) from this, metaphorically, "to walk by rule, to act according to a standard, to behave properly." See also Rom 4:12; Gal 6:16; Phil 3:16 (see ch. 9, n. 59). Here the verb is present subjunctive, "Let us *go on* walking."

20. Ἐνκόπτω: (1) "to dig into," (2) "to hinder." In Gal 5:7 the word is employed in a metaphor from the games—they were "running" and someone had "tripped" (hindered) them (see ch. 12, n. 138). But in 1 Thess 2:18 the thought is more of an obstacle in the road than of dirty tricks in the course of a race. G. Milligan (*St Paul's Epistles to the Thessalonians* [London: Macmillan, 1908], 34) suggests that the idea is of cutting up a road to make it impassable, whereas J. B. Lightfoot (*Saint Paul's Epistle to the Galatians* [London: Macmillan, 1884], 205) maintains that the metaphor is "derived from military operations. The word signifies 'to break up a road' (by destroying bridges, etc.) so as to render it impassable." Sometimes the Holy Spirit prevented Paul from taking a certain direction (Acts 16:6–7). With hindsight, no doubt, he had been able to see the divine purpose in this and to name the author accordingly. But in this instance, the hindrance seemed entirely satanic. In Rom 15:22, the "roadblock" to his coming to Rome appears to have been simply the legitimate demands of his work in the East. The opposite of ἐνκόπτω is προκόπτω

"to cut forward (as through undergrowth in the bush), to blaze a trail, to advance." Paul uses this verb in Rom 13:12; Gal 1:14; 2 Tim 2:16; 3:9, 13 and the noun προκοπή "progress" (properly of a journey, but then generally) in Phil 1:12, 25; 1 Tim 4:15. But in none of these passages is there any suggestion that he used the words as conscious metaphors.

21. Μάχη: "A battle, a battlefield, a quarrel, strife." See also 2 Tim 2:23; Titus 3:9.

22. For troubles experienced by Paul in the Aegean region—the setting of his Corinthian correspondence—see Acts 16:23; 17:5; 1 Cor 15:30–32 (a figurative reference to some human threat; see ch. 12, n. 60); 16:9; Phil 1:30; 1 Thess 2:2.

23. Cf. λογομαχέω (from λόγος "a word" and μάχομαι "to fight"): "To fight with words" in 1 Tim 6:4, and λογομαχία "a fight with words" or perhaps "about words" in 2 Tim 2:14. Controversies between Christians and Jews were perceived by outsiders to be such wars. See Acts 18:15; 23:29; 25:19, where, however, different expressions are used.

24. Ἀντίκειμαι: (1) "to lie opposite to," (2) "to oppose, withstand, resist." The expression in Gal 5:17 is ταῦτα ἀλλήλοις ἀντίκειται "these things [flesh and Spirit] are contrary to one another—they are lined up in combat, face-to-face [the present tense expressing the ongoing conflict], with the result [taking the ἵνα clause in this sense] that we are never able, in this life, to live entirely according to the Spirit." E. de W. Burton (*The Epistle to the Galatians* [Edinburgh: T&T Clark, 1921], 320), however, takes the ἵνα clause in its proper sense as purpose, the purpose being "of both flesh and Spirit, in the sense that the flesh opposes the Spirit that men may not do what they will in accordance with the mind of the Spirit, and the Spirit opposes the flesh that they may not do what they will after the flesh. Does the man choose evil, the Spirit opposes him; does he choose good, the flesh hinders him." For the verb, see also 1 Tim 1:10, and for its use as a participial substantive, "adversary," see 1 Cor 16:9; Phil 1:28; 2 Thess 2:4; 1 Tim 5:14.

25. The form of the Greek is that of a strong negative assertion concerning the future: "Make it your practice to walk [περιπατεῖτε, present imperative] in the Spirit and *you will not fulfill* [οὐ μὴ τελέσητε] the desire of the flesh." If anything, these words express a promise, but I take them as also expressing the goal toward which we must work.

26. Σταυρόω: Notice the aorist tense (ἐσταύρωσαν). The "crucifixion" of the flesh has been accomplished in our identification with Christ (see Rom 6:6; Gal 2:20; 6:14). On crucifixion as a punishment, see ch. 5, nn. 20, 50, for a discussion of this passage in connection with slavery. Crucifixion was a punishment reserved for slaves who had robbed or had been rebellious, but in the provinces it served also as a means of punishing insurrection. Josephus, e.g., tells of mass crucifixions in Judea under several Roman prefects, but especially under Titus during the siege of Jerusalem (*B.J.* 5.449–451).

27. The so-called fruit of the Spirit, i.e., "fruit" that the Spirit helps us (by our own discipline and determination) to produce, but without whose help we could never produce it. For this notion of self-help and Spirit help as components in Christian conduct, see, e.g., Col 1:29.

28. Ὁ παλαιὸς ἡμῶν ἄνθρωπος: "Our old person or self."

29. Νόμος: "Usage, custom, law," used in Rom 7:21, 23, 25; 8:2 of an influence impelling action. One of these influences has been named in v. 18 and elsewhere as the flesh. In v. 23 it is "the law of sin that lies within the faculties" (ὁ νόμος τῆς ἁμαρτίας ὁ ὢν ἐν τοῖς μέλεσιν), the old, sinful nature, which remains a fact of life for the Christian. The other "influence" is "the law of the mind" (ὁ νόμος τοῦ νοός), the "inner man" (ὁ ἔσω ἄνθρωπος) of v. 22. This higher self agrees that the law of God is good (vv. 12, 16, 22). In terms of Gal 5:16–25, it is on the side of the

Spirit of God. It is the Christian conscience in process of being shaped by the Spirit (on conscience, see further p. 197).

30. Ἀντιστρατεύομαι: "To make war against," a rare word found only here in the NT (cf. ch. 5, n. 61).

31. For αἰχμαλωτίζω: "To take or make captive," see ch. 5, n. 62; for the interpretation of Rom 7:7–25, see ch. 5, n. 64.

32. Here Paul speaks of the φρόνημα τῆς σαρκός "the mind of the flesh" (Rom 8:6), where φρόνημα is, strictly, "the content of the mind, its thoughts, its tendency." The tendency of the flesh, he says, is toward ἔχθηρα (from ἐχθρός "hated, hating, hostile" and, as a substantive, "an enemy") "enmity." See also Gal 5:20; Eph 2:15–16. Cf. Paul's references to the sinner himself as God's ἐχθρός in Rom 5:10; 11:28; 1 Cor 15:25; Phil 3:18; Col 1:21.

33. Ὑποτάσσω (from ὑπο "under" and τάσσω "to draw up in order, arrange, etc."; see ch. 10, n. 17): (1) as a military term, "to place or rank under," and so (2) generally, "to subject, put in subjection," and middle, "to subject oneself, obey." See also Rom 8:20 (2x); 10:3; 13:1, 5; 1 Cor 14:32, 34; 15:27 (3x), 28 (3x); 16:16; Eph 1:22; 5:21–22, 24; Phil 3:21; Col 3:18; Titus 2:5, 9; 3:1.

34. Βασιλεύω: See ch. 5, n. 23.

35. Κυριεύω: See ch. 5, n. 24. Here in the future indicative, which I have taken as an imperative, matching the βασιλευέτω of v. 12. It could, however, be "a promise, not a command, . . . pointing to the reason why commands like those he has just given can be obeyed. Believers can present their [faculties] to God for righteousness precisely because sin has no lordship over them. They are free" (L. Morris, *The Epistle to the Romans* [Grand Rapids: Eerdmans, 1988], 259).

36. Ὅπλα (singular ὅπλον): See ch. 10, n. 57.

37. Notice the change of tense in the verb παριστάνω (a late form of παρίστημι; see ch. 11, n. 50) "to present, etc.," from a present (μηδὲ παριστάνετε) to an aorist imperative (παραστήσατε). For the development of this metaphor of armorment, see pp. 219–22, and for the heinous offense of losing one's weapons to the enemy, p. 223 and ch. 10, n. 130.

38. Ἀφορμή (an old word from ἀπό and ὁρμή "rapid motion forward, assault"): "A starting point, a base to rush from," in war "a base of operations," and so generally "occasion, pretext, opportunity for something" (BAGD). Cf. Rom 7:8, 11; 2 Cor 5:12; 11:12 (2x); Gal 5:13. "The enemy" is ὁ ἀντικείμενος "the opposing one." The singular participle may be generic or it may refer to the devil. Paul uses the expression elsewhere of humans and of the antichrist (cf. 1 Cor 16:9; Phil 1:28; 2 Thess 2:4). The particular form of attack that Paul fears is λοιδορία "verbal abuse, reviling, reproach," which might suggest that the enemy is human. But it is sometimes a fine distinction between human actions and the "spiritual forces of evil" that lie behind them. See ch. 10, n. 101, on Eph 6:12.

39. Augustus rightly considered Syria the point of greatest strategic importance in the East. It controlled the natural routes to and across the Euphrates and, since the province of Asia was without a garrison, was the only eastern province with an army. The defense, therefore, of the whole of the Roman East (not only of Syria itself) and the support of the client princes of Galatia, Armenia, and Cappadocia depended on the Syrian army. It appears that at first there were only three legions under the command of the Syrian legate (see Josephus, *B.J.* 2.39, which speaks of Varus leaving in Jerusalem one of the three legions that he had brought with him from Syria), but the number was later increased to four, perhaps at the time of Caligula's expedition to the East, by the transference of the Legio XII Fulminata from Egypt to Syria (see Strabo, *Geog.* 17.1.12, 30; also Parker, *Legions,* 92; Watson, *Soldier,* 13ff.). On the numbers of both legionaries and auxiliaries in Syria, see T. R. S. Broughton, "The Roman Army," *BC* 5:431–41, and on the role of the latter in the Roman army, see ch. 10, n. 98. On Paul's presence in Syria, see Acts 9:8–25,

30; 11:25; 13:1–3; 14:26–28; 15:30–41; 18:23; 22:3; Gal 1:17, 21; at this time Cilicia (Cilicia Pedeias), of which Tarsus was the metropolis, was administered by Syria and was effectively part of that province until about the time of Nero (see A. N. Sherwin-White, *Roman Society and Roman Law in the New Testament* [Oxford: Clarendon, 1969], 56).

40. From Caesarea Paul was removed under military escort to Rome in the charge of a centurion named Julius of "the Augustan cohort" (Acts 27:1). This has been identified as the Cohors I Augusta, a regiment of auxiliaries attested by inscriptions to have been in Syria after 6 CE and in Batanea (Bashan, east of Galilee) in the time of Herod Agrippa II (ca. 50–100 CE). A detachment of the cohort may have been stationed at Caesarea. Cf. Acts 10:1, which refers to the presence of "the Italian cohort" in Caesarea, of which Cornelius was a centurion. The presence of an Italian cohort in Syria in the second half of the first century CE (also in the second century; see Broughton, "Roman Army," 441ff.) is also attested by inscriptional evidence. It is consonant with this for such a cohort to be in Caesarea at the earlier date suggested by Acts. It was almost certainly an auxiliary unit, since the legions were not usually stationed in the smaller provinces, such as Judea. Tacitus (*Hist.* 1.59) does mention an "Italian *legion*," but an inscription found in Austria refers to the second Italian cohort, describing it as belonging to "the archery division of the Syrian army." Since the legionnaires were not archers, the implication is that the Italian cohorts were auxiliary units. See further Sherwin-White, *Roman Society,* 160.

41. See, e.g., Plato, *Apol.* 28D–29A; *Phaedr.* 62D. For other references, see J. Leipolt, "Das Bild vom Kriege in der griechischen Welt," in *Gott und die Götter: Festgabe für Eric Fascher* (ed. G. Delling et al.; Berlin: Evangelische Verlagsanstalt, 1958), 16–30.

42. Seneca, *Ep.* 96.5; cf. Epictetus, *Diatr.* 3.24.31 and 34.

43. For Epictetus, the philosopher's thoughts are his protection (*Diatr.* 4.16.4). In his depiction of the true Cynic, the philosopher's self-respect, αἰδώς, constitutes his fortification. The Cynic must be adorned on every side with self-respect as other men are with walls, doors, and doorkeepers (4.8.33; cf. 3.22.13–19, 94–95; 4.3.7; Dio Chrysostom, *Disc.* 77; 78.40; Marcus Aurelius, *Med.* 3.7.16). On αἰδώς in Epictetus, see B. L. Hijmans, *ASKHSIS: Notes on Epictetus' Educational System* (Assen: Van Gorcum, 1959), 27–30.

44. Seneca shares the Stoic confidence that the wise man withstands every attack and cannot be injured (*Const.* 3.4–5; *Ben.* 5.2.3–4; *Ep.* 59.6–8; 64.3–4). Bravery is his impregnable fortress (*Ep.* 113.27–28), mental toughness his protection (51.5–6; 74.19; *Vit. beat.* 4.2). He therefore girds himself about with philosophy, an impregnable wall that Fortune cannot breach. Come what may to the body, the virtuous (right-thinking) soul stands on unassailable ground (*Ep.* 65.18; 82.5; *Vit. beat.* 15.5). In short, as Seneca says of Stilpo's greatness of soul, "Though beneath the hand of that destroyer of so many cities, fortifications shaken by the battering ram may totter and high towers undermined by tunnels and secret saps may sink in sudden downfall and earthworks rise to match the loftiest citadel, yet no war-engines can be devised that will shake the firm-fixed soul" (*Const.* 6.4). See further J. N. Sevenster, *Paul and Seneca* (Leiden: Brill, 1961), 156–62.

45. Philo, *Conf.* 128–131, makes extensive use of the image of the siege and applies it to the personal lives of individuals. See further ch. 10, n. 59, and Malherbe, "Antisthenes," 143–73.

46. See, e.g., Malherbe, "Antisthenes," who draws attention to the importance of the Odysseus tradition to the Cynics and argues that Paul is answering his critics at Corinth in terms both of that tradition and of the metaphor of the stronghold so favored by these philosophers. S. K. Stowers ("Paul on the Use and Abuse of Reason," in *Greeks, Romans, and Christians* [ed. D. Balch, E. Ferguson, and W. A. Meeks; Minneapolis: Fortress, 1990], 266–67) suggests that Paul portrays himself in 2 Cor

10:3–6 as a rigorist Cynic and his opponents as Stoics. See further, on Paul's medical metaphors, pp. 87–89 and notes, his metaphors of body and head, pp. 89–92 and notes, and his athletic metaphors, pp. 268–69 and ch. 12, n. 106.

47. Στρατεύω: In the NT always deponent. στρατεύομαι (from στρατός "an encamped army"): Used of the general, "to make war, do battle," but more often of the soldiers serving under him, "to serve as a soldier." Found in Paul in 1 Cor 9:7; 2 Cor 10:3; 1 Tim 1:18; 2 Tim 2:4. For the metaphor of walking in 2 Cor 10:2–3, see p. 198.

48. Στρατεία: "An expedition, campaign, warfare." In Paul in 2 Cor 10:4; 1 Tim 1:18. Some MSS read στρατιά, and in this context, the two words must be regarded as synonymous, although strictly the former means "campaign" and the latter "army." For the confused orthography, see A. Deissmann, *Bible Studies* (Edinburgh: T&T Clark, 1901), 132. V. C. Pfitzner (*Paul and the Agon Motif* [Leiden: Brill, 1967], 160) writes that "the image of στρατεία pictures the life and work of the apostle in its totality."

49. A. P. Stanley (*The Epistles of St Paul to the Corinthians* [London: John Murray, 1858], 516) suggests that Paul may have had this particular campaign of Pompey against Mithridates and the pirates in mind in 2 Cor 10:3–6. It is an attractive thought, but there is no evidence to support the proposition (but neither is there any evidence against it). For detailed accounts of ancient sieges, see, e.g., Caesar's descriptions of the siege of Alesia (*Bell. gall.* 7.69–74) and the siege of Massilia (Marseilles) (*Bell. civ.* 2.1–2) and Josephus's report of the siege of Jotapata (*B.J.* 3.132–336).

50. Tacitus, *Ann.* 12.45.4.

51. For a detailed description of this formation, which was employed in a variety of situations, see Dio Cassius, *Rom. Hist.* 49.30.

52. The excavation of saps or galleries under the defenses was common practice. The purpose was to weaken the walls or towers at their foundations or to enable the attackers to gain access to the stronghold. But tunneling could be a defensive measure as well as an offensive one. The towers of the attackers could be undermined by sappers from within the stronghold. There is also the incident in the siege of Massilia, not mentioned by Caesar but recorded by Vitruvius (*Arch.* 10.16.11), in which the defenders dug a large basin inside the walls and filled it with water. When Caesar's sappers unwittingly mined into it, their tunnels were flooded and collapsed.

53. Titus, in the siege of Jerusalem, had three iron-clad towers erected, each about eighty feet in height. One of them unaccountably collapsed one night (Josephus, *B.J.* 7.291).

54. According to Vegetius (*Epitoma rei militaris* 4.13–14), there was also a beam, to which was fastened an iron hook, that was inserted into the hole made by the ram and dragged out the stones. There was also a smaller iron point (*terebrum*) used for dislodging individual stones. Vitruvius gives the history of these machines in *Arch.* 10.13–15.

55. The *onager* ("ass"), so called because of its kick, was, according to Ammianus (*Hist.* 23.4.4–7; see this passage for a detailed description of the device), a relatively late name given to the machine that had formerly been known as the scorpion (*scorpio*). But the *scorpiones* of the late republic and early empire were much smaller machines and should perhaps be distinguished from the *onager*. Vegetius comments that the *onager* threw stones of enormous weight. One used by the Massiliotes hurled huge beams (about twelve feet in length) tipped with iron points at the attacking Romans in the siege of 49 BCE (Caesar, *Bell. civ.* 2.2). At the battle of Cremona in 69 CE Legio XV had a very large machine capable of flinging massive stones at the enemy (Tacitus, *Hist.* 3.23). Josephus states that at the siege of Jerusalem the machines of Legio X Fretensis could catapult stones that weighed a talent

(about 55 pounds) a distance of two furlongs (about 480 yards) or farther (*B.J.* 5.266). *Onager* stones found at High Rochester and Risingham in Northumberland, England, weigh about 110 pounds each. Frontinus (*Strat.* 3) complacently states that the invention of siege weapons had long since reached its limit, and he could see no prospect of improvements.

56. One of the best examples of such a defensive structure can still be seen at Masada. According to Appian (*Hist. rom.* 15.90), it was Scipio Africanus in 134 BCE at Numantia, in Spain, who was the first to build a circumvallation of more than forty-eight stades (six Roman miles).

57. Ὅπλον: An old word for "a tool or instrument" of any kind for shop or war. But in the NT it seems always to mean (in the plural) "arms, armor, weapons." In Paul in Rom 6:13 (2x); 13:12; 2 Cor 6:7; 10:4.

58. His expression is δυνατὰ τῷ θεῷ "powerful before God," in which the dative, τῷ θεῷ, has the sense either "in God's eyes, as it appears to God" (the dative of personal interest) or "on God's behalf," i.e., "God can work powerfully through these weapons, since they are πνευματικά, directed by the Spirit, as in 1 Cor 2:4" (R. P. Martin, *2 Corinthians* [Waco, Tex.: Word, 1986], 305).

59. Ὀχύρωμα (from ὀχυρόω "to fortify" [and this from ὀχυρός, itself from ἔχω "to have, hold fast"]): "A stronghold, fortress," metaphorically of that in which confidence is placed. Found only here in the NT, but καθαιρεῖν τὰ ὀχυρώματα (cf. Paul's πρὸς καθαίρεσιν ὀχυρωμάτων) is the regular LXX phrase for the reduction of a fortress. See Prov 21:22 (also 10:29 for ὀχύρωμα); Lam 2:2; 1 Macc 5:65; 8:10; and Philo, *Conf.* 129. For Philo, the fortress represents a turning away from God, but as Gideon tore down the tower of Peniel (Judg 8:8–9, 17), so this fortress can be demolished by sound argument. The similarity to Paul is striking, but so too is the difference between Paul and Philo. Philo's weapon of assault is human argument; Paul's is the power of God inherent in the gospel. For a more detailed exposition of the differences, see A. J. Malherbe, "Antisthenes and Odysseus, and Paul at War," *HTR* 76 (1983): 146–47.

60. Paul's phrase is πᾶν ὕψωμα ἐπαιρόμενον κατὰ τῆς γνώσεως τοῦ θεοῦ. In this context, it is tempting to want to make something of the root idea of κατά as "down": every *high thing* lifted *up* that looks *down* in enmity on the knowledge of God." Ὕψωμα (from ὑψόω "to lift, raise up") is a late Koine word (in the LXX, Plutarch, Philo, papyri) for height, and this sense of height is reinforced by ἐπαιρόμενον, present passive participle of ἐπαίρω "to lift up, raise." The language is that of military siegecraft. John Chrysostom identified ὕψωμα with πύργωμα "a defensive tower" (*Hom. 2 Cor.* 21), but ὕψωμα with this meaning cannot be found in Greek usage. The word ὕψος, however, for a tall defensive structure, is frequently found, e.g., in the directions of Tacitus (*Hist.* 32.2) to "throw up in opposition wooden towers [πύργους] or other high structures [ὕψη]" (cf. 40.1; Thucydides, *Hist.* 1.90.3; 1.91.1; 2.75.6). Paul's use of the less usual ὕψωμα may have been suggested by its assonance with ὀχύρωμα and νόημα and, in any case, is an example of his predilection for wordplays on nouns ending in μα.

61. For the gospel as powerful, see, e.g., Rom 1:16; 1 Cor 1:17–25; 2:1–5; 1 Thess 1:5; 2:13.

62. Αἰχμαλωτίζω: See ch. 5, n. 62. Cf. 1 Macc 8:10, which has both αἰχμαλωτίζω and ὀχύρωμα (see ch. 10, n. 59).

63. Εἰς τὴν ὑπακοὴν τοῦ Χριστοῦ: Εἰς expresses purpose, and the genitive, τοῦ Χριστοῦ, is objective, "obedience *to* Christ." Such "captivity" is, for Paul, freedom—at last we have become what God intended us to be. See A. Deissmann (*Paul: A Study in Social and Religious History* [London: Hodder & Stoughton, 1926], 161–64) for what he calls "the mystic genitive"; he cites this passage as an example of it.

64. The phrase ἐν ἑτοίμῳ ἔχειν is a common one for military preparedness. Cf. the similar idiom ἑτοίμως ἔχω "I am prepared" in 2 Cor 12:14. Also see Polybius, *Hist.* 2.34.2; Philo, *Legat.* 259; and, without the ἔχειν, Dionysius of Halicarnassus, *Ant. rom.* 8.17.1; 9.35.6; 9.12.14.

65. Δέσμιος (from δεσμός "a band, bond"): Strictly an adjective (1) "binding," (2) "bound, captive," as a substantive, "a prisoner."

66. Συναιχμάλωτος: "A fellow prisoner" (properly of a captive in war), in the NT found only in Paul. Andronicus and Junias, named in Rom 16:7 as Paul's "fellow prisoners," are also called his "relatives," συγγενεῖς, but what he probably meant by this is that they were his "fellow countrymen." From the form of the name, Junias was a woman. She and Andronicus may have been husband and wife. It is generally assumed that Andronicus and Junias had literally shared an imprisonment with Paul, but which imprisonment is unknown (see 2 Cor 6:5; 11:23). It is debatable, in fact, whether they were literally prisoners at all. The term may have been used metaphorically. It has been suggested that Paul's friends could have passed themselves off as his servants and so have shared his incarceration. See F. F. Bruce, in E. K. Simpson and F. F. Bruce, *Commentary on the Epistles to the Ephesians and the Colossians* (Grand Rapids: Eerdmans, 1957), 305.

67. In Roman law, the prisoner of war (i.e., the Roman soldier taken prisoner) forfeited his citizenship. He was effectively dead as far as the state was concerned. Cf. passages that speak of sinners as "dead" (νεκρός, Rom 4:17; 6:13; 8:10; 11:15; Eph 2:1, 5; 5:14; Col 2:13) or as subject to "death" (θάνατος, Rom 1:32; 5:12, 14, 17, 21; 6:9, 16, 21, 23; 7:5, 10, 13, 24; 8:2, 6; 1 Cor 15:21, 56; 2 Cor 2:16; 3:7; 7:10; 2 Tim 1:10). I am not suggesting that these terms are a metaphor from the Roman law, but in a passage such as Col 1:13 the analogy is certainly an interesting one.

68. Ῥύομαι: An old verb, "to draw to oneself," and so "to rescue, deliver." The verb implies both a desperate situation and a great effort needed to remedy it. It is used of rescue in a mundane or physical sense in Rom 15:31; 2 Thess 3:2; 2 Tim 3:11; 4:17–18 (not lit. "from the lion's mouth," but from the worst that his Roman prosecutors might do) and of deliverance from sin and the like, as in Rom 7:24; 11:26; 2 Cor 1:10 (3x, God has delivered, does deliver, and will deliver); Col 1:13; 1 Thess 1:10 (from the wrath of God, the consequence of sin). Compare Acts 26:18 with Col 1:12–14 for a striking agreement of thought and, to some extent, language.

69. Μεθίστημι (and a late form found in 1 Cor 13:2, μεθιστάνω): An old verb meaning "to change, remove." Only here and in 1 Cor 13:2 in Paul. In the sense of Paul's metaphor it is used by Josephus, e.g., of Tiglath-Pileser's removal of Israelites into Assyria (*A.J.* 9.234).

70. Paul's phrase is ἐκ τῆς ἐξουσίας τοῦ σκότους. Ἐξουσία: (1) properly, "liberty or power" to act, (2) later of the power of "right, authority," and (3) by extension, "jurisdiction." The term can also be used of those who exercise the jurisdiction, whether human or supramundane. In Paul in Rom 9:21; 13:1 (3x), 2–3; 1 Cor 7:37; 8:9; 9:4–6, 12 (2x), 18; 11:10; 15:24; 2 Cor 10:8; 13:10; Eph 1:21; 2:2; 3:10; 6:12; Col 1:13, 16; 2:10, 15; 2 Thess 3:9; Titus 3:1. For ἐξουσίαι as one name for the spiritual forces opposed to the Christian and for "the world rulers of this darkness" as another, see ch. 10, n. 101. Σκότος "darkness" is frequently used by Paul of a (negative) moral or spiritual condition. Cf. ch. 1, n. 6.

71. Citizenship is not expressly mentioned in this passage, but it is implied. (On Christians as "citizens of heaven," see p. 150 and ch. 6, n. 69.) By the *jus postliminii*, a former citizen was restored to his citizenship on his (or her) return to Roman territory, that is, when he crossed the "threshold" *(limen)*. See W. W. Buckland, *The Roman Law of Slavery: The Condition of the Slave in Private Law from Augustus to Justinian* (New York: AMS Press, 1969), 304–17. This rescue of a prisoner and his restoration to his former citizenship might be effected by a process known as

redemptio ab hostibus, that is, by the payment of a ransom by a fellow citizen. The freedman then stood under an obligation to his redeemer, as a *libertus* to his *patronus*, until such time as he paid back the amount of his ransom. W. Elert ("Redemptio ab Hostibus," *TLZ* 72 [1947]: 265–70) suggests that this idea lies behind Paul's metaphor of redemption. In support of Elert, it must be conceded that in Col 1:13–14 the ideas of rescue and redemption are juxtaposed in a context in which a metaphor of *redemptio ab hostibus* would be most appropriate. But whatever the merits of Elert's case in respect to Colossians, in general I am inclined to think that Paul's metaphor of redemption is drawn principally from the common practice of the manumission of slaves, as more familiar to his readers, with some further color added from OT. See pp. 122–24.

72. Ζωγρέω (from ζωός "alive" and ἀγρεύω "to take or catch"): "To catch alive, take captive." Found only here in Paul but used metaphorically of Peter "catching people" in Luke 5:10. The qualifying phrase, "by him for his will" (ὑπ αὐτοῦ εἰς τὸ ἐκείνου θέλημα), is variously understood. I have taken both αὐτοῦ and ἐκείνου as referring to the devil. It is possible, however, to take them both as referring to God or, as many prefer, to take αὐτοῦ as referring to the devil and ἐκείνου to God: "That they who have been taken captive by the devil may come to their senses and escape from his trap, in order to serve the will of God."

73. Ἀνανήφω: A late and rare word, "to be sober again," hence "to come to one's senses." Found only here in the NT. On the basis of this word, J. R. W. Stott describes our human condition as a "diabolical intoxication" from which only God can deliver us (sober us up?) (*Guard the Gospel* [Leicester, U.K.: Inter-Varsity Press, 1973], 80).

74. Παγίς: See ch. 2, n. 27, and, for various synonyms, the discussion of Rom 11:9–10 on p. 35.

75. Στήκετε οὖν καὶ μὴ πάλιν ζυγῷ δουλείας ἐνέχεσθε: Ζυγός (from ζεύγνυμι "to yoke") (1) "a yoke," used metaphorically of bondage or submission, as in Gal 5:1; 1 Tim 6:1, and (2) "a balance." Ἐνέχω (1) "to hold in," (2) in the passive, "to be held in, entangled," as in Gal 5:1 (found only here in Paul). Notice the present imperative of both verbs: "Keep on standing . . . stop being entangled." It would seem that Paul's readers were already flirting with Judaism in some form. Paul talks of all human conditions as slavery of some sort. If we are not "slaves" of Christ, we are "slaves" of something else. To go back into Judaism would be to submit again to the yoke of that slavery. To go back to paganism would be to become slaves again of the "elemental spirits" (NIV "weak and miserable principles," Gal 4:9).

76. So Polybius, *Hist.* 4. Cf. Josephus, *B.J.* 3.86: "Their times for sleeping, and watching, and rising, are notified . . . by the sound of trumpets, nor is anything done without such a signal."

77. Σάλπιγξ: "A trumpet" and σαλπίζω "to sound a trumpet." The reference to God's trumpet harks back to several OT and other passages (Exod 19:16, 19; Isa 27:13; Joel 2:1; Zeph 1:14–16; Zech 9:14; cf. *Pss. Sol.* 11:1; 2 Esd 6:17–24; *Apoc. Mos.* 22:37–38). If Matt 24:30–31 represents an authentic tradition, Jesus himself had used the same imagery; this may have influenced Paul. See D. Wenham, *Paul: Follower of Jesus or Founder of Christianity?* (Grand Rapids: Eerdmans, 1995), 331–32; but cf. C. M. Tuckett, "Synoptic Tradition in 1 Thessalonians," in *The Thessalonian Correspondence* (ed. R. F. Collins; Leuven: Leuven University Press, 1990), 177–78. The trumpet call (like the other images sometimes linked with it, e.g., the voice of the archangel and the loud command of 1 Thess 4:16; see the next note) should not be taken literally. It is a figure of God's authority. Cf. ἐξηχέω: "To sound forth (as a trumpet)," used of "the word of the Lord" sounding forth from

Thessalonica (1 Thess 1:8). For the image of successive ranks moving forward (1 Cor 15:23), see the discussion on p. 213.

78. Κέλευσμα (from κελεύω "to command"): "A call, summons, shout of command." F. F. Bruce (*1 and 2 Thessalonians* [Waco, Tex.: Word, 1982], 100) calls it a "military noun." Found only here in the NT, where it is used as a figure of divine authority (cf. the preceding note) but found elsewhere, e.g., LXX Prov 30:27; Aeschylus, *Pers.* 397; Thucydides, *Hist.* 2.92; Philo, *Praem.* 117.

79. See Polybius, *Hist.* 4. Elaborate arrangements were made for the distribution of the watchword, which was written on wooden tablets *(tesserae)*, presumably with waxed surfaces. The patrols collected the *tesserae* from the sentries. If, at daybreak, any *tessera* was found to be missing, it was known that that sentry had been absent from his post. The guilty man was then condemned to the *fustuarium* (see p. 223; Webster, *Army,* 13).

80. Φρουρέω (from φρουρός "a guard"; see ch. 3, n. 119): "To guard." In Paul in 2 Cor 11:32; Gal 3:23; Phil 4:7.

81. Συνκλείω: A word of similar meaning to φρουρέω, "to enclose, shut in on all sides." The preposition σύν adds a certain color to the verb: They are shut in *together*. In the clause ὑπὸ νόμον ἐφρουρούμεθα συγκλειόμονοι, the participle is epexegetical of the verb. They are held in custody *by being shut in together on all sides.* See also Rom 11:32, where God has "confined all people to disobedience, that he might have mercy on all," and Gal 3:22, where the Scripture "has locked up all things under sin, that the promise, which comes through faith in Jesus Christ, might be given to those who believe" (see ch. 3, n. 118).

82. The reference to their hearts as well as to their minds would suggest this. "Heart" in the New Testament is always figurative, but figurative in a broad sense. It includes the emotions (e.g., Rom 9:2; 10:1; 2 Cor 2:4; 6:11; Phil 1:7) and much more. It is the seat of understanding, the source of thought and reflection (e.g., Rom 1:21; Eph 4:18), of moral choice and the will to act (e.g., 1 Cor 7:37; 2 Cor 9:7; see J. Behm, "καρδία, κτλ," *TDNT* 3:605–14, here 611–13). But here Paul couples hearts with minds: "Καρδία very likely has its meaning narrowed simply to that of designating the seat of one's emotions or deepest feelings, or simply to the emotions and feelings themselves" (G. F. Hawthorne, *Philippians* [Waco, Tex.: Word, 1983], 185).

83. Φυλάσσω: "To guard, watch, protect." See also Rom 2:26; Gal 6:13; 1 Tim 5:21; 6:20; 2 Tim 1:12, 14; 4:15. Although this is the only passage in Paul in which φυλάσσω is used of divine protection, it is commonly used in this way in the LXX, especially in the Psalms. See, e.g., Ps 11[LXX 12]:7; 15[16]:1; 40[41]:2; 120[121]:7. C. A. Wanamaker (*The Epistle to the Thessalonians* [Grand Rapids: Eerdmans, 1990], 276) describes the future tense of the verbs in 2 Thess 3:3 as "progressive futures, that is, the Lord 'will *continue* strengthening and guarding them.' "

84. It is not clear whether τοῦ πονηροῦ "the evil" is personal (masculine) or impersonal (neuter). "The Evil One" is a common name for Satan in the NT (cf. Matt 13:19, 38; Eph 6:16; 1 John 2:13f.; 5:18f.), and this reading would give an effective antithesis to the Lord. On this basis, I have taken the view that it is personal, noting the implication that the Evil One stands behind the activities of "the wicked and evil men" of v. 2 and recalling Paul's earlier reference to "the secret power of lawlessness which is already at work" (2 Thess 2:7). See ch. 10, n. 101, and Williams, *1 and 2 Thessalonians,* 141.

85. A provincial governor needed a large staff for administration, guard duties, and other functions. The staff of his *officium* (headquarters or office), normally drawn from the legions, was under the command of a centurion *(princeps praetorii)* and consisted of three secretaries *(cornicularii),* three judicial officers *(commentarienses),* who were also in charge of the prisons and would have their deputies *(adjutores),* and messengers *(speculatores),* the latter serving also as executioners (see

Mark 6:27). These lesser functionaries might be drawn from either the legions or the auxiliaries. In addition, there were other specialists, such as interpreters *(interpretes)*, torturers *(quaestionarii)*, clerks of different kinds, and grooms. The governor's bodyguard was a separate unit of *equites* (mounted troops) and *pedites singulares* (foot soldiers), usually taken from the *auxilia* (for *auxilia*, see ch. 10, n. 98). See Webster, *Army*, 270–71. See also J. Richardson (*Roman Provincial Administration* [London: Gerald Duckworth, 1984], esp. 27–46) for a general description of provincial administration; and D. Engels (*Roman Corinth: An Alternative Model for the Classical City* [Chicago: University of Chicago Press, 1990], 16–21) for the administration of Roman Corinth.

86. Τὰ ὅπλα τοῦ φωτός: For ὅπλον, see ch. 10, n. 57. Here, with a verb of clothing (ἐνδύω; see ch. 4, n. 76), the sense is more likely to be "armor" than "weapons." W. Sanday and A. C. Headlam (*The Epistle to the Romans* [Edinburgh: T&T Clark, 1905], 378) suggest that Paul's image may owe something to the Jewish concept of the last great fight of God's people against the armies of antichrist (Dan 11; *Sib. Or.* 3:663f.; *4 Ezra* 13:33; *1 En.* 90:16). Paul doubtlessly owed much in this metaphor to OT and other Jewish writings (see also Isa 11:4–5; 59:17; Wis 5:17–22), but the more immediate influence of the context in which he was writing cannot be ruled out. Indeed, it appears that Corinth had some association in Paul's mind with armor, for in an earlier letter written from this city he employed the same metaphor in much the same way (1 Thess 5:5–8).

87. For the discussion of this passage as a domestic metaphor, see p. 93.

88. See, e.g., C. E. B. Cranfield, *The Epistle to the Romans* (Edinburgh: T&T Clark, 1979), 2:686, for a discussion of these options.

89. See pp. 93–95 for the different senses in which Paul speaks of "putting on" Christ and for the discussion of Rom 13:11–14 as a domestic metaphor.

90. For this interpretation, see, e.g., A. Oepke, "ʺὅπλον, κτλ," *TDNT* 5:292–315, here 293. There are, however, other interpretations. One is that the right hand signifies good times and the left bad and that the Christian has something to offer at all times (cf. 2 Tim 4:2). Another is that the details of the right hand and the left are not meant to be pressed. They are there simply to make the point that the Christian is fully armed. See, e.g., A. Plummer, *Second Epistle of St Paul to the Corinthians* (Edinburgh: T&T Clark, 1915), 198; C. K. Barrett, *A Commentary on the Second Epistle to the Corinthians* (London: Adam & Charles Black, 1973), 188; R. P. Martin, *2 Corinthians* (Waco, Tex.: Word, 1986), 179.

91. At this time, the Praetorians appear to have worn the same armor, later changing from a strip lorica to a scale *(lorica squamata)*; the legionaries subsequently followed their example. Auxiliaries appear to have continued to use mail *(lorica hamata)*. See Webster, *Army*, 122–25.

92. According to J. W. Wevers ("Weapons and Implements of War," *IDB* 4:825), the breastplate was also secured by being tied to the belt.

93. Trajan's Column depicts this garment worn by soldiers who have stripped off their body armor for work. It appears to be gathered at the waist and fastened with brooches, allowing it to fall in semicircular folds back and front. This formalized treatment of the soldier's dress is also seen on tombstones. For civilian dress, see pp. 94–95.

94. The emperor Gaius owed his nickname, Caligula, to this piece of footwear, having been brought up by his father, Germanicus, among the troops of his command. See Suetonius, *Gaius* 9.

95. On Trajan's Column, *bracae* are worn by legionary and Praetorian standard-bearers and all auxiliaries, but not by the Praetorians and legionaries themselves. This also seems to be the case on the Column of Marcus.

96. In addition to his weapons, each man carried, according to Josephus (*B.J.* 3.95), a saw, a wicker basket (like a small wastepaper basket) for sifting earth, a hook,

a piece of rope or leather (perhaps generally useful but shown on Trajan's Column as being employed by soldiers in handling pieces of turf in the construction of a rampart), and a sickle. He also lists a *dolabra,* which appears to have been a mattocklike tool with a cutting blade at one end and a prong at the other. On Trajan's Column one is used by a soldier felling a tree. It could also be used for digging. Also on this column legionaries crossing the Danube carry some of these items of equipment on long poles. Josephus implies that even in Flavian times each soldier had to carry most of his gear. By the second century, however, the transport system must have improved, for the column has several scenes of baggage being unloaded from carts. The most cumbersome piece of equipment was the leather tent *(papilio)* shared by eight men in the field. This was carried by a mule together with the millstones for grinding the wheat ration (usually enough for three days at a time). See Webster, *Army,* 121–30.

97. In 1 Tim 1:6; 6:21; 2 Tim 2:18, Paul uses a verb that originally referred to such projectiles: ἀστοχέω (from στόχος "a mark") "to miss the mark." He applies it to the activities of false teachers.

98. This description of the Roman soldier is restricted to the legionary of Paul's day, as providing sufficient background to his various references. But the legions were augmented by a range of auxiliary troops (*auxilia*—aids to the legionaries) who were skilled in particular facets of warfare and equipped accordingly. The Romans themselves

> provided first-class heavy infantry in the form of legionaries, but in other types of fighting they were not so adept. In particular, they did not take so easily to the horse and their own cavalry troops were no match against nomadic peoples nurtured in the saddle. There were other notable differences. In some parts of the Mediterranean local conditions had evolved special methods of attack. . . . Among these were the archers from the eastern parts of the Mediterranean and the slingers from the Balearic Islands. (Webster, *Army,* 141)

Livy (*Hist.* 22.37), in describing the engagement of a thousand archers and slingers from Syracuse in 217 BCE for use against Hannibal, implies that the practice of employing auxiliaries was not new even then, and it remained the practice throughout this period. The auxiliaries consisted of cavalry divisions (*alae,* ἶλαι) and of divisions either wholly or in large part made up of infantry (*cohortes,* σπεῖραι). Special corps were also formed to meet special needs, such as slingers, archers, dromedary corps, etc. From the time of Augustus, auxiliaries supplied all the light-armed troops and almost all the cavalry used in the provincial armies. They were a significant component in any military establishment and, in procuratorial provinces such as Judea, probably made up almost the whole of the garrison. Characteristic types of auxiliary weapons included a broad thrusting spear *(hasta)* and a sword *(spatha)* that was longer and narrower than the legionary's *gladius.* At least some of the auxiliaries wore scale armor and helmets. Their oval shield was smaller and lighter than that of the legionary. Some of the mounted auxiliaries carried a light *lancea* that could be thrown from a distance. For further details, see T. R. S. Broughton, "The Roman Army," *BC* 5:427–45; Watson, *Soldier,* 15–16, 24–25; Webster, *Army,* 141–56.

99. Πάλη (from πάλλω "to throw, swing"): "Wrestling," hence generally, "fight or contest," an old word for a contest between two men in which the one attempts to throw the other to the ground (κατέχω) and hold him there. The two would struggle hard and long to get one another off balance in order to achieve the throw. Such struggles are often depicted on vase paintings. In the games each successful throw counted one point in the match, and the first to get three points was the winner. Some commentators think that the word should be given its proper sense here of "a wrestling match" (see ch. 12, n. 104), supposing Paul to have dropped his military metaphor for one from the games. But M. E. Gudorf ("The Use of ΠΑΛΗ in

Ephesians 6:12," *JBL* 117/2 [1998]: 331–35) has shown that the word was some-times used, in a military context, of the heavily armed soldier who was at the same time a formidable opponent at close quarters.

100. The enemy, named elsewhere in Romans and Galatians as "the flesh" (ἡ σάρξ), "the old self" (ὁ παλαιὸς ἄνθρωπος), and "the principle of sin" (ὁ νόμος τῆς ἁμαρτίας), is here called "blood and flesh" (αἷμα καὶ σάρξ). The form αἷμα καὶ σάρξ occurs only here and in Heb 2:14. Elsewhere it is σάρξ καὶ αἷμα "flesh and blood." There is no difference in meaning. In either form, the phrase signifies our human weakness, but perhaps without the suggestion of moral weakness that is gen-erally implied in the other expressions above.

101. In Eph 6:11 Paul states that the ultimate danger facing the Christian, be-yond any danger posed by our own human frailty (or, indeed, others') is the "schemes of the devil" (αἱ μεθοδίαι τοῦ διαβόλου). Μεθοδία: (1) "to treat by rule, method," (2) "to employ craft" (see also Eph 4:14) is not necessarily a military term but in this context might be aptly expressed as the devil's "stratagems." By way of explanation of v. 11 Paul names the enemy in v. 12 as (1) "sovereignties" (ἀρχαί) and (2) "authorities" (ἐξουσίαι; see ch. 10, n. 70); these nouns express, strictly speaking, abstract ideas but are able to include the notion of the person or persons who exercise these functions; (3) "the world rulers of this darkness" (οἱ κοσμοκράτορες τοῦ σκότους τούτου); (4) "the spiritual [things; there is no noun designating what they are] of evil in the heavenly sphere" (τὰ πνευματικὰ τῆς πονηρίας ἐν τοῖς ἐπουρανίοις; the genitive in this phrase is descriptive: "The spiri-tual things which are evil"). These various references should not be seen as indicat-ing different orders of angelic powers or the like but rather as different names by which the forces of evil are called. They may be subsumed under the one name—the devil (v. 11) or Satan (see Rom 16:20; 1 Cor 5:5; 7:5; 2 Cor 2:11; 11:14; 12:7; 1 Thess 2:18; 2 Thess 2:9; 1 Tim 1:20; 5:15; ch. 10, n. 38, for Satan as ὁ ἀντικείμενος and ch. 10, n. 84, for Satan as ὁ πονηρός). The noun κοσμοκράτωρ is, indeed, used elsewhere of Satan in the *Orphic Hymns* 3.3 (cf. 8.11; 11.11) and is a term that was widely used in connection with magic and astrology. On this basis, C. Arnold (*Ephesians—Power and Magic: The Concept of Power in Ephesians in the Light of Its Historical Setting* [Cambridge: Cambridge University Press, 1989], 65–67) supposes κοσμοκράτωρ to be a veiled reference to Ephesian Artemis. Such a notion is certainly appealing in a letter to the Ephesians but is open to question. Some of Paul's readers may have understood this to be his reference, but Paul him-self is much more likely to have been expressing the worldview of Jewish apocalyptic. See further R. Strelan, *Paul, Artemis, and the Jews in Ephesus* (Berlin: de Gruyter, 1996), 155–62.

102. I have interpreted the "evil day" as designating the period of "great tribu-lation" at the end of this era in conformity with Pauline eschatology expressed else-where, e.g., in 2 Thess 2:5–12. It is possible, however, to understand the "evil day" as being any day of which it might be said, "This is your hour when [lit. 'and'] the power of darkness [reigns]" (Luke 22:53).

103. Paul has two verbs in this passage to express the thought of donning one's armor. In v. 11, ἐνδύω "to clothe," middle voice ἐνδύομαι "to put on oneself, to be clothed with" (see ch. 4, n. 76) and, in v. 13, ἀναλαμβάνω "to take up." For the lat-ter, see also Eph 6:16; 1 Tim 3:16; 2 Tim 4:11. Ἀναλαμβάνειν "is the accepted term for taking up arms, as κατατίθεσθαι is for laying them down" (S. D. F. Salmond, "The Epistle of Paul to the Ephesians," *EGT* 3:384).

104. Πανοπλία (from πᾶν "all" and ὅπλον "armor, weapon"; see ch. 10, n. 57): "Full armor," the term used for the full accouterment of the heavily armed foot soldier. See Polybius, *Hist.* 6.23; Thucydides, *Hist.* 3.114.

105. Ἵστημι (cf. the form στήκω, ch. 12, n. 70): (1) transitive, "to make to stand" and in a military context "to bring to a standstill, to check" (see Rom 3:31;

10:3; 14:4 [2x]; 2 Cor 13:1), (2) intransitive, "to stand, stand firm" (see Rom 5:2; 11:20; 1 Cor 7:37; 10:12; 15:1; 2 Cor 1:24; Eph 6:11, 13–14; Col 4:12; 2 Tim 2:19). The verb, especially the intransitive form, "belongs to the language of war and either means 'to take over,' 'to hold a watch post' (Hab 2:1) or 'to stand and hold out in a critical position on a battlefield' " (M. Barth, *Ephesians* [New York: Doubleday, 1974], 2:762). Cf. Thucydides, *Hist.* 5.104; Xenophon, *Anab.* 1.10.1; Polybius, *Hist.* 4.61; LXX Exod 14:13; LXX Nah 2:8; Matt 12:25.

106. Ἀνθίστημι (from ἀντί "over against, opposite" and ἵστημι "to stand"; see the preceding note): (1) transitive, "to set against," (2) intransitive, "to withstand, resist, oppose." See Rom 9:19; 13:2 (2x); Gal 2:11; Eph 6:13; 2 Tim 3:8 (2x); 4:15. It seems that Paul uses the verbs ἵστημι and ἀνθίστημι interchangeably in this passage.

107. This comparison will show, however, that Paul is not slavishly dependent on his sources. His interpretation of the items of armor sometimes differs from that of OT. Barth (*Ephesians*, 2:768) comments, "The varying allegorizations found inside and outside Pauline literature show a certain playfulness. Metaphorical language and allegorizations are an art form in which details cannot be pressed and exploited." Similarly T. K. Abbott (*Epistles to the Ephesians and to the Colossians* [Edinburgh: T&T Clark, 1897], 184) warns against "pressing too minutely" the association of particular attributes with particular pieces of armor.

108. See Barth, *Ephesians*, 2:795–97.

109. See further ch. 10, n. 121 on the "helmet" of salvation.

110. Ἀλήθεια: (1) objectively, "the reality lying at the basis of an appearance; the manifested, veritable essence of a matter" (H. Cremer, *Biblio-theological Lexicon of New Testament Greek* [Edinburgh: T&T Clark, 1886]), (2) subjectively, "truthfulness, truth" not merely in word, "integrity" in all respects, "sincerity." Cf. Ps 51:6; Eph 4:25.

111. No word for "belt" is used (such as ζωστήρ or later ζώνη). The belt is simply implied by the phrase "girding your waist with truth" (περιζωσάμενοι τὴν ὀσφὺν ὑμῶν ἐν ἀληθείᾳ). Περιζώννυμι: Old verb, "to gird," here in the middle, "to gird oneself," with the accusative of the thing girded (τὴν ὀσφύν). Other suggestions besides that of the belt have been made for the object of this verb: (1) The sword belt that was buckled on with the sword (and dagger in the case of an officer) as the last step in preparing for battle. Cf. Exod 32:27; 1 Sam 17:39; 25:13; Neh 4:18. This final step in arming oneself suggests a readiness to fight. But the later mention of the sword in Eph 6:17 makes it unlikely that the sword belt with that implication is in mind here. (2) The sash that distinguished a high official or officer. Since such a sash is in view in Isa 11:5, in describing the Messiah, Barth argues that this is what Paul had in mind, for we have put on none other than Christ (*Ephesians*, 2:767).

112. Δικαιοσύνη: For the Hebrews generally and for Paul in particular, righteousness is not primarily an ethical virtue but a legal standing. It does, however, have an ethical dimension. The righteous (in terms of their standing with God) will be righteous in their conduct. I take the word here in this sense of moral rectitude. Cf. Rom 6:13; 14:17; Eph 5:9. See the discussion ch. 6, n. 28.

113. Θώραξ: Old word for "breast" and then for "breastplate." Cf. Wis 5:18, and see also 1 Thess 5:8, where the breastplate is interpreted as "faith and love."

114. Again, this item of dress is not named (as, e.g., ὑπόδημα or σανδάλιον) but is simply implied by the phrase "having shod the feet with" (ὑποδησάμενοι τοὺς πόδας). Ὑποδέω: Old verb, "to bind under," especially of footwear.

115. Ἑτοιμασία (late word from ἑτοιμάζω "to prepare, make ready"): (1) "readiness, preparation," in the active sense of "making ready," (2) "a state of preparedness," and (3) something fixed, "a foundation, a firm footing." Found only here in the NT.

116. Ἀναλαμβάνω: See ch. 10, n. 103.

117. θυρεός (from θυρα "a door"): (1) in Homer, "a door stone" (put against the door to keep it shut), (2) in late Greek, "a shield," specifically the *scutum* of the legionaries. Found only here in the NT. Cf. Wis 5:19, where ὁσιότης "holiness" is likened to the ἀσπίς, or *clipeus,* the small round shield that had been standard prior to the time of Furius Camillus. See Webster, *Army,* 5.

118. Σβέννυμι: Old verb used of fire or of things on fire, "to quench." See ch. 1, n. 45. The image of God as the "shield" of his people is a familiar one in OT, although it is only found here in the NT. See, e.g., Gen 15:1; 2 Sam 22:3, 31, 36; Ps 3:3; 5:12; 7:10 (and notice the reference to God's "flaming arrows" in v. 13); 18:2, 30; 28:7; 33:20; 59:11; 84:9, 11; 89:18; 115:10; 144:2; Prov 2:7; 30:5; Zech 12:8. We may be sure that this OT material is the source of Paul's metaphor, the more so as "shield" is not found as a figure elsewhere in Greek literature. Given this biblical background, it seems certain that Paul meant more by "faith" than merely our human response. "Above the absence of fear among the people, and higher than their own trust and faith, stands the faithfulness of God himself, and the faithful service of the one who is anointed by God" (Barth, *Ephesians,* 2:773). See Dan 3:22–28 for the faithfulness of "one like a son of the gods" and the faith of the three men in a fiery situation. See also Josephus (*B.J.* 3.173) for his account of rawhides (from recently flayed oxen and therefore still moist) being used on palisades as a protection against various missiles, including incendiary.

119. Βέλος (from βάλλω "to throw"): "A missile, arrow, etc." Found only here in the NT. The noun is qualified by the perfect passive participle of the old verb πυρόω "to set on fire" (cf. ἀναζωπυρέω, ch. 4, n. 97)—τὰ βέλη τὰ πεπυρωμένα "the set-on-fire missiles." What Paul is describing here are the πυρφόροι οἰστοί of Thucydides (*Hist.* 2.75.4), the βέλη πυρφόρα of Diodorus (*Hist.* 20.96), the *malleoli* of Cicero (*Mil.* 24). See also Herodotus (*Hist.* 8.52) and Ps 7:13. Livy describes how these arrows, even when caught by the shield, caused panic. With their shields on fire, the soldiers were tempted to throw them down, thus making themselves more vulnerable to the enemy (*Hist.* 21.8). Heavier loads of burning material were launched by catapults, against which a shield was of little protection.

120. Σωτήριον: The only instance in Paul of the abstract neuter form, but synonymous, as it seems, with his usual word σωτηρία "deliverance, preservation, safety, salvation," especially salvation in relation to God. In this sense, the term embraces the whole work of God in Christ on behalf of sinners and therefore has a past, a present, and a future dimension. For σωτηρία, see Rom 1:16; 10:1, 10; 11:11; 13:11; 2 Cor 1:6 (2x); 6:2 (2x); 7:10; Eph 1:13; Phil 1:19, 28; 2:12; 1 Thess 5:8–9; 2 Thess 2:13; 2 Tim 2:10; 3:15. In Titus 2:11 he uses the adjective σωτήριος in the sense of "saving, bringing salvation."

121. Περικεφαλαία (late word from περί "around" and κεφαλή "a head"): "A helmet." As with "shield," there is no instance of the figurative use of this item in Greek literature outside the Bible. The biblical parallels in Isa 59:17 and 1 Thess 5:8 are therefore the best guide to Paul's meaning. In both, the thought is of a salvation already won. In Isa 59:16 it is after his saving work that God dons the helmet. In 1 Thess 5:8 Paul identifies the helmet with the "hope of salvation," that is, with the expectation that the salvation we now have will have its final outworking in glory at the coming of Christ (cf. Phil 1:6; 1 Pet 1:5). On this basis, Barth thinks it "most likely" that "a helmet of victory is in mind which is more ornate than a battle helmet and demonstrates that the battle has been won: the saints are to 'take' this helmet as a gift from God. They go into battle and stand the heat of the day in full confidence of the outcome . . . for they wear the same battle-proven helmet which God straps on his head. . . . God's victory is passed down to all the saints" (*Ephesians,* 2:775).

122. Μάχαιρα: (1) "a large knife" for sacrificial purposes, (2) "a short sword or dagger," as distinct from a ῥομφαία, a large sword. In this context, it clearly signifies

the short, straight sword of the legionaries, with no clear distinction here between a μάχαιρα and a ξίφος, which was also a straight sword for thrusting. See also Rom 8:35; 13:4. The phrase τὴν μάχαιραν τοῦ πνεύματος "the sword of the Spirit," on the analogy of the preceding genitives ("of righteousness," "of the gospel," "of faith," "of salvation"), all of which define the item in question (the breastplate that is righteousness, etc.), taken on its own, could mean "the sword which is the Spirit." In this case, however, a relative clause is added by way of definition. And since each item of armor, so far, has had only one interpretation, it is likely that the sword is the word of God and that the genitive, "of the Spirit," is not a second definition but subjective—"the sword given by the Spirit, which is the word of God."

123. Here the genitive (θεοῦ) is either possessive or subjective: "the word that belongs to or issues from God." The term ῥῆμα means, in Pauline diction, "a specifically weighty, be it creative, revelatory, prophetic, or otherwise binding pronouncement," such as the words of God in the OT and of Christ in the NT (e.g., 1 Cor 7:10; 1 Thess 4:15) (Barth, *Ephesians*, 2:777). The word of God gives the "cutting edge" to the work of the Spirit, which is essentially christocentric—to have people meet with God in Christ and come to God through Christ. Cf. Isa 49:2; Heb 4:12.

124. I take the injunction to "hold our position" (vv. 11, 13) to be determinative still of the nature of the battle that Paul has in mind. But see, e.g., A. T. Lincoln (*Ephesians* [Dallas: Word, 1990], 451), who suggests that with the sword "the writer's emphasis shifts from the defensive to the offensive."

125. Perhaps we should add (remembering the constant training of the legionaries), "When correctly handled." See 2 Tim 2:15, and compare, e.g., Jesus' use of Scripture against Satan in Matt 4:1–11.

126. Ἀγρυπνέω: "To be sleepless, wakeful." The more common γρηγορέω "to be awake, to watch" is found in the parallel of Col 4:2. It, much more than ἀγρυπνέω, describes the soldier's duty to be vigilant. It is odd, then, that Paul should have chosen the more civilian term for this passage. It may have been to show that he was no longer thinking of a particular item of armor. The more likely explanation is that he regarded the two terms as synonymous.

127. Josephus, *B.J.* 3.72–75. The whole section 3.71–107 should be consulted for his description of the organization of the army. See ch. 10, n. 6, for descriptions of the Roman army in earlier times.

128. E.g., Dio Cassius, *Rom. Hist.* 41.35; 48.42. Just how often is difficult to say. Tacitus, *Ann.* 3.21, recorded an instance in about 20 CE and commented that it was rare in that period. Yet the existence of the word *decumo* "choose one in ten," first attested in this period, suggests that the practice had been common, and other (less convincing) evidence suggests that it did continue. See Watson, *Soldier*, 117ff.

129. "When every tenth man from a defeated army is beaten with clubs, the lot falls also on the brave. Making an example on a grand scale inevitably involves some injustice. The common good is bought with individual suffering" (Tacitus, *Ann.* 14.44). Christians know this very well.

130. This happened to the forces of Paccius Orfitus in the reign of Nero. See Tacitus, *Ann.* 13.36; cf. Frontinus, *Strat.* 4.1.25, 37; Dio Cassius, *Rom. Hist.* 49.38.4; Suetonius, *Aug.* 24. This mark of disgrace often extended over a long period. The survivors of the unfortunate legions that suffered defeat at Cannae were kept together and sent to Sicily. There, in 205 BCE, eleven years later, they were given to Scipio for his African campaign, as a deliberate insult to the commander (see Webster, *Army*, 14). Many soldiers would rather face death than endure dishonor, "refusing to leave their ranks even when vastly outnumbered, owing to the dread of the punishment they would meet with; and again in the battle men who have lost a shield or sword or any other arm often throw themselves into the midst of the enemy, hoping either to recover the lost object or to escape by death from the inevitable disgrace and the taunts of their relations" (Polybius, *Hist.* 6.37.1–4).

131. Three forms derived from the root τάσσω (see ch. 10, n. 17) are employed, each constructed with the α privative: (1) the adjective ἄτακτος "out of order, out of place," frequently of soldiers not keeping ranks or an army in disarray (see 1 Thess 5:14); (2) the adverb ἀτάκτως "disorderly" (see 2 Thess 3:6, 11); (3) the verb ἀτακτέω, primarily of soldiers, "to be out of order, to quit the ranks" (see 2 Thess 3:7). It must be conceded, however, that these words have a wider application than simply to soldiers, and Paul could have used them in the general sense of disorderliness without intending a conscious military metaphor (e.g., as suggested on p. 97, Paul could have employed these terms as a domestic metaphor). On the other hand, there is a distinctly military ring about the context, with Paul's "command," παραγγέλλω, in v. 10 (cf. 1 Thess 4:11; 2 Thess 3:4, 6, 12; 1 Cor 7:10; 11:17; 1 Tim 1:3; 4:11; 5:7; 6:13, 17). Cf. also παραγγελία "command" in 1 Thess 4:2 (also in 1 Tim 1:5, 18), on which L. Morris says, "It is more at home in a military environment, being a usual word for the commands given by the officer to his men. . . . It is probably a command passed along (παρά) a line of soldiers. From this it comes to signify any authoritative order" (*The First and Second Epistles to the Thessalonians* [Grand Rapids: Eerdmans, 1959], 120).

132. Various suggestions as to the cause of this problem have been put forward, including eschatological excitement stemming from a mistaken belief in the imminence of the Parousia, the disdain of the Greeks and Romans for manual labor, and the abuse (or perhaps misunderstanding on Paul's part) of the institution of patronage whereby a poor man, especially a freedman, might be bound to a reciprocal arrangement in which he exchanged expressions of gratitude for the material support of his patron. See further D. J. Williams, *1 and 2 Thessalonians* (NIBC; Peabody, Mass.: Hendrickson, 1992), 149–50. On the relationship between freedman and patron, see pp. 120–21. For the tradition of work as a part of the Christian ethic, see 2 Thess 3:6 and cf. Eph 5:3, where "greed," improper for Christians, is offset by the manual work mentioned earlier in 4:28.

133. I have interpreted Paul's dictum in 2 Thess 3:10 in military terms, but apart from his use of ἄτακτος, etc., in describing these people, there is nothing inherently military about the saying itself. A. Deissmann (*Light from the Ancient East* [London: Hodder & Stoughton, 1908], 314) suggests, rather, that it was probably "a bit of good old workshop morality, a maxim applied no doubt hundreds of times by industrious workmen as they forbade a lazy apprentice to sit down to dinner." On other possible echoes of workplace expressions, see p. 167.

134. Watson, *Soldier*, 133.

135. See Dio Cassius, *Rom. Hist.* 60.24.

136. *Dig.* 24.1.60–62.

137. There were attempts to extend the ban to the highest ranks, such as Augustus's prohibition on senatorial officers taking their wives with them to the provinces (Suetonius, *Aug.* 24). This, however, proved difficult to enforce, as indeed did the ban on the ordinary soldier forming attachments. It was a long-service army, in which the average recruit was eighteen or nineteen years of age and served for at least twenty-five years and often more. Men of such an age are going to form alliances, howbeit unofficially, and many did so. This was known and, in fact, condoned (in the interest, perhaps, of maintaining a supply of potential recruits from their children). See, e.g., the Claudian exemption of soldiers from certain laws in the same way that married men were exempted (Dio Cassius, *Rom. Hist.* 60.24.3; for details of these laws, see H. Last, "The Chronology of the Laws on the Marriage of Roman Citizens," *CAH* 10:441ff.). The general ban on marriages was lifted by Septimus Severus in about 197 CE (Herodian, *Hist.* 3.8.5).

138. Στρατεύομαι: See ch. 10, n. 47.

139. Στρατολογέω (from στρατός "an army" and λέγω "to say"): "To levy a troop, enlist soldiers." Found here as a participle, "the one who has enlisted you,"

and only here in the NT. Presumably Paul is referring to the commander-in-chief himself, whose name and fame has persuaded the recruit to enlist. To his metaphor of the soldier in v. 4, Paul adds that of the athlete in v. 5 (see p. 273) and the farmer in v. 6 (see p. 36 and ch. 2, n. 33). These additions carry his thought from that of commitment to the ministry to the hard work that it entails and the rewards that it brings.

140. See ch. 10, n. 8.

141. Συνστρατιώτης: "A fellow soldier." It could be argued that Paul calls Epaphroditus his "fellow soldier" simply because he had shared, for a time, the difficulties that the apostle had experienced (in Ephesus?) and not because he was a leading light in the church. But the case of Archippus is different. There is nothing to show that he was Philemon's son and much to suggest the contrary: why should the son be addressed in a letter that dealt with one of his father's slaves? The inclusion of his name, therefore, must be due to the fact that he occupied an important position in the local church (cf. the greeting that follows his name, v. 2). Because Philemon was a member of that church, this matter concerning his slave was, in some degree, the responsibility of Archippus also. Cf. Col 4:17. C. S. Wansink (*Chained in Christ: The Experience and Rhetoric of Paul's Imprisonments* [Sheffield, U.K.: Sheffield Academic Press, 1996], 164–74) suggests that Paul's description of himself in Phlm 1, 9 as δέσμιος Χριστοῦ Ἰησοῦ, "[the] prisoner of Christ Jesus," is complementary to his description of Archippus as συστρατιώτης. It too is a military metaphor, expressing his unswerving loyalty (like that of a soldier) to Christ, regardless of cost, whether it be his liberty or even his life.

142. Στρατιώτης: "A soldier." Found only here in Paul and only here in the NT as a figure for the servant of Christ. But see συνστρατιώτης "fellow soldier," the preceding note. The call to endure hardship reiterates the exhortation of 2 Tim 1:8 and is made again in 4:1–5.

143. For στρατεύομαι and στρατεία, see ch. 10, nn. 47 and 48, and for καλός "good," ch. 12, n. 128. It is noteworthy that Timothy is to go into battle ἐν αὐταῖς "in them," i.e., in the "armor" of Paul's instruction concerning his ministry (see vv. 3–11, esp. v. 5), which tallied with what others had said, perhaps at the time when his calling to ministry was first publicly recognized (cf. 4:14; also Acts 13:1–3; 16:1–3).

144. Paul tends to use his military metaphor especially when he is speaking of conflict, either with those who oppose the gospel or with the spiritual powers. Cf. 2 Cor 10:1–6; Eph 6:10–17.

145. Ὀψώνιον: See ch. 5, n. 76.

146. Χάρισμα (from χάρις "grace, kindness, etc.," χαρίζομαι "to show grace, kindness, etc."; cf. ch. 6, n. 59): "A gift of grace, a free gift," in the NT especially of a spiritual endowment. Cf. Rom 1:11; 5:15–16; 11:29; 12:6; 1 Cor 1:7; 7:7; 12:4, 9, 28, 30–31; 2 Cor 1:11; 1 Tim 4:14; 2 Tim 1:6.

147. Tertullian, *Res.* 100.47.

148. Propertius attributes war to avarice (*Eleg.* 3.3.6, 13–15). So also Tibullus: "The cause [of war] is precious gold. There would be no war if the cup that one used at a meal were made simply of wood" (*Corp.*, 1.10.7f.).

149. Thus, e.g., Augustus paid a donative in 8 BCE to mark the entry of his grandson Gaius Caesar into public life (Dio Cassius, *Rom. Hist.* 55.6.4). In his will, with a view to ensuring an easy succession, Augustus left the Praetorians 250 *denarii* each, the members of urban cohorts 125, and the legionaries and those auxiliaries who belonged to the *cohortes civium Romanorum* 75 *denarii* (Tacitus, *Ann.* 1.8; cf. Dio Cassius, *Rom. Hist.* 56.32). Augustus's successors followed his example, which became more and more the means of ensuring the army's loyalty and support. See Watson, *Soldier*, 108–14, for further discussion and references. See also the discussion on the payment of soldiers (pp. 224–25). There is perhaps a hint of this image

of the victorious commander distributing largesse in Paul's application of Ps 68:18 (cf. v. 12) to Christ in Eph 4:8.

150. Paul betrays here an upper-class attitude to manual labor as slavish and demeaning although he chose to work to support his ministry. See R. F. Hock, "Paul's Tentmaking and the Problem of his Social Class," *JBL* 97 (1978): 555–64; and ch. 7, n. 17.

151. Συλάω: An old verb, "to despoil, strip arms from a slain foe," only here in the NT. For a similar metaphor, see the discussion of ἀπεκδύω in Col 2:15 on pp. 259–60 and ch. 4, n. 78.

152. Ὀψώνιον: Cf. p. 224, and see ch. 5, n. 76.

153. Συλαγωγέω (from σύλη "booty" and ἄγω "to lead"; cf. συλάω, ch. 10, n. 151): A late and rare word, this being its first known occurrence in Greek literature, "to carry off as spoil, lead captive." Only in Col 2:8 in the NT, where it appears as a present active articular participle, τις . . . ὁ συλαγωγῶν. Notice the singular. One teacher in particular was doing the damage in leading the Colossians astray. Cf. the similar metaphor in αἰχμαλωτίζω, ch. 5, n. 62.

154. Diodorus Siculus, *Hist.* 14.16.5; Livy, *Hist.* 4.59.11.

155. Polybius (second century BCE) states that the legionary soldier received two obols a day (*Hist.* 6.39). He adds that the centurion was paid four obols and the cavalryman, one drachma a day. What these amounts represented in Roman money is not made clear, but G. R. Watson concludes that "this meant an annual rate of 180 *denarii*, which on the retariffing of the *as* at sixteen to the *denarius* became an annual rate of 112.5 *denarii*. When Caesar doubled the pay the annual rate became 225 *denarii* (Suetonius, *Jul.* 26), and it remained at this level until the time of Domitian" (*Soldier*, 89). In addition, special allowances were sometimes made. Tacitus mentions an allowance called *clavarium* "nail money" for the wear and tear on boots entailed in a long march (*Hist.* 3.50; cf. Suetonius [*Vesp.* 8.3], who mentions possibly the same allowance for *calciarium* "boot money," claimed by the *classiarii*, who had regularly to march from Ostia or Puteoli to Rome). Then there were the donatives—the largess given by the emperor, originally distributed at the conclusion of a successful campaign but subsequently paid to mark special occasions or simply to maintain the goodwill of the troops. On donatives, see the discussion on p. 225 and ch. 10, n. 149; on the whole question of the soldier's pay, see Watson, *Soldier*, 89–114; Webster, *Army*, 264–68.

156. Tacitus, *Ann.* 1.17, contains a list of the grievances of the legionaries: "Body and soul are valued at ten *asses* a day; out of this we have to pay for our clothing, our weapons, and our tents, out of this we have to find sweeteners for brutal centurions or else find ourselves on the roster for extra fatigues." See also Polybius (*Hist.* 6.39) and Plutarch (*Ti. C. Gracch.* 5) for further evidence relating to deductions; see Watson (*Soldier*, 102–4) for an assessment of this evidence.

157. In the passage before us (1 Cor 9:7–14), Paul also speaks of the rewards due the ox, the vineyard owner, the shepherd, the plowman, the thresher, and the priest as illustrating further the application of this principle. See p. 33.

Cultic Observances

TEMPLE

In Eph 2:19–22 Paul speaks of the church as a **temple**. He describes its "construction" in terms that were familiar to the building industry of his day. Its "foundation," he says, is the apostles and prophets, Christ himself is its "cornerstone," and its members, Jews and Gentiles alike, have been "fitted together" into what has become a "holy temple in the Lord."[1] His word for temple is *naos*.[2] When used in connection with the temple in Jerusalem, *naos* served to distinguish the sanctuary from the larger precinct (the *hieron*). In popular belief, if God could be found anywhere, it was in the *naos*, the sanctuary. But Paul implies that the church is now the sanctuary of God[3] and that it is here, in the church (i.e., through the gospel preached and practiced by the church), that God can be found.

The Romans tended to build their temples on raised platforms approached by many steps. (The Greeks generally built their temples at ground level; there were exceptions, such as the Artemisium at Ephesus.) There may be a hint of this architectural phenomenon in 1 Tim 3:13 in Paul's instructions concerning deacons. "Those who have served well as deacons,"[4] he says, "gain for themselves **a step** in the right direction"[5]—not in terms of climbing ambition's ladder or even in the sense of "going up" in the opinion of others. Rather, they advance spiritually in their experience and understanding of God. They step up, so to speak, into the *naos;* they draw ever nearer to the sanctuary in terms of their consciousness and knowledge of God. No Christian service done well is ever done without a sense of the presence and the power of God.[6] Each experience of God's grace gives confidence to go on in God's service and so leads to further experience. Thus faithful Christian service produces Christian maturity. Notice that the "step up" taken by these deacons is coupled with, and perhaps explained by, Paul's second statement: "they gain for themselves . . . great assurance[7] in the faith that they have in Christ"—that is, they gain the Christian maturity that comes with Christian experience.

If these deacons of 1 Tim 3:13 were to literally "step up" into the sanctuary of the Jerusalem temple, they would first have to pass through one of a number of openings in the low wall that surrounded it. Each of these openings was posted with notices in Greek and Latin warning the Gentile visitor not to venture within.[8] This wall, which marked the racial and religious divide between the Jews and the Gentiles, may be what Paul is picturing in Eph 2:14: Christ has "broken down **the dividing wall**,[9] namely, the enmity" between the two peoples. "You see," he says in effect, "by the one stroke of reconciling both to God, Christ has made it possible for each (Jew and Gentile alike) to accept and be at peace with the other."

On the other hand, if these Ephesian deacons were to take the unlikely step of entering the temple of Artemis (for which entrance was unrestricted), having climbed its ten steps, they would find themselves surrounded by a forest of enormous columns. Edward Gibbon describes the Artemisium at Ephesus: "The arts of Greece and the wealth of Asia had conspired to erect a sacred and magnificent structure. It was supported by a hundred and twenty-seven marble columns of the Ionic order, they were the gifts of devout monarchs, and each was sixty feet high."[10]

This temple dominated the city,[11] and Paul, who had spent three years in Ephesus, could not have failed to be impressed by it, although his impression was undoubtedly negative. In writing to Timothy at Ephesus, his thoughts may have turned to the Artemisium and those enormous marble columns. As he laid down rules of conduct for Christians in the house[12] of their God (1 Tim 3:15), he described it as a "column"; their "temple," he said, is "a **pillar**[13] and **support**[14] of the truth."

Some truths of God are written large for all to see: "The heavens declare the glory of God."[15] But Paul is speaking here of *the* truth,[16] namely, the manifestation of God in the person and work of Christ, which is not as accessible to the world as are the truths of general revelation. Hence the church's role. It supports the truth in the sense of promoting it, not in the sense of propping it up. God's truth "is not in danger of collapse. We must not think that if the church does not act as a buttress the truth will lie in ruins. Paul was using a metaphor by which to express the task of the church in the world, and he rightly chose a robust figure."[17] But perhaps the metaphor is not as apt as it might be. Paul might have "rightly chosen" a better figure, since "a pillar and support" does suggest something that is structurally necessary. At any rate, we should be careful not to press the image too closely. As the columns of a temple were an integral part of the whole, so the church has an important role to play (by grace, not of necessity) in the promulgation of God's truth in the world. But the metaphor itself is not clear. If Paul was thinking of the church universal, he must have envisaged one pillar only. If it was the local church, the image is of one among many—the churches together, like so many pillars in a great temple, supporting the truth of the gospel. The latter seems more likely. In the New Testament "the church" usually means the local church, with references to "churches" in the plural not uncommon.

SACRIFICE

Temples were commonly associated with sacrifice. To what extent did the Jewish cultus shape Paul's perception of what Christ did on the cross? Whatever conclusion we draw about the *extent* of that influence, there is no question that the cultus played *some* part in shaping his thoughts.[18] Nowhere is this more apparent than in Rom 3:25, in his declaration that "God put Jesus forward as a *hilastērion*."[19] Many have understood this word, in the light of Heb 9:5 and of its use in the LXX, as the "mercy seat" on the ark of the covenant (its golden covering), which was held to be the very throne of God (see Exod 25:17–22; Lev 16:2) and was where atonement was made by the sprinkling of blood (Lev 16:14–16). But comparing Christ to a piece of furniture ("God put Jesus forward as the mercy seat") does not suit this passage nearly as well as understanding him as the sacrifice itself. It is now generally agreed (not only on the subjective ground of its likelihood but on the much firmer basis of the linguistic data[20]) that Paul meant by *hilastērion* that Jesus was put forward as **"a propitiatory sacrifice,"** that is, a sacrifice that turns away God's wrath by removing its cause (cf. 1 Cor 15:3: "Christ died for our sins"). Paul probably had in mind the **Day of Atonement** (cf. Lev 16). But what was only symbolized on that day has now become a reality. "Sin had been removed *really* . . . not only from the believer's conscience . . . but also from the presence of God."[21]

The phrase that Paul uses in Rom 8:3, speaking of God as sending God's own Son "concerning sin" *(peri hamartias)*, is used many times in the LXX for **the sin offering**.[22] It seems likely, then, that in Rom 8:3 the apostle was deliberately identifying Christ with that particular sacrifice. So too in 2 Cor 5:21, which speaks of Christ as being "made to be sin" on our behalf (*hyper hēmōn;* cf. Gal 3:13, which says he became a curse *hyper hēmōn* "on our behalf"[23]). The statement in Rom 8:32 that God "did not spare his own Son but gave him up on behalf of us all" *(hyper hēmōn pantōn)* may also echo the language of sacrifice.[24] Should we understand these references as literal or as metaphorical? Was Christ an actual sacrifice? Or did his death on the cross for our sins transcend the cultus? It appears the latter: Paul has used the images and language of sacrifice merely to aid us in understanding what Christ has achieved on our behalf.[25]

Paul's reference in Eph 5:2 is clearly metaphorical. Because Christ loved us, says Paul, he gave himself for us as **"an offering**[26] and **a sacrifice**,[27] to be to God **a sweet-smelling fragrance**."[28] The language is that of the Old

Testament, and the image is of the smoke and smell of the sacrificial offering rising up to God as something pleasing.[29] But the truth behind the imagery of a sweet smell is that a sacrifice is only pleasing to God if the one who makes it is pleasing. Although this was certainly the case with Christ, it is beside the point. Paul is not discussing the work of Christ in this passage so much as the conduct of believers. He is counseling his readers how they should live, particularly how they should relate to one another as children of God. Paul introduces Christ into this discussion as an example. Christ "loved us and gave himself for us," says Paul, and we should be like him. We should live as he did and love as he did, with a self-giving love, the nature of which is spelled out in the verses that follow.[30] Elsewhere, in Phil 4:18, Paul uses the same expression, a "fragrant smell," to describe the self-giving love of the Philippian Christians that found expression in their gift of money in support of his missionary work. The Philippians practiced what he was preaching to the Ephesians!

In 1 Cor 5:7 Christ is described our **Passover lamb**.[31] Paul had been speaking of **the leaven** (yeast),[32] every trace of which had to be cleaned out of the house before the Passover was celebrated.[33] On this analogy, he demanded that the Corinthians put their "house" in order by removing from among themselves what he called the "old leaven," a particularly appalling instance of sexual immorality that the church had condoned (vv. 1–5). And there were other failings in that church, their "malice and wickedness" (v. 8), that had to be purged. "It is high time [he says] that you rid yourselves of these remains of your pagan past. Christ, like the Passover lamb, has already been **sacrificed**,[34] and still your house is not clean. You are late in doing what you ought to have done long ago!" The work of Christ calls for a positive response. We have a new Passover, instituted by Christ's "sacrifice for our sins." Let us celebrate that Passover, not for one week of the year but for the whole of our lives, by living according to God's rules, with the "unleavened bread," so to speak, "of sincerity and truth" (v. 8).[35]

At the heart of all sacrifice, whether pagan or Jewish, was the notion of offering—the worshiper, for whatever reason, offering something to the god. It was in this general sense that Paul spoke of himself as being "**poured out [as a libation]**"[36] upon "the sacrifice[37] and service of your faith" (Phil 2:17). Because the Greek nouns for "sacrifice" and "service" here share one article, they should be understood as expressing a single thought: "the sacrificial [i.e., self-giving] service" that flowed from their faith in Christ. But this notion of service takes Paul away from his metaphor, which is of the libation that accompanied a sacrifice. Many peoples, including the Jews, added to a sacrifice a libation of wine that was poured out on top of the altar or at its foot.[38] But what does the metaphor mean? Because he also uses it in reference to his death (2 Tim 4:6), it is commonly thought that he must be speaking of his death here. But the context suggests otherwise. He talks about "running" and "laboring" (v. 16). These are metaphors of ministry, not of death. He refers to his and the Philippians' joy at his being "poured out," and he expresses the hope of visiting Philippi before very much longer (v. 24). It all sounds too hopeful, too full of life, for Paul to be talking of death. This metaphor is actually Paul's picturesque way of describing the hardship of his life as an apostle. The Philippian Christians were making their own sacrificial offering of service to God, and Paul was adding "the libation" of his service to theirs.

PRIESTLY SERVICE

Speaking of the self-giving of the Philippian church (Phil 2:17) and influenced, no doubt, by his thoughts of the cultus, Paul further describes their offering as their **priestly service**.[39] By using this figure, he is saying that the Christians in Philippi—all of them, women no less than men—were priests in the temple of God. He uses the same expression in Phil 2:30 of the service rendered to him by Epaphroditus. This man had come to him with gifts from the church and had stayed on to render whatever assistance he could to the apostle, who was in prison at that time. This stay had almost cost Epaphroditus his life—he "gambled[40] with his life," Paul declares, "to make up for the help you could not give me [in person]." For this service, Paul calls Epaphroditus a *leitourgos,* a **priest of God's sanctuary**[41] (v. 25).

Paul had several objectives in writing to the church in Philippi. One was to send Epaphroditus back to them with his commendation so that the church would not think that he had somehow failed the apostle. By explaining the circumstances of his return, Paul hoped to nip any such mistaken belief in the bud. Epaphroditus had done all that he possibly could, and Paul believed that it was now time for him to go home. "Welcome him in the Lord," he says, "and honor such people as he." Another reason for writing was to thank the church for their gift, which Epaphroditus had brought to Paul in prison. Thus he begins the letter by thanking God for "their partnership [with him] in [turning others toward] the gospel," acknowledging that this "good work" was something that God had inspired in them and would go on doing until Jesus returned (Phil 1:5–6). He ends the letter in businesslike fashion by writing a formal receipt for their gift, echoing the words found in countless commercial documents of that time: "I have received payment in full" (Phil 4:18).[42] But Paul felt he had to go beyond simply acknowledging receipt and say something more about their "good work." In doing so, he again takes his words from the cultus. Their gift, he says, was a "fragrant smell, an acceptable sacrifice, pleasing to God."[43] These expressions are used elsewhere of the work of Christ (Eph 5:2). "Fragrant" means pleasing to God, an idea that is made explicit in Phil 4:18. So the Philippians' gift—money (as is generally supposed) given to him as their "priestly service"—was pleasing to God. And as if he has not already made himself perfectly clear, Paul adds that in God's eyes their gift was an "acceptable sacrifice." The lesson here is that whatever is done for the servant is done no less for the Master.[44] Their gift was as much to God as to Paul.[45]

It seems likely that Paul has already consciously employed cultic language earlier in this letter when he spoke of God as inspiring "the beginning" and "the end" of their good work in supporting his mission (Phil 1:6). Both expressions are associated with sacrifice.[46] In Greek practice, as a prelude to sacrifice, a torch was lit from the altar and then dipped into water, thus cleansing the water. Both the victim and the people were then sprinkled with this purified water for their sanctification. There followed what was known as the *euphēmia*, the sacred silence, during which the worshipers prayed. Finally, a basket of barley was brought, and some grains were scattered on the victim and about the altar. In this passage Paul uses the terms for making this start to the proceedings and for seeing the sacrifice through to the end. The verse may thus be said to move within the scope of the cultus. But no more than that. The metaphor cannot be pressed, since God is the subject and so, strictly speaking, must be the one who would be offering the sacrifice. But the point is sufficiently clear: the Philippians owed their motivation to God, and this is Paul's way of acknowledging his indebtedness to both his human and his divine benefactors ("unless the Lord builds the house, its builders labor in vain," Ps 127:1).

The language of "priestly service" in Rom 15:27 (the verb *leitourgeō*) and 2 Cor 9:12 (the noun *leitourgia*) is applied to the gifts that the Gentile churches gave the Judeans. In serving others, these churches were rendering service to God. And Paul describes himself (Rom 15:16) as a "priest of the sanctuary" in his ministry to the Gentiles (the same term, *leitourgos*, that he used of Epaphroditus in Phil 2:25).[47] Paul goes on to speak of himself as "**performing the sacred rites of the sanctuary**[48] in proclaiming the gospel of God" to the Gentiles. His goal for them was to become "an offering acceptable"[49] to God. This echoes his earlier plea that his readers should **offer**[50] themselves, "their bodies, as a living sacrifice," in contrast with the slain animals of the cultus (cf. Rom 6:8, 11, 13), not as a propitiatory sacrifice but a sacrifice of praise, "holy, acceptable[51] to God, as their spiritual **service**"[52] (Rom 12:1).

NOTES

1. See the discussion of Eph 2:19–22 on p. 18 and ch. 1, n. 74.

2. Ναός (from ναίω "to inhabit"): "A temple." In Paul, found in 1 Cor 3:16–17 (2x); 6:19; 2 Cor 6:16 (2x); Eph 2:21; 2 Thess 2:4. Cf. ἱερόν: (1) strictly an adjective, "marvelous, mighty, divine, sacred," (2) as a substantive (in the plural), "sacrifices, sacred rites, sacred things" and later (in the singular) "a consecrated or sacred place, a temple." In Paul, only in 1 Cor 9:13. Many temples in the ancient world, like medieval cathedrals, were years in the building and some, like the temple of Apollo at Didyma, were never completed. The possibility of such a time frame, if not the fear that the work might be left incomplete through hostile interference (see,

e.g., Acts 20:29–30), may have crossed Paul's mind in using his metaphor. See A. Deissmann, *Paul: A Study in Social and Religious History* (London: Hodder & Stoughton, 1926), 212 n. 4.

3. Cf. 1 Cor 3:16, 17, "you [plural, referring to the church] are God's ναός"; 2 Cor 6:16, "we [the church] are the ναός of God." Cf. Jesus' saying, "Destroy this temple [ναός] and in three days I will raise it up" (John 2:19), where the reference may be in part (but certainly not primarily) to the church. Ναός is used metaphorically in 2 Thess 2:4, not, it would seem, of the church but rather of any sphere that is rightly called God's. See D. J. Williams, *1 and 2 Thessalonians* (NIBC; Peabody, Mass.: Hendrickson, 1992), 125.

4. Διακονέω (from διάκονος "a servant"): "(1) generally, "to serve," (2) "to serve as a deacon," (3) "to supply." See also Rom 15:25; 2 Cor 3:3; 8:19–20; 1 Tim 3:10; 2 Tim 1:18; Phlm 13. In 1 Tim 3:13, it is possible that the participle διακονήσαντες is used in the general sense of "serving," without particular reference to deacons, and could therefore include the ἐπίσκοποι of vv. 1–7 and, indeed, any other member of the church. The immediate context, however, refers to the office of deacon (vv. 8–12), and it is best to take v. 13 as part of that discussion.

5. Paul's phrase is βαθμὸν . . . καλόν "a fine or noble step [up]." Βαθμός (from βαίνω "to step"; cf. βῆμα, ch. 6, n. 43): "A step." Found only here in the NT, but in the LXX used for "a step" or "a threshold," e.g., 1 Sam 5:5 (of the threshold of the temple of Dagon); 2 Kgs 20:9 (of the step of the temple of God). From these references, it appears that the word has cultic association, which is supported by the use of the kindred verb ἐμβατεύω ("to step in or on, to enter on") as a technical expression in the mystery religions with reference to the initiates *entering* the sanctuary on the completion of their rites. W. M. Ramsay (*The Teaching of St Paul in Terms of the Present Day* [London: Hodder & Stoughton, 1914], 289) cites inscriptions from the sanctuary of Apollo at Klaros (Turkey), which record that two inquirers, "having been initiated, *entered* (the sacred precinct)" and that another, "having received the mysteries, *entered*" the sanctuary. See Ramsay's full discussion (pp. 283–305). As for βαθμός, some have suggested that it represents a quite different metaphor from that adopted here, one akin to Paul's figurative use of θεμέλιος, -ον "a foundation," namely, the image of stone being set or "stepped" on stone. From this, it is argued, βαθμός acquires the sense of standing or status: "Deacons who have served well gain for themselves *a good standing*." On this interpretation, it must be supposed that their good standing is with God, that they win God's approval and at the same time and for that reason grow in their confidence in God.

6. Cf., e.g., Acts 14:27; 15:4.

7. Παρρησία (from πᾶς "all" and ῥῆσις "speech"): (1) "freedom of speech, plainness, openness," (2) "confidence, boldness." I have suggested "confidence" as the meaning here, but "boldness" might do just as well: "boldness toward others arising out of their faith in Christ Jesus." See, e.g., 2 Cor 3:12; Phil 1:20; Phlm 8. Elsewhere in Paul, 2 Cor 7:4; Eph 3:12; 6:19; Col 2:15.

8. Josephus (*A.J.* 15.11) describes this wall as a stone barrier about five feet high. Gentiles may have wanted to approach the temple out of curiosity or to offer gifts and sacrifices to the God of the Jews. Hence, warnings were posted at appropriate places to warn them off. Two of these inscriptions have been found. They read, "No man of another nation to enter within the fence and enclosure around this temple. And whoever is caught will have himself to blame that his death ensues" (from J. A. Robinson, *St Paul's Epistle to the Ephesians* [London: Macmillan, 1909], 60). The seriousness with which the Jews regarded any infringement of this regulation may be seen from Acts 21:27ff., where Paul is falsely accused of bringing Greeks, specifically Trophimus the Ephesian, into the ναός, thus defiling "this holy place."

9. Τὸ μεσότοιχον τοῦ φραγμοῦ: "The partition of the fence." Μεσότοιχον (from μέσος "middle" and τοῖχος "a wall"): A late word, found only here in the NT and rare elsewhere (once in a papyrus, once in an inscription), "a partition wall." Φραγμός (from φράσσω "to fence in"): An old word, (1) properly, "a fencing in," (2) = φράγμα "a fence." Found only here in Paul.

10. E. Gibbon, *The Decline and Fall,* cited without reference by J. Romer and E. Romer, *The Seven Wonders of the World* (London: Michael O'Mara, 1995), 129. The archaeological evidence bears out his description, drawn, as it was, from ancient literary sources (see, e.g., ibid., 129ff.). Sadly, there is little to be seen now of this great structure, but the modern traveler can get some sense of what it must have been like by viewing the remains of the temple of Apollo at Didyma, fifty miles south of Ephesus. This temple was about the same width as the Artemisium and just seven feet shorter. Many of its columns still stand to a height of ten feet or so.

11. "From the city behind it and above the plain, you would have seen the form of this great high marble building shining over the walls of its enclosure. From the sea, as you came into port, you would have seen the straight figure of Artemis herself, standing in a central window on its western pediment." And then, every year, by way of reinforcing her presence, the goddess was brought into the city in a great procession "joined by all the townsfolk and their slaves and servants. Powdered boys and girls dancing round the veiled lady." So Artemis "was borne along on general admiration, accompanied with the wealth of her temple, the donations of foreign emperors and kings and local magnates, gold and silver and precious woods and silks, and jewels beyond imagination" (Romer and Romer, *Seven Wonders of the World,* 146, 152). See also R. Strelan (*Paul, Artemis, and the Jews in Ephesus* [Berlin: de Gruyter, 1996], 24–125) for the history and dominance of the cult of Artemis in Ephesus. The reference in 1 Cor 12:2 evokes the scene of just such a cultic procession as that described above (the πομπή). The procession normally made its way through the most public areas of the city, ending at the sanctuary, where sacrifices were offered to the god. Alternatively the culmination of the procession could be other cultic activities, such as a "viewing" of the cult image in the theater or a bathing of the image. See W. Burkert, *Greek Religion* (Cambridge: Harvard University Press, 1985), 99. No one, then, who had lived as long in the city as Paul had (see Acts 19:8–10; 20:31) could have been untouched by, much less unaware of, this pervasive and dominating presence.

12. Οἶκος: See ch. 1, n. 89. I have translated it as "house" in keeping with the reference to the church as "a pillar and a support." But a case can be made for rendering οἶκος as "household," taking up the metaphor of the church as "family" hinted at in 1 Tim 3:4–5.

13. Στύλος: Old word for "a pillar." See also Gal 2:9, where James, Peter, and John are described as "pillars." Cf. Eph 2:20 for the apostles as "foundations," with much the same meaning.

14. Ἑδραίωμα (a late and rare word from ἑδραῖος "sitting," and that from ἕδρα "a seat"): "A support, bulwark, stay." Found only here in the NT and in later ecclesiastical writers. The absence of the definite article in the phrase "a pillar and support" should be noticed. A noun qualified by a genitive, as here, may be deemed to be definite but is certainly not necessarily so. In this instance, I take the indefinite form to be deliberate. The church is *a* pillar of the truth (of Christianity; see ch. 11, n. 16), not *the* pillar, for that truth has other supports (the Scriptures, the resurrection, the witness of the Spirit).

15. Ps 19:1. But see Rom 1:18–32 for the human propensity to turn a blind eye to this glory.

16. Paul's phrase is στῦλος καὶ ἑδραίωμα τῆς ἀληθείας. Ἀλήθεια is found fourteen times in the Pastorals alone (1 Tim 2:4, 7 [2x]; 3:15; 4:3; 6:5; 2 Tim 2:15, 18, 25; 3:7, 8; 4:4; Titus 1:1, 14), always with the sense of "the content of Christian-

ity as the absolute truth" (BAGD), with the exception of 1 Tim 2:7a, and often in Paul elsewhere (cf. Gal 2:5, 14; 5:7; Eph 4:21; Col 1:5; 2 Thess 2:12, 13).

17. R. A. Ward, *Commentary on 1 and 2 Timothy and Titus* (Waco, Tex.: Word, 1974), 62.

18. Nevertheless, I agree with Ramsay that "Paul does not insist much on this sacrificial and priestly side of the relation of man to God," regarding "the old Hebrew dispensation more as a system of law than as a system of sacrifice by priests" (*Teaching of St Paul*, 194), as one might expect of a man trained for the synagogue rather than the temple.

19. Ἱλαστήριος (from ἱλάσκομαι "to be propitious, merciful, to make propitiation," itself from ἵλεως "propitious, merciful"): Strictly an adjective, "propitiatory," but sometimes as a neuter substantive (τὸ ἱλαστήριον) akin in meaning to ἱλασμός "a propitiation" (cf. 1 John 2:2; 4:10). Only in Rom 3:25 and Heb 9:5 in the NT. For a more detailed treatment of Rom 3:21–26, see pp. 145–47.

20. See esp. L. Morris, *The Apostolic Preaching of the Cross* (London: Tyndale, 1965), 125–85. Morris has shown that wherever in the LXX ἱλαστήριον means "mercy seat," it is used with the definite article (as also in Heb 9:5), except in Exod 25:17, where the addition of ἐπίθεμα "cover" has the similar effect of making the reference specific. In Rom 3:25, on the other hand, ἱλαστήριον is anarthrous. There are other considerations that support the interpretation adopted here. Morris has shown, moreover, that in many, if not all, of the passages in which ἱλάσκομαι or related words occur in the LXX the idea of God's wrath is present. He is quick to point out, however, that there is nothing capricious in this wrath. It is the righteous wrath of a holy God—God's unwavering response to human sin. And it is God who put forward the propitiatory sacrifice. Sin is a divine problem (in that God loves the sinner) as well as a human one. God provided God's own solution to the problem in Jesus Christ.

21. F. F. Bruce, *The Letter of Paul to the Romans: An Introduction and Commentary* (Grand Rapids: Eerdmans, 1985), 100. Cf. J. Jeremias, *The Central Message of the New Testament* (London: SCM, 1965), 36.

22. Lev 4:3, 14, 28, 32, 35; 5:5, 6 (2x), 7 (2x), 8–9, 10–11 (2x), 13; 6:25, 30, 37; 7:27; 8:2; 9:2, 3, 7–8, 10, 15, 22; 10:16–17, 19 (2x); 12:6, 8; 14:13 (2x), 19, 22, 31; 15:15, 30; 16:3, 5–6, 9, 11 (2x), 15–16, 25, 27 (2x); 19:22; 23:19; Num 6:16; 7:87; 8:8, 12; 15:24–25, 27; 28:15, 22, 29; 29:5, 11 (2x), 16, 19, 22, 25, 28, 31, 34, 38; Deut 9:18.

23. See further ch. 5, n. 121.

24. In connection with this verse, attention has been drawn to the sacrifice of the "binding" (*'aqedah*) of Isaac (Gen 22), which in early Judaism, particularly in the Palestinian Targumim, was understood to have an atoning efficacy. See R. J. Daly, "The Soteriological Significance of the Sacrifice of Isaac," *CBQ* 39 (1977): 45–75. The currency of this idea in pre-70 CE Judaism, however, has been questioned. See P. R. Davies and B. D. Chilton, "The Aqedah: A Revised Tradition History," *CBQ* 40 (1978): 514–46; and P. S. Alexander, "Aqedah," in *Dictionary of Biblical Interpretation* (ed. R. J. Coggins and J. L. Houlden; Philadelphia: Trinity Press International, 1990), 44–47.

25. "The comparison posits not merely a quantitative superiority of the high-priestly ministry of the New Testament over that of the Old Testament, but also a qualitative distinction between them." In the work of Christ, OT sacrifices are both transcended and ended. See J. Behm, "θύω, κτλ," *TDNT* 3:180–90, here 185. The entire sacrificial or ritual vocabulary of NT, therefore, as it relates to the work of Christ—words such as ἀναφέρω "to offer up," ἱλάσκομαι "to make propitiation," ἱλασμός "a propitiation," καθαίρω "to cleanse," καθαρίζω "to purify" (see ch. 3, n. 34), καθαρισμός "a cleansing," καθαρότης "a cleansing," and the others discussed in this section—should all be regarded as metaphorical rather than actual. Such a

usage, indeed, antedates NT. Already in Ps 50:18–19, e.g., "a crushed and humbled spirit" could be spoken of as an acceptable sacrifice, and DSS, like NT, speak of prayer and praise as a sacrifice to be offered to God (1QS 8:7–9; 9:3–5; 10:6; 4QFlor 1:6–7; cf. Heb 13:15).

26. Προσφορά (from προσφέρω "to bring to, to offer"): (1) "a bringing to, an offering," (2) less frequently in classical Greek, "a present, an offering," in the NT of sacrificial offerings (actual or metaphorical). In Paul in Rom 15:16; Eph 5:2.

27. Θυσία (from θύω, see ch. 11, n. 34): (1) "the act of making an offering, sacrifice," (2) objectively, that which is offered, "a sacrifice." In Paul in Rom 12:1; 1 Cor 10:18; Eph 5:2; Phil 2:17; 4:18.

28. Εἰς ὀσμὴν εὐωδίας: "For an odor of fragrance, a sweet-smelling fragrance." Ὀσμή (from ὄζω "to smell"): "A smell, odor." In Paul in 2 Cor 2:14, 16 (2x); Eph 5:2. Εὐωδία (also from ὄζω): "Fragrance." In Paul in 2 Cor 2:15; Eph 5:2; Phil 4:18.

29. Cf., e.g., Gen 8:21; Exod 29:18, 25, 41; Lev 1:9, 13, 17; 2:2, 9, 12; Ezek 20:41.

30. See also the extended discussion of Gal 4:8–6:10, pp. 62–63, which draws out the distinction between the "moral law," which has a continuing relevance for the Christian, and the "ritual or cultic law," which has been fulfilled in Christ. See also the discussion of Rom 13:8–14, pp. 181–82.

31. Πάσχα: (1) the festival of "the Passover," (2) by extension, "the Passover meal" and "the Passover lamb." The word is common elsewhere, but found only here in Paul. With Paul's reference to Christ as the Paschal lamb, compare the Baptist's description of Christ in John 1:29, 35. Again (as with the offering and sacrifice of Eph 5:2), the reference is only incidental; it expresses the early Christian tradition that Jesus chose to die at Passover time and ate his last supper with the disciples as a Passover meal.

32. Ζύμη (a late word from ζέω "to boil"; see ch. 4, n. 99): "Leaven." See the parables of Jesus for the pervasive power of leaven (Matt 13:33; Luke 13:20–21). Found in Paul in 1 Cor 5:6–8; Gal 5:9. Cf. ἄζυμος (with α privative): Adjective, "unleavened," in Paul only in 1 Cor 5:7–8, and ζυμόω "to leaven," in Paul in 1 Cor 5:6; Gal 5:9. On the metaphor of making bread in 1 Cor 5:6, see p. 96..

33. Exod 12:15f.; 13:7. On ἐκκαθαίρω "to cleanse," see ch. 1, n. 105.

34. Θύω: As in classical Greek, (1) "to make an offering" to a god, (2) "to sacrifice" by slaying a victim, (3) "to slay, kill." In Paul in 1 Cor 5:7; 10:20. Cf. the cognate noun θυσία, ch. 11, n. 27.

35. Ἐν ἀζύμοις εἰλικρινείας καὶ ἀληθείας: Εἰλικρίνεια "sincerity, purity, innocence," but here "in a wider sense than the individual references of 2 Cor 1:12; 2:17." Paul is looking to the church as a whole to display these qualities and to be true to God's moral law. See J. Moffatt, *The First Epistle of Paul to the Corinthians* (London: Hodder & Stoughton, 1938), 59. I have interpreted this passage as a metaphor of Christian living. But some see it as a reference to the Lord's Supper or to a primitive Christian Passover, which Paul is enjoining the Corinthians to observe in a right spirit. See J. Jeremias, "πασχα," *TDNT* 5:896–904, here 901.

36. Σπένδω: "To pour out (as a drink offering), make a libation." Old word, in the NT only here and in 2 Tim 4:6, in both instances in the passive, σπένδομαι.

37. θυσία: See ch. 11, n. 27.

38. See, e.g., Num 28:7; 2 Kgs 16:13; Jer 7:18; Hos 9:4; and especially Sir 50:15, with his description of the temple ministry of Simon the high priest: "He reached out his hand to the cup and poured a libation of the blood of the grape; he poured it out at the foot of the altar, a pleasing odor to the Most High, the King of all" (RSV).

39. Λειτουργία (from λειτουργέω, and that from λειτουργός, which is from λαός "the people" and ἔργον "work"): "A service or ministry." Found in Paul in

2 Cor 9:12; Phil 2:17, 30. Λειτουργία occurs 40 times in LXX, and the corresponding verb λειτουργέω "to serve" 100 times (it is found in Paul in Rom 15:27), all with reference to the cultus and the role of the priests. Less common is the word naming the man who performed the "liturgy," the λειτουργός. Including the Apocrypha, it occurs 14 times in LXX (in Paul in Rom 13:6; 15:16; Phil 2:25). In secular Greek, especially with reference to Athens, these words were usually used of public service, often done at one's own expense. See H. Strathmann, "λειτουργέω," *TDNT* 4:215–31, here 215ff.

40. Παραβολεύομαι (the classical παραβάλλομαι): "To expose oneself to danger, to gamble with or hazard one's life." A. Deissmann (*Light from the Ancient East* [London: Hodder & Stoughton, 1908], 88) cites an inscription at Olbia on the Black Sea, probably second century CE, which employs exactly the same participle as here (παραβολευσάμενος) of a legal advocate who risked his life by taking his clients' cases even up to the emperor himself. It must be doubted that Paul used παραβολεύομαι (= classical παραβάλλομαι, in the NT only in Phil 2:30) as a conscious metaphor from throwing (βάλλω) dice, the original meaning of the word, any more than he employed the word κυβεία "cunning" in Eph 4:14 with an intended reference to "dice" (κύβος). The word *paraboli* "riskers" was later applied to Christians who, in time of plague especially, risked their lives in tending the sick and burying the dead.

41. See ch. 11, n. 39.

42. See ch. 7, n. 20.

43. Πεπλήρωμαι δεξάμενος . . . ὀσμὴν εὐωδίας, θυσίαν δεκτήν, εὐάρεστον τῷ θεῷ "I am full, having received . . . a fragrant smell, an acceptable sacrifice, pleasing to God." For θυσία, see ch. 11, n. 27, for ὀσμὴ εὐωδία, ch. 11, n. 28, and for εὐάρεστος, ch. 11, n. 51. Δεκτός (a verbal adjective from δέχομαι "to receive, accept"): "Acceptable." Cf. 2 Cor 6:2.

44. See G. F. Hawthorne, *Philippians* (Waco, Tex.: Word, 1983), 206f. Cf. Matt 10:40–42; 25:31–40; Acts 9:3–5.

45. On other occasions, Paul enunciated the principle that the minister should have his living from the work of the gospel, a principle that he supported by the cultic analogy (among others) of the priest at the altar receiving his share of the offering. See p. 33 and ch. 2, n. 12. In his own case, however, he consistently waived this right, although he accepted and welcomed gifts when they came.

46. Ἐνάρχομαι: "To begin, make a beginning" (see also Gal 3:3; cf. ἀπάρχομαι, ch. 2, n. 69) and ἐπιτελέω "to complete, accomplish, execute" (see also Rom 15:28; 2 Cor 7:1; 8:6, 11 [2x]; Gal 3:3). On the cultic connotation, see LSJ and G. Delling, "τέλος, κτλ," *TDNT* 8:49–87, here 62.

47. For all of these references, see ch. 11, n. 39.

48. Ἱερουργέω (from ἱερουργός "a sacrificing priest," from ἱερεύς "a priest" and ἔργον "work"): "To perform sacred rites, minister in priestly service." A word found in the LXX, Philo, and Josephus, but only here in the NT.

49. Paul's objective was ἵνα γένηται ἡ προσφορὰ τῶν ἐθνῶν εὐπρόσδεκτος "that the offering of the Gentiles [genitive of apposition; the Gentiles are the offering] might be acceptable." Εὐπρόσδεκτος "acceptable" in Paul in Rom 15:16, 31; 2 Cor 6:2; 8:12. Cf. θυσίαν δεκτήν, ch. 11, n. 43, and εὐάρεστος, ch. 11, n. 51. For προσφορά, see ch. 11, n. 26.

50. Παρίστημι and the late form παριστάνω: (1) transitive, "to place beside, present" (e.g., Rom 6:13, 19 [2x]; 12:1; 1 Cor 8:8; 2 Cor 4:14; 11:2; Eph 5:27 [both here and in 2 Cor 11:2 used in a nuptial context; see pp. 53–54 and ch. 3, n. 26]; Col 1:22, 28; 2 Tim 2:15), a technical term for offering sacrifice, although not in OT (e.g., Josephus, *A.J.* 4.121), (2) intransitive, "to appear, be present, stand by, stand beside" for help or defense (e.g., Rom 14:10; 16:2; 2 Tim 4:17).

51. Εὐάρεστος: "Pleasing, acceptable," in Rom 12:1–2; 14:18; 2 Cor 5:9; Eph 5:10; Phil 4:18; Col 3:20; Titus 2:9. Cf. also εὐπρόσδεκτος, ch. 11, n. 49.

52. Τὴν λογικὴν λατρείαν ὑμῶν: Λογικός, an old word, "reasonable, rational." Here the phrase means "worship rendered by the reason," i.e., inward or spiritual worship. Only here and in 1 Pet 2:2 in the NT. Λατρεία (from λατρεύω "to work for hire, to serve," itself from λάτρις "a hired servant"): "Hired service, service." In the LXX nine times, always, with one exception, in a cultic connection, "divine service, worship," as also in Rom 9:4 and Heb 9:1, 6.

XII

CHAPTER

Public Shows and Sporting Events

THE TRIUMPH

The highest honor that the senate could confer upon a successful commander was a triumph—a triumphal procession through the capital.[1] The commander wrote to the senate detailing his achievements. If his victories were over "worthy enemies," if at least five thousand of them had been slain in a single battle, if he had brought his own troops safely home (their presence was required to show that the war had indeed been won), and if he was himself a magistrate with *imperium* (the authority to raise and command troops), he might be granted his desire.[2] It was an exceptional honor and the one occasion on which a commander could legitimately parade his troops through the streets of Rome. It displayed the splendor of Rome's military might, but at a cost in human lives. The scale of Roman slaughter is reflected in the awarding of over seventy triumphs in the two hundred years from 252 BCE to 53 BCE.[3]

In classical times the procession began at the Campus Martius (the Field of Mars), the traditional mustering site for the army at the beginning of a campaign. From there it passed through the Porta Triumphalis (the Triumphal Arch), the Circus Flaminius, and the Circus Maximus. Then it rounded the Palatine and proceeded along the Via Sacra to the temple of Jupiter on the Capitol.[4] Here a ceremony of thanksgiving was followed by the distribution of largess to the army and the people.[5] At the head of the procession came the magistrates and senators, wearing full ceremonial regalia and accompanied by trumpeters. Then followed the spoils of war, carried on the backs of men or in wagons, in order to be displayed to their best effect (and competitively enumerated in the public records): "golden crowns weighing 112 [Roman] pounds; 83,000 pounds of silver; 243 pounds of gold; 118 Athenian *tetradrachmae;* 12,322 coins called Philippics; 785 bronze statues; 230 marble statues; a great amount of armour, weapons and other enemy spoils, besides catapults, *ballistae* and engines of every kind."[6]

Painted battle scenes, captured standards, models of fortresses that had been breached or ships that had been sunk, and slogans such as Caesar's "I came, I saw, I conquered" might be paraded before the crowd to demonstrate the scale of the victory and the distinction of the triumphator. Musicians accompanied this part of the procession, and after them came the prisoners of war, at least a token number of them, some of whom would be executed as soon as the procession reached the Capitol. The remainder of the prisoners were sold as slaves.

Next came the priests and their attendants, carrying censors of burning incense and bringing with them white bulls, adorned with garlands and gilded horns (and given drugs in their last feed to keep them docile) for the sacrifice to Jupiter. Finally, escorted by his *lictores* (who carried, each on his left shoulder, the *fasces,* the bundles of rods that were their badge of office), came the triumphator himself. He stood erect in a chariot of ebony and silver, hung beneath with a phallic symbol and drawn by four white horses. His face and hands were daubed with red, reflecting the terra-cotta statue of Capitoline Jupiter himself, made long ago by an Etruscan sculptor. Like Jupiter, he was clothed in a purple cloak thrown over a toga sown with golden stars. In one hand he carried a scepter surmounted by an eagle, and in the other a laurel branch. Above his head a slave held the golden wreath of the god and intoned the words "Look behind you and remember that you are but a man." The soldiers were behind him, bringing up the rear. Because they were permitted on this one day to say whatever came to mind, they mingled their repeated cry of "Hurrah, triumph!"[7] with ribald songs and derisive comments aimed at their commander. But for all that, the triumph elevated the commander to a regal, if not a divine, status and dramatized the splendor of his conquests.

It is unlikely that Paul ever witnessed a Roman triumph, but he certainly knew what they were and appears to have known what they entailed. Twice in his letters he uses the verb "to triumph over or to **lead in triumph**."[8] It occurs first in 2 Cor 2:14. Commentators disagree about how the image is applied,[9] but it appears that Christ is the triumphator,[10] processing, as it were, across the world with the apostles in his train, not as captives (as some suggest) exposed to public shame but as participants in Christ's victory, sharing in his triumph. Specifically, it portrays the apostles as the priests, whose censors waft the fragrance[11] of incense throughout the crowd. Paul likens this fragrance to the knowledge of Christ, which God was making known in every place through the apostles. In verse 15 there is a shift in the application of the metaphor. The apostles themselves become "the sweet smell"[12] of Christ (as though Christ were now the incense—Paul is thinking of the apostles as witnesses to Christ), a fragrance, he says, that is offered as their service to God. Their witness is borne both "among those who are being saved and among the perishing." To those who shared in the victory of a victorious general, the incense of the procession had an association with his triumph, whereas to the prisoners, its association was with their own imminent death. Thus the preaching of Christ comes to some as "a fragrance from death to death" and to others as "a fragrance from life to life"[13] (v. 16). There are different responses to the apostolic testimony—some positive, some negative.

The verb "to lead in triumph" occurs again in Col 2:15, but here it is "the sovereignties and authorities"[14] who are marching in Christ's train. This verse raises a number of questions. Who, for example, are "the sovereignties and authorities"? In Eph 6:12 they are "the spiritual things of evil in the heavenly sphere," and that identification has been carried over to this verse. But in Col 2:10 they are referred to in more positive terms as being subject to Christ. (The use of the definite article in v. 15, "*the* sovereignties," etc., suggests that the reference is to the sovereignties and powers introduced in v. 10.) Perhaps they are angelic beings, specifically those who in Jewish thought had mediated the law.[15] Although the law in itself is "holy and righteous and good" (Rom 7:12), it becomes "bad news" to sinners because of their sin. It becomes "the document that stands against us"—in effect, a catalog of our sins and therefore a written acknowledgment of our failure as far as God is concerned (Col 2:14).[16] The angels unwittingly did us a disservice by introducing the law. But they have now been "disarmed,"[17] Paul apparently coining his own verb to express how thoroughly this has been done. But what are we to make of the middle voice of this verb? Some understand it to be reflexive: Christ stripped himself (of "the powers of evil, which had clung like a Nessus robe about his humanity"[18]). But the middle voice need only express an interest in the action, not necessarily that the action is done to oneself. Thus the verb might be understood as Christ stripping others in an action in which he had a personal interest. Christ disarms the mediators of the law in the sense that the law no longer condemns, and so (in the imagery of the triumph) makes a **"show"**[19] of them by leading them as captives in his triumphal procession.

One more question remains. Who is the subject of verse 15? Grammatically it is the implied subject of verse 13, namely, God. On this basis the phrase at the end of the sentence refers to Christ: "God has disarmed the sovereignties and authorities . . . in *him*." But the sentence is a long one, and Paul has probably lost its grammatical thread, finishing with Christ in his mind as the subject. In this event the phrase refers to the cross: "Christ has disarmed the sovereignties and authorities . . . in *it*" (the Greek pronoun is ambiguous; it could be "it," i.e., the cross, or "him"[20]). In this understanding, Paul has given the metaphor a paradoxical twist. Instead of the state chariot of the Roman procession, Christ has ridden to his triumph on "a rough wooden cross." And perhaps there is irony as well as paradox in the verse, for Christ himself had been stripped and put on public display and the powers that be had seemingly triumphed. But from that shame had come glory. The convict's gibbet had become the "chariot" of the victor.

As the triumphal procession ascended the slopes of the Capitol to the temple of Jupiter, some of the prisoners were taken aside into the Tullianum, the prison that stood in the lap of the Arx, the more northern of the two humps of the Capitol hill, and were put to death (a survival of the ancient rite of human sacrifice as a thank offering to the gods), originally by the ax and later by strangulation and occasionally by being thrown into a pit to die a slow death. Other prisoners might be condemned to the arena to fight un-armed, as *bestiarii*, against wild beasts. Condemned criminals commonly suffered this fate as well. The spectacle of men and sometimes women dying often served as the grand finale of the events that were frequently staged in the arenas of Rome and to a lesser extent in cities elsewhere.[21] Paul may have had some such finale in mind (whether of a triumph or of some other event) in 1 Cor 4:8–9, when he declared that God had displayed[22] the apostles "last of all, like **those who are doomed to die.**"[23] Moffatt puts it this way: "God means us apostles to come in at the very end like doomed gladiators in the arena." To the church in Corinth (or at least its leaders), Christianity was about privilege and pride and flaunting their gifts in public.[24] Paul describes them ironically as "kings." But to himself and his colleagues, Christianity was about service, often rendered at great personal cost.

CHARIOT RACES

Public shows, *ludi*,[25] were staged in Rome, in the Italian *municipia*, and in the provincial towns of the empire through the generosity of mag-nates and magistrates (generally prompted more by ulterior political motives than by a genuine altruism). There were three kinds of *ludi*. Chariot races *(ludi circenses)* took place in the circus. The *ludi romani* consisted chiefly of chariot races until 364 BCE, when plays were introduced. Chariot races were included in all of the other regular *ludi*. Theater *(ludi scaenici)* was a second form of *ludus*, and gladiatorial combats *(munera)* were a third form. The second-century CE orator Marcus Cornelius Fronto declared that "the Roman people is absorbed by two things above all others, its food supplies and its shows."[26] He was echoing Juvenal's famous tirade against his degen-erate contemporaries, whom he called "the mob of Remus": "Now that no one buys our votes, the public has long since cast off its cares; the people that once bestowed commands, consulships, legions, and all else, now meddles no more and longs eagerly for just two things—bread and circuses."[27]

The circus, with its chariot races, provided the greatest of all Roman shows, and the Circus Maximus was the first, the greatest, and the prototype of all others. Nature itself had laid it out in the Vallis Murcia, between the Palatine on the north and the Aventine on the south.

The track was originally the shallow depression of the valley itself. The first spectators simply sat on the hillsides that flanked the track. In the center of the valley, two wooden posts *(metae)* were set up, the western one known as the *meta prima*. These were connected by an embankment known as the "backbone" *(spina)*. In time this embankment was embellished, first with statues of gods and later, in 174 BCE, with the *septum ova*, the seven large "eggs," which were moved, like the balls of an abacus, to indicate how many laps had been run. Stables (the first in 329 BCE) were built at the western end of the track next to the Forum Boarium facing the *meta prima*, and seats were added to the sides of the hills. Improvements continued to be made under the emperors, and the Circus Maximus reached its final, imposing form in the time of Trajan. It measured about 650 by 220 yards.

> Its curving exterior displayed three arcades faced with marble, superimposed like those of the Colosseum. . . . Inside, the track was now covered with a bed of sand which sparkled with bright mineral grain. The most striking thing, however, was the *cavea* (where the people sat), whose triple tiers faced each other along the Palatine beneath the imperial *pulvinar* and along the Aventine. The lowest tier of seats was of marble; the second of wood; the third seems to have offered standing places only.[28]

The Circus Maximus had a seating capacity of at least 250,000 people. As it grew in capacity over the years, so did the number and variety of events. By the time of Claudius the Roman calendar included 159 days expressly set aside as holidays, of which ninety-three were devoted to events in the circus at the public expense. The number of races held on any one day increased until, again by the time of Claudius, twenty-four had become the norm. Other events were added for the sake of variety, and the chariot races themselves were diversified by the number of horses in each team: sometimes two, sometimes three, sometimes even six or eight or ten. Most commonly, however, the chariots were *quadrigae*, drawn by four horses. A race started at the sound of a trumpet, which the presiding magistrate signaled.[29] As he stood, the chariots were drawn up for the start below him. "While the horses pawed the ground, branches on their heads, tail held in air by a tight knot, mane starred with pearls, breastplate studded with plaques and amulets, neck bearing a flexible collar and a ribbon died with the colours of their party," all eyes were on the charioteer. "He stood upright in his chariot, helmet on head, whip in hand, leggings swathed round calf and thigh, clad in a tunic the colour of his *factio*, his reins bound round his body, and by his side the dagger that would sever them in case of accident."[30]

The moment of greatest danger occurred when the chariot was turning at the *metae*, which were always on the left (the races ran counterclockwise). The success of this maneuver depended on the strength and agility of the two outside horses, the *funales*. They were not harnessed to the shaft as were the two horses in the middle, but were more loosely attached by a trace (*funis*), the off *funalis* swinging out on the right and the still more vital near *funalis* holding back as a pivot on the left. If the chariot hugged the turning post too closely, it ran the risk of crashing into it; if it swung too widely, it either lost position or was in danger of being overrun and wrecked by the other competitors.

Philippians 3:13–14 describes the charioteer, intent on the race, his eyes fixed on the front, not daring to look behind lest the slightest pressure on the reins (wrapped around his body) produce a false move and cause him to lose the race and possibly his life. Paul declares that his goal is to "know Christ" (v. 10), but he has not yet attained[31] it (v. 12), as some may claim to have done. Nevertheless, it remaines his goal. Thus, "forgetting what lies behind, and **straining forward**[32] to what lies ahead, **I drive on**[33] **toward the finishing line**."[34] He is explaining to his readers, by means of metaphor, that those who long to be like Christ faced danger in looking back. Past achievements (breeding complacency) and past failures (promoting despondency) are best forgotten in the interest of pressing on toward the objective. There is still much to do for Christ, and much to be achieved in the quest to be like Christ. The possibilities both of service and of sanctification are not exhausted until the Christian is summoned to the *pulvinar* of "the presiding magistrate" to receive from him **the prize**[35] that awaits the victor (v. 14).

THEATER

Another place of public concourse was the theater. The theater was both a religious structure and a secular building. It was the venue for a range of public events that had expanded from the Greek drama to include ballet, musical and athletic festivals, gladiatorial shows, fights with wild beasts, and aquatic displays.[36] Here sacrifice was offered—the intrinsic part of any public performance—and here public deliberations, debates, and trials were conducted. For a long time the Romans had resisted the erection of a permanent theater, fearing perhaps that Rome would come to look like a Greek city.[37] Eventually the Romans, like the Greeks, came to regard the theater as an essential part of any self-respecting city,[38] for it played an important role in disseminating Roman culture and Roman ideas.

Although Greek and Roman theaters were distinguishable by their architectural detail, and theaters did have their individual characters, in general, theaters of the Greco-Roman world were constructed along the same lines,[39] with a semicircle of tiered seats looking down to a level area, the orchestra, where the chorus of a Greek drama stood.[40] Beyond this was the stage, which stood higher than the orchestra. The high wall behind the stage was known as the *scaena*. The *scaena* had a facade representing a temple or a palace, and the action of the play took place on the stage in front of the *scaena*. Other scenery of a portable kind might also be used, as well as a variety of mechanical devices to achieve sound and visual effects. To project the sound of the music and the actors' voices, bronze resonating jars (jars of fired earthenware in poorer communities) were, according to Vitruvius,[41] placed in niches around the walls. W. Harris observes that "examples of this kind of device in Hellenistic theatres are cited as normal for the period, as well as the famous second-century BCE example at Corinth which was removed by . . . Lucius Mummius and sold at public auction." He suggests that the Corinthians reinstated the jars when their city was refounded and the theater was rebuilt (by the middle of the first century CE[42]). The fact that Paul speaks of **echoing bronze**[43] in his letter to the Corinthians (1 Cor 13:1) implies that this had again become a notable feature of their city.[44] Those who speak in tongues,[45] says Paul, but have neither love for others nor desire to build them up in Christ are "echoing bronze." They make a sound of sorts, but it is "empty" of any useful purpose. In 1 Thessalonians 1:8 Paul uses a similar expression to congratulate his readers on making the gospel known: "The Word of the Lord has **sounded out**[46] from you [as off a resonating jar] not only in Macedonia and Achaia but everywhere."

Theaters in the Greco-Roman world ranged widely in seating capacity, from the theater at Sepphoris, for example (near Nazareth, in Galilee), which seated about 4,000, to theaters that could hold five or six times that number of people. The theater of Balbus in Rome, laid out in 13 BCE, seated 8,000,[47] and the theater of Marcellus, completed by Augustus in 11 BCE, 14,000.[48] The earlier theater of Pompey (featuring also spectacles proper to the amphitheater), which was dedicated in 55 BCE with the slaughter of five hundred lions and twenty elephants in a *venatio,* seated more than 20,000.[49]

The theaters at Ephesus and Corinth, which were familiar to Paul, compared in size to the theater of Pompey (a figure of 24,000 has been suggested for the theater at Ephesus, 15,000 for that at Corinth). If the performers in Ephesus, Corinth, and Rome played to large "houses," Paul could claim in 1 Cor 4:9 to be playing to an even larger one. The apostles "have become," he says, "**a spectacle**[50] to the whole world, to angels and to humans alike." This is hyperbole, provoked by the pride of the Corinthian Christians in what they were and what they had in the way of spiritual gifts. Over against the Corinthians' pride Paul sets the cost at which the gospel had come to them. Its preachers—the apostles—were held in contempt by the world. Nevertheless, this was the role in which God had cast them. Soon this metaphor of the messengers of God as performers on the world's stage would become a dreadful reality when Christian men and women, in the Neronian and later persecutions, were made to perform in plays and actually suffered the fate—murder, rape, and so on—of the characters they portrayed.[51]

The Greeks took naturally to acting; the Romans did not. They could never quite overcome their sense that surrendering one's own personality to take on another was improper. But they enjoyed the theater and feted its stars. In the time of Augustus, for example, Rome was full of the fame of

Pylades.[52] Under Tiberius the mob came to blows over the comparative merits of rival actors. The riot resulted in a number of soldiers left dead on the streets.[53] Nero envied the notoriety of the actors of his day but was obliged to banish them to put an end to bloody affrays caused by their rivalries. Soon, however, he recalled them and even introduced them into his court.[54] "Though the law still called him an 'actor' and labelled him 'infamous,' the star of the Roman stage inevitably became the hero of the day and the darling of the women"[55]—in law, condemned; in practice, applauded! **Those who applaud**[56] sin, says Paul (taking his figure from the theater), deserve its penalty no less than those who practice it (Rom 1:32).

GLADIATORIAL COMBATS

Gladiatorial combats might be staged in the theater or the circus, but their true home was the amphitheater, a circular or elliptical structure with seats for spectators completely surrounding the arena.[57] Various entertainments were staged in the amphitheater. The *venatio* featured the baiting of wild beasts, either by pitting them against each other or against men *(bestiarii)*, armed or unarmed (as circumstances dictated) and sometimes even bound. From the time of Augustus,[58] this became a common form of public execution. Criminals of low status—men, women, and children—were dragged into the arena as part of the entertainment of the day, to be mauled to death and eaten by the animals (as graphically displayed in a mosaic at Tripoli). Nothing reveals the Roman psyche more clearly than the *venatio*, with its utter brutality to humans and animals alike. The scale of the slaughter of animals is almost beyond belief, and the number of humans who perished in this way is probably of much the same order.[59]

Paul expresses the costliness of Christian service in his reference to **fighting with wild beasts**[60] in Ephesus (1 Cor 15:32). In a passage defending the hope of resurrection for all believers, he asks, If there is no resurrection (as some in Corinth appear to have averred), why do we endanger ourselves every hour? (v. 30). Only the conviction that life is more than merely a period of eating and drinking followed by the oblivion of the grave makes any sense of what we are doing. Otherwise, why waste precious time taking all manner of risks? He then cites a risk he took—an incident at Ephesus in which he appears to have faced considerable danger. "I fought with wild beasts," he says. "Would I have done this for merely human reasons? What would have been the point, if there is no resurrection?" But is his fighting with wild beasts a metaphor? Or could it have actually happened? As a Roman citizen, Paul should have been exempt from the arena, but sufficient evidence exists to demonstrate that citizenship was no ironclad guarantee of safety in this regard.[61] If he had been consigned to such a fate, would he have lived to tell the tale? If so, he would have had an unforgettable tale of deliverance to tell. On balance, the majority opinion that he was using the expression as a figure of speech carries the day, the more so as other instances can be found of such a use.

A similar metaphor (but not *thēriomacheō*) occurs in 2 Tim 4:17. A prisoner once again, Paul was being tried in a Roman court (subsequently to the imprisonment and pending trial of Acts 28). The charge was so serious (presumably; the charge itself is unknown) that no counselor was prepared to take his part.[62] But "the Lord stood beside me," he says, "and I was **rescued from the mouth of the lion**." Paul's exemption as a citizen from such a death (under normal circumstances) points to this being a figure of speech, its language borrowed perhaps from Ps 22:21 (cf. Ps 7:2; 35:17).[63] The "lion" has been variously identified with the prosecutor of the case,[64] the emperor Nero, "on account of his cruelty,"[65] Satan (in light of 1 Pet 5:8), and death. Perhaps it was all of these (see v. 18), and he was a latter-day Daniel, for whose protection the Lord "shut the lion's mouth" (Dan 6:22).

The *venatio* was never the main entertainment.[66] That distinction lay with the *munus gladiatorum,* the gladiatorial combat proper.[67] Sometimes the combat was fought with muffled weapons. Such mock combat was called *prolusio* or *lusio,* according to whether it was merely the prelude to a real fight or filled the entire program. The mock battles were only a foretaste of the *munus,* in which the weapons were not padded. A gladiator's only hope of escaping death lay in dealing death to his opponent unless, as sometimes happened, the combatants were so evenly matched that there was no decisive result. The match was then declared a draw, and the next pair was called on. More often, however, the wounded loser would lie on his back and raise his left arm in mute appeal for quarter. In principle, the right of granting him his life lay with his opponent, but custom demanded that this right be waived in the presence of the patron of the show, the emperor or some other benefactor, who often consulted the crowd. If the fallen man was considered to have fought well enough to deserve a reprieve, the spectators would wave their handkerchiefs, raise their thumbs, and cry, "*Mitte!* Let him go!" and the patron might accede to their wish. If the crowd decided that he deserved to die, their thumbs went down and they cried, "*Jugula!*" lit., "cut his throat!" or "Kill him!" Then the patron passed sentence with inverted thumb.[68] This was the best of all possible conclusions to the contest. The patron could now boast of having decided a man's fate, and the gladiator's execution could be depicted in mosaic, painting, or sculpture to adorn the patron's antechamber or tomb.

Paul could hardly have approved of these bloody contests.[69] Nevertheless, they creep into his letters as metaphor. Thus he appeals to the Philippian Christians to "stand firm[70] in one spirit, **contending together**[71] as one [his compound verb brings out the notion of togetherness] for the faith of the gospel" (Phil 1:27). Like those consigned to the arena, Christians are condemned to fight for their lives (at least in the sense of what undergirds their lives—their Christian faith). Against them is arrayed a hostile world. Paul does not name their opponents, but from Phil 3 they appear to have included the Jews. The Christians' best defense is to stand together and take strength from each other. This support will enable them not to flinch[72] in the face of opposition as they fight to maintain the faith[73] and even to promote the faith in their city, Philippi (1:28). They are assured of the victory in this *munus*. The very fact of *where* they are—in the arena, so to speak—is evidence of *what* they are. They suffer precisely because they are Christians. But being Christians, they are "in Christ," and they can rest assured that they will be saved (see 1:28–29). "The Christian gladiator does not anxiously await the signal of life or death from the fickle crowd. . . . The great ἀγωνοθέτης [the patron and judge of the contest] Himself has given him a sure token of deliverance."[74] In 1:30 Paul describes himself engaging in the same **contest** with his readers, and in 4:3 he speaks of certain women who had also once "fought side by side with him" in the cause of the gospel.[75] Compare Rom 15:30, in which he invites his readers to pray for his deliverance from the unbelievers in Judea. The Roman believers would be **at his side**, through prayer, **in the contest**[76] between Paul and these opponents.

Paul writes to the Corinthians about ministry, specifically about his own role as an apostle and the difficulties that he has encountered (not least those raised by the Corinthians themselves). Again he employs (or appears to employ) the image of the gladiator but emphasizes the combatant's susceptibility to injury and death (together with the power of God). He gives a fourfold description of the apostolic condition, which may be couched in terms of the contests held in the arena:[77] "**hard pressed**[78] yet [because of God] not hemmed in,[79] **in difficulties**[80] yet not in despair,[81] **pursued**[82] yet not abandoned,[83] **struck down**[84] yet not killed"[85] (2 Cor 4:8–9; cf. "**not giving in**,"[86] vv. 1, 16). Verses 10–11 sum up the point that he is making: Christian "gladiators"—the apostles in particular, as Paul believed, but potentially all Christians—are continually exposed to the risk of death (e.g., Rom 8:36). This was the road that Jesus himself had taken (e.g., Col 1:24). Yet, paradoxically, they find their life in this contest, just as Jesus had said they would.[87]

GREEK GAMES

The events that could be witnessed in the amphitheater and the circus were the Roman counterparts of the Greek games.[88] The Olympic games were the earliest and the most celebrated (founded, according to tradition, in 776 BCE and held thereafter every four years at the full moon after the summer solstice until 394 CE). But they were by no means the only games for which the Greeks (and tourists of all nations by Paul's day) assembled. In Greece, the most notable games (other than the Olympic games) were the Pythian at Delphi, which began in 595 BCE as a contest for harp and song. Subsequently athletic contests were added. The Nemean games began about

570 BCE as a kind of military review. The Isthmian games were founded a little earlier than the Nemean (about 581 BCE) and were held in honor of Poseidon at Isthmia, near Corinth, in the first and third years of the four-year Olympiad.[89] They are of particular interest to us because of Paul's long association with Corinth. His stay there must have coincided with the Isthmian games at least once and possibly also with the Caesarean games (established in 30 BCE in honor of Julius Caesar), which were held in every fourth year to coincide with every second Isthmian.[90] A third series of games was also conducted at Isthmia. They were instituted under Tiberius and, like the Caesarean, were quadrennial, falling in the same year as the combined Isthmian and Caesarean games. They were held in honor of the reigning emperor. And the list does not end here. Many cities both in mainland Greece and beyond had their own athletic meets, including several cities with which, again, Paul had some connection, such as Antioch, Tarsus, and Ephesus, the latter being the venue of the famed Panionic games. Even Rome hosted games in the Greek manner and by the third century CE rivaled Olympia itself as a center of athletic competition.

At Olympia

All games had their distinctives, but much was common to them all. Let us visit the Olympic games (as representative of all others), traveling to Olympia on the plain of Elis in the west of the Peloponnese,[91] bounded on the north by the rocky height of Kronos and on the south and west by the rivers Alpheus and Kladeus. Here is the grove of the Altis with the statues of victorious athletes and the temple of Zeus, in whose honor these games are held. The writer of Hebrews, like Paul, was familiar with the games and may have had the Altis or some place like it in mind when he spoke of Christians "running" their "race" with former competitors, "clouds of witnesses,"[92] looking on (Heb 12:1).The white tents that we see against the somber gray-green of the olive trees are those of the *hellanodikai,* the ten umpires of the games, chosen one from each tribe of the Eleians. They have been here for ten months, receiving instruction in their duties. The athletes have been here for a month, exercising in the gymnasium of the Altis. We follow the crowd as it approaches along the Sacred Way. It comprises only men. Apart from the priestess of Demeter, women are forbidden to attend.[93] Conspicuous among the crowd are the *theōroi*—the sacred envoys bearing their gifts for the god.

At last the great day of the games dawns. The athletes present themselves to the umpires at the Bouleuterium (the council house) and prove by witnesses that they are of pure Hellenic stock and of good character. Laying their hands on the sacrificial victim, they swear (1) that they have undergone ten months of preparatory training and a month of exercises in the gymnasium and (2) that they will observe the rules and not play foul in the games.[94] And now they enter the stadium, strip,[95] and anoint themselves with oil. Again the writer of Hebrews shows his familiarity with the games in his plea to those who run a spiritual race to "throw off every encumbrance and the sin which wraps itself around us" and run as Jesus ran his race before them (Heb 12:1–2). The herald proclaims, "Let the runners put their feet to the line." He then calls on the spectators to challenge, on the grounds of race or reputation, the right of any one of them to take part in the games. Once that final preliminary is completed, the program gets under way.

The Events on the Program

Although there were twenty-four Olympic events, not all of them had to be held on any one occasion. Until the seventy-seventh Olympiad the program was completed in one day. Thereafter it was extended to five. The order of the events seems to have followed the order of their introduction into the games. They included footraces for men and boys. For the first thirteen Olympiads the *dromos,* a single lap of the stadium that was about 220 yards long, was the only event. The *diaulos,* in which the course was run twice, was added in the fourteenth Olympiad. The *dolichos,* or long race, which has been variously estimated to have been seven, twelve, or twenty-four laps of the stadium, was added in the fifteenth Olympiad. Paul knew these races well and employed the footrace as a metaphor often and in a variety of ways.[96] In 2 Thess 3:1 he speaks of the word of the Lord as **running**[97] (throughout the world—an idea that goes back to Ps 147:15) and of **being feted**[98] wherever it went, as was the successful competitor in the games.[99] In Acts 13:25 he speaks of John the Baptist as completing his **course**.[100] He sees himself, moreover, as "running" or as having "run" a race like the Baptist's, that is, as adhering to the course prescribed for him by God (Acts 20:24; Gal 2:2; Phil 2:16; 2 Tim 4:7). In Acts 20:24 he speaks as though the "course" still lay before him and in 2 Tim 4:7 as though it were completed (notice the perfect tense of the verbs in this verse). A similar thought is expressed by the past tense of the verb "to run" (*edramon,* the aorist of *trechō*) in Phil 2:16. Paul hopes to look back from the vantage point of the day of Christ to see that he "did not run or labor for nothing." In this context "labor" should be understood as a metaphor of the athlete's training. The combined metaphors of running and training make the point that Paul has worked hard in Philippi and does not want to see that work wasted. He uses the verb "to run" negatively in Rom 9:16 to express the ineffectiveness of human effort. We are not saved by *our* "wishing" or *our* "running,"[101] he declares, but by the sovereign will of God, who chooses on whom to have mercy (v. 15). In 1 Cor 9:24, 26 he uses the verb positively in urging the Corinthian Christians to a greater effort in the running of their **race**[102] (i.e., in applying their salvation to practice by the exercise of discipline—not the strongest point of this church). Finally, in Gal 5:7 he laments that his readers had been running well (specifically, in their obedience to the truth of the gospel) but someone played foul and caused them to stumble.[103]

Wrestling[104] was introduced in the eighteenth Olympiad, and, in the same year, the pentathlon, a combination of running, jumping, wrestling, discus throwing, and javelin throwing. The chariot race was introduced in the twenty-third Olympiad in the hippodrome near the foot of Mount Kronos, the circuit being traversed twelve times. Chariot races with mules, with mares, and with two horses instead of four were successively introduced. Races on horseback date also from the twenty-third Olympiad, as does the introduction of boxing.

Greek boxing resembles the contemporary sport in a number of respects; it also differs. The chief difference, apart from the lack of classification by weight, was that a bout was not divided into rounds. It went on uninterrupted until one of the combatants held up his hand in acknowledgment of defeat. Then, as now, gloves were worn to protect the hands and faces of both fighters.[105] Paul makes a metaphor of this event in 1 Cor 9:26–27 to express his determination to live a disciplined life and especially to keep his natural desires under control: "I am not **boxing**,"[106] he says, "like a man beating the air" (sparring or shadow boxing, *skiamachia*)—I am not making a pretence of Christian discipline—"but I beat my body black and blue[107] [as it were] and make it my slave."[108] In exhorting the Corinthians to a greater effort in their "race," Paul invokes the example of his own "running." He did not run aimlessly, nor (to change the illustration) did he box without a purpose. His aim was to "win." He had his eye on "the crown that lasts for ever" (v. 25)—the final outcome of his salvation—and had every intention of receiving it. To this end, he would not allow anything to interfere with his Christian practice, least of all his body. The body is not sinful in itself, but it does lend itself to sin.[109] Paul was determined to guard against that. He would make of his body a "slave"; he would not allow his body (i.e., his physical needs and natural desires) to dictate the terms by which he lived. He had a higher objective on behalf of which he went into "strict training"[110] (v. 25).

His metaphor continues in verse 27. He pictures himself as **the herald** who has called the athletes to the line (although in his illustration he remains an athlete himself[111]). How sad it would be if, having instructed[112] others in the rules of the contest, he should himself be barred from the crown by a breach of these rules.[113] It is not the ultimate loss—the loss of salvation—that Paul fears, although in the passage immediately following he does remind his readers that those who were saved in the exodus were not spared from the consequence of their misconduct and died in the desert under the displeasure of God (10:1–5). But any diminution in what it meant for him to be a Christian is not a pleasant prospect for Paul. He does see the possibility of some loss if he does not "compete according to the rules."[114] He does not define that loss. He speaks of being *adokimos,*[115] but he does not explain the term. Perhaps he was afraid that some unbecoming conduct or some undisciplined and self-indulgent act could discredit him in the here-and-now and rob him, say, of the satisfaction that he had in his preaching (see v. 18). Or perhaps he was thinking of the hereafter, that he would be reproved by Christ and sustain some loss of joy on the day of Christ. We do not know what he feared, but the emphasis of these verses is not so much on the unpleasant outcome as on its avoidance by the exercise of a rigorous discipline.

Training for the Games

Horace reluctantly acknowledged that the Greek athlete generally performed better than his Roman counterpart. He attributed this to the Greek's training and self-control. "The man," he said, "who wishes to achieve longed-for victory in a race must as a boy have trained long and hard, have sweated and groaned, and abstained from wine and women."[116] Two hundred years later Lucian of Samosata made the same point. "Without hardship," he asserted, the victor's crown "cannot be acquired. The man who covets it must put up with much unpleasantness in the beginning before at last he can expect the profitable and delightful outcome of his exertions."[117] This long, hard exertion required of the athlete in training for his event furnished Paul with the metaphor of Phil 2:16. He was appealing to his readers to remain true to "the word of life," that "in the day of Christ," as he explains, "I may be proud that I did not run in vain or labor in vain." The verb "to labor" means "to work to the point of exhaustion."[118] In this context, juxtaposed as it is to the image of "running," it may be supposed to refer to the **work done by the athlete** on the track and in the gymnasium. Compare this with Acts 24:16, in which Paul says that he has "taken pains" to have a clear conscience, employing a verb that means strictly "**to train as an athlete**"[119] and implies, like the other, that it cost him much in terms of discipline and effort to live and serve as a Christian. But the training is wasted if the athlete does not win. This was Paul's fear in Phil 2:16. In this instance it was more a matter of the Philippians "winning" than of his, although his "success" is caught up in theirs. If they remained true to Christ until Christ's return,[120] in Paul's terms they will have "won" and he will have reason to boast that he had not wasted his efforts in Philippi on their behalf.

The metaphor in Phil 2:16 may extend back to the previous verse. In this case Paul may have seen himself and the Philippian Christians more particularly as runners in **a relay race**. The relay was not included in the regular athletic program at Olympia and elsewhere, but was held at separate festivals.[121] Sometimes the course lay through the streets of the city; there is certainly no evidence that such races were ever run over a course set out for ordinary races. In place of the baton of the present-day relay race, the runners handed on a lighted torch. To win, they had to keep the torch burning to the end of the race.[122] If the Philippians, who were now "shining lights in the world,"[123] were to allow their "torch" to go out, Paul (who had run the first lap, so to speak) would have trained and run his race to no purpose.[124]

The thought of the endurance and the hard work demanded of the athlete is included in the word *agōn,* the general term for any event on the athletic program, and its corresponding verb, *agōnizomai*.[125] Paul uses both verb and noun in 2 Tim 4:7: "I have competed *[agōnizomai],*" he says, with reference to his life and work as a Christian, "in the good contest *[agōn]*." This verse is sometimes rendered, "I have fought the good fight." But it should not be restricted in this way to the combative sports, much less made into a military metaphor.[126] He calls on Timothy to compete in the same event (1 Tim 6:12, again *agōnizomai* and *agōn,* with the verb in the present imperative, "make this your practice," and placed first in the sentence for emphasis) and urges him, moreover, in a figure of speech, "to put in the necessary time in the gymnasium."[127] The rules of the games demanded such training of all who competed, and in any case, it would make him a stronger competitor. In his case (as for all Christians, especially Christian leaders), the training was to be in godliness (1 Tim 4:7). In both 1 Tim 6:12 and 2 Tim 4:7 Paul speaks of the *good*[128] contest. By this he implies that there is only one "event" worth entering, only one that is truly noble (the sense of "good"), namely, that in which "Christ is the path, and Christ the prize" (cf. Heb 12:1–2). This "event" makes considerable demands on the competitors. "We toil and strive,"[129] he says (1 Tim 4:10). It entails pain. But the athlete knows that pain is part of what it means to compete: "It has been granted to you [there is privilege in this as well as pain—the word signifies a gift of God's grace][130] that, for the sake of Christ, you should *not only* believe in him *but also* suffer for his sake, engaged [as you are][131] in the same contest *[agōn]* that you saw and now hear to be mine" (Phil 1:29–30; cf. Acts 16:19–40; 1 Thess 2:2).

THE UMPIRE

The umpire's word was final. The *hellanodikai* were at the games to enforce the rules—both the entry rules and the rules governing the conduct of the events—and enforce them they did. Pausanius tells us that "the six statues of Zeus at Olympia were made from the fines levied on athletes who had not kept the rules."[132] Many vase paintings survive that show umpires with sticks who are ready to beat the offenders.[133] The proper conduct of the games depended on the recognition of their authority, and this is the point of Paul's plea in Col 3:15: "Let the peace of Christ [i.e., the peace that comes through Christ] **umpire**[134] in your hearts." What was at stake here was the unity of the church. Paul has urged them to forgive one another and to love one another (vv. 13–14) and now, as an aid to fostering these virtues, he invites them to consciously allow what God has done for them to "umpire" in their dealings with one another. Since, by God's grace, they have peace with him through Christ (Rom 5:1), should they not act with grace toward one another? If only they would, the Pax Christiana would prevail in the church as the Pax Romana did throughout their world. Paul urges the

Colossian Christians not to succumb to false teaching. If they did, they would be **disqualified**[135] from receiving their prize (Col 2:18).

Certain situations in particular appear to have required the interposition of the umpires. In boxing, for example, if there was holding, the umpire would have to step in to separate the two contestants.[136] In wrestling, when a man was thrown, if his opponent's knee had touched the ground, the throw was disallowed and the umpire would strike the offender with his stick. But it was the footrace more than any other event that demanded the umpires' close attention. The Greek stadium was a rectangle about 220 yards long by 8 to 13 yards wide. A line at each end marked the start and the finish, and there was a turning post in the middle of each line. In races longer than a single lap, the runners had to circle the post. This presented less of a problem in the *dolichos* (the long race). But in the *diaulos*, which was only two laps run at full speed, the turn was of critical importance. When the runners were of comparable ability, bunching at the post was inevitable and interference was likely to occur. A vase in Würzburg shows one of the *hellanodikai*, stick in hand, carefully watching at the post for fouls.[137] In terms of Paul's metaphor, it was at this point that the Galatians had run into trouble. "You were running well," he says, "in your adherence to the truth, but **someone tripped**[138] **you up**" (Gal 5:7). The truth in question is the truth of the gospel. It had set them free from the "slavery" of obedience to a religious system (whether the Jewish system or any other one), but now "another gospel" was threatening to rob them of their freedom in Christ and turn them once again into slaves.[139] The Jews, on the other hand, had **stumbled**[140] over Christ in their "race" to win God's acceptance.[141] They did not believe that God would impute righteousness to disobedient sinners on the grounds that Christ had died for their sins (see Rom 9:16–10:4, esp. 9:31–32).

Paul was confident that he had run his race without infringement. "I have finished the race,"[142] he says, "I have kept the faith" (2 Tim 4:7). His statement echoes the words of inscriptions in which athletes made the same boast about keeping the rules of their events. Thus in a second-century CE inscription in the theater at Ephesus, Marcus Aurelius Agathopus declares, "I kept faith." It is interesting to note that another second-century inscription in the theater attests that "he [not Agathgopus but another] fought three fights, and twice was crowned.")[143] What Paul meant by keeping the faith was that he had been true to the gospel: he had faithfully preached it and had faithfully passed it on to others. Now he would have Timothy, in his turn, do the same (1:14; 2:2). Paul invokes the example of the athlete who "is not crowned unless he competes[144] according to the rules" (*nomimōs*, "lawfully," placed first in the clause for emphasis; 2:5). The rules of the games covered more than the conduct of the events themselves. They governed also the athletes' preparation—the long months spent in training for the events. Thus *nomimōs* could mean not only "according to the rules" but also "with commitment and discipline and a readiness to endure hardship" (cf. 3:12). In 1 Cor 9:25 the competing athlete is exercising self-control, in effect, being a "professional." So Paul wants Timothy to be a "professional" in his ministry, that is, to make the gospel—its preservation and transmission—his life's work.

THE VICTOR'S REWARD

If the rules were kept and the race was won, the winner was rewarded. The victor was crowned with the wreath that belonged to those particular games. At the Olympic games, it was a laurel wreath. The herald would announce the victor's name, his parentage, and his country; the *hellanodikai* would then take the wreath from where it lay on a table of ivory and gold and place it on his head; in his hand they placed a palm branch. At the Pythian games, the wreath was of laurel; at the Nemean, of celery, although some say that the wreath was of parsley. At the Isthmian, it was at first a pine wreath. Later, according to Plutarch, "when the contest was made sacred, they adopted the celery crown of the Nemean games."[145] Still later they appear to have reverted to pine (either way, it was "a crown that would not last," 1 Cor 9:25).[146] In 2 Tim 2:5, Paul speaks of **the athlete being crowned**[147] and, similarly, in 1 Cor 9:24–25: "Do you not know that those who run in the stadium run all, but only one receives the prize?[148] . . . But we compete for a crown that lasts for ever." Each of these passages emphasizes the athlete's preparatory training more than his reward. In Phil 4:1, on the other hand, the thought of the reward is more prominent. Here Paul describes the Philippians as **the wreath**[149] with which he himself will be crowned at the end of his course if only they stand firm, for they will be the living proof (harking back to his earlier discussion in Phil 2:16) that he had neither "run" nor "trained" in vain. Similarly, the Thessalonians will be his "crown of pride,"[150] that is, the victory wreath of which he could boast, as victorious athletes boasted of theirs, at the Parousia of Christ (1 Thess 2:19). Conversely, Paul hopes that the Corinthians will make the same boast of him on that great day (2 Cor 1:14).

In 2 Tim 4:8 Paul declares, "There is laid up[151] for me [as on the ivory and golden table at Olympia] a wreath of righteousness,[152] which the Lord, the umpire who makes no mistakes,[153] will award me on that day." His thought is of imputed righteousness, which is the crown of "all who have longed for [Christ's] appearing." But the more we practice righteousness through discipline and self-control, the more we labor to the point of exhaustion in the contest in which we are involved (but calling all the time on God's resources—the various "means of grace" that God puts at our disposal; Col 1:29[154]), the more that crown will be our reward, without ceasing to be his gift, and the greater our joy at receiving it.

Notes

1. The triumph was Etruscan in origin. To begin with, it was simply the king's return from a victorious campaign with his army and his thanksgiving to the god of the state. It thus had both a military and a religious aspect. The Etruscan kings of the sixth century BCE developed it into a spectacular ceremony, which passed from them in this form to the Romans. See H. H. Scullard, *Festivals and Ceremonies of the Roman Republic* (London: Thames & Hudson, 1981), 213.

2. See esp. Valerius Maximus, *Memor.* 2.8. There was a law forbidding generals to exaggerate the number of enemy killed. On entering Rome, triumphant generals had to swear to the truth of their reports. The rules governing triumphs were, however, gradually relaxed to admit promagistrates (by the first century even *privati* with special *imperia*, like Pompey, and after 45 BCE *legati*) and to allow a mere token presence of the army. But there was always room for intrigue and favor in their interpretation. In the event of a triumph being disallowed, or not even requested, a lesser procession, an *ovatio*, might be granted. This was generally the case if the engagement had been a civil or slave uprising, from which there was no booty to be displayed. It consisted of a procession along the same route as the triumph; the general, however, did not ride in the antique triumphal chariot, did not paint his face, and did not wear triumphal garb. No trumpets sounded, only the less martial tweeting of flutes, and rather than a bull, Jupiter received only a sheep as his offering (see Gellius, *Noct. Att.* 5.6.21, and Scullard, *Festivals,* 217–18). An unofficial triumph might be held outside Rome on the Alban Mount at the triumphator's own expense. Under the empire, triumphs soon became a monopoly of the emperor or his family, and the triumphal costume an official imperial dress (see Velleius, *Rom. Hist.* 2.40.1; Dio Cassius, *Rom. Hist.* 54.4; Plutarch, *Caes.* 61.3; and R. Brilliant, *Gesture and Rank,* 177). For further details, see H. S. Versnel, *Triumphus: An Inquiry into the Origin, Development, and Meaning of the Roman Triumph* (Leiden: Brill, 1970).

3. See K. Hopkins, *Conquerors and Slaves* (Cambridge: Cambridge University Press, 1978), 26. Scullard (*Festivals,* 212) puts the number for approximately the same period at about 100, whereas P. Marshall ("A Metaphor of Social Shame: ΘΡΙΑΜΒΕΥΕΙΝ in 2 Cor. 2:14," *NovT* 25 [1983]: 304) finds that "approximately 350 triumphs are recorded in [Greek and Roman] literature," but he does not make clear whether they include more than one reference to the same event and unofficial as well as official triumphs. Nor does he indicate over what period this number was accumulated.

4. For a more detailed description of the route, see Scullard, *Festivals,* 215.

5. See p. 225 and ch. 10, nn. 149, 155.

6. These are Roman pounds, weight equal to about seven-tenths of a pound weight in our terms. Livy, *Hist.* 39.5; cf. 34.52; 37.46; 45.35ff. The most extravagant of all Roman triumphs was that granted to Aemilius Paulus for his victory over Perseus of Macedonia in 168 BCE. Three days were given over to the procession so that the immense booty plundered from the Greek temples could be exhibited to the admiring populace. Two hundred carts were needed just to carry the priceless pictures and statues. On the second day the captured arms were paraded, together with seven hundred great casks filled with silver coins. The high point was reached on the third day, when the triumphator himself appeared, surrounded by the most valuable items of the booty.

> Now the great casks were filled not with silver, but with the purest gold. The most brilliant amongst the many beautiful works in gold and silver was a great chalice, made from ten talents of gold and studded with precious stones; there was even the gold dinner service and the royal diadem of Perseus, the Macedonian prince. He and his children were paraded be-

fore the Romans as the most valuable of all the human booty. The number of sacrificial animals [permitted for a triumph] was raised to 120 and the number of gold victory wreaths to 400, gifts from the cities of Greece and Asia Minor. (Plutarch, *Aem. 32*)

7. See, e.g., Tibullus (*Corp.* 2.5.115–118): "Crowned with the laurel, the warrior then sings 'Hurrah,' exults 'Triumph,' so that it echoes around."

8. Θριαμβεύω: From θρίαμβος (1) "a festal hymn to Bacchus," (2) the Roman *triumphus*.

9. There are, broadly, three interpretations of Paul's use of θριαμβεύω in this passage. (1) To put someone on show or display. This is the view, e.g., of R. P. Egan, who rejects any association of θριαμβεύω with the Roman triumph and argues that it simply expresses "the idea of openness and visibility on the part of Paul" ("Lexical Evidence on Two Pauline Passages," *NovT* 19 [1977]: 34–62). (2) To lead someone captive in a triumphal procession. This sense has the best lexical support and the support of many modern scholars. This notion has also been enlisted to explain Paul's unique description of himself in Phlm 1, 9 as δέσμιος Χριστοῦ Ἰησοῦ "[the] prisoner of Christ Jesus" (e.g., E. Lohse, *Colossians and Philemon* [Philadelphia: Fortress, 1971], 189). The difficulty of this interpretation, however, whether applied to Phlm or 2 Cor, is in how the procession ended. The prisoners, at best, became slaves, but some of them died. A new twist to this interpretation has been given in a recent study by P. B. Duff, who supposes that Paul is here setting out to answer his detractors at Corinth. On the face of it, says Duff, Paul seems to have been playing into their hands by describing himself as God's prisoner being led to destruction, but, in fact, he has reinterpreted the metaphor in terms of a religious rite, so that "he is a participant not in a military parade but in an epiphany procession. He has been captured, not as a prisoner of war, but as the devotee of the deity" ("Metaphor, Motif, and Meaning: The Rhetorical Strategy behind the Image 'Led in Triumph' in 2 Corinthians 2:14," *CBQ* 53 [1991]: 79–92). This interpretation, however, seems somewhat strained. (3) A better explanation is suggested by the context. Paul is exultant at the news that he has won the day at Corinth and, in that mood, has introduced his metaphor of triumph. He will go on, certainly, to speak of the downside of his ministry, but for the moment, he is "up" and his metaphor reflects his elation. So Paul's use of θριαμβεύω in 2 Cor 2:14 probably means to lead someone on the side of the victor in a triumphal procession. This does not have clear lexical support elsewhere, but it does fit the context, and we must allow to Paul the possibility of some originality.

10. Strictly, it is God who is (1) leading them in triumph in Christ and (2) making manifest the fragrance of the knowledge of Christ through them in every place.

11. Ὀσμή: See ch. 11, n. 28. In the phrase τὴν ὀσμὴν τῆς γνώσεως the genitive is of apposition. The fragrance is the knowledge. Αὐτοῦ "of him," on the other hand, is objective. Its antecedent is almost certainly Christ, so that it is knowledge *about* Christ, but knowledge in the Hebraic sense of intimacy—the apostles' work is to bring people into a relationship with Christ. I have interpreted this passage in terms of the Roman triumph, but R. P. Martin (*2 Corinthians* [Waco, Tex.: Word, 1986], 47) finds that the evidence for the use of incense in the triumph is "weak" and suggests that at this point Paul has slipped into the language of Jewish sacrifice. It is possible that Paul was mixing his metaphors and thinking of his role in Jewish terms as a priestly service (cf. p. 250). But evidence for the use of incense in a triumph is not altogether lacking. See, e.g., Scullard, *Festivals*, 215; and W. L. Knox, *St Paul and the Church of the Gentiles* (Cambridge: Cambridge University Press, 1939), 129.

12. Εὐωδία: See ch. 11, n. 28.

13. In each of these two phrases, the repetition of the word simply serves to emphasize, according to the Hebrew idiom, the thought that is being expressed.

The prepositions ἐκ and εἰς, therefore, should not be labored. Cf. Rom 1:17 and 2 Cor 3:18 for the same idiom. The metaphor of v. 16 was common among Jewish writers, who called the law an *aroma vitae* to the good but an *aroma mortis* to the evil. For details, see T. W. Manson, "2 Cor. 2:14–17: Suggestions towards an Exegesis," in *Studia Paulina* (ed. J. N. Sevenster and W. C. van Unnik; Haarlem: Bohn, 1953), 155–62.

14. Τὰς ἀρχὰς καὶ τὰς ἐξουσίας: See ch. 10, n. 101. Here the sovereignties and authorities are clearly thought of in personal terms, as indicated by the pronoun αὐτούς "them" (v. 15).

15. Cf. Acts 7:53; Gal 3:19; Heb 2:2; Josephus, *A.J.* 15.136.

16. See pp. 182–83 for the discussion of the commercial metaphor of Col 2:14–15.

17. Ἀπεκδύω: See ch. 4, n. 78.

18. J. B. Lightfoot, *Saint Paul's Epistles to the Colossians and to Philemon* (London: Macmillan, 1879), 188. For this as an image of undressing, see p. 95.

19. Δειγματίζω (from δεῖγμα "a thing shown, a specimen, example"): "To make a show of, expose." The verb is found frequently in the papyri, but only here and in Matt 1:19 in the NT. It does not necessarily imply disgrace, but with the qualifying phrase ἐν παρρησιᾳ "in public, openly" may have something of that suggestion here. At any rate, the angels are publicly exhibited, so to speak, as the mediators of a law that has now lost its power to condemn (although it remains as a guide to conduct for those who are saved; see, e.g., the discussion on pp. 63, 92–95, 180–82, 247–48).

20. The pronoun is αὐτῷ, in the phrase ἐν αὐτῷ. Its antecedent could be either Χριστός "Christ," named in v. 11, or ὁ σταυρός "the cross," mentioned in v. 14. Both nouns are masculine.

21. As a rule, combats with wild beasts do not appear to have been common outside of Rome, at least in the eastern provinces, in the early empire. Where Greek culture prevailed, Greek games were more in vogue than the bloody "sports" of the Romans. Corinth, however, was one exception to this rule, reflecting perhaps the Italian cultural influences of the refounded city's first settlers. Here "the populace delighted to watch gladiators in deadly combat, after a matinee at which condemned criminals had been set to fight with wild beasts in the arena" (J. Moffatt, *The First Epistle of Paul to the Corinthians* [London: Hodder & Stoughton, 1938], xviii; cf. Dio Chrysostom, *Disc.* 31.121). In time, neither the theater in Corinth nor the smaller Odeon nearby were able to cater for the demand for such "sports," and in the third century CE a large amphitheater (larger than the Colosseum) was constructed a little over half a mile northeast of the city center exclusively for this purpose. Corinth's obsession with blood sports persisted through the fourth century CE. Julian the Apostate wrote that bears and panthers were still hunted in the arena and that the city had appropriated tax money from Argos to pay for the hunts (*Ep.* 28). The Athenians appear to have been of like mind with the Corinthians in this regard. Indeed, Dio Chrysostom (*Disc.* 31.121) speaks of the Athenians as surpassing the Corinthians and all others in their mad infatuation with gladiatorial displays, which were held in the theater at the foot of the Acropolis. He does not say, however, whether these included *bestiarii*. On the gradual spread of Roman culture eastward, including wild beast shows (normally linked with the imperial cult), see P. Garnsey and R. Saller, *The Roman Empire* (London: Gerald Duckworth, 1987), 190; and C. Wells, *The Roman Empire* (London: Harper-Collins, 1992), 250–51.

22. Ἀποδείκνυμι: (1) "to display," used in a "technical sense for gladiatorial shows" (A. T. Robertson, *Word Pictures in the New Testament* [New York: Richard R. Smith, 1930–1933; repr. Nashville, Tenn.: Broadman & Holman, 1973], 4:107), (2) "to declare," (3) "to prove," (4) "to proclaim" to an office. See also 2 Thess 2:4.

23. Ἐπιθανάτιος: A late and rare word, found only here in the NT. In the LXX Bel 31 it is used of those thrown daily to the lions, which suggests that the word may have had an association with death by wild beasts. Dionysius of Halicarnassus (*Ant. rom.* 7.35) uses it of those thrown from the Tarpeian Rock (a cliff, probably at the southwest corner of the Capitol hill in Rome, from which murderers and traitors were thrown).

24. Evidently this church was greatly blessed. With 1 Cor 4:8, cf. 1:5 and the list of spiritual gifts in ch. 12. But they boasted of their gifts as though they were self-made and not given by God (4:7).

25. These entertainments, and the public holidays on which they were held, had their origin in the religious festivals of an earlier agrarian society. The Latin word for a holiday was *feriae*, a term that belonged originally to the *jus divinum*, the religious law. But with the growth of urban society, the old religious/agrarian festivals were largely neglected or else compacted into festivals of two, three, or more days in which the religious element was minimal, to give time for an elaborate system of public amusement. So the old religious word *feriae* became debased to mean "the holidays of a schoolboy," and its use generally supplanted by *ludi*. The oldest and most imposing of the *ludi* were the *ludi romani* or *magni*, lasting from September 5 to 19 in Cicero's time. These had their origin in the return of a victorious army at the end of the season of war, when king or consul had to carry out vows he had made when entering on his campaign. The usual form of the vow was to entertain the people on his return, in honor of Jupiter. The *ludi plebeii* in November seem to have been a kind of plebian duplicate of the *ludi romani*, probably instituted about the time of the Second Punic War (218–201 BCE). The *ludi apollinares* were vowed by a *praetor urbanus* in 212 BCE, when the fate of Rome was hanging in the balance, and were fixed to a date in July. The *ludi megalenses* were instituted in 204 BCE, the *ludi ceriales* in 202, and the *ludi florales* in 178. These were all annual events, besides which numerous occasional *ludi* were offered from time to time by victorious generals and the like. A striking memorial to a public show staged by a local magnate may be seen in the mosaic of Magerius at Smirat, Tunisia. It depicts a fight between four gladiators and four leopards. It also records the acclamation of the public:

> Magerius! Magerius! May your example serve to instruct those who come after you! May your predecessors also heed the lesson! When has anyone else done so much, and where? You offer a spectacle worthy of Rome, the capital! You pay from your own purse! Today is your great day. Magerius is the donor! That is true wealth! That is true power! The very thing! Now that it is over, give the gladiators something extra to send them on their way!

Magerius agreed to this last wish, and the mosaic shows the four bags of silver (each marked with the amount) that he sent to the gladiators in the arena.

26. Cited without reference by J. Carcopino, *Daily Life in Ancient Rome* (Harmondsworth, U.K.: Penguin, 1956), 204.

27. Juvenal, *Sat.* 10.77–81. Most of the cities of the Roman world were preoccupied with the first of these items (*panem*, bread), but it was the characteristic of the Romans themselves to be preoccupied also with the second (*circenses*, circuses).

28. Carcopino, *Daily Life*, 216.

29. A fourth-century CE figure in the Museum of Conservators, Rome, shows a consul about to throw a handkerchief onto the track to signal the start of a chariot race.

30. Carcopino, *Daily Life*, 218.

31. Καταλαμβάνω: (1) "to lay hold of, seize, appropriate," (2) of an intellectual grasp of something, "to apprehend, comprehend," (3) "to overtake." In the last sense, καταλαμβάνω is a correlative of διώκω (see ch. 12, n. 33) "to pursue and to overtake." Although neither verb is restricted to racing terminology (or to any other

sphere for that matter), both are used in connection with racing. If the chariot race is indeed Paul's metaphor in vv. 13–14, it makes his choice of καταλαμβάνω in vv. 12 (2x) and 13 both understandable and apt. See also Rom 9:30; 1 Cor 9:24 (in the context of a metaphor from the footrace, in which Paul wants the runners "to overtake," that is, to win—his way of urging the Corinthian Christians to greater efforts in their practice of the Christian faith; see ch. 12, n. 102); Eph 3:18; 1 Thess 5:4.

32. Ἐπεκτείνω: "To extend," an old double compound, found only here in the NT and here as a present middle participle, "stretching myself out toward," a graphic word from the arena (see V. C. Pfitzner, *Paul and the Agon Motif* [Leiden: Brill, 1967], 139–56), expressive of any competitor—athlete or charioteer—straining toward the finishing line. "It powerfully describes the need for concentration and effort in the Christian life if one is to advance in the knowledge of Christ. It pictures the ceaseless personal exertion (the force of the present tense), the intensity of the desire (the force of the double compound) of the Christian participant in the contest if he is to achieve the hoped for goal" (G. F. Hawthorne, *Philippians* [Waco, Tex.: Word, 1983], 153).

33. Διώκω: (1) "to put to flight, drive away," (2) "to pursue," without hostility in the sense of "to follow" (see Rom 9:30–31; 12:13; 14:19; 1 Cor 14:1; Phil 3:12, 14; 1 Thess 5:15; 1 Tim 6:11; 2 Tim 2:22); with hostility in the sense of "to persecute" (see Rom 12:14; 1 Cor 4:12; 15:9; 2 Cor 1:13, 23; 5:11; 6:12; Phil 3:6; 2 Tim 3:12). The verb is commonly used of races of one kind or another, including the chariot race.

34. Κατὰ σκοπόν: "Down upon the goal." Σκοπος: (1) "a watchman," (2) "a goal or mark" on which to fix the eye. Found only here in the NT.

35. Βραβεῖον (from βραβεύς "an umpire"): "A prize" for winning an event. A late word in inscriptions and papyri. Only here and in 1 Cor 9:24 in the NT (but cf. βραβεύω, ch. 12, n. 134). Here the prize is defined by the genitive, "of the upward call" (τῆς ἄνω κλήσεως). Because they are "in Christ," those who have endured to the end—who have run with patience the race set before them—are "called up" at last by God to receive the final issue of their salvation: the Christian counterpart of the rewards lavished on the victorious charioteer. "The winner [of the chariot race] was greeted with a storm of applause and the winning driver and his beasts were overwhelmed by the outburst of the crowd's enthusiasm" (Carcopino, *Daily Life*, 220). Most charioteers began their career as slaves, but the more successful won their emancipation and amassed great fortunes from the gifts of magistrates and the emperor himself. See, e.g., *CIL* 6.10048 and the account in Carcopino (*Daily Life*, 220–21) of the monetary and other rewards reaped by the more successful drivers. For a similar thought to that expressed here in Phil 3:14, see Paul's reference to "the crown of righteousness" in 2 Tim 4:8, p. 273 and ch. 12, n. 152.

36. See, e.g., Apuleius (*Metam.* 10.29–32) for the spectacle that he witnessed in the theater at Corinth. The show began with a pyrrhic dance done by choruses of young men and women. Next came an elaborate performance of *The Judgment of Paris*, complete with an artificial wooden mountain turfed and planted with trees. An artificial stream tumbled down the side of the mountain and goats grazed on the grass. A graceful ballet followed, and then the characters of the play entered, Paris and Mercury and the goddesses Juno, Minerva, and Venus, each accompanied by her appropriate attendants: Juno with Ceres and Proserpina; Minerva with Fear and Terror; and Venus with a crowd of cupids, Graces, and seasons. After the thinly clad Venus had done an alluring dance with her attendants, a fountain of wine mixed with saffron burst from the top of the mountain, showering the goats with the golden color associated with the flocks of Mount Ida. Even if the account is not strictly accurate, it gives an impression of the types of entertainment that could be witnessed in the theater. This particular theater was modified about the time of Apuleius's visit to function also as an arena for wild-beast fights and was further modified in the late

third century for aquatic performances. See J. Wiseman, "Corinth and Rome I: 228 BC–AD 267," in *ANRW* 7:521.

37. Temporary stages were set up in the Forum or the Circus, the audience at first standing but afterward accommodated with seats in a *cavea* of wood erected for the occasion. The whole show, including play, actors, and pipe players to accompany the voices where necessary was put out to contract, like all such undertakings, on the occasion of each *ludi scaenici*. An attempt to build a stone theater was made by the censors in 154 BCE, but the senate was persuaded by Scipio Nasica to put a stop to it (see Valerius Maximus, *Memor.* 2.4.2; Livy, *Ep.* 48). Rome continued to be without a stone theater until Pompey built one on a grand scale in 55 BCE in the Campus Martius. But even he did not escape criticism (see Tacitus, *Ann.* 14.20) and had to incorporate in the structure a temple to Venus Victrix to gain acceptance for his theater (see Tertullian, *Spect.* 10; Pliny, *Nat.* 8.20).

38. See Pausanius, *Descr.* 10.4.

39. For a detailed description of the architecture of Roman theaters, see Vitruvius, *Arch.* 5.3–9.

40. In early Greek theatrical productions, the chorus played an important role as dancers, singers, and commentators on the action. Wealthy citizens felt it was something of a duty and certainly a benefaction to their city to defray the costs of the chorus, and thus the verb χορηγέω and its compound, ἐπιχορηγέω, came to mean, by NT times, generally "to supply, provide for." Paul uses them in this sense, without any conscious reference to the theater as far as we can tell, in 2 Cor 9:10 (χορηγέω) and in 2 Cor 9:10; Gal 3:15; Col 2:19 (ἐπιχορηγέω). Another word with theatrical roots is ὑπόκρισις (from ὑποκρίνομαι "to answer, to answer on stage, play a part" and so "to pretend"). It is used of "playacting" in Aristotle, Polybius, etc., and of "hypocrisy" in, e.g., Gal 2:13; 1 Tim 4:2. But there is nothing to suggest that Paul used it as a conscious metaphor from the theater. Cf. ὑποκριτής "an actor" and thus "a hypocrite" (not in Paul).

41. Vitruvius, *Arch.* 5.5.1, 7–8. Vitruvius's description of how these jars worked is, however, questionable, as, indeed, is the need for them at all. On his own admission, none of the stone theaters of Rome had resonance enhancers (he claimed that stone theaters needed them more than did the wooden structures).

42. See Wiseman, "Corinth and Rome I," 521.

43. Χαλκὸς ἠχῶν: Present active participle of ἠχέω (from ἦχος "a sound") "to sound." Found in the NT only here and in Luke 21:25 of the roaring of the sea.

44. W. Harris, "Echoing Bronze," *JASA* 70 (1981): 1184. See also W. Harris, " 'Sounding Brass' and Hellenistic Technology," *BAR* 8 (1982): 38–41. Other suggestions have been made for Paul's reference, such as "clanging armor" (C. K. Barrett, *A Commentary on the First Epistle to the Corinthians* [London: Adam & Charles Black, 1971], 300) or the sounding of musical instruments as the accompaniment of pagan rites—a familiar sight and sound in the streets of Corinth and other cities of that time (Moffatt, *First Corinthians*, 192).

45. His "tongues of men" (ταῖς γλώσσαις τῶν ἀνθρώπων) is probably glossalalia, ecstatic, inarticulate speech, and the following καί takes the description of "tongues" to its climax, "yes, and of angels." That is, this ecstatic utterance, if genuinely of the Spirit, belongs to another world, an echo of heaven. Barrett (*First Corinthians*, 299–300), on the other hand, understands "tongues of men" to be ordinary human speech and only the "tongues of angels" to be glossalalia.

46. Ἐξηχέω: "To sound forth," is found in the NT only in 1 Thess 1:8.

47. See S. B. Platner and T. Ashby, *A Topographical Dictionary of Ancient Rome* (Oxford: Oxford University Press, 1929), 513.

48. Ibid., 513–15.

49. Ibid., 515–17. Some estimates put the capacity of Pompey's theater as high as 40,000 (e.g., W. W. Fowler, *Social Life at Rome in the Age of Cicero* [London:

Macmillan, 1937], 310), but I have given the more conservative figure, which appears to have the consensus. See ch. 12, n. 37 for the importance of this structure in the history of Roman theaters. Although it was an architectural landmark, it did nothing to restore the golden age of Roman tragic and comic drama. Its very size was symptomatic of the degeneracy of the theater. Cicero was at its opening and wrote to a friend,

> The *ludi* had not even that charm which games on a moderate scale generally have; the spectacle was so elaborate as to leave no room for cheerful enjoyment and I think you need feel no regret at having missed it. What is the pleasure of a train of six hundred mules in the *Clytemnestra* [of Accius] or three thousand bowls in the *Trojan Horse* [of Livius] or gay-colored armor of infantry and cavalry in some mimic battle? These things rouse the admiration of the vulgar: To you they would have brought no delight.

Cicero's comment on the five-day *venationes* that accompanied the opening of the theater is also noteworthy:

> Magnificent, no one denies it, yet what pleasure can it be to a man of refinement, when a weak man is torn by a very powerful animal or a splendid animal is transfixed by a hunting-spear? . . . The last day was that of the elephants, about which there was a good deal of astonishment on the part of the vulgar crowd, but no pleasure whatever. Nay there was even a feeling of compassion aroused by them. (*Fam.* 7.1)

Pliny, *Nat.* 8.21, confirms that the people were so moved at the slaughter of the elephants that they actually execrated Pompey.

50. Θέατρον (from θεάομαι "to look at"): (1) "a theater," (2) collective for οἱ θεαταί "the spectators," (3) = θέα, θέαμα, "a spectacle, show." See p. 263 for the discussion of 1 Cor 4:8–9 in terms of the *venatio* or the gladiatorial *munus*. Insofar as these were "theater" and were often staged in theaters, I have included the passage here also. For similar language used by the Stoics, cf., e.g., Seneca (*Prov.* 2.9), who saw Cato as a "worthy spectacle" for God to behold. See further J. N. Sevenster, *Paul and Seneca* (Leiden: Brill, 1961), 115–16.

51. See Suetonius, *Nero* 12; *Cal.* 57; Juvenal, *Sat.* 8.186; Martial, *Epigr.* 8.30; 10.25; *1 Clement* 1.6.

52. See Dio Cassius, *Rom. Hist.*, 54.17.4–5; Suetonius, *Aug.* 45; Macrobius, *Sat.* 2.7.12–19.

53. See Tacitus, *Ann.* 1.77; cf. Suetonius, *Tib.* 37.

54. See Tacitus, *Ann.* 13.25, 28; 14.21; Suetonius, *Nero* 16.2.

55. Carcopino, *Daily Life*, 227.

56. Συνευδοκέω: A late verb, "to heartily approve." "There are thoughts [in this verb] not only of full support, but also of enjoyment. The word certainly includes the encouragement to do wrong" (L. Morris, *The Epistle to the Romans* [Grand Rapids: Eerdmans, 1988], 100). See also 1 Cor 7:12–13; for the same figure of applause, but differently expressed, ζητοῦντες ἐξ ἀνθρώπων δόξαν "seeking praise from men," 1 Thess 2:6. Here δόξα does not have its usual NT meaning of "glory" in a religious sense but the common nonbiblical meaning of popular or good repute. Applause was expressed, much as it is today, by the stamping of feet and the clapping of hands. There might also be cries of approval.

57. The amphitheater is arguably the most characteristic of all Roman structures. "Moderns find it hard to reconcile the positive aspects of Roman civilization with the gladiators, the wild beasts, the savage executions. These were not however a mere aberration. They were fundamental to the culture and to the social systems" (Wells, *Roman Empire*, 248). Indeed, there appears to have been a religious dimension to these events. Certainly slave attendants were sometimes costumed as gods, and Christian victims might be paraded as pagan priests and priestesses (*Martyr.* 18). Amphitheaters came in all sizes, from the Flavian Colosseum at Rome, which seated

45,000 and had room for another 5,000 standing, to the little arenas hollowed out of hillsides beside military camps, which served the garrison for weapon drill as well as for the occasional gladiatorial show. There is just such a one beside the remote Welsh fort of Tomen-y-mur, and another, exemplifying the ubiquity of the structure, at the other end of the empire, at Dura-Europus on the Euphrates. An arena with a capacity of 20–25,000 was not uncommon in many of the provincial cities of the West and Africa especially, such as those at Verona, Arles, Nimes, and El Djem (Tunisia). Jesus once said, "Where your treasure is, there will your heart be also" (Matt 6:21). The reverse is no less true. The amphitheaters represented something close to the heart of Roman culture, and the Romans poured their treasure into their construction and all their architectural skill into their design. The Flavian and post-Flavian amphitheaters are highly sophisticated in terms of crowd control, drainage, provision of awnings (see ch. 9, n. 3), and arrangements for the delivery and storage of props and performers, animal and human. See, e.g., Carcopino (*Daily Life,* 234–37) for a detailed description of the Colosseum, which displayed the typical arrangement of the amphitheater in its most perfect form.

58. Augustus may have unintentionally invented this form of execution when he erected in the Forum a pillory that collapsed and dropped the victim, the criminal Selurus, into a cage of wild beasts. See Strabo, *Geog.* 6.2.6.

59. There are, of course, no total statistics, but see ch. 12, n. 67 for the scale of the human slaughter in man-to-man combat. Of the number of animals killed, occasional references give us some indication. As early as 169 BCE, 63 African animals (probably lions or leopards), 40 bears, and several elephants had been killed in a single show (Livy, *Hist.* 44.18). New species were gradually introduced to Roman spectators—tigers, crocodiles, giraffes, lynxes, rhinoceroses, ostriches, hippopotamuses—and killed for their pleasure (Pliny, *Nat.* 8.65ff.). Pliny tells of single shows that featured 100, 400, and 600 lions respectively, plus other animals (*Nat.* 8.53; cf. Dio Cassius, *Rom. Hist.* 39.38). Augustus is said to have given twenty-six wild beast shows in Rome during his principate, in which 3,500 animals were killed (see K. Hopkins, *Death and Renewal* [Cambridge: Cambridge University Press, 1983], 9). In one day of the *munera* with which Titus inaugurated the Colosseum in 80 CE, 5,000 beasts were killed (Suetonius, *Tit.* 7). In 108–109 CE Trajan celebrated his conquest of Dacia with games, lasting 123 days, in which "some eleven thousand animals wild and tame were killed and ten thousand gladiators fought" (Dio Cassius, *Rom. Hist.* 68.15). Caelius Rufus's badgering of Cicero, at that time the governor of Cilicia, to send him 100 panthers for the games to be held under his aedileship seems, by comparison, a modest request (see Cicero, *Fam.* 8.9)! The emperor Commodus himself killed five hippopotamuses, two elephants, a rhinoceros, and a giraffe in a show that lasted two days (Dio Cassius, *Rom. Hist.* 72.19). On another occasion, he killed 100 animals (lions or bears) in a single morning (Herodian, *Hist.* 1.15). It is not surprising that the lion, the tiger, the hippopotamus, and the elephant became extinct in large areas—within and beyond the borders of the empire—in which once they had freely roamed.

60. Θηριομαχέω (from θηρίον "a wild beast" and μάχομαι "to fight"): "To fight with wild beasts." Found only here in the NT. For the literal meaning of θηριομαχέω, see Diodorus Siculus, *Hist.* 3.43.7; Josephus, *B.J.* 7.38. The literal meaning could be defended, and the difficulty that Paul is unlikely to have survived the ordeal overcome, by understanding the condition, εἰ . . . ἐθηριομάχησα, as contrary to fact: "If I had fought . . . [but, in fact, I didn't]," although the sentence does not conform strictly to the usual pattern of such conditionals. This reading would be consonant with the tradition that Paul suffered an imprisonment in Ephesus and faced the real prospect of death. (Cf. 2 Cor 1:8–11, and see the discussion of this passage in ch. 6, n. 9; Phil 1:19–26 may refer to the same occasion. For the social and political environment of Ephesus at this time, in which even a citizen might be at risk, see

D. J. Williams, *Acts* [NIBC; Peabody, Mass.: Hendrickson, 1990], 341–42. See also
G. S. Duncan, *St Paul's Ephesians Ministry: A Reconstruction* [London: Hodder &
Stoughton, 1929], 126ff.) But if the reading εἰ . . . ἐθηριομάχησα is taken at face
value as a condition based on actual experience, then we must adopt the most likely
interpretation, namely, that Paul is using the expression in a figurative sense. For
such a use, see, e.g., Ign. *Rom.* 5.1 (cf. Ign. *Smyrn.* 4); Appian, *Hist. rom.* 2.61;
Philo, *Mos.* 1.43f. Cf. also the frequent use of θηρίον "the beast" in Revelation, in
view of which, as well as of the reference in 2 Tim 4:17 to the "lion's mouth," it has
been suggested that Paul was employing the "secret language of Christians" to allude to a struggle with the imperial power. For further arguments in support of the
metaphorical interpretation and, specifically, that Paul has taken over the "language
used by the moralists of his day to describe the wise man's struggle against hedo-
nism," see A. J. Malherbe, "The Beasts at Ephesus," *JBL* 87 (1968): 71–80. In all of
this, it is generally (and rightly) supposed that Paul was referring to human adversaries of one kind or another. But another possibility is suggested by Artemidorus
Daldianus, who likens sickness to a wild beast (*Onirocriticus* 2.12). On this basis, it
could be supposed that the "wild beasts" of 1 Cor 15:32 were the "thorn in the
flesh" of 2 Cor 12:7.

61. A Roman citizen could be condemned to the arena for rebellion, but this
entailed the loss of his citizenship, and Paul later claims the privilege of citizenship in
appealing his case to the emperor (Acts 25:11). One of the most notorious cases of a
citizen being forced into the arena as a *bestiarius* is that of the consul Acilius Glabrio,
who had to fight with a lion and two bears in Domitian's private amphitheater, after
which he was exiled. He was put to death four years later in 95 CE (possibly as a
Christian) (Dio Cassius, *Rom. Hist.* 67.14). Cicero also mentions disparagingly the
habit of a certain Balbus, who threw Roman citizens to the beasts despite their cry of
Civis romanus natus sum (*Fam.* 10.32.3). Seneca writes of "youths of the noblest
lineage whose extravagance has flung them into the arena" (*Ep.* 99.13).

62. For the discussion of this passage in terms of the legal processes involved,
see pp. 143–44.

63. Cf. the popular cry of a later date: *Christianos ad leonem*, "to the lion,
Christians!" See Tertullian, *Apol.* 100.40.

64. After describing a scene in the theater depicting the judgment of Paris,
Apuleius has this description of the practitioners of the law: "Why then do you mar-
vel, if the lowest of the people, the lawyers, *beasts of the court,* and advocates that are
but *vultures* in gowns, nay if all our judges nowadays sell their judgments for
money?" (*Metam.* 10.33.1; on the venality of judges, cf. Juvenal, *Sat.* 13.3f.;
16.6–14; Tacitus, *Ann.* 2.34.1).

65. Eusebius, *Hist. eccl.* 2.22.4. Earlier, news of the emperor Tiberius's death
had reached Herod Agrippa as "The lion is dead" (Josephus, *A.J.* 18.228). Cf.
Additions to Esth 14:13 for the same description of Ahasuerus.

66. This is indicated by Pompeian inscriptions in which the *venatio* is classed
with such extra attractions as *athletae, vela,* and *sparsiones* (*CIL* 4.71). Perhaps the
most spectacular of the "other entertainments" was the *naumachia* "sea battle," for
which the arena was flooded and warships brought in to engage in mock sea fights.
The amphitheater had to be purposely built to stage this event. Augustus, e.g., refur-
bished the amphitheater of Taurus beside the Tiber to accommodate *naumachiae,*
and Trajan constructed two other arenas in Rome for that purpose (see Platner and
Ashby, *Topographical Dictionary,* 5–11, 358). At first, the Colosseum had been designed for the dual purpose of the *naumachia* and the ordinary events of the arena
(the *hoplomachia,* armed combat in all its forms, and the *venatio*), but probably in
the time of Trajan the basement area, from which it had been filled and drained, was
converted into pens for animals and housing for the system of ramps and hoists by
which they could be moved quickly into the arena.

67. These appear to have been Etruscan (so Athenaeus, *Deipn.* 4.153) or Campanian in origin and were associated at first with funerals, as part of the funeral games (*ludi novemdiales*, an old religious institution, occurring on the ninth day after the burial), the theory being that blood had to flow to slake the thirst of the *manes*, the deceased ancestors of the underworld. Tertullian speaks of it: "Once upon a time, men believed that the souls of the dead were propitiated by human blood, and so at funerals they sacrificed prisoners of war or slaves of poor quality bought for that purpose" (*Spect.* 12). But the funeral was often merely the pretext, the real intention being to win popularity for the living rather than to serve the dead. The precedent in this regard was set, according to Livy (*Ep.* 16), by one D. Junias Brutus Pera and his brother in 264 BCE, at the beginning of the First Punic War (cf. Cicero, *Fam.* 2.3; Valerius Maximus, *Memor.* 2.4.7). Such *munera* were offered to the public with increasing ostentation and decreasing lip service to their original funerary association (e.g., in 216 BCE by the sons of M. Aemilius Lepidus in honor of their father; in 200; in 183; in 174, in which year "several gladiatorial shows were given"; see Livy, *Hist.* 23.30; 31.50; 39.46; 41.28). These shows were generally staged in the Forum (see Vitruvius, *Arch.* 5.1). The year 105, however, marks a significant development. Hitherto gladiatorial combats had been staged exclusively by private individuals; in this year a show was staged by the ruling consuls, although there is some evidence that it was intended to instruct the soldiers in the better use of their weapons, not to entertain the public. At all events, by the time of Julius Caesar gladiatorial combats were simply one of the entertainments provided for the people by their rulers. Caesar himself, however, maintained the funerary connection by staging gladiatorial exhibitions in 65 and 46 BCE in honor of his dead father and daughter respectively; see Pliny, *Nat.* 33.53; Plutarch, *Caes.* 5; Dio Cassius, *Rom. Hist.* 43.23. Inscriptions on tombs referring to gladiatorial combats and their depiction (also on tombs) is further evidence that the funerary connection was never quite forgotten; see, e.g., *CIL* 11.6366. Sometimes lip service was paid to the religious origins of these shows by dressing the attendant slaves as gods: "Mercury" tested the combatants with red-hot irons to see if they were really dead, and "Pluto" or "Charon" dragged the dead away (see Tertullian, *Apol.* 15). Most gladiators were drawn from three classes of people: prisoners of war, slaves, and criminals, none of whom had any choice in the matter. Some few did volunteer, including the occasional senator and knight, in hope of fame and/or fortune. Gladiators were the sex symbols of their day. In all, enormous numbers were involved. In Caesar's games of 65 BCE, 320 pairs of gladiators fought. Those of 46 BCE included fights between whole detachments of infantry and squadrons of cavalry, some mounted on horses and others on elephants. Five thousand pairs fought in eight different games presented by Augustus (*Res gest.* 22.1). Carcopino (*Daily Life*, 243) cites some figures from a fragment of the *Fasti ostienses*, which cover the period from March 108 CE to April 113 CE. They mention two minor shows, one of 350 pairs of gladiators, the other of 202. The major event was a *munus* lasting 117 days in which 4,941 pairs of gladiators took part. Over the years, some gladiators survived and were rewarded with freedom and wealth (e.g., Martial, *Lib. spect.* 20). Most, however, died prematurely in the arena. Many gladiatorial combats were effectively mass executions. Until the third century, the practice was retained, both in Rome and elsewhere, of proclaiming *munera sine missione*, that is, gladiatorial combats from which none might escape. No sooner had one of the duelists fallen than another took his place, until all were killed. Then there was the practice, described by Seneca (*Ep.* 7), of having criminals paired in the arena, one armed, one not. The one would kill the other, would be disarmed, and would be killed by another in his turn, etc. Gladiators were of four types. (1) The mirmillo, who had a fish for the crest on his helmet, and (2) the Samnite were both heavily armed with large shield (*scutum*), visored helmet, and short sword. (3) The retiarius, who fought with net and trident, and (4) the

Thracian, who fought with round shield *(parma)* and curved dagger *(sica)*, were both lightly clad. The Retiarius was usually pitted against the mirmillo and the Samnite against the Thracian. The interest lay in pitting a heavily armed man, who was necessarily slower in his movements, against a lightly armed man, who was quicker—one depended on speed and agility, the other on defense and close encounter. But sometimes interest was added by some unusual combination, such as a black against a black or a dwarf against a woman.

68. Juvenal, *Sat.* 3.36.

69. In which case he shared the revulsion of some of his contemporaries. Tacitus writes, "There are special vices peculiar to this city that children seem to absorb, almost in their mother's womb: a partiality for the theater and a passion for horse racing and gladiatorial shows" (*Dial.* 29). Seneca tells of a visit he once paid to the arena in Rome. He arrived in the middle of the day, during the entertainment staged in the interval between the wild-beast show of the morning and the gladiatorial show of the afternoon. He expected to find some light relief "from the sight of human blood." Instead, he found himself watching the mass execution of criminals. He describes (*Ep.* 7.2ff.) how degrading he found the whole experience. He went away, he said, feeling "more callous and less human." But Seneca and Tacitus were more the exception than the rule. Either the carnage was rationalized, as by Cicero (*Tusc.* 2.41) and Pliny (*Pan.* 33), who suggest that the spectacle taught courage (but even Cicero sometimes felt something approaching disgust; see ch. 12, n. 49), or it was simply enjoyed, as by the many thousands who, like Claudius, would arrive before dawn and go without their midday meal rather than miss a moment of the day's "entertainment" (see Suetonius, *Claud.* 34).

70. Στήκω: A late present form of ἵστημι (See ch. 10, n. 105). "It conveys the idea of firmness or steadfastness, or unflinching courage like that possessed by soldiers who determinedly refuse to leave their posts irrespective of how severely the battle rages" (Hawthorne, *Philippians,* 56), a not inappropriate word if Paul's metaphor is of gladiators. In the NT found almost exclusively in Paul (the exception is Mark 11:25) in Rom 14:4; 1 Cor 16:13; Gal 5:1; Phil 1:27; 4:1; 1 Thess 3:8; 2 Thess 2:15.

71. Συναθλέω (cf. συναγωνίζομαι, ch. 12, n. 76): "To contend together," as in athletic or other such contests. A late and rare word, found only here and in Phil 4:3. The simple verb ἀθλέω "to contest" is found in 2 Tim 2:5 (see ch. 12, n. 144), where the reference is more likely to Greek games than to Roman gladiatorial combats, although the latter are not entirely ruled out. The word συναθλέω can mean a contest in war or in sport, and the events of the arena had something of the character of both (see ch. 12, n. 125). P. T. O'Brien (*The Epistle to the Philippians* [Grand Rapids: Eerdmans, 1991], 150) points out that most English commentators follow J. B. Lightfoot in regarding συναθλέω and ἀγών (v. 30) as presenting athletic or gladiatorial images (e.g., F. X. Malinowski, "The Brave Women of Philippi," *BTB* 15 [1985]: 62), whereas most German exegetes prefer to see in both no more than the general notions of struggle and hardship. Pfitzner (*Agon Motif,* 115) comes down somewhere between the two. He considers it wrong to take either word in a completely colorless sense; yet it is "equally false to attempt to draw the concrete features of the picture to which Paul supposedly refers by seeing Paul and the Philippians as gladiators in the arena!" Yet if the words are to be allowed some color, that color is of the arena.

72. Πτύρομαι (from πτοέω "to terrify," πτόα "terror"): "To be startled, frightened." Old verb, found only here in the NT. The metaphor (within the metaphor) is of a horse shying at some object.

73. Paul's phrase is τῇ πίστει τοῦ εὐαγγελίου "the faith brought into being by the gospel" (subjective genitive). The dative, τῇ πίστει, is the dative of interest: They are to contend "for the faith," not "with" it (the dative of association, as some

have suggested, governed by the preposition σύν in the compound συναθλοῦντες). "Faith" here may be an early example of the creedal sense of the word—the body of teaching to which Christians subscribe.

74. Lightfoot, *Philippians,* 106.

75. For ἀγών "contest," see ch. 12, n. 125, and for συναθλέω "to contend together," see ch. 12, n. 71.

76. Συναγωνίζομαι (see ἀγωνίζομαι, ch. 12, n. 125): "To strive together with, to help," properly of sharing in a contest. Found only here in biblical Greek. The use of the verb ῥύομαι "to rescue," which implies a situation of great danger (see ch. 10, n. 68), persuades me to include this passage among Paul's possible gladiatorial metaphors rather than among his metaphors from the games (see below).

77. Alternatively, the terms could be taken together as a military metaphor. A. Plummer (*Second Epistle of St Paul to the Corinthians* [Edinburgh: T&T Clark, 1915], 129) is ambivalent. They might be "taken from combatants in battle or in the arena." J. H. Bernard ("The Second Epistle of Paul to the Corinthians," *EGT* 3:62) thinks they are from battle. Parallels with these verses have been found in the language of the Stoics (e.g., Seneca, *Ep.* 71.25ff.). For the sort of concrete experiences to which Paul alludes, see 2 Cor 11:23–33. Cf. also 1 Cor 4:9–13; 2 Cor 6:3–10.

78. Θλίβω: (1) "to press," (2) metaphorically, "to oppress, afflict, distress." In each instance, in these verses, the situation and the exception is expressed by present passive participles, indicating what is characteristic, not merely occasional. For this verb, see also 2 Cor 1:6; 7:5; 1 Thess 3:4; 2 Thess 1:6–7; 1 Tim 5:10.

79. Στενοχωρέω (from στενός "narrow" and χῶρος "space"): (1) "to be hemmed in, compressed," (2) and metaphorically, "to be anxious." The verb is late, in the NT only here and in 2 Cor 6:12. Cf. στενοχωρία: (1) "narrowness of space," (2) and metaphorically, "difficulty, distress," in Rom 2:9; 8:35; 2 Cor 6:4; 12:10.

80. Ἀπορέομαι (from ἄπορος, α negative and πόρος "a way, a resource"): "To be at a loss, perplexed." See also Gal 4:20.

81. Ἐξαπορέομαι (see ἀπορέομαι, the preceding note): "To be utterly at a loss or in despair." See also 2 Cor 1:8.

82. Διώκω: See ch. 12, n. 33.

83. Ἐγκαταλείπω: (1) "to leave behind," (2) "to abandon, desert, forsake," as if overtaken (διώκω). See also Rom 9:29; 2 Tim 4:10, 16.

84. Καταβάλλω: "To strike or put down." Found only here in Paul.

85. Ἀπόλλυμι: "To destroy utterly." See also Rom 2:12; 14:15; 1 Cor 1:18–19; 8:11; 10:9, 10; 15:18; 2 Cor 2:15; 4:3; 2 Thess 2:10.

86. Ἐνκακέω: See ch. 2, n. 56, for the suggestion that it might be an agricultural metaphor. It is certainly not necessarily a metaphor from the arena, but in this context it could be regarded as such.

87. Mark 8:34–35; cf. 2 Cor 1:8–10; Phil 3:10; 4:12–13.

88. This description is generic rather than geographical. Greek games were conducted throughout the hellenized world. In Rome itself the earliest recorded games were promoted by M. Fulvius Nobilior in 186 BCE. We hear of others being offered by Sulla in 81 BCE, by M. Aemilius Scaurus in 58, by Pompey in 55, by C. Curio in 53, and by Julius Caesar in 46.

89. There was a break of more than a century, following the sack of Corinth in 146 BCE, when control of the games passed to the neighboring town of Sicyon, six miles northwest of Corinth. It appears that the games themselves were transferred to the stadium at Sicyon and had not returned to Isthmia when Strabo visited the site in 29 BCE (*Geog.* 8.6.23). Excavations at Isthmia bear this out, showing that the temple of Poseidon lay abandoned in the immediate pre-Roman period (see O. Broneer, *Isthmia, Topography and Architecture* [Princeton, N.J.: American School of Classical Studies at Athens, 1973], 2:2, 4). The administration of the games was restored to Corinth soon after the refounding of the city and, until they

returned to Isthmia (probably in the 50s CE), may have been conducted somewhere in the environs of the city itself. See E. R. Gebhard, "The Isthmian Games and the Sanctuary of Poseidon in the Early Empire," in *The Corinthia in the Roman Period* (ed. T. E. Gregory; Ann Arbor: Cushing-Malloy, 1994), 78–91.

90. O. Broneer ("The Apostle Paul and the Isthmian Games," *BA* 25 [1962]: 1–31) speculates that Paul not only was present in Corinth at the time of the games but actually attended them.

91. Our imaginary visit to Olympia is in its palmy, pre-Roman days, before the Pax Romana was established. In those days, a truce of three months, declared on the announcement of the games by the herald, facilitated travel to the games. See, e.g., Isocrates, *Paneg.*: "Now the founders of our great festivals are justly praised for handing down to us a custom by which, *having proclaimed a truce and resolved our quarrels,* we come together in one place." A city that had failed to observe the truce was barred from being represented by its athletes. A case in point is that of the Spartan, Lichas, who was expected to win the *quadriga,* the four-horse chariot event, in 420 BCE. But he could not enter because his city had failed to pay a fine for a breach of the Olympic truce. Accordingly, he leased his team to the city of Thebes (see Thucydides, *Hist.* 5.50).

92. Νέφος μαρτύρων: Νέφος, an old word (cf. Latin *nubes*), found only here in the NT, for "a mass of clouds." Νεφέλη is a single cloud. It is sometimes argued that this metaphor is of the living spectators watching the race, but they are called μάρτυρες (plural of μάρτυς, see ch. 6, n. 51), "witnesses," not mere spectators (θεαταί, see ch. 12, n. 50 above), suggesting that they have had experience of "competing" themselves. Thus, the image of former competitors is the more likely.

93. It was perhaps the development of sport as an entertainment for spectators that caused the growth in women's athletics that appears to have taken place at about the beginning of the Christian era. Presumably women as well as men could watch these events. The only clear evidence from earlier times of an athletic meeting for women is of that held at Olympia (but separate from the Olympiad). By the first century CE, however, there appear to have been separate meetings for women at Delphi, Isthmia, Nemea, Epidaurus, Athens, and Naples. In the same period, Domitian included races for girls in his Capitoline games at Rome, and a century later girls were competing in wrestling and running events in (mixed?) games at Antioch in Syria (see further H. A. Harris, *Sport in Greece and Rome* [London: Thames & Hudson, 1972], 40–41).

94. See further ch. 12, n. 132.

95. In Homer's day the athletes wore shorts. This was still the practice when the Olympic games were instituted. Two stories are told that account for the change, which appears to have taken place before 700 BCE. One was that in the first race in the Olympiad of 720 BCE a competitor's shorts fell off but he went on to win the race. Thinking that this was his secret of success, the runners in the next race discarded their shorts. The other story is that when a man's pants fell in the Panathenaic games at Athens, he became entangled, fell, and was killed. Because of this, the magistrate ordered that pants should not be worn in the future. See Homer, *Il.* 23.683; Thucydides, *Hist.* 1.6; Pausanius, *Descr.* 1.44.1; Isidorus, *Etym.* 18.17.2.

96. The comparison with the athlete was a commonplace among ethical and religious writers. It was, as V. C. Pfitzner explains, "a popular, traditional metaphor." Even "a single term suffices to recall to mind the whole athletic image in its metaphorical use" (*Agon Motif,* 3). The metaphor appears to have been particularly popular with the Stoics and the Cynics. Thus Musonius Rufus writes, "When we see acrobats face without concern their difficult tasks and risk their very lives in performing them . . . all of which they do for a miserably small recompense, shall we not be ready to endure hardship [in the moral sphere] for the sake of complete happiness?"

(*That One Should Disdain Hardships;* see also C. E. Lutz, "Musonius Rufus, 'The Roman Socrates,' " *YCS* 10 [1947]: 59). And Epictetus:

> Who then is the invincible man? He whom nothing that is outside the sphere of his moral purpose can dismay. I consider the circumstances one by one, as I would do in the case of the athlete.... "This fellow has won the first round. What, then, will he do in the second? ... And what will he do at Olympia?" ... It is the same way in the present case. If you put silver in a man's way, he will despise it. Yes, but what about a beautiful woman, or darkness, or the hope of glory? What about abuse or praise? Or death, what then? All these things he can overcome.... The man who passes all these tests is what I mean by the invincible athlete....

> It is difficulties that show what men are. Consequently, when a difficulty befalls, remember that God, like a physical trainer, has matched you with a rugged young man. "For what purpose?" someone will say. So that you may become an Olympic victor. But that cannot be done without sweat....

> The man who exercises himself against outward appearances is the true athlete in training.... Great is the struggle.... Remember God. Call upon him to help you....

> God says to you, "Give me proof that you have striven by the rules [cf. 2 Tim 2:5], eaten what is prescribed, taken exercise, heeded your trainer." ...

> [The wise man is trained and exercised by Zeus in the "Olympic contest" of life.] Now God says to you, "Come at last to the contest [τὸν ἀγῶνα; on ἀγών, see ch. 12, n. 125] and show us what you have learned and how you have trained yourself. How long will you exercise alone? Now the time has come for you to discover whether you are one of the athletes who deserve victory or belong to the number of those who travel about the world and are everywhere defeated." (*Diatr.* 1.18.21–23; 1.24.1–2; 2.18.27–29; 3.10.8; 3.22.51, 102; 4.4.30)

Cf. also the character and teaching of Diogenes the Cynic in Diogenes Laertius (*Lives of the Philosophers* 6.22.34, 43, 70–71); the "crown" awarded to Titus for his act of self-control in Philostratus (*Vit Apoll.* 6.29); Dio Chrysostom's account of Melancomas, the famous boxer, who was not beaten by any opponent or by "toil, gluttony, or sensuality" (*Melanc.* 1.14; 2.12); and Seneca on boxing (see ch. 12, n. 106). But nowhere is the popular use of the metaphor better illustrated than in Philo, who might be suspected of having been a *habitué* of the stadium at Alexandria. He uses the athletic illustration again and again. He notes, e.g., the training (*Leg.* 3.71) and the diet (1.31). He speaks of the race and of the crown (*Migr.* 24), which he says is the vision of God (*Mut.* 12). In one striking passage he uses language comparable to that of Paul in 1 Tim 6:12: "Strive to win the crown in the contest ... the glorious crown, such as no assembly of men can confer" (*Leg.* 2.26). See further H. A. Harris, *Greek Athletes and Athletics* (London: Thames & Hudson, 1964), 13; M. B. Poliakoff, *Combat Sports in the Ancient World* (New Haven: Yale University Press, 1987), 4, 143. In the light of other parallels between Paul and contemporary philosophers, it is not surprising to find the athlete prominent among the images he employs. Cf. F. G. Downing, "Cynics and Christians," *NTS* 30 (1984): 584–93.

97. Τρέχω: "To run." See also Rom 9:16; 1 Cor 9:24 (2x), 26; Gal 2:2 (2x, with the unusual coupling of a present subjunctive with an aorist indicative to express his fear of present failure and his fear that his past efforts might have been in vain); 5:7; Phil 2:16. Pfitzner (*Agon Motif,* 103) sees τρέχω as "a comprehensive term for the entire missionary labours of the Apostle."

98. Δοξάζω (from δόξα "opinion, repute, splendor"): (1) "to hold an opinion," (2) "to praise, extol," (3) "to glorify." The verbs τρέχω and δοξάζω are only found together here in the NT. In this combination, δοξάζω should be regarded, like τρέχω, as a metaphor from the stadium. Notice also that both verbs occur here in the

present subjunctive. The prayer that Paul is requesting is that the word of the Lord should *keep on* running and being honored. For δοξάζω, see also Rom 1:21; 8:30; 11:13; 15:6, 9; 1 Cor 6:20; 12:26; 2 Cor 3:10; 9:13; Gal 1:24. For a similar notion of the successful athlete's exultation in victory, see 1 Thess 2:19, discussed on p. 273.

99. Victorious athletes were welcomed enthusiastically at home, were allowed to occupy the first rows at festivals, and received free board. In the earlier days of independence from Rome, they were granted the privilege of fighting at the head of the army. Their cities and families basked in their reflected glory.

100. Δρόμος (from δραμέω "to run," whose root supplies the future and aorist of τρέχω; see ch. 12, n. 97): "A course, a race." In the NT in Acts 13:25; 20:24; 2 Tim 4:7.

101. We must supply ἐστὶν ἔλεος with the οὐ of Paul's statement that "*mercy is* not of wishing and running" and should probably understand the genitive of the two articular participles as that of source. Cf. Ps 119:32, where the psalmist says, in effect, that he runs not as a prerequisite to God's mercy but as a result of God's mercy. God has set his heart free, and therefore he runs.

102. Οἱ ἐν σταδίῳ τρέχοντες, πάντες τρέχουσιν, εἷς δὲ λαμβάνει τὸ βραβεῖον: "Those who run in the stadium, run all [of them], but one receives the prize" (βραβεῖον; see ch. 12, n. 35). As much as to say, "Entering the race is not winning the race. Do not be satisfied with running, but make sure of winning [lit., 'overtaking']" (see ch. 12, n. 31). The metaphor is making the point that they should "run" well and see the "race" through to the end. The point is not that only one competitor can receive the crown (unless we think, with Origen, of the whole church as constituting "one body"). Στάδιον "a stadium" can refer to (1) a measure of length, 600 Greek feet (606.75 English feet) or one-eighth of a Roman mile (on the layout of the stadium, see further below), and, this being the length of the Olympic course, (2) a race course. Found only here in Paul.

103. See further on this passage p. 272.

104. Πάλη: Paul's word in Eph 6:12, which he is probably using in its more general sense of "a fight" in the context of a military metaphor. See ch. 10, n. 99.

105. A third- or second-century BCE statue in Rome's Terme Museum shows the boxer's gloves in detail. There was an inner glove over which a pad of leather, about an inch thick and three inches wide, was bound. For full details, see Harris, *Sport*, 22–23.

106. Πυκτεύω (from πύκτης "a boxer," and that from πυγμή "a fist"): An old verb, "to box." Found only here in the NT. There is a striking parallel between Paul's description of himself as a boxer in 1 Cor 9:24–26 and Seneca's exhortation in *Ep.* 78.16: "What blows do athletes receive in their face, what blows all over their body. Yet they bear all the torture from thirst of glory. Let us also overcome all things, for our reward is not a crown or a palm branch or the trumpeter proclaiming silence for the announcement of our name, but virtue and strength of mind and peace acquired ever after." For Paul's familiarity with the images used by the philosophers of his day, see further pp. 87–89 and notes (medical metaphors), 89–92 and notes (metaphors of the body and head), and 215–16 and notes (military metaphors).

107. Ὑπωπιάζω (from ὑπώπιον): (1) "the part of the face below the eyes," (2) "a blow to the face," "to strike under the eye, give a black eye," metaphorically of persistent annoyance or of rigorous self-discipline. Found only here in Paul. Cf. Paul's use of κολαφίζω (from κόλαφος "the knuckles, the closed fist") "to strike with the fist" as a metaphor of some (bodily?) ailment in 2 Cor 12:7 (see ch. 4, n. 13), and either metaphorically or literally of the hardship endured by the apostle in 1 Cor 4:11.

108. Δουλαγωγέω: See ch. 5, n. 67.

109. See Rom 6:13, pp. 214–15, for the potential of the body to be a "weapon" of unrighteousness.

110. Ἐγκρατεύομαι: "To exercise self-control," used by Paul in 1 Cor 7:9 of the control of the sexual urge. Plato, *Leg.* 839E–840A, uses σωφρονέω of the athlete's mastery over sex and, in 840C, the adjective ἐγκρατής of self-control in general (cf. Titus 1:8). But the two terms are probably interchangeable. Paul's self-control did not involve the "mortification" of his body in the manner of some Christian ascetics, who have pleaded this very verse in support of their practice. Paul's was a moral or spiritual discipline. See, e.g., Rom 8:13; Col 2:23 and cf. ch. 12, n. 96.

111. Only one person, Nero, is known to have competed with the heralds. He proclaimed his own success and was crowned as an athlete. See Suetonius, *Nero* 24.

112. In practice it was probably the umpires who instructed the athletes in the rules, not the herald, but for Paul's purposes a reference to the herald was near enough. I have interpreted this verse in terms of Paul's metaphor in the previous verses. Here he simply says ἄλλοις κηρύξας "having preached to others." Κηρύσσω (from κῆρυξ) can mean "to be a herald," but in the NT it is the common word for preaching, with no particular association with the herald of the games (about eighteen occurrences in Paul). Similarly the noun κῆρυξ "a herald" signifies the Christian preacher with no indication that it was a conscious metaphor (see ch. 12, n. 91). In Paul only in 1 Tim 2:7 and 2 Tim 1:11, in each case of himself as a "herald and an apostle and a teacher" of the gospel.

113. Cf. Sir 37:19.

114. See the further discussion of this theme, pp. 272–73.

115. Ἀδόκιμος: "Rejected" (a term commonly applied to materials such as metal, coins, and masonry that were flawed). But the word can also mean "discredited," "reproved" (see LSJ and Moffatt, *First Corinthians,* 128). Could Paul, who grasped so well the doctrine of salvation by grace and penned Rom 8:31–39, ever imagine *himself* as being finally rejected (despite the example of the Hebrews in the desert)? We should certainly not allow the metaphor of the runner's disqualification (from winning, not running) to determine Paul's theology. It simply illustrates the particular point that every effort must be made to keep within the rules. See further pp. 115–16, and on ἀδόκιμος ch. 1, n. 72; ch. 7, n. 8.

116. Horace, *Ars* 412. See also ch. 12, n. 96.

117. Lucian, *Anach.* 10.

118. Κοπιάω: See ch. 7, n. 14, and Deissmann's understanding of this passage, noted on p. 167.

119. Ἀσκέω: (1) "to adorn," (2) "to practice, exercise," and so (3) "to endeavor."

120. Cf. Paul's description of the Thessalonians as a "crown of victory in which we [Paul and his colleagues] will glory in the presence of our Lord Jesus when he comes" (1 Thess 2:19). See p. 273.

121. In the Olympics there was no team competition at all. All contests were between individuals. See M. I. Finley and H. W. Pleket, *The Olympic Games* (New York: Viking, 1976), 22.

122. See, e.g., Aristophanes, *Ran.* 129ff., 1087ff.; Aristophanes, *Vesp.* 1204; Aristophanes, *Frag.* 442; *IG* 7.2871. Alexander included torch races in the games he promoted for his troops. See Arrian, *Anab.* 2.5.8; 2.24.6; 3.16.9.

123. Paul describes them (commentators are divided on whether φαίνεσθε is indicative or imperative—a statement or a command) as "shining as lights," φωστῆρες. A φωστήρ is "a star" (the sense in which the word is understood here by many commentators, on the basis of Dan 12:3), "a torch," "a lantern," even "a harbor beacon." He then speaks of them as "holding out" (ἐπέχω), as one might a torch, the word of life, and then of his own running and training, as though developing a train of thought. Many commentators, however, take ἐπέχω in the sense of "holding fast" rather than "holding out." Christ is the light *of* the world (John 8:12, τὸ φῶς τοῦ κόσμου), and the Philippians are lights (planets reflecting his light?) *in*

the world (φωστῆρες ἐν κόσμῳ). D. Wenham (*Paul: Follower of Jesus or Founder of Christianity?* [Grand Rapids: Eerdmans, 1995], 254) sees in this passage an echo of Jesus' teaching in Matt 5:14–16.

124. O. Bauernfeind ("τρέχω, κτλ," *TDNT* 8:226–35, here 231) suggests that, in light of Gal 2:2, the expression "running in vain" "was a common use of the apostle's." It may be an echo of Isa 49:4. Cf. Gal 4:11: "I fear for you, that somehow I have toiled [κοπιάω] for you in vain." See p. 56.

125. Ἀγών (from ἄγω "to lead, bring, go"): (1) "a gathering," esp. for games, (2) "a place of assembly," (3) "a contest, struggle, trial." In Paul in Phil 1:30; Col 2:1; 1 Thess 2:2; 1 Tim 6:12; 2 Tim 4:7. Ἀγωνίζομαι (from ἀγών and ἄγω): (1) "to contend for a prize," (2) "to contend, struggle, strive." In Paul in 1 Cor 9:25; Col 1:29; 4:12; 1 Tim 4:10 (in some texts); 6:12; 2 Tim 4:7. According to Pfitzner (*Agon Motif,* 109–12, 126–29), this word group (from which we get our "agony" and "agonize") describes Paul's conflict for the faith. It involves untiring labor—an intense wrestling and struggle for the spread, growth, and strengthening of the faith as the goal of his mission—and engagement with both spiritual and human opponents. The thought of suffering is never far from the sense conveyed by these words. And others have shared in Paul's struggle, e.g., Epaphras, who "agonized" in prayer for the Colossians (Col 4:12), and the Christians in Rome, whom Paul invited to "agonize with" him (συναγωνίζομαι) in prayer for his deliverance from the Jews (Rom 15:15, see ch. 12, n. 76). Paul's phrase in 2 Tim 4:7 (coincidentally?) is found almost verbatim in Euripides, *Alc.* 648: καίτοι καλὸν γ' ἂν τόνδ' ἀγὼν ἠγωνίσω "however, I have contested this good contest."

126. But cf. the similarly structured military metaphor in 1 Tim 1:18: στρατεύῃ . . . τὴν καλὴν στρατείαν "wage the good warfare." See ch. 10, n. 143.

127. Γυμνάζω (from γυμνός "naked"; see ch. 1, n. 90 and ch. 12, n. 95): (1) properly, "to exercise naked," (2) generally, "to exercise, train" the body or mind. An old and common verb, but found only here in Paul, where again it is a present imperative—he is to train all the time. Cf. γυμνασία "exercise," also a common and old word, only in 1 Tim 4:8 in the NT, where there is probably an intentional play on the notion of exercise. Timothy is to counter the ascetical practices of the heretics described in vv. 1–5 by "exercising" himself constantly in practical piety (as outlined, e.g., in 2 Cor 6:10). For exercise as a metaphor of moral discipline, see further ch. 12, n. 96. The gymnasium (γυμνάσιον) was a sports ground with various facilities for athletic training, such as a running track, jumping pits, and ranges for throwing the discus and javelin. Its building usually consisted of an open courtyard (*palaestra*) surrounded by a colonnade, off which opened rooms for undressing, dusting (athletes powdered themselves before exercise), bathing, and storing oil. There might also be rooms for boxing practice and other purposes. The availability of rooms for classes led to gymnasia evolving into educational institutions. See, e.g., H. I. Marrou, *A History of Education in Antiquity* (New York: Sheed & Ward, 1956).

128. Καλός: "Good," primarily in appearance but also of ethical goodness in the sense of "right, fair, honorable, noble."

129. Κοπιάω (see ch. 7, n. 14) and ἀγωνίζομαι (see ch. 12, n. 125).

130. Χαρίζομαι: See ch. 6, n. 59. On the privilege of suffering for Christ, cf. Acts 5:41, and on Paul's own call to and acceptance of such suffering, cf. Acts 9:16; 2 Cor 1:3–7; Phil 3:10; Col 1:24, and see also 2 Cor 11:23–27.

131. The metaphor of this verse has been prepared for by the στήκετε ("stand firm") and συναθλοῦντες ("contending together as one") of v. 27. See ch. 12, nn. 70, 71.

132. Pausanius, *Descr.* 5.21. Among the rules of the Olympic games were the following: Competitors had to prove to the umpires that they were freemen, of pure Hellenic stock, not disenfranchised or convicted of sacrilege, and that they had undergone the ten-month preliminary training. They and their fathers, brothers, and

trainers then had to take an oath that they would be guilty of no misconduct in the events. The month of exercises that they undertook in the gymnasium was done under the supervision of the umpires.

133. See Harris, *Sport,* 25. For their pains, the umpires regularly had abuse thrown at them by the competitors, except, Plutarch observes, by the Spartans (*Mor.* 817A–B [*Praec. ger. reipubl.* 21]).

134. Βραβεύω (from βραβεύς "an umpire"): Properly, "to act as an umpire," hence generally, "to arbitrate, decide, control." An old verb, here alone in the NT, where it must be questioned whether Paul was making any conscious reference to the games. Cf. βραβεῖον "a prize," ch. 12, n. 35.

135. Καταβραβεύω (from βραβεύς): "To give judgment against." It is used of a contestant who deserves the prize but is disqualified by the umpire for a breach of the rules, so that another gets the prize instead. Such a ruling was sometimes achieved unfairly by someone bribing the umpire. See further ch. 12, n. 153.

136. Philo (*Contempl.* 43) has an incidental reference to the umpire separating fighters, and Polybius to the umpires ordering a new site for the boxing ring (*Hist.* 1.58).

137. See Plates 4a and 4b in Harris, *Greek Athletes.* The runners are shown strung out in a line, but this is a conventional frieze pattern, not a realistic portrayal.

138. Ἐνκόπτω: (1) "to cut into," as in breaking up a road, hence (2) "to hinder." Similar to our idiom of someone "cutting in" on us. With the figure of the race introduce by ἐτρέχετε "you were running," the verb is clearly used here as a metaphor from the games. See further ch. 10, n. 20.

139. See p. 122 for a fuller discussion of these issues.

140. Προσκόπτω: (1) "to strike (e.g., hand or foot) against," (2) "to stumble." This verb and the corresponding nouns are discussed in ch. 9, n. 62, as a metaphor drawn from the hazards of the road. But in Rom 9:31–32, with its διώκω and καταλαμβάνω ("to pursue" and "to overtake"; see ch. 12, nn. 31, 33) suggesting a race, it appears here to be a figure taken from the games.

141. Paul speaks rather cryptically in Rom 9:31 of "Israel pursuing a righteous law" (Ἰσραὴλ διώκων νόμον δικαιοσύνης). But clearly they were not seeking a law. They would say that they had a law already by which to live—the law of Moses. What they were seeking was the righteousness that came from obedience to that law. The genitive δικαιοσύνης is descriptive of the law. The righteousness that they were seeking is simply understood. The following statement is equally as cryptic: "They did not arrive at a law" (εἰς νόμον οὐκ ἔφθασεν), i.e., "they did not attain what they hoped to have from the law."

142. Δρόμος: See ch. 12, n. 100.

143. From Deissmann, *Light,* 309. Some commentators suggest that, in this third statement, Paul has moved from metaphor to reality, but the inscriptional material allows us to suppose that all three statements constitute a metaphor from the games. The parallels in the inscriptions might suggest that "faith," in this passage, means "loyalty," almost "obedience" (e.g., W. Lock, *Pastoral Epistles,* 111), rather than the body of teaching that constituted "the faith." But in the context of the Pastorals, in which ἡ πίστις so often has that objective sense of "the faith" (see 1 Tim 1:19; 4:1, 6; 5:8; 6:10, 21; 2 Tim 3:8; Titus 1:13), it may be better to understand it so in this verse, with Paul asserting that he had kept the body of teaching intact to pass on to others.

144. Ἀθλέω (from ἆθλος "a contest" in war or in sport): "To contend." An old and common verb, used twice in this verse, but found only here in the NT. For the compound συναθλέω, see ch. 12, n. 71. Second Timothy 2:5 comprises a string of metaphors that carry the thought from commitment through hard work and obedience to reward. See p. 224 and ch. 10, n. 139.

145. Plutarch, *Mor.* 675D–677B (*Quaest. conv.* 5.3.1–3).

146. Lucian writes, "Do you think these prizes are trivial? My dear fellow, it is not the bare gifts that we have in view! They are mere tokens of the victory and marks to identify the winners. But the reputation that goes with them is worth everything to the victors" (*Anach.* 9).

147. Στεφανόω (from στέφανος, στέφω; see ch. 12, n. 149): "To crown," "not infrequently" with "the general meaning 'reward' " (Deissman, *Bible Studies,* 345). Found only here in Paul. Deissmann (*Light,* 309) cites an inscription in the theater at Ephesus relating to an athlete of the second century CE that parallels 2 Tim 4:7–8: "He fought three fights and twice was crowned." The similarity suggests that both Paul and the later athlete were drawing on a familiar formula. Cf. also Philo's use of the metaphor, ch. 12, n. 96.

148. Βραβεῖον: See ch. 12, n. 35.

149. Στέφανος (from στέφω "to encircle): (1) "that which surrounds or encompasses," as a wall (in Homer, etc.), (2) "a crown," i.e., the wreath given as a prize for victory, as a festal ornament, or as a public honor for distinguished service or personal worth. Of all the possible images that Paul might have been evoking with his reference to a crown, the victor at the games is the most likely. Hawthorne (*Philippians,* 178) thinks that it might be a combination of this with the idea of the festal crown, "reinforcing the idea that the Philippians are a cause for his festal-joy, on the one hand, and informing them that they are also a source of great honour for him, on the other." See also 1 Cor 9:25; 1 Thess 2:19; 2 Tim 4:8, and cf. Sir 6:31.

150. Στέφανος καυχήσεως: Καύχησις (from καυχάομαι) "a boasting, glorying," in Paul in Rom 3:27; 15:17; 1 Cor 15:31; 2 Cor 1:12; 7:4, 14; 8:24; 11:10, 17; 1 Thess 2:19. Cf. Καύχημα: (1) "a boast," 2 Cor 5:12; 9:2, (2) "ground or matter of glorying," Rom 4:2; 1 Cor 5:6; 9:15, 16; 2 Cor 1:14; Gal 6:4; Phil 1:26; 2:16. Cf. also καυχάομαι "to boast or glory," thirty times in Paul.

151. Ἀπόκειμαι: "To be laid up, in store, laid away," with dative of person, "to be reserved (for)." An old verb, employed, as numerous inscriptions prove, as "a technical term . . . by Oriental sovereigns when decreeing rewards for loyal service" (J. N. D. Kelly, *The Pastoral Epistles* [London: Adam & Charles Black, 1963], 209). See also Col 1:5. Cf. 2 Macc 12:45.

152. Ὁ τῆς δικαιοσύνης στέφανος: The genitive is of apposition, the crown that consists of righteousness, as in all other instances of ὁ στέφανος with a qualifying genitive (1 Thess 2:19; Jas 1:12; 1 Pet 5:4; Rev 2:10; 12:1). But the phrase may include something of the notion of a reward for righteousness (e.g., N. J. D. White, "The First and Second Epistles to Timothy and the Epistle to Titus," *EGT* 4:178; and W. Grundmann, "στέφανος, στεφανόω," *TDNT* 7:615–36, here 629. Cf. 1 Cor 9:25.

153. Κριτής (from κρίνω "to judge"): "A judge." Found only here in Paul. It has no necessary connection with the games, but in this context "the umpire who makes no mistakes" may be an acceptable rendering of "the righteous judge" (ὁ δίκαιος κριτής). Cf. 2 Cor 5:10. H. A. Harris describes the decline of the games with the influx of money. By Paul's day, "corruption permeated the whole scene. Officials and rivals were bribed to 'fix' matches; collusive agreements between boxers and wrestlers produced tame draws, with the competitors dividing the money" (*Sport,* 40). Paul, on the other hand, knows that the judge of his performance is incorruptible. The judgment will be searching (2 Cor 5:10) but absolutely fair. Meanwhile he is subject to the questionable justice of a Roman court.

154. For the verbs κοπιάω and ἀγωνίζομαι used by Paul in this verse, see ch. 7, n. 14, and ch. 12, n. 125.

Appendix 1: A Select Chronology of the Roman Empire

Emerging Rome

The period from 334 to 264 BCE saw Rome's gradual expansion through colonization, conquest, and alliance into all of Italy south of the Po Valley. Its emergence as a first-class power inevitably brought Rome into conflict with Carthage, which dominated the western Mediterranean. Ultimately Rome would have to deal also with three other great powers: the Seleucid empire in Syria, the Ptolemaic empire in Egypt, and Alexander's original Macedonian empire. Rome found it impossible to live in a world of equals.

264–241 BCE   The First Punic (Carthaginian) War.

237   Roman occupation of Corsica and Sardinia.

218–201   The Second Punic War.

214–205   The First Macedonian War against Philip V.

211–206   Scipio Africanus defeats Hasdrubal in Spain, and Spain is divided into two provinces.

202	Scipio defeats Hannibal, and Carthage becomes a dependent of Rome.
202–191	Roman conquest of Cisalpine Gaul.
200–197	The Second Macedonian War against Philip V.
197–133	Wars in Spain.
196	Rome declares the freedom of the Greeks (from Macedon).
192–188	The Syrian War against Antiochus III.
171–167	The Third Macedonian War against Perseus, Philip's son.
167	Battle of Pydna ends the kingdom of Macedon. Macedonia is divided into four republics.
149–146	The Third Punic War. Carthage is destroyed and Africa becomes a province.
148	The Fourth Macedonian War against the Achaean League. Corinth is sacked and Macedonia becomes a Roman province.

The Late Republic

The history of this period is the history of Roman military dominance. Rome exploited its control of the Mediterranean world, Roman generals leading Roman citizens to even richer conquests. But at home the strains of empire began to destroy republican government.

136–132 BCE	The First Sicilian Slave War.
133	Attalus III of Pergamum bequeaths his kingdom to Rome, and it becomes the province of Asia (129).
121	Gallia Narbonensis becomes a Roman province.
118–117	Roman campaigns in Dalmatia.
112–106	The war against Jugurtha of Mauretania (Numidia) is ended by Gaius **Marius**.
107–100	Marius is elected consul six times. He reforms the army.

104–102	The Second Sicilian Slave War.
102–101	Marius defeats the Teutones and Cimbri in Gaul and Cisalpine Gaul.
100	The birth of **Julius Caesar**.
91–88	The attempted reforms of Marcus Livius Drusus lead to the Social War between Rome and its Italian allies. Under Marius, the Roman forces defeat the allies, and Rome belatedly offers them citizenship.
88–85	Mithradates VI of Pontus massacres Roman citizens in the province of Asia and seeks to free Greece. The First Pontic War.
88	Rivalry between Marius and Lucius Cornelius **Sulla** prompts Sulla, preparing to sail against Mithradates, to march on Rome instead. Marius retreats to Africa.
87	Marius seizes Rome but dies in 86.
86	Sulla defeats Mithradates, reorganizes the province of Asia, and sacks Greek cities that had been allied with Mithradates.
83–80	Sulla returns to Italy. Civil war ensues, with Sulla avenging himself on Marius's followers. He is appointed dictator of Rome and carries through reforms, strengthening the senate. He resigns in 80 and dies in 78.
83–81	The Second Pontic War (inconclusive).
74–64	Rome's annexation of Bithynia in 74 leads to the Third Pontic War.
73–71	The slave revolt led by Spartacus.
70	Consulate of Crassus and Gnaeus Pompeius (**Pompey**). Pompey rescinds the more objectionable of Sulla's laws and does much to restore the power of the plebs.
67	Pompey is given *imperium* to clear the eastern Mediterranean of pirates.
66–63	Pompey defeats Mithradates and Tigranes of Armenia. Since Tigranes controlled Seleucid Syria, this also brings to an end the Seleucid monarchy (64 BCE). It also ends the brief independence of the kingdom of **Judea**. The

provinces of Bithynia, Cilicia, Syria, and Crete are organized by Pompey, and client kingdoms are established elsewhere.

63   The Cataline conspiracy again plunges Rome into disorder.

62   Pompey returns to Italy, but instead of seizing power, he follows tradition and disbands his army. The senate grants him a triumph but refuses to ratify his arrangements in the East.

60–59   The First Triumvirate is formed between Pompey, Crassus, and Caesar, but the latter two are piqued by the treatment they receive from the senate. This arrangement helps each triumvir achieve his own objectives: Pompey gets recognition for his eastern victories, Caesar is given command of Gaul, and Crassus is able to take the field against the Parthians. Pompey marries Julia, Caesar's daughter.

59   Caesar is elected consul.

58–49   Caesar campaigns in Gaul.

56   Agreement between triumvirs is renewed at Luca despite some friction between them.

55–54   Caesar invades Britain.

54   Julia dies. The link between Caesar and Pompey is severed, and friction between them mounts. While Caesar is adding to his political stature in Gaul, Pompey consolidates his power in Rome.

53   Crassus is killed by Parthians at the battle of Carrhae, and his army is destroyed.

51   The Parthians invade Syria.

49   Pompey persuades the senate to order Caesar to disband his army. Caesar crosses the river Rubicon, the southern limit of his command, to march on Rome, thus launching civil war. Pompey, with his army and most of the senate, withdraws to Greece.

48   Caesar defeats Pompey at the battle of Pharsalus. Pompey flees to Egypt and is murdered.

48–47	Caesar takes possession of Egypt. The Alexandrian War ensues. Jewish assistance to Caesar gains for them a number of concessions in succeeding years.
47–44	The dictatorship of Caesar.
47–45	Caesar campaigns against republicans in the East, as well as in Africa and Spain.
45	Caesar returns from Spain.
44	(15 March) Caesar is murdered.

The Early Empire

Caesar's heirs struggled for control of the Roman world. The final victory of his nephew Octavian (later Augustus) saw the establishment of monarchy under the guise of a "restored republic." His long reign was marked by consolidation and reform in every sphere of politics and culture. This period saw the birth of Jesus in what was then the client kingdom of Herod I, and his death and resurrection under the Romans in what had become the province of Judea. It saw also the beginning of the Christian mission.

44 BCE	Marcus Antonius (**Antony**), the surviving consul, controls Rome.
43	**Octavian,** with his army threatening Rome, forces on the senate his own election to the consulate. The Second Triumvirate, Antony, Lepidus, and Octavian, is formed. They divide and rule the empire: Antony takes the East, Lepidus the West, and Octavian Africa. They share control of the Italian homeland.
42	The republicans are defeated at the battle of Philippi; Brutus and Cassius commit suicide. Cisalpine Gaul is incorporated into Italy.
40	Antony marries Octavia, Octavian's sister. Herod is appointed client king of Judea by Rome.
37–4	**Herod I** (the Great), with Roman support, becomes king of Judea.
37	The triumvirate is renewed.
36–35	Campaigns against Sextus Pompeius, son of Pompey.

32	Octavian ousts Lepidus, takes over the African province, and usurps control of Italy. Antony rejects Octavia and marries Cleopatra, an Egyptian. Caesar persuades the senate to support both his annulment of Antony's powers and his declaration of war on Cleopatra.
31	Octavian defeats Antony and Cleopatra in the naval battle of Actium.
30	Antony and Cleopatra commit suicide and Egypt is annexed by Rome.
27–CE 14	The principate of Octavian.
27	The republic is notionally restored in the first constitutional settlement. A grateful senate confers on Octavian the title **Augustus** ("Exalted," rendered in Greek as σεβαστός "Revered").
27–19	Agrippa completes the conquest of northwest Spain.
23	Conspiracy against Augustus and the second constitutional settlement.
20	Settlement with Parthians.
18	Augustan marriage and social reforms.
12	Death of Marcus Agrippa, Augustus's grandson (the son of his daughter Julia by Agrippa) and heir apparent.
12–9	Tiberius, stepson of Augustus, campaigns in Pannonia.
ca. 8/7	John the Baptist is born.
7	**Jesus** is born.
4	Herod I dies, and his kingdom is divided among three sons.
4–CE 39	**Herod Antipas** tetrarch of Galilee.
4–CE 34	Philip tetrarch of Iturea.
4–CE 6	**Archelaus** ethnarch of Judea.
CE 2–4	Tiberius is named heir of Augustus and adopts his nephew Germanicus with a view to the succession.

6–41/44–66	With the deposition of Archelaus, Judea, with Samaria, becomes a Roman province.
6–9	Pannonian revolt.
9	Disaster for the Romans in Germany. The Rhine becomes the frontier between Roman Gaul and Germany.

The Julio-Claudian Dynasty

Despite the excesses of individual emperors, the imperial governmental system was consolidated under a dynasty that claimed hereditary descent from Augustus.

CE 14–37	**Tiberius** emperor.
19	Death of Germanicus.
23	Death of Drusus, the emperor's son.
26	Tiberius retires to Capri and rules the provinces from there, allowing Sejanus, prefect of the Praetorian Guard, to rule Rome. Sejanus aspires to the succession.
ca. 28	Jesus is baptized. John the Baptist dies.
31	Sejanus is executed.
ca. 31	Death and resurrection of Jesus and the Pentecost described in Acts 2.
ca. 34/35	Conversion of **Paul** (Acts 9:1–25; cf. 22:2–21; 26:2–23).
37–41	**Gaius** (nicknamed **Caligula**) becomes emperor. Assassinated by republican senators.
ca. 37/38	Paul returns from Damascus to Jerusalem and retreats to Cilicia (Acts 9:26–31; cf. Gal 1:18–21).
41–54	**Claudius** is proclaimed emperor by the Praetorian Guard to prevent the republicans from regaining control. He dies by poisoning at the hand of his wife, Agrippina, who desires the succession of her son Nero.
41–44	**Herod Agrippa I** (grandson of Herod the Great) is king of Judea.

43	Britain is invaded under Aulus Plautius.
44–66	On the death of Herod Agrippa I (Acts 12:19–23), the Romans resume direct rule of Judea, adding Galilee to the procuratorship. Three of Herod Agrippa's children make fleeting appearances in Acts: Drusilla, the wife of the procurator Felix (Acts 24:24), Bernice, and **Herod Agrippa II**, king of certain adjacent territories and adviser to the Romans on Jewish affairs (Acts 25:13–26:32).
ca. 46–48	Paul's first missionary journey to Cyprus and Asia Minor (Pamphylia and Galatia) (Acts 13:1–14:28).
48	Apostolic council in Jerusalem (Acts 15:1–35).
48–51	Paul's second missionary journey through Galatia, Asia, Macedonia, and Achaia (Greece) (Acts 15:36–18:22). He reaches Corinth, the capital of Achaia, ca. 50 CE, where he writes 1 and 2 Thessalonians ca. 50–51.
52–57	Paul's third missionary journey through Galatia and Asia to Ephesus, where he spends most of this period and corresponds with the church in Corinth. He writes several letters, including 1 Corinthians and possibly Philippians and Galatians at this time. Leaving Ephesus, he writes 2 Corinthians from Macedonia (55 CE) and Romans from Corinth (55–56). He reaches Jerusalem (57 CE) with a delegation from the "Pauline churches" carrying the proceeds of a collection for the relief of the churches of Judea (Acts 18:23–21:16).
54	**Nero** becomes emperor at the age of seventeen.
54–62	Burrus (the prefect of the Praetorian Guard) and Seneca control the young emperor Nero.
57–59	Paul is arrested in Jerusalem, removed to Caesarea, charged with various offenses by the Jews. His case is heard by the procurators Felix and Festus. He appeals to Caesar (Nero), to whose court the case is transferred (Acts 21:17–26:32).
58–62	Conquest and loss of Armenia.
59–60	Paul is transferred to Rome (Acts 27:1–28:31). Here he writes Colossians, Ephesians, and Philemon.

61–65	Paul is acquitted of charges brought against him by the Jews. In his remaining years of ministry he may have visited Spain (cf. Rom 15:24, 28) and appears to have returned to the eastern Mediterranean, with visits to Crete and Ephesus. In these years he writes 1 Timothy and Titus.
61	Revolt of Iceni in Britain under Boudicca.
62	Burrus dies and Seneca's influence over Nero ends.
62–68	Increasing hostility toward Nero in Rome and unrest in the provinces.
ca. 62	**James**, the Lord's brother, is put to death in Jerusalem in a context of mounting Jewish nationalism.
64	Much of Rome is destroyed by fire. Nero is (wrongfully?) blamed and makes the Christians his scapegoats.
65	Paul is arrested, probably in Ephesus, and is removed to Rome, where he is tried and put to death. In the interim between the first and second hearings of his case he writes 2 Timothy. The apostle **Peter** appears to have died in Rome at about the same time.
66–73	Jewish revolt.
68	Nero's reign ends with the senate deposing him in favor of Galba. He commits suicide the next day.

The Flavian Dynasty

With the Flavian dynasty, power shifted to the bourgeoisie of Italy; luxury became unfashionable in Rome as the emperor displayed old-fashioned standards. Literature gave way to government as the art of Rome.

CE 69	The year of the four emperors. **Galba, Otho, Vitellius,** and **Vespasian** struggle for power. It comes down to the eastern and western legions fighting it out. The eastern legions, who support Vespasian, emerge victorious.
69–79	Vespasian emperor.
70	Destruction of the temple at Jerusalem.

78–85	Campaigns of Agricola in Britain.
79–81	**Titus** emperor.
79	The eruption of Vesuvius, destroying Pompeii and Herculaneum.
80	Fire in Rome again, destroying the Capitoline temple.
81–96	**Domitian** emperor. Christians are persecuted in Asia Minor and perhaps elsewhere.
86–92	Domitian's war against the Dacians.
ca. 95	The apostle **John**, who appears to have followed Timothy (at some remove? cf. 1 Tim 1:3; 2 Tim 4:9) at Ephesus, imprisoned on Patmos.

The Age of the Antonines

"If a man were called to fix a period in the history of the world, during which the human race was most happy and prosperous, he would, without hesitation, name that which elapsed from the death of Domitian to the accession of Commodus" (Edward Gibbon). Certainly city life prospered, and there was something of a revival in Greek culture. From a Jewish or a Christian perspective, however, it was not as happy a time as Gibbon makes out. Trajan and Hadrian vigorously promoted the cult of Roma and the emperor. Life was made difficult for those who could not accept the notion that the emperor was divine. The age of the martyrs can be said to have begun under these emperors, reaching its climax two hundred years later under Diocletian (284–305 CE).

CE 96–98	**Nerva** emperor.
98–117	**Trajan** emperor.
ca. 100	The apostle John dies and the apostolic era comes to an end.
101–106	Trajan conquers Dacia.
114–117	Trajan's Parthian War. Armenia and Mesopotamia are annexed.
115–117	Jewish revolt.

117–138	**Hadrian** emperor.
132–135	Bar Kokhba's revolt leads to the final dispersion of the Jews.
138–161	**Antoninus Pius** emperor.
161–180	**Marcus Aurelius** emperor.
162–166	The Parthian Wars of Lucius Verus.
165–167	Plague spreads through the Roman Empire.
168–175	The Germanic Wars.
180–192	**Commodus** emperor.
193	With the murder of Commodus, four emperors contend for power.

The Severan Dynasty

"Our history and the affairs of the Romans descend from an age of gold to one of iron and rust" (Dio Cassius). The causes of the decline and subsequent transformation of the Roman world are complex. As barbarian pressure increased, the empire became militarized, and power shifted from the center to outlying frontiers. The strains caused by these developments started to become apparent under the Severans.

CE 208–211	**Septimus Severus** emperor. He campaigns in Britain and dies at York.
212–217	**Caracalla** emperor.
212	The *constitutio antoniniana* grants citizenship to all inhabitants of the empire.
218–222	**Elagabalus** emperor.
222–235	**Severus Alexander** emperor.
226	Ardashir the Sassanian, crowned king of kings in Iran, inaugurates 400 years of intermittent war with the Roman Empire.

The Late Empire

Fifty years of military anarchy (235–284, with nearly twenty emperors) were ended by Diocletian's reforms and the establishment of the tetrarchy. But intractable problems of frontier defense, heavy taxation, inflation, and excessive bureaucracy remained. This world was different from the one that Paul had known, transforming itself into the Byzantine Empire.

CE 249–251	**Decius** emperor, a persecutor of the Christians.
284–305	**Diocletian** emperor, reestablishes central power and founds the tetrarchy. Christians are persecuted.
306–337	The career of **Constantine** the Great, who establishes Christianity as the supreme religion of the empire.
312	Constantine wins the battle of Milvian Bridge under the sign of the cross. Christianity is declared the official state religion.
324	The city of Constantinople is founded on the site of Byzantium.
360–363	**Julian** the Apostate emperor.
378–395	**Theodosius** the Great emperor. A Christian, he opposes the Arian Christians.
395	The empire is divided between the sons of Theodosius.
410	Sack of Rome by Alaric the Visigoth. Rome formally renounces Britain.
439	The Vandals conquer Carthage and Africa.
476	End of the Roman Empire in the West.
527–565	**Justinian**, the eastern emperor, seeks to reconquer Italy and Africa.
633–655	Arab conquest of Syria, Egypt, and the Sassanid empire.
1453	Conquest of Constantinople by the Turks and the end of the Eastern (Byzantine) Roman Empire.

Appendix 2: Ancient Authors and Texts

(Excluding the books of the Old and New Testaments, the Apocrypha, and the Pseudepigrapha)

Accius, Lucius, born in 170 BCE at Pisaurum in Umbria and lived at least until 90 BCE. He is known to have made an educational tour of Athens and the Greek cities of Asia Minor. Accius is best known as a tragedian, and fragments of forty-six of his plays are extant. He translated some of the works of Euripides, Sophocles, and Aeschylus (on all of whom see below). We have mentioned his *Clytemnestra*.

Achilles Tatius of Alexandria, second-century CE Greek novelist, the author of *The Adventures of Leucippe and Cleitophon*. Also ascribed to him are an *Etymology* and a *Miscellaneous History of Many Great and Illustrious Men;* both works are now lost.

Aeschines, ca. 397–ca. 322 BCE. Athenian orator, whose exchanges with Demosthenes (see below) in the courts in 343 and 330 provide a large part of the evidence for the relations of Athens and Macedon. Two of Aeschines' speeches have been preserved, *Against Timarchus* and *Against Ctesiphon*.

Aeschylus, 525/4–456 BCE, Athenian dramatist. Of his extant plays, *Persae* was produced in 472, *Septem contra Thebas* in 467, and *Oresteia* (*Agamemnon*, *Choephoroe*, and *Eumenides* with the lost satyric *Proteus*) in 458.

Alciphron, second- or third-century CE sophist, whose *Epistles,* which purport to have been written in the fourth century BCE, show a familiarity with classical literature.

Ammianus Marcellinus, fourth century CE, Roman soldier and historian. His *History* was the continuation of the historical works of Tacitus, covering the years 96–378 CE. Books 1–13 have been lost, and the extant narrative begins with the events of 353.

Antiphon, ca. 480–411 BCE, Attic orator. His tetralogies are oratorical exercises designed to show how speeches should be composed for attack and defense. Some of his speeches dealing with real cases survive: *The Murder of Herodes, On the Choreutes,* and *Against a Stepmother.*

Appian, second century CE, a native of Alexandria, where he held public office. He eventually acquired Roman citizenship and moved to Rome. He wrote a *History of Rome,* from Aeneas to the battle of Actium (31 BCE). His main source was probably an imperial annalist who wrote in the early part of the first century CE.

Apuleius, ca. 123–ca. 170 CE, from Madaura in Numidia, Africa. An orator and philosopher, he was educated first at Carthage, then at Athens and Rome. After much travel he returned to Africa, where he appears to have spent the remainder of his life. He became priest of the emperor cult in Carthage. His surviving works include the *Apologia,* the *Metamorphoses* (the *Golden Ass*), the *Florida,* and the *De deo Socratis.*

Aristeas. The *Letter* that bears his name purports to be from an officer at the court of Ptolemy Philadelphus (285–247 BCE) to his brother Philocrates, giving an account of the circumstances that led up to the composition of the LXX. It is commonly dated about the beginning of the Christian era.

Aristides, Aelius, 117–181 CE or later. Son of a priest of Zeus, he became a public speaker and man of letters who spent most of his life as a teacher of rhetoric in Asia Minor but also some time in Egypt (142/143) and in Rome (143/144). Among his public addresses, *To Rome* paints an impressive picture of the Roman achievement as seen by an admiring provincial, while the *Panathenaikos* provides a potted history of Athens, much read in Byzantine times. He wrote a number of polemical works. His *Sacred Writings* record revelations supposed to have been made to him by Asclepius.

Aristophanes, ca. 450–ca. 385 BCE. Regarded as the greatest poet of Old Attic comedy, he may have lived or owned property on Aegina and is said to have written some forty plays, of which eleven are preserved: *Acharnians* (425), *Knights* (424), *Clouds* (423), *Wasps* (422), *Peace* (421), *Birds* (414), *Lysistrata* and *Thesmophoriazusae* (411), *Frogs* (405), *Ecclesiazusae* (392?), and *Plutus* (388). In addition, nearly a thousand *Fragmenta* survive.

Aristotle, 384–322 BCE. Greek philosopher and scientist. Born at Stagirus (later Stagira) in Chalcidice, he may have spent part of his childhood in Pella. At the age of seventeen he entered Plato's school at Athens, where he remained until Plato's death. He then removed to Assos in Mysia, and from there, in 345, to Mytilene on the island of Lesbos. Philip of Macedon invited him to Pella to act as tutor to Alexander (343/342). In 335 he returned to Athens (or at least to its outskirts), where he founded his school and established a library. With the outbreak of anti-Macedonian feeling on the death of Alexander, Aristotle was charged with impiety. He left his school in Theophrastus's hands and retired to Chalcis, where he died. His surviving works cover a great range of subjects, including logic, physics, biology, ethics, and literature. We have cited his *De generatione animalium, Ethica nicomachea* (named after his son, Nicomachus, or possibly edited by him), *Poetica, Politica, Rhetorica,* and *Topica.*

pseudo-Aristotle. A number of spurious works are attributed to Aristotle. In some cases their true author and approximate date can be surmised. The *Oeconomica,* which we have cited, bears evidence of being shaped over a long period, from 300 BCE to 400 CE.

Arnobius, a teacher of rhetoric at Sicca Veneria in proconsular Numidia. Converted to Christianity ca. 295 CE, a year or two later he wrote his *Adversus Nationes,* at the instance of his bishop, as an attack on the pagans.

Arrian (Flavius Arrianus), second century CE. Consul for 130 and governor of Cappadocia under Hadrian. A follower of Epictetus (see below), he preserved his teacher's discourses and produced a number of works in his own right, mainly histories, including his major work, the *Anabasis,* a history of Alexander the Great.

Artemidorus, late second century CE, of Ephesus, but usually known as Daldianus after his mother's native city, Daldis in Lydia. He traveled extensively to collect dreams and wrote an extant treatise, the *Onirocriticus,* on their interpretation.

Athenaeus, early third century CE, Greek writer of Naucratis in Egypt. His only extant work, *Deipnosophists (The Learned Banqueters)* was probably composed after the death of Commodus in 192. It is a vehicle for the discussion of philosophy, literature, law, medicine, and other interests by the supposed guests at a banquet over several days.

Ausonius, Decimus Magnus (died ca. 395 CE) was born at Bordeaux about the beginning of the fourth century. He pursued his studies at Bordeaux and Toulouse. For thirty years he taught in his native town, first as *grammaticus,* then as *rhetor.* His works include the *Ephemeris,* poems dealing with daily life, the *Parentalia,* the *Commemoratio professorum burdigalensium,* and the *Ordo nobilium urbium.*

Caesar (Caius Julius Caesar), 100–44 BCE, consul 59, governor of Gaul 58–49, defeated Pompy at Pharsalus in 48, dictator 47–44. Composed seven books of commentaries on his Gallic campaigns *(Bellum gallicum)* and three books on his Civil Wars *(Bellum civile),* which survive.

Cato the Elder (Marcus Porcius Cato), 234–149 BCE, consul 195, censor 184. An orator and statesman, he also wrote a history in seven books *(Origines)* and a treatise on agriculture. Only fragments of his speeches and of the *Origines* survive, but *De re rustica (On Agriculture)* is preserved.

Catullus, Caius Valerius, ca. 84–ca. 54 BCE, born at Verona in Cisalpine Gaul. His *Poems* fall into three groups: 1–60 are short occasional pieces, 61–64 are longer poems, and 65–116 are all in elegiacs.

Censorinus, third century CE, a Roman grammarian. He is known to have written two works, *De accentibus* (now lost) and *De die natali.* The latter is derived from various sources, especially the works of Varro and Suetonius.

Chrysostom, John, 344/354–407 CE. Born at Antioch in Syria, he studied philosophy and rhetoric before adopting the Christian religious life. He became a hermit ca. 373 but returned to Antioch, where he was made deacon in 381 and priest in 386 and was entrusted with preaching in the cathedral. Over the next decade he delivered most of the series of sermons, chiefly on biblical books, that earned him the sixth-century nickname *chrysostomos,* "golden-mouthed." In 398 he reluctantly became patriarch of Constantinople, where his troubled relationship with the empress Eudoxia and various ecclesiastics twice led to his exile. He died in exile at Comana in Pontus. John's writings have nearly all survived. Besides hundreds of sermons (we have referred to a sermon in the series *Homiliae in epistolam secundam ad Corinthios* and to his *Homiliae in epistolam primam ad Timotheum*), they comprise 236 letters and several practical treatises.

Cicero (Marcus Tullius Cicero), 106–43 BCE, from Arpinum, a town in Latium. Cicero was an orator, writer, and politician. He first appeared for the defense in a major trial in 80. He rose to consul in 63 and was proconsul of Cilicia in 51. A firm defender of the constitution, he was exiled for his opposition to the triumvirate of Caesar, Crassus, and Pompey. Permitted to return after a year, he became friendly with Caesar and Pompey but later approved of Caesar's assassination and urged the senate to oppose Mark Antony. As a gesture to Antony, Octavian had Cicero put to death on 7 December 43 BCE. Among his surviving works are fifty-eight political and legal speeches, some incomplete (we have cited *De domo sua, In verrem, Philippicae, Pro lege manilia, Pro Milone* and *Pro Murena*); sixteen books of letters to his friends *(Epistulae ad familiares),* sixteen to Atticus *(Epistulae ad Atticum;* see Nepos below), three to his brother Quintus *(Epistulae ad Quintum fratrem),* and two to Brutus; twelve philosophical treatises (we have cited *De legibus, De finibus, Tusculanae disputationes, De natura deorum,* and *De senectute*); and six works on oratory (we have cited *De oratore* and *Brutus*). About forty-eight of his speeches are lost.

Cleanthes, 331–232 BCE. Son of Phanias of Assos, he became a disciple of Zeno of Citium and his successor as head of the Stoic school 263–232. His most famous work is the *Hymn to Zeus.*

Clement of Alexandria (Titus Flavius Clement), ca. 155–ca. 220 CE, probably an Athenian, succeeded his teacher Pantaenus as head of the Christian catechetical school at Alexandria in 190. His extant works are the *Protrepticos (Exhortations to Conversion)* the *Paidagogos (The Tutor)* and the *Stromateis (Miscellanies).*

Clement of Rome, flourished ca. 90–100 CE. A prominent early Roman presbyter-bishop. Often identified or connected (as slave or freedman?) with the Titus Flavius Clemens who was executed by Domitian, he is generally regarded as the author of a letter *(1 Clement)* from the Roman to the Corinthian church, written ca. 96.

pseudo-Clement of Rome. The document known as *2 Clement (Second Epistle to the Corinthians)* is a sermon, probably the oldest in postapostolic literature. It appears to have been delivered ca. 140–150 CE in Rome (by bishop Hyginus, ca. 138–142?), Corinth (hence its MS connection with *1 Clement*), or perhaps Alexandria.

Codex justinianus and *Codex theodosianus.* The earliest known collections of imperial *constitutiones* (the generic name for legislative enactments by Roman emperors) were the unofficial *Codex gregorianus* (published ca. 291 CE) and the *Hermogenianus,* a supplementary collection published ca. 194. The *Codex theodosianus* (438), made on the orders of Theodosius II, contained enactments from the time of Constantine. A new compilation was published in 529 on the orders of Justinian but was soon superseded and another published in 534 *(Codex repetitae praelectionis)*. The latter is now referred to as the *Codex justinianus*. At about the same time (30 December 533) the *Digest* and the *Institutes* were also published (see *Digest* and Gaius, below). Unlike the *Codex theodosianus*, the *Codex justinianus* includes both *leges generales* and *rescripta* (imperial decisions upon special points of law), but of the latter none later than Diocletian. The *Codex*, the *Digest*, and the *Institutes*, as well as the *Novels* (*Novellae constitutiones*, constitutions issued by Justinian after the publication of the *Codex*), comprising the *Corpus juris civilis*, are the major source of our knowledge of Roman law.

Columella (Lucius Iunius Moderatus Columella), first century CE, of a Spanish landowning family. He himself held estates in various parts of central Italy and was a successful practical farmer. He is known chiefly for *De re rustica*, a systematic treatise on agriculture in twelve books, written in 60–65 CE.

Cyprian (Thascius Caecilius Cyprianus), ca. 200–258 CE, a prominent Carthaginian master of rhetoric before his conversion to Christianity ca. 246. He became bishop of Carthage ca. 248. His *Epistles* and treatises *The Lapsed* and *The Unity of the Catholic Church* have been preserved.

Demosthenes, 384–322 BCE. Regarded as the greatest Athenian orator, he studied rhetoric and legal procedure and became a *logographos* (professional speech writer) and advocate. His life was spent embroiled in the politics of the day, which was dominated by the emerging power of Macedon, to which he and his adversary, Aeschines (see above), had very different responses. Sixty-one orations, six letters, and a book of fifty-four proems are attributed to Demosthenes. We have cited his *Third Philippic* and *De corona (On the Crown)*, a speech—commonly regarded as his masterpiece—he made in his own defense in 330, in a case brought against him by Aeschines through Ctesiphon.

Digest. *Digest* is a title applied by classical jurisprudence to treatises on the law as a whole and by Justinian to the main part of his codification (see *Codex* above). His *Digest* came into force on 30 December 533 and contains excerpts from the works of jurists of more than three centuries, the earliest being Quintus Cervidius Scaevola, legal adviser of Marcus Aurelius. The excerpts vary in length, but each has an *inscriptio* indicating its author and the work from which it is taken.

Dio Cassius (Cassius Dio Cocceianus) of Nicaea, 155–235 CE. He entered the senate under Commodus, became praetor (194), *consul suffectus* (ca. 205), and consul with Alexander Severus (229). His eighty-volume *Roman History* traces the story from its legendary beginnings to 229 CE. His principle sources were Polybius and Livy and perhaps Tacitus. Only books 36–54 (covering the period 68–10 BCE) have been preserved intact. Books 1–21 exist in a twelfth-century paraphrase by Zonaras (private secretary of Alexis I Comnenus), and books 51–80 were abridged by Xiphilinus, a Constantinopolitan monk of the eleventh century. Dio Cassius also wrote a biography of Arrian and a work on the dreams and portents of Septimus Severus.

Dio Chrysostom (Dio Cocceianus, later called *Chrysostomos*), ca. 40–ca. 111 CE. A Greek orator and popular philosopher born of a wealthy family in Prusa, Bithynia, he began his career as a rhetorician in Rome. After being banished in the early years of Domitian from both Rome and his native Bithynia because of political intrigue, he spent fourteen years as a wandering Stoic-Cynic philosopher. His exile ended in 96. Under Nerva and Trajan he traveled to Rome in the service of his hometown. The last report of him comes from the time when Pliny was proconsul of Bithynia (110/111). Eighty of his *Discourses* survive.

Diodorus Siculus, of Agyrium (Sicily), flourished under Caesar and Augustus (to at least 21 BCE). He wrote (ca. 60–30) a *History* of the world from the earliest times to Caesar's Gallic War (54).

Diogenes, ca. 400–ca. 325 BCE, founder of the Cynic sect. He is said to have come to Athens as an exile from Sinope after 362 but may also have lived in Corinth for many years. He probably wrote some dialogues and tragedies (never acted), but many of the works attributed to him by later authors are almost certainly spurious. We have referred to his supposed *Epistles*.

Diogenes Laertius probably lived in the first half of the third century CE and is the author of an extant compendium, the *Lives of the Philosophers*. It is highly derivative, but he usually names his sources.

Dionysius of Halicarnassus, rhetor and historian, who lived and taught at Rome for many years from 30 BCE. His enthusiasm for all things Roman finds its clearest expression in his *Roman Antiquities,* which began to appear in 7 BCE. The first ten of its twenty books survive. In its complete form, the work went down to the outbreak of the First Punic War.

Dioscorides Pendanius of Anazarbus, a first-century CE army physician, well-versed in pharmacological literature. His *De materia medica,* in which he carefully describes remedies from the vegetable, animal, and mineral worlds, became the standard work of later centuries, superseding all earlier literature of its kind.

Epictetus of Hierapolis, Stoic philosopher, ca. 55–ca. 135 CE. Born in Hierapolis, Phrygia, he grew up as a slave of Epaphroditus (Nero's freedman and secretary, who later served Domitian), who allowed him to attend the lectures of Musonius Rufus (Stoic philosopher; see below) and later set him free. He taught philosophy in Rome, was banished with other philosophers by Domitian in 89, and went to Nicopolis (Epirus), where he continued teaching to the end of his life (interrupted by occasional travel, probably to Olympia and certainly once to Athens). His follower Flavius Arrianus (see Arrian above) collected his lectures, the *Dissertations,* probably in eight books, four of which have come down to us, and later published a summary of his philosophy in the *Manual* or *Enchiridion.* There are also a number of *Fragmenta,* gleaned from the writings of Arrian and others, some of which are of doubtful authenticity. Through these posthumous publications Epictetus had a great influence on the emperor Marcus Aurelius.

Euripides, ca. 480/485–ca. 406 BCE, Greek dramatist. His home was at Phyla, east of Hymettus, and he appears to have been the scion of a well-to-do family that may have owned land on Salamis (he used to compose in a cave on the island). In later life he accepted an invitation to the court of Archelaus at Pella in Macedonia, probably in 408, where he died. He is thought to have written nearly eighty plays, of which twenty-nine have survived along with other literary remains (we have cited his *Alcestis, Bacchae,* and *Electra*).

Eusebius of Caesarea, ca. 265–ca. 339 CE, "the father of church history." Born probably in Palestine, he became bishop of Caesarea about 314. A diverse author, he is remembered most for his histories, the best known of which is the *History of the Church (Historia ecclesiastica),* the most important church history of ancient times.

Favorinus, ca. 80–ca. 150 CE. A rhetor with philosophical interests, he was born at Arles and educated at Marseilles, and later may have heard Dio Chrysostom at Rome. His speaking tours took him to Athens, Corinth, and Ionia. He was the teacher of Herodes Atticus, Aulus Gellius (see below, who cites him in his *Noctes atticae*), and Fronto (see below). At Rome he moved in the circle of the emperor Hadrian. About 130 he fell into disfavor and was banished to Chios. Antonius Pius allowed him to return to Rome, where he recovered his status and influence.

Festus (Sextus Pompeius Festus), late-second-century scholar who abridged the writings of Verrius Flaccus (who was a scholar in the time of Augustus and teacher of Augustus's grandsons).

Frontinus (Sextus Julius Frontinus), ca. 30–104 CE, *praetor urbanus* in 70 and *consul suffectus* in 74(?). After his consulate, he was appointed governor of Britain (probably 74–78). His writings are essentially practical. Of his work on surveying, published under Domitian, only excerpts survive. His work on military science *(De re militari)* is lost, but his *Strategemata,* a more general manual on military strategy, also published in Domitian's reign, survives in four books. Appointed *curator aquarum* by Nerva (97), he wrote a two-volume account of the water supply of Rome, *De aquaeductibus.* He was again *consul suffectus* in 98 and *ordinarius* in 100 with Trajan.

Fronto (Marcus Cornelius Fronto), ca. 100–ca. 176 CE. From Cirta, in Numidia, he became the foremost orator of his day. After passing through the *cursus honorum,* he was *consul suffectus* in 143. Earlier he had been appointed tutor to the future emperors Marcus Aurelius and Lucius Verus and remained in their service until his death. His *Epistulae,* discovered only in the nineteenth century, throw an interesting light on the private life of the Antonines.

Gaius, second century CE, one of the most renowned Roman jurists, although little is known of him other than his writings. Justinian ordered that Gaius's students' textbook, the *Institutes,* be used as the basis for the composition of his own imperial *Institutes* (which also drew on Gaius's *Res cottidianae* and the *Institutes* of other jurists and was given legislative validity on the same day as the *Digest,* 30 December 533; see *Codex* above). Gaius's *Institutes* is the only classical legal work to have come down to us in substantially its original form.

Galen of Pergamum, ca. 129–199 CE. Educated in his hometown, Greece, and Alexandria, he rose from gladiator physician in Asia Minor to court physician in the Rome of Marcus Aurelius. He began his literary career with philosophical works and ended it with medical. We have referred to his treatises *On the Diagnosis and Healing of Faults, On Methods of Healing, On the Mixing and Efficacy of Pure Drugs,* and *That the Best Physician Is Also a Philosopher* and to his glossary of Hippocratic terms entitled *An Explanation of the Words of Hippocrates,* in which he lists the words in alphabetical order with a brief explanation of their meaning.

Gellius (Aulus Gellius), ca. 130–ca. 180 CE. Little is known of him. He was probably born and educated in Rome, but also spent a year studying in

Athens when he was thirty. His *Noctes atticae (Attic Nights)* is a now incomplete collection of mainly short chapters dealing with a great variety of topics, assembled to entertain and instruct his own children.

Gorgias of Leontini, ca. 483–376 BCE, rhetor and Sophist. Two of his works are extant, the *Encomium of Helen* and the *Defense of Palamedes.* There is also the *Epitaphios* fragment. We have noted a reference to him in Aristotle's *Rhetorica.*

Gospel of Truth. A gnostic writing, which may be identified with a work of that name attributed by Irenaeus (see below) to the followers of Valentinus (*Haer.* 3.11.9). It is not properly a "gospel" but a meditation on the truth of redemption. Its theme is that the human state is ignorance and that salvation is through the knowledge imparted by Jesus.

Greek Anthology. The work of an unknown Byzantine scholar (or perhaps a group of scholars), dating from ca. 980 CE. It is sometimes known as the *Palatine Anthology* because the only MS was found in the Count Palatine's library at Heidelberg. The work is based on earlier collections, most notably that of Cephalas, ca. 900 CE. The *Greek Anthology* contains 3,700 epigrams in fifteen books. In modern editions, the collection made by the monk Planudes is added to the *Greek Anthology* as "Book 16."

Harpocration, Valerius, of Alexandria, lexicographer. His dates are unknown. His *Collection of Florid Expressions* is lost, but the *Lexicon of the Ten Orators* is preserved in an early abridgement and in a longer form, closer to the original. It is a dictionary based mainly on works of the imperial age.

Helladios, an otherwise unknown author cited by Photius (see below).

Hermas. Formerly a slave emancipated at Rome, he farmed and prospered, but lost his property and saw his sons apostatize from the Christian faith under the pressure of persecution. He is known almost exclusively from his work the Shepherd of Hermas, which was composed in stages ca. 90–140/150 CE. The work comprises five *Visions,* including one of an angel in the guise of a shepherd, from which the book takes its name, twelve *Mandates,* and ten *Similitudes.* Its major themes are ethical.

Herodian of Syria, third-century CE government official who wrote *Histories of the Emperors* in eight books from Marcus Aurelius to Gordian III (180–238 CE).

Herodotus, ca. 484–ca. 420 BCE. Born at Halicarnassus in Asia Minor, moved to Samos, traveled and lectured in Greece, and visited Athens before joining the Athenian colony at Thurii in Italy (founded 444/443), where he is presumed to have died. But there is also a tradition that, like Euripides, he died at Pella. He wrote a *History* in nine books of the struggle between Asia and Europe, culminating in the Persian Wars.

pseudo-Hippocrates. Although Hippocrates himself, the Asclepiad of Cos and contemporary of Socrates (469–399 BCE), is the most famous of Greek physicians, little is known of him except that he traveled much and probably died at Larissa in Thessaly. There is a considerable literature ascribed to him, but none of it is likely to be genuine. We have cited what purports to be his *Epistles* and his treatise *Concerning Airs*.

Hippolytus, third-century CE (died ca. 236) presbyter and teacher in the church in Rome. Origen heard him preach there in 212. Among his surviving works are his *Refutation of all Heresies* and the *Apostolic Tradition*.

Historia augusta, the modern title given to a collection of biographies of Roman emperors, Caesars and usurpers from 117 to 284 CE (Hadrian to Carinus and Numerianus). The present text is not complete, as there is a lacuna for the years 244–259. The work purports to have had six different authors who lived in the time of Diocletian and Constantine (they are referred to as the *scriptores Historiae augustae*), but this has been questioned and a later date proposed, perhaps during the reign of Theodosius, with the author or authors unknown.

Homer, the traditional author of the *Iliad* and the *Odyssey*. Nothing certain is known about him, but he must be dated at some time before 700 BCE. Chios and Smyrna seem to have the best claims to being his home, and he may have been blind.

Horace (Quintus Horatius Flaccus), 65–8 BCE, from Venusia in Apulia. His father took him to Rome for schooling. He went from there to Athens (45), where he was recruited by Brutus to serve under him as *tribunus militum* until the defeat at Philippi (42). He returned to Italy, obtained a pardon for his political indiscretion, and won the patronage of Maecenas and Augustus (38). He produced four books of *Odes,* two books of *Satires,* seventeen *Epodes,* and two books of *Epistles* (in verse). The *Ars poetica* is also an epistle in verse, addressed to Piso and his two sons, but is not generally included with the other *Epistles*.

Ignatius, second century CE. Bishop of Antioch (died 117), he is known to us almost exclusively from his seven letters, written while he was traveling under armed guard to be executed in Rome. From Smyrna he wrote to the churches in Ephesus, Magnesia, Tralles, and Rome (we have referred to his *Letters to the Romans, the Smyrneans,* and *the Trallians*). Later, from Troas, he wrote to the Philadelphian and Smyrnaean congregations and to Polycarp, bishop of Smyrna.

Institutes. See Gaius and *Codex* above.

Irenaeus, flourished ca. 175–ca. 195 CE. Bishop of Lyons, he was probably a native of Smyrna, where as a boy he had heard Polycarp. He may have studied and taught at Rome before moving to Lyons. His *Adversus Haereses (Against Heresies)* is an attack, in five books, on gnostic teaching, especially that of the Valentinians.

Isidorus Hispalensis, bishop of Seville ca. 602–636 CE, one of the most important links between the learning of antiquity and the Middle Ages. He wrote a number of works, including the *Etymologiae* or *Origines* (now divided into twenty books), a widely used encyclopedia covering a wide range of topics and clearly drawing extensively on other authorities.

Isocrates, 436–338 BCE, Athenian educator and political orator. Of the sixty orations extant under his name in Roman times, twenty-one survive today. Nine of his letters also survive. The most constructive of his political speeches are the *Panegyricus* and the *Philippus.*

Jerome (Eusebius Hieronymus), ca. 345–ca. 419 CE. Biblical scholar and translator, he was born of Christian parents in Stridon in northeastern Italy, studied in Rome, Antioch, and Constantinople, returned to Rome, but finally made his home in Bethlehem. He engaged in a voluminous correspondence, compiled a bibliography of ecclesiastical writers, wrote *De viris illustribus (Of Illustrious Men),* wrote commentaries on virtually all of the books of the Bible (we have referred to his *Commentariorum in epistolam ad Ephesios,* his commentary on Ephesians) and translated the Bible into Latin (the so-called Vulgate, or Bible in the common tongue).

Josephus (Flavius Josephus). Born in the first year of Gaius Caligula's reign (37–38 CE) of the Jewish priestly nobility, he survived to the end of the century. After an unimpressive military career (66–67) as a leader of the Jewish forces in Galilee against Rome, he was taken prisoner (67) but won the favor of the emperor Vespasian, who gave him citizenship and a house in Rome. He was in Titus's entourage at the fall of Jerusalem.

In Rome he wrote, in seven books, the *Wars of the Jews (Bellum judaicum)*, which appeared between 75 and 79, sketching Jewish history from the Maccabean revolt to the outbreak of the Jewish War. His next work, the *Antiquities of the Jews (Antiquitates judaicae)*, in twenty books, is a history of the Jews from creation to immediately before the outbreak of the war, giving a fuller account of the period from the Maccabees to 66 CE. It was published in 93/94. His last works were the *Vita* (his autobiography) and his apologia for Judaism in two books entitled *Against Apion (Contra Apionem)*. He died after 100 CE.

Julian (Flavius Claudius Julianus, Julian the Apostate), born 332 CE, son of Julius Constantius, half brother of Constantine and Basilina. He had a Christian education but fell under the influence of the pagan philosopher Maximus and, on becoming Augustus (emperor), openly professed paganism. His surviving literary works include eight orations, the *Misopogon* (written in Antioch as a satirical defense of his actions), the *Convivium* or *Caesares* (a comic account of Constantine's reception on Olympus), and about eighty letters *(Epistulae)*.

Juvenal (Decimus Junius Juvenalis). He was born between 50 and 60 CE in Aquinum, Campania, and was still writing in 127. He appears to have lived most of his life in Rome, often as a poor man. He may have been banished by Domitian, returning after the emperor's murder. He left sixteen *Satires*, grouped in five books, in which he lampoons, with varying degrees of bitterness, the society in which he lived, focusing chiefly on Domitian's principate.

Libanius, born in Antioch 314 CE and died there ca. 393, a Greek rhetorician and man of letters. He studied in Athens, taught in Constantinople and Nicomedia, and held the official chair of rhetoric in Antioch from 354. Sixty-four of his *Orationes* (speeches) survive, also 1,600 letters, fifty-one school declamations, numerous model rhetorical exercises, and minor rhetorical works composed in the course of his teaching.

Livius Andronicus. Apparently born at Tarentum, he came to Rome as a prisoner of war, perhaps after the surrender of Tarentum in 272 BCE. On manumission, he took his owner's name. The first performance of one of his plays was in 240. In honor of a work written by him in 207, the temple of Minerva on the Aventine was set aside as a meeting place for writers and actors. The titles of eight of his tragedies are known, of which we have mentioned *Equos trojanus (Trojan Horse)*. Of his other writings, the *Odyssia,* a "translation" of Homer's *Odyssey,* is best known.

Livy (Titus Livius), 59 BCE–17 CE or 64 BCE–12 CE. We know little of his life except that he was born in Patavium (Padua), of a well-to-do family, had a daughter and a son (who may also have been a writer), and must have spent much of his life in Rome, although he died in Padua. He gave readings of his work in Rome, where he won Augustus's interest in his historical task. He encouraged Claudius in his historical studies. Livy's *History* was composed in 142 books, from the origins of Rome to the reign of Augustus. Of this immense work, only 35 books are extant (1–10, 21–45). There are a fragment of book 91, other cited fragments, and an epitomized version in the *Periochae* (for all 142 books except 136–137) and in the Oxyrhynchus *Epitomae* (for books 37–40, 48–55). Livy's work probably underlies that of later writers such as Florus, Granius, Licinianus, Aurelius Victor, Eutropius and Festus, Orosius and Cassiodorus, and Julius Obsequens.

Lucian of Samosata, born ca. 120 CE and died after 180. Although his mother tongue was probably Aramaic, he had a good Greek education and became an advocate and later a traveling lecturer, as far afield as Gaul. At about the age of forty he settled in Athens and later accepted a government post in Egypt. He is the author of eighty pieces, chiefly in dialogue form. We have cited his *Anacharsis, De morte peregrini, De Syria dea, Fugitivi, Hermotimus, Navigium, Philopseudes,* and *Vitarum auctio.*

Lysias, son of Cephalus (from Syracuse, in Sicily, whom Pericles persuaded to settle in Athens), ca. 459–ca. 380 BCE. He grew up in Athens, lived in Thurii (Italy) for a time, returned to Athens in 412, fled from the Thirty to Megara in 404, but returned in 403 to spend the remainder of his life in Athens. In this period of his life, he is said to have composed more than two hundred forensic speeches (the *Orations*), of which a number have survived. There were also other speeches, including his *Olympiacus,* delivered in 388 BCE.

Macrobius (Ambrosius Theodosius Macrobius), fourth–fifth century CE. He appears to have been foreign to Italy (he admits that his style is deficient in *nativa Romani oris elegantia*) and may have been African. His works show no trace of Christianity. If he is one of the Macrobii named in the *Codex Theodosianus* (see above), he may have been either *vicarius Hispaniarum* (399) or *proconsul Africae* (410). Of his writings, we have cited his *Saturnalia,* a symposium in seven books, in which the dialogues of imaginary speakers are recorded.

Marcus Aurelius, Roman emperor 161–180 CE, born in 121 and named Marcus Annius Verus, the son of Annius Verus, from a consular family of Spanish origin. He was adopted (as Marcus Aelius Aurelius Verus

Caesar) by Antoninus Pius in 138 and held a number of important posts before becoming emperor himself. His principate was dominated by war. His work as a civil administrator was meticulous but lacked foresight and laid the grounds of later problems. He is one of the few rulers of empire whose writings have outlasted his other achievements. His correspondence with his tutor Fronto has been recovered (see Fronto above), but his fame rests not on this but on the twelve books of his *Meditations,* compiled largely during his military campaigns.

Martial (Marcus Valerius Martialis, born in Bilbilis, Spain, ca. 40 CE (his cognomen would suggest it was on 1 March) and died ca. 104. Educated in Spain, he went to Rome in 64, where his intimacy with his fellow Spaniards Seneca and Lucan was soon cut short by their fate in the Pisonian conspiracy. His life in Rome was largely one of poverty-stricken dependence on patrons not overgenerous in return for complimentary verses. His social, if not his financial, standing gradually improved from contacts with the emperor and his court downwards, and he chronicled succinctly every sort and condition of men. Thanks to Pliny the Younger, who paid his return fare, and his patroness Marcella, who provided him with a rural property, he was able to end his days in the land of his birth (from ca. 98). His works include the *Liber spectaculorum,* commemorating the opening of the Flavian Amphitheater (the Colosseum) (published in 80), the *Xenia* (now book 13 of the *Epigrams*), and the *Apophoreta* (now book 14) (published in 84–85). Of his twelve *Epigrammaton libri (Epigrams),* most appeared at intervals of about a year beginning in 86.

Martyrdom of Perpetua and Felicity. The account of the prison experiences and martyrdom for their faith of Perpetua and others in Carthage in 203 CE. The compiler is unknown but appears to have been a Montanist, as were the martyrs. The book reflects the eschatological expectations, internal tensions, and liturgical customs of contemporary Carthaginian Christianity.

Mekilta, the midrash (commentary) on Exodus (beginning at Exod 12), which originated in Rabbi Ishmael's school. Rabbi Ishmael ben Elisha himself was born in Galilee in the latter half of the first century CE.

Mela (Pomponius Mela) of Tingentera (near Gibraltar), a Latin writer in the time of Gaius or the early years of Claudius. He composed a geographical survey, in three books, of the inhabited world *(De chorographia).*

Menander Rhetor of Laodicea, third century CE, wrote commentaries on Hermogenes and Minucianus. Two set *Orations* (περὶ ἐπιδεικτικῶν) pass under his name. The first deals with hymns, prayers, encomia of

countries and cities, etc.; the second gives rules for ceremonial addresses to the emperor and other officials, various forms of *lalia* "talk,"
epithalamia, etc.

Mishnah (from the Hebrew "to repeat and to study"), a collection of rabbinic laws, arranged in six divisions, which cover agriculture (especially
tithes), public feasts, women (especially their marriage and the concom-
itant economic arrangements), damages, sacrifices at the temple, and
ritual purity. These divisions are, in turn, made up of a total of sixty-
three tractates. The Mishnah represents the deposit of four centuries of
Jewish (Pharisaic) religious history. Its roots are in the Old Testament,
and it grew out of the attempt to apply the Old Testament law (Torah)
to everyday life. The material of the Mishnah (the "tradition," cf. Mark
7:3–13) was transmitted orally until committed to writing in Palestine
ca. 200 CE under Rabbi Judah the Patriarch. The text subsequently underwent some evolution and was interpreted and its teachings modified
by the Palestinian and Babylonian Talmuds.

Modestinus, third-century CE Roman jurist, cited in the *Digest* (see above).

Musonius Rufus, Gaius, of Volsinii (Italy), seems to have been born before
30 CE and to have died before 101/102. About 60, he followed
Rubellius Plautus into exile to Asia Minor, returned to Rome in 65–66,
but, on the discovery of the Pisonian conspiracy, was banished to
Gyaros. He returned to Rome, probably under Galba, but was again
banished by Vespasian, only to return once more under Titus. A Stoic
philosopher, many of whose *Discourses* have been preserved, he included among his pupils other philosophers (most notably Epictetus;
see above) and some notable Roman citizens.

Nepos, Cornelius, ca. 99–ca. 24 BCE. Born in Cisalpine Gaul, he moved to
Rome, where he was familiar with Cicero and Pomponius Atticus. (A
friend of Cicero, whose brother Quintus married Pomponius's sister,
Pomponius himself avoided the troubles in Rome in 85 by residing in
Athens for about twenty years. Hence his cognomen Atticus.) Catullus
(see above), who dedicated his book to Nepos and Fronto (see above),
tells us that Nepos was also a publisher. Nepos's own works include *De
viris illustribus,* in at least sixteen books. It was published before the
death of Atticus ca. 34, but before 27 a second edition appeared, including non-Greeks and expanding the section on Atticus. Some of this
work survives. Other works by Nepos have not.

Odes of Solomon. A collection of hymns of the first or second centuries CE,
Jewish in tone but clearly Christian in origin, in that they joyfully acknowledge the advent of the Messiah (7.1–6; 41.3–7), for whom they

give thanks and express their love. They give thanks also for the eternal life that he has given (3.1–9; 11.1–24; 23.1–3; 26.1–7; 40.1–6).

Origen (Origenes), ca. 185–ca. 254. Born in Egypt of Christian parents, he studied under Clement (see above) in the catechetical school in Alexandria. Origen became the head of the catechetical school and held that office for twenty-eight years. His fame as a teacher grew and many came to hear him. He visited Rome, where he heard Hippolytus (see above) and during the Caracalla persecution in 215 went to Palestine. He was recalled by his bishop to Egypt but was subsequently ordained a priest in Palestine. Demetrios, bishop of Alexandria, took umbrage at this and deprived him of his teaching post. On this Origen established a school in Caesarea. He suffered imprisonment and torture in the persecution of Decius in 250 and died shortly afterwards. He is considered to be one of the first textual critics of the Bible, one of the first to set forth a systematic statement of the faith, and one of the first Bible commentators. Estimates of the number of his works vary from 6,000 (Epiphanius) to 2,000 (Pamphilus) to 800 (Jerome). Most are now lost, although fragments survive and some have been recently discovered. His most famous works include the *Hexapla,* an edition of the OT in Hebrew and various Greek versions. *De principia* is a systematic theology, *De oratione* an argument that prayer is a participation in the life of God, and *Contra Celsum* (which we have cited) a philosophical argument in defense of the faith against one of its critics.

Orphica. Many poems were in circulation at an early date under the name of Orpheus. Euripides (see above) and Hippias hint at their existence, Plato (see below) is the first to quote verses from them, and Aristotle (see above) speaks of the "so-called Orphic epics." A few fragments are preserved.

Ovid (Publius Ovidius Naso), 43 BCE–18 CE. He was born at Sulmo, in the Paeligni, the son of a Roman *eques,* and studied in Rome. The story of his life is told in one of his own poems (*Tristia* 4.10). His father intended him for an official career and he did hold some minor posts, but he abandoned public life for poetry. By 8 CE he was the leading poet in Rome, but in that year he was banished by Augustus to Tomis on the Black Sea, apparently for some indiscretion, which is never explained. Despite repeated appeals to Augustus and later to Tiberius, he was doomed to pass what remained of his life in this remote and insalubrious outpost of empire. Of his surviving works, we have cited the *Amores,* three books of love poems, the *Heroides,* imaginary letters from legendary women to absent husbands and lovers, and the *Metamorphoses,* an epic poem in fifteen books, forming a collection of stories from classical and Near Eastern legends.

Palladius, Rutilius Taurus Aemilianus, fourth century CE, a knowledgeable agriculturist, with estates in Italy and Sardinia. He wrote a practical manual, once thought to comprise fourteen books—an introduction, a book for each month of the year, and an appendix, *De institutione* (to which we have referred). The latter, however, may not be the fourteenth; that distinction may belong rather to *De medicina pecorum.*

Papyri Oxyrhynchus. Oxyrhynchus (Behnesa), to the west of the Nile, has proved to be the richest source of papyri in Egypt so far discovered. Some are Ptolemaic; most are Roman and Byzantine.

Paulus, Julius, flourished ca. 210 CE, one of the greatest Roman jurists, a contemporary of Ulpian, a prolific writer on matters legal (nearly 320 books). The *Pauli sententiae,* which was popular in later centuries and part of which is preserved in the *Lex romana Visigothorum* and elsewhere, was probably a handy anthology of his writings, compiled about 300.

Pausanius of Lydia, born between 111 and 115 CE, apparently in Asia Minor (Lydia). A noted traveler and geographer, he knew Palestine, Egypt, Italy, and Rome, but especially Greece. He wrote his *Description of Greece* (between 160 and 180) as a guidebook (the first known) for those intending to visit that land.

Perseus Flaccus, Aulus, 34–62 CE. An Etruscan knight, rich and well connected. The strongest influence on his character was exercised by the Stoic philosopher Cornutus, who edited Perseus's *Satirae* after his early death.

Petronius. Little is known about him, not even the dates of his birth and death. His praenomen was either Titus or Caius. If this Petronius was the author of the fragmentary novel *Satyricon* (also known as the *Cena Trimalchionis*), he was at one time proconsul in Bithynia and later *consul suffectus* before assuming the post of master of pleasure *(arbiter elegantiae)* at Nero's court. In 66 CE his rival Tigellinus poisoned the emperor's mind against him, and he was driven to commit suicide.

Phaedrus, ca. 15 BCE–ca. 50 CE. A slave of Thracian birth, he received a good schooling, perhaps in Italy, and became a freedman of Augustus. He composed five books of *Fables,* some of which offended Sejanus.

Philo (Philon) of Byzantium, who worked in third-century BCE Alexandria, is best described as a "librarian engineer," a learned man standing in the Alexandrian tradition of scholars specializing in mechanical experiment and written speculation. Not everyone, however, is persuaded that the treatise *On the Seven Wonders* is his.

Philo (or Philon) Judaeus, a Jewish writer, born ca. 30 BCE in Alexandria, who spent all of his life in his native city and died in 45 CE. He devoted the greater part of his career to an exposition of the Pentateuch in terms designed to make it both comprehensible and palatable to those brought up on Greek philosophy. Eventually he became head of the Jewish community in Alexandria and had to deal with the very difficult situation that developed when the Roman governor of Egypt, Aulus Avillius Flaccus (32–38 CE), did not suppress anti-Semitic demonstrations. In 39–41 Philo headed the delegation of Alexandrian Jews to Rome to ask for exemption from the duty of worshiping the emperor. No settlement had been reached when the emperor Gaius was murdered on 24 January 41. It was probably during this period of waiting that Philo completed the *Legatio ad Gaium,* to which we have referred, along with thirteen other of his works.

Philostratus, Flavius, born between 160 and 170 CE. A citizen of Attica, he studied at Athens, Ephesus, and Hierapolis and later joined the philosophical circle patronized by Septimus Severus and his wife, Julia Domna. After 217 he returned to the East to live for the most part in Athens. He died ca. 244–249. At the instance of Julia Domna, Philostratus wrote the *Life of Apollonius of Tyana (Vita Apollonii),* a philosophizing mystic of the first century CE (died under Nerva). He is also the author of a number of other works.

Photius, Byzantine scholar and patriarch of Constantinople 858–867 and 878–886 CE. His most important work is the *Bibliotheca* (or *Myriobiblion*), "a living monument of erudition and criticism" (Edward Gibbon, *Decline and Fall,* ch. 53). It is an account of 280 prose works read by Photius. Theology and history predominate, but oratory, romance, philosophy, science, medicine, and lexicography also come within its scope. It is the best or sole source of information about many lost works.

Pindar, 518–438 BCE, born in Cynoscephalae in Boetia. Of an aristocratic family, he learned his craft as a poet first from his uncle Scopelinus and later, at Athens, from Apollodorus and Agathocles. As his fame increased, he numbered patrons in many different parts of Greece and perhaps reached the pinnacle of his achievement when he wrote *Pythian Odes* 4 and 5 for the king of Cyrene in 462–461. We have cited *Pythian Ode* 2, a dark and unhappy poem, which may have been written in 468. We have also referred to his *Nemean* and *Olympian Odes.*

Plato, ca. 429–347 BCE, son of Ariston and Perictione, both Athenians of
distinguished lineage. His writings show the enormous influence that
Socrates had upon him. After the execution of Socrates in 399, he retired for a time to Megara with other Socratics. He then appears to have
traveled extensively, visiting Italy and Sicily and perhaps Egypt. On returning to Athens he spent the remaining forty years of his life teaching
at a place near the grove of Academus about a mile outside the wall of
the city. During this time he made three more visits to Sicily. His works
have all been preserved, consisting of twenty-five dialogues (of which
we have cited *Alcibiades, Leges, Lysis, Phaedrus, Protagoras, Respublica
[The Republic], Symposium,* and *Timaeus*) and the *Apologia* (which we
have also cited). There are, in addition, thirteen letters, whose genuine-
ness, however, is debated.

Plautus, Titus Maccius. Born at Sarsina in Umbria, died ca. 184 BCE, he is
said to have written 130 plays. The 21 that have come down to us probably represent a select edition produced in the second century CE. Of
these, we have cited *Mercator, Stichus,* and *Truculentus.*

Pliny the Elder (Gaius Plinius Secundus), 23/24–79 CE. Born at Comum
(Como) in Cisalpine Gaul, the son of a wealthy equestrian family, he
was probably educated in Rome. He spent twelve years with the armies
of the Rhine as a cavalry officer. On the completion of his military service, he devoted himself to rhetorical and grammatical studies, pru-
dently withdrawing from public life when the emperor Nero started to
run wild, although he may have done some work in the courts. With the
accession of Vespasian, Pliny's life took a more prosperous turn. His
military service with Titus (Vespasian's son) helped to bring him a series
of procuratorships, one of which is known to have taken him to His-
pania Tarraconensis (ca. 73). At this time he was writing a history in
thirty-one books, completed by 77 but published posthumously (*A fine
Aufidi Bassi,* a continuation of Bassus's *Roman History*), and the
Naturalis historia (Natural History), in thirty-seven books (containing,
he claimed, twenty thousand facts obtained from a hundred principal
authors), dedicated to Titus in 77. Toward the end of his life, Pliny became a counselor *(amicus)* of Vespasian and then of Titus and was appointed commander of the fleet at Misenum. It was from here that he
sailed on 24 August 79 to observe the eruption of Vesuvius, which cost
him his life. In attempting to rescue victims of the eruption, he was
overcome himself by the fumes. He left behind a number of other
books besides those mentioned here, but only the *Natural History* has
survived.

Pliny the Younger (Gaius Plinius Caecilius Secundus), ca. 61–ca. 112 CE.
Son of a landowner of Comum (Como) in Cisalpine Gaul, he was later

brought up by his uncle and adoptive father, Pliny the Elder (see above). He studied advocacy in the schools of Quintilian and Nicetes at Rome, served on the staff of a Syrian legion, entered the senate, and practiced successfully in the civil courts all his life. He held the usual annual offices, becoming praetor in 93 and *consul suffectus* in 100 and receiving a number of longer appointments thereafter. He thrice sat as judicial adviser in the cabinet of Trajan (ca. 104–107), who sent him as *legatus Augusti* to reorganize the disorderly province of Bithynia-Pontus (ca. 110), where he apparently died in office. His career is the best-documented example of the life of a civilian administrator of the early empire. He published nine books of literary *Epistles* between 100 and 109. The tenth book contains his official correspondence with Trajan about the administration of Bithynia and is the only such dossier surviving intact (in *Ep.* 10.96 he gives the earliest outsider's account of Christian teaching and behavior). He also dabbled in versification, publishing two volumes in the manner of his protégé Martial (see above). His surviving speech, the *Panegyricus,* is an expanded version of the original, which he delivered in the Senate as consul, contrasting the actions of Trajan with the misdeeds of Domitian.

Plutarch (L. Mestrius Plutarchus) of Chaeronea (Greece), born before 50 CE and died after 120. He spent most of his life in Chaeronea, about twenty-two miles east of Delphi, but knew Athens well, where he studied in the Platonic Academy (ca. 66), and Corinth and visited both Egypt and Italy, lecturing and teaching at Rome (which he visited twice, in the late 70s and early 90s). His wide circle of influential friends included a number of consulars and Greek men of letters. For the last thirty years of his life he was a priest at Delphi. He may also have held a government office under Trajan and Hadrian. The *Catalogue of Lamprias* (an ancient list of works attributed to Plutarch) contains 227 items. Extant are 78 miscellaneous works, including some not in the *Catalogue,* which are classified under two headings: the *Moralia,* comprising 28 ethical, religious, physical, and political studies (of which we have cited 14, by reference both to the *Moralia* and to the individual treatises), and the *Lives,* biographies of 50 Greek and Roman soldiers and statesmen (of which we have cited 12: *Aemilius Paullus, Alcibiades, Alexander, Caesar, Camillus, Cato Major, Cato Minor, Fabius Maximus, Gaius Gracchus, Pompeius, Pyrrhus, Sulla, Tiberius Gracchus*).

Polybius, ca. 200–after 118 BCE. Born at Megalopolis, after a liberal education, he entered politics and served as a hipparch of the Achaean Confederacy (170/169). After Pydna, he was among 1,000 eminent Achaeans deported to Rome for political investigation and detained without trial. He now became the friend and mentor of Scipio Aemilianus. He probably accompanied Scipio to Spain and to Africa. In 150 the Achaean detainees were released. Polybius witnessed the destruction of Carthage in Scipio's company (146). After the sack of Corinth, he helped to organize Greece and acted as a mediator (146–145). Later he visited Alexandria and Sardes and may have been at Numantia in 133. He wrote his *Histories* in forty books (books 1–5 are extant, together with excerpts, some substantial, from the remainder) with the intention of narrating the history of the fifty-three years (220–168), from the Hannibalic War to Pydna, that left Rome mistress of the world.

Procopius, born in Caesarea (Palestine) ca. 500 CE. After a thorough rhetorical and legal education, he obtained a post as a counselor and later became an assessor on the staff of Justinian's general, Belisarius, whom he accompanied on his Persian (527–531), African (533–536), and Italian (536–540) campaigns. By 540/542 he was back in Constantinople, where he probably continued his official career and became prefect of the city in 562. The date of his death is unknown. His principal work is the *History of the Wars of Justinian* in eight books. He also wrote the *Secret History,* a virulent attack on Justinian, presumably published after his death, and *On Justinian's Buildings,* composed (ca. 553–555) at the emperor's behest, a useful source for the geography, topography, and art of the period.

Propertius, Sextus, born between 54 and 43 BCE in Assisi. He moved to Rome when his family was impoverished by Octavian's land confiscations of 41–40. He became enamored of a lady named Cynthia (ca. 29–24), whose affections were not as fixed as his were, and his turbulent relationship with her inspired most of his four books of *Elegies.* The latest date that can be assigned to any poem of Propertius is 16 BCE. He died about the turn of the century.

Quintilian (Marcus Fabius Quintilianus), born ca. 30–35 CE at Calagurris (Calahorra, Spain). He received most, if not all, of his education in Rome. He returned to Spain, but in 68 Galba brought him back to Rome, where he taught and practiced advocacy for twenty years and was probably the first rhetorician to receive a salary from the *fiscus* (the state treasury). He numbered Pliny the Younger (see above) among his pupils. He retired in 88, presumably to write. Domitian made him tutor to his two great-nephews and heirs, the sons of Flavius Clemens. He died before 100 CE. Of his writings, we have cited the *Institutio oratoria,* published in the 90s and covering the training of an orator from birth to maturity.

Sallust (Gaius Sallustius Crispus), 86–ca. 34 BCE, born at Amiternum. The beginnings of his career are unknown. Our earliest certain information is of his tribunate in 52. His political opponents brought about his expulsion from the senate in 50 on the pretext of immorality. Elected praetor in 47, he took part in the African campaign and was appointed the first governor of Africa Nova. On returning to Rome, he was charged with extortion, only escaping through Caesar's intervention. He retired from public life to write history. We have cited his first and second works, the *Bellum Catilinae* (published probably after 43) and the *Bellum jugurthinum* (published ca. 40).

Seneca the Elder (Lucius Annaeus Seneca), born of an equestrian family at Corduba in Spain about 55 BCE. Little is known about him, but he was certainly in Rome both as a young man and after his marriage and may have spent many years there. Probably through trade, he amassed a considerable fortune. He died between 37 and 41 CE. His *Controversiae* contain recollections of speeches made by others with various digressions and comments of his own. Only five of the original ten books are extant, but a fourth-century CE abridgement gives some idea of the contents of the missing books.

Seneca the Younger (Lucius Annaeus Seneca), one of three sons born to the elder Seneca. (The other sons of Seneca the Elder were Annaeus Novatus, who after adoption by L. Junias Gallio became governor of Achaea [see Acts 18:12–17], and Marcus Annaeus Mela, the father of Lucan, the Roman writer). Born in Corduba, Spain, between 4 BCE and 1 CE. Little is known of his life before 41 CE. He was brought by an aunt to Rome, where his studies turned to philosophy. He achieved the office of quaester and a considerable reputation as an orator and writer. He was banished by Gaius to Corsica in 41 because of his alleged adultery with the emperor's sister, Julia Livilla, but was recalled in 49, made praetor, and appointed tutor to the young Nero. With Nero's accession in 54, Seneca became his advisor and minister. He and Burrus (prefect of the Praetorian Guard) virtually controlled the empire for eight years, but with the death of Burrus in 62 and the change for the worse in Nero, Seneca retired from public life. He committed suicide in 65 because of his implication in the Pisonian conspiracy. The bulk of Seneca's prose work is philosophical in content (we have cited his *Ad Helviam de consolatione, De beneficiis, De clementia, De constantia sapientis, De ira, De providentia, De vita beata, Epistulae morales,* and *Naturales quaestiones*). His most important poetical works are nine tragedies, but some epigrams have also survived. A tenth tragedy, *Octavia,* which we have cited, is attributed to him but, on the internal evidence, was clearly not from his hand. References to Seneca in the current study are to Seneca the Younger.

Sibylline Oracles. The Sibyl was a prophetess. It became a generic term, so that there were, in fact, many Sibyls. Varro's *Res divinae* lists ten. Various collections of their prophecies were made, and fourteen somewhat miscellaneous books of oracles are still extant, their contents owing much to the pious imaginations of Christians and Jews.

pseudo-Socrates. Socrates was born in 469 and died in 399 BCE. In early life he was interested in the scientific philosophy of his time, but by the time that we know most about him he had devoted himself to inquiry into the right conduct of life. He was tried on the pretext of corrupting the young men of Athens and found guilty. (The motives were probably political. He was known to have associated with some of those who had attacked democracy.) He died at his own hand thirty days later. He left nothing written so far as is known. The so-called Socratic *Epistles,* which we have cited, are not his. We have also mentioned a reference to him by Xenophon (see below) in his *Memorabilia.*

Sophocles, born in or about 496 at Colonus, the son of a wealthy industrialist, and died late in 406 BCE. His early life coincided with the expansion of the Athenian empire, and he himself took his share in the duties of citizenship as treasurer for a time, twice as a general, and as a priest. He composed probably 123 plays, 8 of which are extant. We have cited the *Philoctetes,* which was produced in 409 BCE.

Soranus of Ephesus, physician under Trajan and Hadrian (98–138 CE). He studied in Alexandria and practiced in Rome. Of twenty books that he wrote on the history of medicine, terminological problems, and medicine proper, only two survive, together with fragments of another. We have referred to his *Gynaecology.*

Statius, Publius Papinius, ca. 45–96 CE. Born at Naples, he settled in Rome, where he won fame and popularity as a poet and became intimately acquainted with some of the leading men of his day, including the emperor Domitian. Toward the end of his life, he retired to Naples, where he died. The *Silvae,* a collection in five books, from which we have cited, was published at different times from 92 onward. Other works include the *Agave,* a libretto for a *pantomimus,* the epic *Thebais,* in twelve books, and the unfinished *Achilleis.*

Strabo. Born in Amaseia in Pontus in 64 or 63 BCE, he was of mixed Greek and Asiatic descent. His inherited wealth enabled him to dedicate his life to scholarship and travel. He studied grammar under Aristodemus, geography under Tyrannion, and philosophy under Xenarchus and knew Posidonius. He was in Rome in 45–44 and twice again in ca. 31 and 7, in Egypt in 25–ca. 19, and spent the rest of his life in Amaseia until his death in ca. 21 CE. His *Historical Sketches* are now lost, but his *Geography,* in seventeen books, completed ca. 7 BCE and slightly revised ca. 18 CE, has survived.

Suetonius. Little is known of the personal life of Gaius Suetonius Tranquillus, and even the dates of his birth and death are uncertain (ca. 69–140 CE). He was of the equestrian order, probably from Hippo Regius in Numidia, and is mentioned by Pliny the Younger (see above) as a quiet and scholarly man who, after some experience in the courts, settled down as a writer. His connection with Pliny may have helped him to a number of government appointments, culminating in three secretarial posts, the last under Hadrian, by whom he was dismissed in 121/122. His *De viris illustribus,* composed during the reign of Trajan, comprised biographies of Roman literary men arranged by classes. Of these, the *De grammaticis et rhetoribus* is partly preserved, and a few lives, variously abbreviated or corrupted, have come down to us, probably from the *De poetis.* From his *De vita Caesarum,* biographies of the Caesars, we have cited *Julius, Augustus, Tiberius, Gaius, Claudius, Nero, Galba, Vespasian, Titus,* and *Domitian.*

Synesius of Cyrene, ca. 370–413 CE, a Christian orator and poet and sometime bishop of Ptolemais (Libya), who has left behind nine hymns, 156 *Epistles* (we have cited no. 4), and two rhetorical discourses.

Tacitus, Cornelius, ca. 56–ca. 116 CE. Probably from southern Gaul, he began his official career under Vespasian. Away from Rome when Agricola died (he had married Agricola's daughter in 77), he returned to witness the last years of Domitian's rule. His political career reached its zenith with his appointment as *consul suffectus* in 97 and as proconsul of Asia ca. 112/113. He had made a name for himself for his eloquence in the courts but appears to have turned more and more to writing. His works include the *Dialogus* (thought by some to be his first publication, ca. 80), *Agricola* and *De origine et situ Germanorum,* both published in 98, the so-called *Histories* (untitled in the MS), of which only the first four books and part of the fifth survive, tracing the history of Rome from 69 to presumably Domitian's assassination in 96, and the so-called *Annals* (in the MS entitled *Ab excessu divi Augusti [From the Death of the Divine Augustus]*), in eighteen books, not all of which have survived.

Talmud (from the Hebrew "teaching, study, learning, a lesson"), two long collections of Jewish religious literature, one called the Palestinian Talmud and the other the Babylonian. They are largely commentaries on the Mishnah (see above). This component (the commentary) is known as Gemara (from the Aramaic "to learn") and consists of the analysis of words and sentences from the Mishnah, the comparison of traditions from both within and outside the Mishnah, the interpretation of Scripture, stories about rabbis and others, and long digressions on various topics. The Palestinian Talmud covers the first four divisions of the Mishnah (agriculture, public feasts, women, and damages) and was completed in the mid–fifth century CE. The Babylonian Talmud covers the Mishnaic divisions of public feasts, women, damages, and sacrifice and was completed in the sixth century CE, with many additions and modifications being made over the next several centuries. The Babylonian Talmud was more fully edited than the Palestinian and became authoritative for most of Judaism because of the dominance of the Babylonian community until well into the Islamic period.

Terence (Publius Terentius Afer). Born perhaps ca. 190 BCE in North Africa, he came as a slave to Rome to the household of a senator, Terentius Lucanus, and adopted his name when he was manumitted. He died ca. 159, having written, or rather adapted from the Greek, six plays for the Roman stage. We have referred to his *Phormio,* which was produced in 161.

Tertullian (Quintus Septimus Florens Tertullianus), ca. 160–ca. 240 CE. Born in or near Carthage, he was trained in law and was early attracted to Stoicism. Disgust at pagan excesses and admiration for the Christian martyrs, however, won him to Christianity. From then on he used his gifts of advocacy, rhetoric, and irony in favor of the more rigorist wing of the church. It is not certain whether he was ordained. He may have remained a lay teacher. At all events, he became dissatisfied with the state of the church and left it to join the Christian sect of the Montanists ca. 206. His joining of the Montanists coincided with the hardening of attitudes already held and fitted his own eschatological conviction that the end time was near. He may have rejoined the mainstream of the church near the end of his life. His writings span the period roughly from 196 to 212, and all bear the stamp of the brilliant pleader. They include works in defense of the faith, e.g., the *Apologeticus,* works that address moral and ethical issues, e.g., *De spectaculis,* and works that address theological issues, e.g., *De resurrectione carnis* (to name only those we have cited).

Thucydides. He was probably born between 460 and 455 BCE and probably died ca. 400. He was himself a general in the Athenian army in the war of which he writes, and for his failure to save Amphipolis from the Spartan force led by Brasidas, he was exiled in 424, only to return twenty years later when the war was over. He died within a few years of his return, leaving his *History of the Peloponnesian War* unfinished. Three writers—Theopompus, Cratippus, and Xenophon (see below) in the *Hellenica*—wrote completions to Thucydides's work.

Tibullus, Albinus, poet, born between 55 and 48 BCE. He appears to have been of equestrian rank and of modest means (despite his complaints of *paupertas*) and to have done military service under M. Valerius Messalla Corvinus. The *Corpus tibullianum* is made up of three books, of which only two are his. The first deals with his love for his mistress, Delia, the second with another "mistress," whom the poet calls Nemesis. It contains love poems, poems in honor of Messalla, an elegy on the blessings of peace, and a description of a rustic festival.

Tzetzes, Johannes, twelfth-century CE polymath. He wrote allegories in verse on the *Iliad* and *Odyssey*, other works in verse, and scholia on Hesiod, Aristophanes, Lycophron, and others. His chief work was Βίβλος Ἱστορική, named Χιλιάδες by its first editor *(Historiarum variarum chiliades)*, a review of Greek literature and learning, with quotations from over 400 authors.

Ulpian, Domitius, one of the last great Roman jurists, born of a family long established at Tyre. He held a number of important posts in Rome, including that of *praefectus praetorio* at the time of his death. He was killed in 223 CE by the Praetorians, evidently fearing his proposed reform of the guard. Ulpian was an encyclopedic compiler and synthesizer of the work of his predecessors in the law, and Justinian's compilers paid him the compliment of using him far more than any other writer. Nearly a third of the *Digest* (see above) is taken from his copious writings—he produced nearly 280 books, almost all written during the reign of Caracalla (212–217).

Valerius Maximus, a Roman historian in Tiberius's reign. A poor man, he was befriended by Sextus Pompeius (consul 14 CE) and accompanied him to his governorship in Asia ca. 27. After his return, Valerius composed a handbook of illustrative examples for rhetoricians, *Factorum ac dictorum memorabilium libri IX (Memorable Deeds and Words in Nine Books)*, cited as *Memorabilium*. It is dedicated to Tiberius and includes a violent denunciation of Sejanus, which suggests that it was published after Sejanus's downfall in 31.

Varro, Marcus Terentius, 116–27 BCE. Born probably at Reate in Sabine country, he studied in Rome (under the philologist L. Aelius Stilo) and in Athens (under Antiochus of Ascalon). He rose to the office of praetor, served under Pompey in Spain (49), accepted office under Caesar as a librarian, and was outlawed by Antony. When the Civil War was over, he was able to devote himself to his studies. He is said to have edited 490 books by his seventy-eighth year and wrote a number himself, most of which are now lost, but part of his *De lingua* survives and his *De re rustica,* to which we have made reference.

Vegetius (Flavius Vegetius Renatus), author of an *Epitoma rei militaris* in four books, which is the only ancient manual of Roman military institutions to have survived intact. The work is probably to be dated to the years 383–395 CE.

Velleius (Marcus Velleius Paterculus), ca. 19 BCE–ca. 31 CE, of Campanian (southern Italian) descent. After several military campaigns, Velleius served under the younger Tiberius Nero in Germany and Pannonia and was quaestor in 7 CE and praetor in 15 CE. He was enamored of Sejanus and may have met his own death as a consequence of Sejanus's fall in 31. The *Historiae romanae* is a compendium of Roman history addressed to Velleius's friend M. Vinicius (who married Julia, daughter of Germanicus) on attaining the consulship 30 CE.

Vetius Valens, a second-century CE astrological writer and compiler of an anthology of such writings *(Anthologiarum libri).*

Virgil (Publius Vergilius Maro), 70–19 BCE. Born at Andes, near Mantua, in Cisalpine Gaul, of a landowning family rich enough to educate him and prepare him for a senatorial career, he was educated at Mantua, Cremona, Milan, and Rome. During the Civil War he retired to Naples to study philosophy under the Epicurean Siro, whose small villa and holding of land he seems to have inherited before 41 BCE. Virgil was living in Naples in 29 (when he read the *Georgics* to Octavian). In 19 he left Italy, intending to travel in Greece and Asia for three years. At Athens, however, he met Augustus and was persuaded to return home with him. He fell ill at Megara and was brought back as far as Brundisium, where he died. He was buried about two miles from Naples on the road to Puteoli. Besides fourteen short poems and five longer (of these we have referred to his *Moretum*), which are sometimes attributed to Virgil's youth, his works include ten *Eclogues,* four books of *Georgics,* and twelve books of an epic, the *Aeneid,* left almost complete at his death.

Vitruvius Pollio (full name not known), ca. 80–20 BCE. Roman architect and military engineer under the Second Triumvirate and early in Augustus's reign, his fame rests chiefly on his treatise *De architectura,* in ten books, on architecture and engineering, compiled partly from his own experience and partly from similar works by Hermogenes and other noted architects, mostly Greeks. It is the only work of its kind surviving from the ancient world.

Xenophon, ca. 428/427–ca. 354 BCE. He grew up in difficult times in Athens and left the city in 401 to join a mercenary army in Asia Minor in the employ of Cyrus, who aspired to the Persian throne. After the failure of the expedition, the Anabasis, Xenophon was elected a general and brought the army back to Trapezus in 400. He continued to serve as a mercenary in Asia Minor. When Socrates died in 399, because he had belonged to the Socratic circle, Xenophon was formally exiled from Athens. He served under the Spartan king Agesilaus in 396–394 and remained in Sparta when war broke out with Athens. The Spartans presented him with an estate at Scillus, near Olympia. When this region was claimed by Elis in 371, Xenophon and his family were obliged to leave their estate and took up residence near Corinth. As relations between Sparta and Athens improved, the decree of exile was rescinded (ca. 368). In 366–365, when the Athenians were expelled from Corinth, Xenophon returned to Athens, where he lived until his death. Of his many literary works, we have cited the *Anabasis,* an account in seven books of the adventures of the Greek mercenaries under Cyrus, the *Respublica Lacedaemoniorum* (the *Spartan Constitution*), written ca. 388 in a mood of gratitude to the Spartans, the *Memorabilia,* recollections of Socrates in four books written over a number of years from ca. 381 to ca. 355/354, the *Cyropaedia,* a historical novel in eight books with Cyrus the Elder as hero, and *De vectigalibus* (περὶ πόρων, *Ways and Means*), written ca. 355/354, suggesting a policy for Athens of "peace through strength" and practical ways of increasing public resources by stimulating commercial and industrial enterprises.

Xenophon Ephesius. Nothing is known of him, and even his name is suspected of being spurious. He was the author of a novel entitled *Ephesiaca* (or *Anthia and Habrocomes*). He can be dated sometime later than Trajan (98–117 CE) and before the destruction of the Artemisium in Ephesus in 263.

Bibliography

Abbott, G. F. *Songs of Modern Greece*. Cambridge: Cambridge University Press, 1900.

Abbott, T. K. *Epistles to the Ephesians and to the Colossians*. Edinburgh: T&T Clark, 1897.

Alexander, P. S. "Aqedah." Pages 44–47 in *Dictionary of Biblical Interpretation*. Ed. R. J. Coggins and J. L. Houlden. Philadelphia: Trinity Press International, 1990.

Alford, H. *Greek Testament: An Exegetical and Critical Commentary*. 6 vols. London: Rivingtons & Deighton, Bell, 1871.

Andreau, J. "The Freedman." Pages 175–98 in *The Romans*. Ed. A. Giardina. Chicago: University of Chicago Press, 1993.

Arma, J. H. d', and E. C. Kopff, eds. *The Seaborne Commerce of Ancient Rome: Studies in Archaeology and History*. Memoirs of the American Academy in Rome 36. Rome: American Academy in Rome, 1980.

Arnim, J. von. *Stoicorum veterum fragmenta, I*. Leipzig: Terbner, 1903.

Arnold, C. *Ephesians—Power and Magic: The Concept of Power in Ephesians in the Light of Its Historical Setting*. Cambridge: Cambridge University Press, 1989.

Backman, G. *Meaning by Metaphor: An Exploration of Metaphor with a Metaphoric Reading of Two Stories by Stephen Crane*. Uppsala: Almquist & Wiksell International, 1991.

Bailey, D. R. S. *Two Studies in Roman Nomenclature*. New York: American Philological Association, 1976.

Baird, W. "Letters of Recommendation: A Study of 2 Cor. 3:1–3." *JBL* 80 (1961): 166–72.

Balch, D. L., E. Ferguson, and W. A. Meeks, eds. *Greeks, Romans, and Christians: Essays in Honor of Abraham J. Malherbe*. Minneapolis: Fortress, 1990.

Ball, W. E. B. *St Paul and the Roman Law*. Edinburgh: T&T Clark, 1901.

Bandstra, A. J. *The Law and the Elements of the World: An Exegetical Study in Aspects of Paul's Teaching.* Grand Rapids: Eerdmans, 1964.

Banks, R., ed. *Reconciliation and Hope: New Testament Essays on Atonement and Eschatology Presented to L. L. Morris on His 60th Birthday.* Exeter, U.K.: Paternoster, 1974.

_____. "Walking as a Metaphor of the Christian Life." Pages 303–13 in *Perspectives on Language and Text.* Ed. E. W. Conrad and E. G. Newing. Winona Lake, Ind.: Eisenbrauns, 1987.

Baron, S. W. *A Social and Religious History of the Jews.* 14 vols. New York: Columbia University Press, 1962.

Barrett, C. K. *A Commentary on the Epistle to the Romans.* New York: Harper & Row, 1957.

_____. *A Commentary on the First Epistle to the Corinthians.* London: Adam & Charles Black, 1971.

_____. *A Commentary on the Second Epistle to the Corinthians.* London: Adam & Charles Black, 1973.

_____. *Freedom and Obligation.* London: SPCK, 1985.

Barrow, R. H. *The Romans.* Harmondsworth, U. K.: Penguin, 1949.

Bartchy, S. S. *Mallon Chresai: First-Century Slavery and the Interpretation of 1 Corinthians 7:21.* Missoula: Scholars Press, 1973.

Barth, M. *Ephesians.* 2 vols. New York: Doubleday, 1974.

Batey, R. "Paul's Bride Image: A Symbol of Realistic Eschatology." *Int* 17 (1963): 176–82.

Beker, J. C. *Paul the Apostle: The Triumph of God in Life and Thought.* Edinburgh: T&T Clark, 1980.

Bengel, J. A. *Gnomon Novi Testamenti.* Edinburgh: T&T Clark, 1877.

Benjamin, B. "The Urban Background to Public Health Changes in England and Wales, 1900–1950." *Population Studies* 17 (1964): 225–48.

Bernard, J. H. *The Pastoral Epistles.* Cambridge: Cambridge University Press, 1899.

_____. "The Second Epistle of Paul to the Corinthians." Pages 4–119 in vol. 3 of *Expositor's Greek New Testament.* Ed. W. R. Nicoll. 5 vols. London: Hodder & Stoughton, 1897–1910.

Betz, H. D. *2 Corinthians 8 and 9: A Commentary on Two Administrative Letters of the Apostle Paul.* Philadelphia: Fortress, 1985.

_____. *Galatians: A Commentary on Paul's Letter to the Churches in Galatia.* Philadelphia: Fortress, 1979.

Birdsall, J. N. "ΠΡΕΣΒΥΤΗΣ in Philemon 9: A Study in Conjectural Emendation." *NTS* 39 (1993): 625–30.

Blaiklock, E. M. *The World of the New Testament.* London: Ark, 1981.

Blanchette, O. A. "Does the *Cheirographon* of Col. 2:14 Represent Christ Himself?" *CBQ* 23 (1961): 306–12.

Bogaert, R. *Banques et banquiers dans les cités grecques.* Leiden: A. W. Sijthoff, 1968.

_____. "Gelt (Geldwirtschaft)." *RAC* 9 (1976): 797–907.

Bonner, S. *Education in Ancient Rome: From the Elder Cato to the Younger Pliny.* Berkeley: University of California Press, 1977.

Booth, A. "The Art of Reclining and Its Attendant Perils." Pages 105–20 in *Dining in a Classical Context.* Ed. W. J. Slater. Ann Arbor: University of Michigan Press, 1991.

Boswell, J. E. "*Expositio* and *oblatio:* The Abandonment of Children and the Ancient and Medieval Family." *AHR* 89 (1984): 10–33.

Bowerstock, G. W. *Greek Sophists in the Roman Empire.* Oxford: Clarendon, 1969.

Bradley, K. R. *Slaves and Masters in the Roman Empire: A Study in Social Control.* New York: Oxford University Press, 1987.

_____. "Wet-Nursing at Rome: A Study in Social Relations." Pages 201–29 in *The Family in Ancient Rome.* Ed. B. Rawson. London: Croom Helm, 1986.

Brewer, R. R. "The Meaning of *politeuesthe* in Philippians 1:27." *JBL* 73 (1954): 76–83.

Brilliant, R. *Gesture and Rank in Roman Art: The Use of Gesture to Denote Status in Roman Sculpture and Coinage.* New Haven: Connecticut Academy of Arts and Sciences, 1963.

Broneer, O. "The Apostle Paul and the Isthmian Games." *Biblical Archaeologist* 25 (1962): 1–31.

_____. *Isthmia, Topography and Architecture.* 2 vols. Princeton: American School of Classical Studies at Athens, 1973.

Broughton, T. R. S. *The Magistrates of the Roman Republic.* 2 vols. New York: American Philological Association, 1951–1952.

_____. "The Roman Army." Pages 431–41 in vol. 5 of *The Beginnings of Christianity.* Ed. F. J. Foakes Jackson and K. Lake. 5 vols. London: Macmillan, 1920–1933.

Bruce, F. F. *1 and 2 Thessalonians.* Waco, Tex.: Word, 1982.

_____. *The Acts of the Apostles.* Grand Rapids: Eerdmans, 1990.

_____. *The Epistle to the Galatians.* Grand Rapids: Eerdmans, 1982.

_____. *The Letter of Paul to the Romans: An Introduction and Commentary.* Grand Rapids: Eerdmans, 1985.

_____. "The New Testament and Classical Studies." *NTS* 22 (1976): 229–42.

_____. *Paul: Apostle of the Free Spirit.* Exeter, U.K.: Paternoster, 1977. Also published as *Paul: Apostle of the Heart Set Free.* Grand Rapids: Eerdmans, 1977.

Buckland, W. W. *The Roman Law of Slavery: The Condition of the Slave in Private Law from Augustus to Justinian.* New York: AMS Press, 1969.

_____. *A Testbook of Roman Law from Augustus to Justinian.* Cambridge: Cambridge University Press, 1963.

Burkert, W., *Greek Religion.* Cambridge: Harvard University Press, 1985.

Burrows, M. "The Marriage of Boaz and Ruth." *JBL* 59 (1940): 445–54.

Burton, E. de W. *The Epistle to the Galatians.* Edinburgh: T&T Clark, 1921.

Byrne, B. *"Sons of God"—"Seed of Abraham": A Study of the Idea of the Son-ship of God of All Christians against the Jewish Background.* Rome: Biblical Institute Press, 1979.

Cadbury, H. J. "Roman Law and the Trial of Paul." Pages 297–338 in vol. 5 of *The Beginnings of Christianity.* Ed. F. J. Foakes Jackson and K. Lake. 5 vols. London: Macmillan, 1920–1933.

Caird, G. B. *The Language and Imagery of the Bible.* Philadelphia: Westminster, 1980.

_____. *Paul's Letters from Prison.* Oxford: Oxford University Press, 1976.

Calder, W. M. "Adoption and Inheritance in Galatia." *JTS* 31 (1930): 372–74.

Campbell, A. C. *The Rhetoric of Righteousness in Romans 3:21–26.* Sheffield, U.K.: Sheffield Academic Press, 1992.

Carcopino, J. *Daily Life in Ancient Rome.* Harmondsworth, U.K.: Penguin, 1956.

Cartledge, P. A., and F. D. Harvey, eds. *Crux: Essays Presented to G. E. M. de Ste. Croix on His 75th Birthday.* London: Imprint Academic, 1985.

Casson, L. *Ancient Trade and Society.* Detroit: Wayne State University Press, 1984.

Cervin, R. S. "Does ΚΕΦΑΛΗ Mean 'Source' or 'Authority over' in Greek Literature? A Rebuttal." *TJ* 10 (1989): 85–112.

Chevalier, R. *Roman Roads.* London: B. T. Batsford, 1976.

Chow, J. K. *Patronage and Power: A Study of Social Networks in Corinth.* Sheffield, U.K.: Sheffield Academic Press, 1992.

Cohen, B. *Jewish and Roman Law: A Comparative Study.* 2 vols. New York: Jewish Theological Seminary of America, 1966.

Cohn, M. "Blood-Avenger." Pages 530–31 in *The Principles of Jewish Law.* Ed. M. Cohn. Jerusalem: Ktav, 1975.

_____. "City of Refuge." Pages 531–32 in *The Principles of Jewish Law.* Ed. M. Cohn. Jerusalem: Ktav, 1975.

_____. *The Principles of Jewish Law.* Jerusalem: Ktav, 1975.

Connolly, P. *Pompeii.* Oxford: Oxford University Press, 1990.

Corbett, P. E. *The Roman Law of Marriage.* Oxford: Clarendon, 1930.

Couch, H. N. *The Treasures of the Greeks and Romans.* Menasha, Wis.: George Banta, 1929.

Cranfield, C. E. B. *The Epistle to the Romans.* 2 vols. Edinburgh: T&T Clark, 1979.

Cremer, H. *Biblio-Theological Lexicon of New Testament Greek.* Edinburgh: T&T Clark, 1886.

Crook, J. A. *Law and Life in Rome.* London: Thames & Hudson, 1967.

_____. "Patria Potestas." *CQ* 17 (1967): 113–22.

Dahl, N. A. *Studies in Paul: Theology for the Early Christian Mission.* Minneapolis: Augsburg, 1977.

Daly, R. J. "The Soteriological Significance of the Sacrifice of Isaac." *CBQ* 39 (1977): 45–75.

Daube, D. *The New Testament and Rabbinical Judaism.* London: Athlone, 1956.

_____. *Studies in Biblical Law.* Cambridge: Cambridge University Press, 1947.

Davies, G. N. *Faith and Obedience in Romans: A Study of Romans 1–4.* Sheffield, U.K.: Sheffield Academic Press, 1990.

Davies, O. *Roman Mines in Europe.* Oxford: Clarendon, 1935.

Davies, P. R., and B. D. Chilton. "The Aqedah: A Revised Tradition History." *CBQ* 40 (1978): 514–46.

Deissmann, A. *Bible Studies.* Edinburgh: T&T Clark, 1901.

_____. *Light from the Ancient East.* London: Hodder & Stoughton, 1908.

_____. *Paul: A Study in Social and Religious History.* London: Hodder & Stoughton, 1926.

Delling, G., et al., eds. *Gott und die Götter: Festgabe für Eric Fascher.* Berlin: Evangelische Verlagsanstalt, 1958.

Denney, J. "St Paul's Epistle to the Romans." Pages 554–725 in vol. 2 of *Expositor's Greek New Testament.* Ed. W. R. Nicoll. 5 vols. London: Hodder & Stoughton, 1897–1910.

Derrett, J. D. M. "The Footwashing in John 13 and the Alienation of Judas Iscariot." *Revue internationale des droits de l'antique* 24 (1977): 3–19.

_____. "The Function of the Epistle to Philemon." *ZNW* 79 (1988): 63–91.

_____. *Law in the New Testament.* London: Darton, Longman & Todd, 1970.

Dibelius, M., and H. Conzelmann. *The Pastoral Epistles.* Philadelphia: Fortress, 1972.

Dill, S. *Roman Society from Nero to Marcus Aurelius.* New York: Meridian, 1956.

Dixon, S. *The Roman Family.* Baltimore: Johns Hopkins University Press, 1992.

_____. *The Roman Mother.* London: Croom Helm, 1988.

_____. "The Sentimental Ideal of the Roman Family." Pages 99–113 in *Marriage, Divorce, and Children in Ancient Rome.* Ed. B. Rawson. Oxford: Clarendon, 1991.

Dodd, C. H. *The Epistle of Paul to the Romans.* London: Hodder & Stoughton, 1932.

Downing, F. G. "Cynics and Christians." *NTS* 30 (1984): 584–93.

Duff, A. M. *Freedmen in the Early Roman Empire.* Oxford: Clarendon, 1928.

Duff, P. B. "Metaphor, Motif, and Meaning: The Rhetorical Strategy behind the Image 'Led in Triumph' in 2 Corinthians 2:14." *CBQ* 53 (1991): 79–92.

Duncan, G. S. *St Paul's Ephesians Ministry: A Reconstruction.* London: Hodder & Stoughton, 1929.

Duncan-Jones, R. *The Economy of the Roman Empire: Quantitative Studies.* Cambridge: Cambridge University Press, 1982.

Dunn, J. D. G. *Romans.* 2 vols. Dallas: Word, 1988.

Dupont, F. *Daily Life in Ancient Rome.* Oxford: Blackwell, 1992.

Earnshaw, J. D. "Reconsidering Paul's Marriage Analogy in Romans 7:1–4." *NTS* 40 (1994): 66–88.

Edersheim, A. *Sketches of Jewish Social Life in the Days of Christ.* London: Religious Tract Society, 1876.

Egan, R. P. "Lexical Evidence on Two Pauline Passages." *NovT* 19 (1977): 34–62.

Elert, W. "Redemptio ab Hostibus." *TLZ* 72 (1947): 265–70.

Ellis, E. E. "Sōma in First Corinthians." *Int* 44 (1990): 132–44.

_____. "Traditions in 1 Corinthians." *NTS* 32 (1986): 481–502.

Engels, D. *Roman Corinth: An Alternative Model for the Classical City.* Chicago: University of Chicago Press, 1990.

Eyben, E. "Family Planning in Graeco-Roman Antiquity." *AncSoc* 11–12 (1980–1981): 1–82.

_____. "Fathers and Sons." Pages 114–45 in *Marriage, Divorce, and Children in Ancient Rome.* Ed. B. Rawson. Oxford: Clarendon, 1991.

Falk, Z. W. *Introduction to Jewish Law of the Second Commonwealth.* 2 vols. Leiden: Brill, 1972.

Fee, G. D. *1 and 2 Timothy, Titus.* NIBC. Peabody, Mass.: Hendrickson, 1984.

Findlay, G. G. "St Paul's First Epistle to the Corinthians." Pages 729–953 in vol. 2 of *Expositor's Greek New Testament.* Ed. W. R. Nicoll. 5 vols. London: Hodder & Stoughton, 1897–1910.

Finley, M. I. *The Ancient Economy.* London: Hogarth, 1985.

_____. *Ancient Slavery and Modern Ideology.* New York: Viking, 1980.

_____. "Was Greek Civilization Based on Slave Labour?" Pages 53–72 in *Slavery in Classical Antiquity: Views and Controversy.* Ed. M. I. Finley. Cambridge: Heffer, 1974.

_____, ed. *Slavery in Classical Antiquity: Views and Controversy.* Cambridge: Heffer, 1974.

Finley, M. I., and H. W. Pleket. *The Olympic Games.* New York: Viking, 1976.

Fitzmyer, J. A. "Another Look at ΚΕΦΑΛΗ in 1 Corinthians 11:3." *NTS* 35 (1989): 506–10.

_____. "Κεφαλή in 1 Corinthians 11:3." *Int* 47 (1993): 52–59.

Flory, M. B. "Family in *Familia:* Kinship and Community in Slavery." *AJAH* 3 (1978): 78–95.

Forbes, C. A. "The Education and Training of Slaves in Antiquity." *TAPA* 86 (1955): 321–60.

Fowl, S. "A Metaphor in Distress: A Reading of νήπιοι in 1 Thessalonians 2:7." *NTS* 36 (1990): 469–73.

Fowler, W. W. *Social Life at Rome in the Age of Cicero.* London: Macmillan, 1937.

Fox, R. L. *Pagans and Christians.* Harmondsworth, U.K.: Penguin, 1988.

Frank, T. "Race Mixture in the Roman Empire." *AHR* 21 (1916): 689–708.

Frier, B. W. "Natural Fertility and Family Limitation in Roman Marriage." *CP* 89 (1994): 318–33.

Furnish, V. P. *II Corinthians.* New York: Doubleday, 1984.

Gale, H. M. *The Use of Analogy in the Letters of Paul.* Philadelphia: Westminster, 1964.

Galsterer, H. "Roman Law in the Provinces: Some Problems of Transmission." Pages 13–28 in *Sources for Ancient History.* Ed. M. H. Crawford. Cambridge: Cambridge University Press, 1983.

Gardner, J. F. *Women in Roman Law and Society.* London: Croom Helm, 1986.

Garnsey, P. *Social Status and Legal Privilege in the Roman Empire.* Oxford: Clarendon, 1970.

_____, ed. *Non-Slave Labour in the Graeco-Roman World.* Cambridge: Cambridge University Press, 1980.

Garnsey, P., and R. P. Saller. *The Roman Empire.* London: Gerald Duckworth, 1987.

Garnsey, P., K. Hopkins, and C. R. Whittaker, eds. *Trade in the Ancient Economy.* Berkeley: University of California Press, 1983.

Gebhard, E. R. "The Isthmian Games and the Sanctuary of Poseidon in the Early Empire." Pages 78–84 in *The Corinthia in the Roman Period.* Ed. T. E. Gregory. Ann Arbor: Cushing-Malloy, 1994.

Gempf, C. "The Image of Birth Pangs in the New Testament." *TB* 45 (1994): 119–35.

Giardina, A., ed. *The Romans.* Chicago: University of Chicago Press, 1993.

Gibbon, E. *The History of the Decline and Fall of the Roman Empire.* Repr., 3 vols. Ed. D. Womerlsey. New York: Penguin, 1995.

Gill, D. W. J. "Corinth: A Roman Colony of Achaea." *BZ* 37 (1993): 259–64.

_____. "Macedonia." Pages 397–417 in *The Book of Acts in Its Greco-Roman Setting.* Vol. 2 of *The Book of Acts in Its First Century Setting.* Ed. D. W. J. Gill and C. Gempf. Grand Rapids: Eerdmans, 1994.

Ginzberg, L. *The Legends of the Jews.* Philadelphia: Jewish Publication Society, 1954.

Glass, D. V. "Some Indicators of Differences between Urban and Rural Mortality in England and Wales and Scotland." *Population Studies* 17 (1964): 263–67.

Godet, F. *Commentary on St Paul's Epistle to the Romans.* 2 vols. Edinburgh: T&T Clark, 1895.

Goodenough, E. R. "Paul and Onesimus." *HTR* 22 (1929): 181–83.

Gordon, T. D. "A Note on Παιδαγωγός in Gal. 3:24–25." *NTS* 35 (1989): 150–54.

Gorman, M. J. *Abortion and the Early Church.* Downers Grove, Ill.: InterVarsity Press, 1982.

Grant, M. *A Social History of Greece and Rome.* New York: Scribner's, 1992.

Grudem, W. "Does ΚΕΦΑΛΗ Mean 'Source' or 'Authority over' in Greek Literature? A Survey of 2,336 Examples." *TJ* 6 (1985): 38–59.

Gudorf, M. E. "The Use of ΠΑΛΗ in Ephesians 6:12." *JBL* 117 (2, 1998): 331–35.

Gunton, C. E. *The Actuality of Atonement: A Study of Metaphor, Rationality, and the Christian Tradition.* Grand Rapids: Eerdmans, 1989.

Guthrie, D. *The Pastoral Epistles: An Introduction and Commentary.* Grand Rapids: Eerdmans, 1990.

Hanson, A. T. "The Origin of Paul's Use of ΠΑΙΔΑΓΩΓΟΣ for the Law." *JSNT* 34 (1988): 71–76.

_____. *Studies in Paul's Technique and Theology.* London: SPCK, 1974.

Harrill, J. A. *The Manumission of Slaves in Early Christianity.* Tübingen: Mohr, 1995.

Harris, H. A. *Greek Athletes and Athletics.* London: Thames & Hudson, 1964.

_____. *Greek Athletics and the Jews.* Cardiff: University of Wales Press, 1976.

_____. *Sport in Greece and Rome.* London: Thames & Hudson, 1972.

Harris, H. W. "Towards a Study of the Roman Slave Trade." Pages 117–40 in *Roman Seaborne Commerce.* Ed. J. H. d'Arma and E. C. Kopff. Rome: American Academy, 1980.

Harris, W. "Echoing Bronze." *JASA* 70 (1981): 1181–86.

_____. " 'Sounding Brass' and Hellenistic Technology." *BAR* 8 (1982): 38–41.

Harris, W. V. *War and Imperialism in Republican Rome, 327–70 BC.* Oxford: Clarendon, 1979.

Hassall, M. "Romans and Non-Romans." Pages 685–98 in *The Roman World.* Ed. J. Wacher. Vol. 2. London: Routledge & Kegan Paul, 1987.

Hawthorne, G. F. *Philippians.* Waco, Tex.: Word, 1983.

Heichelheim, F. M. "Banks." Pages 160–61 in *The Oxford Classical Dictionary.* Ed. N. G. L. Hammon and H. H. Scullard. Oxford: Clarendon, 1970.

Hemer, C. *The Book of Acts in the Setting of Hellenistic History.* Tübingen: Mohr, 1989.

Hendricksen, W. *Philippians.* Grand Rapids: Baker, 1962.

Hertzog, I. H. *The Main Institutions of Jewish Law.* 2 vols. New York: Soncino, 1967.

Hester, J. D. *Paul's Concept of Inheritance: A Contribution to the Understanding of Heilsgeschichte.* Edinburgh: Oliver & Boyd, 1968.

Hicks, R. D., trans. *Diogenes Laertius: Lives of Eminent Philosophers.* 2 vols. London: Williams Heinemann, 1959.

Hijmans, B. L. ΑΣΚΗΣΙΣ: *Notes on Epictetus' Educational System.* Assen: Van Gorcum, 1959.

Hobson, D. W. "House and Household in Roman Egypt." *YCS* 28 (1985): 211–29.

Hock, R. F. "Paul's Tentmaking and the Problem of His Social Class." *JBL* 97 (1978): 555–64.

———. *The Social Context of Paul's Ministry: Tent Making and Apostleship.* Philadelphia: Fortress, 1980.

Hopkins, K. *Conquerors and Slaves.* Cambridge: Cambridge University Press, 1978.

———. *Death and Renewal.* Cambridge: Cambridge University Press, 1983.

Horowitz, G. *The Spirit of Jewish Law.* New York: Central Book, 1963.

Hort, F. J. A. *The Christian Ecclesia.* London: Macmillan, 1898.

Howson, J. S. *The Metaphors of St Paul.* London: Strahan, 1868.

Hubbard, R. L. "The *Go'el* in Ancient Israel: Theological Reflections on an Israelite Institution." *BBR* 1 (1991): 3–19.

Hughes, P. E. *Paul's Second Epistle to the Corinthians.* Grand Rapids: Eerdmans, 1962.

Humphreys, A. E. *The Epistles to Timothy and Titus.* Cambridge: Cambridge University Press, 1895.

Hvalvik, R. "A 'Sonderweg' for Israel: A Critical Examination of a Current Interpretation of Romans 11:25–27." *JSNT* 38 (1990): 88–107.

Jeremias, J. *The Central Message of the New Testament.* London: SCM, 1965.

Johnson, D. G. "The Structure and Meaning of Romans 11." *CBQ* 46 (1984): 98–99.

Johnson, L. T. "Rom. 3:21–26 and the Faith of Jesus." *CBQ* 44 (1982): 77–90.

Jolowicz, H. F. *Historical Introduction to the Study of Roman Law.* Cambridge: Cambridge University Press, 1952.

Jolowicz, H. F., and B. Nicholas. *Historical Introduction to the Study of Roman Law.* Cambridge: Cambridge University Press, 1972.

Jones, A. H. M. *The Greek City.* Oxford: Clarendon, 1940.

———. "Slavery in the Ancient World." *EHR* 9 (1956): 185–99.

Jones, H. S. " Ἀπαρχὴ πνεύματος." *JTS* 23 (1922): 282–83.

Jones, J. W. *The Law and Legal Theory of the Greeks: An Introduction.* Oxford: Clarendon, 1956.

Kee, H. C. *Medicine, Miracle, and Magic in New Testament Times.* Cambridge: Cambridge University Press, 1986.

Keener, C. S. "Man and Woman." Pages 583–92 in *Dictionary of Paul and His Letters.* Ed. G. Hawthorne and R. P. Martin. Downers Grove, Ill.: InterVarsity Press, 1993.

Kelly, J. N. D. *The Pastoral Epistles.* London: Adam & Charles Black, 1963.

Kennedy, G. "Classical and Christian Source Criticism." Pages 125–55 in *The Relationships among the Gospels: An Interdisciplinary Dialogue*. Ed. W. O. Walker. San Antonio: Trinity University Press, 1978.

Kennedy, H. A. A. "The Epistle of Paul to the Philippians." Pages 399–473 in *Expositor's Greek New Testament*. Ed. W. R. Nicoll. 5 vols. London: Macmillan, 1897–1910.

Kent, J. H. "The Temple Estates of Delos, Rheneia, and Mykonos." *Hesperia* 17 (1948): 243–338.

Keyes, C. W. "The Greek Letter of Introduction." *AJP* 56 (1935): 28–44.

Kinross, Lord. *Europa Minor: Journeys in Coastal Turkey*. London: Travel Book Club, n.d.

Kirschenbaum, A. *Sons, Slaves, and Freedmen in Roman Commerce*. Washington: Catholic University of America Press, 1987.

Knight, G. W. *The Pastoral Epistles*. Grand Rapids: Eerdmans, 1992.

Knox, W. L. *St Paul and the Church of the Gentiles*. Cambridge: Cambridge University Press, 1939.

Kruse, C. G. *Paul, the Law, and Justification*. Leicester, U.K.: Inter-Varsity Press, 1996.

Kurylowicz, Marek. *Die adoptio im klassischen römischen Recht*. Studia Antiqua 6. Warsaw: University Warszawskiego, 1981.

Ladd, G. E. *A Theology of the New Testament*. Grand Rapids: Eerdmans, 1974.

Lang, M. *Cure and Cult in Ancient Corinth: A Guide to the Asklepieion*. Princeton: American School of Classical Studies at Athens, 1977.

Laslett, P., ed. *Household and Family in Past Time*. Cambridge: Cambridge University Press, 1972.

Last, H. "The Chronology of the Laws on the Marriage of Roman Citizens." Pages 441–43 in vol. 10 of *The Cambridge Ancient History*. Ed. S. A. Cooke, F. E. Adcock, and M. P. Charlesworth. 12 vols. Cambridge: Cambridge University Press, 1953–1965.

Leipolt, J. "Das Bild vom Kriege in der griechischen Welt." Pages 16–30 in *Gott und die Götter: Festgabe für Eric Fascher*. Ed. G. Delling et al. Berlin: Evangelische Verlagsanstalt, 1958.

Leon, H. J. *The Jews of Ancient Rome*. Philadelphia: Jewish Publication Society, 1960.

Levick, B. *The Government of the Roman Empire: A Sourcebook*. Totowa, N.J.: Barnes & Noble, 1985.

Lightfoot, J. B. *Notes on the Epistles of St Paul*. London: Macmillan, 1895.

_____. *Saint Paul's Epistle to the Galatians*. London: Macmillan, 1884.

_____. *Saint Paul's Epistle to the Philippians*. London: Macmillan, 1868.

_____. *Saint Paul's Epistles to the Colossians and to Philemon*. London: Macmillan, 1879.

Lincoln, A. T. *Ephesians*. Dallas: Word, 1990.

_____. *Paradise Now and Not Yet*. Cambridge: Cambridge University Press, 1981.

Little, J. A. "Paul's Use of Analogy: A Structural Analysis of Romans 7:1–6." *CBQ* 46 (1984): 82–83.

Littleton, A. C., and B. S. Yamey, eds. *Studies in the History of Accounting.* Homewood, Ill.: Association of University Teachers of Accounting/ American Accounting Association, 1956.

Liversidge, J. *Everyday Life in the Roman Empire.* New York: Putnam's, 1976.

Loane, H. J. *Industry and Commerce of the City of Rome.* Baltimore: Johns Hopkins University Press, 1938.

Lock, W. *The Pastoral Epistles.* Edinburgh: T&T Clark, 1924.

Lohmeyer, E. *Die Briefe an die Philipper, Kolosser, und an Philemon.* Göttingen: Vandenhoeck & Ruprecht, 1964.

Lohse, E. *Colossians and Philemon.* Philadelphia: Fortress, 1971.

Longenecker, B. W. "Πίστις in Romans 3:25: Neglected Evidence for the 'Faithfulness of Christ'?" *NTS* 39 (1993): 478–80.

Longenecker, R. N. *Galatians.* Dallas: Word, 1990.

———. "The Pedagogical Nature of the Law in Galatians 3:19–4:7." *JETS* 25 (1982): 53–56.

Lull, D. J. " 'The Law Was Our Pedagogue': A Study in Galatians 3:19, 25." *JBL* 105 (1986): 489–95.

Lutz, C. E. "Musonius Rufus, 'The Roman Socrates.' " *YCS* 10 (1947): 3–147.

Lyall, F. "Of Metaphors and Analogies: Legal Language and Covenant Theology." *SJT* 32 (1979): 1–17.

———. "Roman Law in the Writings of Paul—Adoption." *JBL* 88 (1969): 458–66.

———. *Slaves, Citizens, Sons: Legal Metaphors in the Epistles.* Grand Rapids: Zondervan, 1984.

MacMullen, R. *Roman Social Relations.* New Haven: Yale University Press, 1974.

Macve, R. H. "Some Glosses on Greek and Roman Accounting." Pages 233–64 in *Crux: Essays Presented to G. E. M. de Ste. Croix on His 75th Birthday.* Ed. P. A. Cartledge and F. D. Harvey. London: Imprint Academic, 1985.

Malherbe, A. J. "Antisthenes and Odysseus, and Paul at War." *HTR* 76 (1983): 143–73.

———. "The Beasts at Ephesus." *JBL* 87 (1968): 71–80.

———. "Medical Imagery in the Pastoral Epistles." Pages 19–35 in *Texts and Testaments.* Ed. W. E. March. San Antonio: Trinity University Press, 1980.

———. *Social Aspects of Early Christianity.* Baton Rouge: Louisiana State University Press, 1977.

Malinowski, F. X. "The Brave Women of Philippi." *BTB* 15 (1985): 60–64.

Manson, T. W. "2 Cor. 2:14–17: Suggestions towards an Exegesis." Pages 155–62 in *Studia Paulina.* Ed. J. N. Sevenster and W. C. van Unnik. Haarlem: Bohn, 1953.

Marrou, H. I. *A History of Education in Antiquity.* New York: Sheed & Ward, 1956.

Marshall, I. H. "The Development of the Concept of Redemption." Pages 153–69 in *Reconciliation and Hope: New Testament Essays on Atonement and Eschatology Presented to L. L. Morris on His 60th Birthday.* Ed. R. Bank. Exeter, U.K.: Paternoster, 1974.

Marshall, P. *Enmity in Corinth: Social Conventions in Paul's Relations with the Corinthians.* Tübingen: Mohr, 1987.

_____. "A Metaphor of Social Shame: ΘΡΙΑΜΒΕΥΕΙΝ in 2 Cor. 2:14." *NovT* 25 (1983): 302–17.

Martin, D. B. *Slavery as Salvation.* New Haven: Yale University Press, 1990.

Martin, R. P. *Colossians and Philemon.* London: Oliphants, 1981.

_____. *2 Corinthians.* Waco, Tex.: Word, 1986.

Maxey, M. *Occupations of the Lower Classes in Roman Society.* Chicago: University of Chicago Press, 1938.

McKay, A. K. *Houses, Villas, and Palaces in the Roman World.* Ithaca, N.Y.: Cornell University Press, 1975.

McKeown, T., and R. G. Record. "The Reason for the Decline of Mortality in England and Wales during the Nineteenth Century." *Population Studies* 16 (1962): 94–122.

McLean, B. H. "The Absence of an Atoning Sacrifice in Paul's Soteriology." *NTS* 38 (1992): 531–53.

_____. "Christ as Pharmakos in Pauline Soteriology." Pages 187–206 in *SBL Seminar Papers, 1991.* SBLSP 30. Atlanta, Ga.: Scholars Press, 1991.

Meecham, H. G. *Light from Ancient Letters.* London: George Allen & Unwin, 1923.

Meeks, W. A. *The First Urban Christians: The Social World of the Apostle Paul.* New Haven: Yale University Press, 1983.

_____. *The Moral World of the First Christians.* Philadelphia: Westminster, 1986.

Meijer, F., and O. Nijf. *Trade, Transport, and Society in the Ancient World: A Sourcebook.* London: Routledge, 1992.

Mendelsohn, I. *Slavery in the Ancient Near East: A Comparative Study of Slavery in Babylonia, Assyria, Syria, and Palestine from the Middle of the Third Millennium to the End of the First Millennium.* Oxford: Oxford University Press, 1949.

Millar, F. G. B. "The World of the Golden Ass." *JRS* 71 (1981): 65–75.

Miller, E. C. "Πολιτεύεσθε in Philippians 1:27: Some Philological and Thematic Observations." *JSNT* 15 (1982): 86–96.

Miller, J. C., ed. *Slavery and Slaving in World History: A Bibliography, 1990–1991.* Milford, N.Y.: Kraus International, 1993.

_____. *Slavery: A Worldwide Bibliography, 1900–1982.* White Plains, N.Y.: Kraus International, 1985.

Milligan, G. *The New Testament Documents: Their Origin and Early History.* London: Macmillan, 1913.

_____. *St Paul's Epistles to the Thessalonians.* London: Macmillan, 1908.

Mitchell, M. M. "New Testament Envoys in the Context of Graeco-Roman Diplomatic and Epistolary Conventions." *JBL* 4 (1992): 641–62.

Moffatt, J. *The First Epistle of Paul to the Corinthians.* London: Hodder & Stoughton, 1938.

Momigliano, A. "Procum Patricium." *JRS* 56 (1966): 16–24.

Monro, H. *Digest 17.2: Pro Socio.* Cambridge: Cambridge University Press, 1902.

Morris. L. *The Apostolic Preaching of the Cross.* London: Tyndale, 1965.

_____. *The Epistle to the Romans.* Grand Rapids: Eerdmans, 1988.

_____. *The Epistles of Paul to the Thessalonians.* Leiceser, U.K.: Inter-Varsity Press, 1984.

_____. *The First and Second Epistles to the Thessalonians.* Grand Rapids: Eerdmans, 1959.

Morrison, J. S., and R. T. Williams. *Greek Oared Ships.* Cambridge: Cambridge University Press, 1968.

Mosley, D. J. *Envoys and Diplomacy in Ancient Greece.* Wiesbaden: Steiner, 1973.

Moule, C. F. D. *The Epistles of Paul the Apostle to the Colossians and to Philemon.* Cambridge: Cambridge University Press, 1957.

_____. *The Phenomenon of the New Testament.* London: SCM, 1967.

Moule, H. C. G. *Ephesian Studies.* London: Hodder & Stoughton, 1900.

_____. *The Second Epistle to Timothy.* London: Religious Tract Society, 1905.

Murphy-O'Connor, J. *St Paul's Corinth.* Wilmington, Del.: Michael Glazier, 1983.

Nauck, W. "Salt as a Metaphor in Instructions for Discipleship." *ST* 6 (1952): 165–78.

Nicholas, B. *An Introduction to Roman Law.* Oxford: Clarendon, 1987.

_____. "Patria Potestas." Page 789 in *The Oxford Classical Dictionary.* Ed. N. G. L. Hammond and H. H. Scullard. Oxford: Clarendon, 1970.

Noonan, J. T. *Contraception: A History of Its Treatment by the Catholic Theologians and Canonists.* Cambridge, Mass.: Belknap, 1965.

Nygren, A. *Commentary on Romans.* Philadelphia: Fortress, 1949.

O'Brien, P. T. *Colossians, Philemon.* Waco, Tex.: Word, 1982.

_____. *The Epistle to the Philippians.* Grand Rapids: Eerdmans, 1991.

Oke, C. C. "A Suggestion with Regard to Romans 8:23." *Int* 11 (1957): 455–60.

Packer, J. E. "Housing and Population in Imperial Ostia and Rome." *JRS* 57 (1967): 80–95.

_____. *The Insulae of Imperial Ostia.* Memoirs of the American Academy of Rome 31. Rome: American Academy in Rome, 1971.

Paoli, U. E. *Rome: Its People, Life, and Customs.* London: Gerald Duckworth, 1990.

Parker, H. M. D. *The Roman Legions.* Cambridge: Cambridge University Press, 1958.

Parkin, T. G. *Demography and Roman Society.* Baltimore: Johns Hopkins University Press, 1992.

Pate, C. M. *Adam Christology as the Exegetical and Theological Substructure of 2 Corinthians 4:7–5:21.* Lanham, Md.: University Press of America, 1991.

Perriman, A. C. "The Head of a Woman: The Meaning of ΚΕΦΑΛΗ in 1 Corinthians 11:3." *JTS* 45 (1994): 602–22.

Pfitzner, V. C. *Paul and the Agon Motif.* Leiden: Brill, 1967.

Pilch, J. J. "Beat His Ribs While He Is Young (Sirach 30:12): A Window on the Mediterranean World." *BTB* 23 (1993): 101–13.

Piper, J. "The Demonstration of the Righteousness of God in Romans 3:25, 26." *JSNT* 7 (1980): 2–32.

Platner, S. B., and T. Ashby. *A Topographical Dictionary of Ancient Rome.* Oxford: Oxford University Press, 1929.

Pleket, H. W. "Urban Elites and Business in the Greek Part of the Roman Empire." In *Trade in the Ancient Economy.* Ed. P. Garnsey, K. Hopkins, and C. R. Whittaker. Berkeley: University of California Press, 1983.

Plummer, A. *The Pastoral Epistles.* London: Hodder & Stoughton, 1888.

_____. *Second Epistle of St Paul to the Corinthians.* Edinburgh: T&T Clark, 1915.

Poliakoff, M. B. *Combat Sports in the Ancient World.* New Haven: Yale University Press, 1987.

Pomeroy, S. B. *Goddesses, Whores, Wives, and Slaves: Women in Classical Antiquity.* New York: Schocken, 1975.

_____. "The Relationship of the Married Woman to Her Blood Relatives in Rome." *AncSoc* 7 (1976): 215–37.

Preisendanz, K. *Griechische Zauberpapyri, I–II.* 2 vols. Leipzig: Teubner, 1928–1931.

Pringsheim, F. *The Greek Law of Sale.* Weimar: Bohlaus Nachfolger, 1950.

Pusey, P. E. *Sancti patris nostri Cyrilli archiepiscopi Alexandrini in D. Joannis evangelium.* 3 vols. Oxford: Clarendon, 1872.

Ramsay, W. M. *The Church in the Roman Empire.* London: Hodder & Stoughton, 1897.

_____. "Ephesus." Pages 720–25 in vol. 1 of *Dictionary of the Bible.* Ed. J. Hastings. 5 vols. Edinburgh: T&T Clark, 1898.

_____. *A Historical Commentary on St Paul's Epistle to the Galatians.* New York: Putnam's, 1900.

_____. *Pauline and Other Studies in Early Church History.* New York: A. C. Armstrong, 1906.

_____. *The Teaching of St Paul in Terms of the Present Day*. London: Hodder & Stoughton, 1914.

Ranft, J. "Depositum." *RAC* 3 (1957): 778–84.

Rapske, B. M. "The Prisoner Paul in the Eyes of Onesimus." *NTS* 37 (1991): 187–203.

Rawson, B. "Adult-Child Relationships in Roman Society." Pages 7–30 in *Marriage, Divorce, and Children in Ancient Rome*. Ed. B. Rawson. Oxford: Clarendon, 1991.

_____. "The Roman Family." Pages 1–57 in *The Family in Ancient Rome*. Ed. B. Rawson. London: Croom Helm, 1986.

_____, ed. *The Family in Ancient Rome*. London: Croom Helm, 1986.

_____. *Marriage, Divorce, and Children in Ancient Rome*. Oxford: Clarendon, 1991.

Rensberger, D. "2 Corinthians 6:14–7:1—a Fresh Examination." *SBT* 8 (1978): 25–49.

Richardson, J. *Roman Provincial Administration*. London: Gerald Duckworth, 1984.

Richter, G. M. A. *Ancient Furniture, Greek, Etruscan, and Roman*. Oxford: Oxford University Press, 1926.

Riddle, J. M. *Contraception and Abortion from the Ancient World to the Renaissance*. Cambridge: Harvard University Press, 1992.

Rives, J. "The *iuno feminae* in Roman Society." *EMC* 36 (1992): 39–42.

Roberts, R. "Old Texts in Modern Translation: Philippians 1:27." *ExpT* 49 (1937–1938): 325–26.

Robertson, A., and A. A. Plummer. *First Epistle of St Paul to the Corinthians*. Edinburgh: T&T Clark, 1914.

Robertson, A. T. *Word Pictures in the New Testament*. 6 vols. New York: Richard R. Smith, 1930–1933. Repr. Nashville, Tenn.: Broadman & Holman, 1973.

Robinson, J. A. *St Paul's Epistle to the Ephesians*. London: Macmillian, 1909.

Robinson, J. A. T. *The Body*. London: SCM, 1952.

_____. *Wrestling with Romans*. London: SCM, 1979.

Romer, J., and E. Romer. *The Seven Wonders of the World*. London: Michael O'Mara, 1995.

Rossell, W. H. "New Testament Adoption—Graeco-Roman or Semitic?" *JBL* 71 (1952): 233–34.

Rostovzeff, M. *The Social and Economic History of the Roman Empire*. 2 vols. Oxford: Clarendon, 1957.

Roth, J. "The Size and Organization of the Roman Imperial Legion" *Historia* 43 (1994): 346–62.

Saller, R. P. "*Familia, Domus,* and the Roman Conception of the Family." *Phoenix* 38 (1984): 336–55.

_____. "Men's Age at Marriage and Its Consequences in the Roman Family." *CP* 82 (1987): 21–34.

_____. *Personal Patronage under the Early Empire*. Cambridge: Cambridge University Press, 1982.

Salmond, S. D. F. "The Epistle of Paul to the Ephesians." Pages 203–395 in vol. 3 of *Expositor's Greek New Testament*. Ed. W. R. Nicoll. 5 vols. London: Hodder & Stoughton, 1897–1910.

Sampley, J. P. *Pauline Partnership in Christ*. Philadelphia: Fortress, 1980.

Sanday, W., and A. C. Headlam. *The Epistle to the Romans*. Edinburgh: T&T Clark, 1905.

Sanders, E. P. *Paul and Palestinian Judaism*. London: SCM, 1977.

Sawatzky, S. "Church Images and Metaphorical Theology." *TJT* 6 (1984): 109–30.

Schulz, F. *Classical Roman Law*. Oxford: Clarendon, 1951.

_____. *History of Roman Legal Science*. Oxford: Clarendon, 1963.

Scott, J. M. *Adoption as Sons of God: An Exegetical Investigation into the Background of* ΥΙΟΘΕΣΙΑ *in the Pauline Corpus*. Tübingen: Mohr, 1992.

Scullard, H. H. *Festivals and Ceremonies of the Roman Republic*. London: Thames & Hudson, 1981.

Sevenster, J. N. *Paul and Seneca*. Leiden: Brill, 1961.

_____. *The Roots of Pagan Anti-Semitism in the Ancient World*. Leiden: Brill, 1975.

Sevenster, J. N., and W. C. van Unnick, eds. *Studia Paulina*. Haarlem: Erven F. Bohn, 1953.

Shaw, B. "The Age of Roman Girls at Marriage: Some Reconsiderations." *JRelS* 77 (1987): 30–46.

Sherwin-White, A. N. *The Roman Citizenship*. Oxford: Clarendon, 1973.

_____. *Roman Society and Roman Law in the New Testament*. Oxford: Clarendon, 1969.

Sieder, R., and M. Mitterauer. *The European Family*. Cambridge: Cambridge University Press, 1982.

Simpson, E. K. *The Pastoral Epistles*. London: Tyndale, 1954.

Simpson, E. K., and F. F. Bruce. *Commentary on the Epistles to the Ephesians and the Colossians*. Grand Rapids: Eerdmans, 1957.

Spicq, C. " ΆΠΑΡΧΗ: Note de lexicographie néotestamentaire." Pages 493–510 in *The New Testament Age: Essays in Honor of Bo Reike*. Ed. C. Weinrich. Vol. 2. Macon, Ga.: Mercer, 1984.

Stanley, A. P. *The Epistles of St Paul to the Corinthians*. London: John Murray, 1858.

Starr, C. G. "Ships." Page 984 in *The Oxford Classical Dictionary*. Ed. N. G. L. Hammon and H. H. Scullard. Oxford: Clarendon, 1970.

_____. "Trireme." Page 1095 in *The Oxford Classical Dictionary*. Ed. N. G. L. Hammon and H. H. Scullard. Oxford: Clarendon, 1970.

Ste. Croix, G. E. M. de. *The Class Struggle in the Ancient World from the Archaic Age to the Arab Conquest*. London: Gerald Duckworth, 1987.

————. "Greek and Roman Accounting." Pages 14–74 in *Studies in the History of Accounting*. Ed. A. C. Littleton and B. S. Yamey. Homewood, Ill.: Association of University Teachers of Accounting/American Accounting Association, 1956.

Stott, J. R. W. *Guard the Gospel*. Leicester, U.K.: Inter-Varsity Press, 1973.

————. *The Message of Galatians*. London: Inter-Varsity Press, 1968.

Stowers, S. K. " ᾽ΕΚ ΠΙΣΤΕΩΣ and ΔΙΑ ΤΗΣ ΠΙΣΤΕΩΣ in Romans 3:30." *JBL* 108 (1989): 665–74.

————. *Letter Writing in Graeco-Roman Antiquity*. Philadelphia: Westminster, 1986.

————. "Paul on the Use and Abuse of Reason." Pages 253–86 in *Greeks, Romans, and Christians*. Ed. D. Balch, E. Ferguson, and W. A. Meeks. Minneapolis: Fortress, 1990.

Strelan, R. *Paul, Artemis, and the Jews in Ephesus*. Berlin: Gruyter, 1996.

Stroud, R. S. "The Sanctuary of Demeter on Acrocorinth in the Roman Period." Pages 65–77 in *The Corinthia in the Roman Period*. Ed. T. E. Gregory. Ann Arbor: Cushing-Malloy, 1994.

Taylor, L. R. "Freedmen and Freeborn in the Epitaphs of Imperial Rome." *AJP* 82 (1961): 113–32.

Tellbe, M. "The Sociological Factors behind Philippians 3:1–11 and the Conflict at Philippi." *JSNT* 55 (1994): 97–121.

Thebert, Y. "The Slave." Pages 138–74 in *The Romans*. Ed. A. Giardina. Chicago: University of Chicago Press, 1993.

Thomas, J. A. C. *Textbook of Roman Law*. Amsterdam: North Holland, 1973.

Thompson, W. E. "Insurance and Banking." Pages 829–36 in *Civilization of the Ancient Mediterranean: Greece and Rome*. Vol. 2. Ed. M. Grant and R. Kitzinger. New York: Scribner's, 1988.

Tigay, H., and H. J. Tigay. "Adoption." *EncJud* 2:298–301.

Tod, M. N. "Epigraphical Notes on Freedmen's Professions." *Epigraphica* 12 (1950): 3–26.

Treggiari, S. M. "Divorce Roman Style: How Easy and How Frequent Was It?" Pages 31–46 in *Marriage, Divorce, and Children in Ancient Rome*. Ed. B. Rawson; Oxford: Clarendon, 1991.

————. "Jobs in the Household of Livia." *PBSR* 43 (1975): 48–77.

————. *Roman Freedmen during the Late Republic*. Oxford: Clarendon, 1969.

————. *Roman Marriage: Iusti Coniuges from the Time of Cicero to the Time of Ulpian*. Oxford: Clarendon, 1991.

————. "Urban Labour in Rome: *Mercennarii* and *Tabernarii*." Pages 48–64 in *Non-Slave Labour in the Graeco-Roman World*. Ed. P. Garnsey. Cambridge: Cambridge University Press, 1980.

Tuckett, C. M. "Synoptic Tradition in 1 Thessalonians." Pages 160–82 in *The Thessalonian Correspondence*. Ed. R. F. Collins. Leuven: Leuven University Press, 1990.

Unnick, W. C. van. "Tarsus or Jerusalem: The City of Paul's Youth." Pages 259–320 in *Sparsa Collecta I*. Ed. W. C. van Unnick. Leiden: Brill, 1974.

Verner, D. C. *The Household of God: The Social World of the Pastoral Epistles*. Chico, Calif.: Scholars Press, 1983.

Versnel, H. S. *Triumphus: An Inquiry into the Origin, Development, and Meaning of the Roman Triumph*. Leiden: Brill, 1970.

Veyne, P. "The Roman Empire." Pages 6–233 in vol. 1 of *A History of Private Life*. Ed. P. Ariès and G. Duby. 5 vols. Cambridge: Harvard University Press, 1987.

Vincent, M. R. *A Critical and Exegetical Commentary on the Epistles to the Philippians and to Philemon*. Edinburgh: T&T Clark, 1945.

Vogt, J., and H. Bellen, eds. *Bibliographie zur antiken Sklaverei: Im Auftrag der Kommission für Geschichte des Altertums der Akademie der Wissenschaften und der Literatur*. Rev. E. Herrmann and N. Brockmeyer. Bochum, Germany: N. Brockmeyer, 1983.

Wacher, J., ed. *The Roman World*. 2 vols. London: Routledge & Kegan Paul, 1987.

Waele, F. J. de. "The Roman Market North of the Temple at Corinth." *AJA* 34 (1930): 432–54.

Wanamaker, C. A. *The Epistle to the Thessalonians*. Grand Rapids: Eerdmans, 1990.

Wansink, C. S. *Chained in Christ: The Experience and Rhetoric of Paul's Imprisonments*. Sheffield, U.K.: Sheffield Academic Press, 1996.

Ward, R. A. *Commentary on 1 and 2 Timothy and Titus*. Waco, Tex.: Word, 1974.

Watson, A. *Roman Slave Law*. Baltimore: Johns Hopkins University Press, 1987.

Watson, G. R. *The Roman Soldier*. London: Thames & Hudson, 1969.

Weaver, P. R. C. "Where Have All the Junian Latins Gone? Nomenclature and Status in the Early Empire." *Chiron* 20 (1990): 275–305.

Webster, G. *The Roman Imperial Army*. London: Black, 1979.

Weingrod, A. "Patrons, Patronage, and Political Parties." *Comparative Studies in Social History* 10 (1968): 377–400. Reprinted in *Friends, Followers, and Factions*. Ed. F. W. Schmidt, L. Guasti, C. H. Land, and J. C. Scott. Berkeley: University of California Press, 1977.

Wells, C. *The Roman Empire*. London: Harper-Collins, 1992.

Wengst, K. *Pax Romana and the Peace of Jesus Christ*. London: SCM, 1987.

Wenham, D. *Paul: Follower of Jesus or Founder of Christianity?* Grand Rapids: Eerdmans, 1995.

Westbrook, R., "Jubilee Laws." *ILR* 6 (1971): 206–26.

———. "Redemption of Land." *ILR* 6 (1971): 367–75.

Westermann, W. L. *The Slave System of Greek and Roman Antiquity*. Philadelphia: American Philosophical Society, 1955.

_____. "Slavery and the Elements of Freedom in Ancient Greece." Pages 17–32 in *Slavery in Classical Antiquity: Views and Controversy*. Ed. M. I. Finley. Cambridge: Heffer, 1974.

_____. "Warehousing and Trapezite Banking in Antiquity." *JEBH* 3 (1930–1931): 30–54.

Wevers, J. W. "Weapons and Implements of War." Pages 820–25 in vol. 4 of *Interpreter's Dictionary of the Bible*. Ed. G. A. Buttrick. 4 vols. Nashville: Abingdon, 1962.

White, K. D. *Greek and Roman Technology*. London: Thames & Hudson, 1984.

White, N. J. D. "The First and Second Epistles to Timothy and the Epistle to Titus." Pages 57–202 in vol. 4 of *Expositor's Greek New Testament*. Ed. W. R. Nicoll. 5 vols. London: Hodder & Stoughton, 1897–1910.

Wiedemann, T. E. J. *Greek and Roman Slavery: A Source Book*. London: Croom Helm, 1988.

_____. *Slavery*. Oxford: Clarendon, 1987.

Wilken, R. L. *The Christians as the Romans Saw Them*. New Haven: Yale University Press, 1984.

Williams, A. L. *The Epistle of Paul the Apostle to the Colossians and to Philemon*. Cambridge: Cambridge University Press, 1928.

Williams, D. J. *1 and 2 Thessalonians*. NIBC. Peabody, Mass.: Hendrickson, 1992.

_____. *Acts*. NIBC. Peabody, Mass.: Hendrickson, 1990.

_____. *The Promise of His Coming*. Homebush West, Australia: Anzea, 1990.

Williams, T. Review of C. E. Gunton, *The Actuality of Atonement*. *SJT* 43 (1990): 401–3.

Williamson, L. *God's Work of Art*. Richmond: CLC Press, 1971.

Winter, B. W. "1 Corinthians." Pages 1161–87 in *New Bible Commentary*. Ed. D. A. Carson et al. Leicester, U.K.: Inter-Varsity Press, 1994.

_____. *Seek the Welfare of the City: Christians as Benefactors and Citizens*. Grand Rapids: Eerdmans, 1994.

Winter, S. "Methodological Observations on a New Interpretation of Paul's Letter to Philemon." *USQR* 35 (1984): 3–12.

_____. "Paul's Letter to Philemon." *NTS* 33 (1987): 1–15.

Wiseman, J. "Corinth and Rome I: 228 BC–AD 267." Pages 438–548 in vol. 7 of *Aufstieg und Niedergang der römischen Welt*. Ed. H. Temporini. Berlin: de Gruyter, 1972–.

Witherington, B. *Conflict and Community in Corinth*. Grand Rapids: Eerdmans, 1995.

Woodhouse, W. J. "Adoption (Roman)." Pages 111–14 in vol. 1 of *Encyclopedia of Religion and Ethics*. Ed. James Hastings. 13 vols. New York: Scribner's, 1908–1926.

Wright, F. A., and L. B. Lawler. "Dress." Pages 364–65 in *The Oxford Classical Dictionary*. Ed. N. G. L. Hammon and H. H. Scullard. Oxford: Clarendon, 1970.

Yates, R. "Colossians 2:14: Metaphor of Forgiveness." *Bib* 71 (1990): 248–59.

Yorke, G. L. O. *The Church as the Body of Christ in the Pauline Corpus.* Lanham, Md.: University Press of America, 1991.

Young, N. H. "The Figure of the Παιδαγωγός in Art and Literature." *BA* 53 (1990): 80–86.

_____. "Παιδαγωγός: The Social Setting of a Pauline Metaphor." *NovT* 29 (1987): 150–76.

Youtie, H. C. "The Κλίνη of Seraphis." *HTR* 41 (1948): 9–29.

Ziesler, J. A. *Paul's Letter to the Romans.* London: SCM, 1989.

Zulueta, F. de. *The Roman Law of Sale.* Oxford: Clarendon, 1966.

Scripture Index

Ancient Source Index

Modern Author Index